The Church O
Publishi

Bishop Charles E. Blake, Sr.
Presiding Bishop of the Church Of God In Christ

We Are Called To Minister and Witness to a Deeply Distressed and Troubled World (Acts 26:15-18)

Order materials today from the Power for Living Series:

Church Of God In Christ Publishing House
2500 Lamar Avenue, Memphis, Tennessee 38114
P.O. Box 140636, Memphis, Tennessee 38114
Toll Free: 1-877-746-8578 | Fax: (901) 743-1555
Website: www.cogicpublishinghouse.net
Email: sales@cogicpublishinghouse.net

CHURCH OF GOD IN CHRIST, INC.
ANNUAL SUNDAY SCHOOL LESSON COMMENTARY 2014–2015
INTERNATIONAL SUNDAY SCHOOL LESSONS
COMMEMORATIVE EDITION

Mark A. Ellis

Chairman, Publishing Board

Bible art: Aaron and Alan Hicks

Copyright © 2014 by Urban Ministries, Inc.

Item No.: 1-2011. ISBN-13: 978-1-60997-170-0. ISBN-10: 1-60997-170-1,
PFL Large Print Item No.: 1-2612. ISBN-13: 978-1-60997-174-8. ISBN-10: 1-60997-176-0
Publishers: COGIC Publishing House, Memphis, TN 38114
To place an order, call 877-746-8578 or visit our website at www.cogicpublishinghouse.net

TABLE OF CONTENTS

Fall Quarter 2014

Winter Quarter 2014-2015

TABLE OF CONTENTS

Spring Quarter 2015

Summer Quarter 2015

FROM THE PRESIDING BISHOP'S DESK

To all sons and daughters of God's Kingdom,

The institution of Sunday School has been a long-standing tradition within our great church; it was started by Professor L.W. Lee in 1908. Later, Sunday School became an international department under the leadership of Elder F.C. Christmas (Father Christmas); however, Sunday School goes even farther back. It was started in Great Britain during the 1780s by English Anglican evangelical Robert Raikes (1725–1811) to help teach children how to read and write; most children during that time period had to work long hours to help provide for their families. That offered little time for education for the working class, and when the Industrial Revolution took place, children were forced to work longer hours, driving them further down and forcing many of them to abandon their education altogether.

Sunday School teachings eventually travelled over to the United States, where missionaries made sure that children were taught how to read and write. With God at the focal point of the teaching, it helped spread the Gospel to the lowest of the low, and encouraged parents to attend so they could help them learn how to read and write as well. However, teaching children how to read and write in Sunday School all came to an end in 1870, when both the United States of America and Great Britain instituted state schools and mandated that all children attend them. However, because of the dedication and help that Sunday School had offered children through teachings, parades, fairs, and prizes, it continued to encourage children and parents to grow in the Word of God.

Now Sunday School has transformed into something more than just education; it teaches us the building blocks of the Bible, of the importance of being a Christian—why to live holy lives, why to live sanctified lives, why to treat your fellow man with dignity and respect. In Sunday School, our country's children and its leaders were taught values and morals; it teaches us how to respect humanity and how to respect God and His working plan for man. In Sunday School, we are taught how to hold on to hope when all else seems to fail; moreover it teaches us how to worship the Lord with all of our might, about the Holy Ghost and what He brings to our lives. More importantly, it teaches us how to stand when no one else will stand with you, that with God on your side, the world against you still is not enough to take you down.

I want to applaud the wonderful work of our International Sunday School Department for their fine and hard, dedicated work to our church. They are the ones that keep Sunday School in the front of the public's eye; I also would like to thank the Publishing House for the excellent work in bringing us the quality quarter by quarter. Our church deserves the best, and because we have the best working on our course material, I promise that we will continue putting our best foot forward. I also want to thank the partnership that we have with UMI (Urban Ministries, Inc.) out of Chicago; they have made sure that the Church Of God In Christ is put first when it comes to making sure that our materials come out with their own flair and own presence.

Finally I want to thank all Sunday School superintendents, teachers, and most of all the students; without your dedication and your thirsting for the Word of God, there would be no Sunday School. Everyday people make our Sunday School Department what it is, for history has taught us without a Sunday School, we would not have a country built on moral ethics, and we know that "a child saved is a soul saved plus a life."

Bishop Charles E. Blake Sr.

Presiding Bishop

The Seventh in Succession

Church of God in Christ Inc.

FROM THE DESK OF CHAIRMAN MARK ELLIS

This year the 2014–2015 Annual Commentary is focused on four areas: Sustaining Hope, Acts of Worship, The Spirit Comes, and God's Prophets Demand Justice. I pray as teachers and students of the Word of God that you will be inspired to study in advance of the lessons and prepare the people of God for discipleship ministry.

Sustaining Hope: Sometimes God gives us more than we can handle … alone. Perhaps the greatest human question of all is the question of suffering: If God is good, why does He allow so much pain in the world? This is a question not often talked about in church, but Sunday School addresses it head on and doesn't offer trite answers. Our Sunday School material offers insight and hope to explore how, in the face of personal pain or the suffering of those we love, that we can trust in the Lord at all times. Ralph Waldo Emerson wrote, "For every minute you are angry you lose sixty seconds of happiness."

I like to be a bearer of good news. I like to be able to be positive about situations, especially when those situations involve the people of God. At the same time, I refuse to deny reality. Such denial can only lead to a worsened condition.

Acts of Worship: If you are a pastor, Sunday School superintendent, teacher, or student, you need a healthy and theologically sound attitude for dealing with the people of God. In addition to prayer and study, Sunday School can greatly improve your knowledge of worship. When we worship and adore Christ Jesus our Lord, who is perfect and flawless in every way, we are simply showing our intelligence and good taste. Our words do matter. And I have a concern with the way that we use a couple of particular words: We are not just a "Sunday School teacher/student" anymore; we become worshipers through reading and studying the Word of God.

The Spirit Comes: I have personally always found reassurance knowing that God is with us each and every moment. When Jesus was asked about His leaving the earth in a human form, He explained that He would ask the Father to send a Comforter to be with us. This invisible Comforter, the Holy Spirit, means we never walk alone. The pain we feel and the hurts we carry are not solely ours, but the Bible teaches us that the work of the Spirit is present in each moment. As you study the lessons during the spring quarter of 2015, you will see how the Holy Spirit comes to be that Comforter in your life and for your family and children. How do we engage with this in our daily lives? Have you developed rhythms in your life to focus on the daily work of the Holy Spirit? How does this help us engage people in a deeper understanding of God's loving character?

God's Prophets Demand Justice: "Injustice anywhere is a threat to justice everywhere," said Dr. Martin Luther King Jr. Therefore, we need to understand God's heart for justice and the poor if we are to fully understand the Good News of the Gospel. Justice is part of the very nature of God; it is represented in how He acts toward us and is the foundation of His rule and reign. As people created in His image, we need to reflect our Creator and care about the things He cares about. One of those primary concerns is justice.

Let me invite you to become a part of this great journey for the 2014–2015 year of our Annual Sunday School Commentary. Many thanks to Urban Ministries, Inc., for their collaboration with the Church Of God In Christ Publishing House.

Mark Ellis

Chairman

Church Of God In Christ

Publishing House

FROM THE CHAIRMAN OF MARKETING

To all teachers, students, and workers of Jesus Christ,

I have discovered throughout the years that we all have many roles to fill in our lives: an adult, a parent, a friend, a brother or sister, a co-worker, and a provider. Yet those same roles we have in our natural lives we also carry in our spiritual lives. A spiritual adult gaining maturity in the Word of God; a parent leading and guiding our children in the church and in God's Word and Law. A friend in prayer to help heal a broken heart, or to help celebrate when a soul has found deliverance. A brother and sister in the Kingdom of God, for knowing that we are all God's children makes us bonded together in the spirit of unity and love. A worker in the church as an evangelist, a teacher, preacher, pastor, prophet, or even apostle; and also a provider of our gifts from God to the world.

In this 2014–2015 commentary, we are going to cover the roles we share in both our natural lives and spiritual lives. Just like the seasons throughout the year bring different elements, the different spiritual seasons also bring change into our lives. In the fall, we harvest crops; in the winter, we lie dormant; in the spring, we began to grow with the fresh rain; in the summer, we produce fruit, so that when the fall comes again, it can be harvested.

That same pattern can be found in our spiritual lives. In the fall, we will learn how to sustain our hope in our faith. Then, in the winter, we will discover different acts of worship, followed by the spring, when we will encounter the fresh rain from the Spirit of God. Finally, in the summer, we will learn that God's prophets will demand justice. These four subjects will teach us how to stand when times get hard; how to press through to God in our darkest moments; how to understand that after sustaining and pressing, God's Spirit will reward us; and also how to stand for holiness and godliness in an unloving and unfeeling society.

This year's commentary is a beacon of hope to the hopeless, a cry to experience change within our worship, a push to feel the move of God's Spirit, and a chain to anchor our souls when times get hard. This tool, along with your Bible, is a weapon that God wants to use to equip His people, to spread the Gospel, to grasp a better understanding of what God wants from all of us. So when you look at this commentary, do not look at it as a way of saving money, but a weapon that will teach you how to fight off the enemy. Look at it as a ray of light to help pierce the darkness in a place that you never knew existed. Look at it as a way of spreading God's love to those who feel no love, who feel no warmth because they've been forgotten; share this with your friends and family, and use this tool to spread God's Gospel and His compassion toward man.

However, many thanks to the Church Of God In Christ Publishing House and UMI (Urban Ministries, Inc.) for their continued hard work and love for this work. But most of all, I want to thank you, the people of God who continue to purchase our literature. Remember, without you, this dream wouldn't have become a reality, and a church without its people is just an empty shell.

Yours for service,

Evangelist Sandra Smith Jones

Chairman of Marketing for the Publishing Board

Church Of God In Christ

FROM THE SENIOR ADVISOR TO THE PUBLISHING HOUSE

Combat Biblical Illiteracy

I want the teachers and officials of Sunday School classes to realize they are the front line against biblical illiteracy. Too many Christians no longer take time to study the Word of God, or attend mid-week Bible study classes. Whether by choice or circumstance, modern-day Christians know less of the Bible today than their predecessors ten years ago. Not even the convenience of the Internet and other technological advances encourage in-depth study of the Word. Every pastor is pressed to insist that members take his admonitions as recorded in the Scriptures: "If thou put the brethren in remembrance of these things, thou shalt be a good minister of Jesus Christ, nourished up in the words of faith and of good doctrine, whereunto thou hast attained. But refuse profane and old wives' fables, and exercise thyself rather unto godliness" (1 Timothy 4:6–7). Add to that reference, "All scripture is given by inspiration of God, and is profitable for doctrine, for reproof, for correction, for instruction in righteousness" (2 Timothy 3:16). Our goal is to provide excellent curriculums and classic instruction to gain the best results. Believers need to be reinforced and prepared to face the challenges that come daily.

The Sunday School class is where the needs of fledgling and mature Christians are nourished in the Word. The task may seen daunting but is so rewarding. The Sunday School Superintendent and staff are truly owed a debt of gratitude for their devotion. Teaching is Kingdom work, and strong doctrinally prepared members make effective witnesses for our Lord.

The Power For Living series is thoughtfully prepared in order to make the objective of defeating biblical illiteracy a reality. Therefore, take our booklets, helps, and suggestions to heart. The local church is considered part and parcel of "Team Jesus," who are disciples of Christian education and character building. Make it your goal to encourage the students that weekly sit under your instruction to apply themselves, and create the discipline and mindset to study for a purpose. Everybody has something to give! Make certain those who sit under your tutelage are prepared to serve Christ in this world. Being biblically literate is the first step.

I can't end this note without using that most appreciated and recited Scripture: "Study to shew thyself approved unto God, a workman that needeth not to be ashamed, rightly dividing the word of truth" (2 Timothy 2:15).

Bishop David Allen Hall

Sunday School Teacher

FROM THE INTERNATIONAL SUNDAY SCHOOL PRESIDENT

Greetings saints of God,

It is again a great honor and pleasure to greet you in another Annual Sunday School Commentary.

We thank God for each of you and the tremendous ministry of Sunday School. Can you imagine life without it?

For many of us in the Church Of God In Christ, we were raised in Sunday School from the "Cradle Roll Class" on up. Every Sunday morning, we found ourselves in our classes being fed the Word by men and women of God who loved us and His Word. In fact, it was almost a given that everybody went to Sunday School. But not so today!

Lives have become too busy, burdens so heavy that many have eliminated the core foundation of their walk with the Lord: the ministry of Sunday School.

Our leader, Presiding Bishop Charles E. Blake Sr., has so clearly presented to us in our annual theme how *we*, the church, are to respond to the challenges of this world. He reminds us that "we are called to minister and witness to a deeply distressed and troubled world" (based on Acts 26:15–18).

The ministry of Sunday School is a core foundation to every church. Through its teaching core, we must *minister* to the saints through creative, current, and relevant Sunday School instruction and course offerings. Through Sunday School's outreach and winning cores, we must *effectively witness* to the world that there is hope; there is a better, new, and living way, and that way is Jesus!

Our contributions to the 2014–15 Church Of God In Christ Annual Commentary are designed to strengthen local Sunday School leadership and ministries by providing *tools, strategies,* and *solutions* that will enhance and grow your Sunday Schools in this *distressed* and *troubled* world.

Without a vision, the people perish! Our prayer is that these articles will empower, equip, and motivate your local Sunday School to dig deeper, flourish, and grow as a result of your labors and the information provided.

Faithfully yours,

Bishop Alton Gatlin, President

International Sunday School Department

FROM THE COGIC-UMI SUNDAY SCHOOL LIAISON

Greetings Sunday School Students,

I want to compliment you for adding the Church Of God In Christ Commentary to your library. The Church Of God In Christ and Urban Ministries, Inc., team work together to ensure a quality of study materials and helps that will enable you to achieve an understanding of the Word of God not obvious to most students.

The Sunday School material provides several levels of training. The student book is written so a person can read it anytime and anywhere and be edified. The teacher's manual goes a few steps further, with information and suggested teaching methods that empower the instructor to more effectively educate his or her students. The COGIC Commentary is almost equivalent to having a theological library in your home. The only difference is some of our most important scholars do the research for us.

The lessons for this year will bring focus on "Sustaining Hope," "Acts of Worship," "The Spirit Comes," and "God's Prophets Demand Justice."

- The **first quarter** will teach us how to sustain what we know is right in our lives; it will teach us how to not succumb to the pressures of this world, and understand that hope is more important than water, for it is truly our life source.
- The **second quarter** will focus on pressing beyond the veil, finding out the very thing that will move God and take us to a higher level in our worship with Him.
- The **third quarter** shows us the results of holding on and taking our worship further and higher, by learning how to entertain the Spirit of God when He comes.
- Finally, in the **fourth quarter**, we will learn about the prophets and that they demanded justice, but more so, we will learn how we too should stand like the prophets of old, and that God's Word is absolute and that no part of it should be compromised nor explained away.

We are asking all teachers to be sure that all lessons relate somehow to the theme that our Presiding Bishop Charles Blake gave us at the beginning of the year:

"We are called to minister and witness to a deeply distressed and troubled world" (based on Acts 26:15–18).

Our nation is experiencing the worst period of moral and spiritual corruption in our history. Our only hope in the past and our only hope for the future is the Power and the Word. Therefore, any reading and research you do to help you teach the Word with authority is worth having. It is our hope this commentary will do this for you.

Sincerely,

Bishop James L. Whitehead Jr., A.A., B.A., M.Div.

Research Team:
Dr. Charles Hawthorne, Ph.D., Dr. Herman Hullum, D.Min.,
Evang. Iretha Sanford, Th.D. (candidate), Elder Avery Brown, M.A., M.Div.,
Elder Scott Bradley, B.A.

COGIC PUBLISHING BOARD 2014-2015

Mark Ellis
Chairman of the Board

Uleses Henderson
1st Vice Chairman
(Incumbent)

Sandra S. Jones
Vice Chairman
(Incumbent)

Dr. Joe Chase, Jr.
Secretary
(Incumbent)

Bishop E. Charles Connor
(Incumbent)

Bishop David Hall, Sr.

Bishop Welton Lawrence
(Incumbent)

Bishop O.L. Meadows
(Incumbent)

Stephen Savage
COGIC Photographer
(Incumbent)

Reggie Witherspoon
(Incumbent)

Superintendent
Tony Campbell

Dr. Sabrina Ellis

Supervisor
Gracie Davis Harris

Administrative Assistant
Dr. Philip Jackson

HISTORIC EXECUTIVE COMMISSION OF BISHOP MASON

The Church Of God In Christ celebrates its historic 107–108th year as a primary classical Holiness-Pentecostal body and global voice of holiness. These men of God took their mandates seriously and set the standards we all enjoy today. They believed as a collective body in holiness, evangelizing the world and edifying believers through our faith, worship, and commitment to biblically based tenets. ***"Their legacy and hard work continues today."***

(Seated, left to right): Bishop Barker; Bishop O.M. Kelly; Bishop J.O. Patterson, Sr.; Bishop U.E. Miller; Bishop J.S. Bailey; Bishop C.H. Mason (***Centered***); Bishop A.B. McEwen; Bishop O.T. Jones, Sr.; Bishop S.E. Crouch; Bishop W. Wells; Bishop F.D. Washington.

(Standing, left to right): Bishop L.H. Ford; Bishop C.L. Anderson; Bishop J. White; Bishop C.E. Bennett; Bishop R.E. Ranger; Bishop F.L. Haynes; Bishop B. Lyles; Bishop C.D. Love; Unknown; Bishop T.D. Iglehart; Bishop A. M. Cohen.

This was the Executive Board of Bishop C. H. Mason, men of power and influence; men who helped begin the process in the life of the Church Of God In Christ.

THE HISTORY AND LEGACY OF THE CHURCH OF GOD IN CHRIST

Celebrating Bishop Charles Harrison Mason Sr. Founder 150th Birthday

Bishop Charles Harrison Mason and our **Church Of God In Christ** patriarchs and matriarchs boldly challenged us to courageously ascend to new heights and expand toward new horizons, while embracing our original witness. As we reflect upon our heritage and legacy, we continue to declare that we are unashamedly Pentecostal and unapologetically committed to living and reflecting the fruit of sanctification. The Church Of God In Christ Annual Commentary front matter is designed to expose present and future generations to the rich traditions of our faith and develop effective witnessing disciples of our Lord Jesus Christ. Included in this edition are select articles, leadership portraits and profiles, and a short history of the Church Of God In Christ from its inception to the present.

The Church Of God In Christ is committed to making relevant its message and witness for twenty-first century impact as we celebrate our glorious past, while embracing a promising future. It is our hope that this devotional and Bible Study Commentary will instruct, inspire, impact, and illumine future generations to embrace the God of our forefathers who were empowered and anointed by the Holy Spirit. I implore members of the Body of Christ to study the Word and to earnestly contend for the faith once delivered to the saints.

The Most Reverend Charles Edward Blake Sr.

Presiding Bishop

According to the late Bishop Ithiel Clemmons, Church of God In Christ chronicler and General Board Member, "the phenomenal growth of the Church Of God In Christ can be traced to a covenant-promise that the Lord gave Bishop Mason." During his pilgrimage, God fulfilled a promise to Bishop Mason that the "sun would never set upon the expanse of the Church Of God In Christ a.k.a. COGIC." Historians for years to come will continue to probe the unique spiritual dynamism and mystique of Bishop Charles Harrison Mason and the legacy of the Church Of God In Christ, the charismatic movement from the Word Church and Deliverance Movement evolved, as did the Full Gospel Baptist Movement; and finally the Holy Spirit Renewal in a global context. All these movements are indebted to the pioneering and seminal influence of Bishop Charles Harrison Mason, of the Church Of God In Christ.

As a result of the impact of Bishop Mason's vision and ministry, the face of modern Christianity would never be the same. The Church Of God In Christ reports having over five million members in the United States; the **National Council of Churches** ranks it as the largest Pentecostal denomination and the fifth largest Christian denomination in the U.S. Internationally, its worldwide membership is estimated to be between six and eight million members and more than 15,000 congregations throughout the world. COGIC spans more than six continents with vital missionary, evangelistic, teaching, and social ministries. With the United States as its hub, COGIC ministry reaches a variety of communities throughout the global village. COGIC membership consists of various nationalities and in nearly sixty countries. The Church Of God In Christ has grown from its fledgling beginnings in 1895 to become a leading global Christian denomination within the world. Hence, the covenant-promise of God has been fulfilled.

The Legacy Begins

Charles Harrison Mason (1864-1961 corrected birthday verified by census) - founder of the Church Of God In Christ, is one of the most significant figures in the rise and spread of the modern Pentecostal movements. Mason was born on Prior Farm, just outside of Memphis, in an area that is today the town of Bartlett, Tennessee. His parents, Jerry and Eliza Mason, former slaves, were members of the Missionary Baptist Church, a source of the strength for them in the distressing times that followed the Civil War.

Even as a young boy, it is said that Mason had a religious bent. He prayed earnestly that God would give to him above all things a religion like the one he had heard about from the old slaves and seen demonstrated in their lives. It was this yearning for the God of his forebears that became the dynamic of his life.

When he was twelve years old, a yellow fever epidemic forced Jerry Mason and his family to leave Memphis for Plumersville, Arkansas, where they lived on John Watson's plantation as tenant farmers. The plague claimed his father's life in 1879. During those fearful and difficult days, the younger Mason worked hard and had little chance for schooling.

In 1880, just before his fourteenth birthday, Charles Mason fell ill with chills and fever. His mother despaired for his life. However, in an astounding turn of events, on the first Sunday in September 1880, he was miraculously healed. He and his mother went to the Mt. Olive Baptist Church near Plumersville, where the pastor, Charles Mason's half-brother, the Reverend I. S. Nelson, baptized him in an atmosphere of praise and thanksgiving. Charles Mason then traveled throughout the area of southern Arkansas as a lay preacher, giving his testimony and working with souls on the mourner's bench, especially during the summer camp meetings.

Charles Harrison Mason was licensed and ordained in 1891 in Preston, Arkansas, but held back from full-time ministry to marry. After two years, however, she divorced him—his greatest disappointment and distress—because she bitterly opposed his ministerial plans. This was a dark time in his life and some say it forced him to become even more consecrated to God. However, in 1893 came a crucial turning point in his life: following his heart-rending divorce, he was determined to get an education. That year, Meyer and Brothers of Chicago published a significant and widely read volume, "An Autobiography: The Story of the Lord's Dealing With Mrs. Amanda Smith, The Colored Evangelist." Evangelist Smith was one of the most widely respected Black holiness evangelists of the nineteenth century. Her life story led many African Americans into the Holiness movement. Her autobiography deeply impressed the Rev. Charles Mason. Evangelist Smith (1839–1915) was a disciple of John Inskip, and became one of the most influential, widely traveled, and respected Black Holiness Evangelists of the nineteenth century. Her life story gave hope to many Blacks and brought them into the Holiness movement, including the Rev. Charles Mason.

Mason claimed the grace of divine sanctification after reading her book and in Preston, Arkansas, preached his first sermon on the subject of Holiness. He chose as his text 2 Timothy 3:12–13, which begins, "Thou therefore endure hardness as a good solider of Jesus Christ." This sermon stayed with him throughout his life.

Bishop Mason married Leila Mason; they were married for thirty-one years and she was the mother of their seven children. In 1936, Lela Mason's death brought another period of adjustment to Bishop Mason's life; however, she had been extremely instrumental in his ministry and gave a great contribution to the Church Of God In Christ.

In 1942, Mason married Missionary Elsie Washington, another strong woman active in ministry.

In November 1893, Mason entered Arkansas Baptist College. But he became deeply disturbed by the hermeneutical and cultural suspicions of their methods and philosophy, and concluded that the school would not help his task of preserving the vitality of slave religion. He left there in January 1894.

In 1895, Rev. Mason met Charles Price Jones and they became fast friends. Like Mason, Rev. Charles Price Jones had come under the influence of the Holiness movement and in 1894 claimed the experience of sanctification while pastoring Tabernacle Baptist Church in Selma, Alabama; they both preached that sanctification was a second definite work of grace subsequent to conversion. From 1896–99, the Holiness conventions, revivals, and periodicals of Rev. Mason and Rev. Jones split the Baptists and, in a few cases, the Methodist Churches, causing the development of independent "sanctified" or "holiness" congregations and associations. Eventually they and their colleagues were expelled from the Baptist churches (the National Baptist Convention).

After being expelled from preaching in Baptist churches, Rev. Mason founded the St. Paul Church in Lexington, Mississippi, the first and oldest COGIC church in the world. However, in 1897, the group was originally known simply as the "Church of God." Many Christian groups forming at the time wanted biblical names such as "Church of God, Church of Christ, or Church of the Living God" and rejected terms such as Baptist, Methodist, or

Episcopal as not being scriptural names for the church. Now there were so many new holiness groups organizing and using the name "Church of God" that Rev. Mason looked for a name to distinguish this holiness organization from others. Later in 1897, while in Little Rock, Arkansas, Mason believed that God had given him such a name for the group, the "Church Of God In Christ." Mason believed that the name taken from 1 Thessalonians 2:14 and 2 Thessalonians 1:1 was divinely revealed and biblically inspired. He believed that God said, "If you take the name that I give you, they would never build a building that would hold all those who would come." The group adopted the name and COGIC began to grow throughout the South. Rev. C. P. Jones was elected the General Overseer, while the Rev. Charles Harrison Mason was selected as Overseer of Tennessee, and J.A. Jeter was selected as Overseer of Arkansas. A major Black denomination was born.

This was a significant event because from the 17th through 19th centuries, most Blacks had encountered Christianity under the control of Baptist or Methodist churches. These two brave and devoted men changed the religious landscape in the Black community and broadened the Black religious experience. As the new work progressed, Mason continued to seek a more complete consecration of his life. In 1906, he received reports of the Pentecostal revival in Los Angeles. He traveled to California, and under the ministry of W. J. Seymour, Rev. Mason received the baptism of the Holy Spirit and spoke in tongues. After five weeks in Los Angeles, he returned to Memphis and Jackson eager to share his additional experience of the Lord with his brethren.

However, when he presented his Pentecostal message and his experience with the Lord, not everyone in the church was willing to accept it; his message was rejected. Rev. C. P. Jones and Mason had many intensive debates, but eventually Jones rejected the doctrine of speaking in tongues, that it was the initial evidence of Spirit baptism, and sought to resolve the issue at the upcoming general assembly; needless to say, the church split.

At the 1907 General Assembly in Jackson, those men led by Jones wanted Mason and his followers to acknowledge other initial evidences of Spirit baptism besides speaking in tongues. Mason refused and was expelled from the church. Those who agreed with Mason met in September 1907 to organize the Church Of God In Christ. They elected the Elder C. H. Mason as General Overseer and appointed D. J. Young—his most constant companion—as editor of the new periodical, *The Whole Truth*. From Elder Young's earliest ministry, his evangelistic endeavors ran counter to mainstream religion and brought him under religious persecution. A converted cotton gin warehouse became a sanctuary of praise.

In 1907, the early pioneers of this newly formed Pentecostal body were E. R. Driver, J. Bowe, R. R. Booker, R. E. Hart, W. Welsh, A. A. Blackwell, E. M. Blackwell, E. M. Page, R. H. I. Clark, D. J. Young, James Brewer, Daniel Spearman, and J. H. Boone. These elders became the first Pentecostal General Assembly of the Church Of God In Christ, where they also adopted Pentecostalism at this time.

Overseer (Bishop) Mason began to ordain ministers of all races; he performed an unusually important service to the early twentieth-century Pentecostal movement. It appears that he was the only early convert who came from a legally incorporated church body who could thus ordain people whose status as clergymen was recognized by civil authorities. As a result, scores of White ministers sought ordination at the hand of Bishop Mason. In the years of 1909–14, there were as many White churches as Black churches carrying the name COGIC.

But by 1913, it had become increasingly clear that as Pentecostals moved toward denominationalism, they would follow the segregating practices of American culture. The color line which had been washed away in the blood of Jesus at the Azusa Street revival had reappeared. Therefore, in April 1914, Bishop Mason traveled to Hot Springs, Arkansas, to invoke God's blessings on the newly formed General Council of the Assemblies of God. By the 1930s, its ministry among Whites had ended.

Bishop Mason was investigated by the FBI along with others because of his pacifism and interracialism. Mason's commitment to the preaching of Hebrews 12:14, *"Follow peace with all men, and holiness, without which no man shall see the Lord,"* drew the ire of the FBI. In 1918, some White followers in Los Angeles were identified as being of German extraction, and Mason was jailed in Lexington, Mississippi, for allegedly preaching against the war; however, he did sell bonds to help the war efforts. They even confiscated his briefcase for incriminating evidence, but found only a bottle of anointing oil, a handkerchief, and a Bible.

But William B. Holt, one of the White brethren targeted by the FBI as suspicious, was a lawyer and former Nazarene Preacher, and traveled to Lexington and posted a two-thousand-dollar cash bond for Mason's release. Hence, the 1918 FBI report comments: "It is clear that Charles Harrison Mason and his followers were felt to be of far reaching significance that one of the great religious movements of the twentieth century was founded by a member of the African race." Later many scholars have voiced the same conclusion as the FBI report.

There are many reports of persecution against Mason; he traveled all over the country preaching the gospel of Jesus Christ and the Holy Ghost. The U.S. District Court in Jackson, Mississippi, could never prosecute a case against him. A "kangaroo court" in Paris, Texas tried to no avail to convict him. A prosecutor en route to try a case against him in Jackson, Mississippi, was killed in a train incident. A mob in Arkansas tried to interrupt a baptism in Arkansas by using a pistol to intimidate the crowd of worshipers. Each time the pistol was pointed toward Bishop Mason, it misfired. Isaiah 54:17 says, *"No weapon that is formed against thee shall prosper."* As in the New Testament era, the Church grew under persecution, and so it was with the Church Of God In Christ during its infancy.

The Leader and Chief Apostle of the Church Of God In Christ

Bishop Charles Harrison Mason and his first Executive Board was awarded the original charter. The Church Of God In Christ became the first legally chartered Pentecostal body incorporated in the United States. The Jones faction continued as a Holiness church, changing its name to the Church of Christ (Holiness) U.S.A. The members of the church referred to themselves as "the Saints," believing that they were set apart for holiness.

Despite this obstacle, Bishop Mason traveled across the nation preaching and establishing COGIC churches. As African Americans relocated north during the Great Migration, converted members spread the church north and west. In addition to his own efforts, Mason sent dozens of preachers and evangelists to cities and urban areas outside the South to spread COGIC, including William Roberts (Chicago), O. M. Kelly (New York), O. T. Jones Sr. (Philadelphia), E. R. Driver (Los Angeles), and Samuel Kelsey (Washington, D.C.) Therefore, from these major cities, the denomination spread throughout the country. However, in 1926, Bishop Mason authorized the Church's constitution, outlining the organization's bylaws, rules, and regulations. In 1933, Mason set apart five overseers to the office of bishop in the Church; the first five bishops of the Church Of God In Christ (COGIC) consecrated were I. S. Stafford (Detroit, Michigan), E. M. Page (Dallas, Texas), W. M. Roberts (Chicago, Illinois), O. T. Jones Sr. (Philadelphia, Pennsylvania), and R. F. Williams (Cleveland, Ohio).

In 1951, Mason was nearing 85 years of age, and set up a "Special Commission" to help with the administration and oversight of the Church. On June 5, 1951, he selected Bishop A. B. McEwen, Bishop J. S. Bailey, and Bishop O. M. Kelly as his assistants. On May 19, 1952, he added Bishop J. O. Patterson Sr.; Bishop Mason revised the constitution to determine the leadership and succession of the Church Of God In Christ after his demise. Three years later, on October 12, 1955, three more bishops were added: Bishop U. E. Miller, Bishop S. M. Crouch, and Bishop O.T. Jones Sr. This group became known officially as the Executive Commission and assumed greater control over church affairs until Mason's death.

The church has experienced great growth since its inception in 1907 with ten churches. By the time of Mason's death in 1961, COGIC had spread to every state in the United States and to many foreign countries with more than 400,000 members and more than 4,000 churches. At least ten other Churches (denominations) owed their origins to Bishop Mason and the Church Of God In Christ. Bishop Charles Harrison Mason lived to see the Church Of God In Christ become a major denomination and one of the largest Pentecostal bodies in the world, with a graduate seminary to its credit. Bishop Mason traces the Church's phenomenal growth to a covenant-promise that the Lord gave to him. He died at the age of 95 in Harper's Hospital, Detroit, Michigan, on November 17, 1961. Dr. Martin Luther King Jr. preached his last sermon from Bishop Mason's pulpit in Mason Temple, headquarters of the Church Of God In Christ, in Memphis, Tennessee, where Bishop Mason's remains are entombed to this day.

The Organization

Leadership has to do with the exercise of influence. Bishop Mason's leadership and authority was grounded in his spirituality and total commitment to God. He gave himself to fasting and praying for many days and nights. He was stripped bare of all pretenses as he sought to do the will of God. Such influence often crossed racial lines.

The Church Of God In Christ experienced tremendous growth and expansion worldwide through Bishop Mason's vision for Church growth through the development of Departmental Ministries, from local churches to the national Church. Societal change invariably impacts the Church. Therefore, as a visionary leader trusting the promises of God, Bishop Mason saw the need to institutionalize the various ministries of the Church. He accepted women as an integral part of ministry and demonstrated it in the way he appointed leadership.

The Women's Department

Mother Lizzie Robinson
General Mother
Church Of God In Christ

Bishop Mason, being intuitive and sensitive to ministry, understood that in order to expand, women definitely needed to be involved. In 1911 Bishop Mason appointed Mother Lizzie Woods Robinson (1860–1945) from Omaha, Nebraska, as the first leader of the Women's Department based on Jeremiah 9:17–20. Mother Robinson was the first "General Mother" of the church. Under her leadership, Bible Band, Sunshine Band, Sewing Circle, and later the Home and Foreign Missions were founded by women in ministry. As the church continued to grow, she began state organizations and appointed the first state mothers. Robinson was a staunch advocate for holiness and taught strict guidelines for the women with regard to dress and worldliness. She was greatly interested in the building of Mason Temple and she kept her national building fund drives functioning until she knew the building was ready for dedication. When she died in 1945, she had laid an impressive foundation for the Women's Ministry in Church Of God In Christ.

Mother Lillian B. Coffey
General Supervisor
Church Of God In Christ

Great women of God continued in succession to lead this department, including **Mother Lillian B. Coffey**, who succeeded Mother Robinson from 1945–1964. Mother Coffey was the organizer of the Women's International Convention. The first convention was held in Los Angeles, California, in 1951. Today the International Women's Convention/Crusade meets annually in May in different cities throughout the nation drawing thousands of women from around the world. Mother Coffey was a child convert to the Church Of God In Christ under the preaching and teaching of Bishop Mason. She was influential in organizing many of the auxiliaries, bands, and units that exist within the COGIC Women's

Department even today. The most active women's auxiliaries include: Prayer and Bible Band, Christian Women's Council, Home and Foreign Mission Bands, Young Women's Christian Council, Purity Class and the Sunshine Band. Mother Coffey also began the use of the title "Jurisdictional Supervisor" for state mothers as more jurisdictions were forming in each state.

Mother Annie L. Bailey
General Supervisor
Church Of God In Christ

Mother Annie L. Bailey assumed the position as General Supervisor after the death of Mother Coffey in 1964. Mother Bailey (1964–1975) became the third General Supervisor. She was the wife and companion of Bishop John Seth Bailey, a trusted adviser of Bishop Mason, and later the First Assistant Presiding Bishop of the Church Of God In Christ. The pair modeled the pastor and wife ministry team in COGIC. Mother Bailey developed the International Women's Convention into a training institute for women in the ministry. She served as the Jurisdictional Supervisor of several states, helping to establish and stabilize struggling jurisdictions.

Mother Mattie C. McGlothen
General Supervisor
Church Of God In Christ

Mother Mattie C. McGlothen was the fourth General Supervisor in succession of the International Women's Department. She was a tremendous organizer with a great impact on the development of the Women's Department. She was the Jurisdictional Supervisor of Women for California Northern First Jurisdiction. Mother McGlothen established several new auxiliaries including the International Hospitality Unit, the Educational and Bishop's Wives Scholarship funds, WE-12, and Lavender Ladies. She built a home for missionaries in the Bahamas, as well as a pavilion for senior citizens and unwed mothers in Port-au-Prince, Haiti. She also established the Mattie McGlothen Library and Museum in Richmond, California, as a resource for COGIC historical facts and memorabilia. Finally, she changed the visible presence of women in ministry with the introduction of the ministry "Habit." Therefore, today thousands of COGIC women, when ministering the gospel or serving in official capacities are seen in their civic (black) or ceremonial (white) Habits.

Mother Emma Crouch
General Supervisor
Church Of God In Christ

Mother Emma Crouch (1994–1997) succeeded Mother McGlothen. Mother Crouch of Dallas, Texas, served as the fifth General Supervisor. She was the Jurisdictional Supervisor of Women for Texas Southwest Jurisdiction. In her brief tenure, she encouraged the women to stay focused and supportive to the leadership of the church. One of her contributions was to divide the women's fellowship in the local congregations into two groups: the Christian Women's Council for the middle-aged and senior women and the YWCC for the younger women.

Mother Willie Mae Rivers
Current General Supervisor
Church Of God In Christ

Today **Mother Willie Mae Rivers**' (1997–present) leadership continues to contribute to the legacy of the Church Of God In Christ. Mother Rivers is also the Jurisdictional Supervisor of Women for the South Carolina Jurisdiction. She served as International Marshall, Secretary, and Assistant General Supervisor for the Department of Women. A local church mother since the age of 21, she is committed to strengthening the auxiliaries in the local churches and to prepare the younger women to carry the mission of the Church Of God In Christ into the twenty-first century. Mother Barbara McCoo Lewis serves as the Assistant General Supervisor of the Department of Women appointed by Bishop Blake. She is the Jurisdictional Supervisor for the First Jurisdiction, Southern California.

The National Youth Department

Under the leadership of Bishop Mason, the first youth denomination was organized under Elder M.C. Green. However, in 1917, the National Youth Department was formally organized by Elder (Bishop) Ozro Thurston Jones Sr. (1891–1972). The current president is Dr. Ben Stephens.

The National Sunday School

Appointed in 1908 by Bishop Mason, the first Superintendent of Sunday School was Professor L. W. Lee (1908–1916). In 1916, Father F. C. Christmas formally organized the Sunday School Department. The current president is Bishop Alton Gatlin.

The National Music Department

Leaders of the Music Department in succession were Mother Deborah Mason Patterson, Anna Crocket Ford (First Organizer and Director), and Dr. Mattie Moss Clark (1968, 1970–1994). The current president is Dr. Judith McAllister.

The National Evangelism Department

In the early years, this ministry was led by Overseer S. T. Samuel. Later Bishop Mason appointed Bishop L. C. Page to formally organize the Church Of God In Christ Department of Evangelism. From 1951 to 1999, National Evangelist Reatha Herndon served as the Department's Elect Lady. The current president is Dr. Elijah Hankerson.

The National Missions Department

Bishop Mason knew that the call of Jesus Christ was "to evangelize all nations." Elder

Searcy began Missions in 1925. In 1926 Elder C. G. Brown was appointed the first Executive Secretary. Bishop S. M. Crouch took up the mantle and served from 1937 to 1968. The current president is Bishop Corlis Moody.

The Department of Education

In 1918 Sister Pinkie Duncan and Professor James Courts established the first institution of learning in the Church Of God In Christ Saints Industrial and Literary School. Dr. Arenia C. Mallory (1905–1977), at the request of Bishop Mason, developed the school into an accredited Junior College. The current director is Dr. David Daniels.

International Conventions

These were formed for the growth of the International Departmental Ministries and were held annually for the designated purpose of training and promotion of Auxiliary Ministry on the local, district, and jurisdictions or state level.

The Church Of God In Christ Publishing House

In the earlier years, the Church found the publishing ministry of D. J. Young and family an extremely valuable resource for local churches. In 1968, through the vision of Presiding Bishop J. O. Patterson, the church would establish the COGIC Publishing House, with oversight provided for many years by Bishop Roy L. H. Winbush and Bishop Norman Quick as the Chairman of the Board with Dr. David Hall as the CEO of the Publishing House.

In 2009, a new Chairman and Publishing House Board were appointed by Presiding Bishop Charles E. Blake Sr. under the leadership of: John Daniels, Esq., Chairman of the Board. Inspired by the vision of Presiding Bishop J. O. Patterson, the laborious task of publishing provided a new face to the further institutionalization of COGIC influence. The Publishing House has provided local churches with literature for Sunday School, Y.P.W.W. (Young People's Willing Workers), Bible Band, and Home and Foreign Missions, as well as established the COGIC Bookstore, which has proven to be critical and invaluable in the expansion of the Church Of God In Christ. In 2013, Superintendent Mark Ellis was appointed as Chairman of the Publishing Board by Presiding Bishop Charles E. Blake Sr. The Publishing House has grown over the years and is now considered to be one of the most prestigious entities of the Church Of God In Christ.

New Departments and Conferences of Appointment

- Superintendent Linwood Dillard, Chairman of Auxiliaries In Ministry
- Bishop Darrell L. Hines, Chairman of the SIMUL Conference, Chairman of the Men's Conference
- Bishop Matthew Williams, Adjutant General
- Mother Willie Mae Rivers, General Supervisor of Women

- Mark Ellis, Chairman of the Publishing Board
- Sunday School Department, Bishop Alton Gatlin
- Evangelism Department, Dr. Elijah Hankerson
- Home & Foreign Missions, Bishop Carlis Moody
- Board of Education, Dr. David Daniels
- Music Department, Dr. Judith McAllister
- Department of Public Relations, Robert Coleman
- Department of Urban Initiatives, Bishop Edwin Bass

Annual Events

- Leadership Conference (January)
- General Assembly and Call Meeting (April) Memphis, TN
- International Women's Convention (May)
- National Judicial Conference (June)
- Auxiliaries in Ministry (AIM) Conference (June-July)
- General Council of Pastors and Elders (May)
- National SIMUL Conference (September) Memphis, TN
- Bishop Mason's Birthday (September) Memphis, TN
- Bishop's Conference (September)
- International Holy Convocation and General Assembly (November)

The Church Of God In Christ's Beliefs

The Church of God In Christ is a Trinitarian Pentecostal-holiness denomination. The church believes and teaches that there are three works of grace (salvation, sanctification, and Spirit baptism) that God bestows on believers. This is often testified by COGIC members in an affirmation: "I am saved, sanctified, baptized, and filled with the Holy Ghost." The church is considered Protestant and identified as a classical Pentecostal organization. COGIC is earnestly evangelical in its mission, fervently fundamental in doctrine, and purely Pentecostal in worship. The church is conservative in social, political, and cultural issues.

Our Affirmation of Faith

The beliefs of the Church Of God In Christ are briefly articulated in its Statement of Faith, which is reproduced below:

- We believe the Bible to be the inspired and only infallible written Word of God.

- We believe that there is One God, eternally existent in three Persons: God the Father, God the Son, and God the Holy Spirit.
- We believe in the Blessed Hope, which is the rapture of the Church of God, which is in Christ, at His return.
- We believe that the only means of being cleansed from sin is through repentance and faith in the precious Blood of Jesus Christ.
- We believe that the regeneration by the Holy Ghost is absolutely essential for personal salvation.
- We believe that the redemptive work of Christ on the Cross provides healing for the human body in answer to believing prayer.
- We believe that the Baptism of the Holy Ghost, according to Acts 2:4, is given to believers who ask for it.
- We believe in the sanctifying power of the Holy Spirit, by whose indwelling the Christian is enabled to live a Holy and separated life in the present world. Amen.

Bishop Charles Harrison Mason's legacy has been preserved through his successors. After his death, according to the 1952 Church Constitution, the control of the church reverted to the Board of Bishops, but the constitution did not specifically outline a clear successor or the powers granted to the leadership after his death. The General Assembly vested authority in an Executive Board composed of twelve bishops. Hence, Bishop O.T. Jones Sr. was unanimously acclaimed Senior Bishop by the General Assembly because of his seniority and remained until 1965.

The Legacy is Preserved and Continues

Bishop Ozro T. Jones Sr. (1962-1968)

Bishop O. T. Jones was the only remaining of the five original bishops. However, what many didn't know was that his health was failing him at the time of his elevation. Bishop Jones was born March 26, 1891 and died September 23, 1972 in Fort Smith, Arkansas; he was the son of Baptist parents, Marion and Mary Jones. As a young man, in 1912, he experienced and confessed salvation and "spirit baptism" or "infilling" as a second work of grace. He answered a call to the ministry under the guidance of Elder Justus Bowe, a COGIC pioneer. Soon afterwards, he, his older sister, and a brother developed into an evangelistic team in North Arkansas and the surrounding states. Over the next few years, 18 congregations were established as a direct result of their evangelistic endeavors.

His educational ability and passion for Bishop Mason's style and expression of sanctified living and doctrinal underpinnings inspired Bishop Jones to preserve and codify the teachings and doctrines as taught by Bishop Mason. In 1914, Jones organized the youth department of the Church Of God In Christ and served as its first president. Two years later, he founded and edited the Y.P.W.W. Quarterly Topics, an education-oriented journal. Because of this curriculum, countless Church Of God In Christ children have been raised.

Bishop Jones was one of the first men Bishop Mason consecrated as a Jurisdictional Prelate. In 1920, he was appointed assistant to the state overseer in Oklahoma.

Assuming his power as the Senior Bishop in 1961 upon Mason's death, Bishop O. T. Jones Sr. became the Senior Bishop of the Church Of God In Christ. He inherited a seemingly fragmented and shocked organization. His tenure proved problematic because he felt his authority was the same as Bishop Mason's power when he was alive; Bishop Jones made decisions and appointments without collaboration and consensus of the Board of Bishops, General Assembly, or the Executive Board.

Because of this, disagreement soon arose over the power and the authority of the Senior Bishop and of the Executive Board at the Fifty-Seventh Holy Convocation in 1964. Factions developed and controversy engulfed the organization as executive and administrative decisions were being made with the Senior Bishop and the Executive Board often conflicting with one another. In 1966, Bishop O. T. Jones was removed from the office of Senior Bishop by the General Assembly for misuse of power and misrepresentation of the office of Senior Bishop; however, he continued to be honored as the "Senior" Bishop of the church and he remained steadfast and faithful to his calling as the leader of the growing denomination and as a premier preacher and educator.

Therefore, in 1966, suits were filed in the Chancery Court of Shelby County, Tennessee, to resolve the legitimate authority controversy of the denomination. The court ordered COGIC to convene a Constitutional Convention in February 1968. The Constitutional Convention drafted and approved a new constitution that dissolved both the office of the Senior Bishop and the Executive Board. These were replaced by the office of the Presiding Bishop and a General Board who would be elected every four years to preside over the church. The General Assembly would have the supreme authority over the church to decide matters of faith and practice. On November 14, 1968, the General Assembly of the COGIC elected the first General Board and Presiding Bishop of the church.

First General Board 1968–1972

- Bishop J. O. Patterson Sr.—Presiding Bishop
- Bishop J. S. Bailey—First Assistant Presiding Bishop
- Bishop S. M. Crouch—Second Assistant Presiding Bishop
- Bishop W. N. Wells
- Bishop L. H. Ford
- Bishop O. M. Kelly
- Bishop C. E. Bennett
- Bishop J. A. Blake
- Bishop J. W. White

- Bishop D. L. Williams
- Bishop F. D. Washington
- Bishop J. D. Husband

Our founder and Chief Apostle, Bishop Charles Harrison Mason, was succeeded by men of vision with an ear for God and a passion for people. After a long court struggle, the General Board emerged as the new leadership structure for the executive branch of the church. Our leaders since that time have been:

Senior and Presiding Bishops

- Bishop Charles Harrison Mason, 1907–1961—Founder and First Senior Bishop
- Bishop Ozro Thurston Jones Sr., 1962–1968—Second Senior Bishop
- Bishop James Oglethorpe Patterson Sr., 1968–1989—First Elected Presiding Bishop (elected six times)
- Bishop Louis Henry Ford, 1990–1995—Second Elected Presiding Bishop (elected twice)
- Bishop Chandler David Owens, 1995–2000—Third Elected Presiding Bishop (elected once)
- Bishop Gilbert Earl Patterson, 2000–2007—Fourth Elected Presiding Bishop (elected twice)
- Bishop Charles Edward Blake, 2007–Present—Fifth Elected Presiding Bishop (elected twice)

Bishop James O. Patterson Sr. (1968–1989)

Bishop J. O. Patterson Sr. became the first Presiding Bishop of the Church Of God In Christ, which ended a seven-year crisis in the Church. A native of Derma, Mississippi, he was born July 21, 1912. He had four sisters, Argie, Alice, Retha, and Lillian, and one brother, William. He was educated in the public school system in Memphis, Tennessee, and received further training in religious studies at the Howe School of Religion, which later became a part of LeMoyne-Owen College in Memphis, Tennessee. In 1934, he married Deborah Mason, the daughter of Bishop C. H. Mason, the founder of the Church Of God In Christ. Deborah M. Patterson died in 1985, and in 1989, Bishop Patterson married Mary Peak Patterson. Bishop Patterson acknowledged his call to preach in 1932 and was ordained an Elder in the COGIC in 1935 by Bishop A. B. McEwen Sr. The Elder (Bishop) J. O. Patterson pastored congregations in Gates, Brownsville, and Memphis, Tennessee, and he served a congregation in East Orange, New Jersey. In 1941, he became pastor of Woodlawn Church of God in Christ (now known as Pentecostal Temple Institutional Church of God in Christ), in Memphis, Tennessee. During his 48-year tenure, the church grew in membership from fewer than twenty to more than three thousand. During this time, Patterson was also owner of the successful J. O. Patterson Funeral Home and was heavily involved in community activities. Church leaders noticed his spiritual leadership, business acumen, and ability to communicate. He was also the pastor of Pentecostal Temple COGIC.

Bishop Louis Henry Ford (1990–1995)

Bishop Louis Henry Ford became the fourth succeeding Presiding Bishop of the Church Of God In Christ and was know as a man of inexhaustible energy.

Named after Henry Ford, the American car maker and automobile industrialist, Bishop Louis Henry Ford was born in 1914 in Chicago, Illinois. From the very start, having been raised in the COGIC, Bishop Ford wanted to be a preacher for the Church Of God In Christ and wanted to "use the church as a platform to spread the unadulterated Gospel of Jesus Christ," as he said in the Holy Convocation in Memphis, Tennessee in 1992. He began preaching in the countryside around Lexington, Miss., while attending college there in the early 1930s. He moved to Chicago in 1933 and preached on the street until founding St. Paul's in Chicago in 1935.

As a son the ministry of Bishop Mason, Bishop Ford never forgot his Mississippi roots. He walked with Bishop Mason as a youthful and dedicated pastor. Ford often utilized the past as a point of reference for present decisions. He came into office when the Church Of God In Christ was in transition from its traditional past to an era of modernity. The formation and emergence of charismatic renewal and the Word Churches challenged the orthodoxy of the Church Of God In Christ. What made Ford's tenure as Presiding Bishop very memorable was his stand and his views on the Biblical doctrine of holiness. Bishop Ford was a strong and powerful advocate for biblical holiness and he encouraged all the members of the church to adhere to the teachings of holiness in the Old Testament and New Testament of the Holy Bible. He also taught that after you get saved and start living holy, you must have the Holy Ghost. Bishop Ford was the main person who introduced the doctrine that besides being saved by the grace of God through Jesus Christ, that being baptized and filled with the Holy Ghost in biblical standards was one of the most important things of being a good, saved Christian.

After being elected to the office of Presiding Bishop, Ford began spreading missions to help the poor and the needy throughout the United States and built homeless shelters throughout Tennessee and the rest of the United States. He was succeeded by Bishop Chandler D. Owens.

Bishop Chandler D. Owens (1995–2000)

Bishop Chandler D. Owens (October 1, 1931—March 6, 2011) was an American minister, youth organizer, and ordained pastor. Bishop C.D. Owens was the fifth in succession of the Presiding Bishop of the Church Of God In Christ. He was a talented child and credits the church for saving his life from the extreme poverty found in the South. His attentiveness and participation in the ministry of the Church at an early age prepared him for leadership.

All over the world he was know for his eloquent, big, beautiful, baritone voice. Preachers wanted to be able to speak just like him because he gradually became a favorite of the Church. He served as pastor, the International Youth President, Jurisdictional Prelate, Constitutional Committee Chairman, as well as other ecclesiastical roles. He led the Constitutional Convention of 1972, which proved to be a milestone in the organizational life of the Church Of God In Christ. During the time that he served as Presiding Bishop, he brought the Church into a new era of wealth and development.

In 1996, Bishop Owens was invited to give the official prayer for worldwide leaders at the 1997 Presidential Inaugural. He was also selected to serve as co-chairman of the President's Summit for America's Future Committee and was honored by *Ebony* Magazine in April 1997 as one of the 100 most influential Black men in America. Bishop Owens was a prototype leader who expanded the prerogatives of leadership wherever he served. He was succeeded by Bishop Gilbert Earl Patterson. Bishop Chandler died March 2011.

Bishop Gilbert Earl Patterson (2000–2007)

Bishop Gilbert Earl Patterson (September 22, 1939–March 20, 2007) affectionately known as G. E. Patterson brought to the office of the Presiding Bishop a wealth of experience as a telecommunications minister. He was the sixth in succession as the Presiding Bishop of the Church Of God In Christ. Bishop Patterson's parents were Bishop William Archie "W. A." (1898–1991) and Mary Louise Williams Patterson (1901–1981). He was born in the parsonage next door to the Church of God in Christ in Humboldt, Tennessee and is the youngest of six children. Bishop Patterson accepted Christ as his Savior at 11 years old at Holy Temple COGIC in Memphis, Tennessee. Shortly after, the family moved to Detroit, Michigan. He accepted his call to ministry in 1956 while he was only 16 years old at the church his father pastored. Bishop J. S. Bailey ordained him in 1958 as an elder in the Church Of God In Christ. In 1962, Bishop Patterson became co-pastor with his father at Holy Temple Church of God in Christ in Memphis. However, he continued his pastorate in 1975 as the founder and pastor of Temple of Deliverance, the Cathedral of the Bountiful Blessings near downtown, where it is said that he had 18,000 on its membership roll.

Bishop G. E. Patterson was a well-known evangelist and preacher; some called him the preacher's preacher par excellence. He had weekly local telecast and was viewed by millions of individuals around the world. The reach and scope of Bishop Patterson's ministry is unparalleled in the Church Of God In Christ. In the year of 2000, Calhoun Street where Bountiful Blessing is located was renamed G. E. Patterson Ave., in honor of the bishop.

Bishop G. E. Patterson was the representative of something old and something new as he bridged two centuries. When he came to the leadership of the Church, there was a need for coalition building around spiritual unity, organizational peace, and the need to refocus the Church as the pentecostal entity of relevance. He would occasionally say the Church must remain true to the past, but embrace the future! In his prerogative as leader, he reinforced our position in charitable giving and social ministries with the creation of COGIC Charities.

Bishop Charles Edward Blake Sr. (2007–Present)

The Church Of God In Christ experienced a transitional period with the passing of Bishop G. E. Patterson. Bishop Blake is the seventh in succession as the Presiding Bsihop of the Church Of God In Christ. Bishop Blake was born August 5, 1940, in Little Rock, Arkansas. In November 2007, a special election was conducted, and he was elected to complete the unexpired term of Bishop G.E. Patterson as the Presiding Bishop. In November 2008, Bishop Charles E. Blake Sr. was re-elected to serve a four-year term as Presiding Bishop of the Church Of God In Christ. Bishop Blake brings a blended and unique combination of administrative skills, global vision, and spiritual focus. Clearly, he represents the contemporary face of a global Pentecostalism by advancing spiritual, economic, educational, and familial initiatives within the denomination. As a seasoned churchman, his inclusive leadership style has provided the opportunity for broad-based participation of membership in the Church Of God In Christ.

Bishop Blake became the Jurisdictional Bishop of Southern California First in 1985 where he served as the Ecclesiastical Jurisdictional Prelate until 2009, overseeing more than 250 churches that comprised the jurisdiction. He was succeeded by Bishop Joe L. Ealy.

Bishop Blake is a spiritual motivator who is astute in world business systems. He leads by example and has transformed church culture throughout the denomination. He is a consummate visionary and knows how to inspire others who share his vision. He is the pastor of West Angeles Church Of God In Christ with a membership of more than 26,000. West Angeles is deeply involved in providing not only for the spiritual life of its people, but also provides more than 80 programs for psychological, social, and economic enhancement of the community. Bishop is the founder and CEO of Save Africa's Children. He oversees the support of more than 100,000 children in 340 orphan care programs throughout more than 123 nations on the continent of Africa.

Before Bishop Blake ascended to the office of Presiding Bishop, he was the First Assistant Presiding Bishop to Bishop G. E. Patterson. In addition, he was a General Board member for several years, served as founding Chairman of the Board of Directors for C.H. Mason Theological Seminary and served as editor of the Young People's Willing Workers (Y.P.W.W.) topics. He has served as an Executive Committee Member on the Board of Directors of the Interdenominational Theological Seminary; Chairman of Oral Roberts

University Board of Directors; and Executive Committee and Director of the International Charismatic Bible Ministries. Bishop Blake has received numerous awards, commendations, and accolades from government, civic, and ecumenical entities.

Again in November 2012, Bishop Charles Edward Blake Sr. was re-elected to serve another four-year term as the Presiding Bishop of the Church Of God In Christ by General Assembly delegates who also elected four new members to the General Board, with seven returning incumbents.

Branches of Governing of the Church Of God In Christ and Their Descriptions

We, the members of the Constitution Committee Commission of the Church Of God In Christ, count serving our great church a privilege. As we continue to move forward the mandate of our Chairman Hunt, that every member of the Church Of God In Christ understand and fully appreciate all the rights afforded them by our constitution. In addition to understanding our constitutional rights, it is significantly important that every member of our great church understand its mechanism, which consist of the Legislative Branch (General Assembly), the Executive Branch (Executive Board), and the Judicial Branches (Judiciary Board) of government. Their descriptions are as follows:

General Assembly

Chairman Superintendent James Hunt, Vice-Chairman Bishop L.H. Thuston

The General Assembly is the sole entity to create legislation for the governance of the Church Of God In Christ, including but not limited to expressing doctrine, creating law, and electing officials. It is the only Branch with these enumerated powers. Its laws shall be binding on all members of the Church Of God In Christ, Inc.

General Board

The Presiding Bishop is the spiritual leader of the Church of God in Christ, Inc.

The General Board shall exercise all powers, expressed and implied, which shall be necessary and proper to execute the day-to-day operations of the church and all powers vested in it by the constitution and bylaws of the church, regardless of whether the General Assembly is in session.

Judicial Branch

Chief Justice Thomas Jackson

The Judiciary Board is (1) the final court of appeals, hearing disputes appealed from decisions of subordinate tribunals and (2) an ecclesiastical court of first instance as prescribed by the constitution and (3) the ultimate authority on matters of constitutional interpretation.

The Legislative Branch does not execute the laws; the Executive Branch does not make the laws and the Judicial Branch does not execute the laws.

The description of each branch of government constitutes separation of power, the prevention of any entity's motivation of self-interest to violate the rights of others.

Members of the General Board, Quadrennial 2012–2016

- Bishop Charles E. Blake Sr.—Presiding Bishop (2007–present)
- Bishop Phillip A. Brooks—First Assistant Presiding Bishop (1984–present)
- Bishop Jerry W. Macklin—Second Assistant Presiding Bishop (2004–present)
- Bishop Roy L. H. Winbush—Secretary of the General Board (1988–present)
- Bishop Frank O. White—Assistant Secretary of the General Board (2008–present)
- Bishop George D. McKinney—Board Member (2000–present)
- Bishop Nathaniel W. Wells—Board Member (2000–present)
- Bishop Sedgwick Daniels—Board Member (2008–present)
- Bishop J. Drew Sheard—Board Member (2012–present)
- Bishop Brandon B. Porter—Board Member (2012–present)
- Bishop Ted G. Thomas Sr.—Board Member (2012–present)
- Bishop Lawrence Wooten—Board Member (2012–present)

Executive Elected Officers of the Board of Bishops, *Quadrennial 2012–2016*

- Bishop John H. Sheard, Chairman
- Bishop Donald R. Murray, 1st Vice Chairman
- Bishop Albert Galbraith Jr., 2nd Vice Chairman
- Bishop Larry L. Shaw, Secretary to the Board of Bishops

General Assembly Elected Officers, 2011–2015

- Superintendent James Hunt, Chairman
- Bishop Lemuel Thuston

National Trustee Board, *Quadrennial 2012–2016*

- Superintendent Dwight Walls, Chairman
- Supervisor Mildred Linzy, Ph.D., 1st Vice Chairman
- Assistant Supervisor Sylvia Law, 2nd Vice Chairman
- Pastor Melton Timmons, Secretary

- Evangelist Cari Barnes
- Pastor Darin Burns
- Superintendent Joseph Chase, Ph.D.
- Pastor Michael Golden
- Elder David Hall Jr.
- Evangelist Sandra S. Jones
- Evangelist Georgia Lowe
- Elder Joseph Shepherd
- Elder Amos Smith
- Dr. Ailene Stingley
- Bishop William Watson Jr.

Elected Judiciary Board

- Superintendent Thomas Jackson Jr., Chief Justice
- Bishop E. Charles Connor
- Bishop F. E. Perry
- Judge Cassandra Lewis
- Dr. Valda Slack
- Elder Talbert Swan

Elected Officers of Pastors & Elders

- Administrative Assistant Michael Eaddy, Chairman
- Administrative Assistant Destry Bell, Vice Chairman
- Superintendent Prince E. Bryan II, Secretary
- Elder Thomas May, Treasurer

Annual Events

- Leadership Conference (January)
- General Assembly and Call Meeting (April), Memphis, TN
- International Women's Convention (May)
- National Judicial Conference (June)
- Auxiliaries in Ministry (AIM) Conference (June-July)

- General Council of Pastors and Elders (May)
- National SIMUL Conference (September), Memphis, TN
- Bishop Mason's Birthday (September), Memphis, TN
- Bishop's Conference (September)
- International Holy Convocation and General Assembly (November)

The impact and influence of the Church Of God In Christ is global in the twenty-first century. The very essence and mark of the original vision of our founder and Chief Apostle Bishop Charles Harrison Mason continues to be the three branches of governance. It is this unique polity of the Church Of God In Christ's organizational structure that gives local churches the freedom and authority to exercise their creativity in ministry. Pastors are responsible to superintendents, who are responsible to bishops, in a network of mutual responsibility and accountability as each seeks to implement the original vision of our founder. Global ministries make their impact from "sea to shining sea" as new ministries are spawned as we enthusiastically make known God's deeds among the nations.

Writings were taken from the following contributors: Bishop Ithiel Clemmons, Dr. David Daniels, Bishop Davvid Hall, Sr., Mother Francis A. Curtis, Elder Talbert Swann II, Bishop Jack Whitehead Jr., Mother Dr. Barbara McCoo Lewis, Mother Pearl Page Brown, Bishop Robert Asberry, Bishop George D. McKinney, Bishop Martin Luther Johnson, Elder Scott Bradley, Bishop Bob Jackson, and Mother Mae Winbush, Professor Alonzo Johnson, Mother Clara C. Clemmons, M.Ed.

Submitted by: Sandra S Jones, Chair of Marketing – Church Of God In Christ, Publishing Board/Vice President

ABOUT THE ARTIST

Curtis Lewis is an extraordinary artist considered to be one of the most renowned contemporary artists in the art world today. Lewis has been called "The Artist of Champions and Icons." He is the grandson of Church Of God In Christ pastor Mack Davis and nephew of Bishop Fred Lewis of Michigan.

Lewis was born in 1952 in Grand Rapids, Michigan. He began demonstrating his artistic talents early and began illustrating at the age of five. By junior high school, he was painting and excelled at honors art courses; during this time, he received several Scholastic Arts awards. While in high school, he took courses at the Detroit Institute of Art (DIA) and was invited to lecture and exhibit his work at the University of Detroit Mercy and Wayne State University.

In 1968, after a class at the DIA, Lewis had a prophetic encounter in an elevator with U.S. Congressman John Conyers Jr. at the J.L. Hudson building in Detroit. Conyers observed Lewis' sketchbook and asked to see his work, then said, "You have a great gift, and one day you will be a prolific artist." Lewis never forgot that encounter and determined at that moment that it was up to him to make that prophecy come true—not knowing that Congressman Conyers would one day become a subject of one of Lewis's most prestigious collections, "The Executive Collection."

In 1970, Lewis was awarded a full art scholarship to the School of the Art Institute of Chicago and the University of Chicago, where he studied fine and commercial art. Lewis became a highly skilled illustrator, portraiture painter, and muralist.

His first commission was the portrait of sports legend Spencer Haywood, 1968 Olympic gold medalist with the United States men's basketball team. Haywood later became a member of the NBA Championship Lakers team. It was the start of Lewis' immortalizing notable figures on canvas. Lewis received subsequent commissions to paint prominent judicial, political, sports, and society figures, including Rev. Jesse Jackson, C.L. Franklin, Aretha Franklin, Angela Davis, Bishop David Ellis, PAW Presiding Bishop Charles Ellis, Heisman Trophy winner and #1 1980 Detroit Lions draft pick Billy Sims, MLB Hall of Famer Willie Horton, NBA superstar and former mayor Dave Bing, NHL champion Steve Yzerman, Muhammad Ali, Justice Stephen Cooper, CEO Bob Gillette, Bernice King, civil rights icon Rosa Parks, and many more.

Inspired by the works of Diego Rivera, Lewis began painting murals and added to his body of work more than 200 murals. Lewis's works often reflect his passions for sports, icons, champions, history, and social issues. Among his most celebrated achievements and murals, Lewis was the first artist to unveil a mural saluting Joe Louis at Joe Louis Arena, the first major arena named after a Black man. Lewis also was the first artist to unveil a championship mural during an NBA World Championship game in 1990 at the Palace of Auburn Hills for the World Champion Pistons. He also unveiled the second championship Piston Mural in 2004 at the Pistons Hoop City Restaurant. In 2000, GM sponsored Lewis' Tiger Woods mural "Eye of the Tiger" at the Buick Open two weeks after Woods won the Grand Slam of Golf. Woods also signed the mural. Lewis was the first artist to unveil a mural of the first African American President at the Church Of God In Christ Holy Convocation in the FedExForum. In 2004, Lewis received a presidential call from the White House, congratulating him for his one-man show "The Southfield Heritage Dream Ball," qualifying him for the Guinness Book of World Records by being the first artist to unveil leaders of five levels of government simultaneously: Mayor Brenda Lawrence, Governor Jennifer Granholm, Congressman John Conyers, Senator Carl Levin, and President George W. Bush. Congressman Conyers was the keynote speaker for the evening, years after encouraging Lewis.

Lewis is also founder and CEO of World Class Icon Publishing LLC. He has published over 22 children's coloring and reading books. His books have gone into school districts, as well as religious and retail markets as far north as Alaska and as far south as Australia. Lewis is grateful to the Lord for his gifts and recognizes that only what you do for Christ will last.

TEACHING TECHNIQUES

A RECIPE FOR HOPE

One thing we can count on is that sometime in our lives we will go through hard times. As a part of a community or as an individual, you do not need a prophet to predict that you will experience trouble in this journey of life. This is one of humanity's lowest common denominators, and many do not know how to sustain hope during the seasons of hardship and suffering that we all experience. When it comes to sustaining hope, the most basic principle is to place your hope in someone or something that is worthy of hope. Many place their hope in the next political candidate, only to have their hopes dashed when the candidate's promises fail. Others place their hope in relationships, only to see their trust and love abused or taken for granted. Often people place their hope in money, and the economy shows them how unstable riches and wealth can be. The surest way to sustain hope is to place it in God. Even when we do this, our hope can diminish and we can falter along the way. Sustaining hope is about persevering for the long haul. There is a recipe for sustaining hope during the hard times and it consists of four ingredients: promises, people, prayer, and presence.

We Need Promises (Romans 15:4)

Paul explains to the church in Rome that we can persevere and continue in our walk with Christ because of the promises of Scripture. He says that the ultimate goal of the things that were written is that we would have encouragement and hope. These Scriptures written in the past sustain us in the present as we wait for their fulfillment in the future. We can only gain more hope as we learn and think on the fulfillment of what God has promised. What has He promised? He has promised us a kingdom where we live with Him forever (see Matthew 19:29). He has promised that we would have resurrected bodies and overflowing joy (see Psalm 16:9-11). Meditating on promises like these can only serve to steer us toward hope in God.

We Need People (1 Thessalonians 4:13–18)

In 1 Thessalonians 4:13–18, Paul lets the believers know that they do not have to grieve as those who have no hope. He then goes on to explain the hope of the resurrection and the second coming of Jesus. He describes how the Lord will come and that all who believe, whether living or dead, will rise to be with Him forever. Then He says to encourage each other with these words. The way that we can sustain hope is by being surrounded by others who have the same hope. The people we have around us can either discourage us so that we throw that hope away, or encourage us so that we keep that hope in our hearts alive. This does not mean that we should avoid at all costs people who have no hope, for Jesus calls us to love and care for those in need. Instead, we must continue to remind each other of the hope in Jesus so that we can make it through the difficulties that we and others face.

We Need Prayer (Psalm 65:5)

The psalmist declares that God faithfully answers the prayers of His people. Then he further adds that the Lord is the hope of everyone on the face of the earth. Prayer, especially answered prayer, increases our hope. When we have seen God do amazing things in our lives, our hope is more steadfast and resilient. We know what God has done and this enables us to trust Him more for future acts. As we lean into prayer, we recall a big God who does big things and our small hope is enlarged to handle the storms of life.

We Need Presence (Romans 5:5, 15:13)

Paul explains in Romans 5 that we have a hope that doesn't disappoint us. Why? Because the love of God is overflowing in our hearts. We experience God's love. We experience that we are His and He will never leave us or forsake us. How does this happen? Through the presence of his Holy Spirit in our hearts, we know that God loves us. Later, in Romans 15:13, Paul prays that God would give the church in Rome joy and peace and that they would overflow with confident hope through the power of the Holy Spirit. Through the presence of God filling us with joy and peace, we have confident hope as we face the many trials of life.

That is the recipe for hope. When disaster strikes and crisis invades our lives, we can sustain hope through God's promises, people, prayer, and presence. Many things may trouble us and douse the fire of our hope. Every day we read of terrorist attacks, unstable economies, and unspeakable crimes, but we have a hope that will outlast the present age. With this kind of hope we can say like Jeremiah in Lamentations 3:21–23: "This I recall to my mind, therefore have I hope. It is of the LORD's mercies that we are not consumed, because his compassions fail not. They are new every morning: great is thy faithfulness."

TEACHING TECHNIQUES

INTERNATIONAL SUNDAY SCHOOL DEPARTMENT

YOUNG ADULT & COLLEGIATE SUNDAY SCHOOL MINISTRY

BY PASTOR A.L.SHAW-DIRECTOR

INTRODUCTION

The life of the 18- to 29-year-old young adult is a time of enormous emotional, mental, and spiritual challenge. The purpose of this information is to share an understanding of the growth potential these young adults possess. During this season in life, these young souls are challenged to learn how to live on their own, establish careers, choose life partners, and most vitally, start to own and develop their faith apart from the life experiences of their childhood.

In light of this tremendous ministry opportunity, many traditional Sunday Schools are experiencing a difficult time. More than half of the young people who went to church as teens drop out of attending church after leaving high school. Today, the style of ministry that appeals to older generations is becoming less and less popular among young adults. It is the mandate of ministry everywhere to provide solutions that address the question of why so many young people aged 18–29 leave the church and question the faith they embraced as children.

It is my belief that the answer to this dilemma of building successful Young Adult & Collegiate Sunday School Classes at the local church or building a campus Sunday School ministry is found in developing strategies which include the following key components:

- actively promoting intimate relationships
- utilizing social media models to connect and communicate with collegiate young adults
- developing innovative church service formats

The good news is that the potential for churches desiring to engage in collegiate young adult Sunday School ministry is incredible. People are recognizing that the young adult and collegiate stage of life is a time of searching, establishing new relationships, and discovering purpose.

Our Mission: To support and strengthen young adult and collegiate believers in their walk of faith with God during college.

Our Vision: To connect young adult and collegiate believers to the resources needed to nurture their spiritual growth during the college and young adult years of life.

The focus of the International Sunday School Department's Young Adult & Collegiate Sunday School Ministry is to *effectively present* the Gospel of Christ while developing engaging, Spirit-filled, Word-empowered college-age believers.

THE CHARACTERISTICS OF AN EFFECTIVE YOUNG ADULT & COLLEGIATE SUNDAY SCHOOL MINISTRY:

- Be flexible, relevant, transparent, supportive, and participatory
- Be Bible-based, Jesus-focused, and Spirit-led
- Be both evangelistic and discipleship-driven
- Involve students in leadership roles
- Be rooted in love and designed to build genuine relationships

EXAMINE THE CULTURE YOU PLAN TO REACH

Some churches may find that they are only able to connect with students who grew up with them. This is perfectly appropriate for part of a college student strategy, but those churches hoping to involve students from local colleges in their ministry must get to know the students and the mission fields they plan to reach.

Examining the local campus contexts involves spending time there, walking the campus, and talking with those already ministering there and connecting with both present and former students.

Every campus is unique. As you get to know a campus, your understanding of this unique "tribe" will grow. **What are the unique characteristics of this campus?** Many characteristics—everything from the spiritual climate to the number of students who commute to school—could have drastic effects on your church's specific eventual college student strategy.

KEYS FOR LAUNCHING YOUNG ADULT & COLLEGIATE SUNDAY SCHOOL MINISTRY

1. The Key is Leadership. Whoever leads the ministry can either sink it or make it steam ahead. There are probably two key qualities for leading a Young Adult & Collegiate Sunday School ministry: being relational and being authentic. You have to build your group through authentic relational leadership.

2. Build Through Relationships. This can't be overstated. Collegiate young adults are students who are rational. It's what drives them. College-age students are critical thinkers and want to know if you're in it for them or if you really do care. Trust comes in increments, and you need to earn it before you give insight into their lives.

3. Engage in the Culture. This means more to them than denominational traditions. Young adult and collegiate students don't want to run away from their world, but rather they want to challenge and change it. They possess a faith that will help them to decide for themselves about critical life issues.

4. Nurture a Community Environment. It takes time to develop a group of young people to see outside their own world. That is why some activities involve local service projects and support ministries at local churches.

5. Be Consistent. As with any age group, young people will trust you more if you are consistent. Don't start a midweek study and then drop it after two weeks. They need an anchor, even if they don't say so at this point. So be consistent, even if they are not.

These ministry solution ideas are designed to provide a construct to launch your Young Adult & Collegiate Sunday School ministry. Further, these tips provide insight to assist your local church to become successful in ministering to this group of young people.

Every church that encounters college students must decide how it plans to impact them. As you spend the necessary time to understand your mission field and the practical possibilities for reaching it, God will lead your church to a specific Young Adult & Collegiate Sunday School Ministry strategy that fits it best. Young adults aren't in this age range long, so you have a short time frame to connect with them and integrate them into your local church.

10 QUESTIONS BEFORE YOU BEGIN OR EXPAND YOUR SUNDAY SCHOOL MINISTRY TO COLLEGE YOUNG ADULTS.

1. Are young adults attracted to your church and ministry?

2. Does your church view college ministry as part of its church outreach?

3. Does your church have an established and effective ministry to young adults?

4. Does your church have young adults in leadership/decision-making roles?

5. Is your church helping students transition from high school to college?

6. Is the ministry of collegiate young adults in line with the vision of the pastor?

7. Does your church have the capacity to start a ministry on a college campus?

8. Do you have young adults who are willing to be part of the leadership team?

9. Does your church have the financial resources to sustain a campus ministry?

10. Will your church collaborate with other churches to support campus ministry?

BEGIN WITH THE END IN MIND

Do everything with your end goal in mind. Determine and define the purpose and develop the structure of a college ministry that fits your congregation.

Church-based Ministry: Primarily provides support to young adults who are members of your church.

Campus-based Ministry: Primarily provides ministry on the college campus.

Church-based Campus Ministry: Provides ministry on campus with opportunities to connect to the local church.

Campus Ministry Support: Supports a partner church's ministry on campus.

DETERMINE WHO YOU ARE TRYING TO REACH

Determine if you want to provide ministry to everyone or target niche groups. Besides athletes, Greek organizations, international students, and ethnic-specific ministries, there are other strong candidates for niche-based ministry at many campuses.

It is important to set goals or establish success factors for the Young Adult & Collegiate Sunday School ministry. This will help the church know if you are making progress. Measurements should be based on the type of campus ministry the church chooses to become.

Examples could include: how many 18–29-age students attend Sunday service, how many college students attend special events, how students are engaged by the college ministry coordinator, student feedback, salvations, etc.

Programs to draw attention and attract a crowd are not what will make your Young Adult & Collegiate Sunday School ministry succeed with college students. You don't need another church service especially designed for them. Therefore, we must learn to develop other ideas and strategies on how to help young people develop and maintain a vibrant faith that they embrace throughout their college years and beyond.

The chief element needed for effective young adult and collegiate ministry is the presence and participation of dedicated church members who are willing to spend time supporting and encouraging these young adults, teaching and helping them live out the principles and the biblical truths found in Sunday School instruction. All of us—pastors, lay leaders, and parents—must equip young people with the resources to live *"in the world, but not of the world"* and to avoid the mishaps which occur during this period of transition from teenagers to adults.

Typically, believers who are older and seasoned in their faith and walk with God need to show what it means to be deeply committed to the simple truths of holiness and the Word of God. Spiritual individuals are needed who are willing to open up their lives to these young people and give them glimpses into real life experiences. Jesus shared of Himself by imparting wisdom into the lives of those He met. He showed them what it meant to be faithful by letting people into His life.

CONDUCT RESEARCH BEFORE YOU DEVELOP A STRATEGY

As you spend time discerning your ultimate plan, consider these final ideas:

Consult with other local college ministry leaders. If you plan to reach out to a local campus, one of the best ways to put the plan together is to discuss the possibilities with other college ministry leaders there. If they believe your church wants the same thing, they usually respond favorably and will help your church think about the unique role it might play.

Consider potential partnerships. Every church should be open to a college student strategy that involves partnering with other ministries—either other local churches or campus-based groups. Partnership can enable college ministries to more easily reach a dynamic size, display unity to a watching campus, learn from experienced college ministers, and share resources, leadership, and other ideas.

It's okay to be small. A church doesn't have to build a full-fledged ministry to make a difference. Anything a church does to provide solutions to the needs of these young people is valuable.

Formulate a long-term ministry strategy. The church must also be willing to invest enough financially to give the ministry room to grow. Once the strategy and leader are in place, the church must be patient; healthy college ministries often take several years to show much growth or identity.

Make your college student strategy unique and specific. It is my hope that many churches who purposefully work out their college student plan will arrive at an altogether unique solution for their church. Just as every college campus is different, so is every church different.

Therefore, whether your church is "traditional" or "non-traditional," your approach to Young Adult & Collegiate Sunday School ministry should be based on what you have discovered about your church and its unique role in the kingdom and the mission of ***"Taking Sunday School EVERYWHERE."***

Bomar, Chuck. *College Ministry 101: A Guide to Working with 18-25 Year Olds.*

Boyd, Damian L. *College Impact: Empowering Collegiate Christians for Campus Influence.*

Lutz, Stephen. *College Ministry in the Post-Christian Culture.* (*Highly Recommended:* This book is a wake-up call for the campus ministries and churches that are failing miserably to engage emerging adults. Steve Lutz clearly explains why college ministry is so desperately needed and offers a paradigm to effectively minister to today's students.)

Additional Resources

Presenter: Tyrone Roderick Williams. Email: tyrone.williams@hotmail.com. Cell: 404-519-6837

Building Church Leaders. Resources from Christianity Today's *Leadership Journal.* www.buildingchurchleaders.com

Cru Church Partners Handbook. crupartners.wikidot.com

APPENDIX A

"THE SHIFT"

Young Adult & Collegiate Sunday School Ministry Training For Church Leaders

By Pastor A.L. Shaw

Director – COGIC ISSD *"Love Alive"* Campus Ministries

Texas South Central Jurisdiction

INTRODUCTION

The college student is a young, energetic, and innovative individual who is an asset to the kingdom of God. It is our mission as leaders to address their concerns regarding this new phase of life as they approach full adulthood. They serve a vital and necessary component of growth in the local church.

In order to achieve this missive, ministry leaders must adhere to a systematic way of pulling together the various components of the local, district, and jurisdictional work in order to develop a balanced college ministry approach.

The Local Congregation and Leadership

The local church and its congregation provide a foundation and support system during this important time in the life of the college student.

The college institution serves as the source for their educational development, social network, and introduction to community involvement. However, the local church provides the source of spiritual and emotional well-being as the college student transitions to adulthood.

You must first identify young adult and collegiate ministry within the vision and scope of the pastor and the local congregation. Do the characteristics of your church in term of age, education, location near a local campus, and church culture provide a basis for a Sunday School college ministry?

The Importance of Leadership

Leaders must embrace all ministry for the purpose of fulfilling the Great Commission mandate given by Jesus Christ (Matthew 28:19–20). This includes young adult and collegiate ministry. Leaders are admonished to teach the members of the local congregation not to view college ministry with disdain or misunderstanding based on misconception, but rather with the approach of understanding that it is the plan of God that no one *"should perish, but that all should come to repentance"* (from 2 Peter 3:9). When this vision is fully communicated, then the members will be willing to serve and embrace the Young Adult & Collegiate Sunday School ministry concept.

Your college ministry will grow as leaders model kingdom living within the local congregation. Strong, healthy interpersonal relationships must be exemplified within the local church among all leaders. The college student is very observant and any indication of confusion or discord among the leadership will discourage their involvement.

College ministry will grow as leaders are developed. Every member of the local church must be challenged to embrace this ministry as the vision of the pastor and the plan of God.

UNDERSTANDING THE YOUNG ADULT & COLLEGIATE

MINISTRY MODEL

Student	Church	College
Young	Foundation	Educational Development
Energetic	Support System	Friends
Innovative	Spiritual Basis	Community Involvement

Leadership Equirements

- Leaders understand that activities are vital for the strength of your young adult and col legiate ministry.
- Leaders provide proper guidance and structure.
- Leaders set parameters for church involvement and participation.
- Leaders must establish a system of good communication.
- Leaders must be willing to provide support and networking opportunities.

"DEVELOPING YOUNG ADULT & COLLEGIATE SUNDAY SCHOOL MINISTRY"

Essentials of Developing, Implementing, and Building Young Adult & Collegiate Ministry Within The Local Church.

By Tyrone Williams

Family Life Church in Dallas, Georgia

THE GOAL: To develop Spirit-filled, Word-empowered believers who are bold ambassadors for the kingdom of God.

CHARACTERISTICS OF AN EFFECTIVE YOUNG ADULT & COLLEGIATE MINISTRY:

• College ministry should be contemporary, relevant, transparent, and supportive.

• College ministry should be Bible-based (using study guides to complement teaching), Spirit-led, and Jesus-focused.

• College ministry should have both evangelistic and discipleship components.

• College ministry should have student involvement in the leadership.

TOPICS WHICH SHOULD BE COVERED IN COLLEGE MINISTRY:

• Basic principles of salvation and Christian living (assurance of salvation, forgiveness, the love of God, the importance of the Word of God, giving, witnessing, the role of the church)

• The Holy Ghost and the fruit of the Spirit

• Faith (what it is and how it works)

• Prayer

• Worship

KINGDOM PRINCIPLES FOR ABUNDANT LIVING IN THE NEW COVENANT

Purpose, passion and calling, healing and deliverance, success and prosperity in the mind, body, and spirit, the authority of the believer.

"UNDER PRESSURE, BUT NOT PERSUADED"

CAMPUS MINISTRY SWAG

(**S**AVED **W**ILLING **A**GENTS FOR **G**OD)

How to maintain your Christian "swag" during college life challenges.

By Evangelist Alethea Nichols

Michigan Southwest #3 Jurisdiction

THE THREE E'S NEEDED IN MINISTRY: ENCOURAGE, EQUIP, AND EMPOWER

I. **ENCOURAGE**—KNOW YOUR TRUE IDENTITY

a. I am a new creature (2 Corinthians 5:17)

b. I am FREE (John 8:36)

c. I am chosen (1 Peter 2:9)

d. I am holy, oh so holy… (Romans 12:1–2)

e. I am more than a conqueror (Romans 8:37)

f. I can do all things through Christ (Philippians 4:13)

g. I am unashamedly Christian (1 Peter 3:14)

II. **EQUIP** YOURSELF TO DO MINISTRY

a. Study the Word (2 Timothy 2:15)

b. Put on the whole armor (Ephesians 6:10–18)

c. Take a stand (1 Corinthians 15:58)

d. Expect suffering (1 Peter 4:1, 14–16)

e. Believe the power of forgiveness (Mark 11:25; Romans 12:17–21; Ephesians 4:32)

f. Love God with your whole heart! (Mark 12:30)

g. Be strong and very courageous (Joshua 1:7–8)

III. **EMPOWERED** TO MAKE A DIFFERENCE

a. Saved, willing agents for God empower others to become disciples

b. Remember you have SWAG!!!

c. Transformation leads to a renewed mind (Romans 12:2)

d. Dare to be different (Leviticus 10:10)

e. Teach others (Matthew 28:19–20)

Empowerment Tools: If the church is to be all God intends it to be, we must mentor and empower those around us.

1. Prayer and fasting
2. Word of God
3. Courage
4. Holy living
5. Obedience
6. Love
7. Anointing
8. Patience and perseverance
9. Forgiveness and longsuffering

Evangelist Alethea Nichols serves as the Jurisdictional Sunday School Field Representative for the Michigan Southwest #3 Jurisdiction. Bishop Samuel Duncan is her prelate and Mother Earlie Peppers, her Supervisor of Women. Evangelist Nichols also serves the International Sunday School Department as the Regional Field Representative for the Michigan Great Lakes Region.

Join the "COGIC College Network" Sunday School group via Facebook. To receive updated information via text message about the ISSD "Love Alive" Campus Ministries upcoming events, text the word "collegeministry " to 55469.

QUARTERLY QUIZ

The questions on this page may be used in several ways: as a pretest at the beginning of the quarter; as a review at the end of the quarter; or as a review after each lesson. The questions are based on the Scripture text of each lesson (King James Version).

LESSON 1

1. What did the Lord promise to return to His people of Israel and Judah (**Jeremiah 30:3**)?

____

____

2. Complete Jeremiah 30:22: "And ye ______ be ___ people, and ____ will be ____ ___."

____

____

LESSON 2

1. The Lord made a new ______ with the people (**Jeremiah 31:31**).

____

____

2. God will forgive their ______ and (will/will not) remember their ______ (**Jeremiah 31:34**).

____

____

LESSON 3

1. Whom did Jeremiah buy the land from (**Jeremiah 32:8**)?

____

____

2. How many shekels did Jeremiah pay for the land (**Jeremiah 32:9**)?

____

____

LESSON 4

1. God promises Jeremiah that He will bring ____ and ____ to the people (**Jeremiah 33:6**).

____

____

2. _______ and _______ were left desolate (**Jeremiah 33:10**).

____

____

LESSON 5

1. Where did Habakkuk stand to wait for God's answer to his question (**Habakkuk 2:1**)?

____

____

2. God told Habakkuk to write the vision on _______ (**Habakkuk 2:2**).

____

____

QUARTERLY QUIZ

LESSON 6

1. How many times did Job accuse his friends of bothering him **(Job 19:3)?**

____

____

2. How did Job want his words recorded **(Job 19:23)?**

____

____

LESSON 7

1. The wicked take ____ ____ of the poor in **Job 24:9.**

____

____

2. The injustice and wickedness of the wicked affect the agricultural society and the ______ **(Job 24:12)**.

____

____

LESSON 8

1. God spoke directly to Job. Read **Job 42:1–2** and record Job's initial response to the Lord.

____

____

2. What were the sacrifices that Job's friends had to offer because of their responses to Job **(Job 42:8)**?

____

____

LESSON 9

1. How did Ezekiel enter into the inner court **(Ezekiel 43:5)**?

____

____

2. God said the Children of Israel had even defiled His name—true or false **(Ezekiel 43:8)**?

____

____

LESSON 10

1. What were the ordinances of the altar **(Ezekiel 43:18)**?

____

____

2. Who should receive the offerings **(Ezekiel 43:19)**?

____

____

LESSON 11

1.The fishermen will stand along the shore from ____ ______ to ______ _______ **(Ezekiel 47:10).**

____

____

2. There will be many new fish, but the _____ and ______ will not become fresh **(Ezekiel 47:10–11).**

____

____

QUARTERLY QUIZ

LESSON 12

1. Read **Ezekiel 47:17** and fill in the blanks: "And the border from the sea shall be Hazarenan, the border of ________, and the north northward, and the border of _____. And this is the _____ side."

____

____

2. The Lord wants the land to be divided among the Levitical tribe, the priests, and the tribe of Benjamin.

____

____

LESSON 13

1. The people are to celebrate with joy and _____ together **(Isaiah 52:9)**.

____

____

2. The Children of Israel need not hurry to leave because God will _____ ______ ______ **(Isaiah 53:12)**.

____

____

ANSWERS TO THE QUARTERLY QUIZ

LESSON 1 1. The land that their forefathers possessed; 2. shall, my, I, your, God

LESSON 2 1. covenant; 2. wickedness and will not remember their sin

LESSON 3 1. Hanamel, his cousin; 2. seventeen shekels

LESSON 4 1. health and cure; 2. Judah and Jerusalem

LESSON 5 1. He stood on the tower; 2. tablets

LESSON 6 1. ten times; 2. written on a scroll

LESSON 7 1. a pledge; 2. city

LESSON 8 1. "1 Then Job answered the LORD, and said, 2 I know that thou canst do every thing and that no thought can be withholden from thee."; 2. seven bullocks and seven rams

LESSON 9 1. The Spirit took him into the inner court. 2. True

LESSON 10 1. To offer burnt offerings and then to sprinkle blood on it; 2. The offerings should be given to the Levitical priests.

LESSON 11 1. Engedi to Eneglaim; 2. swamps and marshes

LESSON 12 1. Damascus, Hamath, north; 2. False

LESSON 13 1. sing; 2. make intercession for transgressors

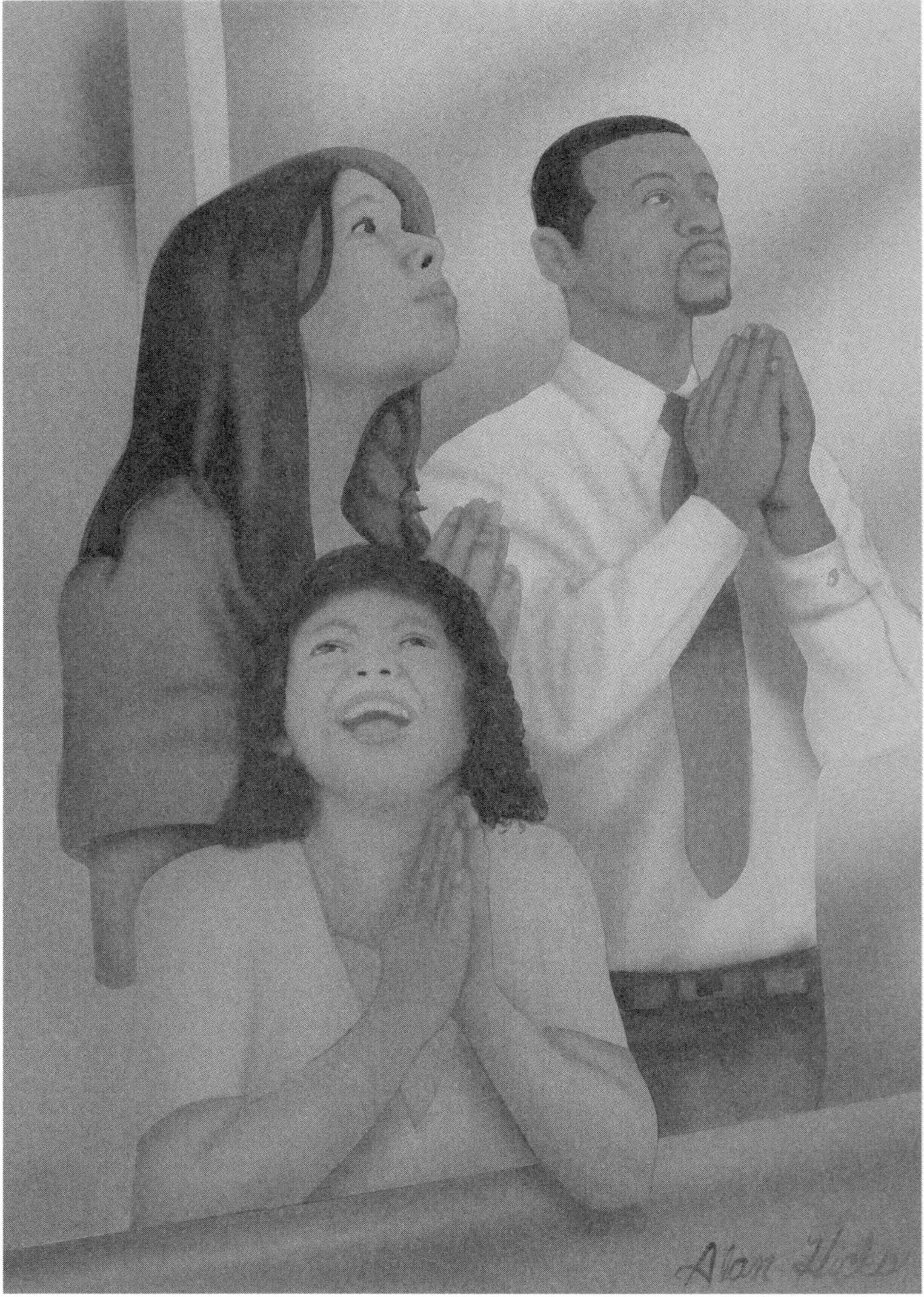

A VISION OF THE FUTURE

BIBLE BASIS: JEREMIAH 30:1–3, 18–22

BIBLE TRUTH: God's promise to restore the fortunes of the people, Israel and Judah, and to reestablish the covenant with them.

MEMORY VERSE: "For, lo, the days come, saith the LORD, that I will bring again the captivity of my people Israel and Judah, saith the LORD: and I will cause them to return to the land that I gave to their fathers, and they shall possess it" (Jeremiah 30:3).

LESSON AIM: By the end of the lesson, your students will: review God's written promise to restore the people and the land of Israel and Judah as of old; imagine and express the feelings of safety in a community that has great promise for the future; and plan a way to invite people who are not part of the covenant community to become members of the church and Sunday School.

TEACHER PREPARATION

MATERIALS NEEDED: Quarterly Commentary/Teacher Manual, Adult Quarterly, Adult resources—charts, worksheets, and other teaching tools, paper, pens, pencils, Bibles (several different versions)

OTHER MATERIALS NEEDED / TEACHER'S NOTES:

____

____

LESSON OVERVIEW

LIFE NEED FOR TODAY'S LESSON
People often find themselves in situations when they feel lost and alone.

BIBLE LEARNING
God promises to bring the people back to their ancestors' lands so they can possess them.

BIBLE APPLICATION
People of faith look to divine justice as their hope.

STUDENTS' RESPONSES
Students will find comfort in the covenant promise: "you shall be my people, and I will be your God" (30:22).

LESSON SCRIPTURE

JEREMIAH 30:1–3, 18–22, KJV

1 The word that came to Jeremiah from the LORD, saying,

2 Thus speaketh the LORD God of Israel,

JEREMIAH 30:1–3, 18–22, NIV

1 This is the word that came to Jeremiah from the Lord:

2 "This is what the Lord, the God of Israel,

saying, Write thee all the words that I have spoken unto thee in a book.

3 For, lo, the days come, saith the LORD, that I will bring again the captivity of my people Israel and Judah, saith the LORD: and I will cause them to return to the land that I gave to their fathers, and they shall possess it.

18 Thus saith the LORD; Behold, I will bring again the captivity of Jacob's tents, and have mercy on his dwelling places; and the city shall be builded upon her own heap, and the palace shall remain after the manner thereof.

19 And out of them shall proceed thanksgiving and the voice of them that make merry: and I will multiply them, and they shall not be few; I will also glorify them, and they shall not be small.

20 Their children also shall be as aforetime, and their congregation shall be established before me, and I will punish all that oppress them.

21 And their nobles shall be of themselves, and their governor shall proceed from the midst of them; and I will cause him to draw near, and he shall approach unto me: for who is this that engaged his heart to approach unto me? saith the LORD.

22 And ye shall be my people, and I will be your God.

says: 'Write in a book all the words I have spoken to you.

3 The days are coming,' declares the LORD, 'when I will bring my people Israel and Judah back from captivity and restore them to the land I gave their ancestors to possess,' says the LORD."

18 "This is what the LORD says: "'I will restore the fortunes of Jacob's tents and have compassion on his dwellings; the city will be rebuilt on her ruins, and the palace will stand in its proper place.

19 From them will come songs of thanksgiving and the sound of rejoicing. I will add to their numbers, and they will not be decreased; I will bring them honor, and they will not be disdained.

20 Their children will be as in days of old, and their community will be established before me; I will punish all who oppress them.

21 Their leader will be one of their own; their ruler will arise from among them. I will bring him near and he will come close to me—for who is he who will devote himself to be close to me?' declares the LORD.

22 "'So you will be my people, and I will be your God.'"

LIGHT ON THE WORD

Located between the Mediterranean Sea and Dead Sea, Judah lies in southern Palestine. Following the death of King Solomon, the united kingdom of Israel split into two. Two tribes, Judah and Benjamin, remained loyal to King Rehoboam and became the Southern Kingdom of Judah. The other ten tribes followed King Jeroboam and are generally referred to as the Northern Kingdom of Israel. Judah's capital city and central place of worship was the city of Jerusalem. Prior to its destruction by the Babylonians in 587 B.C., Judah was ruled by a succession of nineteen kings, all from the line of David.

TEACHING THE BIBLE LESSON

LIFE NEED FOR TODAY'S LESSON

AIM: Students will often find themselves in situations when they feel lost and alone.

INTRODUCTION

Jeremiah's Prophecy

In the book that bears his name, Jeremiah declared the sins of the people (including idolatry) and God's judgment against them. One cannot fail to see the prophet's sadness and sympathy as he denounced Judah's ungodly behavior and the impending doom it would bring about. While Jeremiah frequently issued harsh denunciations, the prophet's love for the people was evident. His prophecies, however, fell on deaf ears. The people of Judah were using the Temple as a good luck charm. They mistakenly believed that no real harm could befall the city that housed the magnificent Temple of Jerusalem.

BIBLE LEARNING

AIM: Students will know that God promises to bring the people back to their ancestors' lands so they can possess them.

I. THE PROPHET CALLED TO WRITE THE VISION (Jeremiah 30:1–2)

Prior to the destruction of Jerusalem, Jeremiah, who continues to speak out against false priests and prophets, is imprisoned for treason. It is important to note that God no longer has the prophet speaking directly with the people. His people still have access to His Word even though they will no longer have access to His messenger. God tells Jeremiah to write all the words that He had given him in a book. Here we see a loving God making a way for a people who have been continually unfaithful to Him.

Instructed by God (verses 1–2)

1 The word that came to Jeremiah from the LORD, saying, 2 Thus speaketh the LORD God of Israel, saying, Write thee all the words that I have spoken unto thee in a book.

For most of the preceding chapters of his book, Jeremiah has been instructed by God to speak words of condemnation to the nation of Israel for their behavior. Beginning with this chapter, however, Jeremiah receives "word" (Heb. *dabar*, **daw-VAWR**, meaning message or edict) from the Lord to "write" (Heb. *kathab*, **kaw-THAV**, meaning to register or record in writing) his message to the nation of Israel. God wants Jeremiah to write down the prophecy instead of speaking it because His message is to be preserved for future generations to read and understand. God knew that Jeremiah would not be taken into captivity with the rest of the Jewish nation, and by having him write the prophecy instead of speaking it, those Jews in captivity to the Babylonians could have a source of hope that even their bondage was in accord with God's divine plan for them. Later, while a captive of the Babylonian empire, Daniel would read and take heed of Jeremiah's prophecy, responding with a repentant heart (cf. **Daniel 9:2–4**).

SEARCH THE SCRIPTURES

QUESTION 1

How did God instruct Jeremiah to communicate with the people?

LIGHT ON THE WORD

The Fall of Jerusalem

Just as God said, and just as Jeremiah prophesied, Jerusalem fell to the Babylonians in 587 B.C. The city was utterly destroyed and many of the people were deported. Jeremiah emphasizes that God had not forgotten nor forsaken His people—a people who had failed to heed the Word of God, refused to repent, and were now suffering the consequences of their sin. God's love for His people was enduring. Even in captivity, His thoughts were turned toward them. Yes, they were being punished, but God intended that the people of Judah would be restored to Him and returned to their land.

II. A FUTURE OF RESTORATION (v. 3)

In this verse, we see Jeremiah delivering a more specific message of hope to the people of Judah. His message is not simply one that contains words of comfort and consolation to a suffering people. It is, actually, a vision for their future! Even though it is their fault that they have come into captivity, we will see that God still loves His people and that He cares deeply for them. We must be careful to remember that it is only a trick of the enemy to make us believe that our sins separate us from the loving care and concern of God. Through the blood of His Son Jesus Christ, we are always in the thoughts of God, and there is nothing that can separate us from His love.

The Consolation of God's Promise (verse 3)

3 For, lo, the days come, saith the LORD, that I will bring again the captivity of my people Israel and Judah, saith the LORD: and I will cause them to return to the land that I gave to their fathers, and they shall possess it.

Through Jeremiah, God wants His chosen people to understand that their "captivity" (Heb. *shebuwth*, **sheh-VOOTH**, meaning exile or ill fortune) to the Babylonians will come to an end. Many scholars assert that this chapter of Jeremiah begins a Book of Consolation to the Jewish nations held in captivity. God has promised that He "will bring again the captivity" (Heb. *shuwb*, **SHOOB**, meaning turn back or ever turn away), the exile of His chosen people. Jeremiah is to write the prophecy so that when the captivity has ended and the nations of Israel and Judah are restored to their former land in Palestine, there will be no doubt how the restoration came about and that God was the source of that restoration. Through Jeremiah, God pledges to the Jewish nations that the promise He made to "their fathers" (Heb. *'ab*, **AWV**, meaning father or ancestor), that they would "possess" (Heb. *yarash*, **yaw-RASH**, meaning to seize, inherit, or occupy) the land of Palestine, would one day be a reality.

III. A FUTURE WITH A KINGDOM (v. 18)

In this verse we see that God's vision for His people's future includes their liberation and restoration. Jeremiah's referral to "Jacob" informs us that God is addressing Israel as a united nation and not just the Southern Kingdom of Judah. The prophet references "tents" and "dwellingplaces" as a reminder to the people of both Israel and Judah that they have now become wanderers and sojourners in foreign and alien lands, but this is coming to an end.

Jeremiah continues to show that even more acts of mercy for the people of God are forthcoming. God will once again rebuild Jerusalem, and He will do it on the "heap" or ruins of their former capital. Although Jerusalem had been destroyed, remnants of its foundations and portions of the walls surrounding the city remained. God would use these painful physical reminders to restore the city.

A Permanent Dwelling Place (verse 18)

18 Thus saith the LORD; Behold, I will bring again the captivity of Jacob's tents, and have mercy on his dwellingplaces; and the city shall be builded upon her own heap, and the palace shall remain after the manner thereof.

Through Jeremiah, the Lord continues His promise to the Jewish nations now in bondage. The nations are to understand and believe that they will not always feel like nomads or wanderers living in "tents" (Heb. *'ohel*, **O-hel**, meaning nomadic dwelling thus symbolic of wilderness life) like their forefathers Abraham, Isaac, and Jacob had to do. Tents will one day give way to permanent dwelling places in the land that God has promised to them. God also promises to "have mercy" (Heb. *racham*, **raw-KHAM**, meaning to have pity or compassion) on those dwellings, a promise of divine protection. Further, the city will be rebuilt upon her own "heap" (Heb. *tel*, **TEL**, meaning former ruins). In ancient times, sites for cities were often chosen for their strategic importance, whether commercial or military, and for that reason, when a city was destroyed, a new city would often be erected on the exact same spot. Finally, God promises that the "palace" (Heb. *'armown*, **ar-MONE**, meaning royal citadels or Temple) will once again be "after the manner thereof" (Heb. *mishpat*, **mish-PAWT**, meaning what is proper and right). It will once more be a place of righteousness and judgment. Even the palace is to be rebuilt to its former glory and in its former spot and will once more be the host of sacred feasts with offerings of sacrifice to the Most High God.

SEARCH THE SCRIPTURES

QUESTION 2

Where did God tell Jeremiah the city of Jerusalem would be rebuilt?

LIGHT ON THE WORD

A Joyful Thanksgiving

Jeremiah prophesies that following their restoration the people of Israel would finally give the appropriate response to the God of their salvation—thanksgiving. Recognizing, at last, the source of their joy, the people would now worship God honestly and joyfully. Jeremiah goes on to prophesy that God would increase their numbers. This would be a sign to the pagan nations around them that the blessing of God rested once again on the nation He had called out of nothingness.

IV. A FUTURE WITH JOY AND A RENEWED COVENANT (vv. 19–22)

Here, we are now given even further glimpses of God's vision for His people. No longer would foreign and ungodly rulers govern the people of God. Instead, their ruling class would rise from among them. The God-appointed "nobles" would be men who both knew and understood their prior suffering and afflictions. More importantly, we are now presented with a clear pre-figuration of Christ as both our Mediator and Righteous Judge. Like the governors, Jeremiah predicts in this verse, Christ knew the full suffering of mankind. As Mediator, it is the role of Christ to "draw near" or to go to the Father, not for Himself, but for the express purpose of intervening on behalf of man.

God's Faithfulness (verses 19–22)

19 And out of them shall proceed thanksgiving and the voice of them that make merry: and I will multiply them, and they shall not be few; I will also glorify them, and they shall not be small. 20 Their children also shall be as aforetime, and their congregation shall be established before me, and I will punish all that oppress them.

All of these promises (permanent dwellings,

divine protection, increase of children, the restoration of the cities and Temple in their original places) were to result in the people offering "thanksgiving" (Heb. *towdah*, **toe-DAW**, meaning hymn of praise) to the Lord God. This thanksgiving would be accompanied by voices expressing great joy and happiness. God would have demonstrated His faithfulness and love for His chosen people. In their present state of bondage, such an occurrence would have been hard to imagine, but the nations were to have faith in God. Their sufferings were to be mixed with hope for their future. As in many African societies children in Israelite culture were a valuable possession and a sign of prosperity. Thus the the size and fortunes of the various tribes of Israel would be restored and increased and children would be "as aforetime" (Heb. *qedem*, **KEH-dem**, meaning from of old)—bountiful, playing in the streets of their cities, and inheriting their parents' estates. Further, God will sit and watch over their "congregation" (Heb. *'edah*, **eh-DAW**, meaning assembly) to protect their worship practices and will "punish" (Heb. *paqad*, **paw-KAD**, meaning to impose a penalty on) any who would seek to "oppress" (Heb. *lachats*, **law-KHATS**, meaning to force themselves upon or afflict) His chosen nation.

21 And their nobles shall be of themselves, and their governor shall proceed from the midst of them; and I will cause him to draw near, and he shall approach unto me: for who is this that engaged his heart to approach unto me? saith the LORD.

It must have pleased Jeremiah to be writing a prophecy that was intended to assure the Children of Israel that at the end of their captivity to the Babylonians, their leadership structure would once again be in place. This is because the leaders were primarily responsible for the nation's exile. Their "nobles" (Heb. *'addiyr*, **ad-DEER**, meaning leading men or rulers) would be selected from their own tribes. Moreover, their "governor" (Heb. *mashal*, **maw-SHAL**, meaning king or one who exercises authority over) will come from one of their tribes and the Lord God will cause him to "draw near" (Heb. *qarab*, **kaw-RAB**, meaning to approach or be brought close) to Him. God, who sees and judges on the basis of the "heart" (Heb. *leb*, **LEV**, meaning the seat of the affections, intellect, and memory), is mindful of any who would seek to approach Him. Only Christ the Messiah would be found worthy for such a task. Only Christ, acting as the High Priest of the people, could have so "engaged" (Heb. *'arab*, **aw-RAWV**, meaning pledged as security) His heart.

22 And ye shall be my people, and I will be your God.

God will accept the sacrifice of this King and Ruler, thus ensuring the continuing relationship between Himself and the Jewish nations. Christ as High Priest and King will be the Mediator between God and the people. As the people accept Christ, God will accept the people.

SEARCH THE SCRIPTURES

QUESTION 3

What were some of the signs of restoration that would accompany God's people?

BIBLE APPLICATION

AIM: Students will look to divine justice as their hope.

We need only walk down the streets of any major urban city to see ruin and decay. Once-prosperous cities and towns are full of abandoned and boarded-up buildings. There are no signs of thriving businesses, and entire neighborhoods are blighted and empty. The people who remain in these areas sometimes look as forlorn as the property surrounding them. These are all signs of hopelessness. Through

Jesus Christ, there is hope for the restoration and renewal of the communities and the people who live in them. We must be as diligent as Jeremiah in sharing the Word that God not only loves but also cares for His people and that He has a plan for their future.

STUDENTS' RESPONSES

AIM: Students will find comfort in the covenant promise: "you shall be my people, and I will be your God" (30:22).

Consider ministries that are helping to rebuild and restore communities that have been devastated by crime, poverty, or natural disaster. Pray and ask God to show you where there is time in your busy schedule to demonstrate His love through you. Next, ask Him to give you a tender and understanding heart.

PRAYER

Lord, thank You for being faithful, loving, and holding true to Your promises. We know that Your plans and thoughts for us are far greater than we can ever imagine. We are blessed that You care for us even when we sin and have strayed from Your ways. Thank you for Your mercy and goodness toward us everyday. In Jesus' Name we pray. Amen.

HOW TO SAY IT

Aforetime. a-**FOR**-time.

Captivity. cap-**TI**-vit-ee.

PREPARE FOR NEXT SUNDAY

Read **Jeremiah 31:31–37** and study "Restoration."

DAILY HOME BIBLE READINGS

MONDAY
Act with Justice and Righteousness
(Jeremiah 22:1–9)

TUESDAY
Hear the Words of This Covenant
(Jeremiah 11:1–10)

WEDNESDAY
Only the Lord Will Be Exalted
(Isaiah 2:10–19)

THURSDAY
Turn from Your Evil Way
(Jeremiah 18:1–10)

FRIDAY
A Future with Hope
(Jeremiah 29:10–14)

SATURDAY
Hope for Israel's Neighbors
(Jeremiah 12:14–17)

SUNDAY
The Days are Surely Coming
(Jeremiah 30:1–3, 18–22)

Sources:

Alexander, David, et al. Eerdman's Handbook to the Bible. Grand Rapids, MI: Wm. B. Eerdmans Publishing Company, 1994. 398–405.

Dunn, James D. G. and John W. Rogerson. Commentary on the Bible. Grand Rapids, MI: Wm. B. Eerdmans Publishing Company, 2003.

Elwell, Walter A. Baker Theological Dictionary of the Bible. Grand Rapids, MI: Baker Book House Company, 1996. 389–390.

English, E. Schuyler and Marian Bishop Bower, eds. The Holy Bible: Pilgrim Edition. New York: Oxford University Press, 1952.

Howley, G.C.D., F.F. Bruce, and H. L. Ellison. The New Layman's Bible Commentary. Grand Rapids, MI: Zondervan, 1979.

Keener, Craig S. The IVP Bible Background Commentary: New Testament. Downers Grove, IL: InterVarsity Press, 1993.

RESTORATION

BIBLE BASIS: JEREMIAH 31:31–37

BIBLE TRUTH: Jeremiah assures the people that God will make a new covenant with God's people that will nurture and equip them for the present and the future.

MEMORY VERSE: "Behold, the days come, saith the LORD, that I will make a new covenant with the house of Israel, and with the house of Judah" (Jeremiah 31:31).

LESSON AIM: By the end of the lesson, your students will: know God's new covenant to reveal Himself to all the people, forgive their sins, and hold them accountable; sense the relief and joy that come from starting over in agreement with someone; and make plans for renewing our personal covenant with God.

TEACHER PREPARATION

MATERIALS NEEDED: Quarterly Commentary/Teacher Manual, Adult Quarterly, Adult resources—charts, worksheets, and other teaching tools, paper, pens, pencils, Bibles (several different versions)

OTHER MATERIALS NEEDED / TEACHER'S NOTES:

____

____

LESSON OVERVIEW

LIFE NEED FOR TODAY'S LESSON
Sometimes agreements and relationships must be revised and renewed.

BIBLE LEARNING
The new covenant is a relational knowledge of God.

BIBLE APPLICATION
Christians confess their sins believing that God is willing and able to forgive them and renew the divine-human relationship.

STUDENTS' RESPONSES
Christians renew their commitments to God in formal and informal ways.

LESSON SCRIPTURE

JEREMIAH 31:31–37, KJV

31 Behold, the days come, saith the LORD, that I will make a new covenant with the house of Israel, and with the house of Judah:

32 Not according to the covenant that I made with their fathers in the day that I

JEREMIAH 31:31–37, NIV

31 "The days are coming," declares the LORD, "when I will make a new covenant with the people of Israel and with the people of Judah.

32 It will not be like the covenant I made with their ancestors when I took them

took them by the hand to bring them out of the land of Egypt; which my covenant they brake, although I was an husband unto them, saith the LORD:

33 But this shall be the covenant that I will make with the house of Israel; After those days, saith the LORD, I will put my law in their inward parts, and write it in their hearts; and will be their God, and they shall be my people.

34 And they shall teach no more every man his neighbour, and every man his brother, saying, Know the LORD: for they shall all know me, from the least of them unto the greatest of them, saith the LORD: for I will forgive their iniquity, and I will remember their sin no more.

35 Thus saith the LORD, which giveth the sun for a light by day, and the ordinances of the moon and of the stars for a light by night, which divideth the sea when the waves thereof roar; The LORD of hosts is his name:

36 If those ordinances depart from before me, saith the LORD, then the seed of Israel also shall cease from being a nation before me for ever.

37 Thus saith the LORD; If heaven above can be measured, and the foundations of the earth searched out beneath, I will also cast off all the seed of Israel for all that they have done, saith the LORD.

by the hand to lead them out of Egypt, because they broke my covenant, though I was a husband to them," declares the LORD.

33 "This is the covenant I will make with the people of Israel after that time," declares the LORD. "I will put my law in their minds and write it on their hearts. I will be their God, and they will be my people.

34 No longer will they teach their neighbor, or say to one another, 'Know the LORD,' because they will all know me, from the least of them to the greatest," declares the LORD. "For I will forgive their wickedness and will remember their sins no more."

35 This is what the Lord says, he who appoints the sun to shine by day, who decrees the moon and stars to shine by night, who stirs up the sea so that its waves roar— the Lord Almighty is his name:

36 "Only if these decrees vanish from my sight," declares the LORD, "will Israel ever cease being a nation before me."

37 This is what the LORD says: "Only if the heavens above can be measured and the foundations of the earth below be searched out will I reject all the descendants of Israel because of all they have done," declares the LORD.

LIGHT ON THE WORD

A covenant is not simply an agreement between two parties. Covenants are not arbitrary; they are binding. Covenants are special relationships by which the parties enter into a binding commitment with one another. This committed relationship makes a demand on each party. In the Bible, we see all types of covenants. There are the covenants that are made between groups and nations, as is the case in **Joshua 9** when the people of Gibeon covenant with the Children of Israel (**Joshua 9:6, 15**). Still another type of covenant is demonstrated in the relationship between David and Saul's son Jonathan. This relationship is not a trivial friendship. The Scriptures tell us "that the soul of Jonathan was knit with the soul of David, and Jonathan loved him as his own soul" (**1 Samuel 18:1**). Throughout the Old Testament, the covenant between God and the Children of Israel provides that God offers His love and protection, and in return His people pledge to worship and serve Him alone.

TEACHING THE BIBLE LESSON

LIFE NEED FOR TODAY'S LESSON

AIM: Students will know that sometimes agreements and relationships must be revised and renewed.

INTRODUCTION

Jeremiah's Prophecy of a New Relationship

Jeremiah, the final prophet to the Southern Kingdom of Judah, was from Anathoth, a priestly community belonging to the tribe of Benjamin. Under the instruction of the Lord, Jeremiah wrote to people of Judah who had been captured and taken into captivity by the powerful nation of Babylonia. Despite admonitions and warnings delivered by the godly prophets like Jeremiah, the people of Judah had shown themselves unwilling to change and unrepentant.

Jeremiah continued to prophesy to the people of Judah. He let them know that God would restore their relationship with Him through a new covenant. This new covenant would bind them to the Lord in a unique and different way. It would also give them the ability to obey the stipulations of the covenant and to experience the Lord in their midst.

BIBLE LEARNING

AIM: Students will learn that the new covenant is a relational knowledge of God.

I. GOD OFFERS A NEW COVENANT (Jeremiah 31:31–32)

We must keep in mind that Judah's continued unfaithfulness and failure to return to God was a national breach of their covenant with Him. This initial covenant was made on Mount Sinai after the Exodus of the Children of Israel from Egypt. Now, Jeremiah declares that God is instituting a new covenant. There is to be a change in the relationship between God and His chosen people. Jeremiah clearly names the nations or "houses" of Israel and Judah as parties and ultimate recipients of this new covenant.

A New Beginning (verses 31–32)

31 Behold, the days come, saith the LORD, that I will make a new covenant with the house of Israel, and with the house of Judah: 32 Not according to the covenant that I made with their fathers in the day that I took them by the hand to bring them out of the land of Egypt; which my covenant they brake, although I was an husband unto them, saith the LORD.

Beginning with this passage, the "LORD" (Heb. *Yehovah*, **yeh-ho-VAW**, the self-existing One) would continue His message of hope to the nations of Israel and Judah. God's promise includes the making of a "new covenant" with the nations of Israel and Judah (cf. **Hebrews 8:8–9**). Previously God had covenanted with the people at Mount Sinai. Moses was given God's laws for the nations to observe. These laws required effort on the part of the Israelites and could be understood in a more material sense. The new covenant that God will make in "days" (Heb. *yowm*, **YOME**, sometime later or the future) to "come" (Heb. *ba'*, **BO**) looks forward to the time of Christ and the grace of God that will be available only through Him. Even though God took the Children of Israel by the hand, led them out of Egypt, and walked with them in the wilderness the way a husband would guide his wife, they would be unfaithful to Him and break their covenant. This Mosaic covenant the Israelites were able to "brake" (Heb. *parar*, **paw-RAR**, meaning to make void or annul) because it demanded a particular behavior. However, the new covenant that God was promising through Jeremiah to make with the nations, would be grounded in the work of Christ and require only acceptance of Christ to trigger God's grace.

SEARCH THE SCRIPTURES

QUESTION 1

With whom is God making the new covenant?

LIGHT ON THE WORD

From Brokenness to Restoration

Jeremiah points out that this new covenant will be quite different from the previous Mosaic covenant. We will recall that while Moses was talking to God, the Children of Israel had grown impatient and subsequently constructed a golden calf to worship (**Exodus 32**). Thus the initial covenant was broken before Moses could even come down from Mount Sinai.

Moreover, the phrase "I took them by the hand" shows us the parental approach God used toward Israel. It is very interesting to note that the imagery Jeremiah uses to denote God's faithfulness toward Israel is that of a "husband." While a husband-wife relationship certainly makes the point of faithfulness, it is a bit odd that such an analogy would be used to describe the relationship between the Creator and His obviously inferior creation. Here we see the loving quality of God's character exemplified. As the Children of Israel wandered through the hostile desert, God, like a loving husband, had protected them and provided for Israel. This imagery also foreshadows Christ's fulfillment in the New Testament as a loving husband of His bride, the church (cf. **Ephesians 5:23**).

II. A COVENANT OF LOVE (vv. 33–34)

Jeremiah goes on to point out a major difference between the Mosaic and the new covenant: its character. The previous covenant had been written on stone tablets. It had been a legalistic mechanism whereby the people would follow the laws and statutes of God. This new covenant would be intrinsic in nature, and so it would be inscribed in their hearts. Here we see that God wants His people to recognize the corrupting effects of their sin: that it actually destroys them both externally and internally.

A New Covenant (verses 33–34)

33 But this shall be the covenant that I will make with the house of Israel; After those days, saith the LORD, I will put my law in their inward parts, and write it in their hearts; and will be their God, and they shall be my people.

Because God's new "covenant" (Heb. *beryth*, **be-REETH**) would be located in the "inward parts" of each person and written upon the "hearts" (Heb. *qereb*, **KEH-rev**) it differentiates itself from the old covenant that was written on stone. The old covenant was written by the finger of God on stone tablets, and through Moses, was laid before the people for them to accept or reject. Under the old covenant, if God's laws were accepted, then they would be followed and could be received into their hearts. However, the possibility remained that they could reject God's law. Embedded within the old covenant were the kernels of righteousness that would be the fruit of obedient adherence to the commands of the law, but those kernels were presented externally to the people. The new covenant was to be internal and righteousness would come on the basis of belief in the Messiah, Jesus Christ. The promise of a new covenant should be understood as a completion of the old covenant where God pledged this special relationship between Himself and His people (cf. **Exodus 29:45** and **Leviticus 26:12**).

34 And they shall teach no more every man his neighbor, and every man his brother, saying, Know the LORD: for they shall all know me, from the least of them unto the greatest of them, saith the LORD: for I will forgive their iniquity, and I will remember their sin no more.

The light and knowledge of God will be freely available to all who believe. Under the new covenant, it will no longer be necessary for anyone to receive individual instruction and have others "teach" (Heb. *lamad*, **law-MAD**, to instruct) the ways of God, because everyone will personally have access to God and His wisdom. Nothing of God will be hidden from His people because His laws and precepts will be written internally upon each individual heart, and all will know for themselves what pleases or displeases God. In the event that errors in judgment are made, God will forgive their "iniquity" (Heb. *'avon*, **aw-VONE**, meaning wrongdoing or transgressions) and in forgiving will remember the offense no more. This is a glorious promise to future Israel and to all who come to God through Christ because of them.

SEARCH THE SCRIPTURES

QUESTIONS 2 & 3

Rather than a law on tablets, where will the new covenant be written?

What assurances does God offer the people about their former transgressions and sins?

LIGHT ON THE WORD

God is in Control

In these verses, Jeremiah offers even greater hope to the captives to whom he is writing. It is God, the prophet posits, who can control the uncontrollable. The intricate cycles of day and night and the motion and movement of seas are under the sovereign control of God. God alone orders and controls nature. Jeremiah now presents a powerful image for his reader. In order for Israel not to belong to God, God would have to discard His control of nature itself—something that clearly cannot happen since God alone is sovereign.

III. A COVENANT OF EVERLASTING INTIMACY (vv. 35–37)

Only God is all knowing, or "omniscient." Since there is no one who can know these marvelous secrets of nature, then the captives could rest in their assurance that Israel would again be a nation of God's chosen people. God and God alone, the prophet declares, is able to restore His people and only He can hold any power against them.

A Promise of Restoration (verses 35–37)

35 Thus saith the LORD, which giveth the sun for a light by day, and the ordinances of the moon and of the stars for a light by night, which divideth the sea when the waves thereof roar; The LORD of hosts is his name: 36 If those ordinances depart from before me, saith the LORD, then the seed of Israel also shall cease from being a nation before me for ever.

These verses proceed to show why God by His intrinsic nature cannot fail in the fulfillment of the the covenant He has made with Israel. God created, God controls, and God sustains. God put the sun in place and established its purpose to give light and heat to the earth.

He then put the moon in place and the stars with it. According to His "ordinances" (Heb. *chuqqah*, **khook-KAW**, limits, enactments or something prescribed), they have their regular duties and functions. God "divideth" (Heb. *raga'*, **raw-GAH**, to cause to rest) the bounds for the sea, and when the waves threaten to overrun its bounds, He quiets those waves with a word. These things must be so because they all exist to serve Him (cf. **Psalm 119:90–91**). God's people and His church need only look around and observe nature to understand that as it is subject to His ordinances and relies on His faithfulness for its continuance, so too His holy people and His church, "the seed of Israel," will not cease or come to an end without His sanction.

37 Thus saith the LORD; If heaven above can be measured, and the foundations of the earth searched out beneath, I will also cast off all the seed of Israel for all that they have done, saith the LORD.

It is nearly impossible for man to measure the heavens or to determine the foundations of the earth. God's Word established the heavens and the earth, and that same Word declares that they are hung upon nothing (cf. **Job 26:7**). Believing this to be true, God's people and His church can be assured that He has the power and the goodness to be faithful to the promises He has made. Iniquities will be pardoned and forgotten, nations will be rebuilt, future generations will be enlarged and protected, and God will be their God through all eternity. This is the gift of grace to all "the seed" (Heb. *zera'*, **ZEH-rah**, meaning descendants, offspring, or posterity) of Israel who embrace Christ as Lord and Savior.

LIGHT ON THE WORD

Blessings of God's New Covenant

Jeremiah is clear that the blessings of God's new covenant will be experienced by a fully restored nation. More importantly, present-day believers have the assurance through Christ Jesus that the blessings of God's new covenant have been extended to us.

BIBLE APPLICATION

AIM: Students will confess their sins believing that God is willing and able to forgive them and renew the divine-human relationship.

In today's world, agreements are constantly made and broken. It seems that no one's word can be trusted. Corporations make agreements with their customers that they readily break. Governments make agreements with their citizens and with other nations, only to break those as well. God gives us more than just a flimsy human agreement. His new covenant is backed by Jesus' death on the Cross. This was His demonstration and pledge of His love for us. Our response ought to be one of gratitude and sharing this love with others.

STUDENTS' RESPONSES

AIM: Students will renew their commitments to God in formal and informal ways.

The Lord told His people that "I will remember [your] sin no more" (from **Jeremiah 31:34**). Again and again we see that God continues to forgive and love His people despite their sins. As recipients of this amazing love, we do not want to take it for granted. We need to pray and examine our lives. If there is any old anger, hurt, betrayal, or heartbreak, it only means that God is presenting us with an opportunity to forgive and be forgiven. Only then can we renew our relationship with Him.

PRAYER

Lord, forgive us as we forgive others. Let us not hold grudges or become envious or prideful in our thoughts, actions, or deeds. As we help to mend the broken pieces of so many shattered lives, we look to You for our peace, comfort, and care. In Jesus' Name we pray. Amen.

HOW TO SAY IT

Iniquity. in-**IH**-qui-tee.

Ordinance. **OR**-din-ans.

PREPARE FOR NEXT SUNDAY

Read **Jeremiah 32:2–9, 14–15** and study "A New Future."

DAILY HOME BIBLE READINGS

MONDAY
A Better Covenant
(Hebrews 8:1–7, 13)

TUESDAY
Mediator of a New Covenant
(Hebrews 9:11–15)

WEDNESDAY
Ministers of a New Covenant
(2 Corinthians 3:4–11)

THURSDAY
I Will Gather Them
(Jeremiah 31:7–11)

FRIDAY
Hope for Your Future
(Jeremiah 31:12–17)

SATURDAY
Set Up Road Markers
(Jeremiah 31:18–25)

SUNDAY
I Will Make a New Covenant
(Jeremiah 31:31–37)

Sources:

Alexander, David, et al. *Eerdman's Handbook to the Bible*. Grand Rapids, MI: Wm. B. Eerdmans Publishing Company, 1994. 398–405.

Dunn, James D. G. and John W. Rogerson. *Commentary on the Bible*. Grand Rapids, MI: Wm. B. Eerdmans Publishing Company, 2003.

Elwell, Walter A. *Baker Theological Dictionary of the Bible*. Grand Rapids, MI: Baker Book House Company, 1996. 389–390.

English, E. Schuyler and Marian Bishop Bower, eds. *The Holy Bible: Pilgrim Edition*. New York: Oxford University Press, 1952.

Howley, G.C.D., F.F. Bruce, and H. L. Ellison. *The New Layman's Bible Commentary*. Grand Rapids, MI: Zondervan, 1979.

Keener, Craig S. *The IVP Bible Background Commentary: New Testament*. Downers Grove, IL: InterVarsity Press, 1993.

COMMENTS / NOTES:

A NEW FUTURE

BIBLE BASIS: JEREMIAH 32:2–9, 14–15

BIBLE TRUTH: While Jerusalem was under siege, God instructed the prophet Jeremiah to purchase property as a sign that there was a future for the people and their land beyond defeat and exile.

MEMORY VERSE: "For thus saith the LORD of hosts, the God of Israel; Houses and fields and vineyards shall be possessed again in this land" (Jeremiah 32:15).

LESSON AIM: By the end of this lesson, your students will: retell the hopefulness of Jeremiah's purchase of a field while he awaits the invasion and siege of Jerusalem; appreciate hope and hopeful actions in the face of deep hardship; and review our personal times of hardship in the past that held, and hold, hope for the future.

TEACHER PREPARATION

MATERIALS NEEDED: Quarterly Commentary/Teacher Manual, Adult Quarterly, Adult resources—charts, worksheets, and other teaching tools, paper, pens, pencils, Bibles (several different versions)

OTHER MATERIALS NEEDED / TEACHER'S NOTES:

____

____

LESSON OVERVIEW

LIFE NEED FOR TODAY'S LESSON
Even in difficult circumstances, some people take hopeful actions.

BIBLE LEARNING
God promised to gather the people from the lands in which they had been scattered and to bring them back together and settle them in the city, in safety.

BIBLE APPLICATION
Christians believe they have hope based in a spiritual heritage established in Jesus Christ.

STUDENTS' RESPONSES
Christians embrace hope for the future in times of personal hardship.

LESSON SCRIPTURE

JEREMIAH 32:2–9, 14–15, KJV

2 For then the king of Babylon's army besieged Jerusalem: and Jeremiah the prophet was shut up in the court of the

JEREMIAH 32:2–9, 14–15, NIV

2 The army of the king of Babylon was then besieging Jerusalem, and Jeremiah the prophet was confined in the courtyard

prison, which was in the king of Judah's house.

3 For Zedekiah king of Judah had shut him up, saying, Wherefore dost thou prophesy, and say, Thus saith the LORD, Behold, I will give this city into the hand of the king of Babylon, and he shall take it;

4 And Zedekiah king of Judah shall not escape out of the hand of the Chaldeans, but shall surely be delivered into the hand of the king of Babylon, and shall speak with him mouth to mouth, and his eyes shall behold his eyes;

5 And he shall lead Zedekiah to Babylon, and there shall he be until I visit him, saith the LORD: though ye fight with the Chaldeans, ye shall not prosper.

6 And Jeremiah said, The word of the LORD came unto me, saying,

7 Behold, Hanameel the son of Shallum thine uncle shall come unto thee saying, Buy thee my field that is in Anathoth: for the right of redemption is thine to buy it.

8 So Hanameel mine uncle's son came to me in the court of the prison according to the word of the LORD, and said unto me, Buy my field, I pray thee, that is in Anathoth, which is in the country of Benjamin: for the right of inheritance is thine, and the redemption is thine; buy it for thyself. Then I knew that this was the word of the LORD.

9 And I bought the field of Hanameel my uncle's son, that was in Anathoth, and weighed him the money, even seventeen shekels of silver.

14 Thus saith the LORD of hosts, the God of Israel; Take these evidences, this evidence of the purchase, both which is

of the guard in the royal palace of Judah.

3 Now Zedekiah king of Judah had imprisoned him there, saying, "Why do you prophesy as you do? You say, 'This is what the LORD says: I am about to give this city into the hands of the king of Babylon, and he will capture it.

4 Zedekiah king of Judah will not escape the Babylonians but will certainly be given into the hands of the king of Babylon, and will speak with him face to face and see him with his own eyes.

5 He will take Zedekiah to Babylon, where he will remain until I deal with him, declares the LORD. If you fight against the Babylonians, you will not succeed.'"

6 Jeremiah said, "The word of the LORD came to me:

7 Hanamel son of Shallum your uncle is going to come to you and say, 'Buy my field at Anathoth, because as nearest relative it is your right and duty to buy it.'

8 "Then, just as the LORD had said, my cousin Hanamel came to me in the courtyard of the guard and said, 'Buy my field at Anathoth in the territory of Benjamin. Since it is your right to redeem it and possess it, buy it for yourself.' "I knew that this was the word of the LORD;

9 so I bought the field at Anathoth from my cousin Hanamel and weighed out for him seventeen shekels of silver.

14 'This is what the LORD Almighty, the God of Israel, says: Take these documents, both the sealed and unsealed copies of the deed of purchase, and put them in a clay jar so they will last a long time.

15 For this is what the LORD Almighty,

sealed, and this evidence which is open; and put them in an earthen vessel, that they may continue many days.

15 For thus saith the LORD of hosts, the God of Israel; Houses and fields and vineyards shall be possessed again in this land.

the God of Israel, says: Houses, fields and vineyards will again be bought in this land.'

LIGHT ON THE WORD

Zedekiah was the last king of Judah and son of King Josiah. His birth name was actually Mattanyahu, but it was changed by Nebuchadnezzar when he appointed Zedekiah king of Judah. Zedekiah attempted a revolt against Babylon, which prompted the military turmoil that is present in our text. Ultimately, Zedekiah was captured in a very gruesome manner; he was forced to watch the killing of his children and spent the remainder of his life as a prisoner in Babylon. These events mark the beginning of the Babylonian exile. The Judeans were deported to Babylonia and the Temple was destroyed (**2 Kings 24–25; 2 Chronicles 36**).

Jeremiah is known as the weeping prophet, so much so that there is an entire book of the Bible dedicated to his sorrow: the book of Lamentations. Most of the anguish he experienced was due to the sinful nature of the Israelites and their rejection of God. Subsequently, this also led to their captivity. But, Jeremiah also experienced grief because both he and his message were rejected by the people.

TEACHING THE BIBLE LESSON

LIFE NEED FOR TODAY'S LESSON

AIM: Students will know that in difficult circumstances, some people take hopeful actions.

INTRODUCTION

The Prophets of the Bible

Jeremiah is the longest book in the Bible and is a part of the biblical category known as the "prophets." This genre can be divided in two sub-categories: major and minor. The major prophets are Isaiah, Jeremiah, Ezekiel, and Daniel, and then the minor prophets comprise the last twelve books of the Old Testament. The distinguishing factor between major and minor is based solely on the length of the books. It has nothing to do with importance or status.

A prophet is one who serves as a medium of communication between the human and divine worlds. Prophets helped to shape Judaism and Christianity. Over the course of time, they became a mainstay as much-needed divine messengers for the nation as well as for individuals. Not all prophets have biblical books of the same name. The Bible is actually full of prophets; the only difference is that some wrote while others didn't. Various types of prophets existed in both the Old and New Testaments, and their delivery and characters were uniquely different. Biblical prophets were concerned with things of the past, present, and future. Not only did some have the gift of foresight (prediction), but they also had the "forthsight" to discern present times and admonish wrongdoing. Prophets did not have superstar appeal; most were not eloquent or charismatic and their messages were contrary to what popular culture wanted to hear.

BIBLE LEARNING

AIM: Students will know that God kept His promise to gather the people from the lands in which they had been scattered and to bring them back together and settle them in the city, in safety.

I. THE PLOT (Jeremiah 32:2–5)

Jeremiah was going to Anathoth to take care of the land deal when he was accused of desertion and thus imprisoned in the palace of the king. Based on the information provided, at the time of the text the year is between 588–587 B.C. and Nebuchadnezzar is the king of Babylon. Judah is still free but has been surrounded by the Babylonian army for eighteen months. Now that King Zedekiah has Jeremiah in his custody, the king asks a question, or rather interrogates him. The question is in fact a quote previously spoken by Jeremiah that has evidentially ravished the emotional well-being of the king.

Jeremiah is Imprisoned (verses 2–5)

2 For then the king of Babylon's army besieged Jerusalem: and Jeremiah the prophet was shut up in the court of the prison, which was in the king of Judah's house.

The siege by Babylon's army had begun a year earlier (cf. **2 Kings 25:8**) and would last for an additional six months. Jeremiah had predicted that King Nebuchadnezzar of Babylonia would be successful in his efforts to capture Israel and Judah and take its inhabitants captive back to Babylonia. Now even in the midst of being "besieged" (Heb. *tsur*, **TSOOR**, meaning to shut up or enclose) by the foreign invaders, King Zedekiah hardened his heart against Jeremiah and imprisoned God's prophet in the court of his palace. This court was probably the courtyard of the palace guards and located within the palace grounds. Jeremiah was not bound and had the freedom to have visitors and to walk the courtyard, but he was "shut up" (Heb. *kala'*, **kaw-LAW**, meaning to restrain or restrict or forbid) in the court and would have been unable to have an audience for any more of his prophecies. King Zedekiah imprisoned Jeremiah even though it was obvious that he was a prophet of God.

3 For Zedekiah king of Judah had shut him up, saying, Wherefore dost thou prophesy, and say, Thus saith the LORD, Behold, I will give this city into the hand of the king of Babylon, and he shall take it; 4 And Zedekiah king of Judah shall not escape out of the hand of the Chaldeans, but shall surely be delivered into the hand of the king of Babylon, and shall speak with him mouth to mouth, and his eyes shall behold his eyes.

Zedekiah was incensed that Jeremiah would "prophesy" (Heb. *naba'*, **naw-VAW**, meaning to be under the influence of divine spirit) as he did. The phrase "wherefore dost thou prophesy" is better understood as "how dare you prophesy" such a disaster upon Jerusalem and its king. Jeremiah prophesied that Nebuchadnezzar would capture Jerusalem as an agent of God's displeasure with His chosen nation and its leadership. Even though Jerusalem was at that moment under siege by the Babylonians, Zedekiah would not humble himself before God or His prophet (cf. **2 Chronicles 36:12**). Further, Jeremiah indicated that even though King Zedekiah would try to "escape" (Heb. *malat*, **maw-LAT**, meaning to slip away or flee), he would not be able to do so. Instead, he would be delivered into the hands of the Babylonians, where he would stand before their king, look into his eyes, and hear from his mouth the punishment to be exacted upon him. In some older African cultures the phrase "mouth to mouth and eye to eye" is used as a reference to wrestling or a swordfight. It carries the nuance of the fear and terror exuding from another warrior in close proximity. No wonder Zedekiah was furious. Jeremiah speaking in the name of Yahweh had implied that the King will be coward groveling with fear when he meets the King of Babylon.

5 And he shall lead Zedekiah to Babylon, and there shall he be until I visit him, saith the LORD: though ye fight with the Chaldeans, ye shall not prosper.

Once captured by the Babylonians, King Zedekiah would be led in chains to Babylon. He would be forcibly removed from his throne and dragged along by horses. This is a picture of complete and utter humiliation. There in Babylon he would remain a prisoner until God "visit[ed] him" (Heb. *paqad*, **paw-KAD**, meaning to punish) with death. Some scholars assert that Zedekiah found a degree of favor with Nebuchadnezzar in Babylon because he was not put to death but rather died of natural causes, even receiving some honor at his funeral (cf. **Jeremiah 34:4–5**). This suggest that Zedekiah repented of his sin sometime before his death.

SEARCH THE SCRIPTURES

QUESTION 1

How was the king of Babylon going to be able to capture Jerusalem?

LIGHT ON THE WORD

Zedekiah Loses His Kingdom

The Lord makes it clear that although the Babylonians will hold Zedekiah captive, God will administer the punishment. Even more discouraging is the warning that fighting will prove futile because there is no chance for Judah to win. The king is shaken by the prophecy and wants an explanation for why Jeremiah spoke the dispiriting words.

II. THE PROPHECY (vv. 6–9)

When Hanameel says, "By law you have the right to buy it" (**v. 7**), he is speaking of the law of redemption, which can be explained as a "keep it in the family" clause. If an owner was not able to care for the family land or didn't want it for whatever reason, the closest relative had the first right to purchase the property. One may attribute Jeremiah's diligence to wanting to ensure there was no disputing the authenticity of the transaction. His prophecy was for all of Judah, so he ensured that all the men who were in the courtyard could bear witness and hear as he spoke the words of the Lord.

Jeremiah Becomes a Landowner (verses 6–9)

6 And Jeremiah said, The word of the LORD came unto me, saying, 7 Behold, Hanameel the son of Shallum thine uncle shall come unto thee saying, Buy thee my field that is in Anathoth: for the right of redemption is thine to buy it. 8 So Hanameel mine uncle's son came to me in the court of the prison according to the word of the LORD, and said unto me, Buy my field, I pray thee, that is in Anathoth, which is in the country of Benjamin: for the right of inheritance is thine, and the redemption is thine; buy it for thyself. Then I knew that this was the word of the LORD.

God instructed Jeremiah to be prepared for a visit from his nephew Hanameel, who would approach Jeremiah to purchase his property located in Anathoth. The right of redemption was spelled out in **Leviticus 25:24–34** and illustrated in **Ruth 4:3–4** and would have been known to most Israelites of the time. It is probable that Hanameel's father Shallum was dead and the property had passed to his son. It is also probable that the siege by the Assyrians had made money a scarce possession throughout the region and Hanameel needed money. Jeremiah was not married (cf. **Jeremiah 16:2**) and had already been told by God that the Babylonians would be victorious over Israel and Judah and take possession of all the lands of those nations. For that reason, there was not much value in purchasing land within Israel or Judah at that time. Because Jeremiah did not have a wife or children, he would only be able to use the property while he lived and then could leave it only to a relative until the time of Jubilee, when the land would revert back to the original owner. Still, he knew that when Hanameel visited him in prison and requested that he purchase the land, he had been sent by God.

9 And I bought the field of Hanameel my uncle's son, that was in Anathoth, and weighed him the money, even seventeen shekels of silver.

Scholars estimate a shekel of silver to be worth about five dollars in 2010 money and seventeen shekels would be equivalent to about seven ounces of silver. Jeremiah, as a priest, would not have had a lot of money, but by being frugal, he could have had sufficient funds to purchase the field from his cousin. The prophet knew that God had sent Hanameel to him and therefore did not haggle over the price. Rather, in front of the appropriate witnesses (cf. **v. 12**), Jeremiah counted out the seventeen shekels of silver and purchased the field in accord with God's further purpose.

LIGHT ON THE WORD

An Obedient Prophet

The previous section was centered on the king asking Jeremiah about his prophecy. Oddly Jeremiah provides an extensive response, but never answers Zedekiah's question. Instead Jeremiah goes into what the reader assumes is an explanation of a revelation God has given him. God told Jeremiah about a proposition that his cousin would present to him concerning a portion of land in their hometown. When the event transpired just as the Lord said it would, Jeremiah was very diligent concerning the transaction. Not that it wasn't necessary, but this particular manifestation of God's words was confirmation that the revelations he received really were from God.

III. THE PURPOSE (vv. 14–15)

People buy when they are planning to stay and settle. The actions of Jeremiah signify something far greater than words; like the old saying goes . . . put your money where your mouth is.

An Earthen Vessel (verses 14–15)

14 Thus saith the LORD of hosts, the God of Israel; Take these evidences, this evidence of the purchase, both which is sealed, and this evidence which is open; and put them in an earthen vessel, that they may continue many days.

The land purchase agreement between Jeremiah and Hanameel, witnessed by those present, would have been written down on two documents. These documents or "evidences" (Heb. *sepher*, **SAY-fer**, meaning missive or writing) of the purchase were to be placed in a clay pot to be retrieved at some future date. One document was to be sealed (this was probably the original document which contained the terms and conditions of the agreement), while the second document that summarized the agreement was to remain "open" (Heb. *galah*, **gaw-LAW**, meaning uncovered or exposed) so that it could be housed in a public register for any person to have access to.

15 For thus saith the LORD of hosts, the God of Israel; Houses and fields and vineyards shall be possessed again in this land.

God then reveals the reason that Jeremiah was to purchase the field from his cousin. Jeremiah had already been told that the Babylonians would be successful in their siege of Jerusalem and would lay the land to waste. During the seventy years that the Children of Israel would be in bondage in Babylonia, the land that made up the nations of Israel and Judah would be desolate and in ruin. Houses and fields and vineyards would all be destroyed. In purchasing Hanameel's field, God was communicating to future generations through Jeremiah that His chosen people will once again possess the land promised to them.

SEARCH THE SCRIPTURES

QUESTION 2

What was the purpose of putting the sealed deeds in a pottery jar?

LIGHT ON THE WORD

Hope in Action

God's purpose is revealed here. This is not just a foolish transfer of land from one family member to another during a time of military occupation, but a sign of hope. Jeremiah took care in preserving the deeds as a sign that the day would come when the land would once again be of value. It is very likely that during this time everyone wanted to sell and no one wanted to buy because all of the land could any day become the property of Babylon. This is yet another message given to the prophet from God. This time the message is of hope and comes in the form of action, not just words. It was so during ancient times and still holds true today: when a country is in despair, the housing and real estate market is a gauge used to measure recovery and stability.

BIBLE APPLICATION

AIM: Students will believe they have hope based in a spiritual heritage established in Jesus Christ.

Jeremiah speaks regarding the faith and future of a nation. The same way God sent prophets to the nation of Israel, He sends messages and messengers to the nations of today. What are some of the things that we do as a nation that God may be displeased with? Now think about it on a smaller level. What are some of the things your local community may do that are displeasing to God? When the appointed messenger, your pastor, speaks doom and hope, does it affect the actions of the community?

STUDENTS' RESPONSES

AIM: Students will embrace hope for the future in times of personal hardship.

Think about a past experience in your life that was filled with despair. Even though you may not have been hopeful at the time, try to remember if there were any signs of hope that everything would work out in the end.

PRAYER

Dear God, our hope in You gives us fresh air to breathe Your Word. Our hope in You allows us to listen and feel Your presence in our lives. Help us to care for others and restore relationships with others as we discover how to develop a deeper relationship with You. In Jesus' Name we pray. Amen.

HOW TO SAY IT

Chaldean.	chal-**DEE**-en.
Zedekiah.	ze-de-**KAY**-ah.
Hanameel.	ha-na-**MEEL**.
Anathoth.	a-na-**THOTH**.

PREPARE FOR NEXT SUNDAY

Read **Jeremiah 33:2–11** and study "Improbable Possibilities."

DAILY HOME BIBLE READINGS

MONDAY
The Steadfast Love of God
(Jeremiah 32:16–23)

TUESDAY
Provoking God
(Jeremiah 32:26–35)

WEDNESDAY
Very Soon My Anger Will End
(Isaiah 10:20–25)

THURSDAY
I Will Surely Gather Them
(Jeremiah 32:36–44)

FRIDAY
The Wolf and Lamb Live Together
(Isaiah 11:1–12)

SATURDAY
Surely God is My Salvation
(Isaiah 12)

SUNDAY
Hope for a Distant Future
(Jeremiah 32:2–9, 14–15)

Sources:

Brueggmann, Walter. *To Build, To Plant: Jeremiah 26–52*. Grand Rapids, MI: Wm. B. Eerdsmans Publishing Company, 1991.

Dunn, James D. G. and John W. Rogerson. *Commentary on the Bible*. Grand Rapids, MI: Wm. B. Eerdmans Publishing Company, 2003.

English, E. Schuyler and Marian Bishop Bower, eds. *The Holy Bible: Pilgrim Edition*. New York: Oxford University Press, 1952.

Howley, G.C.D., F.F. Bruce, and H. L. Ellison. *The New Layman's Bible Commentary*. Grand Rapids, MI: Zondervan, 1979.

Keener, Craig S. *The IVP Bible Background Commentary: New Testament*. Downers Grove, IL: InterVarsity Press, 1993.

Keown, Gerald L., Pamela J. Scalise, and Thomas G. Smothers. *Word Biblical Commentary, Volume 27: Jeremiah 26–52*. Dallas, TX: Word Books Publisher, 1995. 169.

COMMENTS / NOTES:

IMPROBABLE POSSIBILITIES

BIBLE BASIS: JEREMIAH 33:2–11

BIBLE TRUTH: God is willing to forgive and bring recovery, healing, and restoration.

MEMORY VERSE: "Call unto me, and I will answer thee, and show thee great and mighty things, which thou knowest not" (Jeremiah 33:3).

LESSON AIM: By the end of this lesson, your students will: realize that God's promise to follow punishment with forgiveness and restoration is still a valid promise; affirm that with God, punishment, forgiveness, and healing come as a package; and design a thanks offering for hope, healing, and forgiveness we receive from God.

TEACHER PREPARATION

MATERIALS NEEDED: Quarterly Commentary/Teacher Manual, Adult Quarterly, Adult resources—charts, worksheets, and other teaching tools, paper, pens, pencils, Bibles (several different versions)

OTHER MATERIALS NEEDED / TEACHER'S NOTES:

____

____

LESSON OVERVIEW

LIFE NEED FOR TODAY'S LESSON
We do not always know which way to go or where to turn at certain points in our lives.

BIBLE LEARNING
God promised His people renewed abundance, prosperity, and security.

BIBLE APPLICATION
Christians struggle to act on the faith that God will fulfill promises of restoration.

STUDENTS' RESPONSES
Christians show gratitude to God for the promises of restoration in difficult times.

LESSON SCRIPTURE

JEREMIAH 33:2–11, KJV

2 Thus saith the LORD the maker thereof, the LORD that formed it, to establish it; the LORD is his name;

3 Call unto me, and I will answer thee, and show thee great and mighty things, which thou knowest not.

JEREMIAH 33:2–11, NIV

2 "This is what the LORD says, he who made the earth, the LORD who formed it and established it—the LORD is his name:

3 'Call to me and I will answer you and tell you great and unsearchable things you do not know.'

4 For thus saith the LORD, the God of Israel, concerning the houses of this city, and concerning the houses of the kings of Judah, which are thrown down by the mounts, and by the sword;

5 They come to fight with the Chaldeans, but it is to fill them with the dead bodies of men, whom I have slain in mine anger and in my fury, and for all whose wickedness I have hid my face from this city.

6 Behold, I will bring it health and cure, and I will cure them, and will reveal unto them the abundance of peace and truth.

7 And I will cause the captivity of Judah and the captivity of Israel to return, and will build them, as at the first.

8 And I will cleanse them from all their iniquity, whereby they have sinned against me; and I will pardon all their iniquities, whereby they have sinned, and whereby they have transgressed against me.

9 And it shall be to me a name of joy, a praise and an honour before all the nations of the earth, which shall hear all the good that I do unto them: and they shall fear and tremble for all the goodness and for all the prosperity that I procure unto it.

10 Thus saith the LORD; Again there shall be heard in this place, which ye say shall be desolate without man and without beast, even in the cities of Judah, and in the streets of Jerusalem, that are desolate, without man, and without inhabitant, and without beast,

11 The voice of joy, and the voice of gladness, the voice of the bridegroom, and the voice of the bride, the voice of them that

4 For this is what the LORD, the God of Israel, says about the houses in this city and the royal palaces of Judah that have been torn down to be used against the siege ramps and the sword

5 in the fight with the Babylonians: 'They will be filled with the dead bodies of the people I will slay in my anger and wrath. I will hide my face from this city because of all its wickedness.

6 "'Nevertheless, I will bring health and healing to it; I will heal my people and will let them enjoy abundant peace and security.

7 I will bring Judah and Israel back from captivity and will rebuild them as they were before.

8 I will cleanse them from all the sin they have committed against me and will forgive all their sins of rebellion against me.

9 Then this city will bring me renown, joy, praise and honor before all nations on earth that hear of all the good things I do for it; and they will be in awe and will tremble at the abundant prosperity and peace I provide for it.'

10 "This is what the LORD says: 'You say about this place, "It is a desolate waste, without people or animals." Yet in the towns of Judah and the streets of Jerusalem that are deserted, inhabited by neither people nor animals, there will be heard once more

11 the sounds of joy and gladness, the voices of bride and bridegroom, and the voices of those who bring thank offerings to the house of the LORD, saying, "Give thanks to the LORD Almighty, for the LORD is good; his love endures forever."

shall say, Praise the LORD of hosts: for the LORD is good; for his mercy endureth for ever: and of them that shall bring the sacrifice of praise into the house of the LORD. For I will cause to return the captivity of the land, as at the first, saith the LORD.

For I will restore the fortunes of the land as they were before,' says the LORD.

LIGHT ON THE WORD

Nebuchadnezzar's father, who was a Chaldean, seized Babylon around 626 B.C., and at some point in ancient history Chaldean and Babylonian became synonymous. More correct, however, is the term Neo-Babylonian, which marks the period Chaldeans ruled Babylon. Babylon was located in the lower regions of the Tigris and the Euphrates Rivers, which is present-day Iraq. The larger area to which Chaldea belonged is Mesopotamia. Aside from the aforementioned Iraq, parts of present-day Iran, Syria, and Turkey comprise Mesopotamia. The region is known for its desert terrain.

TEACHING THE BIBLE LESSON

LIFE NEED FOR TODAY'S LESSON

AIM: Students will acknowledge that we do not always know which way to go or where to turn at certain points in our lives.

INTRODUCTION

Yahweh—My Provider

The word "LORD" in this text is translated from the Hebrew word Yahweh. Whenever the Bible uses the name of Yahweh, there's a prevailing promise for God's people. The name Yahweh is used for God whenever His personal relationship with His people is highlighted.

Throughout the Bible, God reminds the Children of Israel several times: "I am Yahweh your God, who brought you out of the land of Egypt, out of the house of bondage. You shall have no other gods before me" (**Deuteronomy 5:6–7**, World English Bible). This consistent declaration reminded the Children of Israel, and us today, of an offer of partnership, provision, and a potent prescription for power!

In Jeremiah, the Judeans are on the brink of captivity, but this would not be the first time the Israelites experienced oppression. They were enslaved in Egypt, and Yahweh provided them a passage to freedom. Yahweh is willing to make the same provisions for us today!

BIBLE LEARNING

AIM: Students will know God promised them renewed abundance, prosperity, and security.

I. A POINT OF CLARITY (Jeremiah 33:2–6)

Chapter 33 serves as a reassurance that the covenant God had with Israel was still binding despite what was going on currently and about to happen. This text begins with a point of clarity. God is saying, if you want to know something, be sure you call on the right God. One of Judah's transgressions was that they were faithless and had gone astray by entertaining other deities. God wanted to ensure there was no confusing the author of the message. In essence, God's message is "I alone, the One who created the Earth, am capable of revealing things beyond your knowledge."

Our Call and God's Response (verses 2–6)

2 Thus saith the LORD the maker thereof, the LORD that formed it, to establish it; the LORD is his name; 3 Call unto me, and I will answer thee, and show thee great and mighty things, which thou knowest not.

A second time God visits Jeremiah while he is imprisoned and speaks to him. The "LORD" (Heb. *Yahweh*, **yah-WAY**, meaning the self-existing One) God who is addressing this prophecy through Jeremiah is the same one who was the "maker" (Heb. *'asah*, **aw-SAW**, meaning to produce, fashion or make to come to pass) of the earth. He formed it so that He could establish it. The message from God is simple: if He was able to make, "form" (Heb. *yatsar*, **yaw-TSAR**, meaning to shape clay or metal), and "establish" (Heb. *kuwn*, **KOON**, meaning to make secure) the earth and all that is in it, He is able to accomplish any request Israel and Judah might make to Him. They need only to "call" (Heb. *qara*, **kaw-RAW**, meaning to cry out for help) upon Him and He has promised to "answer" (Heb. *'anah*, **aw-NAW**) them. God even offers to extend what they might pray for by showing (Heb. *nagad*, **naw-GAD**, to announce) them great and mighty things of which they "knowest" not (Heb. *yada'*, **yaw-DAH**, meaning to understand).

4 For thus saith the LORD, the God of Israel, concerning the houses of this city, and concerning the houses of the kings of Judah, which are thrown down by the mounts, and by the sword.

The Lord affirms for Israel that He is their God and has been watching their plight. He wants them to know that He is aware that the attack by the Babylonians has destroyed their homes and left the palace in a heap of rubble. The Chaldean army was famous for its use of the battering ram, and other instruments of war had been used to siege the city of Jerusalem for over a year. In order to patch the holes in the wall that fortified the city, the inhabitants of Jerusalem were using the rubble from the homes and royal dwellings that had been destroyed in the fighting. Some commentators suggest that "mounts" (Heb. *solelah*, **so-lel-AW**, meaning siege ramps) refers to the ramparts that the soldiers within the city built in order to fight the Babylonians.

5 They come to fight with the Chaldeans, but it is to fill them with the dead bodies of men, whom I have slain in mine anger and in my fury, and for all whose wickedness I have hid my face from this city.

The normal practice of taking the dead bodies of the slain and placing them on a heap outside of the city gate was not possible during the siege by the Babylonians. The bodies could not be left in the homes or on the street, so they were piled up and left by the walls where the battle was raging. Seeing all the dead and rotting bodies would have been visible evidence to the Israelites within the city of God's great displeasure with them. Jeremiah is telling the people that God in his "anger" (Heb. *'aph*, **AF**, meaning to be enraged) also has permitted the slaying of His chosen people because of their sin. His righteousness has caused Him to hide his face from the city, or turn His back on it and its plight (cf. **Micah 3:4**).

6 Behold, I will bring it health and cure, and I will cure them, and will reveal unto them the abundance of peace and truth.

The Lord initially healed them with the cure of bringing the exiles back from Babylon and rebuilding the city and Temple. Through Jeremiah, God continues to speak to future generations of the Children of Israel (also to us who are heirs to the promises), stating that He will bring both health and the cure for the disease of sin that has caused Him to turn His back on His chosen people. God is promising that He will "reveal" (Heb. *galah*, **gaw-LAW**, meaning to uncover) to them just how deep and full His "peace" (Heb. *shalom*, **shaw-LOME**, meaning welfare, health, prosperity) and "truth" (Heb. *'emeth*, **EH-meth**, meaning faithfulness, reliableness) are.

SEARCH THE SCRIPTURES

QUESTION 1

What did God say happened because of Judah's wickedness?

LIGHT ON THE WORD

Judah is Defeated

The text is clear that Judah's effort will be in vain and their defeat will be great. The entire nation will suffer destruction; every dwelling from the smallest cottage to the grandest palace of the king will be affected. The loss will extend beyond possessions and wealth; there will even be death. God will turn aside while the Chaldeans wreak havoc on them and the consequences of their wickedness unfold. God reiterates the terms of their punishment prior to confirming the promise.

II. LAUGHTER SHALL RETURN (vv. 7–11)

God's actions are similar to a parent. If a child does something wrong, the parent reprimands the child. God makes it clear that once Judah has been corrected, He will come and restore the relationship. The restoration will come in many forms: land revitalization, healing, peace, truth, liberation, forgiveness, and unity again with God. God will bring Judah back not only from physical but emotional discipline, and things of the heart such as joy, singing, and laughter shall return.

From Captivity to Freedom (verses 7–11)

7 And I will cause the captivity of Judah and the captivity of Israel to return, and will build them, as at the first.

What joy it must have been for Jeremiah to write this promise of God to bring the captives of the nations of Israel and Judah back to their Promised Land and to restore them to a status and situation that equaled their state before their bondage to the Babylonians. And what faith it must have prompted in the prophet to believe God's promise while he himself was being held prisoner in Zedekiah's courtyard.

8 And I will cleanse them from all their iniquity, whereby they have sinned against me; and I will pardon all their iniquities, whereby they have sinned, and whereby they have transgressed against me.

God's promise to His chosen people and to His church is that though they at present are reprehensible to Him because of sin, He will cleanse them from that sin. But not that sin only; He will cleanse them from all their "iniquities" (Heb. *'awon*, **aw-VONE**, meaning violations or offenses). Further, God will "pardon" (Heb. *salach*, **saw-LAKH**, meaning to release or forgive) all of the wrong and evil done against His holy person. Only then would His people be fit to reoccupy the land that had been promised.

9 And it shall be to me a name of joy, a praise and an honour before all the nations of the earth, which shall hear all the good

that I do unto them: and they shall fear and tremble for all the goodness and for all the prosperity that I procure unto it.

The suffering that the Israelite nations would undergo and all the pain and misery of God's chosen people would cause the other nations of the earth to take note. Then, once the Children of Israel had repented, been forgiven, and been restored to their own land and the land repopulated, their homes rebuilt, and their worship of God renewed, all the nations would hear of the good that God had done for His chosen people. In response, those nations would "fear" (Heb. *pachad*, **paw-KHAD**, meaning to be in dread) and "tremble" (Heb. *ragaz*, **raw-GAZ**, meaning to shake with fear) before the God of the Israelites, and He would receive honor from this. Additionally, the Jews thus being restored and noting the reactions of the other nations would glorify God by being obedient to His will. The "prosperity" Jeremiah mentions in this verse is the same word in the original text as "peace" in **verse 6**.

10 Thus saith the LORD; Again there shall be heard in this place, which ye say shall be desolate without man and without beast, even in the cities of Judah, and in the streets of Jerusalem, that are desolate, without man, and without inhabitant, and without beast, 11 The voice of joy, and the voice of gladness, the voice of the bridegroom, and the voice of the bride, the voice of them that shall say, Praise the LORD of hosts: for the LORD is good; for his mercy endureth for ever: and of them that shall bring the sacrifice of praise into the house of the LORD. For I will cause to return the captivity of the land, as at the first, saith the LORD.

As the Babylonians besieged Jerusalem and the surrounding nations of Judah and Israel and were about to completely overrun its fortifications, all one could see was "desolate" ruins. Jeremiah had prophesied that the people of the land would be carried off as captives of war and that the land would appear to be without a single "inhabitant" (Heb. *yashab*, **yaw-SHAV**, meaning people who live in a certain area). But God here promises that voices of sadness will one day be turned to voices of joy and gladness. God promises that the voice of the bridegroom and the voice of the bride will ring out in praises to the Lord of hosts. In His "mercy" (Heb. *chesed*, **KHEH-sed**, meaning favor, faithfulness or loyal love), God will return the inhabitants of the land and restore them to a condition that will equal their state when they first occupied the Promised Land. Then their weeping will be turned to joy, and they will bring their "sacrifice of praise" to the house of the Lord. This wondrous promise is intended to give hope and encouragement to the Children of Israel and, by extension, to all who will share in God's favor because of them.

SEARCH THE SCRIPTURES

QUESTION 2

"The voice of _______, and the voice of ________, the voice of the bridegroom, and the voice of the bride, the voice of them that shall say, Praise the LORD of hosts" (KJV).

LIGHT ON THE WORD

A New Day Will Come

God's message seems like an improbable possibility to the Children of Israel. The nation is on the brink of captivity. God avows that not only will they be freed from captivity and reclaim what is rightfully theirs, but they will experience abundant peace. God's love is just and all encompassing. It is inclusive of everything we need to take our rightful place in God's kingdom.

BIBLE APPLICATION

AIM: Students will learn that Christians struggle to act on the faith that God will fulfill promises of restoration.

Although incarceration rates are high, more and more we are becoming a society that does not fear punishment. God's punishment, healing, and forgiveness are all a part of His love for us. No one should expect to commit a crime and not have to suffer the repercussions. On a more personal level, when we take our relationships for granted, mistreat someone, or don't own up to our responsibilities, there is a consequence.

STUDENTS' RESPONSES

AIM: Students will show gratitude to God for the promises of restoration in difficult times.

Think about an instance when you did something wrong. What were the ways in which God extended hope, healing, and forgiveness to you afterward? Use these thoughts to assist you in completing the last section of the Lesson Aim.

PRAYER

Oh God of restoration, we need You in our lives each and everyday. The empty spaces in our lives or the pain of wrong choices, keep us from experiencing the depth of Your promises for us. Lord, give us this day, and everyday, the opportunity to know the love that You renew in us again and again. Forgive us for our sins as we repent and turn to You. In Jesus' Name we pray. Amen.

HOW TO SAY IT

Procure.	**PRO**-kyur.
Desolate.	de-**SO**-let.

PREPARE FOR NEXT SUNDAY

Read **Habakkuk 2:1–5, 3:17–19** and study "Rejoice Anyway."

DAILY HOME BIBLE READINGS

MONDAY
In Returning You Shall Be Saved
(Isaiah 30:9–17)

TUESDAY
Where Are Your Gods?
(Jeremiah 2:26–32)

WEDNESDAY
I Will Bring You to Zion
(Jeremiah 3:11–15)

THURSDAY
I Will Heal Your Faithlessness
(Jeremiah 3:19–23)

FRIDAY
The Hope of Israel
(Jeremiah 17:12–17)

SATURDAY
The Lord Acts with Steadfast Love
(Jeremiah 9:17–24)

SUNDAY
Voices of Mirth and Gladness
(Jeremiah 33:2–11)

Sources:

Achtemeier, Paul J., Roger S. Boraas, Michael Fishburne, et al. eds. *Harper Collins Bible Dictionary.* New York: HarperCollins Publishers, 1996. 154, 550.

Brueggmann, Walter. *To Build, To Plant: Jeremiah 26–52.* Grand Rapids, MI: Wm. B. Eerdsmans Publishing Company, 1991.

Dunn, James D. G. and John W. Rogerson. *Commentary on the Bible.* Grand Rapids, MI: Wm. B. Eerdmans Publishing Company, 2003.

English, E. Schuyler and Marian Bishop Bower, eds. *The Holy Bible: Pilgrim Edition.* New York: Oxford University Press, 1952.

Howley, G.C.D., F.F. Bruce, and H. L. Ellison. *The New Layman's Bible Commentary.* Grand Rapids, MI: Zondervan, 1979.

Keener, Craig S. *The IVP Bible Background Commentary: New Testament.* Downers Grove, IL: InterVarsity Press, 1993.

Strong, James. *Strong's Exhaustive Concordance.* Grand Rapids, MI: Zondervan, 2001.

REJOICE ANYWAY

BIBLE BASIS: HABAKKUK 2:1–5, 3:17–19

BIBLE TRUTH: Job, the psalmist, and Habakkuk all affirm that—no matter what calamities might come their way—they will trust God, rejoice in God's presence in their lives, and praise God for strength to carry on.

MEMORY VERSE: "Although the fig tree shall not blossom, neither shall fruit be in the vines; the labour of the olive shall fail, and the fields shall yield no meat; the flock shall be cut off from the fold, and there shall be no herd in the stalls: Yet I will rejoice in the LORD, I will joy in the God of my salvation" (Habakkuk 3:17–18).

LESSON AIM: By the end of the lesson, your students will: hear God's message of patience for the people and assurance that God will act with justice; experience the feeling of joy when we have patiently awaited God's promises; and practice responding to difficulties by trusting in God's presence and by praising God for strength to endure.

TEACHER PREPARATION

MATERIALS NEEDED: Quarterly Commentary/Teacher Manual, Adult Quarterly, Adult resources—charts, worksheets, and other teaching tools, paper, pens, pencils, Bibles (several different versions)

OTHER MATERIALS NEEDED / TEACHER'S NOTES:

LESSON OVERVIEW

LIFE NEED FOR TODAY'S LESSON

Some people experience so many difficulties in life that they lose all hope for the future.

BIBLE LEARNING

Habakkuk recognized that God rejected Israel's justice system as corrupt.

BIBLE APPLICATION

Believers experience joy when they have patiently waited for God's promises to be revealed.

STUDENTS' RESPONSES

Believers hold accountable those who abuse political and economic power.

LESSON SCRIPTURE

HABAKKUK 2:1–5, 3:17–19, KJV

1 I will stand upon my watch, and set me upon the tower, and will watch to see what he will say unto me, and what I shall answer when I am reproved.

HABAKKUK 2:1–5, 3:17–19, NIV

1 I will stand at my watch and station myself on the ramparts; I will look to see what he will say to me, and what answer I am to give to this complaint.

2 And the LORD answered me, and said, Write the vision, and make it plain upon tables, that he may run that readeth it.

3 For the vision is yet for an appointed time, but at the end it shall speak, and not lie: though it tarry, wait for it; because it will surely come, it will not tarry.

4 Behold, his soul which is lifted up is not upright in him: but the just shall live by his faith.

5 Yea also, because he transgresseth by wine, he is a proud man, neither keepeth at home, who enlargeth his desire as hell, and is as death, and cannot be satisfied, but gathereth unto him all nations, and heapeth unto him all people.

3:17 Although the fig tree shall not blossom, neither shall fruit be in the vines; the labour of the olive shall fail, and the fields shall yield no meat; the flock shall be cut off from the fold, and there shall be no herd in the stalls:

18 Yet I will rejoice in the LORD, I will joy in the God of my salvation.

19 The LORD God is my strength, and he will make my feet like hinds' feet, and he will make me to walk upon mine high places. To the chief singer on my stringed instruments.

2 Then the LORD replied: "Write down the revelation and make it plain on tablets so that a herald may run with it.

3 For the revelation awaits an appointed time; it speaks of the end and will not prove false. Though it linger, wait for it; it will certainly come and will not delay.

4 "See, the enemy is puffed up; his desires are not upright—but the righteous person will live by his faithfulness—

5 indeed, wine betrays him; he is arrogant and never at rest. Because he is as greedy as the grave and like death is never satisfied, he gathers to himself all the nations and takes captive all the peoples.

3:17 Though the fig tree does not bud and there are no grapes on the vines, though the olive crop fails and the fields produce no food, though there are no sheep in the pen and no cattle in the stalls,

18 yet I will rejoice in the LORD, I will be joyful in God my Savior.

19 The Sovereign LORD is my strength; he makes my feet like the feet of a deer, he enables me to tread on the heights. For the director of music. On my stringed instruments.

LIGHT ON THE WORD

Habakkuk was a prophet of the late seveneth century. His name in Hebrew means "embrace" or "ardent embrace." As the chosen human instrument for God, he spoke the Word of God to the people. Not much is known about Habakkuk the person other than he may have been a Levite who was familiar with the Temple singers. This is due to the musical notation that is found at the conclusion of the book that bears his name.

A prophet is one called to receive and declare a Word from God after being prompted by the Holy Spirit. Prophets were usually called to speak a word concerning the present and the future. Their words could be addressed to nations as well as individuals. God used prophets to speak of injustice and wickedness in the nation of Israel. This was accomplished not only through verbal means; sometimes prophets were called to demonstrate their message through physical acts. Habakkuk was a prophet. Other known prophets are Moses, Samuel, Elijah, and Elisha.

TEACHING THE BIBLE LESSON

LIFE NEED FOR TODAY'S LESSON

AIM: Students will know that some people experience so many difficulties in life that they lose all hope for the future.

INTRODUCTION

Habakkuk Questioned God

As with many righteous religious leaders, Habakkuk faced a lot of wickedness and injustice during his time. This was a time when, after a period of reform under King Josiah, many in Israel had fallen back into godlessness and idolatry. Instead of speaking out against national sin and addressing the perpetrators of wickedness, Habakkuk addressed himself to God. He could not stand to see the wicked get away with their crimes and sinful actions. He complained to God and asked, "How long, O Lord...?" (from **1:2**). Habakkuk's personal plea was a radical departure from the usual activity of the prophets who pronounced judgement and encouraged the people to repent of their ways. This time he questioned the justice of God.

BIBLE LEARNING

AIM: Students will know that Habakkuk recognized that God rejected Israel's justice system as corrupt.

I. HABAKKUK TRUSTS GOD FOR AN ANSWER (Habakkuk 2:1–2)

Habakkuk has asked questions of God and now stands like a watchman waiting for an answer. This attitude and posture shows that Habakkuk had faith and trust in God. His questions were not questions based on doubt, but a rock-solid faith in God. He embraced the hard questions and is willing to receive the answer that God would give.

Waiting for God's Response (verses 1–2)

1 I will stand upon my watch, and set me upon the tower, and will watch to see what he will say unto me, and what I shall answer when I am reproved.

Habakkuk looks around and sees all sorts of wickedness among his own people. He sees them perpetrating violence and destruction on one another. He asks God to show him why He is allowing these things to go on. God's answer is even more shocking: He will punish His people, the Israelites, by allowing the Babylonians (Chaldeans, KJV) to conquer them. This amazes Habakkuk. It seems to him that the sins of Israel were baby stuff in comparison with the extreme violence and destruction of the Babylonians. We can see some parallels among some African American communities. Black-on-Black crime seems to be abundant, and yet, when the police force, etc. of the mainstream move in, we may see things that are even worse for our people.

Habakkuk, whose name in Hebrew is *Chabaqquwq* (**kha-bawk-KOOK**) and means "to embrace," fully embraces his people and his faith in Yahweh, the God of Israel, and yet he has questions. He figuratively stands at the watchtower and waits to see what God will do in answer to his doubts. "When I am reproved" may not be the best translation. The Hebrew for "reproved" is *tokhakhat* (**toe-khaw-KHAWT**) and does mean correction, but whether this refers to a rebuke of Habakkuk or by him is not clear. But it is certain that Habakkuk is patiently waiting for God's answer to his complaint.

2 And the LORD answered me, and said, Write the vision, and make it plain upon tables, that he may run that readeth it.

Israel lay at the crossroads for many cultures; thus they learned to write on papyrus scrolls, inscribe on soft clay tablets, and chisel on stone tablets. The picture here is probably writing on a large, wooden tablet with large, clear letters that could be easily read, so legible that even hurried passersby could read the message and pass it on. Picture the billboard on an interstate expressway, and you will get the idea. Not only is the message clear, but the message is meant to be shared.

SEARCH THE SCRIPTURES

QUESTION 1

What is the significance of Habakkuk standing on a tower to hear God answer?

LIGHT ON THE WORD

Write the Vision

This is the second time Habakkuk receives a response from God: "And the LORD answered me, and said" (**v. 2**). God instructs Habakkuk to write down the vision as he receives it. The written vision gives Habakkuk credibility before speaking it to the people. The written vision also serves as a guarantee God will act and does act.

The Lord also assures Habakkuk of the vision's timing. The vision would come to pass in a future time. God says that the vision will be delayed, but it will come to pass. It will not be delayed indefinitely. It will be delayed but not denied! Habakkuk is given assurance that the vision will come to pass in God's timing. Then the Lord encourages him to wait for the vision to be fulfilled. The assurance that what God has spoken will come to fruition will enable Habakkuk to wait and endure the injustice of the present.

II. HABAKKUK MUST CONTINUE TO TRUST (vv. 3–5)

In the vision, God assures Habakkuk to remain committed to God in the midst of the injustice and violence taking place around him. "Behold, his soul which is lifted up is not upright in him: but the just shall live by his faith" (**v. 4**). God gives Habakkuk the right way to respond to the wickedness around him: trust. Trust will separate the righteous from the wicked. Trust in the Lord distinguishes God's people from those who trust in themselves. God lets Habakkuk know that he is supposed to live by faith. Faith should permeate all aspects of his life. His whole way of being should be characterized by trusting in God, not himself.

Wait for the Vision (verses 3–5)

3 For the vision is yet for an appointed time, but at the end it shall speak, and not lie: though it tarry, wait for it; because it will surely come, it will not tarry. 4 Behold, his soul which is lifted up is not upright in him: but the just shall live by his faith.

Habakkuk lives between the times of the promise and the fulfillment. Although God is using the Babylonians to punish His own people, in the end the Babylonians will be judged for their excessive cruelty to the Israelites. Habakkuk wants God to bring judgment on the Babylonians right away, but he has to wait. In **verse 3** God assures Habakkuk that the prophecy will come to pass. This is not unlike our own lives, as we learn to wait patiently for the Lord to act. But what should Habakkuk do in the meantime? He is to continue living a life of faith.

The Hebrew word used for faith in **verse 4** is *'emunah* (**eh-moo-NAW**). The synonym for this is literally firmness and can be translated as faith, faithfulness, or moral fidelity. This reminds us that very few words can be translated exactly into another language. The Hebrew word for faith here encompasses both faith and faithfulness.

"The just shall live by faith" was the standard upon which the Protestant Reformation was started—the phrase that helped Martin Luther see that buying indulgences, performing good deeds, or living a moral life could not give us salvation. Paul quotes this phrase in **Romans 1:17** and in **Galatians 3:11**. **Hebrews 10:37–38** quotes **verses 3–4** in this way: "For yet a little while, and he that shall come will come, and will not tarry. Now the just shall live by faith: but if any man draw back, my soul shall have no pleasure in him." The New Testament writers clearly saw this as referring to the second coming of our Savior. **Habakkuk 2:3** refers to "it," but the writer of Hebrews makes clear that "it" is not a thing but a "He"—Jesus Christ, the promised Messiah. Biblical prophecy is often that way; there is a partial fulfillment soon after the prophecy—the Babylonians were already poised to conquer Israel, but they would be totally out of the picture in seventy years, when the people of Judah had the opportunity of returning to their land. Then there is a grander fulfillment of biblical prophecy, often referring to the first or second coming of Jesus. The life of the believer, whether in the Old Testament or the New, is to be a life of faith, putting our full trust in our Lord.

The fourth verse begins with the phrase "Behold, his soul which is lifted up is not upright in him." This refers to the Babylonian king or the Babylonian people who would soon conquer Judah. In so many words, this description calls them arrogant, which contrasts with Habakkuk and God's chosen people who are to humbly trust and wait for God.

5 Yea also, because he transgresseth by wine, he is a proud man, neither keepeth at home, who enlargeth his desire as hell, and is as death, and cannot be satisfied, but gathereth unto him all nations, and heapeth unto him all people.

The Babylonians and other imperial powers were well-known for their over-indulgence in alcoholic beverages and drunkenness. For example, Babylonia was overthrown while their leaders were in the midst of a drunken feast (**Daniel 5**). The Bible warns in several places of the dangers of drinking, especially drinking to excess (**Proverbs 23:31–32**). Secondly, the Babylonians are called "proud" (Heb. *yahiyr*, **yaw-HERE**), which also means arrogant or haughty, just as the accusation in **verse 4**. And thirdly, the Babylonians are portrayed as rapacious, seeking to devour all the surrounding nations, just as death and hell seek to swallow everyone.

SEARCH THE SCRIPTURES

QUESTION 2

What does it mean for the just to live by faith?

LIGHT ON THE WORD

The Character of the Wicked

The Lord then describes the character of the wicked. They drink excessively and are full of pride. They have an insatiable greed and attempt to bring everything under their ownership. This is also a picture of the Babylonian ruler who will come to conquer Judah. It is a picture of someone who is not in a relationship with God but is against God and His people. This is not the way the righteous live. The righteous are called to live by faith in a God who takes care of them and will remedy every injustice.

III. HABAKKUK TRUSTS GOD ENOUGH TO REJOICE (vv. 17–19)

Habakkuk describes utter disaster for an agricultural way of life (**v. 17**). Nothing that is planted grows and the animals fail to reproduce. It is a sad picture that spoke to the mostly agricultural society in those times. The first hearers would have seen this as the worst thing that could happen to someone. It is a scene where there is no sign of life or growth. There is no provision that the land can give. It is barren. This is a picture of poverty and devastation.

Rejoice in the Midst of Barrenness (verses 17–19)

3:17 Although the fig tree shall not blossom, neither shall fruit be in the vines; the labour of the olive shall fail, and the fields shall yield no meat; the flock shall be cut off from the fold, and there shall be no herd in the stalls: 18 Yet I will rejoice in the LORD, I will joy in the God of my salvation.

Habakkuk is not an unrealistic optimist. He knows that God is going to bring awful judgment upon His people through the Babylonians. This ruthless army will not only take all the food that God's people are growing, but they will destroy the trees and vines so that for years to come, no olives, grapes, or figs will grow. In addition they will take all the herds—the sheep, the goats, and other animals. But in the midst of all this, Habakkuk gives a ringing testimony that he will trust in the Lord, no matter what the situation. So in spite of everything, Habakkuk will rejoice.

The third and last chapter of Habakkuk is a prayer in the form of a psalm. After all the questions, Habakkuk sings of the power and justice of God that bring him to the triumph of faith. We tend to think that the beauty of psalms lies in their ability to express the feelings that are in our own hearts, and they certainly do that. But our singing can be a spiritual discipline in which the very character and feelings of God's people become impressed within us. As we take within ourselves the words of Habakkuk, the inspired words of God are being planted in our hearts. Imagine composing a tune to go with **verses 17 and 18**—what increasing faith will grow in our hearts, even in the midst of difficult circumstances!

19 The LORD God is my strength, and he will make my feet like hinds' feet, and he will make me to walk upon mine high places. To the chief singer on my stringed instruments.

The reason for Habakkuk's confidence in the midst of the expectations of great horrors for the Israelites is his trust in the Lord God. The Hebrew for "LORD" is Yahweh, which is the personal name by which God identifies Himself to His chosen people. Vowels were not written in ancient Hebrew and so the translators of the KJV Bible surmised that the pronunciation for "LORD" was Jehovah.

The hind can be a variety of animals that are swift and sure-footed, such as deer or gazelles. These animals can confidently climb up the mountains with their nimble feet and strong legs. Habakkuk is imagining himself climbing upon spiritual mountaintops because God is giving him the strength and confidence so that even when troubles come he can trust in the Lord.

Evidently this chapter was written for the levitical choir, accompanied by stringed instruments.

Habakkuk himself may have been a Levite, one of the official Temple workers, but not descended directly from the Aaronic priestly line. Two of the stringed instruments mentioned in the Old Testament are the lyre and the harp. The lyre was shaped like a rectangle or a trapezoid and had a varied number of strings. It was used to accompany singing, either sacred or secular. The harp had its origins in Egypt and was used primarily in Temple music. So you can imagine whatever your favorite string instruments—guitar, violin, or harp—being used to accompany these beautiful verses.

LIGHT ON THE WORD

Rejoice in the Lord!

After painting this scene, the next words are surprising. "Yet I will rejoice in the LORD, I will joy in the God of my salvation" (**v. 18**). Habakkuk says that in the midst of utter devastation and loss, he will rejoice. Habakkuk does not say he will rejoice in this situation, but that He will rejoice in the Lord. Habakkuk rejoices because the Lord is his strength and will support him and make him firm and stable as a deer on a high mountain.

BIBLE APPLICATION

AIM: Students will experience joy when they have patiently waited for God's promises to be revealed.

There are two types of people in this world: those who trust in themselves and those who trust in God. When life comes crashing down, those who trust in themselves have no reason to rejoice. They cannot sustain joy in times of disappointment. Belief, hope, and trust in God are prerequisites for enduring the daily challenges of life. When disappointment and suffering appear, our trust in God is the primary factor that can sustain our joy. In this world full of crime, economic crisis, and terrorism, we can rejoice in knowing God, who is sovereign over all.

STUDENTS' RESPONSES

AIM: Students will know that believers hold accountable those who abuse political and economic power.

The problems and trials of life can bring us down. Sometimes our patience can wear thin and our joy can decrease. Think of one thing that you have been waiting God to act on. It could be a job opportunity or a loved one coming to know Jesus. It has to be something that hasn't happened yet. Praise and thank God as an act of faith that He will bring it to pass. Let God be your joy in the absence of the thing that you have been waiting for.

PRAYER

Lord, we praise You and we rejoice in knowing who You are. Your patience, forgiveness, and justice are amazing and wonderful. God, You have given us Jesus, who sacrificed His life for our sins. Your justice prevailed. May we live and strive to seek Your justice in all that we do and say. In Jesus' Name, we pray. Amen.

HOW TO SAY IT

Babylonian.	bab-y-**LO**-ni-an.
Chaldean.	kal-**DE**-an.
Habakkuk.	ha-**BA**-kuk.

PREPARE FOR NEXT SUNDAY

Read **Job 19:1–7, 23–29** and study "Even So, My Redeemer Lives."

DAILY HOME BIBLE READINGS

MONDAY
How Long Shall I Cry Out?
(Habakkuk 1:1–5)

TUESDAY
Why Are You Silent?
(Habakkuk 1:12–17)

WEDNESDAY
The Lord Has Turned Against Me
(Ruth 1:12–21)

THURSDAY
Blessed Be the Name
(Job 1:13–21)

FRIDAY
Be Gracious to Me, O God
(Psalm 56:1–7)

SATURDAY
In God I Trust
(Psalm 56:8–13)

SUNDAY
Yet I Will Rejoice
(Habakkuk 2:1–5, 3:17–19)

Sources:

Brand, Chad, Charles Draper, and Archie England, eds. *Holman Illustrated Bible Dictionary*. Nashville, TN: Holman Bible Publishers, 2003.

Guthrie, Steven R. "Love the Lord with All Your Voice." *Christianity Today*. June 2013.

Keck, Leander, gen. ed. *The New Interpreter's Bible*. Vol. 3. Nashville, TN: Abingdon Press, 1999.

Meyers, Allen C., ed. *The Eerdmans Bible Dictionary*. Grand Rapids, MI: Wm. B. Eerdmans Publishing Company, 1996.

Morgan, G. Campbell. *The Minor Prophets: The Men and Their Messages*. Old Tappan, NJ: Fleming H. Revell, 1960.

Pfeifer, Charles F. and Everett F. Harrison, eds. *The Wycliffe Bible Commentary*. Chicago, IL: Moody Press, 1962.

Rachmacher, Earl D., Th.D., gen. ed. *The Nelson Study Bible New King James Version*. Nashville, TN: Thomas Nelson Publishers, 1997.

Smith, Ralph L. *Micah–Malachi. Word Biblical Commentary*. Vol. 32. Dallas, TX: Word Books Publisher, 1984.

Today's Parallel Bible. Grand Rapids, MI: Zondervan, 2000.

Walvoord, John F. and Roy B. Zuck, eds. *The Bible Knowledge Commentary: Old Testament*. Wheaton, IL: Victor Books, 1985.

COMMENTS / NOTES:

EVEN SO, MY REDEEMER LIVES

BIBLE BASIS: JOB 19:1–7, 23–29

BIBLE TRUTH: God, the Redeemer, lives and constantly sends forth steadfast love to all people.

MEMORY VERSE: "For I know that my redeemer liveth, and that he shall stand at the latter day upon the earth" (Job 19:25).

LESSON AIM: By the end of the lesson, your students will: understand that Job had unwavering belief in God's redemption even as he was made to suffer; affirm that, though we suffer much, God loves us and offers us redemption; and acknowledge ways we are loved and blessed during times of trouble.

TEACHER PREPARATION

MATERIALS NEEDED: Quarterly Commentary/Teacher Manual, Adult Quarterly, Adult resources—charts, worksheets, and other teaching tools, paper, pens, pencils, Bibles (several different versions)

OTHER MATERIALS NEEDED / TEACHER'S NOTES:

____

____

LESSON OVERVIEW

LIFE NEED FOR TODAY'S LESSON

Even when people admit their shortcomings, they are often ostracized by others and receive no justice.

BIBLE LEARNING

God's steadfast love and presence is demonstrated in the lives of those who take refuge in Him.

BIBLE APPLICATION

People of faith know that relentless pursuits of justice, particularly for those who are powerless and voiceless, help redeem corrupt and compromised systems.

STUDENTS' RESPONSES

Believers learn that asking questions of God is part of the healing process.

LESSON SCRIPTURE

JOB 19:1–7, 23–29, KJV

1 Then Job answered and said,

2 How long will ye vex my soul, and break me in pieces with words?

3 These ten times have ye reproached me: ye are not ashamed that ye make yourselves strange to me.

JOB 19:1–7, 23–29, NIV

1 Then Job replied:

2 "How long will you torment me and crush me with words?

3 Ten times now you have reproached me; shamelessly you attack me.

4 And be it indeed that I have erred, mine error remaineth with myself.

5 If indeed ye will magnify yourselves against me, and plead against me my reproach:

6 Know now that God hath overthrown me, and hath compassed me with his net.

7 Behold, I cry out of wrong, but I am not heard: I cry aloud, but there is no judgment.

23 Oh that my words were now written! oh that they were printed in a book!

24 That they were graven with an iron pen and lead in the rock for ever!

25 For I know that my redeemer liveth, and that he shall stand at the latter day upon the earth:

26 And though after my skin worms destroy this body, yet in my flesh shall I see God:

27 Whom I shall see for myself, and mine eyes shall behold, and not another; though my reins be consumed within me.

28 But ye should say, Why persecute we him, seeing the root of the matter is found in me?

29 Be ye afraid of the sword: for wrath bringeth the punishments of the sword, that ye may know there is a judgment.

4 If it is true that I have gone astray, my error remains my concern alone.

5 If indeed you would exalt yourselves above me and use my humiliation against me,

6 then know that God has wronged me and drawn his net around me.

7 "Though I cry, 'Violence!' I get no response; though I call for help, there is no justice.

23 "Oh, that my words were recorded, that they were written on a scroll,

24 that they were inscribed with an iron tool on lead, or engraved in rock forever!

25 I know that my redeemer lives, and that in the end he will stand on the earth.

26 And after my skin has been destroyed, yet in my flesh I will see God;

27 I myself will see him with my own eyes—I, and not another. How my heart yearns within me!

28 "If you say, 'How we will hound him, since the root of the trouble lies in him,'

29 you should fear the sword yourselves; for wrath will bring punishment by the sword, and then you will know that there is judgment."

LIGHT ON THE WORD

Job is a man from the land of Uz (ancient Edom). Although not an Israelite, we do know that Job has a relationship with God. He is wealthy and is blessed with many children. Job experienced great prosperity until he is tested by God and loses everything. In the midst of his suffering and doubt, Job remains faithful to God.

TEACHING THE BIBLE LESSON

LIFE NEED FOR TODAY'S LESSON

AIM: Students will learn that when people admit their shortcomings, they are often ostracized by others and receive no justice.

INTRODUCTION

Job's Situation

Job had experienced the destruction of his wealth, his children, and his health. His wife had told him to curse God but he refuses. Job accepted that everything he has experienced has come from the hand of God. Soon his friends came to his side and sat with him. As they sat, they began to try to explain Job's situation. In trying to explain his current calamities, they began to blame Job and say that he is responsible for everything that has happened to him. The rest of the book (chapters 3–37) is a back and forth between Job and his friends which culminates in the final verdict given by God in chapters 38–42. Job is restored and given double what he had before.

BIBLE LEARNING

AIM: Students will affirm that God's steadfast love and presence is demonstrated in the lives of those who take refuge in God.

I. JOB SPEAKS TO HIS FRIENDS' VERBAL ATTACK (Job 19:1–7)

Job speaks to his friends' verbal attacks. "How long will you torture me?" He is frustrated with the way his friends have talked to him. They have accused him of wrongdoing and it has been insulting. This shows us the power of our words, especially when people are dealing with tragedy and hardship in their life.

How Long, God, Must I Suffer? (verses 1–7)

1 Then Job answered and said, 2 How long will ye vex my soul, and break me in pieces with words? 3 These ten times have ye reproached me: ye are not ashamed that ye make yourselves strange to me.

What is Job's mood at this point? His three friends are unable to see that suffering might not be caused by the sin of the sufferer, and Job is trying to tell them that he is sure from his personal experience that this is not so. Do you think someone remains sick because they lack faith? This is just the same situation—we need to be careful not to judge the heart of another or how God is working in their lives. God does not always heal and He often allows suffering to come into our lives to strengthen us.

Job is often credited with patience, but this is not the case. Job perseveres in spite of it all, but he is not feeling very patient! "How long?" he asks. The Hebrew is *'ad* (**AD**), which is almost as if asking if it will last forever. Job seems to be feeling angry here—do you blame him? All three of his friends are ganging up against him. They are trying to vex him and break him in pieces with their words. "Break" in Hebrew is *dakka'* (**dak-KAW**), which literally means to crush into powder. This is not used here in the literal, physical sense, but a psychological sense of to humiliate or oppress.

Job says that his so-called friends have tried ten times to accuse him. He is not literally counting the number of times with his ten fingers, but this is a Hebrew idiom meaning many times and completely, and Job is saying that it is too many times to accuse a friend.

4 And be it indeed that I have erred, mine error remaineth with myself.

Scholars have interpreted this verse in a variety of ways. "With myself" (Heb. *'iytiy*, **ee-TEE**) is an emphatic expression; in other words, it is as if Job had underlined it. So the most logical interpretation is that Job says he alone is responsible to God for his own sin. No one else can see what transpires between Job and the Lord. If Job has sinned, his sin is not hurting his friends; it only hurts Job, so he thinks they should stop bothering him about it. And by using the word "erred" (Heb. *shagah*, **shaw-GAW**), Job is intimating a smaller sin, probably done in ignorance, not the huge sin that would be expected to bring on the great suffering that Job is enduring.

5 If indeed ye will magnify yourselves against me, and plead against me my reproach.

Job's accusers are acting as if they are his moral superiors—they are magnifying themselves. They think that they are pure, because obviously God is not punishing them. A "reproach" (Heb. *cherpah*, **kher-PAW**) is a condition of disgrace in which Job feels he is being treated like a terrible sinner.

6 Know now that God hath overthrown me, and hath compassed me with his net.

Job feels that it is God who has unjustly caused his suffering, which makes Job's friends view him as a great sinner, and he finds that humiliating. The word "overthrown" (Heb. *'avat*, **aw-VAWT**) means to bend or pervert the cause of someone or something. Job thinks that God has ruined his reputation as an upright man. He says that God has compassed or surrounded him with a net like a hunter catching his prey.

7 Behold, I cry out of wrong, but I am not heard: I cry aloud, but there is no judgment.

The picture here is like the person being assaulted in broad daylight, but no one listens to his or her cries for help. In this case, Job is crying out for God's help, but seemingly God has His ears shut. Job is not accusing God of being unjust. He is just complaining that he has not received a fair and equitable response from God; God is not answering.

SEARCH THE SCRIPTURES

QUESTION 1

How did Job defend himself against the accusations of his friends?

LIGHT ON THE WORD

Job's Friends

Job states that if he has done wrong, then that is his concern and not theirs. It is not for them to show him his sin, because his sin is for him alone to deal with. Job clarifies to his friends they are unable to humiliate him because God already has. He says God is like a hunter who has trapped him in a net. He doesn't need them to do the same.

II. JOB'S RESPONSE TO HIS SITUATION (vv. 23–29)

Job desires for his words to be written down. Why? So his testimony of innocence could be recorded for future generations. By saying this, Job is stating his innocence not only to his friends but for those to come and ultimately to God. He states that he wants his words to be engraved with an iron pen. This way the message could last forever and not changed. Job was confident of his innocence and wanted everyone to know, even those who had not existed yet.

The Book of Job's Life and Misfortunes (verses 23–29)

23 Oh that my words were now written! oh that they were printed in a book! 24 That they were graven with an iron pen and lead in the rock for ever!

Job desires vindication and it certainly does not seem to be happening. He wishes that the facts of his life could be written down for the future—so it could be seen that he is not guilty of horrendous sins. First he thinks of the facts being written down in a scroll, the book format of his day. Then he thinks he really desired a permanent record, inscribed in stone with the letters filled in with lead so in the future, it could be seen that he is innocent. Job's desire is answered by God in far greater ways than Job could ever imagine. The story of his suffering and his godly life is recorded in the book of Job, and many more are reading it than were even alive on earth in his days.

25 For I know that my redeemer liveth, and that he shall stand at the latter day upon the earth: 26 And though after my skin worms destroy this body, yet in my flesh shall I see God: 27 Whom I shall see for myself, and mine eyes shall behold, and not another; though my reins be consumed within me.

In these verses, Job is speaking under the inspiration of the Holy Spirit of the wonderful truth that he would someday see his living Redeemer. Old Testament prophets often spoke of things that they didn't fully understand, especially in the references to Jesus, our Messiah. But with this statement we seem to see a turning in the attitude of Job—yes, in the end God will vindicate him.

A redeemer (Heb. *ga'al*, **gaw-AL**) in Israelite society was the next of kin and had certain responsibilities and privileges, such as buying back family property which had been lost as a result of indebtedness, marrying a widow, avenging, delivering, purchasing, ransoming, and redeeming. David spoke of God being his Redeemer (**Psalm 19:14**) and so did Isaiah (**44:6**), and it is certainly in this sense that Job speaks of his Redeemer. Only God could vindicate him of his sins. And since Job expects to die soon, he saw the only hope of God declaring him innocent as happening after he died. So if God vindicated Job after he died, would that really help him? Job expresses in these verses the belief that even though his physical body would be eaten by worms as it lay in the grave, his physical body would also be resurrected and he would be face to face with his Redeemer.

We read the word "reins" in the KJV and wonder what this is referring to. This is how the KJV translates the Hebrew word *kilyah* (**kil-YAW**), which actually refers to the kidneys, which were viewed as the seat of the emotions. The NIV translation renders this as: "How my heart yearns within me!" Particularly as we get older or as we experience terminal diseases, the thought that excites us is that we will soon see Jesus.

28 But ye should say, Why persecute we him, seeing the root of the matter is found in me? 29 Be ye afraid of the sword: for wrath bringeth the punishments of the sword, that ye may know there is a judgment.

Now Job returns to his complaints concerning his so-called friends. We think of the ninth commandment: "Thou shalt not bear false witness against thy neighbour" (**Exodus 20:16**). Job knows in his heart that he is not guilty of the gross sins his friends are accusing him of. We, too, should remember that whether in a court of law or a whisper of gossip, we should not accuse someone of doing anything wrong unless we have seen it for ourselves, or we will suffer punishment from God. When we get to the end of the book of Job, we will see that God judges the three for their accusations against Job. They had repeatedly harassed an innocent victim. The root of the matter was not found in Job.

SEARCH THE SCRIPTURES

QUESTION 2

Why did Job refer to God as his Redeemer (**v. 25**)?

LIGHT ON THE WORD

Our Redeemer Lives!

Job reaffirms his unconditional faith and trust in God in all situations. "For I know that my redeemer liveth, and that he shall stand at the latter day upon the earth: and though after my skin worms destroy this body, yet in my flesh shall I see God" (**vv. 25–26**). Job knows God will remove him from his circumstance even if it happens after his death. He knows that only God can redeem him from death and take up the cause of his innocence. Job sees beyond his present situation and look to the time when he will be able to stand in the presence of God.

BIBLE APPLICATION

AIM: Students will know that relentless pursuits of justice, particularly for those who are powerless and voiceless, help redeem corrupt and compromised systems.

There is so much suffering in the world we live in. During these times, many people turn to many things to medicate the pain. Some turn to drugs, alcohol, and sex. Others turn to milder things like shopping and food. Those who believe in Christ look to Him as their redemption and hope. In our suffering we can be assured that God is for us and not against us. Whether or not we are freed from our suffering, we will be able to see our Redeemer and be in His presence forever.

STUDENTS' RESPONSES

AIM: Students will learn that asking questions of God is part of the healing process.

Think about the times that you have experienced God's blessing even amid suffering. Maybe it was during a time of illness or the loss of income. Make a list of the ways that God showed you His love and care in times of suffering. It could have been through the words of a friend or a sermon. It could have been through unexpected provision or a small comfort. As you make the list, thank God that He does not leave us alone in our suffering.

PRAYER

God of mercy who sees all, grant us what we need to help those who are suffering for Your sake. Allow us to stand up for truth and Jesus as our redeemer. Bless us so that we can bless others as we witness to others. In Jesus' Name we pray. Amen.

HOW TO SAY IT

Persevere.	per-se-**VERE**.
Intimation.	in-ti-**MA**-shun.
Vindication.	vin-di-**CA**-shun.

PREPARE FOR NEXT SUNDAY

Read **Job 24:1, 9–12, 19–25** and study "Hope Complains."

DAILY HOME BIBLE READINGS

MONDAY
Forsaken by Family and Friends
(Job 19:13–21)

TUESDAY
Why Do You Stand Far Off?
(Psalm 10:1–11)

WEDNESDAY
Do Not Fear
(Isaiah 44:1–8)

THURSDAY
God's Purpose for Me
(Psalm 57:1–6)

FRIDAY
My Heart Is Steadfast
(Psalm 57:7–11)

SATURDAY
Loves That Endures Forever
(1 Chronicles 16:28–34)

SUNDAY
My Redeemer Lives!
(Job 19:1–7, 23–29)

Sources:

Andersen, Francis I. *Job: Introduction and Commentary.* Tyndale Old Testament Commentaries. Downers Grove, IL: InterVarsity Press, 1976.

Brand, Chad, Charles Draper, and Archie England, eds. *Holman Illustrated Bible Dictionary.* Nashville, TN: Holman Bible Publishers, 2003.

Clines, David J.A. *Job 1–20.* Word Biblical Commentary, Vol. 17. Dallas, TX: Word Books Publisher, 1989.

Gray, John. *The Book of Job.* Sheffield, England: Sheffield Phoenix Press, 2010.

Keck, Leander, gen. ed. *The New Interpreter's Bible.* Vol. 3. Nashville, TN: Abingdon Press, 1999.

Meyers, Allen C., ed. *The Eerdmans Bible Dictionary.* Grand Rapids, MI: Wm. B. Eerdmans Publishing Company, 1996.

Rachmacher, Earl D., Th.D., gen. ed. *The Nelson Study Bible New King James Version.* Nashville, TN: Thomas Nelson Publishers, 1997.

Today's Parallel Bible. Grand Rapids, MI: Zondervan, 2000.

Walvoord, John F. and Roy B. Zuck, eds. *The Bible Knowledge Commentary: Old Testament.* Wheaton, IL: Victor Books, 1985.

COMMENTS / NOTES:

HOPE COMPLAINS

BIBLE BASIS: JOB 24:1, 9–12, 19–25

BIBLE TRUTH: God takes care of the unjust and saves the needy and gives the poor hope in the battles they are waging.

MEMORY VERSE: "Why, seeing times are not hidden from the Almighty, do they that know him not see his days?" (Job 24:1).

LESSON AIM: By the end of this lesson, your students will: explore Job's complaint about the appearance that God does nothing to call wicked people to account; appreciate that, although the timing of God's justice is often inscrutable to us, it is certain; and determine ways to help God bring justice to the poor and weak.

TEACHER PREPARATION

MATERIALS NEEDED: Quarterly Commentary/Teacher Manual, Adult Quarterly, Adult resources—charts, worksheets, and other teaching tools, paper, pens, pencils, Bibles (several different versions)

OTHER MATERIALS NEEDED / TEACHER'S NOTES:

LESSON OVERVIEW

LIFE NEED FOR TODAY'S LESSON

Sometimes it seems that wicked people get all the breaks and cannot be stopped from doing terrible things.

BIBLE LEARNING

God hears the needy and poor cry out and redeems them from their sorrows.

BIBLE APPLICATION

Believers patiently await the administration of God's justice on behalf of those who suffer.

STUDENTS' RESPONSES

Students will embrace the call to participate in God's purpose to bring justice to the poor and weak of society.

LESSON SCRIPTURE

JOB 24:1, 9–12, 19–25, KJV

1 Why, seeing times are not hidden from the Almighty, do they that know him not see his days?

9 They pluck the fatherless from the breast, and take a pledge of the poor.

10 They cause him to go naked without clothing, and they take away the sheaf from the hungry;

JOB 24:1, 9–12, 19–25, NIV

1 "Why does the Almighty not set times for judgment? Why must those who know him look in vain for such days?

9 The fatherless child is snatched from the breast; the infant of the poor is seized for a debt.

10 Lacking clothes, they go about naked; they carry the sheaves, but still go hungry.

11 Which make oil within their walls, and tread their winepresses, and suffer thirst.

12 Men groan from out of the city, and the soul of the wounded crieth out: yet God layeth not folly to them.

19 Drought and heat consume the snow waters: so doth the grave those which have sinned.

20 The womb shall forget him; the worm shall feed sweetly on him; he shall be no more remembered; and wickedness shall be broken as a tree.

21 He evil entreateth the barren that beareth not: and doeth not good to the widow.

22 He draweth also the mighty with his power: he riseth up, and no man is sure of life.

23 Though it be given him to be in safety, whereon he resteth; yet his eyes are upon their ways.

24 They are exalted for a little while, but are gone and brought low; they are taken out of the way as all other, and cut off as the tops of the ears of corn.

25 And if it be not so now, who will make me a liar, and make my speech nothing worth?

11 They crush olives among the terraces; they tread the winepresses, yet suffer thirst.

12 The groans of the dying rise from the city, and the souls of the wounded cry out for help. But God charges no one with wrongdoing.

19 As heat and drought snatch away the melted snow, so the grave snatches away those who have sinned.

20 The womb forgets them, the worm feasts on them; the wicked are no longer remembered but are broken like a tree.

21 They prey on the barren and childless woman, and to the widow they show no kindness.

22 But God drags away the mighty by his power; though they become established, they have no assurance of life.

23 He may let them rest in a feeling of security, but his eyes are on their ways.

24 For a little while they are exalted, and then they are gone; they are brought low and gathered up like all others; they are cut off like heads of grain.

25 "If this is not so, who can prove me false and reduce my words to nothing?"

LIGHT ON THE WORD

A pledge is a security given for future payment. Pledges were often oppressive to the poor. Many times wicked men would take pledges from the poor of things they could hardly do without. Legislation can be found in the Bible regarding the proper taking of pledges. A man's clothing could not be taken (**Amos 2:8**; **Job 24:10**) although his outer garment could be taken for the day and returned at night (**Exodus 22:26**; **Deuteronomy 24:12–13**). A widow's clothing could not be taken as a pledge (**Deuteronomy 24:17**). Additionally, a mill for breadmaking could not be taken for a pledge (**Deuteronomy 24:6**). Those who took pledges were not allowed to enter into the debtor's house to take the pledge (**Deuteronomy 24:10**).

Uz is the poetic name for Edom (the southernmost part of Transjordan) according to Jewish tradition. According to the description of Job's friends, it seemed to be inhabited or bordered by Temanites, Namathites, and Buzites. Due to lack of archaeological evidence, Uz is sometimes thought of as part of Edom, but the Bible is not explicit about the location of Uz, and a more general location of east of Palestine would make it accessible to the Sabateans and Chaldeans (**Job 1:15–17**).

TEACHING THE BIBLE LESSON

LIFE NEED FOR TODAY'S LESSON

AIM: Students will think that sometimes it appears that wicked people get all the breaks and cannot be stopped from doing terrible things.

INTRODUCTION

Job's Situation

Job was a wealthy and righteous man who, through a series of events, lost his possessions, his children, and his health. As a result, Job began to question God about suffering. Job's friends (Eliphaz, Bildad, and Zophar) mourned with him over his great loss. After the time of mourning had ended, Job's friends wrongly assumed that all suffering is the result of sin and began to persuade Job to repent of his sins. Job, however, was not suffering because of sin. God was orchestrating the circumstances in Job's life to prove Satan wrong.

BIBLE LEARNING

AIM: Students will know God hears the needy and poor cry out and redeems them from their sorrows.

I. JOB'S QUESTIONS (Job 24:1)

Almighty, Powerful, Mighty One are all names for God that can be used in this verse. It is fitting that Job uses the term Almighty in reference to God. Injustice has been committed, and Job looks to the ultimate power and authority in the universe to right the wrongs on earth. Yet, the wicked seemed to be in control and the godly had no defender from these evil men.

A Judicial Calendar (verse 1)

1 Why, seeing times are not hidden from the Almighty, do they that know him not see his days?

Job is wondering why God doesn't make some sort of judicial calendar so people could clearly understand His plan for justice. This is the way we humans think; we want justice to be done right away. But God's justice is different from ours (cf. **Isaiah 55:8–9**). There is a time of final justice—judgment day— but no one knows when that will be. God does not deal with us as parents deal with toddlers. We may not be punished for wrong immediately or rewarded for good right away. That would make us just God's toddler-puppets, but He desires for us to do what is good, no matter what the consequences may be.

Job is speaking of justice for those who know God. The Hebrew for "know" is *yada'* (**yaw-DAH**), and it means more than just an intellectual understanding that there is a God; it means to respond to Him, to recognize His rights as God Almighty, and to esteem Him as God. Job thought that especially those who worship God and obey Him deserve to have Him answer them in regard to punishment and reward for the things they do. "Why?" (Heb. *maddua'*, **mad-DOO-ah**) asks Job, not seeking the answer, but expressing sorrow that he does not know the answer.

LIGHT ON THE WORD

Why, God, Why?

In anguish, Job cries out to the Almighty, but God's silence only compounds his suffering. Job asks the question "Why?" He believes God is the Almighty One, and he also believes that God is righteous and just. If this is the case, then why are the wicked allowed to oppress the poor and innocent? Job asks the age-old question of humanity: "If God is all-powerful and always good, how can He allow evil to flourish?" Bewilderment is beginning to set in. Justice has not been served.

II. THE PLIGHT OF THE OPPRESSED (vv. 9–12)

Job is concerned about injustice in this diatribe to the Almighty. He is crying out in anguish at the cruelty of this world.

The Pain of the Oppressed (verses 9–12)

9 They pluck the fatherless from the breast, and take a pledge of the poor. 10 They cause him to go naked without clothing, and they take away the sheaf from the hungry; 11 Which make oil within their walls, and tread their winepresses, and suffer thirst. 12 Men groan from out of the city, and the soul of the wounded crieth out: yet God layeth not folly to them.

Job begins to look at the suffering of others who seem innocent and powerless also (**vv. 2–8**). He wonders why they, too, suffer unjustly. The theological term for this is theodicy, and it deals with the question of why an omnipotent God, a God of love and justice, allows suffering in this world, particularly when bad things happen to good people. The entire book of Job wrestles with this problem. Christians have come up with several answers. One is that God allows pain because it refines and purifies us, so that the end result outweighs the suffering endured. Second, if good were the only choice open to us human beings, we would not have a genuine choice. So our evil choices cause much of the suffering in this world. Although these reasons do not fully explain all the problems in this world, God calls upon us as His followers to trust in His sovereign design and His love for us, even when things seem upside down to us.

Job is beginning to grow and look beyond his own problems to see that others are in similar situations. This is one area where we definitely should be growing spiritually when we ourselves are suffering—it should make us more sensitive to the plight of others. The first example Job mentions is the cruel person snatching an infant to pay for a debt. The example is exaggerated in **verse 9**, a hyperbole; it would not make sense to take an infant as a slave. A baby would have to be fed and cared for until old enough to do any worthwhile work, but Job is making the point of the cruelty that would cause a person to snatch a child from his or her mother. The next example is likely an exaggeration also. While those in poverty may not be running around naked, they are destitute and dressed in rags.

And the next three examples show extreme worker exploitation. Farm workers carry the sheaves of grain but do not have enough to eat. Others crush olive oil, but it is implied that they receive no oil for their work. They stomp on the grapes, but they don't get any grape juice or even water to drink. Job sees that people are wounded and dying; they are crying out for help, but God doesn't seem to be doing anything about it. In each of these examples, we see suffering that is not caused by God, but is caused by the wealthy owners of the agricultural businesses. But Job says that injustice is not confined to agriculture; there are cries from those in the city as well. Not only does God want us to trust Him to bring about justice in the end, but He also wants us to help others in their distress as we are able.

SEARCH THE SCRIPTURES

QUESTION 1

How does God seem to respond to injustice at times?

LIGHT ON THE WORD

Injustice Rules

Job complains that justice does not prevail in the world because the wicked are prosperous and successful. God is allowing this wickedness to thrive. Job takes it a step further and says that God is ignoring the cries of the dying and the wounded. No one is brought to justice for this wrong. There is no relief. Job is in anguish because of this great wrong.

III. CHANGE IN PERSPECTIVE (vv. 19–25)

Finally, Job begins to argue that the wicked will not get away with their sin. He realizes that the wicked are punished in death. This is a fact of life as much as "drought and heat consume snow" (**v. 19**).

God's Justice Does Prevail (verses 19–25)

19 Drought and heat consume the snow waters: so doth the grave those which have sinned. 20 The womb shall forget him; the worm shall feed sweetly on him; he shall be no more remembered; and wickedness shall be broken as a tree.

Job's side of the debate so far has been that God ignores the wicked and they are not punished for their sins, while the innocent face suffering as God turns His face away. But Job seems to be changing his ideas, since we read in **19:25–27** that he is expecting to meet his Redeemer face to face in the afterlife. Although he does not have a clear idea of hell for the wicked, he realizes that the faithful can expect a glorious future after death, and there will be punishment for evildoers in the end. Job acknowledges that just as snow is melted away by heat and dry air, so the wicked will come to the end of their lives and be remembered no more (**vv. 19–20**). Even if they have a well-attended funeral, they will soon be forgotten.

21 He evil entreateth the barren that beareth not: and doeth not good to the widow. 22 He draweth also the mighty with his power: he riseth up, and no man is sure of life. 23 Though it be given him to be in safety, whereon he resteth; yet his eyes are upon their ways. 24 They are exalted for a little while, but are gone and brought low; they are taken out of the way as all other, and cut off as the tops of the ears of corn.

Again Job returns to the idea that the wicked are brutal to the poor and helpless. This time it is not to the widowed mother but to the woman who faces great problems alone—maybe she has no children, a disgrace in that era, or maybe she is a widow without anyone to help her. In most societies, lone women are at a disadvantage. We all know elderly women and single moms who are in poverty, but in the ancient patriarchal society, things were even worse for women. People think they can get away with taking advantage of women who are alone because they have no one to stand up for them. But in spite of the ancient context, God commended women who spoke up for themselves. Read **Numbers**

36 to see how God defended the rights of the daughters of Zelophehad.

Job says he feels like doing the right thing is not worth it, because in spite of the good things he did, he is suffering. Then God gives him spiritual insight and he understands the final end of the wicked. Instead of Job standing on slippery ground, the wicked will be feeling the ground pulled out from under them. God is helping him and guiding him. Even if his physical health and strength may fail, God is his strength forever. Yes, and the unfaithful will finally be destroyed. Job has not reached the end of his wrestling match with his friends and with God, but he will get there!

25 And if it be not so now, who will make me a liar, and make my speech nothing worth?

Job is very sure of himself here—he says that no one can prove wrong what he has just said. How could his friends insist that the wicked are always immediately punished and the good never suffer? Job gives examples from real life that prove otherwise. And yet he is not saying things are just backward of what they say. Yes, evildoers are punished, we just don't know when—it could be upon their death. Yes, God will reward those who follow Him, but again, we don't know when, and the greatest rewards will surely come after we die.

SEARCH THE SCRIPTURES

QUESTION 2

What is the cost of wickedness?

LIGHT ON THE WORD

The Wicked are Forgotten

The wicked will soon be forgotten by family members and friends. Though they were once rich, secure and great, God will strip them of their riches and they will die like everyone else. Job likens their demise to a tree being destroyed in a storm. From the outside they look like they will stand strong, but they are not what they appear to be. In death, they will be broken by the power and judgment of God. Job is convinced that judgment for the wicked is certain and harsh, and that there will be no relief for them. The downfall of the wicked will be swift and brutal. God will answer the cries of the oppressed and deliver them from evil. Job has renewed hope in God the Deliverer.

BIBLE APPLICATION

AIM: Students will discover how believers patiently await the administration of God's justice on behalf of those who suffer.

The Civil Rights Act of 1964 outlaws discrimination based on race, color, religion, sex, or national origin in specific settings. Additional civil rights acts have expanded the specific settings of the Civil Rights Act of 1964 to general settings across a wide variety of American life and have expanded the categories of protection to cover age and disability. These legislations were passed to protect vulnerable people from injustice.

The laws in Uz to protect people from oppression were not enforced in this passage of Job. However, Job's final conclusion was that God will judge those who oppress other people. The oppressors will lose their riches, status, and even their own lives.

STUDENTS' RESPONSES

AIM: Students will embrace the call to participate in God's purpose to bring justice to the poor and weak of society.

Are there widows and poor people in the neighborhood to whom your church can minister? Are there lawyers in your church who can help the oppressed fight against discrimination based on the Civil Rights Act of 1964? Is your group praying for God to bring justice on the wicked? Pray and act in the fight against oppression of the widows and the poor in your community.

PRAYER

Dear Gracious God, help us to see the needs of those around us, and for those we cannot see. Allow us to make a difference in the lives of those who struggle. Help us to open our hearts, eyes, minds, and hands to do what You have called us to do for others and for ourselves. In Jesus' Name we pray. Amen.

HOW TO SAY IT

Theodicy. thee-**AH**-di-see.

Hyperbole. hi-**PER**-bo-lee.

PREPARE FOR NEXT SUNDAY

Read **Job 42:1–10** and study "Hope Satisfies."

DAILY HOME BIBLE READINGS

MONDAY
Set a Time to Remember Me
(Job 14:7–13)

TUESDAY
You Destroy the Hope of Mortals
(Job 14:14–22)

WEDNESDAY
Why is My Pain Unending?
(Jeremiah 15:10–18)

THURSDAY
Our Hope is in God
(Jeremiah 14:14–22)

FRIDAY
Shelter from the Storm
(Psalm 55:1–8)

SATURDAY
I Call Upon God
(Psalm 55:12–23)

SUNDAY
The Poor and the Mighty
(Job 24:1, 9–12, 19–25)

Sources:

Adelson, Eric. "Dorchester, Death and a New England Patriot." http://sports.yahoo.com/news/nfl--dorchester--death-and-a-new-england-patriot-184406099.html. Accessed July 1, 2013.

Adeyemo, Tokunboh, ed., et al. *Africa Bible Commentary: A One-Volume Commentary Written by 70 African Scholars*. Nairobi, Kenya: Word Alive Publishers, 2006.

Andersen, Francis I. *Job: An Introduction and Commentary*. Tyndale Old Testament Commentaries. Downers Grove, IL: Inter-Varsity Press, 1976.

Archaeological Study Bible, New International Version. Grand Rapids, MI: Zondervan, 2005. 732–734.

Ferguson, Sinclair B., ed., et al. "Theodicy." *New Dictionary of Theology*. Downers Grove, IL: InterVarsity Press, 1988.

Jewish Study Bible, Tanakh Translation. New York: Oxford University Press, 2004. 1499–1505, 1535–1536.

Key Word Study Bible, New International Version. Chattanooga, TN: AMG International, 1996. 584, 608–609.

Life Application Study Bible, New International Version. Wheaton, IL: Tyndale House Publishers, 1997. 764–765.

Quest Study Bible, New International Version. Grand Rapids, MI: Zondervan, 2003. 733–734.

COMMENTS / NOTES:

HOPE SATISFIES

BIBLE BASIS: JOB 42:1–10

BIBLE TRUTH: God can do all things, prevails over all things, and hears our prayers in trying situations.

MEMORY VERSE: "And the LORD turned the captivity of Job, when he prayed for his friends: also the LORD gave Job twice as much as he had before" (Job 42:10).

LESSON AIM: By the end of this lesson, your students will: explore the satisfactory conclusion of Job and God's conversation; affirm that God will answer our questions in ways best for us; and become involved in an active and hopeful prayer life.

TEACHER PREPARATION

MATERIALS NEEDED: Quarterly Commentary/Teacher Manual, Adult Quarterly, Adult resources—charts, worksheets, and other teaching tools, paper, pens, pencils, Bibles (several different versions)

OTHER MATERIALS NEEDED / TEACHER'S NOTES:

LESSON OVERVIEW

LIFE NEED FOR TODAY'S LESSON

People often wonder who or what controls the final outcome in life's many challenges.

BIBLE LEARNING

The psalmist pleads with God to send help in a time of great need.

BIBLE APPLICATION

People of faith understand and accept that they cannot know everything about God's motives and actions.

STUDENTS' RESPONSES

People of faith respond in obedience to God's correction.

LESSON SCRIPTURE

JOB 42:1–10, KJV

1 Then Job answered the LORD, and said,

2 I know that thou canst do every thing and that no thought can be withholden from thee.

3 Who is he that hidest counsel without knowledge? therefore have I uttered that I

JOB 42:1–10, NIV

1 Then Job replied to the LORD:

2 "I know that you can do all things; no purpose of yours can be thwarted.

3 You asked, 'Who is this that obscures my plans without knowledge?' Surely I spoke of things I did not understand, things too wonderful for me to know.

understood not; things too wonderful for me, which I knew not.

4 Hear, I beseech thee, and I will speak: I will demand of thee, and declare thou unto me.

5 I have heard of thee by the hearing of the ear: but now mine eye seeth thee.

6 Wherefore I abhor myself, and repent in dust and ashes.

7 And it was so, that after the LORD had spoken these words unto Job, the LORD said to Eliphaz the Temanite, My wrath is kindled against thee, and against thy two friends: for ye have not spoken of me the thing that is right, as my servant Job hath.

8 Therefore take unto you now seven bullocks and seven rams, and go to my servant Job, and offer up for yourselves a burnt offering; and my servant Job shall pray for you: for him will I accept: lest I deal with you after your folly, in that ye have not spoken of me the thing which is right, like my servant Job.

9 So Eliphaz the Temanite and Bildad the Shuhite and Zophar the Naamathite went, and did according as the LORD commanded them: the LORD also accepted Job.

10 And the LORD turned the captivity of Job, when he prayed for his friends: also the LORD gave Job twice as much as he had before.

4 "You said, 'Listen now, and I will speak; I will question you, and you shall answer me.'

5 My ears had heard of you but now my eyes have seen you.

6 Therefore I despise myself and repent in dust and ashes."

7 After the LORD had said these things to Job, he said to Eliphaz the Temanite, "I am angry with you and your two friends, because you have not spoken the truth about me, as my servant Job has.

8 So now take seven bulls and seven rams and go to my servant Job and sacrifice a burnt offering for yourselves. My servant Job will pray for you, and I will accept his prayer and not deal with you according to your folly. You have not spoken the truth about me, as my servant Job has."

9 So Eliphaz the Temanite, Bildad the Shuhite and Zophar the Naamathite did what the LORD told them; and the LORD accepted Job's prayer.

10 After Job had prayed for his friends, the Lord restored his fortunes and gave him twice as much as he had before.

LIGHT ON THE WORD

To sit or to lie in dust and ashes was often a sign of repentance and humiliation in the ancient Near East. Dust represented man's frailty, and to lie in dust was to recognize the frailty of one's humanity in committing a wrong or experiencing grief due to the loss of a loved one, famine, or other calamity. Ashes symbolized worthlessness; to throw ashes on one's head was to humble oneself and acknowledge one's worthlessness in the sight of God. These gestures were not mandated by God but originated in the culture of the time.

Job's friends Eliphaz, Bildad, and Zophar mourned with him for seven days after he suffered great loss. They then encouraged Job to confess his sin of pride, as they believed that it was the reason for his suffering. Eliphaz appealed to personal experience, Bildad pointed to universal wisdom, and Zophar declared what he felt was common sense. They all agreed that Job's problems were his own doing and that questioning God simply made matters worse.

TEACHING THE BIBLE LESSON

LIFE NEED FOR TODAY'S LESSON

AIM: Students will know some people often wonder who or what controls the final outcome in life's many challenges.

INTRODUCTION

The Trouble with Friends

After Eliphaz, Bildad, and Zophar finished speaking to Job concerning his suffering, a young man named Elihu spoke. Elihu rebuked the three friends for being unable to give Job a reasonable answer for why he was suffering. However, Elihu was only able to give a partial answer to Job's question by saying that people cannot understand all that God allows but must trust Him. This was the best answer that a human could give, yet it was incomplete because Elihu did not have all of the facts.

BIBLE LEARNING

AIM: Students will know that the psalmist pleads with God to send help in a time of great need.

I. JOB'S RESPONSE TO THE LORD (Job 42:1–6)

Job understands his humanity in a new way. He has an encounter with God that causes him to re-evaluate his perspective. Job repents of complaining, as he now knows that God is sovereign. His spiritual eyes have been opened, and he humbles himself in dust and ashes.

Job's Reply (verses 1–6)

**1 Then Job answered the LORD, and said,
2 I know that thou canst do every thing,
and that no thought can be withholden
from thee. 3 Who is he that hideth counsel without knowledge? therefore have I
uttered that I understood not; things too
wonderful for me, which I knew not.**

Now we come to the end of the book. When Job says "I know" (Heb. *yada'*, **yaw-DAH**), he is acknowledging the omnipotence of God. God knows everything and He is all powerful. Job has had the amazing experience of God Himself speaking to him. Instead of speaking about justice issues, God spoke of His mighty creation. Job and his friends had thought of God as the great moral accountant, chalking up our rights and wrongs, and dishing out appropriate punishments and rewards.

In **verse 3**, Job quotes what God said in **Job 38:2**, intensifying the action with the verb "hideth" which is more complete than "darkeneth" (Heb. *chashach*, **haw-SHAWKH**). In this verse God said that Job was speaking out of ignorance when he brought his complaints before Him. "Hideth" in verse 3 is *'alam* (Heb. **aw-LAM**), which is speaking of God's grand designs for the universe that are concealed from us human beings. These are things that Job cannot speak of, because they are hidden from him and from us. God is the great I AM—He exists in the past, the present, and the future, all simultaneously. His plans take all of these things into account.

So what did Job say after hearing what God had to say about Himself? First of all, he discovered that God is much more than some superior human being. When we pray, we often think we know just what God should do to answer our prayers, when in reality, God has the whole picture and we do not.

4 Hear, I beseech thee, and I will speak: I will demand of thee, and declare thou unto me. 5 I have heard of thee by the hearing of the ear: but now mine eye seeth thee. 6 Wherefore I abhor myself, and repent in dust and ashes.

Job begins **verse 4** by quoting God as He had spoken to him (**38:3**). God says that He wants to question Job, and Job must answer Him. This is a rhetorical question—one that Job answers in his mind, not aloud. But in **verse 5**, Job is ready with his answer, or non-answer in this case. When Job brought all his questions to God, he only asked from the point of view of a man who had a rather superficial knowledge of God—things that he had heard from others. But now that God Himself has talked with Job, Job's view of God has greatly expanded. Now Job knows God's voice, and he sees God with his very eyes and takes Him to heart.

To see our holy God as He really is always causes us to realize how sinful we are in comparison. We think of Isaiah in the Temple as God in His holiness appeared to him. Isaiah said, "Woe is me! for I am undone; because I am a man of unclean lips, and I dwell in the midst of a people of unclean lips: for mine eyes have seen the King, the LORD of hosts" (from **Isaiah 6:5**). We find Job saying a similar thing in **verse 6**. "I abhor myself" can have several different meanings. The verb in Hebrew is *ma'as* (**maw-AS**) and can also mean to melt or submit. Although his three friends had accused him of doing terrible things, Job is not agreeing to their accusations. He still maintains that he has done nothing so awful that he deserves the troubles he has experienced. He is aware of his arrogance before the Lord. When coming face to face with God, all these things must have been going through Job's mind. The last words that we hear from Job show his desire to "repent in dust and ashes." The Hebrew word for "repent" is *nacham* (**naw-KHAM**), in which we see him sighing, breathing strongly with a sense of sorrow, and regretting his ignorant and hasty words before God.

SEARCH THE SCRIPTURES

QUESTION 1

How was Job able to see God when God did not make a physical appearance?

LIGHT ON THE WORD

Job's Faith is Deeper

Job is now conscious of the fact that he did not speak in the right way concerning God. His speech only served to hide God's true purposes rather than reveal them. He sought to understand God and his ways but fell short. His repentance is an acknowledgment that God is in control and that He alone knows what is best for His creation.

II. THE LORD RESPONDS TO JOB'S FRIENDS (vv. 7–9)

The Lord is angry with Job's friends. They are deserving of His wrath. He demands a sacrifice from Job's friends as a payment for defaming the name of the Almighty. Seven bulls and seven rams, which represent a sin offering, must be taken to Job, who will pray for his friends. Only then will the Lord forgive Job's friends and not treat them as their sins deserve.

God Reprimands Job's Friends (verses 7–9)

7 And it was so, that after the LORD had spoken these words unto Job, the LORD said to Eliphaz the Temanite, My wrath is kindled against thee, and against thy two friends: for ye have not spoken of me the thing that is right, as my servant Job hath. 8 Therefore take unto you now seven bullocks and seven rams, and go to my servant Job, and offer up for yourselves a burnt offering; and my servant Job shall pray for you: for him will I accept: lest I deal with you after your folly, in that ye have not spoken of me the thing which is right, like my servant Job. 9 So Eliphaz the Temanite and Bildad the Shuhite and Zophar the Naamathite went, and did according as the LORD commanded them: the LORD also accepted Job.

Now we switch from poetry to prose as we come almost to the end of the book. God defends Job by speaking to his friends. Evidently Eliphaz was the oldest of the three men, and so he is chosen by God as the representative. The three friends have the very narrow view of God mentioned earlier—that God is the great moral police officer, a God of immediate retribution, quickly meting out punishment when people sin and quickly bestowing material riches on the righteous. Sometimes this is true, but often it is not. When we accuse people of wrongdoing, just because they are suffering, we are imputing to God a very limited character. We read in **Hebrews 12:6** that the one "the Lord loveth he chasteneth, and scourgeth every son whom he receiveth." Yes, those who suffer are more likely to be God's favorite children. This is similar to the way good parents treat their children. They do not ignore them and let them do whatever they want.

When we look at people who seem successful even though they are very immoral, we may be forgetting God's grace and mercy to sinners as He waits for them to repent. Often people die without ever turning to God and then they are punished, because they have ignored the great grace of God. The book of Job should open our eyes to see more of the sovereign greatness of God. He alone does what He wants, because He alone sees the whole picture. Hopefully, this study has helped us to catch a greater vision of the greatness of our God.

Job was certainly not perfect, but he passionately desired to communicate honestly with God. His friends, on the other hand, just mouthed platitudes that they had heard. But even worse, they arrogantly thought they knew why Job was suffering, even though they had no real evidence for sin on his part. So God commanded them to make a sacrifice for their sins of spiritual pride and their lack of kindness toward Job. Eliphaz, Bildad, and Zophar must have felt humiliated. They had thought they were the righteous ones, but God accuses them of sin and validates Job's righteousness. To make things even worse, they need Job's prayers of intercession for their own sakes. And the Lord accepts Job's prayer for them.

SEARCH THE SCRIPTURES

QUESTION 2

Why was the Lord's wrath kindled against Eliphaz, Bildad, and Zophar?

LIGHT ON THE WORD

Unwise Counsel

The Lord calls Job's friends to account for their bad advice and counsel. They spoke for God when they too did not understand God. In fact, God says they did not speak about Him correctly. They accused Job and did not have the right to do so. As a result, their sins must be atoned for and they must rely on the prayers of the one whom they sought to accuse.

III. THE LORD REVERSES JOB'S SITUATION (v. 10)

Job prays for his friends, and the Lord accepts his prayer. Job is accepted because he has already repented of his arrogance and pride. God reverses Job's situation and brings him out of "captivity." It is also recorded that the Lord gives Job twice as much as he had before. This is all detailed in the rest of the chapter (**vv. 11–17**). All this happened as a result of Job's prayer for his friends.

10 And the LORD turned the captivity of Job, when he prayed for his friends: also the LORD gave Job twice as much as he had before.

Here God has asked Job to take a step of faith. He first has to intercede for his so-called friends, and then the Lord gives him twice as much as he had before. Job had no idea that this would be the result, and he surely had to wait many years for this to happen. He lived 140 years more and in this time he had seven sons and three daughters, the same number as he had lost. Although children cannot be replaced with other children, nevertheless, these were amazing children. We look at the names of the daughters—Jemima, which means dove; Kezia, which means cinnamon; Kerenhappuch, which means a container of expensive black eye makeup. Job lived to see his children grow up and have his grandchildren, and his grandchildren grow up and have his great-grandchildren. His herds grew from nothing to double the number of sheep, camels, oxen, and donkeys than he had before. Not only did Job's material blessings increase, but because of his experiences he gained the privilege of knowing God in a unique and powerful way.

LIGHT ON THE WORD

Spiritual Eyes Opened

Throughout the story of Job, we see him questioning God and His goodness. Now we see God giving Job even more than what he had before. The Lord knew the whole story while Job only knew a piece of it. Amid the wrestling, Job comes to have his spiritual eyes opened—not after he is blessed, but during the time of his trial. When Job first experienced his troubles, he had no idea that the Lord would restore him. When he began to pray for his friends, he had no idea that God was about to bless him with twice as much as he had before.

BIBLE APPLICATION

AIM: Students will understand and accept that they cannot know everything about God's motives and actions.

There are many people in our society who are experiencing the trials of life. Because of this, their hope grows thin and they resort to relieving the pain they feel through addictive and destructive behaviors. Even as believers, we often question God's ways and whether He is good to us. This lesson shows us that the Lord can sustain us in our hope when we maintain intimate communication with Him. When our hope fades, He can strengthen us until His purpose is finally revealed.

STUDENTS' RESPONSES

AIM: Students will respond in obedience to God's correction.

Evaluate the circumstances in your life and pray that the Lord would open your spiritual eyes to see what He is doing. But do not stop there! Pray that the Lord would show you how to respond to your family and friends who are going through circumstances that are beyond their control. Offer wisdom, prayer, and silence. We as humans cannot know what God is doing in someone's life unless we seek God for our friend in need. Only speak when your friend is in danger or when the Lord shows you, then remain silent and let the Lord reveal an answer.

PRAYER

Speak to my mind and heart, Lord, and let me understand what You would have me to do in caring for others. Speak to my ears, hands, feet, and eyes, Lord, as You guide me where to go and what to say and do. In Jesus' Name we pray. Amen.

HOW TO SAY IT

Eliphaz.	el-ee-**FAWZ**.
Bildad.	bill-**DAWD**.
Zophar.	zoh-**FAWR**.
Jemima.	dzheh-mee-**MAW**.
Kezia.	keh-zee-**AH**.
Kerenhappuch.	**KEHR**-ehn-**HAP**-ouk.

PREPARE FOR NEXT SUNDAY

Read **Ezekiel 43:1–12** and study "God's Divine Glory Returns."

DAILY HOME BIBLE READINGS

MONDAY
I Wait for You, O Lord
(Psalm 38:9–15)

TUESDAY
You Alone are God
(Psalm 86:1–10)

WEDNESDAY
Give Strength to Your Servant
(Psalm 86:11–17)

THURSDAY
God Has Called You to Hope
(Ephesians 1:11–19)

FRIDAY
My Hope is from God
(Psalm 62:1–8)

SATURDAY
You are the Hope of All
(Psalm 65:1–5)

SUNDAY
Wonderful Things I Did Not Know
(Job 42:1–10)

Sources:

Adeyemo, Tokunboh, ed., et al. *Africa Bible Commentary: A One-Volume Commentary Written by 70 African Scholars*. Nairobi, Kenya: Word Alive Publishers, 2006.

Andersen, Francis I. *Job: An Introduction and Commentary*. Tyndale Old Testament Commentaries. Downers Grove, IL: InterVarsity Press, 1976.

Archaeological Study Bible, New International Version. Grand Rapids, MI: Zondervan, 2005. 732–734.

Clines, David J. A. *Word Biblical Commentary: Job 38–42*. Vol. 18B. Nashville, TN: Thomas Nelson, 2011.

Jewish Study Bible, Tanakh Translation. New York: Oxford University Press, 2004. 1499–1505, 1561–1562.

Key Word Study Bible, New International Version. Chattanooga, TN: AMG International, 1996. 584, 627.

Life Application Study Bible, New International Version. Wheaton, IL: Tyndale House Publishers, 1997. 764–765, 779, 805, 813, 820.

Quest Study Bible, New International Version. Grand Rapids, MI: Zondervan, 2003. 755–756.

COMMENTS / NOTES:

GOD'S DIVINE GLORY RETURNS

BIBLE BASIS: EZEKIEL 43:1–12

BIBLE TRUTH: God's calming presence can be felt in sacred places where He is truly worshiped.

MEMORY VERSE: "So the spirit took me up, and brought me into the inner court; and, behold, the glory of the LORD filled the house" (Ezekiel 43:5).

LESSON AIM: By the end of the lesson, your students will: comprehend the vision of God's holy and merciful glory in the Temple; associate a sense of holiness of place with the presence and mercy of God; and grow in respect for the sacredness of worship settings.

TEACHER PREPARATION

MATERIALS NEEDED: Quarterly Commentary/Teacher Manual, Adult Quarterly, Adult resources—charts, worksheets, and other teaching tools, paper, pens, pencils, Bibles (several different versions)

OTHER MATERIALS NEEDED / TEACHER'S NOTES:

____

____

LESSON OVERVIEW

LIFE NEED FOR TODAY'S LESSON
People look for a place where they can experience some sense of release and order, away from the chaos that surrounds them.

BIBLE LEARNING
God was angry about the way the leaders and people of Judah had defiled His Temple.

BIBLE APPLICATION
Believers receive visions of hope and assurances of peace that sustain them through the most trying times.

STUDENTS' RESPONSES
Believers accept God's discipline and correction that sets them on the right pathway when they have strayed.

LESSON SCRIPTURE

EZEKIEL 43:1–12, KJV

1 Afterward he brought me to the gate, even the gate that looketh toward the east:

2 And, behold, the glory of the God of Israel came from the way of the east: and his voice was like a noise of many waters: and the earth shined with his glory.

EZEKIEL 43:1–12, NIV

1 Then the man brought me to the gate facing east,

2 and I saw the glory of the God of Israel coming from the east. His voice was like the roar of rushing waters, and the land was radiant with his glory.

3 And it was according to the appearance of the vision which I saw, even according to the vision that I saw when I came to destroy the city: and the visions were like the vision that I saw by the river Chebar; and I fell upon my face.

4 And the glory of the LORD came into the house by the way of the gate whose prospect is toward the east.

5 So the spirit took me up, and brought me into the inner court; and, behold, the glory of the LORD filled the house.

6 And I heard him speaking unto me out of the house; and the man stood by me.

7 And he said unto me, Son of man, the place of my throne, and the place of the soles of my feet, where I will dwell in the midst of the children of Israel for ever, and my holy name, shall the house of Israel no more defile, neither they, nor their kings, by their whoredom, nor by the carcases of their kings in their high places.

8 In their setting of their threshold by my thresholds, and their post by my posts, and the wall between me and them, they have even defiled my holy name by their abominations that they have committed: wherefore I have consumed them in mine anger.

9 Now let them put away their whoredom, and the carcases of their kings, far from me, and I will dwell in the midst of them for ever.

10 Thou son of man, shew the house to the house of Israel, that they may be ashamed of their iniquities: and let them measure the pattern.

11 And if they be ashamed of all that they have done, shew them the form of the house, and the fashion thereof, and the

3 The vision I saw was like the vision I had seen when he came to destroy the city and like the visions I had seen by the Kebar River, and I fell facedown.

4 The glory of the LORD entered the temple through the gate facing east.

5 Then the Spirit lifted me up and brought me into the inner court, and the glory of the LORD filled the temple.

6 While the man was standing beside me, I heard someone speaking to me from inside the temple.

7 He said: "Son of man, this is the place of my throne and the place for the soles of my feet. This is where I will live among the Israelites forever. The people of Israel will never again defile my holy name—neither they nor their kings—by their prostitution and the funeral offerings for their kings at their death.

8 When they placed their threshold next to my threshold and their doorposts beside my doorposts, with only a wall between me and them, they defiled my holy name by their detestable practices. So I destroyed them in my anger.

9 Now let them put away from me their prostitution and the funeral offerings for their kings, and I will live among them forever.

10 "Son of man, describe the temple to the people of Israel, that they may be ashamed of their sins. Let them consider its perfection,

11 and if they are ashamed of all they have done, make known to them the design of the temple—its arrangement, its exits and entrances—its whole design and all its regulations and laws. Write these down

goings out thereof, and the comings in thereof, and all the forms thereof, and all the ordinances thereof, and all the forms thereof, and all the laws thereof: and write it in their sight, that they may keep the whole form thereof, and all the ordinances thereof, and do them.

12 This is the law of the house; Upon the top of the mountain the whole limit thereof round about shall be most holy. Behold, this is the law of the house.

before them so that they may be faithful to its design and follow all its regulations.

12 "This is the law of the temple: All the surrounding area on top of the mountain will be most holy. Such is the law of the temple.

LIGHT ON THE WORD

The inner court was a separate area in the Temple reserved only for the priests. This separate area contained ten golden lampstands. It also contained twelve tables for the shewbread, which was constantly on display and replaced every Sabbath. An altar of incense stood in the inner court before the entrance into the Holy of Holies, where the glory of the Lord was manifested. As a member of the priesthood, Ezekiel was qualified to have access to this area of the Temple (**1:2**).

The Chebar was a river that ran through the land of the Chaldeans. Many of the captive Jews settled here. Many believe that the Chebar was the royal canal of Nebuchadnezzar that joined the Tigris and Euphrates. Ezekiel sat here among the captives and received many of his visions and prophetic words at this location (**1:1–3**).

TEACHING THE BIBLE LESSON

LIFE NEED FOR TODAY'S LESSON

AIM: Students will look for a place where they can experience some sense of release and order, away from the chaos that surrounds them.

INTRODUCTION

Visionary Narratives

During the final section of the book of Ezekiel, there is a special focus on the coming restored Temple. These visionary narratives provide a glimpse of God's plans for His land and His people. Here we can see Ezekiel's priestly concerns and knowledge come into play. The Temple was described in architectural terms in the previous chapters and as such it is empty and lifeless. Now the glory of God came to the Temple. As a result, the Temple was full of life. Ezekiel then begins to talk of what that means for those who serve and worship in the Temple. Since the glory of God is now present in the Temple, its worshipers must be holy. It must not continue to be business as usual. As a priest, Ezekiel stressed the holiness that is required by God and the putting away of all things that would defile the Temple.

BIBLE LEARNING

AIM: Students will learn that God was angry about the way the leaders and people of Judah had defiled His Temple.

I. THE RETURN OF THE GLORY (Ezekiel 43:1–5)

After describing the measurements and the physical description of the Temple, Ezekiel is brought to the gate of the east. There he has a vision of the glory of the Lord with both an aural component (the "noise of many waters") and a visual component ("the earth shined with his glory"). He notices that this vision is similar to the ones in previous chapters where the Lord called him to destroy the city (**Ezekiel 9:5–11**) and the one that he received at the river Chebar (**Ezekiel 1–3**). The Spirit takes Ezekiel up into the inner court of the Temple, and he observes that the glory of the Lord fills the house.

God's Glory is Glorious (verses 1–5)

1 Afterward he brought me to the gate, even the gate that looketh toward the east: 2 And, behold, the glory of the God of Israel came from the way of the east: and his voice was like a noise of many waters: and the earth shined with his glory.

God's actions and symbols are never accidental, and the emphasis here on the east is significant for several reasons in addition to the prophetic context. This is the direction to which God's presence departed in **Ezekiel 11:23**. The sun rises in the east, so God's glory followed the path of the rising sun as it cast its light on the Temple. Entering the east gate led directly to the main entrance to the Temple, which was a direct path to the Holy of Holies. Directly to the east of the Temple mount is the Mount of Olives and the Garden of Gethsemane, both of which have momentous biblical significance, including both Jesus' agony (**Matthew 26:36–39**) and His parting ascension (**Acts 1:9–12**). This gate is also the one into which Jesus rode on a donkey on Palm Sunday (**Mark 11:1–11**)—another example of God's incarnate glory entering the Temple from the east. The word for east in Hebrew (*qedem*, **KEH-dum**) also means first or at the beginning, indicating that God's glory has existed since the beginning and is primal (first and fundamental).

3 And it was according to the appearance of the vision which I saw, even according to the vision that I saw when I came to destroy the city: and the visions were like the vision that I saw by the river Chebar; and I fell upon my face. 4 And the glory of the LORD came into the house by the way of the gate whose prospect is toward the east. 5 So the spirit took me up, and brought me into the inner court; and, behold, the glory of the LORD filled the house.

Ezekiel had two prior experiences with God's glory: 1) he saw in a vision the destruction of Jerusalem when the glory left, moving toward the east (**10:1–22**; **11:22–25**), and 2) he saw a vision of the glory when he was called to the ministry of prophecy by the river Chebar (Kebar River), where the glory had come from the north (**1:25–3:15**). Nothing could be more natural than to fall prostrate before such brilliant radiance (cf. **1:28**).

Since Ezekiel witnessed the glory departing, it was altogether fitting that he is given a preview of its return. For Old Testament believers, the glory of the Lord was a tangible reality that wasn't witnessed often, but whenever it appeared, it was unforgettable and beyond description. Numerous Scriptures attempt to capture it, e.g., **Psalm 24:9–10**, which seems appropriate for Ezekiel's vision: "Lift up your heads, O ye gates; even lift them up, ye everlasting doors; and the King of glory shall come in. Who is this King of glory? The LORD of hosts, he is the King of glory."

For New Testament believers, God's glory is usually "an intangible concept" per Iain Duguid (492), but we are not without examples of New Testament references to His tangible glory, e.g., "who [is] the brightness of his glory, and the express image of his person" (**Hebrews 1:3**), among others from the beginning to the end of the New Testament (cf. **Matthew 1:23**; **Revelation 21:23**). One would be correct to say that in the Christian era, Jesus' veil of humanity was removed momentarily during His transfiguration, revealing the glory of God (**Matthew 17:2**).

SEARCH THE SCRIPTURES

QUESTION 1

What was Ezekiel's reaction to seeing the glory of the Lord?

LIGHT ON THE WORD

God's Glory in the Temple

This is the return of God's glory to the Temple. It is important to note that without the glory of God, the Temple is just another building. The glory of God animates it and gives it life. Ezekiel recognizes this and falls on his face. The proper response to experiencing the glory of God is authentic worship. Notice that Ezekiel didn't sing a song or begin to preach. He fell on his face because it was God who was there and took center attention.

II. RETURN TO THE GLORY (vv. 6–8)

Next, as Ezekiel is face down in submission to God and His glory, God speaks to him. He lets Ezekiel know that the Temple must not be defiled by Israel anymore. They must treat the glory of God with reverence. It is not enough that God's glory has returned to them; they also must return to Him. They must put away their whoredom and the carcasses or memorials of their kings. This word is not just for the common people of Israel but also her kings and leaders.

Return to God (verses 6–8)

6 And I heard him speaking unto me out of the house; and the man stood by me.
7 And he said unto me, Son of man, the place of my throne, and the place of the soles of my feet, where I will dwell in the midst of the children of Israel for ever, and my holy name, shall the house of Israel no more defile, neither they, nor their kings, by their whoredom, nor by the carcases of their kings in their high places.

Even in a vision, Ezekiel does not behold God directly, but rather he hears Him from within the Holy of Holies; His glory makes it beyond man's ability to perceive Him directly. Although God dwells in Heaven and earth cannot contain Him, still He chooses to dwell on earth. **Isaiah 66:1** captures the balance, "Thus saith the LORD, The heaven is my throne, and the earth is my footstool: where is the house that ye build unto me? and where is the place of my rest?" (cf. "throne" in **Jeremiah 3:17, 17:12**, with "footstool" in **Psalm 99:5, 132:7**). In this speech, God dedicates the restored Temple Himself, essentially saying that the soles of His feet are on the same ground as the soles of mankind. The difference is that wherever God chooses to make His earthly habitation must be holy and sacred.

The word "dwell" in Hebrew is *shakan* (**shaw-KAN**), which means "reside," "inhabit," or "rest" and is the root of the word "Shekinah" (which does not appear in Scripture), referring to the glory of God that appeared in a cloud to guide the Israelites (**Exodus 16:10**). Some theologians connect this dwelling or settling of the divine presence with the New Testament use of the Greek *parousia* (**par-oo-SEE-ah**), which means "presence" or "coming" (cf. **2 Thessalonians 2:8; 2 Peter 1:16**).

Christopher Wright notes that the Lord's speech "begins and ends with words of reassurance," declaring that His return is permanent, which provides "wonderful words of hope" (334). From the beginning, God's presence marked and accompanied every move of the nation of Israel, and by itself distinguished Israel from all other nations, and her God from all other gods. Israel was not complete without God's presence, and now it not only will return, but this time it will be home "forever." Wright observes, "It remains the ultimate vision of the new creation."

8 In their setting of their threshold by my thresholds, and their post by my posts, and the wall between me and them, they have even defiled my holy name by their abominations that they have committed: wherefore I have consumed them in mine anger.

God reminds Ezekiel why His presence had departed from the people: because of their cumulative and collective sins, represented by their spiritual "whoredom" (**v. 7**) and the provided Temple example. Lamar Cooper asserts that "a corrupt temple was the sad witness of a corrupt nation" (cf. **36:23**). Apparently, the Temple authorities had permitted either actual burials of deceased kings on the Temple mound or had erected memorials to them, neither of which glorified the living God, the King of glory, in what was supposed to be His sacred Temple. The notion that only the thickness of a wall separated such profane things from God's exalted sacred place was both defiling and an abomination against God's holiness. Robert Jensen posits, "The arrogance of the king has inflicted the presence of death . . . on the incorporated temple" (307).

LIGHT ON THE WORD

God's Promise to His People

God's glory would return to the Temple, but Israel needed to return to Him. Without His glory, they would be just like the Temple in the absence of His glory—a lifeless shell. God promises them that if they would return to Him by putting away these abominations, then He would dwell with them forever. This is God's desire and plan, and this is the true reason the Temple is to be rebuilt. God wants to be with His people in a life-giving and sustaining way!

III. THE REQUIREMENTS FOR THE GLORY (vv. 9–12)

Ezekiel is now commanded to show the Temple or "house" to the "house of Israel," so that they would be ashamed of their sins and the things that they have done to defile God's name. Ezekiel is instructed to show them the pattern of the house. The Lord says that if they see the pattern and are ashamed of their sins, then he is to show them all the measurements and architectural design of the Temple. He is to show them the decorations and the ritual acts that are to be performed in the Temple. This is what they are to do in order to maintain the presence of God's glory in the Temple.

Change Your Ungodly Ways (verses 9–12)

9 Now let them put away their whoredom, and the carcases of their kings, far from me, and I will dwell in the midst of them for ever. 10 Thou son of man, shew the house to the house of Israel, that they may be ashamed of their iniquities: and let them measure the pattern.

As Peter Craigie observes, "The prophet's vision so many centuries ago carries a perpetual message" (288). The message of the prophets has taken similar forms throughout the history of faith, but the theme barely varies—turn from the death of evil and turn to the life of God; put sin out of your heart and purify your Temple so God may dwell within you—culminating in today's ultra-succinct Gospel in a nutshell, "repent and be saved."

The Temple, per Craigie, is God's "symbolic dwelling" (289). It is His earthly residence, which is not to be defiled in any way. It is the ultimate paradox that the infinite, uncontainable God chooses to be present among mortal, finite humanity—a paradox perfectly embodied in the life of Jesus Christ: "who is the image of the invisible God" (from **Colossians 1:15**). This same paradox creates the ultimate tension in humanity—at any given time, how much is the profane rejected and the glory of the sacred presence welcome in our hearts? In Duguid's words, "God will live in our midst only as King, nothing less" (497).

The use of the word "ashamed" as the purpose of the vision stands in stark contrast to modern thinking that tends to avoid the subject at all costs. Yet shame, like guilt or fear, can be a valuable emotion if it leads one to transformation—much like the sensation of burning helpfully teaches one to withdraw from or avoid things that burn. Only from within the healthy experience of shame in confessing one's sins can one truly repent and thus fully experience God's mercy and grace.

11 And if they be ashamed of all that they have done, shew them the form of the house, and the fashion thereof, and the goings out thereof, and the comings in thereof, and all the forms thereof, and all the ordinances thereof, and all the forms thereof, and all the laws thereof: and write it in their sight, that they may keep the whole form thereof, and all the ordinances thereof, and do them. 12 This is the law of the house; Upon the top of the mountain the whole limit thereof round about shall be most holy. Behold, this is the law of the house.

The ultimate disaster for Israel was the Lord's departure. Even captivity by her enemies did not compare to His absence. Conversely, the ultimate blessing for Israel would be His permanent return. The element on which both departure and return hinged was Israel's faithlessness or her faithfulness. As a result, it is not enough that the people be aware of God's return. They must know everything involved with the Temple, including its design (both exits and entrances) and the laws and teachings associated it, which refer to the instructions originally laid out through Moses. Just as Jesus came not to destroy the law and the prophets but to fulfill them (**Matthew 5:17**), so Ezekiel promises that God will restore the blessings associated with Him originally through Moses (both His presence and worship of Him). Ezekiel was exhorted to deliver the message of hope both orally and in hard copy. One can only imagine the depth of meaning and significance that his vision would have brought for the languishing exiles. Many today are in self-imposed exile, imprisoned by their own bondages, and held in bondage by their addictions and profane habits. Not so different from the people of Ezekiel's time, they are in desperate need of the hope of God's glory entering their Temple and evicting their darkness and sin. By receiving Him, they experience the sacred place of God's glorious presence within their hearts.

SEARCH THE SCRIPTURES

QUESTION 2

What did the Lord ask the Children of Israel to remove and put away?

LIGHT ON THE WORD

Seeing and Living God's Vision

Craigie insightfully perceives that Ezekiel's vision of hope for exiled Israel could be compared to Martin Luther King Jr.'s vision for a racially torn America, which he cast for a downtrodden people who desperately needed to be infused with hope for the future. Just as Ezekiel's vision superseded his people and his time, so King's "I Have a Dream" speech also was a timeless message and vision for all humanity, for any who could see with new eyes the difference that a holy God could make in an evil world. Perhaps King had Solomon's words in mind that "where there is no vision, the people perish" (**Proverbs 29:18**).

BIBLE APPLICATION

AIM: Students will know that believers receive visions of hope and assurances of peace that sustain them through the most trying times.

Our society has lost the sense of the sacred. Most people live as if everything is banal and trivial. This type of attitude has even spread to the church. Our worship of God sometimes can be dull and lifeless and treated as something that is man-made and common. God's presence is always near when His people gather. His glory is meant to be experienced in these settings. The attitude of sacredness and sensitivity to the presence of God ought to permeate our gatherings and continue with us once we go our separate ways. God is a holy God and deserves to be treated as such.

STUDENTS' RESPONSES

AIM: Students will accept God's discipline and correction that sets them on the right pathway when they have strayed.

How can you grow in respect for the sacredness of worship settings? One of the ways you can do this is to begin to pray when you step through the doors of your church. Say a prayer to calm your heart and focus your mind on God. In this way you can remind yourself of the reason you are there and go in with a desire to experience the glory of God and to worship Him.

PRAYER

God, thank You for allowing us the opportunity to share in Your desire for justice and peace. Let us speak and act boldly to bring Your kingdom here on earth. In Jesus' Name we pray. Amen.

HOW TO SAY IT

Chebar.	keh-**VAR**.
Shekinah.	sheh-kee-**NAW**.

PREPARE FOR NEXT SUNDAY

Read **Ezekiel 43:13–21** and study "The Altar, A Sign of Hope."

DAILY HOME BIBLE READINGS

MONDAY
God's Glory and Greatness
(Deuteronomy 5:23–29)

TUESDAY
God's Exalted Name
(Psalm 138)

WEDNESDAY
Standing on Holy Ground
(Exodus 3:1–6)

THURSDAY
God's Holy Place
(Psalm 24)

FRIDAY
Worshiping in Awe
(Psalm 5)

SATURDAY
God Examines Humankind
(Psalm 11)

SUNDAY
God's Glory Returns to the Temple
(Ezekiel 43:1–12)

Sources:

Allen, Leslie C., ed. *Word Biblical Commentary: Ezekiel 20–48*. Dallas, TX: Word Book Publishers, 1990.

Barlow, Rev. George. *The Preacher's Homiletic Commentary: Lamentations and Ezekiel*. Grand Rapids, MI: Baker Books, reprint 1996.

Blenkinsopp, Joseph. *Ezekiel. Interpretation: A Bible Commentary for Teaching and Preaching*. Louisville: John Knox Press, 1990. 210–216.

Bryant, T. Alton, ed. *The New Compact Bible Dictionary*. Grand Rapids, MI: Zondervan, 1967.

Cooper, Lamar Eugene, Sr. *Ezekiel*. The New American Commentary, vol. 17. Nashville, TN: Broadman and Holman Publishers, 1994. 374–390.

Craigie, Peter C. *Ezekiel*. Louisville, KY: Westminster John Knox Press, 1983. 286–293.

Duguid, Iain M. *Ezekiel. The NIV Application Commentary*. Grand Rapids, MI: Zondervan, 1999. 487–497.

Jensen, Robert W. *Ezekiel*. Brazos Theological Commentary on the Bible. Grand Rapids, MI: Brazos Press, 2009. 305–312.

Strong, James. *The New Strong's Exhaustive Concordance of the Bible*. Nashville, TN: Thomas Nelson Publishers, 1990.

Wright, Christopher J. H. *The Message of Ezekiel: A New Heart and a New Spirit*. Downers Grove, IL: InterVarsity Press, 2001. 333–348.

THE ALTAR, A SIGN OF HOPE

BIBLE BASIS: EZEKIEL 43:13–21

BIBLE TRUTH: The Israelites could hope for release from their iniquities by making sin sacrifices in the sacred space of the altar that stood before the Temple.

MEMORY VERSE: "And when these days are expired, it shall be, that upon the eighth day, and so forward, the priests shall make your burnt offerings upon the altar, and your peace offerings; and I will accept you, saith the Lord GOD" (Ezekiel 43:27).

LESSON AIM: By the end of this lesson, your students will: review the instructions Ezekiel received for building a new altar and making offerings; reflect on the value of finding personal sacred spaces for atonement and renewal; and identify and use personal sacred spaces for atonement and renewal.

TEACHER PREPARATION

MATERIALS NEEDED: Quarterly Commentary/Teacher Manual, Adult Quarterly, Adult resources—charts, worksheets, and other teaching tools, paper, pens, pencils, Bibles (several different versions)

OTHER MATERIALS NEEDED / TEACHER'S NOTES:

____

____

LESSON OVERVIEW

LIFE NEED FOR TODAY'S LESSON

Sometimes people seek space in which they can find direction for making the most of life.

BIBLE LEARNING

The Israelites considered the Temple in Jerusalem the place of God's divine presence.

BIBLE APPLICATION

Christians believe that they can seek God for forgiveness of their sins and find release from guilt.

STUDENTS' RESPONSES

People of faith make meaningful contact with God and find renewal and restoration through the power of praise and worship.

LESSON SCRIPTURE

EZEKIEL 43:13–21, KJV

13 And these are the measures of the altar after the cubits: The cubit is a cubit and an hand breadth; even the bottom shall be a cubit, and the breadth a cubit, and the border thereof by the edge thereof round

EZEKIEL 43:13–21, NIV

13 "These are the measurements of the altar in long cubits, that cubit being a cubit and a handbreadth: Its gutter is a cubit deep and a cubit wide, with a rim of one span around the edge. And this is the height of the altar:

about shall be a span: and this shall be the higher place of the altar.

14 And from the bottom upon the ground even to the lower settle shall be two cubits, and the breadth one cubit; and from the lesser settle even to the greater settle shall be four cubits, and the breadth one cubit.

15 So the altar shall be four cubits; and from the altar and upward shall be four horns.

16 And the altar shall be twelve cubits long, twelve broad, square in the four squares thereof.

17 And the settle shall be fourteen cubits long and fourteen broad in the four squares thereof; and the border about it shall be half a cubit; and the bottom thereof shall be a cubit about; and his stairs shall look toward the east.

18 And he said unto me, Son of man, thus saith the Lord GOD; These are the ordinances of the altar in the day when they shall make it, to offer burnt offerings thereon, and to sprinkle blood thereon.

19 And thou shalt give to the priests the Levites that be of the seed of Zadok, which approach unto me, to minister unto me, saith the Lord GOD, a young bullock for a sin offering.

20 And thou shalt take of the blood thereof, and put it on the four horns of it, and on the four corners of the settle, and upon the border round about: thus shalt thou cleanse and purge it.

21 Thou shalt take the bullock also of the sin offering, and he shall burn it in the appointed place of the house, without the sanctuary.

14 From the gutter on the ground up to the lower ledge that goes around the altar it is two cubits high, and the ledge is a cubit wide. From this lower ledge to the upper ledge that goes around the altar it is four cubits high, and that ledge is also a cubit wide.

15 Above that, the altar hearth is four cubits high, and four horns project upward from the hearth.

16 The altar hearth is square, twelve cubits long and twelve cubits wide.

17 The upper ledge also is square, fourteen cubits long and fourteen cubits wide. All around the altar is a gutter of one cubit with a rim of half a cubit. The steps of the altar face east."

18 Then he said to me, "Son of man, this is what the Sovereign LORD says: These will be the regulations for sacrificing burnt offerings and splashing blood against the altar when it is built:

19 You are to give a young bull as a sin offering to the Levitical priests of the family of Zadok, who come near to minister before me, declares the Sovereign LORD.

20 You are to take some of its blood and put it on the four horns of the altar and on the four corners of the upper ledge and all around the rim, and so purify the altar and make atonement for it.

21 You are to take the bull for the sin offering and burn it in the designated part of the temple area outside the sanctuary.

LIGHT ON THE WORD

An altar is a place where sacrifices can be made. It was an object that assisted in worship in ancient Near Eastern culture. Two types of altars can be found in the Bible. One type of altar was made of earth or unhewn stones piled up into a heap. This type of altar was mostly used by God's people during pre-Mosaic times and was readily available for the average worshiper. The second kind of altar was one made of metal or hewn stone and had horns attached to it. This type of altar could be found in the Temple and only the levitical priests could make sacrifices on these.

A sin offering was an expiatory sacrifice to cleanse from sin. Various animals were used depending on the status of the worshiper. The priest or the whole community used a young bullock (**Leviticus 4:3–12**). A male goat was used for an Israelite ruler (**4:22–26**). The common person would use a lamb or female goat, while a poorer person would use two turtledoves (**4:27–5:13**). The animal was killed, and the blood was sprinkled over the altar. Sin offerings were made for unintentional sins that if done consciously or willingly would have caused someone to be executed.

A cubit was the length from the elbow to the tip of the middle finger. A span was a measurement of half a cubit or the distance between a thumb and the little finger on an outstretched hand. A handbreadth was the distance between the index finger and the little finger. All of these measurements are approximate.

TEACHING THE BIBLE LESSON

LIFE NEED FOR TODAY'S LESSON

AIM: Students will seek space in which they can find direction for making the most of life.

INTRODUCTION

The Future Temple

Ezekiel's vision of a future Temple is described beginning in **Ezekiel 40**. This future Temple would be the ideal place for the worship of God. Ezekiel described the general architectural design and measurements of the Temple. Once he described this, he was approached by a heavenly messenger who took him toward the East Gate. Here Ezekiel witnessed the return of the glory of the Lord. As he saw the shining presence of God, he immediately fell down prostrate in worship and submission. Then the heavenly messenger spoke to him regarding the holiness of the Temple. Based on this, Israel was called on to repent of their sins and remove anything that would defile the Temple. Finally, the basic law of the Temple is given: holiness.

BIBLE LEARNING

AIM: Students will see that the Israelites considered the Temple in Jerusalem the place of God's divine presence.

I. THE DETAILS OF THE ALTAR OFFER HOPE (Ezekiel 43:13–17)

Ezekiel communicates the precise measurements of the altar. The altar is specifically designed for the sacrificial offerings and also for symbolic teaching on the nature and ways of God. Ezekiel gives the measurements of the altar. Two things can be observed concerning the construction and measurements of the altar for the future Temple. The first thing that we notice is there is a sump for cleansing the inner court of the sacrificial blood (**v. 13**). The second thing is that the priest who performs the sacrifices approaches it on stairs that faced east (**v. 17**).

The Sacred Altar (verses 13–17)

13 And these are the measures of the altar after the cubits: The cubit is a cubit and an hand breadth; even the bottom shall be a cubit, and the breadth a cubit, and the border thereof by the edge thereof round about shall be a span: and this shall be the higher place of the altar. 14 And from the bottom upon the ground even to the lower settle shall be two cubits, and the breadth one cubit; and from the lesser settle even to the greater settle shall be four cubits, and the breadth one cubit.
15 So the altar shall be four cubits; and from the altar and upward shall be four horns. 16 And the altar shall be twelve cubits long, twelve broad, square in the four squares thereof. 17 And the settle shall be fourteen cubits long and fourteen broad in the four squares thereof; and the border about it shall be half a cubit; and the bottom thereof shall be a cubit about; and his stairs shall look toward the east.

Commentators variously interpret the modern equivalent of an ancient "long" cubit (cf. **40:5**) to translate the physical description of the altar shown to Ezekiel—ranging 24–32 square feet at the base, and ranging 10–16 feet in height. According to Joseph Blenkinsopp, a cubit is "the distance from the elbow to the fingertips plus a hand-breadth, and the handspan" (213)—inexact at best. Scholars collectively agree, however, that it is a large altar, four times larger than the one in the wilderness tabernacle (**Exodus 27:1–8**), and on par with the bronze altar in Solomon's Temple (**2 Chronicles 4:1**). Also, the simple construction—four layers of progressively smaller squares with a stairway facing east and horns at each of the four corners at the top—belies the divine intent and symbolism.

Throughout Israel's history, even proper sacrifices were meaningless without a proper attitude and lifestyle that was congruent with the ritual. Various prophets address this core truth: Amos forever and poetically captures the concept (**Amos 5:21–24**, especially **v. 24**); Isaiah writes about offerings made in vain (**Isaiah 1:12–17**); Micah makes a memorable statement similar to the classic passage in Amos (**Micah 6:6–8**, especially **v. 8**); and David also writes many memorable and often-quoted words on the subject (e.g., **Psalm 51:16–17**). In the New Testament, Paul continues the unabated theme of offering one's body, i.e. life, as a spiritual worship (**Romans 12:1**); and Peter echoes a similar thought to offer spiritual sacrifices that are acceptable to God (**1 Peter 2:5**).

SEARCH THE SCRIPTURES

QUESTION 1

Where were the altar's stairs placed?

LIGHT ON THE WORD

The Sacred Space

Both of these things symbolize the holiness of God and the holiness that God requires of His people. The sump was put there to cleanse the court of blood. The inner court was to be holy and free from all defilement. This sump would remove the leftover sacrificial blood which was considered holy. Due to its sacredness this blood was to be used for no other purpose and would defile any common person or thing it came into contact with. It was definitely a reminder that this was sacred space. The stairs facing east would insure that the priest approached the Lord facing the Holy of Holies and not toward the sun. Facing the sun was a prominent feature of worship in many idolatrous cultures of the time. These small details let Israel know that the worship of God is a holy thing and something not to be taken lightly.

II. THE PRIESTS OF THE ALTAR OFFER HOPE (vv. 18–19)

Ezekiel's vision then describes the type of

priests who will minister at the altar. The priests will come from the line of Zadok. Zadok was the joint high priest during David's reign and the high priest during the reign of Solomon. When Abiathar the high priest conspired against Solomon, he was put into retirement and Zadok was made sole high priest because of his loyalty to the king.

The Purity of the Priest and the Altar (verses 18–19)

18 And he said unto me, Son of man, thus saith the Lord GOD; These are the ordinances of the altar in the day when they shall make it, to offer burnt offerings thereon, and to sprinkle blood thereon.
19 And thou shalt give to the priests the Levites that be of the seed of Zadok, which approach unto me, to minister unto me, saith the Lord GOD, a young bullock for a sin offering.

The priests, as well as the altar, were to be consecrated and pure. The purity of the priests was even evident in their bloodline, as they were to be Levites from the seed of Zadok. The seed of Zadok had been loyal to King David and King Solomon, and thus their line continued on to be priests. They were seen as not only loyal to these particular kings but also loyal to God. The priests were also to be set apart through the offering of a young bullock. A sin offering was given for sins that were committed unconsciously. The purity of the priests who would minister at the altar would not be taken for granted. Every measure would be taken to ensure that they remained pure and their sins were atoned for.

LIGHT ON THE WORD

The Righteous High Priest

Choosing priests from the line of Zadok points to the desire for a righteous high priest. In fact, in Hebrew, Zadok's name is from the same root as the word for righteousness (*tsedeq*, **TSEH-duk**). As believers we have a righteous High Priest who is sinless: Jesus Christ. He has access and authority with God the Father because of His righteousness. Just like the priests in Ezekiel's vision, He can approach God and minister to Him on our behalf (**v. 19**, see **Hebrews 5:1–2**)

III. THE SACRIFICE ON THE ALTAR OFFERS HOPE (vv. 20–21)

The priests were charged with presenting a sin offering to God for the people. This sin offering was to be a young bullock or male steer. As a sin offering it would be offered to God for the unwilling and unconscious sins of the people. It would be the first step in dedicating the altar and making it holy to God. The blood of the sacrifice would be sprinkled on corners of the altar and on the horns of the altar. The rest of the animal would be taken outside of the sanctuary and burned.

A Blood Offering (verses 20–21)

20 And thou shalt take of the blood thereof, and put it on the four horns of it, and on the four corners of the settle, and upon the border round about: thus shalt thou cleanse and purge it. 21 Thou shalt
take the bullock also of the sin offering, and he shall burn it in the appointed place of the house, without the sanctuary.

When speaking of the Hebrew sacrificial system, to "purge" is translated "make atonement" in most versions (Heb. *khaphar*, **kaw-FAR**) and also means "expiate," "forgive," or "reconcile." Once the sacrificial lifeblood had been used for atonement, the animal had to be burned in another area (cf. **Leviticus 8:17**)—just as Jesus was put to death outside of the Temple (**Hebrews 13:11–13**). Today, our acceptance into

God's presence comes because of Jesus' atoning blood on the Cross, which each of us symbolically sprinkles on the altar of our heart. We, like Ezekiel's people, then are cleansed and forgiven, and God accepts us. Blenkinsopp insightfully observes, "The institution continues its life cycle as metaphor" (216).

Even in Jesus' day, Jews continued to practice the rituals prescribed by Moses and reinstated by Ezekiel. In fact, Jesus Himself only addresses those who take advantage of observers of the sacrificial laws (**Matthew 21:12–13**), and not those who practice these laws. It was not until the Temple was destroyed again in A.D. 70 that Jews abandoned the sacrificial system completely. Hebrews states clearly that it was the blood of Jesus, not the blood of animals, that sealed the new covenant (**Hebrews 10:1–8**; cf. **Matthew 26:28**), and Ezekiel's vision does not contradict this eternal truth. Lamar Cooper helpfully writes that both "systems of worship were intended to employ rituals to commemorate spiritual truths" (381). All the passages about a kingdom of priests in both the Old and New Testaments finally will have converged, and all the Old Testament typology will have found ultimate fulfillment.

SEARCH THE SCRIPTURES

QUESTION 2

What was the purpose of the sin offering?

LIGHT ON THE WORD

The Symbols of Christ

We can see in these verses that the altar is a symbol of hope for the Children of Israel and for us. Dedicating the altar to the service of God represents renewed closeness to God for His people. The altar, the sacrifice, and as stated earlier, the high priest are symbols of Christ. The altar symbolizes Christ because, in order to get to the Holy of Holies where God dwells, one must pass by the altar. The only way to get to God is through Jesus Christ. The sacrifice is also a symbol of Christ as He is our sin offering and cleanses us from sin that we consciously or unconsciously commit. The high priest symbolizes Christ because he is righteous and represents the people before God. Christ is our High Priest who represents us before the Father. In this way, the altar symbolizes our hope in Christ.

BIBLE APPLICATION

AIM: Students will believe that they can seek God for forgiveness of their sins and find release from guilt.

Many in our society long for a place where they can go to find peace and refreshment. Our 24/7 busy world is yearning for a sacred space to keep out the noise and pollution of life. Constant attention to technology, overwhelming workloads, and endless recreational distractions make it hard to carve out space for God. As believers, we can always go to Christ in prayer and worship. He is our sacred space and an altar that brings us near to God.

STUDENTS' RESPONSES

AIM: Students will learn that people of faith make meaningful contact with God and find renewal and restoration through the power of praise and worship.

Many times in our lives we experience a need for atonement and renewal. There are many ways that we can go about setting apart space and time for this. Try taking a personal retreat for a day. We can also make special appointments with God to praise and thank Him, even if only for a moment. We can use our time before work or going to bed for prayer, praise, and confession.

PRAYER

Gracious Lord, we praise You, we bless You, we worship You, and we confess our sins before You. Thank you for redeeming us through the blood of Jesus Christ. In Jesus' Name we pray. Amen.

HOW TO SAY IT

Zadok. tsaw-**DOKE**.

Abiathar. ab-yaw-**THAR**.

PREPARE FOR NEXT SUNDAY

Read **Ezekiel 47:1, 3–12** and study "A Transforming Stream."

DAILY HOME BIBLE READINGS

MONDAY
Quest for a True Altar
(Joshua 22:21–34)

TUESDAY
Pulling Down False Altars
(Judges 6:24–32)

WEDNESDAY
A Costly Altar and Sacrifice
(2 Samuel 24:17–25)

THURSDAY
You, O Lord, are My Hope
(Psalm 71:1–8)

FRIDAY
Hope in the Lord Forevermore
(Psalm 130–131)

SATURDAY
I Will Accept You
(Ezekiel 43:22–27)

SUNDAY
The Ordinances for the Altar
(Ezekiel 43:13–21)

Sources:

Allen, Leslie C., ed. *Word Biblical Commentary: Ezekiel 20–48*. Dallas, TX: Word Books, 1990.

Barlow, Rev. George. *The Preacher's Homiletic Commentary: Lamentations and Ezekiel*. Grand Rapids, MI: Baker Books, reprint 1996.

Blenkinsopp, Joseph. *Ezekiel. Interpretation: A Bible Commentary for Teaching and Preaching*. Louisville, KY: John Knox Press, 1990. 210–216.

Bryant, T. Alton. *The New Compact Bible Dictionary*. Grand Rapids, MI: Zondervan, 1967.

Cooper, Lamar Eugene, Sr. *Ezekiel*. The New American Commentary, vol. 17. Nashville, TN: Broadman and Holman Publishers, 1994. 374–390.

Duguid, Iain M. *Ezekiel*. The NIV Application Commentary. Grand Rapids, MI: Zondervan, 1999. 487–497.

Strong, James. *The New Strong's Exhaustive Concordance of the Bible*. Nashville, TN: Thomas Nelson Publishers, 1990.

Wright, Christopher J. H. *The Message of Ezekiel: A New Heart and a New Spirit*. Downers Grove, IL: InterVarsity Press, 2001. 333–348.

COMMENTS / NOTES:

A TRANSFORMING STREAM

BIBLE BASIS: EZEKIEL 47:1, 3–12

BIBLE TRUTH: In Ezekiel's vision, water is the symbol of God's presence and blessings that flow God's sanctuary and are available to the earth and its people.

MEMORY VERSE: "And it shall come to pass, that every thing that liveth, which moveth, whithersoever the rivers shall come, shall live: and there shall be a very great multitude of fish, because these waters shall come thither: for they shall be healed; and every thing shall live whither the river cometh" (Ezekiel 47:9).

LESSON AIM: By the end of the lesson, your students will: know about Ezekiel's vision of life-giving water; appreciate our covenant with God as an ever-deepening river of blessings; and commit to communing with God daily.

TEACHER PREPARATION

MATERIALS NEEDED: Quarterly Commentary/Teacher Manual, Adult Quarterly, Adult resources—charts, worksheets, and other teaching tools, paper, pens, pencils, Bibles (several different versions)

OTHER MATERIALS NEEDED / TEACHER'S NOTES:

LESSON OVERVIEW

LIFE NEED FOR TODAY'S LESSON

Sometimes people feel like they are stranded on a high cliff and are forced to leap into dangerous and unknown water.

BIBLE LEARNING

The vision indicates that covenant with God is an ever-deepening river of blessings.

BIBLE APPLICATION

Believers are encouraged with images and symbols of God's enduring provisions of the water and the bread of life.

STUDENTS' RESPONSES

Believers find signs of God's presence and blessings in their surroundings.

LESSON SCRIPTURE

EZEKIEL 47:1, 3–12, KJV

1 Afterward he brought me again unto the door of the house; and, behold, waters issued out from under the threshold of the house eastward: for the forefront of the house stood toward the east, and the

EZEKIEL 47:1, 3–12, NIV

1 The man brought me back to the entrance to the temple, and I saw water coming out from under the threshold of the temple toward the east (for the temple faced east). The water was coming down

waters came down from under from the right side of the house, at the south side of the altar.

3 And when the man that had the line in his hand went forth eastward, he measured a thousand cubits, and he brought me through the waters; the waters were to the ankles.

4 Again he measured a thousand, and brought me through the waters; the waters were to the knees. Again he measured a thousand, and brought me through; the waters were to the loins.

5 Afterward he measured a thousand; and it was a river that I could not pass over: for the waters were risen, waters to swim in, a river that could not be passed over.

6 And he said unto me, Son of man, hast thou seen this? Then he brought me, and caused me to return to the brink of the river.

7 Now when I had returned, behold, at the bank of the river were very many trees on the one side and on the other.

8 Then said he unto me, These waters issue out toward the east country, and go down into the desert, and go into the sea: which being brought forth into the sea, the waters shall be healed.

9 And it shall come to pass, that every thing that liveth, which moveth, whithersoever the rivers shall come, shall live: and there shall be a very great multitude of fish, because these waters shall come thither: for they shall be healed; and every thing shall live whither the river cometh.

10 And it shall come to pass, that the fishers shall stand upon it from Engedi even unto Eneglaim; they shall be a place

from under the south side of the temple, south of the altar.

3 As the man went eastward with a measuring line in his hand, he measured off a thousand cubits and then led me through water that was ankle-deep.

4 He measured off another thousand cubits and led me through water that was knee-deep. He measured off another thousand and led me through water that was up to the waist.

5 He measured off another thousand, but now it was a river that I could not cross, because the water had risen and was deep enough to swim in—a river that no one could cross.

6 He asked me, "Son of man, do you see this?" Then he led me back to the bank of the river.

7 When I arrived there, I saw a great number of trees on each side of the river.

8 He said to me, "This water flows toward the eastern region and goes down into the Arabah, where it enters the Dead Sea. When it empties into the sea, the salty water there becomes fresh.

9 Swarms of living creatures will live wherever the river flows. There will be large numbers of fish, because this water flows there and makes the salt water fresh; so where the river flows everything will live.

10 Fishermen will stand along the shore; from En Gedi to En Eglaim there will be places for spreading nets. The fish will be of many kinds—like the fish of the Mediterranean Sea.

11 But the swamps and marshes will not become fresh; they will be left for salt.

to spread forth nets; their fish shall be according to their kinds, as the fish of the great sea, exceeding many.

11 But the miry places thereof and the marishes thereof shall not be healed; they shall be given to salt.

12 And by the river upon the bank thereof, on this side and on that side, shall grow all trees for meat, whose leaf shall not fade, neither shall the fruit thereof be consumed: it shall bring forth new fruit according to his months, because their waters they issued out of the sanctuary: and the fruit thereof shall be for meat, and the leaf thereof for medicine.

12 Fruit trees of all kinds will grow on both banks of the river. Their leaves will not wither, nor will their fruit fail. Every month they will bear fruit, because the water from the sanctuary flows to them. Their fruit will serve for food and their leaves for healing."

LIGHT ON THE WORD

What we know about Ezekiel as a person is found only in the book of Ezekiel. He was born to a priestly family during a time of political upheaval both nationally and within the surrounding kingdoms. Among the Israelites exiled to Babylon, Ezekiel was called to be a prophet of God while in Babylon and was active for twenty-two years. The destruction of the Temple in Jerusalem in 587 B.C. occurred during his lifetime.

Ezekiel's vision of the river is the third major vision in the book of Ezekiel. Visions are, in essence, waking dreams. They were seen by numerous Bible characters including Abraham, Peter, and Paul (**Genesis 15**; **Acts 10**; **2 Corinthians 12**). Visions contain messages from God concerning the individual experiencing the vision or for the larger community of His people. Most of the time visions contain things that are beyond the scope of what could happen in real life. They are rich with symbolism and usually have to be interpreted in much the same way as dreams. The Lord seemed to communicate to Ezekiel major portions of his prophecy through visions.

TEACHING THE BIBLE LESSON

LIFE NEED FOR TODAY'S LESSON

AIM: Students will understand that sometimes people feel like they are stranded on a high cliff and are forced to leap into dangerous and unknown water.

INTRODUCTION

The Book of Ezekiel

The first three chapters of Ezekiel detail the calling and commissioning of Ezekiel as a prophet of God. The rest of the book of Ezekiel can be divided into three main sections. The first section, **chapters 4–24**, is prophetic messages of judgment upon Israel and Jerusalem, ending with the prediction of the fall of Jerusalem in **chapter 24**. The second section, **chapters 25–32**, is prophetic messages of God's judgment of foreign nations. The third section, **chapters 33–48**, is predictions of Israel's restoration and redemption, and include details concerning the Temple, the sacrificial system, and the rebuilding of Jerusalem. These last chapters also point toward the re-establishment and exaltation of the kingdom of God.

It is in the context of this last section that Ezekiel receives a multi-part vision of the new Temple of God that is to come during the future thousand-year reign of Christ on earth. In today's lesson, we will examine the last part of Ezekiel's "Temple tour" where Ezekiel is standing just inside the gate of the Temple and sees the river flowing from under the Temple.

BIBLE LEARNING

AIM: Students will see that the vision indicates that covenant with God is an ever-deepening river of blessings.

I. THE RISE OF THE RIVER (Ezekiel 47:1, 3–7)

Ezekiel's third vision begins as he is standing in the inner court of the new Temple in Jerusalem. He sees water coming out from under the Temple, flowing from the side of the altar. In **Revelation 22:1**, we also see "the river of the water of life, as clear as crystal, flowing from the throne of God and of the Lamb" (NIV). It is significant that this river proceeds from where God dwells. God's presence has been associated with water elsewhere in Ezekiel (**1:24, 43:2**). Likewise, the flow of God's Spirit, through Jesus, brings energizing life and healing to those who will accept Him.

The Water of Life (verses 1, 3–7)

1 Afterward he brought me again unto the door of the house; and, behold, waters issued out from under the threshold of the house eastward: for the forefront of the house stood toward the east, and the waters came down from under from the right side of the house, at the south side of the altar.

After Ezekiel's guided tour of the Temple (Heb. *bayith*, **BAH-yith**), he is brought back to the entrance of the Temple building to the inside of the inner court. Upon reaching the gate of the Temple, he sees waters that has their spring under the threshold of that gate. These waters, which look toward the east and pass to the south of the altar of burnt offerings on the right of the Temple, run from the west to the east. The most important fact about the river is its Source. The river issues directly from the presence of God Himself. This is the reason it is able to give life and sustenance, for they are both gifts of the living God. The river has its spring out of sight—the fountainhead is invisible—but it proceeds out of the sanctuary of God. We need to remember that all renewal in the church and the world flows by God's wonderful grace from His presence and is not something that can be generated or controlled by humans.

3 And when the man that had the line in his hand went forth eastward, he measured a thousand cubits, and he brought me through the waters; the waters were to the ankles. 4 Again he measured a thousand, and brought me through the waters; the waters were to the knees. Again he measured a thousand, and brought me through; the waters were to the loins. 5 Afterward he measured a thousand; and it was a river that I could not pass over: for the waters were risen, waters to swim in, a river that could not be passed over.

The divine messenger takes Ezekiel to explore the extent of this stream. A measuring line is used to mark off four one-thousand-cubit intervals, approximately one-third of a mile each. At each interval, Ezekiel is taken out into the stream to examine its depth. The waters increase so that they become a river in which one could swim. What an amazing transformation that a river so tiny at its source could become a mighty river in just over a mile! The depth increases at each interval from ankle-deep to knee-deep to waist-deep, and finally to a depth in which one must swim. At the four-thousand-cubit mark, the stream has become a river of such magnitude that it cannot be crossed. The river appears so torrential or so wide that it is not possible to swim across it. A miracle is no doubt at work, something like the unspent jar of meal and unfailing cruse of oil in **1 Kings 17:12–16** or like the growth of the kingdom of God from mustard seed to a spreading tree (**Mark 4:31–32**).

We all have plenty of room for improvement! With each step of obedience, Ezekiel finds himself going deeper into dependence upon the grace of God. With each venture of forward progress, more of Ezekiel is submerged in the river with less of him being visible. The Christian life is progressive in nature, showing growth that is both measurable and discernible. God does not make us grow. We must choose to walk on into greater maturity.

Ezekiel has gone so far from the shore that he can no longer walk back. Wherever the river flows, that is where he is going. The current is so strong and the volume of water is so great that Ezekiel is in over his head. Still God is carrying him and there is no danger of the prophet drowning. God is still in control of the water and the life of the prophet.

6 And he said unto me, Son of man, hast thou seen this? Then he brought me, and caused me to return to the brink of the river. 7 Now when I had returned, behold, at the bank of the river were very many trees on the one side and on the other.

Ezekiel must have been left in such utter amazement that he continues to stare at the scene. He is brought right back to the brink—back to the starting point. But there is more to see. Ezekiel is a new sight that he had not noticed before. Both sides of the river are lined with trees. The purpose of the river is becoming clearer. Its basic purpose is to bring life. Many trees line its sides. Every kind of fruit tree grow on both sides. There is an oasis of trees growing in the wilderness of Judah, between Jerusalem and the Dead Sea. What a sight, and what a miracle!

SEARCH THE SCRIPTURES

QUESTIONS 1 & 2

Where did Ezekiel's vision of the river begin?

Who is guiding Ezekiel through this vision?

LIGHT ON THE WORD

The Strength of the River

As the river flowed from the Temple and over the mountains, instead of eventually waning to a trickle, it gained in depth and strength. Ezekiel, in his vision, waded into the river. It was ankle-deep (**v. 3**). A little farther downstream, the river was knee-deep, then waist-deep (**v. 4**). One final check revealed that the river was so deep that "no one could cross" (**v. 5**, NIV).

And so it is with our spiritual life. When we first begin our relationship with God, we wade out ankle-deep. We learn the first things about God. As we begin to mature, we search out the deeper things of God that require some "knee-deep" wading into the river. And then there are some things that we will never fully understand, and we must be content to say with the Apostle Paul, "Oh, the depth of the riches of the wisdom and knowledge of God! How unsearchable his judgments, and his paths beyond tracing out!" (**Romans 11:33**, NIV). When we are in covenant with God, His river in our lives grows ever deeper as we spend time communing with Him and getting to know Him better.

II. THE RESULT OF THE RIVER (vv. 8–12)

The waters that proceed from God have a healing, restorative effect. Even the lowest, saltiest body of water in the world, the Dead Sea, will be made fresh by the healing river of God (**v. 8**). In place of this "dead" water where no life can be sustained, there will be "swarms of living creatures" (**v. 9**, NIV). This signifies great provision for humankind—fishermen will stand along the shore from one end of the country to the other to fill their nets with the abundance of fish (**v. 10**). Fruit trees of all kinds will bear bountiful crops—a different kind of fruit every month, because "the water from the sanctuary flows to them. Their fruit will serve for food and their leaves for healing" (**v. 12**, NIV).

The Healing Waters (verses 8–12)

8 Then said he unto me, These waters issue out toward the east country, and go down into the desert, and go into the sea: which being brought forth into the sea, the waters shall be healed.

The guide does not leave the prophet in doubt concerning the interpretation of what he has just seen. Ezekiel learns that the river, which he has just seen, eventually flows into the sea. "The sea" is a term commonly applied to the Dead Sea (cf. **Deuteronomy 3:17**). The waters are miraculously healed. The word "healed" (Heb. *rapha'*, **raw-FAW**) normally refers to the healing of a diseased body. However in this case, the miracle involves the neutralizing of the corrupting chemicals in the water so it becomes fresh and life is no longer suppressed.

9 And it shall come to pass, that every thing that liveth, which moveth, whithersoever the rivers shall come, shall live: and there shall be a very great multitude of fish, because these waters shall come thither: for they shall be healed; and every thing shall live whither the river cometh.

The thoroughness of the healing is evident in the phrase "whithersoever the rivers shall come." Everywhere else, the river brought its life-giving power. Every living thing will abound in the "healed" waters. The absence of living creatures in the Dead Sea has been remarked by ancient and modern writers. In the same way, the living water that Jesus gives brings life to those dead in trespasses and sins (cf. **John 4:14**). Ezekiel's river is similar to the rivers in the Garden of Eden and the eternal state (cf. **Revelation 22:2–3**).

10 And it shall come to pass, that the fishers shall stand upon it from Engedi even unto Eneglaim; they shall be a place to spread forth nets; their fish shall be according to their kinds, as the fish of the great sea, exceeding many.

Ordinarily, the salt and minerals of the Dead Sea permit no life in it of any kind, but in the ideal (coming) age, it will miraculously teem with life. The entire Dead Sea and Arabah plain, where the Dead Sea is located, are healed by these waters, causing the Dead Sea to swarm with marine life to the extent that fishermen fish its entire length from Engedi to Eneglaim, catching a great variety of fish.

11 But the miry places thereof and the marishes thereof shall not be healed; they shall be given to salt.

The guide informes Ezekiel that there will be exceptions to the remarkable picture of life that he has just seen. The Arabah blooms (cf. **Isaiah 35:1–2, 6–7**; **Joel 3:18**); only the swamps and marshes are not healed. They are left to provide salt for the people. These are places to which the living water does not reach and indicate that life and health are solely due to the stream, which proceeds from beneath the throne of God.

12 And by the river upon the bank thereof, on this side and on that side, shall grow all trees for meat, whose leaf shall not fade, neither shall the fruit thereof be consumed: it shall bring forth new fruit according to his months, because their waters they issued out of the sanctuary: and the fruit thereof shall be for meat, and the leaf thereof for medicine.

The vision comes to a conclusion with a focus on the abundance of the growth of the trees and their benefits for human use. Both banks are filled with "all" (Heb. *kol*, **KOLE**), literally "every" tree, to suggest profusion and variety. Their fruit provides food, and their leaves provide healing. The source of the land's redemption and healing comes from God and His throne. He will heal the land in the time of the consummation of the kingdom. Ultimately, the river of life in Ezekiel, as in Revelation, anticipates the new creation. In this new creation, God will have lifted the curse from the earth forever and will dwell in life-giving abundance with His redeemed people gathered from all nations.

SEARCH THE SCRIPTURES

QUESTION 3

What was growing on both sides of the river?

LIGHT ON THE WORD

The Flowing Waters

How we wish the water of the sanctuary would flow over us—that healing, reviving presence of God in our lives. How we need His grace, His healing, His forgiveness to wash away the stagnant, dead waters of our lives. Only when we bask in His presence and soak up the living water of His words will we become bountifully fruitful servants of God.

Our fruitfulness is not just for us. The fruit we bear is to serve as food to those who are hungry for the Gospel. Our green leaves of revival and purity will be for the healing of others who are sick or wounded. Wash us in Your living water, O God!

BIBLE APPLICATION

AIM: Students will be encouraged with images and symbols of God's enduring provisions of the water and the bread of life.

According to scientists, 97 percent of all water on Earth is salty. Another 2 percent of Earth's water is ice, leaving about 1 percent of all water on Earth for human use. Water conservation and pollution are major concerns in our world today, yet this is approximately the same quantity of water that has cycled continuously for centuries. God has blessed all of mankind—both saved and sinner—with the life-giving gift of water.

We've all seen the pleas for help from poverty-stricken countries where people are dying for lack of pure water. God's people should not be hardened to the plight of these nations, but we should do what we can to help. God calls believers to hold out a cup of cold water to those who are thirsty—both literally and spiritually (cf. **Matthew 25:35**).

God's living water is available to quench the thirsty souls of those around us. God's well will never run dry; His river will never be dammed up. But it is up to us to lead the lost and dying to the water's Source.

STUDENTS' RESPONSES

AIM: Students will find signs of God's presence and blessings in their surroundings.

What is happening in your life spiritually? Is your stream growing stronger and deeper over time, or is it drying up and becoming stagnant? This week, examine your life. Compare your life today to where you were spiritually a year ago. Are you in ankle-deep? Knee-deep? Ask God for a desire to go deeper into His river and commit to commune with Him daily.

PRAYER

Dear Lord, we bask in Your flowing water that refreshes our spirits every day as we experience You healing, forgiving, and renewing us. Your tender care refreshes our spirits every day. In Jesus' Name we pray. Amen.

HOW TO SAY IT

Engedi. eyn-ge-**DEE**.

Eneglaim. eyn-eg-**LA**-im.

PREPARE FOR NEXT SUNDAY

Read **Ezekiel 47:13–23** and read "Transformation Continued."

DAILY HOME BIBLE READINGS

MONDAY
Forsaking the Living Water
(Jeremiah 2:5–13)

TUESDAY
Living Water Shall Flow from Jerusalem
(Zechariah 14:1–8)

WEDNESDAY
Let the Thirsty Come to Me
(John 7:37–44)

THURSDAY
Guided to the Water of Life
(Revelation 7:13–17)

FRIDAY
Give Me This Water
(John 4:7–15)

SATURDAY
Planted by Streams of Water
(Psalm 1)

SUNDAY
Water Flowing from the Sanctuary
(Ezekiel 47:1, 3–12)

Source:

Buttrick, George Arthur, ed. *The Interpreter's Bible*. Vol. 6. Nashville, TN: Abingdon Press, 1956. 327.

Cooper, Lamar Eugene Sr. *Ezekiel*. The New American Commentary, Vol. 17. Nashville, TN: Broadman and Holman Publishers, 1994. 39.

Henry, Matthew. *Matthew Henry's Complete Commentary on the Bible*. http://www.biblestudytools.com/commentaries/matthew-henry-complete/ezekiel/47.html. Accessed August 22, 2013.

Keil, C. F., and F. Delitzsch. *Ezekiel and Daniel*. Commentary on the Old Testament, Vol. 9. Peabody, MA: Hendrickson Publishers, 1996. 7.

NIV Study Bible, 10th Anniversary Edition. Grand Rapids, MI: Zondervan, 1995. 1219, 1285.

COMMENTS / NOTES:

TRANSFORMATION CONTINUED

BIBLE BASIS: EZEKIEL 47:13–23

BIBLE TRUTH: God provides opportunities for new beginnings throughout the Bible, today, and for future generations to share with one another.

MEMORY VERSE: "So shall ye divide this land ... unto you, and to the strangers that sojourn among you" (from Ezekiel 47:21–22).

LESSON AIM: By the end of the lesson, your students will: know what God's Word says about sharing our inheritance with all those who live among us; feel the importance of affirming and appreciating one another as children of God who have made, or can make, new beginnings together; and embrace new beginnings as gifts from God to be enjoyed with others.

TEACHER PREPARATION

MATERIALS NEEDED: Quarterly Commentary/Teacher Manual, Adult Quarterly, Adult resources—charts, worksheets, and other teaching tools, paper, pens, pencils, Bibles (several different versions)

OTHER MATERIALS NEEDED / TEACHER'S NOTES:

LESSON OVERVIEW

LIFE NEED FOR TODAY'S LESSON
There are times in life when people need a new beginning.

BIBLE LEARNING
Believers overcome their transgressions through repentance and forgiveness.

BIBLE APPLICATION
Believers understand and appreciate that all they possess is an inheritance from God.

STUDENTS' RESPONSES
Believers embrace the concept of sharing with others for the sake of God.

LESSON SCRIPTURE

EZEKIEL 47:13–23, KJV

13 Thus saith the Lord GOD; This shall be the border, whereby ye shall inherit the land according to the twelve tribes of Israel: Joseph shall have two portions.

14 And ye shall inherit it, one as well as another: concerning the which I lifted up mine hand to give it unto your fathers: and

EZEKIEL 47:13–23, NIV

13 This is what the Sovereign LORD says: "These are the boundaries of the land that you will divide among the twelve tribes of Israel as their inheritance, with two portions for Joseph.

14 You are to divide it equally among them. Because I swore with uplifted hand

this land shall fall unto you for inheritance.

15 And this shall be the border of the land toward the north side, from the great sea, the way of Hethlon, as men go to Zedad;

16 Hamath, Berothah, Sibraim, which is between the border of Damascus and the border of Hamath; Hazarhatticon, which is by the coast of Hauran.

17 And the border from the sea shall be Hazarenan, the border of Damascus, and the north northward, and the border of Hamath. And this is the north side.

18 And the east side ye shall measure from Hauran, and from Damascus, and from Gilead, and from the land of Israel by Jordan, from the border unto the east sea. And this is the east side.

19 And the south side southward, from Tamar even to the waters of strife in Kadesh, the river to the great sea. And this is the south side southward.

20 The west side also shall be the great sea from the border, till a man come over against Hamath. This is the west side.

21 So shall ye divide this land unto you according to the tribes of Israel.

22 And it shall come to pass, that ye shall divide it by lot for an inheritance unto you, and to the strangers that sojourn among you, which shall beget children among you: and they shall be unto you as born in the country among the children of Israel; they shall have inheritance with you among the tribes of Israel.

23 And it shall come to pass, that in what tribe the stranger sojourneth, there shall ye give him his inheritance, saith the Lord God.

to give it to your ancestors, this land will become your inheritance.

15 "This is to be the boundary of the land: "On the north side it will run from the Mediterranean Sea by the Hethlon road past Lebo Hamath to Zedad,

16 Berothahand Sibraim (which lies on the border between Damascus and Hamath), as far as Hazer Hattikon, which is on the
border of Hauran. 17 The boundary will
extend from the sea to Hazar Enan, along the northern border of Damascus, with the border of Hamath to the north. This will be the northern boundary.

18 "On the east side the boundary will run between Hauran and Damascus, along the Jordan between Gilead and the land of Israel, to the Dead Sea and as far as Tamar. This will be the eastern boundary.

19 "On the south side it will run from Tamar as far as the waters of Meribah Kadesh, then along the Wadi of Egypt to the Mediterranean Sea. This will be the southern boundary.

20 "On the west side, the Mediterranean Sea will be the boundary to a point opposite Lebo Hamath. This will be the western boundary.

21 "You are to distribute this land among yourselves according to the tribes of Israel.

22 You are to allot it as an inheritance for yourselves and for the foreigners residing among you and who have children. You are to consider them as native-born Israelites; along with you they are to be allotted an inheritance among the tribes of Israel.

23 In whatever tribe a foreigner resides, there you are to give them their inheritance," declares the Sovereign LORD.

LIGHT ON THE WORD

The land of Israel's borders have changed over the years and have differed from the Bible's description. In Ezekiel's vision, the western boundary of the Mediterranean Sea has been the most stable permanent boundary. The eastern boundary is in Syria. The northern boundary is Lebanon. The southwest border goes along Syria and the Jordan River to the western bank of the Dead Sea. It later follows the desert of Kadesh Barnea and then goes along the Brook of Egypt to the Mediterranean.

TEACHING THE BIBLE LESSON

LIFE NEED FOR TODAY'S LESSON

AIM: Students will affirm that there are times in life when people need a new beginning.

INTRODUCTION

Starting Anew

Ezekiel received numerous visions from God regarding the future restoration of Israel. In **chapter 47**, he received a vision of a river of life flowing from the Temple. This river would produce an abundance of fish and trees, which possessed leaves of healing. This river symbolized the Holy Spirit and its life-giving vitality to God's people.

After Ezekiel received this vision, he received another regarding the boundaries of the nation of Israel. The boundaries would be the same general boundaries that were given when the Israelites approached the Promised Land. The big difference when it came to this inheritance is that it would be available to strangers as well. The Gentiles would have a share in the inheritance of Israel along with the native-born Israelites. This points toward the fellowship and mutual sharing within the life of the church.

BIBLE LEARNING

AIM: Students will overcome their transgressions through repentance and forgiveness.

I. INSTRUCTIONS FOR THE INHERITANCE (Ezekiel 47:13–14)

Ezekiel receives instructions from God on dividing the inheritance of the land among the twelve tribes. First, God lets them know that He is the one who gives the border or boundaries of the inheritance. It is not determined by man or by chance. Israel's inheritance comes from God and God alone. Next, he is given instruction that Joseph will inherit two portions of the land. These two portions would be given to the tribes of Ephraim and Manasseh, tribes descended from the two sons of Joseph. Joseph was the older son of Jacob's favorite wife, Rachel. The double portion is because his two sons were adopted by Jacob, so they became two tribes of Israel and therefore each get a portion in the inheritance (**Genesis 48**). The Lord reminds Ezekiel of the equal participation of all the tribes in the inheritance. No one would be left out. They all would be included in what God gave to Israel.

God's Land Allotment (verses 13–14)

**13 Thus saith the Lord GOD; This shall be the border, whereby ye shall inherit the land according to the twelve tribes of Israel: Joseph shall have two portions.
14 And ye shall inherit it, one as well as another: concerning the which I lifted up mine hand to give it unto your fathers: and this land shall fall unto you for inheritance.**

It is noteworthy that the land allotment begins and ends with "Thus saith the Lord GOD," making it clear that this isn't Ezekiel's interpretation or a later editor's compilation. Rather, this is a "prophetic-messenger word" from God (Jensen 338). God made a "unilateral promise" to Israel's forefathers, and now that promise inexplicably is inserted into Ezekiel's vision (339). There is no explanation provided of how the northern tribes will reassemble, or why whole tribes are uprooted and arbitrarily planted elsewhere. Moreover, the straight east-west lines pay no attention to the natural topography of the land. Robert Jensen observes, "What determines the map is not history but what God promised" (ibid.).

Because the Levites have no portion, having provision within the "holy" areas (**45:4, 48:13**), Joseph is given two portions for his sons, Ephraim and Manasseh (**48:4–5**), which then retains the original number of twelve tribes who would own land. Even in Ezekiel's utopian vision, the number of tribes must be twelve, just as other numbers of twelve were critical in other parts of biblical history, e.g., the apostles replacing Judas rather than being content with eleven (**Acts 1:26**). Many Bible students are aware of the significance of the number twelve, particularly throughout the book of Revelation, e.g., **chapter 21**.

The stress is on the principle of equality for "one as well as another" (Heb. *'ach*, **AWKH**, meaning brother or kindred), which is preserved with the allotment for the priests even though they aren't numbered among the twelve tribes. In this renewed Israel, any inequities would be a distant memory. It wasn't that Israel deserved this grace, but it was about God fulfilling His promise to Abraham (**Genesis 12:7, 15:7, 17:8**).

SEARCH THE SCRIPTURES

QUESTION 1

How many shares of land would be given to the descendants of Joseph?

LIGHT ON THE WORD

The Promised Inheritance

The Lord also reminds the Israelites that they are receiving the inheritance based on His promise "concerning the which I lifted up mine hand to give it unto your fathers." This means that His giving of the land of Israel was sealed with a binding oath. It was a sure thing and would not be taken away. The inheritance was a promise from God, and He is faithful to do what He promised.

II. ILLUSTRATING THE INHERITANCE (vv. 15–20)

Ezekiel then receives details concerning the borders of the land of Israel. This is in anticipation of the next chapter, where he will receive the boundaries of the tribes. First, the borders of the entire nation are given because God promised the whole land to a whole Israel. They were promised this land not as isolated tribes but as a community. This was their portion together as a people.

Boundaries of the Tribes (verses 15–20)

15 And this shall be the border of the land toward the north side, from the great sea, the way of Hethlon, as men go to Zedad;
16 Hamath, Berothah, Sibraim, which is between the border of Damascus and the border of Hamath; Hazarhatticon, which is by the coast of Hauran. 17 And the border
from the sea shall be Hazarenan, the border of Damascus, and the north northward, and the border of Hamath. And this is the north side. 18 And the east side ye
shall measure from Hauran, and from Damascus, and from Gilead, and from the land of Israel by Jordan, from the border unto the east sea. And this is the east side. 19 And the south side southward, from Tamar even to the waters of strife in Kadesh, the river to the great sea. And

this is the south side southward. 20 The west side also shall be the great sea from the border, till a man come over against Hamath. This is the west side.

The borders are listed in clockwise order, starting with the north (the parallel passage in **Numbers 34** starts in the south), basically from the Mediterranean (the "great sea") heading east to somewhere between Damascus to the south and Hamath (modern Hama) to the north, following a somewhat unclear line of several cities that long ago disappeared into history. As John Taylor notes, "The place-names are impossible to identify with any certainty" (273). The eastern border is clearer, from the Jordan River to the Dead Sea. The southern border starts in northern Sinai at the oasis of Kadesh Barnea, also called the "waters of strife" (**Numbers 27:14**), and winds westward to the river (also known as the "brook of Egypt") to the Mediterranean, which of course is the western border (Blenkinsopp 233).

LIGHT ON THE WORD

Foreigners and Strangers in Israel

The Lord then goes on to give Ezekiel the northern border, which reached the border of Damascus and Hamath. This is the land of Lebanon. Then the Lord gives the eastern border, which runs along Syria then follows the Jordan River and the Dead Sea. The land to the east of the Jordan is not mentioned, probably because it is regarded as unclean (**Joshua 22:19, 25, 27**). Next, the border south travels southwest to the desert of Kadesh Barnea. This has been the most southerly border in Israel's biblical history. The land then spreads out toward the river of Egypt, which has been the most common border with Egypt (**Joshua 15:4; 1 Kings 8:65**). The western border of the nation of Israel is the Mediterranean Sea. This border was actually never realized in Old Testament history. All of these borders indicate that the inheritance was a real tangible thing and that it coincided with the original boundaries for the land (**Numbers 33:50–34:15**).

III. INCLUDED IN THE INHERITANCE (vv. 21–23)

Next, God reiterates the goal of dividing the land among the twelve tribes. Then we see further instructions regarding those who were not Israelites by birth. The Lord says that they are to receive a share in the inheritance. This is unprecedented. Earlier Old Testament passages regarding foreigners and strangers talk about fair treatment and showing hospitality. This takes it a step further and includes them in the citizenship of Israel. This foreshadows the Gentiles being included in the family of God and receiving the blessings of citizenship in the kingdom of God. This can be seen in **Acts 2:42–47**, where those who are part of the church all share and have everything in common.

The Division of the Land (verses 21–23)

21 So shall ye divide this land unto you according to the tribes of Israel.

As noted, the division of land in Ezekiel's vision is neither practical according to Israel's geography, nor does it fit with the actual history of the nation and its tribes. As Wright notes, "It seems unmistakable that Ezekiel is making a theological statement, not providing a functional map" (363). This theological statement includes sweeping provisions for long-awaited and much-needed equality and security. Wright further asserts that "the intention was that every household should have sufficient for economic viability" and "the equality of all people reflects their covenantal unity" (ibid.). Ezekiel's vision was the definition of a new beginning, the essence of a new start, the picture of a new lease on life.

22 And it shall come to pass, that ye shall divide it by lot for an inheritance unto you, and to the strangers that sojourn among you, which shall beget children among you: and they shall be unto you as

born in the country among the children of Israel; they shall have inheritance with you among the tribes of Israel. 23 And it shall come to pass, that in what tribe the stranger sojourneth, there shall ye give him his inheritance, saith the Lord GOD.

The "strangers" (Heb. *ger*, **GARE**, meaning a foreigner), translated "sojourners" or "aliens" in other versions, were a familiar presence in Israel's history and, according to Hebrew laws, they were a people "in need of special protection as part of a powerless class, subject to exploitation" (Duguid 542). Israel held unforgettable memories of having been "strangers" who had been enslaved and exploited in Egypt, which would be expected of any people with such a history. Indeed, God Himself reminds them often of how He delivered them from bondage while they were foreigners (e.g., **Deuteronomy 6:12**; **Judges 6:8**; **1 Samuel 10:18**)—and that memory was the basis for Israel's laws regarding the just treatment of strangers or aliens who sojourned among them (e.g., **Leviticus 19:33–34**, the last verse of which includes another reminder of why they are to obey this law). Those resident aliens who had adopted the Hebrew laws and religion became proselytes, which entitles them to the rights and privileges of native Israelites (**Isaiah 56:3–8**). This reference includes the portion of Isaiah that describes God's house as a "house of prayer for all people" (**v.** 7).

SEARCH THE SCRIPTURES

QUESTION 2

What was the qualification for foreigners and strangers to receive a share of the land?

LIGHT ON THE WORD

God's Justice and Righteousness

Ezekiel's vision included, per Lamar Cooper, "a new temple, a new way of life, a new quality of life, and in the final vision a new land" (415). He adds that the new allotments "will preserve the laws of equity that eliminated discrimination ... making the new land a model for justice and righteousness" (417). If any theme dominates the Old Testament, it is justice and righteousness (e.g., **Psalm 99:4**; **Isaiah 9:7**; **Amos 5:24**). If any phrase describes God's character, it is just and righteous (cf. **Exodus 34:6–7**; **Numbers 14:18**; **Psalm 145:17**; **2 Thessalonians 1:6**), and by extension this also should describe each of God's people. In the end, after every human form of government ultimately has failed to secure an equitable and righteous common good, in God's kingdom described by Ezekiel, "there will be a political community of perfect mutual love—glorious with the Lord's own glory, of which the supply is infinite" (Jensen 342).

BIBLE APPLICATION

AIM: Students will understand and appreciate that all they possess is an inheritance from God.

Life is full of new beginnings. Some new beginnings are planned, joyful occasions: a wedding, a birth, a new home, a new career opportunity. But sometimes people need new beginnings for reasons that are anything but planned or joyful: the loss of a spouse or child, the loss of a job or relationship, or the onset of a devastating health issue. The church is a place that should be a haven for people seeking a new beginning. Just as Christ provides redemption and salvation for all, His church should provide acceptance, support, and fellowship to those who need a new start in life.

STUDENTS' RESPONSES

AIM: Students will embrace the concept of sharing with others for the sake of God.

The members of the early church shared everything with each other—food, possessions, prayer, work, and fellowship. From this example and God's instruction in Ezekiel for even the "outsiders" to be included in the inheritance, we see that God values His people supporting one another through life's ups and downs. As believers, we need to make sure that we share our "inheritance" with one another as well as with those who are outside the Body of Christ. Ask God to show you how you can share with those both inside and outside your church. Donate food and clothing to a local food bank or homeless shelter. Volunteer to cook meals for those who are sick or mothers who have just given birth. God has given you a new beginning; make sure you are available to help others who are in desperate need of the new beginning that only Christ can offer.

PRAYER

O Sovereign God, Your mercy is everlasting. Grant us a new beginning that allows us to have the resources that we need to make a difference in this world. In Jesus' Name we pray. Amen.

HOW TO SAY IT

Hethlon.	kheth-**LONE**.
Zedad.	tseh-**DAWD**.
Hamath.	khah-**MAWTH**.
Berothah.	be-ro-**THAW**.
Sibraim.	siv-**RAH**-yim.
Hazarhatticon.	kha-**TSER** hat-tee-**KONE**.
Hauran.	khav-**RAWN**.
Hazarenan.	khah-**TSAR** ey-**NONE**.
Kadesh.	kaw-**DESH**.

PREPARE FOR NEXT SUNDAY

Read **Isaiah 52:1–2, 7–12** and study "Let Zion Rejoice."

DAILY HOME BIBLE READINGS

MONDAY
God Declares New Things
(Isaiah 42:5–9)

TUESDAY
A New Song, a New Way
(Isaiah 42:10–16)

WEDNESDAY
A New and Right Spirit
(Psalm 51:1–13)

THURSDAY
New Mercies Every Morning
(Lamentations 3:19–26)

FRIDAY
A New Birth, a Living Hope
(1 Peter 1:1–7)

SATURDAY
All Who Believed Were Together
(Acts 2:37–47)

SUNDAY
Inheritance for You and the Immigrants
(Ezekiel 47:13–23)

Sources:

Blenkinsopp, Joseph. *Ezekiel. Interpretation: A Bible Commentary for Teaching and Preaching*. Louisville, KY: John Knox Press, 1990. 232–237.

Cooper, Lamar Eugene, Sr. *Ezekiel*. The New American Commentary, vol. 17. Nashville, TN: Broadman and Holman Publishers, 1994. 415–417.

Duguid, Iain M. *Ezekiel*. The NIV Application Commentary. Grand Rapids, MI: Zondervan, 1999. 538–551.

Jensen, Robert W. *Ezekiel*. Brazos Theological Commentary on the Bible. Grand Rapids, MI: Brazos Press, 2009. 338–342.

Strong, James. *The New Strong's Exhaustive Concordance of the Bible*. Nashville, TN: Thomas Nelson Publishers, 1990.

Taylor, John B. *Ezekiel: An Introduction and Commentary*. Tyndale Old Testament Commentaries. Vol. 22. Downers Grove, IL: IVP Academic, 1969. 272–273.

Wright, Christopher J. H. *The Message of Ezekiel: A New Heart and a New Spirit*. Downers Grove, IL: InterVarsity Press, 2001. 359–362.

LET ZION REJOICE

BIBLE BASIS: ISAIAH 52:1–2, 7–12

BIBLE TRUTH: The psalmist and Isaiah tell God's people that God, who reigns above, is their help, shield, and salvation, and that they can put their hope in God and rejoice.

MEMORY VERSE: "How beautiful upon the mountains are the feet of him that bringeth good tidings, that publisheth peace; that bringeth good tidings of good, that publisheth salvation; that saith unto Zion, Thy God reigneth!" (Isaiah 52:7).

LESSON AIM: By the end of the lesson, we will: know Isaiah's words of hope, good news, and rejoicing; express great joy through heartfelt worship for the Lord's salvation; and respond to God's blessings with exuberant worship.

TEACHER PREPARATION

MATERIALS NEEDED: Quarterly Commentary/Teacher Manual, Adult Quarterly, Adult resources—charts, worksheets, and other teaching tools, paper, pens, pencils, Bibles (several different versions)

OTHER MATERIALS NEEDED / TEACHER'S NOTES:

____

____

LESSON OVERVIEW

LIFE NEED FOR TODAY'S LESSON
Everyone needs to hear words of hope.

BIBLE LEARNING
All the earth is to witness to God's magnificent acts of salvation of the faithful.

BIBLE APPLICATION
Believers are comforted and assured by the Holy Spirit that God is constantly working things out to the benefit of all.

STUDENTS' RESPONSES
Believers praise and glorify God at all times for all good things.

LESSON SCRIPTURE

ISAIAH 52:1–2, 7–12, KJV

1 Awake, awake; put on thy strength, O Zion; put on thy beautiful garments, O Jerusalem, the holy city: for henceforth there shall no more come into thee the uncircumcised and the unclean.

2 Shake thyself from the dust; arise, and

ISAIAH 52:1–2, 7–12, NIV

1 Awake, awake, Zion, clothe yourself with strength! Put on your garments of splendor, Jerusalem, the holy city. The uncircumcised and defiled will not enter you again.

2 Shake off your dust; rise up, sit enthroned, Jerusalem. Free yourself from

sit down, O Jerusalem: loose thyself from the bands of thy neck, O captive daughter of Zion.

7 How beautiful upon the mountains are the feet of him that bringeth good tidings, that publisheth peace; that bringeth good tidings of good, that publisheth salvation; that saith unto Zion, Thy God reigneth!

8 Thy watchmen shall lift up the voice; with the voice together shall they sing: for they shall see eye to eye, when the LORD shall bring again Zion.

9 Break forth into joy, sing together, ye waste places of Jerusalem: for the LORD hath comforted his people, he hath redeemed Jerusalem.

10 The LORD hath made bare his holy arm in the eyes of all the nations; and all the ends of the earth shall see the salvation of our God.

11 Depart ye, depart ye, go ye out from thence, touch no unclean thing; go ye out of the midst of her; be ye clean, that bear the vessels of the LORD.

12 For ye shall not go out with haste, nor go by flight: for the LORD will go before you; and the God of Israel will be your reward.

the chains on your neck, Daughter Zion, now a captive.

7 How beautiful on the mountains are the feet of those who bring good news, who proclaim peace, who bring good tidings, who proclaim salvation, who say to Zion, "Your God reigns!"

8 Listen! Your watchmen lift up their voices; together they shout for joy. When the LORD returns to Zion, they will see it with their own eyes.

9 Burst into songs of joy together, you ruins of Jerusalem, for the LORD has comforted his people, he has redeemed Jerusalem.

10 The LORD will lay bare his holy arm in the sight of all the nations, and all the ends of the earth will see the salvation of our God.

11 Depart, depart, go out from there! Touch no unclean thing! Come out from it and be pure, you who carry the articles of the LORD's house.

12 But you will not leave in haste or go in flight; for the LORD will go before you, the God of Israel will be your rear guard.

LIGHT ON THE WORD

Zion is synonymous with Jerusalem, but most commonly referred to a specific mountain near Jerusalem, Mount Zion. It is also regarded as a synonym for the people of God. It later became a term that denoted the church (**Hebrews 12:22–23**) as well as the heavenly city (**Revelation 14:1**).

Jerusalem's name means the Foundation of Peace. It is located in the Judean mountains and was the ancient capital of Israel (and specifically Judah during the divided monarchy). Its elevation is remarkable, and there were two main approaches to the city (from the Jordan Valley by Jericho and the Mount of Olives). It is full of pools and fountains, including the Well of Job, the Pool of Hezekiah, and the Pool of Bethesda. There are many gates and gardens there; most famous is the Garden of Gethsemane. During its long history, it is said to have been destroyed twice, besieged 23 times, attacked 52 times, and captured and recaptured 44 times.

TEACHING THE BIBLE LESSON

LIFE NEED FOR TODAY'S LESSON

AIM: Students will affirm that everyone needs to hear words of hope.

INTRODUCTION

The Babylonian Captivity

Remember the movie *Taken*? It features a scene where the father tells his daughter that she is going to be kidnapped, but he gives her instructions on what to do when she is, and he tells her that he will rescue her. **Isaiah 52** is reminiscent of that scene. First, it is written about Jerusalem's captivity before it even happens! Then, it offers encouragement because it tells of her future deliverance.

Jerusalem was taken captive as a consequence of disobedience (and idolatry). There were three deportations of Israelites to Babylon, probably 597 B.C., 587 B.C., and 582 B.C. God allowed them to be held by the Babylonians for seventy years! Most of the captives were treated as colonists. The Babylonian captivity was brought to a close after the fall of Babylon to Cyrus the Great. Cyrus issued a decree at approximately 536 B.C. for the Jews to return and rebuild Jerusalem (**Ezra 1:2**).

BIBLE LEARNING

AIM: Students will know all the earth is to witness to God's magnificent acts of salvation of the faithful.

I. GET ON YOUR MARK (Isaiah 52:1–2)

Seventy years is a long time to be in a bad situation. By then, hope would be long gone and replaced by the slumber of complacency, apathy, and resentment. Forecasting the depression, heaviness, and lack of energy to do nothing more than sleep, **Isaiah 52:1** commands the captive representing the exiles taken to Babylonia to wake up. With freedom arriving seven decades later, the sleeping captives might have mistaken it for a dream and missed out on the opportunity to return home. So, the first order of business is to arouse the captive. Loosely translating the verse, it might read, "Wake up! Stretch! Get out of your pajamas and put on some clothes. The captor will not bother you anymore!" Isaiah further declares that "there shall no more come into thee the uncircumcised and the unclean." This means that Jerusalem would not have foreigners ruling over her.

Jerusalem, the Holy City (verses 1–2)

1 Awake, awake; put on thy strength, O Zion; put on thy beautiful garments, O Jerusalem, the holy city: for henceforth there shall no more come into thee the uncircumcised and the unclean. 2 Shake thyself from the dust; arise, and sit down, O Jerusalem: loose thyself from the bands of thy neck, O captive daughter of Zion.

Isaiah uses the same dual or double imperative in **51:9** (also "Awake, awake") and **v. 17** (also translated "Rouse yourself"), which in Hebrew is *'ur* (**OOR**), and means to wake, rise, or stir up. Zion variously refers to God's people, Jerusalem or Israel. From Hanson, both Zion and Jerusalem "depict the Holy City as a mother of the children of Israel" (147). In this case, it clearly refers to Jerusalem, and her strength refers to the power of her God. For such a great occasion, it is time for her to dress her best. In Hebrew, strength is *'wz* (**OZE**), and means might or power, while beauty is *tiph'arah* (**tif-aw-RAW**), which means comeliness or glory, as in fine garments (cf. **Psalm 96:6**). John Goldingay pens, "There is a beauty about strength and a strength about beauty" (447).

As sovereign, God is the one who determines the future, and God has heard the cry of His people from bondage—now it is time to wake up, for freedom has arrived. In times past, Israel has drunk from the cup of God's wrath, but now that time has passed and the time of comfort has come. Now is the time to stand up and prepare for a time of celebration. This time, Israel's enemies will not be permitted entrance, as all unholiness will be prohibited—the holy city will be kept holy. Claus Westermann writes, "Jerusalem is holy as the city chosen by God, and by him freed and destined for new life" (247).

A biblical parallel can be seen in Matthew 10:14, referencing the disciples shaking the dust off their feet from places where they were not welcome. There is a clear sense of the people of God being set free or liberated and leaving behind the chains of bondage. Also evident is the fact that God's love reaches out to people in their bondage (cf. Romans 5:8).

LIGHT ON THE WORD

Arise!

Isaiah further instructs the Israelites in verse 2, in case they cannot believe their ears. He tells them to shake off the dust that has settled on them from sitting so long. They are so used to sitting that he has to tell them to get up. "Arise!" he commands, and tells them to take their place as the children of the Most High God. Instead of sitting down in the dirt, they are to take a position more suitable to their status as children of the King of the universe. They are to release themselves from the yoke that held them captive. As believers, we are also called to arise and take our rightful position as children of God. We are to no longer live in bondage and under the yoke of spiritual slavery.

II. GET SET (vv. 7–10)

The captives do not have to go out to find word of God's salvation; He sends the news to them! In our text, the prophet assures that a messenger will come to bring the good tidings. The watchmen proclaims salvation, and the sound will be so beautiful that the captives will break forth in song. Isaiah makes reference to the feet of the messenger and says they are beautiful because of the message that he is running to give to the captives. It is a message of peace, salvation, and good news.

The Beauty of the Mountain (verses 7–10)

7 How beautiful upon the mountains are the feet of him that bringeth good tidings, that publisheth peace; that bringeth good tidings of good, that publisheth salvation; that saith unto Zion, Thy God reigneth! 8 Thy watchmen shall lift up the voice; with the voice together shall they sing: for they shall see eye to eye, when the LORD shall bring again Zion.

To describe the feet of the good news runner or messenger, Isaiah selects the Hebrew word *na'ah* (**naw-AW**), also meaning to be pleasant or comely, which is only used twice elsewhere in the Old Testament (cf. **Psalm 93:5** referring to the beauty of God's house, and **Song of Solomon 1:10** referring to adorned cheeks). This verse is a direct parallel to **Nahum 1:15**, "Behold upon the mountains the feet of him that bringeth good tidings, that publisheth peace!" Goldingay reminds us of the poet's literary tool: "Feet is metonymy for steps" (452). The passage also restates **Isaiah 40:9**.

As Isaiah has inspired many modern songs from

his poetic prowess, this portion is well known. Many believe that he wrote in lyrical mode with the intent for the verses to be sung, much like the Psalms. Because of God's trustworthiness and reliability, just the news of the coming event is as good as the event. Using "prophetic" perfect tense, Israel's release has come to pass—in Goldingay's words, it is "as-good-as-done" (454). He writes that this is "a matter of . . . imminent historical reality" (453). Such "future is here" language dovetails with **2 Corinthians 5:17**, "all things have become new" (NKJV).

From Westermann, "These are the feet that bring words that thrill the heart longing for just this announcement, 'Your God reigns!'" (149). Even Jesus was not handsome, but rather plain in appearance (**Isaiah 53:2**) and certainly on the Cross He was a repulsive sight—yet how beautiful those pierced, bleeding feet that carried the message from His day to today: our God reigns.

News is not always good, but in this case the adjective makes all the difference. This is "good tidings," a phrase almost synonymous today with the Gospel. The remaining descriptors in the verse further reinforce that this isn't an ordinary victory by any means.

9 Break forth into joy, sing together, ye waste places of Jerusalem: for the LORD hath comforted his people, he hath redeemed Jerusalem. 10 The LORD hath made bare his holy arm in the eyes of all the nations; and all the ends of the earth shall see the salvation of our God.

At first, it is the voice of a lone arriving messenger, and then those on the watchtower join in, and now the city will raise its voice in song as a choir. The people of the "waste places" (cf. **51:3**) per Goldingay are "the suffering, bewildered and weary remnant of the nation in the exile and the Diaspora" (251). Now all that has changed, as God has returned to comfort His people with His strong arm of deliverance and salvation (cf. **40:10, 51:9**). This is a "strongly symbolic statement" (Goldingay 457), an anthropomorphism indicating both strength and preparation for action. Surely such reassurances spell divine comfort for all of God's people (cf. **40:1–2**), starting in Jerusalem and including the whole world (cf. **42:1–12**).

They hear first and then see, just as Israel first heard about the coming Messiah, and then finally saw Him with their eyes (e.g., **Simeon, Luke 2:25–32**). Similarly, today, most everyone has heard about Christ's second coming, and one day every eye will see Him (**Revelation 1:7**). Isaiah's prophecy about God's triumphant return to Zion runs parallel to Ezekiel's account of God's glory returning to the Temple from a recent lesson exploring **Ezekiel 43:1–12**. Another parallel today is the Body of Christ waiting expectantly for Jesus to return triumphantly to the Mount of Olives from which He ascended, which is due east of the Temple mound from which direction Ezekiel saw the glory of God returning to His Temple.

SEARCH THE SCRIPTURES

QUESTIONS 1 & 2

What makes the messenger's feet beautiful?

What will the watchmen do when they see the messenger?

LIGHT ON THE WORD

The Joy of the Watchmen

The watchmen will see the messenger coming and begin to sing for joy. Isaiah states that they would see eye to eye. They would see the same thing. This may have been a reference to the prophets as Ezekiel called them "watchmen" in a later prophecy (**Ezekiel 3:17, 33:1–11**). The prophets and leaders will have the same good news and be in unity. They will relay their joy to the people, and the people will break forth in song.

The content of the messenger's message has to do with redeeming Jerusalem. After a seventy-year captivity, Isaiah states, the waste or ruined places of Jerusalem will begin to sing. This is because Jerusalem will be rebuilt and restored and will be the Lord's possession, not under foreign rule. After seventy years of captivity, this will be a comfort to God's people. This is definitely good news to make them sing and shout for joy!

Isaiah further describes the redemption of Jerusalem. He states that the "LORD hath made bare his holy arm in the eyes of all the nations." This will not be a private event. It will be known among all the nations. They will see that the Lord is still looking out for His people. They will see His power and His salvation. The Lord does not want to keep the salvation of His people a secret. Why? He wants other nations to worship and serve Him as well.

III. GO (vv. 11–12)

The Israelites are instructed to depart from Babylon. During their departure, they are to touch nothing that is unclean. They are in a foreign land, surrounded by a culture of idolatry and wickedness. The Lord instructs them to stay holy even though they have been exposed to the wickedness of a foreign people. They are to return to Him as worshipers bearing the holy vessels of the Temple. They are to remain holy and get rid of anything that would defile them.

The New Exodus (verses 11–12)

11 Depart ye, depart ye, go ye out from thence, touch no unclean thing; go ye out of the midst of her; be ye clean, that bear the vessels of the LORD. 12 For ye shall not go out with haste, nor go by flight: for the LORD will go before you; and the God of Israel will be your reward.

Now comes the climax of Isaiah's message with another dual imperative. His intention is to "make clear that this miraculous departure [from 'thence' is from Babylon] is distinctive in its holiness" (Westermann 253). This is a religious, not a military march, "a ceremonial procession that requires the avoidance of anything that compromises purity" (Goldingay 458). There will be no more defiling or staining of Zion; the sins that brought judgment will be left behind.

The "vessels" are speculated to be either: 1) the actual vessels that had been stolen from the Temple by King Nebuchadnezzar (see **2 Chronicles 36:7, 10, 18**; **Ezra 1:7–11**; **Jeremiah 27:16–22**), or 2) symbolic of the total worship experience that had been stopped since the Babylonian exile.

As stated, the actual victory is declared in prophetic perfect tense, and the outcome is certain even though the battle is still ongoing. This reminds us of a common expression of the hope of the ages, "We're on the winning team." For believers, this is not pie-in-the-sky wishful thinking but present inspiration from tomorrow's, future perfect, as-good-as-done, coming reality. In a real sense, Isaiah—even before Christ's time—captured the Christian's irrepressible hope that stands strong regardless of circumstances and the direness of one's present reality.

The passage evokes an unmistakable comparison to the Exodus, but Isaiah reverses it. The "new Exodus," writes Westermann—unlike the original flight in fear—"is to be a journey in peace and security" (253). Flight implies seeking safety, but here safety is guaranteed. Here, God both leads and protects; there is no Pharaoh chasing them, and the former anxiety and fear are left in the dust. All is well—the King has returned in victory to His people—all is well (cf. **51:16**).

SEARCH THE SCRIPTURES

QUESTION 3

How are the people of God told to depart?

LIGHT ON THE WORD

Leave in Peace and Confidence

Although the Israelites may have been brought into captivity in haste and uncertainty, it will not be the way they will leave. They are instructed to depart in peace, in confidence, and not as one being pursued. It seems contradictory—to be told to leave a place of bondage but not so fast. Imagine being trapped in an elevator for hours and being told to walk out slowly when the door finally open. Why are they told to exit slowly? This instruction is similar to customary evacuation procedures—to stay calm and exit carefully. They are to depart in peace knowing that the Heavenly Father has delivered them, gone before them, and that this is a place where they will never have to be again.

BIBLE APPLICATION

AIM: Students will be comforted and assured by the Holy Spirit that God is constantly working things out to the benefit of all.

Our society is bombarded with bad news. The newspaper and television are filled with stories of terrorist attacks and collapsing economies. We are constantly seeing the embarrassing sins of celebrities and high-profile preachers. This bad news saturation ought to make us hungry and thirsty for good news that brings hope. As believers, we have the good news that brings hope: the Gospel. There is enough hope in the Good News of the Gospel to drown out all of the bad news that the world throws at us. This kind of hope is enough to make us go all out in praising God and rejoicing.

STUDENTS' RESPONSES

AIM: Students will praise and glorify God at all times for all good things.

Think of a situation you can't wait to get out of—your job, single parenthood, financial hardship, or a relationship. Now, consider today's lesson and apply what you've learned. This might include: warding off complacency, rejoicing with deliverance in mind, and leaving confidently knowing that God's deliverance is sure.

PRAYER

O God, You are marvelous and wonderful to behold. You care for us even when we find ourselves held captive by our own thoughts or the deeds of others. Deliver us and keep us in the arms of Jesus. In Jesus' Name we pray. Amen.

HOW TO SAY IT

Zion. **ZEYE**-on.

Bethesda. Beh-**THEZ**-duh.

PREPARE FOR NEXT SUNDAY

Read **Hebrews 1:1–9** and study "Worship Christ's Majesty."

DAILY HOME BIBLE READINGS

MONDAY
Hope in God!
(Psalm 42:5–11)

TUESDAY
Fear, Awe, and Praise
(Psalm 33:1–9)

WEDNESDAY
O Lord, We Hope in You
(Psalm 33:10–22)

THURSDAY
Hope Set on the Living God
(1 Timothy 4:4–11)

FRIDAY
The God of Our Salvation
(Psalm 85:1–7)

SATURDAY
God is Our Shield
(Genesis 15:1–6)

SUNDAY
God Before Us, God Behind Us
(Isaiah 52:1–2, 7–12)

Sources:

Goldingay, John. *The Message of Isaiah 40–55: A Literary-Theological Commentary.* New York: T&T Clark International, 2005. 417–460.

Grogan, Geoffrey W. *Isaiah—Ezekiel.* The Expositor's Bible Commentary, vol. 6. Grand Rapids, MI: Zondervan, 1986. 296–297.

Hanson, Paul D. *Isaiah 40–66. Interpretation: A Bible Commentary for Teaching and Preaching.* Louisville, KY: John Knox Press, 1995. 142–153.

Smith's Bible Dictionary. Peabody, MA: Hendrickson Publishers, 2000. 292–303.

Strong, James. *The New Strong's Exhaustive Concordance of the Bible.* Nashville, TN: Thomas Nelson Publishers, 1990.

Westermann, Claus. *Isaiah 40–66: A Commentary.* The Old Testament Library. Philadelphia, PA: The Westminster Press, 1969. 246–258.

COMMENTS / NOTES:

TEACHING TECHNIQUES

ACTS OF WORSHIP

BY ELDER ELIJAH HILL

INTRODUCTION

The winter quarter deals with Acts of Worship, and the Publishing Board would like to share with you about the necessity of teaching your students what being in the presence of God truly is. When one speaks of the awe of God, one is speaking of the overwhelming experience of His presence, and the adoration one has for the God of our salvation.

When the Christian is literally in the presence of God Almighty, this experience alone teaches us to appreciate, respect, and worship God. This experience is key to a vibrant spiritual and practical church community.

In the life of the believer, worship is a vital part of the way we express our adoration to God. It is essential to our inner spiritual stewardship to express ourselves in praise and prayer, to dedicate our bodies daily as a living sacrifice. Romans 12:1 compels us to "present your bodies a living sacrifice, holy, acceptable unto God, which is your reasonable service."

In Awe of God As God's people, we can do nothing but greatly admire His presence. To come before Him means that we acknowledge Him and thank Him for Jesus. God knew His creation was in trouble, and so He gave His Son for humanity, redeeming us all from our transgressions. The psalmist wrote in Psalm 4:4, "Stand in awe and sin not: commune with your heart upon your bed, and be still. Selah."

Psalm 4:4 encourages us to be in awe of God's mercy and grace towards us as His human creation, and by that, encourages us to live with godly standards. He sent Christ, His expressed image, and through grace expunged our sins. The love of God is expressed in the sinner's life through worship, and encourages them to know their sins can be forgiven, For example, any parent would want their children to know that no matter what they've done, they can come into their presence and talk to them, and the parent will let them know their mistakes, errors, or wrongdoings have been forgiven. God is much better than any parent!

Jesus Christ achieved this goal of reconciliation on behalf of the Father in Heaven. Therefore, we worship Him in His majesty, lifting up that excellent Name that redeemed us back to right standing with God.

What can we give to God for His unmerited favor? "Let us come before his presence with thanksgiving, and make a joyful noise unto him with psalms" (Psalm 95:2). When we come to church, we should not come looking to receive joy or a feel-good experience, but we should be participants coming before Him to demonstrate our appreciation for His goodness toward us.

I remember my grandfather telling me when he used to attend revival service, he would be walking toward the church, but then when he heard the joyful praises and worship of God he would start running, because he wanted to become a participant in the joyful worship with the saints of God. Psalm 95:6 declares, "O come, let us worship and bow down: let us kneel before the LORD our maker." It is something about God's goodness and grace that should motivate one's heart to desire to make a joyful noise to God whenever one goes into His Holy Temple.

Make certain through this quarter you continually remind people that worship is where they make that personal connection with God. It is vital for them to worship God, and Sunday School should be a constant reminder of what worship should be.

The greatest gift that we can give to God is to give Him the glory for the things that He has done. The lesson guide demonstrates the birth of the Christ child. The lessons are a vivid portrayal of how the angels received Him, and they make certain to enlighten the reader about what the sustaining hope in their life is. When Jesus was born, there appeared a heavenly host, praising and glorifying God for the gift of His Son. Heaven and the angels established a pattern for humanity to show them how to give glory and honor to God for Him giving His only begotten Son.

The shepherds, after seeing the heavenly celebration (Luke 2:13–14), were excited after they visited the Christ child and worshiped Him. It is equally important for today's Christian to know that when we gather together, we should likewise be so inspired. It is important that we narrow our focus to the one significant being, Jesus Himself, when we come into the house of God.

The Lord gave to us His highest gift that walked in the flesh on this earth, and yet He took dominion over the earthly things while walking among us. The Greek word for worship is *proskuneo* (**pros-koo-NEH-oh**), which means to kiss the hand as token of reverence or to bow down to make obeisance that expresses respect in making supplication. In this context, supplication is not us coming to God just to receive from Him, but it is our need to come to Him in all humility, and give Him glory, honor, and praise.

Jesus knew how to minister to God's people, and He showed us how to have a personal prayer life. Matthew 14:23 begins, "And when he had sent the multitudes away, he went up into a mountain apart to pray." Jesus demonstrated to us how to unbusy ourselves and worship God. After the disciples experienced the miracle of Jesus calming the storm, "they

… worshipped him, saying, Of a truth thou art the Son of God" (from Matthew 14:33). When we think of God's deliverance and the help He gives us daily, we will be constrained to bow down and worship the Son of God.

Learning to Pray One of the important things Jesus demonstrated to His disciples was not just the working of miracles, the healing of the lame, and the teaching of the Word of God. He also demonstrated how a true disciple of Christ should let prayer be an essential part of their walk with God. On many occasions, Jesus' disciples saw Him taking time out to pray (Matthew 14:23; Luke 11:1). One of the duties of a Christian is not just to perform religious duties, but to demonstrate a commitment to prayer.

In Luke 11:1, the Scripture states, "And it came to pass, that, as he was praying in a certain place, when he ceased, one of his disciples said unto him, Lord, teach us to pray, as John also taught his disciples." Do we demonstrate that a prayer life is an important part of our walk with the Lord within our family? It is important for the leader of the family to be looked upon as an authority when it comes to prayer. Christ's disciples saw Him as their leader walking in commitment, having a disciplined life of prayer and spending time before the Lord. They observed this so much that they asked, "Lord, teach us to pray, as John also taught his disciples." In this quarter we want to do as Jesus did, and teach people how to pray as a part of worship.

I was invited to a country church, and the person who invited me told me that the people loved to hear his cousin Johnny pray. Every Sunday they were poised to listen to Johnny pray. So I asked Johnny's cousin, "What do you do when he prays?" He answered, "When Johnny drops down on one knee, all of us go up in praise." I praise God that I witnessed that day how Johnny's prayer brought the whole church together, and everyone was praising God together, when Johnny dropped to his knees in prayer.

The founder of the Church Of God In Christ was a praying man who demonstrated a life of prayer before his constituents and God, and he did it so that others within COGIC desired to know God with a deeper walk in prayer. Many individuals, because of his commitment to praying long hours, sought God in a deeper way. Individuals like Mother Dabney and Mother Shaw led strong prayer lives that modeled the prayer life of our founder, Bishop Charles Harrison Mason. The founder prayed as Daniel in the Old Testament prayed, three times a day, demonstrating a continual stewardship and commitment toward having a life of prayer (Daniel 6:10).

In John 17, not only is Jesus praying for His disciples, He is giving them an example of how to pray. One of the unsung commitments of Christ's spiritual principles as a leader was that He prayed for His disciples. Christ said, "For I have given unto them the words which thou gavest me; and they have received them, and have known surely that I came out from thee, and they have believed that thou didst send me. I pray for them: I pray not for the world, but for them which thou hast given me; for they are thine" (John 17:8–9). Let us be reminded that this was a prayer that Jesus prayed during the most dire time of His life and ministry. The act of prayer in Jesus Christ's life was a very important component to His spiritual leadership traits.

The Master felt that one of His commitments to being a covering over His disciples was that He had to pray for them and lift them up before God. Why should we pray for those that God has given us charge over? So that those who are under your supervision can see you seeking God's direction before making a decision. Whenever one is in a role of authority, prayer is always in order. Jesus showed us an example that when you are in the leadership role, you should take on the responsibility to pray for those God has given you to care for.

Prayer during worship helps one release stress about those you are concerned about. King David once wrote, "Cast thy burden upon the LORD, and he shall sustain thee" (from Psalm 55:22). We should give all of our problems to God and let him handle them. The effectual and fervent prayer of the righteous brings results. Just as cousin Johnny came to church every Sunday and led the people in prayer, so too did the pioneer saints of the Church Of God In Christ. Mother Dabney wrote a book entitled *What It Means To Pray Through*. In her book, she tells us how to intercede in prayer for others and believe in God for deliverance.

One of Christ's roles to the church was to become the priest "after the order of Melchisedec" (see Hebrews 5:10). His purpose as a priest over God's people is to make intercession for them. Just as Jesus prayed for His disciples (John 17:9), He never ceases to pray for us as we face different trials and persecutions in the world (John 17:20).

We can be thankful that "we have not a high priest which cannot be touched with the feeling of our infirmities" (Hebrews 4:15). While He walked on earth, Jesus experienced and faced the same temptation, trials, and persecution that we face in our daily lives, and He is our constant reminder that it is important for us to pray daily so that the will of God can be done on earth. When we pray, it sends a sweet-smelling savor up to God in the midst of the sin and shame on this earth.

The Apostle Paul writes, "Likewise the Spirit also helpth our infirmities: for we know not what we should pray for as we ought: but the Spirit itself maketh intercession for us with groanings which cannot be uttered" (Romans 8:26). The importance of prayer in the life of the believer is a vital part of stewardship as a true disciple of Christ. Where our words end, the Spirit of God supports and upholds the prayers for the righteous.

The Apostle James tells us, "Is any sick among you? let him call for the elders of the church; and let them pray over him, anointing him with oil in the name of the Lord" (James 5:14). The Lord Jesus Christ left it in place for His church to be an extension of His healing ministry within the earth. Through our faith, the healing ministry of Jesus Christ can be demonstrated (James 5:15). My grandmother and I boldly practiced this healing ministry, because she believed in what the Bible says in Mark, that "these signs shall follow them that believe... they shall lay hands on the sick, and they shall recover" (from Mark 16:17–18).

The Apostle James also states, "Elias was a man subject to like passions as we are, and he prayed earnestly that it might not rain" (from James 5:17); this passage of Scripture is a constant reminder to us that even though we are human with human limitations, through our earnest prayer, God can and will do mighty things in our midst by trusting in the power of prayer (James 5:18).

Stewardship for Life A part of the life of the believer in Christ Jesus is to not live after the flesh. Paul warns, "For if ye live after the flesh, ye shall die: but if ye through the Spirit do mortify the deeds of the body, ye shall live" (Romans 8:13). When an individual lives a consecrated life of fasting and prayer, this mortifies or crucifies our flesh so that we can live an abundant life over what we forsook when we accepted Christ.

When we walk in a life of consecration by practicing the discipline of fasting and praying, we commit ourselves to decrease so Christ may increase within our beings. When Jesus' disciples wanted to know how Christ was able to access God's supernatural power, especially when it came to demonstrating great miracles or casting out demons, Christ answered, "Howbeit, this kind goeth not out but by fasting and prayer" (Matthew 17:21).

Living a life of fasting and prayer takes a personal commitment on the part of the individual to make a decision to live a life of self-sacrifice. A great example is Daniel, who "purposed in his heart that he would not defile himself with the portion of the king's meat, nor with the wine which he drank" (from Daniel 1:8). Even though it is easier to feast and eat without taking the time to sacrifice your appetite in crucifying your flesh, Daniel decided to do it God's way. Daniel decided to take a stand concerning the former standards of fasting and prayer that existed in Israel before he became a slave in Babylon. He remembered the old ways of fasting and prayer, and the health that it brought to his people. The eating methods instituted by the Levitical priest far surpassed the eating habits of the prince of the eunuchs in Babylon (Leviticus 11:4, 7, 8).

Even today the physician has identified that the methods of Christian fasting bring better health to the human body. The art of fasting, which has existed for millennia as a spiritual practice of decreasing one's food intake, can do what the Bible confirms in Isaiah: "thine health shall spring forth speedily: and thy righteousness shall go before thee" (from Isaiah 58:8).

When we fast and pray and dedicate our lives to Christ, we should do so not to be as the Pharisee for an outward display; but this denial of self should be practiced so that we can die to self, and the love of God can be displayed in our lives to others. The beloved disciple states, "Beloved, let us love one another: for love is of God; and every one that loveth is born of God, and knoweth God" (1 John 4:7). The expression of love toward one another as our neighbor is a mandate for validating that we know God.

We cannot confess Christ without demonstrating our compassion for others' needs and not just our own. It is easier to focus just on our own self-interest and overlook opportunities where we can help someone else that may be less fortunate than we are. The reality is that love is not love until it is given away. You have to give in order to prove that true, godly love exists within your heart. Again, John tells us, "Beloved, if God so loved us, we ought also to love one another" (1 John 4:11). This Scripture reveals that when we express love toward another, we are also demonstrating how God also loves us.

A Jewish lawyer interrogated and cross-examined Jesus regarding showing love to one's neighbor (Luke 10:25–37). Christ told the lawyer a parable of the good Samaritan who was moved with compassion and assisted a person who had been robbed and wounded on the road. Two religious persons passed the man and did nothing to help. Jesus asked the lawyer a question that we should consider a lesson today: "Which now of these three, thinkest thou, was neighbor unto him that fell among the thieves?" (Luke 10:36). The question we should ask ourselves today is, "Which one of these three individuals do we want to pattern ourselves after in our walk with Christ?"It is obvious that, in the teachings of Christ, the theme of serving the least is an important aspect of the Christian journey. Religious people looked down upon the ones that Christ said for us to extend our hand to help. If we are not careful, religious status and position can make us forget where we came from, and cause us to not want to help those who are less fortunate than us.

To drive home the seriousness of how important helping each other is to the life of the Christian believer, in a parable, the Lord Jesus bases His judgment of whether an individual will be accepted into Heaven upon how compassionate they have been in serving the least of these, which He called those hungry, thirsty, homeless, naked, sick, and imprisoned (Matthew 25:31–46). This was to relay the message to the Christian church that the mistreatment of those that are less fortunate than you is not His example of true Christianity. Taking out the time to feed the hungry, clothe the naked, and help the homeless is a part of the mandate to the Body of Christ; we are to help with the social needs of the disadvantaged community, not to look down on them.

In the parable's conclusion, Jesus says, "Then he shall answer them, saying, Verily I say unto you, Inasmuch as ye did it not to one of the least of these, ye did it not to me" (Matthew 25:35). On Christ's throne of judgment, it will be taken personally if those that are in Christ fail to demonstrate their concern for the less fortunate as they walk with God.

The Christian life is inundated with spiritual battles that deal with the opposition, those opposing forces of evil that make our walk a constant challenge. The Apostle Paul states, "Put on the whole armour of God, that ye may be able to stand against the wiles of the devil" (Ephesians 6:11). The enemy of Heaven and our Savior is constantly presenting challenges to our faith and commitment to God's plan for our lives.

The Apostle Paul tells of an armor that one must use to be effective against the wiles of the devil. He utilizes strategies in spiritual warfare, and the Holy Spirit is intelligent enough to have an armor that will assist us in standing for God in the midst of this world's spiritual wickedness in high places.

Without this spiritual equipment, we will be susceptible to defeat at the hand of our spiritual enemy. The Scripture warns us who the enemy is: "For we wrestle not against flesh and blood, but against principalities, against powers" (from Ephesians 6:12). It is easy to begin to focus on those in the flesh who are being weak to the works and strategies of the wicked one, and take our focus off of our real enemy, the devil. To combat the devil, the Apostle Paul lets us know that a continual prayer life is the characteristic of a truly dedicated Christian solider. He tells us what to do to remain clothed and ready for battle: "Praying always with all prayer and supplication in the Spirit, and watching thereunto with all perseverance and supplication for all saints" (Ephesians 6:18).

Bibliography

The New Testament Greek Lexicon. Nelson, 2003.

MOTIVATION: HOW TO INSPIRE AND MOTIVATE OTHERS TO DO THEIR BEST

By Dr. Jeannette H. Donald

INTRODUCTION

People are progressing through life and affecting other people's lives. This thought is echoed by individuals like John Maxwell, a great motivational speaker and leadership management author, who has touched many people's lives, or Bishop T. D. Jakes, who ministers to people all over the world to help them improve their self-esteem. When people feel good about themselves, they will feel good about other people. In other words, people can only appreciate and motivate others after they see themselves as worthwhile.

Leaders must ...

Motivate, inspire, be energetic and enthusiastic, encourage, encourage, and encourage

"No one can make you feel inferior

without your consent." —Eleanor Roosevelt

I. Know Your Beginning *(Genesis 15:5–6)*

A. See the big picture.

a. God gave Abraham a picture of what it meant when He promised Abraham children. His offspring would number more than the stars in the sky and the sands of the sea.

b. How many times have you dreamed or thought, *What does God's plan for me look like?* Many times there are so many distractions clouding the way that you couldn't clearly see the picture of the life God has given you.

B. Learn to be still and step outside of life's distractions and let God show you the big picture He has for your life.

II. You are Not a Mistake *(Jeremiah 1:5)*

A. God planned your life.

a. You are important. Your existence means God wants you to exist. You are somebody simply because you were born.

b. God designed you to be somebody.

c. All His plans for your life were set out long before you took your first breath.

d. God indeed wrote out the order of your days before you lived even one day *(Psalm 139:16).*

10 WAYS TO MOTIVATE OTHERS TO BE THEIR BEST:

1. **Treat People Kindly.** As leaders, you need to treat the people helping you with the utmost respect and kindness.

2. **Be a Good Example.** People watch what you do more than they listen to what you say. Be someone worth emulating.

3. **Care about Others**. People don't care about how much you know until they know how much you care. Take interest in people.

4. **Be a Good Listener.** No one likes to feel unappreciated. People enjoy feeling like they matter or make a difference.

5. **Encourage People.** Everyone goes through tough times. Support and encourage people through rough times; you will inspire them to see the best in themselves.

6. **Share.** Share from your experiences; you may be the only one who can touch someone with your inspiring message.

7. **Be Vulnerable.** Be willing to share your failures as well as your successes.

8. **Get to Know People.** Keep the lines of communication open and pay attention to others' wants; let them know you care.

9. **Keep Everyone in the Know.** Nobody likes to be kept in the dark. Make sure that you are open about your decisions with the people you motivate.

10. **Be a Good Communicator**. Watch how you speak to others. It is important to communicate effectively to inspire others.

Always remember when you are motivating others,

it's very important to strengthen their sense of belonging.

Field Representative Dr. Jeannette Donald serves under the leadership of Bishop James E. Gordon and Supervisor Dorothy Richardson. She serves as Dean of W.K. Gordon Institute (Jurisdiction #1) and associate professor of Life Christian University (Zachary, Louisiana). She also serves as First Lady and Sunday School teacher of Gospel Temple COGIC. Nationally, she serves in the International Sunday School Department as Director of Education–Leadership Ministry. Her motto is "Each One, Reaching One." She feels it is a tremendous and rewarding opportunity to teach and affect the lives of others through the teaching ministry of Sunday School.

"FORMULATING A WORKING STRATEGY FOR SUNDAY SCHOOL GROWTH"

By Evangelist Betty J. Byrd

Introduction/Overview: *Are you planning to fail? This seems like an absurd question to ask a leader. But a quote from Benjamin Franklin says, "If you fail to plan, you are planning to fail!" For our Sunday Schools, failure is not an option.*

DO YOU KNOW where your Sunday School is going? What will your Sunday School be like in two or three years? If you do not change anything, will the future be any different than the past? One sure way to impact your Sunday School's future is to use an old tool called the ***Strategic Plan****.*

Formulating a working strategy is simply the process of choosing the best course of action to achieve the goals and objectives set by an organization, group, or individual. No one strategic model fits all organizations, but the planning process includes certain basic elements that all churches, organizations, and individuals can use to explore their vision, goals, and their most effective course of action.

WHY USE A STRATEGIC PLAN?

Strategic planning is a process that helps to focus or organize the unique gifts and resources that God has given your organization in order to take advantage of all possible opportunities. The Scripture says, "Be very careful, then, how you live—not as unwise but as wise, making the most of every opportunity" (Ephesians 5:15–16, NIV). As you do the planning, let God do the directing.

For the Church, this is not simply making a projection, but it is the realization that through prayer and obedience, you can be a promoter to help bring about a future that is in alignment with God's will. Through prayer, the framework for a plan can be established. Remember, we do the planning, but God does the directing.

WHAT IS STRATEGIC PLANNING?

Simply put, a strategic plan is the formal road map that describes how your organization will achieve a specific goal or objective. A plan spells out where an organization is going over the next year or more and how it is going to get there. A strategic plan is a management tool that serves the purpose of helping an organization do a better job, and it improves organizations by focusing the energy, resources, and time of everyone in the organization in the same direction.

A strategy is the total of all the activities needed to achieve an objective. The process of developing a strategy involves several steps.

1. **Develop Goals & Objectives.** The first mission is to define the organization's purpose. Why does your organization exist? The primary objectives of the organization, group, or individual must be delineated. After a clearly outlined set of goals have been set, then the strategy (the method, means, and resources to be used to realize and achieve these objectives) is developed.
2. **Evaluate the Goals & Objectives.** Review the goals and objectives to make sure they are feasible and obtainable. You want to make sure the goals and objectives are realistic; otherwise, you set yourself up for discouragement and failure. Careful evaluation of your goals will increase the possibility that the factors important for success can be discovered. Likewise, vision (or a clear understanding of the organization's goals) is necessary in order to explain where you are headed. Where do we want to be in five years? When you plan, you will need to set goals to build on your church's strengths, strengthen or correct the weaknesses, capitalize on the opportunities, and recognize the threats. Assess your strengths and weaknesses by answering these questions: What do we do well, and where could we improve?
3. **Analyze Performance.** In this step, you must review your goals and determine how you will achieve them by analyzing the past performance strengths and weaknesses of your organization. Take a critical evaluation of the organization's past performance, present condition, and the desired future conditions.
4. **Choose A Strategy.** This is the ultimate step in Strategy Formulation. This will be your best course of action to carry out the organizational goals, looking at the organization's strengths, potential, and limitations.

CONCLUSION

A vision is a picture of what your future Sunday School will be and where the organization is headed. Vision provides a clear mental picture, by faith, of what your Sunday School will look like in a couple of years. Forming a strategic vision should provide long-term direction, delineate the organizational activities to be pursued, encourage the capabilities it plans to develop, and infuse the church with a sense of purposeful action. A strategic vision serves as a unifying focal point for the organization. It pointedly captures a picture of how you want your Sunday School to look in the future.

A godly vision is based on God's will for the church. It is a picture of seeking the needs of other people and meeting those needs. It is vitally connected to the heart of God and His perspective. A vision inspired by God will require His power to fulfill. A godly vision makes your heart surge, carries you to heights you never dreamed possible, and causes growth. You are empowered and motivated by it. It seizes hold of you and orders your thoughts and actions. The Scripture says, "Record the vision and inscribe it on tablets, that the one who reads it may run" (Habakkuk 2:2, NASB).

To write a plan to carry out the vision (goals and objectives), pray and seek God's wisdom by asking the following questions:

- What will our church look like ten years from now?
- Where is God directing our church?
- What is God's vision for our church?

Simply put, your strategic plan for the Sunday School's future can be developed by answering three questions:

- Where are we now?
- Where are we going?
- How will we get there?

Evangelist Betty J. Byrd is a member of the Fairfield First Church of God in Christ, in Fairfield, Alabama, where her pastor is Elder James Brinkley Jr. There she serves as Sunday School teacher, president of the Young Women's Christian Council (YWCC), corresponding secretary, and coordinator of public relations. Jurisdictionally, she serves as the State YWCC President for Alabama First Jurisdiction, where her Jurisdictional Prelate is Bishop O. L. Meadows, and Mother Mattie Taylor is her Jurisdictional Supervisor. In the State Women's Department, she serves as assistant marshal. Nationally she serves as a member of the International YWCC Advisory Board under the leadership of International President Mother Maxine Billingsley.

QUARTERLY QUIZ

The questions on this page may be used in several ways: as a pretest at the beginning of the quarter; as a review at the end of the quarter; or as a review after each lesson. The questions are based on the Scripture text of each lesson (King James Version).

LESSON 1

1. Complete **Hebrews 1:9:** "Thou hast loved _______, and hated _______; therefore God, even thy God, hath anointed thee with the ____ of ________ above thy fellows" (KJV).

2. The name of the Son is (greater than/less than) the names of others **(Hebrews 1:4)**.

LESSON 2

1. God is great and above all _____ **(Psalm 95:3)**.

2. According to the psalmist, what do the hands of God form **(Psalm 95:4)**?

LESSON 3

1. How many angels were praising God **(Luke 2:13)**?

2. What did the shepherds do after they saw the Savior, the Messiah lying in a manger **(Luke 2:20)**?

LESSON 4

1. In **Matthew 14:23**, Jesus sends the people ____, and goes up into the ______ by Himself to _______.

2. Why did so many want to see Jesus **(Matthew 14:35)**?

LESSON 5

1. How did Jesus tell His disciples to begin their prayer **(Luke 11:2)**?

2. What analogy does Jesus use in **Luke 11:11** to compare God caring for His children?

QUARTERLY QUIZ

LESSON 6

1. What does Jesus pray for among believers **(John 17:21)**?

____

____

2. Who is Jesus sending into the world as God sent Him into the world **(John 17:18)**?

____

____

LESSON 7

1. Who is the great High Priest **(Hebrews 4:14)**?

____

____

2. Jesus as the High Priest has been called by God after the _______ _______ _______ **(Hebrews 5:10)**.

____

____

LESSON 8

1. James states that those who are sick should ask for who to respond to their sickness **(James 5:14)**?

____

____

2. What were the elders responsibilities do to care for those who are sick **(James 5:14)**?

____

____

LESSON 9

1. The king appointed the captive young men to eat and drink what for how many years **(Daniel 1:5)**?

____

____

2. Who was concerned for Daniel not following the king's diet? Why **(Daniel 1:10)**?

____

____

LESSON 10

1. Who questioned Jesus about inheriting eternal life **(Luke 10:25)**?

____

____

2. How did Jesus respond to the question about who is his neighbor **(Luke 10:30)**?

____

____

LESSON 11

1. The sheep sit on the _____ ______ of Jesus and the _____ on the ______ **(Matthew 25:33)**.

____

____

2. Complete this section of **Matthew 25:35:** Jesus said that when "I was thirsty, and ___ gave ___ ______."

____

____

QUARTERLY QUIZ

LESSON 12

1. Should believers put on some armor or the whole armor of God **(Ephesians 6:13)**?

____

____

2. Paul states that the "feet shod" are for what **(Ephesians 6:15)**?

____

____

ANSWERS TO THE QUARTERLY QUIZ

LESSON 1 1. righteousness, iniquity, oil, gladness; 2. more excellent

LESSON 2 1. gods; 2. sea and dry land

LESSON 3 1. a multitude; 2. The shepherds told everyone what had happened and what the angel said about this child.

LESSON 4 1. home, mountain (hills), pray; 2. The people wanted to be healed.

LESSON 5 1. Our Father which art in heaven, Hallowed by thy name.; 2. A child who asks for bread, but the father gives him a stone instead, or asks for a fish, but receives a snake.

LESSON 6 1. That they all may be one, that they also may be one in u; 2. Jesus sent the disciples.

LESSON 7 1. Jesus; 2. order of Melchisedec

LESSON 8 1. The elders; 2. The elders were pray for them and anoint the person with oil.

LESSON 9 1. They were to eat the king's meat and drink red wine for three years.; 2. The eunuch was concerned for Daniel's life and his own.

LESSON 10 1. A lawyer; 2. Jesus tells a story that has been titled "The Good Samaritan."

LESSON 11 1. right hand, goats, left; 2. ye, me drink

LESSON 12 1. whole armor; 2. "The preparation of the gospel of peace."

WORSHIP CHRIST'S MAJESTY

BIBLE BASIS: HEBREWS 1:1–9

BIBLE TRUTH: Jesus Christ is the gift of salvation that God's people respond to with worship.

MEMORY VERSE: "[Jesus] being the brightness of his glory, and the express image of his person, and upholding all things by the word of his power, when he had by himself purged our sins, sat down on the right hand of the Majesty on high" (Hebrews 1:3).

LESSON AIM: By the end of this lesson, your students will: consider why Jesus is worthy of adoration and worship; affirm that Jesus' superiority and God's anointing of Him "with the oil of gladness" leads to our response of worship; and lead adults to practice meaningful worship.

TEACHER PREPARATION

MATERIALS NEEDED: Quarterly Commentary/Teacher Manual, Adult Quarterly, Adult resources—charts, worksheets, and other teaching tools, paper, pens, pencils, Bibles (several different versions)

OTHER MATERIALS NEEDED / TEACHER'S NOTES:

____

____

LESSON OVERVIEW

LIFE NEED FOR TODAY'S LESSON
People give praise and honor in various ways.

BIBLE LEARNING
Jesus Christ fulfills the three offices of the Hebrew Scriptures—prophet, priest, and king.

BIBLE APPLICATION
Believers acknowledge that Jesus is God's Son.

STUDENTS' RESPONSES
Students will acknowledge that they have a deep desire to worship God.

LESSON SCRIPTURE

HEBREWS 1:1–9, KJV

1 God, who at sundry times and in divers manners spake in time past unto the fathers by the prophets,

2 Hath in these last days spoken unto us by his Son, whom he hath appointed heir of all things, by whom also he made the worlds;

HEBREWS 1:1–9, NIV

1 In the past God spoke to our ancestors through the prophets at many times and in various ways,

2 but in these last days he has spoken to us by his Son, whom he appointed heir of all things, and through whom also he made the universe.

3 Who being the brightness of his glory, and the express image of his person, and upholding all things by the word of his power, when he had by himself purged our sins, sat down on the right hand of the Majesty on high:

4 Being made so much better than the angels, as he hath by inheritance obtained a more excellent name than they.

5 For unto which of the angels said he at any time, Thou art my Son, this day have I begotten thee? And again, I will be to him a Father, and he shall be to me a Son?

6 And again, when he bringeth in the first-begotten into the world, he saith, And let all the angels of God worship him.

7 And of the angels he saith, Who maketh his angels spirits, and his ministers a flame of fire.

8 But unto the Son he saith, Thy throne, O God, is for ever and ever: a sceptre of righteousness is the sceptre of thy kingdom.

9 Thou hast loved righteousness, and hated iniquity; therefore God, even thy God, hath anointed thee with the oil of gladness above thy fellows.

3 The Son is the radiance of God's glory and the exact representation of his being, sustaining all things by his powerful word. After he had provided purification for sins, he sat down at the right hand of the Majesty in heaven.

4 So he became as much superior to the angels as the name he has inherited is superior to theirs.

5 For to which of the angels did God ever say, "You are my Son; today I have become your Father"? Or again, "I will be his Father, and he will be my Son"?

6 And again, when God brings his firstborn into the world, he says, "Let all God's angels worship him."

7 In speaking of the angels he says, "He makes his angels spirits, and his servants flames of fire."

8 But about the Son he says, "Your throne, O God, will last for ever and ever; a scepter of justice will be the scepter of your kingdom.

9 You have loved righteousness and hated wickedness; therefore God, your God, has set you above your companions by anointing you with the oil of joy."

LIGHT ON THE WORD

The book of Hebrews was written to a predominantly Jewish-Christian audience, the proclamation that Jesus "cleansed us from our sins" would have had profound meaning for them (v. 3, NLT). It would have served as a powerful reminder that no longer must they spill the blood of an animal to be in God's presence. Rather, Jesus' sacrifice, once and for all, allows them to have access to a holy God (**Hebrews 9:11–14**). No longer must a priest serve on their behalf to enact purification rituals, either. As the author of Hebrews explains, Jesus not only replaces the animal sacrifice, but the high priest as well (**chapters 7–8**). No longer are the old rituals necessary. Jesus' sacrifice for their sins is lasting and completely effectual. The key point is that with the sacrifice of Jesus, a new type of purification of sins has been established.

TEACHING THE BIBLE LESSON

LIFE NEED FOR TODAY'S LESSON

AIM: Students will discuss that people praise and honor in various ways.

INTRODUCTION

Instruction to the New Christians

Many of the references to Jewish history are to instruct the new Christians. By drawing on language and themes that would have had significance for the audience, the author is instructing and encouraging these fledgling Christians to press forward in their new faith. The author contrasts their Jewishness to their Christian identity and explains how being a follower of Christ is similar to and different from Judaism. The author is careful to point out that because Christ is superior to figures in their Jewish history, including highly esteemed angels, He is worthy of their faith and worship.

BIBLE LEARNING

AIM: Students will know that Jesus Christ fulfills the three offices of the Hebrew Scriptures—prophet, priest, and king.

I. THE SON OF GOD (Hebrews 1:1–3)

You will notice that in verses 1–3 the name Jesus is not mentioned; neither is the title Christ (Messiah). Almost startlingly, "Jesus" is not invoked until **Hebrews 2:9**. Not mentioning Jesus in this section seems most likely to do with the focus of the author. By not mentioning His name until later, the author wishes to draw the attention of the readers to who Jesus is. And for this author, discussion of Jesus' identity begins not with His name but with the fact that He is God's Son, and thus God Himself. Jesus' divinity is highlighted.

God's Revelation (verses 1–3)

1 God, who at sundry times and in divers manners spake in time past unto the fathers by the prophets, 2 Hath in these last days spoken unto us by his Son, whom he hath appointed heir of all things, by whom also he made the worlds;

In this epistle, the writer begins with God. God is the initiator of revelation; therefore, the focus is on Him, not man. The first and second verses contrast the methods of communication God used in the past with the method He used then. The phrase "at sundry times and in divers manners spake" refers to the fact that God chose the times and methods to communicate. The Old Testament records the clouds, dreams, visions, etc. that God used to communicate with His people. God also used the prophets to reveal His Word. The reference to "prophets" here is not limited to the traditional prophets but includes men of God like Moses, David, and Solomon, to mention a few.

The phrase "in these last days" refers to both the present and end times. There is a clear sense that God has reached the climax of His self-revelation. He has saved the best for last. There is a definite intention to show that this last revelation of God is superior to what He has done in the past. The fact that God has already "spoken unto us by his Son" suggests that, at the time of writing this epistle, the revelation had been completed.

Even though most English translations say "his son" or "the Son," the Greek has no definite article. It simply says "son." Instead of identifying whom God spoke through, it emphasizes the nature of the one whom God spoke through. Unlike the prophets, the Son is more than a messenger. His divine nature makes Him the right and only capable bearer of God's complete revelation. The rest of Hebrews elaborates on this truth about the identity and the superiority of the revelation of God through Jesus Christ.

The phrase "appointed heir of all things, by whom also he made the worlds" indicates that Christ embodies a dual motif of sonship and creation. He is eternal and therefore superior to any other revelation of God. The word translated as "worlds" (**Hebrews 1:2**, KJV) or "universe" (NIV) is *aionas* (Gk. **eye-OWN-as**). It literally means ages or times. The preferred interpretation is "ages," which suggests that Jesus not only created the world but also controls the events of history.

3 Who being the brightness of his glory, and the express image of his person, and upholding all things by the word of his power, when he had by himself purged our sins, sat down on the right hand of the Majesty on high;

In **verse 3**, we get a complete Christology. The first part of the verse talks about the Son's relationship with God, the second part deals with the work of the Son, and the third part refers to His exaltation—the pre-existence, incarnation, and exaltation of Christ. The phrase "brightness of his glory" could mean that Jesus is either the reflection or the radiance of the glory of God. The Bible tells us that God is inapproachable, but that Jesus makes it possible to know Him truly and intimately. What a blessing! The "express image of his person" means "the imprint or seal of God's nature," and the word translated as "person" connotes "the reality or actuality of His being." Thus, Jesus fully represents God (cf. **Colossians 2:9**), and upholds all things by the word of His power. This is not a passive holding up but an active sustaining. Jesus is not only Creator of the universe, but He is also sustaining it by His Word. The exaltation of Christ is an allusion to **Psalm 110:1**. Jesus used this verse in silencing the Pharisees concerning his position of Messiah (**Matthew 22:41–46**). The Son of David who is also the pre-incarnate God would come down to earth to die and then be raised to Heaven in triumph over all of God's enemies including death. "The Majesty on high" is a title for God. It is a sign of kingship and royal authority.

SEARCH THE SCRIPTURES

QUESTIONS 1 & 2

Who has appointed Jesus the heir of all things?

How does Jesus sustain all things?

LIGHT ON THE WORD

Jesus is God

If the readers forget that Jesus is God, then they will forget the importance of His message and His life, and they will not offer Him the worship He deserves. If Jesus was just a man, then His message was just a good word spoken by a human being. If Jesus' actions were just human actions, then He was just a good human being. But this is not so, says the author in these opening verses. Jesus' message is connected to the very mind of God. Jesus' actions are connected to the very will of God. Jesus is God.

II. SUPERIOR TO THE ANGELS (vv. 4–9)

In this set of verses, the author continues to build upon the description of Jesus. Let me sketch you a picture, the author seems to say. Imagine the angels. They're pretty important, aren't they? Pretty powerful. Pretty amazing creatures. Well, where do you think Jesus stands in comparison? Higher, the author contends! Jesus is more important, more powerful, and more amazing.

The Superiority of Christ (verses 4–9)

4 Being made so much better than the angels, as he hath by inheritance obtained a more excellent name than they.

The phrase "better than" or "superior to" is used thirteen times in the Christology presented in Hebrews. Christ is the revelation that is superior to all others. He is the One we are to serve and worship. His revelation holds more sway in our lives than any other. In the Old Testament, a name (Gk. *onoma*, **AWN-o-maw**) is associated with reputation, and Christ's name/reputation is superior to the angels.

Verse 4 introduces the major subjects of the discussion that is to follow: Christ and the angels. To counter the worship of angels, the writer shows the real position of the angels in contrast to Christ. Christ is directly related to the Father and the angels are not. Christ inherited the universe and the angels are under His dominion. Christ has a more excellent name due to His pre-existence, incarnation, and exaltation to the right hand of God.

5 For unto which of the angels said he at any time, Thou art my Son, this day have I begotten thee? And again, I will be to him a Father, and he shall be to me a Son?

Hebrews 1:5–14 continues the explanation of who Jesus Christ is, and **Hebrews 2:1–4** challenges the reader to respond appropriately. The author follows this pattern throughout the epistle. He always gives the explanation of who Jesus is and then the challenge to respond appropriately. Beginning with **verse 5**, we find frequent references to, or quotations from, the Old Testament (thirty or more), especially the Psalms. **Verse 5** is a combination of two Old Testament quotations: **Psalm 2:7** and **2 Samuel 7:14**. The truth from **Psalm 2:7** ("Thou art my Son; this day have I begotten thee") concerning Jesus' relationship to God was very significant for the early church's understanding of Christ. This truth was announced from Heaven at Jesus' baptism (**Mark 1:10–11**) and preached by Paul (**Acts 13:33–34**). The reference to **2 Samuel 7:14** is taken from the promise to David that he will always have a son to reign on the throne. This passage carries messianic expectation that the Messiah would be a son of David. The verse in particular shows that not only would the Messiah be a son of David but also a son of God. None of the kings of Israel could claim both of these titles in reality. The only true fulfillment of this was through Christ the son of David and the Son of God.

6 And again, when he bringeth in the firstbegotten into the world, he saith, And let all the angels of God worship him. 7 And of the angels he saith, Who maketh his angels spirits, and his ministers a flame of fire.

The term "first begotten" is translated from the Greek word *prototokos* (**pro-TOE-toe-kose**). It does not mean the first to be created. Rather, it indicates privilege, authority, and inheritance. Its meaning centers on the firstborn son's rights and position. Christ has the highest authority. The phrase "all the angels of God worship him" emphasizes His exalted state as God because only God can be worshiped. Since the angels worship Him, do not worship the angels. Worship Christ. This seals the exaltation of Christ over the angels. Even the angels know that He is superior, and therefore they bow down and worship Him. This is not an exaltation of His human nature but the recognition of who He truly is as the Son of God.

Verse 7 contains an Old Testament quotation from **Psalm 104:4**. It further shows the superiority of Christ over angels. They not only worship Him, but serve Him. **Psalm 104:4** is taken from a passage about creation. While Christ created the world, the angels were just instruments in the overall act of creation. They are servants and agents of God in creating the world. The angels are subordinate to Christ. They are spirits and flames of fire. This suggests their temporality and transient nature. This is placed in contrast to the eternality of the Son.

8 But unto the Son he saith, Thy throne, O

God, is for ever and ever: a sceptre of righteousness is the sceptre of thy kingdom. 9 Thou hast loved righteousness, and hated iniquity; therefore God, even thy God, hath anointed thee with the oil of gladness above thy fellows.

These verses are a quotation of **Psalm 45:6–7. Psalm 45** is a marriage psalm calling a princess to heed the king's call and "forget also thine own people and thy father's house" (**v. 10**) in order to enter the king's palace, where there is great joy. This king loves righteousness and hates sin. This psalm has many messianic applications. **Hebrews 1:8–9** refers to the Son as God and says that His throne is exalted forever. Christ is superior to the angels—"anointed with the oil of gladness above thy fellows."

LIGHT ON THE WORD

Jesus is Inseparable from God

The most important point to realize here is the same as in the previous verses. Jesus is superior to the angels because His identity is connected directly and inseparably to God. "The name he has inherited is superior to theirs" (**v. 4**, NIV). Next the author asks, "For to which of the angels did God ever say, 'You are my Son; today I have become your Father'? Or again, 'I will be his Father, and he will be my Son'?" (**v. 5**, NIV). The answer to these rhetorical questions is "none." But the author doesn't stop there. He continues to hammer the point of Jesus' divinity home for the audience. As if he hasn't been clear, "And again, when God brings his firstborn into the world, he says, 'Let all God's angels worship him'" (**v. 6**, NIV). In **verses 7–9**, the author elaborates even more on the deity (divinity) of Jesus, God's Son.

The author reiterates Jesus' divinity to caution his readers to heed His message and live lives faithful to God. As the letter unfolds, the author continues discussing who Jesus is as a reason to worship Him through obedience.

BIBLE APPLICATION

AIM: Students will acknowledge that Jesus is God's Son.

People in society often esteem other people. Presidents, kings, queens, athletes, and celebrities receive praise for their status and achievements. When President Obama was elected, for example, many thought he would take the "presidential throne" as a type of savior.

Today's passage draws our attention to the one who is most deserving of all our praise and worship: Jesus, God's Son. How often do we find ourselves worshiping Him instead of finding ourselves at the feet of a person in society?

STUDENTS' RESPONSES

AIM: Students will acknowledge that they have a deep desire to worship God.

Sometimes when we read the Bible, it is tempting to view Jesus as a man. Even Christians can forget the significance of Jesus being God. How can you shape your worship of Jesus to start with the fact that He is God instead of what He's done for you?

PRAYER

God, our Father, we thank you for giving us Jesus. For Jesus is higher than the angels and us. He is superior to all people and anything that has or will be created or made. We worship and adore You for allowing us to have fellowship with Jesus, our redeemer, and our savior. In Jesus' Name we pray. Amen.

HOW TO SAY IT

Superior. Soo-**PEE**-ri-or.

Subordinate. Su-**BOR**-din-it.

Allusion. Uh-**LOO**-shin.

PREPARE FOR NEXT SUNDAY

Read **Psalm 95:1–7a** and study "Make a Joyful Noise."

DAILY HOME BIBLE READINGS

MONDAY
Great and Awesome God
(Daniel 9:3–10)

TUESDAY
O Lord, Hear and Forgive
(Daniel 9:11–19)

WEDNESDAY
God the Almighty Reigns
(Revelation 19:1–8)

THURSDAY
First and Last, Beginning and End
(Revelation 22:8–14)

FRIDAY
My Son, the Beloved
(Matthew 3:13–17)

SATURDAY
Honor and Glory Forever
(1 Timothy 1:12–17)

SUNDAY
The Son Reflects God's Glory
(Hebrews 1:1–9)

Sources:

Hamilton, Victor P. *Handbook on the Pentateuch: Genesis, Exodus, Leviticus, Numbers, Deuteronomy.* Grand Rapids, MI: Baker Academic, 2005.

Keener, Craig S. *The IVP Bible Background Commentary.* Downers Grove, IL: Intervarsity Press, 1993

COMMENTS / NOTES:

MAKE A JOYFUL NOISE

BIBLE BASIS: PSALM 95:1–7a

BIBLE TRUTH: God is the rock of our salvation and is worthy of praise and worship.

MEMORY VERSE: "O come, let us sing unto the LORD: let us make a joyful noise to the rock of our salvation" (Psalm 95:1).

LESSON AIM: By the end of the lesson, your students will: discern that God is the Creator of the earth and the maker of humankind, and God is truly worthy of praise; experience the enthusiasm, power, and excitement that comes when believers praise God as their divine King; and shed inhibitions in worship and praise God exuberantly.

TEACHER PREPARATION

MATERIALS NEEDED: Quarterly Commentary/Teacher Manual, Adult Quarterly, Adult resources—charts, worksheets, and other teaching tools, paper, pens, pencils, Bibles (several different versions)

OTHER MATERIALS NEEDED / TEACHER'S NOTES:

____

____

LESSON OVERVIEW

LIFE NEED FOR TODAY'S LESSON
Many people realize that a power beyond them gives meaning to their lives.

BIBLE LEARNING
In Psalms, calls to worship were often hymns sung by the ancient community.

BIBLE APPLICATION
Believers worship God as the Creator of Heaven and earth.

STUDENTS' RESPONSES
Worship is a vital response by believers to the awesome power of God.

LESSON SCRIPTURE

PSALM 95:1–7a, KJV

1 O come, let us sing unto the LORD: let us make a joyful noise to the rock of our salvation.

2 Let us come before his presence with thanksgiving, and make a joyful noise unto him with psalms.

3 For the LORD is a great God, and a great King above all gods.

PSALM 95:1–7a, NIV

1 Come, let us sing for joy to the LORD; let us shout aloud to the Rock of our salvation.

2 Let us come before him with thanksgiving and extol him with music and song.

3 For the LORD is the great God, the great King above all gods.

4 In his hand are the deep places of the earth: the strength of the hills is his also.

5 The sea is his, and he made it: and his hands formed the dry land.

6 O come, let us worship and bow down: let us kneel before the LORD our maker.

7a For he is our God; and we are the people of his pasture, and the sheep of his hand.

4 In his hand are the depths of the earth, and the mountain peaks belong to him.

5 The sea is his, for he made it, and his hands formed the dry land.

6 Come, let us bow down in worship, let us kneel before the LORD our Maker;

7a for he is our God and we are the people of his pasture, the flock under his care.

LIGHT ON THE WORD

In the ancient Near East, different nations worshiped a variety of gods. The Israelite worship of Yahweh was unique in that the people were commanded to worship only one God as opposed to the surrounding nations, who worshiped a roster of different deities dedicated to different aspects of life. Although the Israelites did not worship these deities, they often declared their one God to be supreme over the many other gods of the nations.

Many times the Bible refers to God as a Rock or the Rock of our salvation. This may have been because during their trek in the wilderness God gave Israel water from a rock (**Numbers 20:1–13**). It also could have been due to the benefits of a rock as a shade during the heat (**Isaiah 32:2**) and the safety of a rock when hiding from or fighting an enemy (**Psalm 31:2, 3; 104:18**).

Shepherds would keep their sheep in a pen during the night and let them out into the pasture during the day. These were areas where they could find grass and vegetation to eat freely. In ancient Palestine, pasture was not necessarily an abundant field of greenery but the rocky bare hills. The shepherd led the sheep to eat just what they needed for that day. The best pasture was usually on the plateaus east of the Jordan and the mountains of Palestine and Syria.

TEACHING THE BIBLE LESSON

LIFE NEED FOR TODAY'S LESSON

AIM: Students will understand that many people realize that a power beyond them gives meaning to their lives.

INTRODUCTION

An Invitation to Worship

Psalm 95 is an invitation to worship. Perhaps the crowd or congregation had grown weary. It seemed that they'd stopped believing, and were no longer expecting God to fulfill His promises. The author who tired of their passivity essentially said, "Don't just stand there; do something!" Through the psalm, the psalmist exhorted the people to serve God.

One cannot worship God with a hardened heart, as this psalm warns. In **verse 8**, the psalmist used the testing at Meribah (also known as Massah) as an example. At Meribah, the Israelites sinned against God (**Exodus 17:1–7**). "Is the Lord among us or not?" they complained. Not trusting God in the wilderness kept them out of the Promised Land. In our text, the psalmist admonished the congregation to not let the same happen to them. "Come, let us sing to the one who'll save us," he urged. The same testing is referenced in **Hebrews 3:7** and **4:7** as a warning to believers.

BIBLE LEARNING

AIM: Students will learn that in Psalms, calls to worship were often hymns sung by the ancient community.

I. PRAISE HIM (Psalm 95:1–2)

Praising God was as natural to the psalmist as breathing. Psalms is full of praises, adoration, and worship to God. Even when things were bad, the psalmist poured out his heart to the Rock of his salvation. The "Rock" is a recurrent metaphor for God in Psalms, used over 20 times.

The psalmist sees the worship of God as something to be done corporately. He exhorts the congregation with the words "Come, let us sing together." It is an invitation to praise the Rock of our salvation, but at the same time the psalmist is also leading the way by including himself in the invitation. He says "us" so that the call is personal as well as corporate.

Joyful Thanksgiving (verses 1–2)

1 O come, let us sing unto the LORD: let us make a joyful noise to the rock of our salvation. 2 Let us come before his presence with thanksgiving, and make a joyful noise unto him with psalms.

The psalm begins the call to worship with an imperative (come), followed by four verbs exhorting the people to sing and rejoice in God's presence. It is more than an invitation to worship the Lord, the Rock our salvation; it is a powerful summons to worship God with a joy that compels His people to shout. The psalmist is filled with such jubilation at God's power that words are not enough. Music is necessary to express such wonderment.

The people are urged to enter God's presence. In the Old Testament, God's presence is described as His very face. God is not just a transcendent Creator and Ruler who is not involved personally with His creation. God interacts face to face with those who worship Him, and since their worship brings them face to face with their Creator, they must sing!

SEARCH THE SCRIPTURES

QUESTION 1

How should we come into His presence?

LIGHT ON THE WORD

Shout Joyfully

The psalmist says, "Let's shout joyfully." Praising God should be joyful and exuberant, not a solemn and sad occasion. Our deepest joy is to be found in God, and this joy must have full expression. Shouting joyfully was a way of celebrating God and all that He had done for His people.

The tools that the psalmist prescribes to be used in worship are thanksgiving and psalms of praise. Our worship of God is to be permeated by thanksgiving. We have received nothing outside of what God has given us. This is enough motivation for thanks. Psalms of praise were songs written for the express purpose of praising and adoring God in small and large settings.

II. ADORE HIM (vv. 3–5)

As if the people had asked why they should

praise the Lord, the psalmist answered. "Because He is great." Then, he gave evidence of God's greatness by recalling that He held the deep places of the earth in His hand. Essentially he challenged, "If things that are out of sight and out of reach are in His hands, how much more so are your problems?"

A Great God (verses 3–5)

3 For the LORD is a great God, and a great King above all gods.

The psalm begins the explanation of the reasons for worshiping God. Not only is the Lord a great God, but He is also greater than all other gods. In antiquity, the Israelites always had neighbors who worshiped other gods, and the Old Testament narrates many times when the Israelites were tempted to, and sometimes did, worship those false deities. Here the psalm contains a metaphor the people would comprehend because they were ruled by kings and understood the authority and power that a king had. Just as David, Solomon, and the other Israelite kings had authority and power over the people, so the Lord has authority and power over all gods. For anyone tempted to worship other gods, this psalm reminds them that their God is the one with power over everything.

4 In his hand are the deep places of the earth: the strength of the hills is his also. 5 The sea is his, and he made it: and his hands formed the dry land.

God is the Creator of all things. The deep places and the hills represent creation from top to bottom. Similarly, **v. 5** mentions water and dry land. These opposite pictures of the depths and the hills, as well as water and dry land, form an all-encompassing picture of God's creation. In addition, the reference to the sea and the dry land echoes the Exodus, reminding the people of the miraculous ways in which God saves those of faith. Bookending these verses with God's hands also creates an image of His hands encompassing all of creation. God created everything and cares for everything.

In the Old Testament, God's hand represents not only the things He touches and tends to, but also His power and strength. Literally, God's hand touches all parts of the earth, including the heights of the mountains. Metaphorically, God's power and strength as Creator are reflected in the very foundations and heights of creation. God's hand is both powerful and caring, and tends to all of His creation.

LIGHT ON THE WORD

God's Power

Scripture often used Creation as evidence of God's power. The Lord made the sea and dry land, and both are under His control. No matter how much an angry sea rages, it can go no farther than the boundary the Lord sets. It's as if the psalmist set a challenge: "If the Lord set an end to something seemingly uncontrollable, would He not have an end to this?"

III. WORSHIP HIM (vv. 6–7)

The psalmist recognized pride can hinder our relationship with God. The antidote to pridefulness is worship. By showing God how much He is worth to us, we realize our true worth in relationship to Him. This is a surefire cure for pride: "Bow down and worship the Lord who made us." **Psalm 100:3** also points to God as our Creator, saying, "... it is he that hath made us, and not we ourselves."

Bow Before the Lord (verses 6–7a)

6 O come, let us worship and bow down: let us kneel before the LORD our maker.

Parallel to **verse 1** in structure, this verse once again commands the people to worship God, adding new forms of worship to the noisy singing and rejoicing of **vv. 1–2**. Although the first exhortative verb, *shachah* (Heb. **shah-KHAH**), is translated "worship," it also means to bow down because it carries the connotation of submitting to someone in authority. As a result, all three verbs describing worship in this verse indicate physical bowing before God the Creator. The final verb for kneeling, *barak* (Heb. **bah-RAHK**), can also indicate blessing in other contexts where God blesses the faithful, establishing a relationship between God as the one who blesses and the people as worshipers. In addition, the epithet for God as our Maker reminds the people that God has created not only the earth and the sea but also the people, and they should worship Him by surrendering to Him.

7a For he is our God; and we are the people of his pasture, and the sheep of his hand.

Similar to **v. 3**, **7a** explains why the people should worship with submission. Quite simply, the Lord is our God. The metaphor shifts from God as Creator to God as Shepherd. Now God's hand of care and power is involved in tending to His flock. The remainder of the psalm carries out this metaphor by reminding the people that their ancestors did not always follow God, even though they knew about His works. Amid a psalm of praise and worship, the final verses serve as a reminder of the need for such psalms. Even God's faithful can forget how to worship God, so the psalm calls the people to keep worshiping God with song and submission lest they too forget His power and mighty deeds.

SEARCH THE SCRIPTURES

QUESTION 2

What is the posture for worship?

LIGHT ON THE WORD

God is the Shepherd

Who tells the maker what to do? **Isaiah 45:9** echoes, "Does the clay say to the potter, 'What are you making?'" (NIV). Further, in **verse 7**, the psalmist challenged the reader to know that He is their God, not the other way around. We are His sheep, in His pasture, and cannot be plucked out of His hand.

Jesus further illustrated the sheep-shepherd relationship when He proclaimed Himself The Good Shepherd (**John 10**). There, Jesus confronted the Pharisees who had set themselves up as shepherds of the people.

BIBLE APPLICATION

AIM: Students will worship God as the Creator of Heaven and earth.

Our society promotes pridefulness, often concealing it as self-confidence. Bestseller lists tout titles that reveal seven or ten steps to self-promotion. The Bible shows us that promotion comes from the Lord (**Psalm 75:6**). Our text reminds us that one must come before the Lord humbly and with thanksgiving—certainly not positions of pride, especially while on bended knee.

STUDENTS' RESPONSES

AIM: Students will learn to shed inhibitions in worship and praise God exuberantly.

This week, practice joyfulness. No matter how challenging your days get, sing songs of praise to God. Remember that you belong to God, not the other way around. Instead of standing, complaining, and prolonging your pain, get on your knees and worship. Bow down and thank Him for the things that are good and right.

PRAYER

Lord, we praise You with great thanksgiving.

We worship You in reverence and with great anticipation of Your marvelous acts in all of creation. In Jesus' Name we pray. Amen.

HOW TO SAY IT

Exhortation. eks-or-**TAY**-shun.

Transcendent. tran-**SEN**-dent.

PREPARE FOR NEXT SUNDAY

Read **Luke 2:8–20** and read "Glory to God in the Highest."

DAILY HOME BIBLE READINGS

MONDAY
Hold Fast to God
(Deuteronomy 13:1–8)

TUESDAY
Devote Yourselves to the Lord
(1 Kings 8:54–62)

WEDNESDAY
Worship with Reverence and Awe
(Hebrews 12:22–29)

THURSDAY
Sing Praises to God
(1 Chronicles 16:7–15)

FRIDAY
Ascribe Greatness to Our God
(Deuteronomy 32:1–7)

SATURDAY
A Sacrifice of Praise to God
(Hebrews 13:6–15)

SUNDAY
Let Us Worship and Bow Down
(Psalm 95:1–7a)

Sources:

Bellinger, W. H. *Psalms: Reading and Studying the Book of Praises*. Peabody, MA: Hendrickson Publishers, 1990.

Mays, James Luther. *Psalms. Interpretation: A Bible Commentary for Teaching and Preaching*. Edited by James Luther Mays, Patrick D. Miller, Jr. and Paul J. Achtemeier. Louisville, KY: Westminster John Knox Press, 1994.

McCann, J. Clinton, Jr. "The Book of Psalms." *Vol. IV of The New Interpreter's Bible*. 12 vols. Edited by Leander E. Keck, et al. Nashville, TN: Abingdon Press, 1996. 641–1280.

The Word in Life Study Bible. Nashville, TN: Thomas Nelson, 1993. 149.

The New Spirit Filled Life Bible. Nashville, TN: Thomas Nelson, 2002. 687–688, 760.

COMMENTS / NOTES:

GLORY TO GOD IN THE HIGHEST

BIBLE BASIS: LUKE 2:8–20

BIBLE TRUTH: The angels announced the birth of the Savior and a multitude of the heavenly host praised God.

MEMORY VERSE: "And the shepherds returned, glorifying and praising God for all the things that they had heard and seen, as it was told unto them" (Luke 2:20).

LESSON AIM: By the end of this lesson, your students will: explore the events that led to the angels' spontaneous joy and the shepherds' pilgrimage to see Jesus; feel the unrestrained joy that comes with the good news of the Savior's birth; and participate in worship events of Christmas and Epiphany.

TEACHER PREPARATION

MATERIALS NEEDED: Quarterly Commentary/Teacher Manual, Adult Quarterly, Adult resources—charts, worksheets, and other teaching tools, paper, pens, pencils, Bibles (several different versions)

OTHER MATERIALS NEEDED / TEACHER'S NOTES:

____

____

LESSON OVERVIEW

LIFE NEED FOR TODAY'S LESSON

There are events in people's lives that cause spontaneous celebration.

BIBLE LEARNING

Jesus' birth was to an unlikely audience in a way that made God's glory visible.

BIBLE APPLICATION

Christians know that God sent Jesus into the world as the Redeemer of lost people.

STUDENTS' RESPONSES

Believers respond to the birth of Christ by glorifying and praising God and by telling others.

LESSON SCRIPTURE

LUKE 2:8–20, KJV

8 And there were in the same country shepherds abiding in the field, keeping watch over their flock by night.

9 And, lo, the angel of the Lord came upon them, and the glory of the Lord shone round about them: and they were sore afraid.

LUKE 2:8–20, NIV

8 And there were shepherds living out in the fields nearby, keeping watch over their flocks at night.

9 An angel of the Lord appeared to them, and the glory of the Lord shone around them, and they were terrified.

10 But the angel said to them, "Do not

10 And the angel said unto them, Fear not: for, behold, I bring you good tidings of great joy, which shall be to all people.

11 For unto you is born this day in the city of David a Saviour, which is Christ the Lord.

12 And this shall be a sign unto you; Ye shall find the babe wrapped in swaddling clothes, lying in a manger.

13 And suddenly there was with the angel a multitude of the heavenly host praising God, and saying,

14 Glory to God in the highest, and on earth peace, good will toward men.

15 And it came to pass, as the angels were gone away from them into heaven, the shepherds said one to another, Let us now go even unto Bethlehem, and see this thing which is come to pass, which the Lord hath made known unto us.

16 And they came with haste, and found Mary, and Joseph, and the babe lying in a manger.

17 And when they had seen it, they made known abroad the saying which was told them concerning this child.

18 And all they that heard it wondered at those things which were told them by the shepherds.

19 But Mary kept all these things, and pondered them in her heart.

20 And the shepherds returned, glorifying and praising God for all the things that they had heard and seen, as it was told unto them.

be afraid. I bring you good news that will cause great joy for all the people.

11 Today in the town of David a Savior has been born to you; he is the Messiah, the Lord.

12 This will be a sign to you: You will find a baby wrapped in cloths and lying in a manger."

13 Suddenly a great company of the heavenly host appeared with the angel, praising God and saying,

14 "Glory to God in the highest heaven, and on earth peace to those on whom his favor rests."

15 When the angels had left them and gone into heaven, the shepherds said to one another, "Let's go to Bethlehem and see this thing that has happened, which the Lord has told us about."

16 So they hurried off and found Mary and Joseph, and the baby, who was lying in the manger.

17 When they had seen him, they spread the word concerning what had been told them about this child,

18 and all who heard it were amazed at what the shepherds said to them.

19 But Mary treasured up all these things and pondered them in her heart.

20 The shepherds returned, glorifying and praising God for all the things they had heard and seen, which were just as they had been told.

LIGHT ON THE WORD

In the story of Jesus' birth, Bethlehem is the key town. Historically, Bethlehem was known as the city of David, referring to the famous King David who ruled the people of Israel hundreds of years before Jesus' birth. Bethlehem was not a large town, so when the shepherds arrived, they probably had little difficulty finding Joseph, Mary, and Jesus. Also there is evidence that Joseph had a significant connection to Bethlehem, perhaps being an owner of a piece of land, which is the reason he and Mary journeyed there for the census. It was also known as the city that was prophesied to be the birthplace of the Messiah (**Micah 5:2, Matthew 2:5–6**).

TEACHING THE BIBLE LESSON

LIFE NEED FOR TODAY'S LESSON

AIM: Students will discover that people have events in their lives that causes spontaneous celebration.

INTRODUCTION

The Lowly Shepherds

By the time we arrive at the story of the angel of the Lord bringing news of Jesus' birth to the shepherds, several events have already occurred. The angel Gabriel had been sent by God to inform Mary that God was giving her a son named Jesus, who would be "the Son of the Highest" and would rule a kingdom that would be established forever (**Luke 1:26–38**). Pregnant Mary and her fiancé Joseph had traveled at least 70 miles (from Nazareth to Bethlehem) to register under a census by Quirinius, governor of Syria. After no suitable room could be found for her to deliver the child, Mary delivered Jesus into a manager where animals stayed nearby (**Luke 2:1–7**).

BIBLE LEARNING

AIM: Students will know that Jesus' birth was to an unlikely audience in a way that made God's glory visible.

I. THE ANGEL OF THE LORD DELIVERS A MESSAGE (Luke 2:8–14)

In these six verses, the angel of the Lord appeared. The angel of the Lord is commonly referenced as a heavenly being who is a special messenger or servant of God. Typically, the angel comes to accomplish the explicit will of the Lord. Beside the stories of Jesus' birth, the angel of the Lord also appears in the Old Testament, for example, to Moses at the burning bush (**Exodus 3**). The angel of the Lord came to (or stood before) the shepherds who were tending to their flock at night. The nighttime setting gives an interesting contrast when the glory (Gk. doxa, **DAW-ksa**) of the Lord appears with the angel of the Lord. The glory is said to have "shone round about them," suggesting an image of radiating light. No wonder the shepherds became afraid. Imagine walking at night and a comet suddenly appearing before you. Fear would seem like the natural response.

Watching the Sheep (verses 8–14)

8 And there were in the same country shepherds abiding in the field, keeping watch over their flock by night. 9 And, lo, the angel of the Lord came upon them, and the glory of the Lord shone round about them: and they were sore afraid.

As the shepherds watched their flock that night, the angel suddenly appeared to them. The glory of the Lord shone around them. The "glory" *doxa* (Gk. **DOX-ah**) is used here as in the Old Testament. It often symbolizes the presence of God (**Exodus 24:16; 1 Kings 8:11; Isaiah 6:1–6**). It describes the radiating splendor and majesty of God's presence. The glory of God, or God's presence, is seen or felt in different forms. To the Israelites in the wilderness, it was seen as a pillar of cloud and fire (**Exodus 13:21**). To Moses, it was seen as a burning bush (**Exodus 3:1–2**). To the worshipers in the Temple, it was felt as the radiance of His glory (**1 Kings 8:10–11**). This same radiance appeared to Peter, James, and John on the Mount of Transfiguration (**Matthew 17:1–2**). This phenomenon was often associated with the appearance of an angel. There is a luminous aspect of glory, as described by the phrase "shone round about them." The reaction of the shepherds was consistent with Zacharias' and Mary's reactions when Gabriel visited them (**Luke 1:12, 29**). Moses, too, was terrified when he encountered the burning bush (**Exodus 3**). The shepherds were all overwhelmed by fear and wonder because of the strange supernatural happening. "They were sore afraid" underlies this fact.

10 And the angel said unto them, Fear not: for, behold, I bring you good tidings of great joy, which shall be to all people. 11 For unto you is born this day in the city of David a Saviour, which is Christ the Lord.

Here the reassuring words of the angel, "Fear not" (cf. **1:13, 30**), were echoed. The angel told them not to fear and gave them the reason not to. He was bearing "good tidings (news) of great joy, which shall be to all people." "Bring good tidings," *euaggelizo* (Gk. **ehoo-ang-ghel-EED-zo**), is a verb which means to announce, to declare good news. The English verb "evangelize" is a transliteration of the Greek and can mean to preach, especially the Gospel. Hence, evangelism is the act of preaching, and evangelists are those who preach or proclaim the Good News of the Gospel. Euaggelizo referred to any type of happy news in the Greek translation of the Old Testament, but in the New Testament it is used for the Gospel of salvation, which is through Christ's redemptive sacrifice. The angel qualified the Good News that he announced to the shepherds. It was "good tidings of great joy (Gk. *megale*, **me-GAH-lay,** great; *chara*, **kha-RAH,** joy) ... to all people." The great news was not only for all people, but also it will bring joy to all people. The words "all people" (Gk. pas to laos, **PAS toe la-OSE**) have the idea of all people groups everywhere. Therefore, this Gospel is for people (all nationalities) and is intended by God to bring joy to all people universally. What is the good news? The angel announced that the long-expected Messiah, the hope of Israel, the Savior, was born "this day in the city of David." Notice how the angel described this newborn Babe that was born.

First, He is a "Saviour," *soter* (Gk., **so-TARE**), which means a deliverer, a preserver. It was a name given by the ancients to deities, princes, kings, and men who had brought deliverance to their country. It is used repeatedly for both God and His Christ, the medium of God's salvation to men.

Secondly, He is Christ. The word "Christ" is a direct transliteration of the Greek, *Christos* (**khris-TOS**), which means anointed (the anointed one). The equivalent in Hebrew is Messiah, which is another epithet of Jesus. In Jewish thought, there were a number of different forms the Messiah might take. For some the Messiah would be the king of the Jews, a political leader who would defeat their enemies and bring in a golden era of peace and prosperity. In Christian thought, the term Messiah refers to Jesus' role as a spiritual deliverer, setting His people free from sin and death.

During the time of Daniel, the 6th century B.C., the word Messiah was used as an actual title of the future king (**Daniel 9:25–26**). Even later, as the Jewish people struggled against their political enemies, the Messiah came to be thought of as a political, military ruler. Because Jesus' humble birth did not coincide with most understandings of Messiah, the majority of modern Jews still do not accept Jesus as the Messiah and are still waiting for one. However, the angel announced to the shepherds that the cause of the strange event they observed is the birth of the Christ—the long-anticipated Messiah of Israel. The Gospels show how many were eagerly hoping and watching out for the Messiah. Andrew met Jesus and told Simon Peter his brother, "We have found the Messias, which is, being interpreted, the Christ" (**John 1:41**). The woman at the well said to Jesus, "I know that Messias cometh, which is called Christ: when he is come, he will tell us all things" (**John 4:25**).

Thirdly, He is the "Lord." The word is a translation of the Greek, *kurios* (**KOO-ree-os**), meaning master. It signifies ownership, one with supreme authority over a person or a group. It is a title of honor expressive of servants' respect and reverence to their masters. It was used in reference to princes, chiefs, and the Roman emperor. In the African context, servants, students, or apprentices call their owners, teachers, or instructors "master" as a sign of respect, never their names. "Lord" is often used in the New Testament for God and the Messiah—the Christ. It was the usual way of referring to Yahweh in Greek. Because God's name was considered too holy to pronounce, Jews instead said Adonai ("my Lord"), which is kurios in Greek. Here the angel's designation of the newborn babe as the Lord identified Him as the possessor and supreme owner of all creation. Later in the Bible, the Apostle Peter declared that God made Jesus "both Lord and Christ" (**Acts 2:36**). While "Messiah," or Christ (the Anointed One), refers to Jesus' humanity, Kurios, "Lord," refers to His deity as the Supreme Being.

There seems to be a number of reasons and theological implications for the role of the shepherds in the events of that night. The main reason is probably for the purpose of identification. Shepherding in the Jewish tradition was a lowly occupation usually reserved for slaves. Therefore, the announcement was to identify Christ's humility with the shepherds (cf. **Philippians 2:7–8**). The announcement also identified His mission—caring and protecting. In both the Old and New Testaments, shepherds can symbolize those who care for God's people. Christ later identifies Himself in John's Gospel as the "Good Shepherd" (**John 10:2, 11, 12, 14, 16**). David writes, "The Lord is my shepherd" (**Psalm 23:1**). A number of passages in both Testaments use imagery to identify the Lord as the Shepherd of His people (**Isaiah 40:11; Jeremiah 23:1–4; Hebrews 13:20; 1 Peter 2:25; 5:2**).

Shepherds at the time of Jesus were not only poor, but also considered outsiders. Their work, like that of the tax collectors, made them ceremonially unclean. Therefore, the implication is that the Gospel came first to the social outcasts of Jesus' day. This accounts for the recurring emphasis in Luke of Jesus' identification with both the poor and the societal outcasts of His day. He ate with "sinners" (**Luke 7:37–39; 19:7**). He said that He did not have a place to lay His head (**Luke 9:58**; cf., **Matthew 8:20**). He declared that He was commissioned to preach and care for the poor, the sick, and the less privileged in the society (**Luke 4:18–19**). Even at death He was buried in a borrowed grave (**Matthew 27:57–60**).

12 And this shall be a sign unto you; Ye shall find the babe wrapped in swaddling clothes, lying in a manger. 13 And suddenly there was with the angel a multitude of the heavenly host praising God, and saying, 14 Glory to God in the highest, and on earth peace, good will toward men.

After the announcement, the angel did not instruct the shepherds to go and see the Child.

He assumed they would. However, he did inform them how they would recognize Him. They would find Him, rather than being surrounded by grandeur and glory, wrapped in swaddling clothes and lying in a manger. This information was necessary because there are probably other children born in Bethlehem on this same day, but no others would be lying in a manger. As the angel announced the news to the shepherds, he was suddenly joined by "a multitude of the heavenly host praising God." The word "host" (Gk. *stratia*, **stra-tee-AH**) means an army. "Multitude," *plethos* (Gk. **PLAY-thos**), quantifies the number of these angels that appear before the shepherds as a great or large number, probably too many to count. The host is described as "heavenly," which means they are celestial beings or angels. The heavenly host filled the air with praises to God singing, "Glory to God in the highest, and on earth peace, good will toward men." What does this host of angels mean by the song? What message do they convey through this chorus?

By the phrase "glory to God in the highest," the angels seem to declare the purpose of the birth of the newborn Child. His birth brings the highest degree of glory to God. Here the angels foresaw the ultimate purpose of Christ on earth, i.e., to glorify God through His death and resurrection. Creation glorifies God, but not so much as redemption. The heavenly hosts not only praise God but they also bless those on earth with peace. The NLT more clearly captures the sense of the Greek here than KJV: "and peace on earth to those with whom God is pleased." Jesus' birth brings a blessing of peace to such people. Isaiah said centuries before that He shall be called "the Prince of Peace" (**Isaiah 9:6**). Thirdly, the birth of Christ reveals God's "good will" for humankind. Right from Creation, God has never willed otherwise. His desires for humanity have always been for our good or wellbeing, and He seeks to convince us of that desire. We can see this through the creation narrative (**Genesis 1:28–31**). The psalmist said, "The LORD God is a sun and shield ... no good thing will he withhold from them that walk uprightly" (**Psalm 84:11**). The Lord through Jeremiah assured Israel of His desire for them, "For I know the thoughts that I think toward you, saith the LORD, thoughts of peace, and not of evil, to give you an expected end" (**Jeremiah 29:11**). God's wish for mankind is to "have all men to be saved" (**1 Timothy 2:4**). Peter wrote, "The Lord is not ... willing that any should perish, but that all should come to repentance" (**2 Peter 3:9**). Here the angels proclaim the wish of God for all for us.

SEARCH THE SCRIPTURES

QUESTION 1

How did the angels say the shepherds would find the baby?

LIGHT ON THE WORD

The Good News

The angel of the Lord quickly reassured these fearful shepherds by announcing good news of "great joy." The angel told the shepherds that he brought a message that should evoke the opposite feelings. Whereas the shepherds were afraid after having been startled by the angel, the angel said the message of Jesus' birth should turn their fear into joy!

II. THE SHEPHERDS SPREAD THE MESSAGE (vv. 15–18)

After receiving the news of Jesus' birth from the angel of the Lord and witnessing the multitude of angels praising God, the shepherds did two things: they believed the message was from God, and they went to see this child. Their excitement is obvious! "Let us now go even unto Bethlehem, and see this thing which is come to pass, which the Lord hath made known to us" (from **v. 15**). Then instead of delaying, the shepherds acted "with haste" (**v. 16**). The shepherds' belief in the angel's message and their prompt journey to Bethlehem are remarkable.

The Strange Event (verses 15–18)

15 And it came to pass, as the angels were gone away from them into heaven, the shepherds said one to another, Let us now go even unto Bethlehem, and see this thing which is come to pass, which the Lord hath made known unto us. 16 And they came with haste, and found Mary, and Joseph, and the babe lying in a manger.

After these spectacular and supernatural happenings, the shepherds decided to go to Bethlehem to see for themselves what the angels had told them. They never questioned or doubted the story, but went rather to see this strange event which the Lord had revealed to them through the angels. The clause "which the Lord hath made known unto us" confirms the fact that they accepted the message of the angels as truth from God. Hence, they hurried with excitement into Bethlehem to visit the newborn child. They find not only what the angel has told them concerning the child (**v. 12**), but they also saw Mary and Joseph with the baby in the manger. What happened to their flocks, whether the shepherds left them by themselves under the protection of God or under the care of some other people, the Bible does not tell us. How they found the right manger, the Bible does not say. However, the verb used here, "found" (Gk. *aneurisko*, **an-yoo-RIS-ko**), seems to show that they searched before they found the child.

17 And when they had seen it, they made known abroad the saying which was told them concerning this child. 18 And all they that heard it wondered at those things which were told them by the shepherds.

The shepherds were the first to hear the Good News of the birth of the Savior; they were also the first to proclaim it to others. Their message was simple; they declared what the angels told them concerning the child, and what they had seen. Their message left the listeners with wonder and marvel. However, "Mary kept all these things, and pondered them in her heart." "All these things" includes the story the shepherds told—the appearance of the angel and the heavenly host. This story adds to the chain of miraculous events regarding the Christ, which began with the initial visit of Gabriel announcing to Mary that she would be the mother of the Messiah. The word "kept" is the Greek *suntereo* (**soon-tay-REH-oh**), and means to preserve, to conserve something of great importance. Hence, it is translated as "treasured" by New American Standard Bible and New International Version.

SEARCH THE SCRIPTURES

QUESTION 2

Where did the angels go after they appeared before the shepherds?

LIGHT ON THE WORD

The Angel of the Lord

When the shepherds saw Jesus and realized that things were as the angel of the Lord had announced (**v. 17**), they could not contain what they heard; they shared it with those present, who reacted with wonder. It is not clear what they were most surprised by: perhaps by their receiving this message, or the message itself—that is, perhaps they wondered how this baby in the manger would be the Savior and the Messiah they anticipated from the Lord.

III. MARY AND THE SHEPHERDS RESPOND (vv. 19–20)

Mary's response to the shepherds' statements was different from the others'. Whereas they wondered at the shepherds' words, Mary pondered them "in her heart." The language here might suggest that unlike the others, Mary's reaction was internal and private, while the others outwardly responded.

Mary and the Shepherds' Responses (verses 19–20)

19 But Mary kept all these things, and pondered them in her heart. 20 And the shepherds returned, glorifying and praising God for all the things that they had heard and seen, as it was told unto them.

Mary preserved the words of the shepherds in her heart with all the strange things that had been taking place, and she meditated upon them as future events unfolded.

After visiting the newborn, and finding the child as the angels had told them, the shepherds returned, glorifying and praising God. The object of their joyful praise is obvious—the long-expected Messiah is born and they have been witnesses. The birth of a Redeemer brings joy and peace to those who accept Him. Here the shepherds accepted the good tidings. Therefore, they praised and worshiped the Lord, and proclaimed to others the wonders of God's dealing with mankind. Like the shepherds, we are called to declare the birth of the Savior and His purpose to the world. Christ was born to bring peace and redemption. This event occurred over two thousand years ago, but it is still as relevant today as it was then. He came that we might have peace, He suffered that we might be healed, and He died that we might live. That is the message of Christmas.

LIGHT ON THE WORD

The Shepherds Praise the Lord

Following Mary's reaction is the shepherds' response to the unfolding events. Like the angels who had appeared before them, the shepherds now glorify and praise God to others. Like the angels, they experience the same joy and thankfulness to God, and they respond with worship.

BIBLE APPLICATION

AIM: Students will know that God sent Jesus into the world as the Redeemer of lost people.

"News is like the new reality show," it has been said. Our culture has become so obsessed with news that you can find it anywhere and at anytime you want. News has almost become entertainment. You can get rapid news updates on your smartphone, Facebook, and Twitter. The unfortunate thing is that we often pay too much attention to stories that don't matter; and the stories that do matter hardly affect us because we've become so numb to hearing them all the time. In our news society, how are we hearing the "good news" of Jesus' birth that the angel of the Lord announced to the shepherds?

STUDENTS' RESPONSES

AIM: Students will respond to the birth of Christ by glorifying and praising God and by telling others.

How can you read the story of Jesus afresh and with joy? Take time during this season to read through the story in different ways, each time concentrating on what Jesus' coming into the world truly means. Try reading it aloud. Another time, try doing a slow reading (concentrating on each word). Read it at home with your family. Read it outside in an open field or area. Read it in a public place, focusing on what the "good news" might mean to the people around you. And finally, remember what it means in your life, and allow yourself to be drawn to worship and praise God.

PRAYER

Glory to our God! There is no other God like

Him. The Lord refreshes our spirit. Let us rejoice and be exceedingly glad that we serve a God who cares about all of creation. In Jesus' Name we pray. Amen.

HOW TO SAY IT

Historicity.	Hi-sto-**RI**-ci-tee.
Caesar.	**CEE**-zer.
Augustus.	au-**GU**-stus.

PREPARE FOR NEXT SUNDAY

Read **Matthew 14:22–36** and study "In Awe of Christ's Power."

DAILY HOME BIBLE READINGS

MONDAY
Give Thanks to God's Holy Name
(1 Chronicles 16:35–41)

TUESDAY
Praising and Thanking God Together
(2 Chronicles 5:2–14)

WEDNESDAY
The Heavens Proclaim God's Handiwork
(Psalm 19)

THURSDAY
God's Glory Over All the Earth
(Psalm 108:1–6)

FRIDAY
Our Hope of Sharing God's Glory
(Romans 5:1–5)

SATURDAY
Expecting a Child
(Luke 2:1–7)

SUNDAY
A Savior Born This Day
(Luke 2:8–20)

Sources:

Alexander, David and Pat Alexander. *Eerdmans Handbook to the Bible*. Grand Rapids, MI: Wm.B. Erdmans Publishing Co., 1992.

Green, Joel B and Scot McKnight. *Dictionary of Jesus and the New Testament*. Downers Grove, IL: InterVarsity Press, 1992.

COMMENTS / NOTES:

IN AWE OF CHRIST'S POWER

BIBLE BASIS: MATTHEW 14:22–36

BIBLE TRUTH: Matthew tells about the times when Jesus miraculously walked on water to meet his disciples in a boat, which led them to worship him as truly the Son of God, and when Jesus healed the sick.

MEMORY VERSES: "And when they were come into the ship, the wind ceased. Then they that were in the ship came and worshipped him, saying, Of a truth thou art the Son of God" (Matthew 14:32–33).

LESSON AIM: By the end of the lesson, your students will: review the disciples' response to Jesus' miracles; be inspired by the miracles of Jesus and yearn to become faithful worshipers; and believe in Jesus' miracles and commit to being prayerful encouragers of others.

TEACHER PREPARATION

MATERIALS NEEDED: Quarterly Commentary/Teacher Manual, Adult Quarterly, Adult resources—charts, worksheets, and other teaching tools, paper, pens, pencils, Bibles (several different versions)

OTHER MATERIALS NEEDED / TEACHER'S NOTES:

LESSON OVERVIEW

LIFE NEED FOR TODAY'S LESSON
Many things inspire awe in people.

BIBLE LEARNING
Jesus' miracles are evidence of His divinity.

BIBLE APPLICATION
Christians should be inspired by the miracles of Jesus and yearn to become faithful worshipers.

STUDENTS' RESPONSES
Christians are comforted and encouraged by Jesus.

LESSON SCRIPTURE

MATTHEW 14:22–36, KJV

22 And straightway Jesus constrained his disciples to get into a ship, and to go before him unto the other side, while he sent the multitudes away.

23 And when he had sent the multitudes away, he went up into a mountain apart to pray: and when the evening was come, he was there alone.

MATTHEW 14:22–36, NIV

22 Immediately Jesus made the disciples get into the boat and go on ahead of him to the other side, while he dismissed the crowd.

23 After he had dismissed them, he went up on a mountainside by himself to pray. Later that night, he was there alone,

24 But the ship was now in the midst of the sea, tossed with waves: for the wind was contrary.

25 And in the fourth watch of the night Jesus went unto them, walking on the sea.

26 And when the disciples saw him walking on the sea, they were troubled, saying, It is a spirit; and they cried out for fear.

27 But straightway Jesus spake unto them, saying, Be of good cheer; it is I; be not afraid.

28 And Peter answered him and said, Lord, if it be thou, bid me come unto thee on the water.

29 And he said, Come. And when Peter was come down out of the ship, he walked on the water, to go to Jesus.

30 But when he saw the wind boisterous, he was afraid; and beginning to sink, he cried, saying, Lord, save me.

31 And immediately Jesus stretched forth his hand, and caught him, and said unto him, O thou of little faith, wherefore didst thou doubt?

32 And when they were come into the ship, the wind ceased.

33 Then they that were in the ship came and worshipped him, saying, Of a truth thou art the Son of God.

34 And when they were gone over, they came into the land of Gennesaret.

35 And when the men of that place had knowledge of him, they sent out into all that country round about, and brought unto him all that were diseased;

24 and the boat was already a considerable distance from land, buffeted by the waves because the wind was against it.

25 Shortly before dawn Jesus went out to them, walking on the lake.

26 When the disciples saw him walking on the lake, they were terrified. "It's a ghost," they said, and cried out in fear.

27 But Jesus immediately said to them: "Take courage! It is I. Don't be afraid."

28 "Lord, if it's you," Peter replied, "tell me to come to you on the water."

29 "Come," he said. Then Peter got down out of the boat, walked on the water and came toward Jesus.

30 But when he saw the wind, he was afraid and, beginning to sink, cried out, "Lord, save me!"

31 Immediately Jesus reached out his hand and caught him. "You of little faith," he said, "why did you doubt?"

32 And when they climbed into the boat, the wind died down.

33 Then those who were in the boat worshiped him, saying, "Truly you are the Son of God."

34 When they had crossed over, they landed at Gennesaret.

35 And when the men of that place recognized Jesus, they sent word to all the surrounding country. People brought all their sick to him

36 and begged him to let the sick just touch the edge of his cloak, and all who touched it were healed.

36 And besought him that they might only touch the hem of his garment: and as many as touched were made perfectly whole.

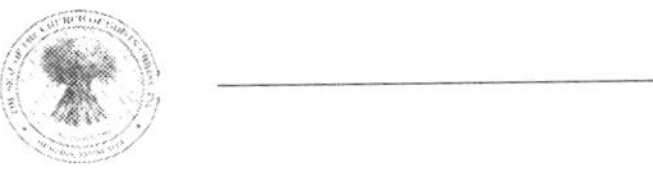

LIGHT ON THE WORD

Although not explicit in Matthew's account, it is more clear on Mark's Gospel (**6:45–53**) that Jesus walked on the Sea of Galilee, located north of Jerusalem. Scholars estimate that Jesus did many of His most notable miracles, at least eighteen, in and around the communities bordering this body of water.

TEACHING THE BIBLE LESSON

LIFE NEED FOR TODAY'S LESSON

AIM: Students will learn that many things inspire awe in people.

INTRODUCTION

His Unquestionable Power

In the preceding verses, Jesus dealt with the devastating news of the imprisonment and execution of his cousin John the Baptist at the hands of Herod the tetrarch (**Matthew 14:1–13**). He sought to get away from the crowd and retreated by Himself to a remote place to rest. However, crowds of people from surrounding towns began to seek after Jesus. As the evening set in, the disciples sought to send the people on their way to fend for themselves for dinner, but Jesus objected. He ordered His disciples to give the people something to eat. The disciples were perplexed at Jesus' command, but it was all a setup for a display of His unquestionable power and convincing proof of His ability to defy natural law. With five loaves and two fishes, Jesus blessed His Father and turned little into overflow, feeding five thousand men, not including women and children (**Matthew 14:13–21**). After this, Jesus sent the disciples away by boat to the other side of the Sea of Galilee while He recharged in prayer.

BIBLE LEARNING

AIM: Students will know Jesus' miracles are evidence of His divinity.

I. JESUS REPLENISHES HIS POWER (Matthew 14:22–23)

Jesus, after His exhausting time of ministry and meeting the spiritual and natural needs of the people, again seeks to commune alone with His Father in prayer. Jesus sends the disciples ahead of Him by boat while dismissing the crowds that gathered to see Him. He sought to be alone with His Father to recharge and regroup.

Time to Leave (verses 22–23)

22 And straightway Jesus constrained his disciples to get into a ship, and to go before him unto the other side, while he sent the multitudes away.

Jesus multiplied bread for five thousand people in a desert place (**vv. 13–21**) where He had retreated with His disciples. His withdrawal was motivated by a report of Herod's beheading of His cousin John the Baptist and by the king's comments about Him and the miracles He was performing (**vv. 1–2, 13**). After feeding the people with the bread, they were overwhelmed and wanted to appoint Him king (**John 6:15**). Jesus rejected this as a potential threat to His mission on earth. Jesus' purpose on earth was to serve, not to be served (**Matthew 20:28; Mark 10:45**, NLT).

This situation led Jesus to constrain His disciples to leave the scene immediately while He dismissed the crowd. The Greek word for constrained is *anagkazo* (**aw-nawng-KAD-zo**) which means to physically or mentally compel or force somebody to do something. It is derived from *anagke* (Gk. **aw-NAWNG-kay**), which means necessity or need. There was an imperative motive for Jesus to send His disciples ahead. Carson states that Jesus wanted to "tame a messianic uproar" (Matthew, 343).

The disciples had to go to "the other side," which according to scholars refers to the western side of the Sea of Galilee. However, the synoptic parallel in Mark adds "to Bethsaida" (**6:45**), where **Luke 9:10** also locates the feeding of the five thousand. Some scholars suggest that the desert place where the feeding took place was closer but separated from Bethsaida by a bay. Jesus intended the disciples to wait for Him at Bethsaida, but the contrary wind took them to Gennesaret. A similar situation happened in **Acts 27:15**, where the boat driving Paul and the other crew members was carried away from its initial course by a strong wind.

23 And when he had sent the multitudes away, he went up into a mountain apart to pray: and when the evening was come, he was there alone.

After He has sent them away, He climbed the mountain to communicate with the Father. At some critical periods of Jesus' earthly ministry, He isolated Himself from the crowd and even His disciples to pray. **Luke 5:16** explains that Jesus was withdrawing in the wilderness for prayer in periods of great popularity. In **Matthew 6:6**, Jesus entreats us to withdraw in our closet to pray to God. It is therefore important for us Christians today to emulate our Lord and retreat ourselves from noise and busyness at times to pray.

He was alone at evening. We should not be confused about the use of "evening" twice in this chapter in the narrative sequence. The Jews divided the day into three periods: morning, noon, and evening (cf. **Psalm 55:17**). The evening was in turn subdivided into two parts: the first evening began at sunset (twilight) and the second began when the sun was fully set (dusk) (cf. **Exodus 12:6,** literally "between the evenings"). The Greek word for evening was *opsios* (**OP-see-os**) which could refer either to the period before sunset or right after sundown, but was sometimes used for the two. In context, however, it is logical to ascribe the first mention of evening (**Matthew 14:15**) to the first evening and the current one after sunset. Jesus was left praying alone when it was night.

LIGHT ON THE WORD

A Time for Empowerment

In this scene, we see the humanity of Jesus and the dependency that He had on the Father and the Holy Spirit in His daily life and ministry. Through Jesus, we have a model for how we should carve out time away from the busyness of life to steal away with the Father. In His presence we are refreshed, renewed, and empowered to continue on with His purpose. It sets the perfect stage for the next scene, in which we see the perfect exhibition of the divinity of Jesus Christ.

II. JESUS DEFIES THE LAWS OF NATURE (vv. 24–27)

Matthew shifts the scene. While on the boat, the disciples encounter torrential winds and waves in their travel, which is very unsettling even for the trade fishermen to navigate. In this brewing storm, between 3 and 6 o'clock in the morning, the disciples see a figure walking toward them and become terrified. Out of fear, their imaginations take them to the worst possible scenario, and they conclude that it was a threatening figure. They begin to scream out with terror, "It's a ghost!" not realizing that it was Jesus (**v. 26**, NLT). Upon their reaction, Jesus immediately calls on His disciples to calm down and "take courage" (**v. 27**, NLT) because He has arrived on the scene among the waves and wind.

The Strength of Contrary Winds (verses 24–27)

24 But the ship was now in the midst of the sea, tossed with waves: for the wind was contrary.

While Jesus was on the mountain praying, the disciples were on the sea tossed with waves. They encountered a contrary wind that would eventually lead them to Gennesaret. **Mark 6:48** tells us that Jesus saw that the disciples were battling with the contrary wind. We cannot be certain if Jesus saw them physically or supernaturally. The current event is taking place after they had left the desert place for quite a long time. Still, John states that it was already night when they encountered the wind. It would have been difficult for Jesus to see from such a long distance. Some suggest that it was the full moon and Jesus could see from the mountain. In any case, if Jesus in the beginning of His ministry could see Nathanael (**John 1:50**) from afar, it is not unlikely that He could see the disciples by the divine endowments of the Holy Spirit.

25 And in the fourth watch of the night Jesus went unto them, walking on the sea.

The Jews divided the night into three watches and the Romans divided it into four between 6 p.m. and 6 a.m. Jesus therefore came to the disciples between three and six o'clock in the morning. Around this time, Jesus appeared to them in an unprecedented fashion by walking on the sea. Great figures of Old Testament history such as Moses, Joshua, Elijah, and Elisha did miracles involving parting of water bodies, but never has it been recorded that anyone walked on water (**Exodus 14:21, 22; Joshua 3:15–17; 2 Kings 2:8, 14**). This action of Jesus clearly portrays His divine nature. There was probably no boat left for Him to join the disciples.

26 And when the disciples saw him walking on the sea, they were troubled, saying, It is a spirit; and they cried out for fear.

The disciples saw someone walking on water at night and with a contrary wind. The disciples could not fathom this scene, assuming the being they saw was a spirit. The Greek word for spirit here is *phantasma* (**FAN-tas-mah**), meaning phantom or "a ghost" (NLT). Our perception of reality always shapes our responses and reactions. They expressed their inner feelings of fear outwardly by a strident noise. Their fear could have been due to prevailing cultural beliefs of the time. In the ancient Near East, the sea was thought to be the realm of powerful, chaotic beings (cf. **Job 41; Revelation 13:1**). They undoubtedly thought Jesus was a "ghost" that would do them harm. Their deduction that it was a ghost led them to fear, *phobos* (**FOB-os**), which means fear, dread, terror—that which is caused by intimidation or adversaries. Hagner compares the "fear of the disciples" to that of "all who are threatened by insecurity in the face of the unknown" (425).

27 But straightway Jesus spake unto them, saying, Be of good cheer; it is I; be not afraid.

The Lord is always prompt in coming to rescue us. "Be of good cheer" or "do not be afraid" (NLT) are phrases of encouragement and comfort. It resonates when we have a challenging task ahead; it will re-echo if we are in peril or in the face of danger, such as the current case facing the disciples.

The Lord wants us to "be of good cheer" and not be afraid because of His presence. "It is I" is the translation of *ego eimi* (Gk. **eg-O ay-MEE**), which echoes the "I am" God's self-revelation to Moses in **Exodus 3:14** and other similar passages like **Isaiah 43:12**. We have this promise of Jesus in **Matthew 28:20**: "I am with you always, even to the end of the age" (NLT). We should therefore not be afraid even in our darkest circumstances or the most violent storm of our lives.

LIGHT ON THE WORD

Faith in Jesus

Jesus' appearance on the water is not an everyday occurrence, and it is not something that has been repeated. He defies all natural laws by walking on the water. Scholars are still trying to rationalize how this could have happened, and if it really occurred as recorded. However, as Christians, we accept it as truth because the One who created the seas has the power to walk on them and is sovereign over all the earth.

III. JESUS CALLS PETER TO STEP OUT (vv. 28–29)

Peter, being often the spokesman of the group and bold enough to ask the tough questions, puts Jesus to the test after hearing His voice. Peter responds, "Lord, if it's really you, tell me to come to you, walking on the water" (**v. 28**, NLT). It was Peter's personality to take Jesus at His word and take risks of faith which would prove to be invaluable for his future role in the church.

Peter's Faith (verses 28–29)

28 And Peter answered him and said, Lord, if it be thou, bid me come unto thee on the water.

Peter's request was not portraying a doubt about the identity of the one walking on water. Carson suggests the phrase "since it is you" is an acceptable rendering of "if it be thou." Peter is an extrovert as far as personality is concerned. His request might have been guided by the delegation of power Jesus granted them in **Mark 6:12, 13, 30** over sicknesses and demons. Since it was the Lord, He can grant Peter with this authority over physical laws also.

29 And he said, Come. And when Peter was come down out of the ship, he walked on the water, to go to Jesus.

Jesus granted Peter's request by the word "come." It should not be perceived here as a mere invitation but rather as a delegation of power or a transfer of authority. Peter therefore took the first step and came out of the ship. Once he was out of the boat and on the sea, he could walk just as Jesus was doing. **John 14:12** says that "anyone who believes in me will do the same works I have done..." (NLT).

SEARCH THE SCRIPTURES

QUESTION 1

What was Peter's response to the sight of Jesus walking on water?

LIGHT ON THE WORD

Walking on Water

No one since has successfully walked on water, but in the Spirit, as we receive a word from the Lord to do something, we have the ability to defy the odds through the power of the Holy Spirit. Jesus said: "Verily, verily, I say unto you, He that believeth on me, the works that I do shall he do also; and greater works than these shall he do; because I go unto my Father. And whatsoever ye shall ask in my name, that will I do, that the Father may be glorified in the Son" (**John 14:12–13**, KJV).

IV. JESUS' POWER DECLARED (vv. 30–36)

We can only imagine what the other disciples were thinking as Peter launched out into the deep. As he continued, he began to notice within his natural senses what was happening around him and became afraid. The wind got stronger, and as it pressed his body, he began to get nervous, which caused him to take his eyes off Jesus. Again, how often do we take our eyes off Jesus when things don't look like what we expect, even though we have been given a word from the Lord to go forward in faith?

Peter's Fear (verses 30–36)

30 But when he saw the wind boisterous, he was afraid; and beginning to sink, he cried, saying, Lord, save me.

We can perform greater works by faith as long as we keep on looking at the Lord who instructs us. Anytime we shift our focus from the Lord to the challenge, we will start to experience failure. Here Peter fails to look at the Lord, who instructed him to come, but rather focused on the wind.

When Peter realized he was sinking, he cried to Jesus, saying, "Lord save me." Our faith may fail us at times, but ultimately Jesus is our last recourse in peril or danger. Instinctively, Peter cried out of fear and despair for the rescue of the Lord.

31 And immediately Jesus stretched forth his hand, and caught him, and said unto him, O thou of little faith, wherefore didst thou doubt?

Jesus did not tarry in rescuing Peter. Without any delay, He stretched His hand to seize the drowning Peter. Peter walked quite a distance since Jesus could just stretch His hand to get hold of Him.

Jesus rebuked him after He got hold of him. The Greek word for "little faith" is *oligopistos* (**o-lee-GO-pis-tos**), and it is used only by the Lord to gently rebuke His disciples for their anxiety. Our cry of desperation will always be heard, and God will swiftly deliver us from our trouble, but we must expect a gentle rebuke from our loving Lord. This word suggests a quantification of faith just as Jesus explained the amount of faith required to move mountains in **Matthew 17:20**.

32 And when they were come into the ship, the wind ceased.

This verse indicates that Peter walked back with Jesus into the boat. When they (Jesus and Peter) entered the ship, the wind ceased.

33 Then they that were in the ship came and worshipped him, saying, of a truth thou art the Son of God.

When the wind ceased, the disciples realized the true personality of Jesus. This man could multiply five loaves of bread for five thousand people, walk on water, and still the wind. Who could that person be except the promised Son of God? The Roman officer and the soldiers made the same confession when they witnessed the events at Jesus' death and were filled with awe (**Matthew 27:50–54**).

The term used for worship is *proskunein* (**pros-KOO-nayn**), which signifies to fall prostrate in front of the one being worshiped. The same word is used when Cornelius welcomed Peter into his house. Peter's objection that he was also a man points to the fact that the term is used only for divine being (**Acts 10:25–26**).

34 And when they were gone over, they came into the land of Gennesaret.

After crossing the lake, they landed at Gennesaret, described as a triangular coastal land on the western side of the lake.

35 And when the men of that place had knowledge of him, they sent out into all that country round about, and brought unto him all that were diseased;

Jesus was already very famous and He could not move unnoticed. John even records that the people who were fed the previous day went after Jesus to the other side of the lake (**John 6:24–25**). The people of that area spread the news about Jesus' arrival in their territory, and they brought sick people to Jesus for healing. The term used to describe the sick people could mean physical or mental illness (Gk. *kakos*, **kaw-KOSE**).

36 And besought him that they might only touch the hem of his garment: and as many as touched were made perfectly whole.

The hem of His garments probably refers to the fringes or tassel at the corner of Christ's mantle; it was a Jewish religious requirement in **Numbers 15:37–39** and **Deuteronomy 22:12**. The request to only touch the fringe of the garments might be due to the crowds at the place. Anyone who was able to touch Him was made perfectly whole, meaning a complete restoration, similar to the woman with the blood issue (**Luke 8:44, 48**).

SEARCH THE SCRIPTURES

QUESTION 2

How did Jesus react to the disciples and Peter's trouble on the water?

LIGHT ON THE WORD

Jesus' Healing Power

After this, Jesus landed on the opposite shore in Gennesaret. The people immediately heard that Jesus was there and sought out His healing and miracles. Jesus' power is evident in the fact that people desired to touch the fringes of His robe in order to be healed. These fringes are actually the tassels spoken of in **Numbers 15:37–41**. For the Jews, they were a reminder to obey God's Word and also a symbol of authority. The passage records that those who touched the fringes were healed. This is a small window into the awesome power of Jesus.

BIBLE APPLICATION

AIM: Students will be inspired by the miracles of Jesus and yearn to become faithful worshipers.

God is still performing signs and wonders today as we call on the name of His Son Jesus. We should seek the Lord's will for our lives to receive vision and be empowered by the Holy Spirit to get in alignment to make the miraculous happen in our age. The same power that raised Jesus from the dead lives within us. Just as the apostles turned the world upside down at the word of the Lord to establish the church, we live on as His fruit on the earth.

STUDENTS' RESPONSES

AIM: Students will be comforted and encouraged by Jesus.

We are encouraged to fix our eyes on Jesus, the Author and Finisher of our faith, who for the sake of the joy set before Him endured the Cross and is seated at the right hand of the throne of God (**Hebrews 12:2**). If we truly believe that Jesus ever lives to make intercession for us, we must trust that we are safe in His arms and follow His lead.

PRAYER

Jesus, thank You for providing for us and protecting us. You are truly a loving and forgiving Savior. In Jesus' Name we pray. Amen.

HOW TO SAY IT

Gennesaret. juh-**NES**-uh-ret.

Galilee. **GAL**-uh-lee.

Bethsaida. beth-**SAY**-uh-duh.

PREPARE FOR NEXT SUNDAY

Read **Luke 11:1–13** and study "A Model for Prayer."

DAILY HOME BIBLE READINGS

MONDAY
By Faith We Please God
(Hebrews 11:1–6)

TUESDAY
Where is Your Faith?
(Luke 8:19–25)

WEDNESDAY
I Believe; Help My Unbelief
(Mark 9:15–24)

THURSDAY
The Light Overpowers Darkness
(John 1:1–9)

FRIDAY
A Mustard-Seed-Sized Faith
(Matthew 17:14–20)

SATURDAY
Great is Your Faith
(Matthew 15:21–31)

SUNDAY
Oh, You of Little Faith
(Matthew 14:22–36)

Sources:

Attridge, Harold et. al. *The Harper Collins Study Bible New Revised Standard Version*. New York: Harper One, 2006. 1693, 1694, 1736.

Bromiley, G. W. *Theological Dictionary of the New Testament*. 7th Edition. Grand Rapids, MI: Eerdmans, 1978.

Carson, D. A. *The Expositor's Bible Commentary with the New International Version*. Grand Rapids, MI: Zondervan Publishing House, 1995.

Fullam, E. L. *Living the Lord's Prayer*. Lincoln, VA: Chosen Books, 1980.

Green, J. B. *The New International Commentary on the New Tesstament: The Gospel of Luke*. Grand Rapids, MI: Eerdmans, 1997.

Hagner, D. A. *Word Biblical Commentary: Matthew 14-28 Vol. 33*. Dallas, TX: Word Books Publisher, 1995.

Hendriksen, W. *New Testament Commentary: Luke*. Carlisle, PA: The Banner of Truth Trust, 1978.

Howard, F. D. *The Gospel of Matthew: A Study Manual*. Grand Rapids, MI: Baker Book House, 1961.

Howard, M. J. *The New International Greek Testament Commentary: The Gospel of Luke*. Grand Rapids, MI: Eerdmans, 1978.

Keener, C. S. *The IVP Bible Background Commentary: New Testament*. Downers Grove, IL: Inter Varsity Press, 1993.

Morris, L. *Tyndale New Testament Commentary: Luke*. Grand Rapids, MI: Eerdmans, 1984.

Nolland, J. *Word Biblical Commentary: Luke 9:21–18:34. Vol. 35B*. Dallas, Texas: Word Books, 1993.

Ryrie, C. C. *The Ryrie Study Bible: New Testament, King James Version*. Chicago, IL: The Moody Bible Institute, 1976.

Tasker, R. V. *Tyndale New Testament Commentaries: Matthew*. Grand Rapids, MI: Wm. Eerdmans Publishing Company, 1961.

Unger, Merrill. *Unger's Bible Dictionary*. Chicago, IL: Moody Press, 1981. 387, 388, 847, 848.

Vine, W. E. *An Expository Dictionary of New Testament Words*. Old Tappan, NJ: Fleming H. Revell, 1966.

Vine, W. E. *An Expository Dictionary of the New Testament Words*. 7th Edition. Old Tappan, NJ: Fleming H. Revell, 1966.

Wilson, N. S., and L. K. Taylor. *Tyndale Handbook of Bible Charts and Maps*. Wheaton, IL: Tyndale House Publisher, 2001.

Zodhiates, Spiros, Baker, Warren. eds. *Hebrew Greek Key Word Study Bible King James Version*. 2nd ed. Chattanooga, TN: AMG Publishers, 1991. 1749, 1766, 51.

COMMENTS / NOTES:

A MODEL FOR PRAYER

BIBLE BASIS: LUKE 11:1–13

BIBLE TRUTH: Jesus teaches that nurturing a relationship with God requires persistent prayer.

MEMORY VERSE: "And he said unto them, When ye pray, say, Our Father which art in heaven, Hallowed be thy name. Thy kingdom come. Thy will be done, as in heaven, so in earth" (Luke 11:2).

LESSON AIM: By the end of the lesson, your students will: understand the Lord's Prayer as a model for praying various kinds of prayers; accept the need for constant prayer; and develop a more disciplined prayer life as a means of growing a relationship with God.

TEACHER PREPARATION

MATERIALS NEEDED: Quarterly Commentary/Teacher Manual, Adult Quarterly, Adult resources—charts, worksheets, and other teaching tools, paper, pens, pencils, Bibles (several different versions)

OTHER MATERIALS NEEDED / TEACHER'S NOTES:

LESSON OVERVIEW

LIFE NEED FOR TODAY'S LESSON
People build intimate, trust-filled relationships by having open communication with one another.

BIBLE LEARNING
Jesus' example for guidance on how to pray in the Gospel of Luke is also found in an example in the Gospel of Matthew.

BIBLE APPLICATION
Christians express faith that they can turn to God in prayers of petition.

STUDENTS' RESPONSES
Students will affirm that God answers prayer.

LESSON SCRIPTURE

LUKE 11:1–13, KJV

1 And it came to pass, that, as he was praying in a certain place, when he ceased, one of his disciples said unto him, Lord, teach us to pray, as John also taught his disciples.

2 And he said unto them, When ye pray, say, Our Father which art in heaven,

LUKE 11:1–13, NIV

1 One day Jesus was praying in a certain place. When he finished, one of his disciples said to him, "Lord, teach us to pray, just as John taught his disciples."

2 He said to them, "When you pray, say: "'Father, hallowed be your name, your kingdom come.

Hallowed be thy name. Thy kingdom come. Thy will be done, as in heaven, so in earth.

3 Give us day by day our daily bread.

4 And forgive us our sins; for we also forgive every one that is indebted to us. And lead us not into temptation; but deliver us from evil.

5 And he said unto them, Which of you shall have a friend, and shall go unto him at midnight, and say unto him, Friend, lend me three loaves;

6 For a friend of mine in his journey is come to me, and I have nothing to set before him?

7 And he from within shall answer and say, Trouble me not: the door is now shut, and my children are with me in bed; I cannot rise and give thee.

8 I say unto you, Though he will not rise and give him, because he is his friend, yet because of his importunity he will rise and give him as many as he needeth.

9 And I say unto you, Ask, and it shall be given you; seek, and ye shall find; knock, and it shall be opened unto you.

10 For every one that asketh receiveth; and he that seeketh findeth; and to him that knocketh it shall be opened.

11 If a son shall ask bread of any of you that is a father, will he give him a stone? or if he ask a fish, will he for a fish give him a serpent?

12 Or if he shall ask an egg, will he offer him a scorpion?

13 If ye then, being evil, know how to give good gifts unto your children: how much more shall your heavenly Father give the Holy Spirit to them that ask him?

3 Give us each day our daily bread.

4 Forgive us our sins, for we also forgive everyone who sins against us. And lead us not into temptation.'"

5 Then Jesus said to them, "Suppose you have a friend, and you go to him at midnight and say, 'Friend, lend me three loaves of bread;

6 a friend of mine on a journey has come to me, and I have no food to offer him.'

7 And suppose the one inside answers, 'Don't bother me. The door is already locked, and my children and I are in bed. I can't get up and give you anything.'

8 I tell you, even though he will not get up and give you the bread because of friendship, yet because of your shameless audacity he will surely get up and give you as much as you need.

9 "So I say to you: Ask and it will be given to you; seek and you will find; knock and the door will be opened to you.

10 For everyone who asks receives; the one who seeks finds; and to the one who knocks, the door will be opened.

11 "Which of you fathers, if your son asks for a fish, will give him a snake instead?

12 Or if he asks for an egg, will give him a scorpion?

13 If you then, though you are evil, know how to give good gifts to your children, how much more will your Father in heaven give the Holy Spirit to those who ask him!"

LIGHT ON THE WORD

In this passage, Jesus speaks of the kingdom of Heaven. The kingdom of God is God's manifested rule on earth as it is in Heaven, bringing forth His way of doing and being in the earth. The theocracy was God's original intent at creation (**Genesis 1:26–31**). The kingdom also refers to the reign of God, which through prayer brings humanity in partnership with God to bring forth His divine rulership in every realm. In Mark and Luke's Gospel, it is mentioned 46 times and is synonymous with the term "kingdom of heaven" in the Gospel of Matthew.

TEACHING THE BIBLE LESSON

LIFE NEED FOR TODAY'S LESSON

AIM: Students will affirm that people build intimate, trust-filled relationships by having open communication with one another.

INTRODUCTION

The Importance of Prayer

Prayer is a major theme of Luke's Gospel. Scholars note that Luke records at least eleven instances of Jesus praying and two times where He teaches His disciples how to pray (**Luke 11:1–13, 18:1–14**). The placement of this discourse on the Lord's Prayer is interesting to note because in the last verses of the previous chapter, Luke shares Jesus' sending out the seventy (**Luke 10:1–12**), where He calls on them to "pray for the Lord of the harvest" to increase the harvest for more laborers in the kingdom. We learn from today's lesson is how prayer and being still enough to listen enable us to tap into God's power.

BIBLE LEARNING

AIM: Students will know that Jesus' example for guidance on how to pray in the Gospel of Luke is also found in an example in the Gospel of Matthew.

I. THE STRUCTURE OF PRAYER (Luke 11:1–4)

This particular text is traditionally noted as a passage taught to be recited, rather than a model for prayer, hence the words "when you pray say." However "The Lord's Prayer" is actually "the disciple's prayer." Many of the men who followed Jesus were first followers of John the Baptist, so they were familiar with the forerunner's practices of spiritual retreats in the wilderness (fasting, prayer, repentance). After walking with Jesus they sensed that there was something different about His posture of prayer, and just as John taught his disciples, they too wanted to be taught by their leader.

Jesus' Prayer Life (verses 1–4)

1 And it came to pass, that, as he was praying in a certain place, when he ceased, one of his disciples said unto him, Lord, teach us to pray, as John also taught his disciples.

The impression Jesus' prayer life created has motivated a disciple to request a teaching on the subject. The identity of the particular disciple is not given in the text and the geographical location of the scene is not stated either. As it would have appeared discourteous and irreverent for the disciple to interrupt Jesus, he therefore waited for Him to finish. The disciple added "as John also taught his disciples," showing that religious leaders taught their followers how to pray. The scenario echoes the centrality of prayer in Jesus' life and presents the disciple's willingness to learn (Green, 438, 440). This suggests that they wanted to grow in the likeness of their Master (**Luke 6:40**).

2 And he said unto them, when ye pray, say, Our Father which art in heaven, Hallowed be thy name. Thy kingdom comes. Thy will be done, as in heaven, so in earth.

Jesus introduced the prayer with the phrase "Our Father which art in heaven." The Greek word for Father is *Pater* (**PA-tair**) with the corresponding Aramaic term *abba* (**AH-bah**). The use of the first person plural "our" suggests that the prayer should be conducted in community with others and it also means that there is a personal relationship between the one praying and God. Christians have a personal God, not an impersonal one.

After the address comes a clause with utmost importance: "hallowed be thy name." Hallowed means "made holy, reverenced." The name is not only a label but also communicates something essential or substantive about the nature of its bearer. The sanctification of the name of God implies two responsibilities. God should sanctify His name, which He never fails to do. It also calls on the one praying to sanctify the name of God by their life (**Isaiah 29:23**). "Thy kingdom come" is a petition for God's reign to be manifested in the world. This has an immediate dimension in everyday life and a future eschatological dimension when God will establish His kingdom at the restoration of all things. In this verse the KJV includes the phrases "which art in heaven" and "Thy will be done, as in heaven, so in earth" but NLT does not. This is because some ancient manuscripts of Luke include these phrases, while others do not. Most scholars think that the manuscripts that add these phrases did so because they are included in Matthew's version (**6:9–10**), so the scribes wanted to harmonize the two passages.

3 Give us day by day our daily bread.

The bread could be anything necessary for the sustenance of physical life, or the provision for human need. The Greek word *epiousios* (**eh-pee-OO-see-os**), translated as "daily," is however difficult to convey because the word has no other known usage. Its only usage in the New Testament is found in **Matthew 6:11** and **Luke 11:3**. Basically it could have two meanings. The traditional one related to time is translated as "daily." In this case it portrays a total dependence on God. The example of the rich fool fits the situation where we are no longer dependent on God but ourselves; he said: "you have enough stored away for years to come. Now take it easy! Eat, drink, and be merry!" (from **Luke 12:19**, NLT). The word also recalls Jesus' warning to let "tomorrow worry about itself" (**Matthew 6:34**, NIV). Others, however, conceived *epiousios* in terms of measure or quantity and therefore assume that it speaks of the appropriate amount for the individual, like in the case of the manna. Both conceptions are important because even in the case of the manna, God wanted to teach the people of Israel to depend on Him. The leftovers from the day before went rotten apart from the reserve for the Sabbath (**Exodus 16:15–24**).

4 And forgive us our sins; for we also forgive every one that is indebted to us. And lead us not into temptation; but deliver us from evil.

The word for forgive here is *aphiemi* (Gk. **ah-FEE-eh-mee**), and it is composed of two words: apo (**ah-POE**), meaning from, and *hiemi* (**HEE-eh-mee**), meaning to send. It therefore means to send forth or send away. When used for debts, it means a complete cancellation, and when used for sins, it means the remission of punishment due to sinful conduct. The clause on forgiveness in the context of this prayer does not suggest that God's forgiveness depends on human activity as we may suppose. We should be mindful as Christians that our salvation is not dependent on our good deeds. However, for our prayers to be answered, we need to be cleansed from our sins, because they might be a barrier to God hearing our prayer (**Isaiah 59:1–2**). The context probably suggests therefore that we forgive our offenders so that God will not hold our sins against us and generate a barrier to the answer.

The Greek word for temptation is *peirasmos* (**pey-ras-MOS**). It also means "trial or test." The petition "lead us not into temptation" is not a suggestion that God tempts His people into sin, for James clearly defeats this conception: "for God cannot be tempted with evil, neither tempteth he any man" (from **James 1:13**, KJV). The source of our temptation is our own desires (**v. 14**). Marshall suggests that "to enter into temptation" does not mean "to be tempted" but rather "to succumb to temptation" (461–462). Keener also, on the basis of other ancient Jewish prayers, suggests a similar reading: "let us not sin when we are tested." This fits with **1 Corinthians 10:13**, which states that when we are tempted, God in His faithfulness will provide us a way out (NIV).

SEARCH THE SCRIPTURES

QUESTION 1

What was Jesus doing before His disciples asked Him to teach them how to pray?

LIGHT ON THE WORD

Key Points of Prayer

Jesus outlines the structure or pattern of prayer for His disciples placing emphasis on five key points: adoration (honoring the Father, coming in humble reverence), submission (His will/kingdom first, His way of doing and being), supplication (asking for His daily provision), repentance (forgiveness of sins, ours and others), and protection (from the evil one and awareness of our own selfishness).

II. PERSISTENT IN PRAYER (vv. 5–8)

What Jesus taught His disciples about prayer was a significant departure from Jewish and other surrounding ancient religious cultures because He reveals God in a personable way. By sharing an example they can relate to, how friends and neighbors treat each other in the time of need, Jesus lets His disciples (and ultimately us) know that God is good, merciful, compassionate, and would not turn us away if we pursue Him for what we need.

Prayer and Friendship (verses 5–8)

5 And he said unto them, Which of you shall have a friend, and shall go unto him at midnight, and say unto him, Friend, lend me three loaves; 6 For a friend of mine in his journey is come to me, and I have nothing to set before him? 7 And he from within shall answer and say, Trouble me not: the door is now shut, and my children are with me in bed; I cannot rise and give thee.

It is suggested that these three verses all constitute one question. The beginning of the question can be rephrased, "Can you imagine..." In other words, Jesus is asking which of them would do what the character portrayed in the example does or wanted to do.

The scenario pictures a single-room peasant home. The father shares the same bed or sleeping mat with the children. For the father to get up and satisfy his friend's request, he must disturb the whole family. The friend who came to ask is short of bread and has a visitor in the middle of the night. It is suggested that three loaves is the appropriate number for an evening meal. The basis for the request is friendship. It is evident from the scenario that none of the hearers will do as the character portrayed. The story suggests that in extreme challenge, when we appeal to friends, they will naturally assist us. It also implies that prayer is an issue of relationship. Indeed, Jesus is our friend (**John 15:15**), and will never let us down when we call on Him. In our need we will find God yet more reliable than any friend, which prepares us for the challenge to trust Him.

8 I say unto you, Though he will not rise and give him, because he is his friend, yet because of his importunity he will rise and give him as many as he needeth.

Friendship should be a sufficient reason for the friend to give a hand of assistance. In case the friend does not value the friendship that much, he will act to avoid the embarrassment to the one seeking or for his "shameless persistence" (NLT). In Nolland's view, God's reliability in comparison to a friend "prepares the challenge to venture with God" (632).

LIGHT ON THE WORD

God Answers Prayer

Jesus taught in **Luke 18:1–8** that as we cry out to God for help and are persistent in looking to Him to meet our needs, He will answer. We do not need to be persistent because God cannot hear, He is toying with us, or He is in need of the attention; the purpose of prayerful persistence is for us to get our minds in accord with His. Hence within Matthew's account following of the Lord's Prayer, we also find Jesus teaching to take no thought for our lives but to seek first the Kingdom and everything else will be added (**Matthew 6:25–33**).

III. PURSUING THROUGH PRAYER (vv. 9–13)

Jesus teaches us how to ask, seek, and knock for the things of God. To ask God for something is to come to Him knowing that He is able to supply. The writer of Hebrews teaches us that we have to come to God with faith believing that He is God and a rewarder of those who diligently seek Him (**Hebrews 11:6**). Jesus teaches that we must come to God knowing He is able to grant or supply our need, and (if we are asking in alignment with His Word) that He will do it for His glory (**John 14:12–14**). If we seek after God, His way of doing and being, we will find Him. Searching for Him is intentional and requires focus.

Seeking God for Help (verses 9–13)

9 And I say unto you, Ask, and it shall be given you; seek, and ye shall find; knock, and it shall be opened unto you. 10 For every one that asketh receiveth; and he that seeketh findeth; and to him that knocketh it shall be opened.

From this example, Jesus entreats the disciples to ask, seek, and knock. To ask is to make a request for something that we do not possess, and it may not require an effort from us to receive it when granted. To seek is to look for something that is lost; it might require effort from us to get it. To knock implies that a closed door needs to be opened. It happens when we want to get access to something which is locked. These three may suggest variants or levels of prayers. Green explains that the instruction to ask, seek, and knock is universal. It is an encouragement "to recognize God's fidelity and expansiveness of his goodness to respond" (The Gospel of Luke, 449).

11 If a son shall ask bread of any of you that is a father, will he give him a stone? or if he ask a fish, will he for a fish give him a serpent? 12 Or if he shall ask an egg, will he offer him a scorpion?

After the example with friendship and the encouragement to ask, seek, and knock, Jesus uses the illustration of a father-son relationship. This means that prayer is above all about relationship. Here Jesus demonstrates a human father's willingness to answer his child's request in spite of his innate wickedness. Human beings are evil by nature; however, they demonstrate kindness to their children. It is very hard to conceive of a father who will do such evil to his child by giving him something that would harm him instead of what he asked for.

13 If ye then, being evil, know how to give good gifts unto your children: how much more shall your heavenly Father give the Holy Spirit to them that ask him?

Jesus then draws the conclusion and proves, as Nolland puts it, that "the fatherhood of God is more dependable than the flawed human fatherhood" (632). God will bestow the Holy Spirit to whomever asks Him. Morris believes this gift of the Spirit refers to the work of the Spirit in Christian life as generally found in **Romans 8** (196). In this case, it may imply an issue of relationship because **Romans 8:9** states "...those who do not have the Spirit of Christ living in them do not belong to him at all" (NLT). Finally, **1 Corinthians 2:12** states that we have received God's Spirit to "know the wonderful things God has freely given us" (NLT). The suggestion is that we should first seek the Spirit, who will lead us to discover all that God has in store for us.

SEARCH THE SCRIPTURES

QUESTION 2

What example does Jesus give to reveal how God the Father responds to our prayers?

LIGHT ON THE WORD

Seeking After God

In a parable, Jesus likens seeking after the kingdom to one who is in pursuit of something valuable and precious (**Matthew 13:44–45**). To seek after God is to esteem Him above all, and Jesus reiterates what Jeremiah prophesied: that God is willing to be found by one in honest pursuit (**Jeremiah 29:13**). Finally, to knock is to approach expecting a welcomed entry.

BIBLE APPLICATION

AIM: Students will express faith that they can turn to God in prayers of petition.

Our Lord encourages us in the prayer of faith as the key to a vibrant relationship with His Father. The Holy Spirit is available to us to guide into truth and reveal the nature and character of God; all we have to do is ask, seek, and knock. What would happen in our communities if we really took God at His word, and through the power of prayer we received the strategy to go into the streets to stop the violence through the power of love?

STUDENTS' RESPONSES

AIM: Students will affirm that God answers prayer.

Jesus says if we "being evil know how to give good gifts to our children how much more will the heavenly Father give the Holy Spirit to those who ask Him!" (**Luke 11:13** paraphrase). As the old saying goes, "much prayer, much power; little prayer, little power; no prayer, no power." We must not be slack in the posture of prayer. As the Lord has taught His disciples, take this lesson and examine your prayer pattern and times of intimacy with the Lord. See where there is room for improvement in your relationship with God.

PRAYER

Precious Lord, we are grateful that You give us the opportunity to pray. You listen to our prayers and respond in Your way, Your time, and in Your mercy. Thank You for Your everlasting love. Hear our prayers O Lord today and the many tomorrows to come. In Jesus' Name we pray. Amen.

HOW TO SAY IT

Persistence. Per-**SIS**-tenz.

PREPARE FOR NEXT SUNDAY

Read **John 17:6–21** and study "Jesus Prays for His Disciples."

DAILY HOME BIBLE READINGS

MONDAY
Whenever You Pray
(Matthew 6:1–8)

TUESDAY
You Shall Not Profane My Name
(Leviticus 22:26–33)

WEDNESDAY
Bless God's Holy Name
(Psalm 103:1–13)

THURSDAY
God's Kingdom Has Come Near
(Luke 10:1–11)

FRIDAY
Do Not Worry about Your Life
(Matthew 6:25–34)

SATURDAY
The Lord Will Not Abandon You
(Psalm 37:27–34)

SUNDAY
Lord, Teach Us to Pray
(Luke 11:1–13)

Sources:

Abraham, Kenneth A. *The Matthew Henry Study Bible, King James Version*. Dallas, TX: World Bible Publishers, 1994. 1990.

Attridge, Harold et al. *The Harper Collins Study Bible New Revised Standard Version*. New York: Harper One, 2006. 1770, 1785–1786.

Cabal, Ted et al. *The Apologetics Study Bible, Holman Christian Standard*. Nashville, TN: Holman Bible Publishers, 2007. 1509, 1536.

Fullam, E. L. *Living the Lord's Prayer*. Lincoln, VA: Chosen Books, 1980.

Green, J. B. *The New International Commentary on the New Testament: The Gospel of Luke*. Grand Rapids, MI: Eerdmans, 1997.

Hendriksen, W. *New Testament Commentary: Luke*. Carlisle, PA: The Banner of Truth Trust, 1978.

Keener, C. S. *The IVP Bible Background Commentary: New Testament*. Downers Grove, IL: Inter Varsity Press, 1993.

Marshall, I. H. *The New International Greek Testament Commentary: The Gospel of Luke*. Grand Rapids, MI: Eerdmans, 1978.

Morris, L. *Tyndale New Testament Commentary: Luke*. Grand Rapids, MI: Eerdmans, 1984.

Nolland, J. *Word Biblical Commentary: Luke 9:21–18:34*. Vol. 35B. Dallas, Texas: Word Books, 1993.

Unger, Merrill. *Unger's Bible Dictionary*. Chicago, IL: Moody Press, 1981. 632.

Vine, W. E. *An Expository Dictionary of the New Testament Words*. 7th Edition. Old Tappan, NJ: Fleming H. Revell, 1966.

Zodhiates, Spiros, Baker, Warren. eds. *Hebrew Greek Key Word Study Bible, King James Version*. 2nd ed. Chattanooga, TN: AMG Publishers, 1991. 1681, 1743.

COMMENTS / NOTES:

JESUS PRAYS FOR HIS DISCIPLES

BIBLE BASIS: JOHN 17:6–21

BIBLE TRUTH: Jesus prayed that the disciples would be united as they brought new people into their community in an unsafe world protected by God.

MEMORY VERSE: "That they all may be one; as thou, Father, art in me, and I in thee, that they also may be one in us: that the world may believe that thou hast sent me" (John 17:21).

LESSON AIM: By the end of the lesson, your students will: review Jesus' prayer for the unity of all who believe in Him; experience intimacy with Jesus and God the Father through prayer; and unite in prayer for one another and for unity in Jesus Christ.

TEACHER PREPARATION

MATERIALS NEEDED: Quarterly Commentary/Teacher Manual, Adult Quarterly, Adult resources—charts, worksheets, and other teaching tools, paper, pens, pencils, Bibles (several different versions)

OTHER MATERIALS NEEDED / TEACHER'S NOTES:

____

____

LESSON OVERVIEW

LIFE NEED FOR TODAY'S LESSON
Small, intimate groups exist within a larger community.

BIBLE LEARNING
Jesus gave God glory for the disciples given to Him.

BIBLE APPLICATION
Christians testify of Christ when nonbelievers ask them about their faith.

STUDENTS' RESPONSES
Through Christ, believers work in unity as God's agents in proclaiming the Gospel of salvation in the world.

LESSON SCRIPTURE

JOHN 17:6–21, KJV

6 I have manifested thy name unto the men which thou gavest me out of the world: thine they were, and thou gavest them me; and they have kept thy word.

7 Now they have known that all things whatsoever thou hast given me are of thee.

JOHN 17:6–21, NIV

6 "I have revealed you to those whom you gave me out of the world. They were yours; you gave them to me and they have obeyed your word.

7 Now they know that everything you have given me comes from you.

8 For I gave them the words you gave me

8 For I have given unto them the words which thou gavest me; and they have received them, and have known surely that I came out from thee, and they have believed that thou didst send me.

9 I pray for them: I pray not for the world, but for them which thou hast given me; for they are thine.

10 And all mine are thine, and thine are mine; and I am glorified in them.

11 And now I am no more in the world, but these are in the world, and I come to thee. Holy Father, keep through thine own name those whom thou hast given me, that they may be one, as we are.

12 While I was with them in the world, I kept them in thy name: those that thou gavest me I have kept, and none of them is lost, but the son of perdition; that the scripture might be fulfilled.

13 And now come I to thee; and these things I speak in the world, that they might have my joy fulfilled in themselves.

14 I have given them thy word; and the world hath hated them, because they are not of the world, even as I am not of the world.

15 I pray not that thou shouldest take them out of the world, but that thou shouldest keep them from the evil.

16 They are not of the world, even as I am not of the world.

17 Sanctify them through thy truth: thy word is truth.

18 As thou hast sent me into the world, even so have I also sent them into the world.

and they accepted them. They knew with certainty that I came from you, and they believed that you sent me.

9 I pray for them. I am not praying for the world, but for those you have given me, for they are yours.

10 All I have is yours, and all you have is mine. And glory has come to me through them.

11 I will remain in the world no longer, but they are still in the world, and I am coming to you. Holy Father, protect them by the power of your name, the name you gave me, so that they may be one as we are one.

12 While I was with them, I protected them and kept them safe by that name you gave me. None has been lost except the one doomed to destruction so that Scripture would be fulfilled.

13 "I am coming to you now, but I say these things while I am still in the world, so that they may have the full measure of my joy within them.

14 I have given them your word and the world has hated them, for they are not of the world any more than I am of the world.

15 My prayer is not that you take them out of the world but that you protect them from the evil one.

16 They are not of the world, even as I am not of it.

17 Sanctify them by the truth; your word is truth.

18 As you sent me into the world, I have sent them into the world.

19 For them I sanctify myself, that they too may be truly sanctified.

19 And for their sakes I sanctify myself, that they also might be sanctified through the truth.

20 Neither pray I for these alone, but for them also which shall believe on me through their word;

21 That they all may be one; as thou, Father, art in me, and I in thee, that they also may be one in us: that the world may believe that thou hast sent me.

20 "My prayer is not for them alone. I pray also for those who will believe in me through their message,

21 that all of them may be one, Father, just as you are in me and I am in you. May they also be in us so that the world may believe that you have sent me.

LIGHT ON THE WORD

One of the sons of Zebedee, this apostle and his brother James were among the first handpicked by Jesus to walk alongside Him and carry on His earthly ministry, as well as establish the church. He is the disciple who is noted in his own Gospel as "the one whom Jesus loved" (**John 13:23, 19:26**), but his weaknesses were also portrayed in the Gospels, such as seeking to call down fire on those who did not receive Jesus (**Luke 9:53–54**).

TEACHING THE BIBLE LESSON

LIFE NEED FOR TODAY'S LESSON

AIM: Students will discover how small, intimate groups exist within a larger community.

INTRODUCTION

The Public and Private Ministry of Jesus

John's Gospel provides a more intimate account of both the public and private ministry of Jesus Christ. The apostle's editorial slant is focused on highlighting Jesus' deity (God incarnate) and His humanity (the Word made flesh who dwelt among humanity). John's Gospel was the last one written, and he does not repeat many of the accounts noted in the other synoptic Gospels (i.e., Matthew, Mark, and Luke). He does still provide convincing proofs of Jesus' messianic authority as "the Christ," Son of the Living God, Savior and Lord. Throughout John's account, Jesus is portrayed as one who stays in complete oneness with His Father and is singularly focused on accomplishing the Father's will. In the chapters leading up to this time of prayer before the Crucifixion, Jesus is careful to prepare His disciples for what is to come: both sorrow and triumphant joy. Most notably, He informs the disciples of the coming Holy Spirit who will be their Helper, Comforter, and Advocate (**John 14:16–17, 26, 15:26, 16:7–8**), and through this unbroken fellowship He will continue to reveal Himself and remain in contact henceforth.

BIBLE LEARNING

AIM: Students will know that Jesus gave God glory for the disciples given to Him.

I. PRAYER FOR UNITY (John 17:6–12)

Jesus acts in His role as High Priest by praying on behalf of His disciples. In the preceding verses, He opens His intimate conversation with His Father by calling attention to the fact that He has accomplished the Father's will on earth, having brought glory to His name as the only true God by using His authority (**John 17:1–5**).

Prayer for Disciples (verses 6–12)

6 I have manifested thy name unto the men which thou gavest me out of the world: thine they were, and thou gavest them me; and they have kept thy word. 7 Now they have known that all things whatsoever thou hast given me are of thee. 8 For I have given unto them the words which thou gavest me; and they have received them, and have known surely that I came out from thee, and they have believed that thou didst send me.

Jesus makes a transition here from praying for Himself (**vv. 1–5**) to praying for His disciples. He begins with a rehearsal of His ministry to them. In His three and half years with the disciples, He had given them the words that God had given to Him. He had revealed to them the glory of God—the glory about which John says, "We beheld [Jesus'] glory, the glory as of the only begotten of the Father" (from **1:14**). And He manifested—revealed—to the disciples the name of the Father. This language of "the name of the Father" appears three more times in this chapter (**vv. 11–12, and 26**) in addition to three other times in the Fourth Gospel (**5:43, 10:25, and 12:28**). The word used here for "name" is *onoma* (Gk. **OH-no-ma**), which means more than just a person's name, but functions more like a title to encompass the person's entire identity and character. Such usage of someone's name is still common in most Middle Eastern and African cultures. In John's language, the name of the Father is the Father Himself, and includes all His attributes (Brown 754–756). In the Old Testament, we find "the name of the Lord" occasionally used in place of "the Lord" (**Isaiah 30:28, 55:13; Psalm 20:7**). Therefore, in revealing the name of the Father to the disciples, Jesus was really revealing the essential nature of who God is and what God does. Indeed, He had told Philip earlier that night, "He that hath seen me hath seen the Father" (**John 14:9**). Jesus came to make God known.

In His prayer, Jesus reveals further that the disciples were given to Him by the Father. Thus, the disciples were God's gift to Jesus—and a means through which Jesus would be glorified (**17:10**). Carson observes that, "Christians often think of Jesus as God's gift to us; we rarely think of ourselves as God's gift to Jesus" (184). The disciples were given to Him by the Father might seem strange since the Gospels tell of Jesus choosing His disciples (**Matthew 4:18–22; Mark 1:16–20, 2:13–14; Luke 5:1–11; John 1:35–51**). However, even for our leaders today, disciples—a title that is closer to students or followers than to members—are given by the Father.

The disciples had received the Father's words, and they had kept them. This is a presumptive statement though, since the disciples evidently did not understand Jesus' mission until much later. However, Jesus was confident that the powerful Word that He had shared with them in the previous months had taken roots. Carson adds, "They may not yet enjoy massive comprehension and profound faith; but at least Jesus can say that the disciples have come to know 'with certainty that I [Jesus] came from you [the Father], and they believed that you sent me" (184). In receiving and keeping Christ's words, the disciples recognized everything Jesus gave them was indeed from God. These words are spirit and life (**6:63**) and are also the word of eternal life (**6:68**).

9 I pray for them: I pray not for the world, but for them which thou hast given me; for they are thine. 10 And all mine are thine, and thine are mine; and I am glorified in them. 11 And now I am no more in

the world, but these are in the world, and I come to thee. Holy Father, keep through thine own name those whom thou hast given me, that they may be one, as we are. 12 While I was with them in the world, I kept them in thy name: those that thou gavest me I have kept, and none of them is lost, but the son of perdition; that the scripture might be fulfilled.

When He offered this prayer, Jesus had come to the very last few hours of His earthly ministry. He had taught His disciples everything He needed to teach them, and now, in the mood of a farewell conversation—one that started in **John 13**—He needed now to pray for them. This prayer takes the form of intercession, *erotao* (**eh-row-TAH-oh**), a Greek word that is translated "to ask, request, or beseech, sometimes on behalf of someone else." Jesus' intercession in this chapter covers not only the 11 disciples who were there with Him, but also many who had believed in Him in the course of His ministry, and many more who would believe in Him in the years to follow (**17:20**). It should encourage the believers of our day that both Christ and the Spirit have continued to intercede for us (**Romans 8:26–27, 34; Hebrews 7:25**). In addition, God expects us to intercede for one another (**Isaiah 59:16**). In interceding for His disciples, Jesus sets a good example of spiritual leadership. Leonard Ravenhill, in Why Revival Tarries, said, "A pastor who is not praying is playing." Leading God's people ought to be first achieved in prayer. Leaders must pray for their followers.

Jesus prayed for the protection of His disciples from disunity and from the evil one. He had been present among them as their leader, but He was soon to leave them as lambs in a world filled with wolves (**Luke 10:3**). There was a real danger of the sheep scattering after the shepherd was taken away. Jesus wants them to stay together, and here, He goes beyond the new commandment—love one another (**John 13:34**)—to loving them in a specific way by praying for them. Jesus is showing us here that there are issues in life that teaching and counseling will not resolve without the help of prayer. Even though all disciples belong to Christ and to the Father (**v. 10**) and are therefore covered and protected in this never-changing relationship with God, praying for them was still very necessary. In this belonging to God, they would glorify Christ (Gk. *doxazo*, **dok-SAHD-zo**: "to lift up, bring honor to, and make glorious," **v. 10**). The lives of the disciples would be a testimony to God's goodness to the world, and through this testimony, Jesus would be glorified, drawing many people to Himself (**John 12:32**).

SEARCH THE SCRIPTURES

QUESTION 1

Did the disciples know that Jesus came from God?

LIGHT ON THE WORD

Jesus Prays for His Disciples

The time has come for Him to return to His Father in Heaven, but before the end of His of earthly ministry, He intercedes on behalf of His chosen disciples who would go on to carry out His ministry. Jesus prays for their deliverance, and He prays for them to be one with Him as He is one with His Father. He prays that through them, His name would continue to be made great. In the power of this unity with God the Father and the Son, the church was born at Pentecost.

II. PRAYER FOR PROTECTION (vv. 13–19)

Jesus was there to guard and protect His disciples from the world and the evil one. Now Jesus intercedes on their behalf that they would be protected, recognizing that all but one would be covered. That one was Judas Iscariot, whom He calls the "son of perdition" or destruction, that the Scripture would be fulfilled.

Prayer of Assurance (verses 13–19)

13 And now come I to thee; and these things I speak in the world, that they might have my joy fulfilled in themselves. 14 I have given them thy word; and the world hath hated them, because they are not of the world, even as I am not of the world. 15 I pray not that thou shouldest take them out of the world, but that thou shouldest keep them from the evil. 16 They are not of the world, even as I am not of the world.

The theme of joy was critical in the tough circumstances around this chapter. However, Jesus prayed in the hearing of the disciples to strengthen their assurance of their relationship with God, and that in being so assured, the joy which Jesus finds in the Father's love may be fully reproduced in the disciples' hearts (Bruce 333). This joy, which is their strength (**Nehemiah 8:10; Hebrews 12:2**), would come through the Word that Jesus had given them and from the memory that He prayed for them on the night He was betrayed. Living in a world that would hate them as it had hated their master, they would need the joy to remain wholehearted in their obedience to His commands (Morris 674). This obedience should not imply that the disciples were robotic followers of Christ. Prior to this prayer, Jesus had called them friends (**John 15:15**).

This small community of believers would be persecuted in the world, but Jesus does not wish them to be spared from the hostility. He only asks the Father to protect them from the evil one through the power of the Father's name, just as he had taught them to pray, "deliver us from the evil one" (**Matthew 6:13**). Of course, in the Jewish thought, the name of the Lord is a strong, protective tower (**Proverbs 18:10**). Sometimes, in the face of persecution and martyrdoms, it seems that they were not protected at all. However, their protection is guaranteed, they are the apple of the Lord's eye, and whatever persecution they encounter, God was always in control. Since they do not belong to this world, God will not leave them alone.

17 Sanctify them through thy truth: thy word is truth. 18 As thou hast sent me into the world, even so have I also sent them into the world. 19 And for their sakes I sanctify myself, that they also might be sanctified through the truth.

To be sanctified is to be set aside for God's purposes. This sanctification involves their consecration for the task entrusted to them; it involves their further inward purity and endowment with all the spiritual resources for carrying out the task (Bruce 334). This work is done by the Holy Spirit through the Word of truth—in John, Jesus is both the Word and Truth—and is directed toward their mission. Jesus was sent by the Father into the world, and now He sends His disciples into the same world. The disciples need to be consecrated to serve as apostles—the "sent ones." The Greek word here is *apostello* (**ah-po-STEL-lo**), which means "to order to go to an appointed place" or "to send away." The entire Christian community is, thus, to be sanctified, as it is an apostolic community sent by Christ to be His witnesses in the world.

As Christ was sent by the Father, He also sent the disciples into the world. The mission of the Christ informs and shapes the mission of the disciples. The Father has sanctified and sent Christ into the world (**John 10:36**), and here we see Jesus praying for the sanctification of the disciples whom He then sends into the world. But the Father had sent Christ in the power of the Holy Spirit. His ministry was inaugurated by His own encounter with the Spirit during

His baptism. The disciples' going into all the world would wait as well for the coming of the Spirit upon them (**Acts 2**). Jesus commanded them not to depart from Jerusalem—not to go anywhere—until they had been endowed with the Spirit's power. Brown observes that even though the Spirit is not mentioned in **John 17**, this whole prayer can be interpreted in terms of the role of the Spirit (766). Indeed, both the sanctification and the sending of the disciples is a work of the Spirit, for without the Spirit, there is no mission.

Jesus also sanctifies Himself for the same purpose of God's mission in the world. This is not sanctification for the remittance of sin or personal holiness, for Christ is the spotless Lamb of God. "His sanctification does not make him any holier, but rather establishes the basis for the disciples' sanctification (Carson, 192). Jesus meant, "For them, I sanctify myself." With the impending Cross on His mind and the disciples hearing Him pray, Jesus sets a basis for the disciples' obedience later by resolving afresh to do the Father's will—which in His case meant death on the Cross. Jesus sets Himself apart to perform the redemptive work on the Cross so that the beneficiaries of that work might set themselves apart for the work of mission (Carson 193). He shows the disciples that the Father's will reigns supreme, and the disciples' best response to God's will is surrender. In this sense, Christ's sanctification resembles the sacrificial lamb being prepared for the offering (Brown 766–767). Christ Himself would later say, "Not my will, but yours be done" (**Luke 22:42**, NIV; see also **Matthew 26:42, John 18:11**).

LIGHT ON THE WORD

A Living Sacrifice

He knows just as He has suffered hatred and rejection, believers would also experience enemy attacks and rejection because of His name, but He has us covered. Jesus also asks that followers past, present, and future be made holy in His truth. For their sakes, He has consecrated Himself as a living sacrifice and stood in the gap on our behalf.

III. PRAYER FOR FUTURE BELIEVERS (vv. 20–21)

Jesus also prays for those who would believe in Him based on their witness. This prayer can be summed up as a desire for a unity that would mimic the unity that Jesus has with the Father. It is a mutual connection where Jesus is one with the Father, and the Father is one with Jesus. Jesus is "in" the Father, and the Father is "in" Jesus. Jesus prays that they would be as close as He and the Father are. This is a huge, all-encompassing prayer that borders on asking for a miracle.

Jesus Prays for all Believers (verses 20–21)

20 Neither pray I for these alone, but for them also which shall believe on me through their word; 21 That they all may be one; as thou, Father, art in me, and I in thee, that they also may be one in us: that the world may believe that thou hast sent me.

Jesus continues to pray even for the future disciples who would believe in Him through the ministry of the apostles. He especially prays for their unity, that they may all be one just like He and the Father are one. He had already taught them that by their love toward one another, the world would know that they are His disciples (**John 13:35**). In this love, they would form a nucleus of a new apostolic community that would live its life through the Holy Spirit while preaching the Good News of salvation to others. Their manifest oneness would give public confirmation both of their relationship with Jesus and that of Jesus with the Father (Bruce 335). This expanding unity would generate a multiplying witness throughout the world, and that is how the church grows (Carson 199). While debates about what this unity looks like continue (see Brown 775), it is helpful to realize that such love is possible through God's power and not only human effort.

SEARCH THE SCRIPTURES

QUESTION 2

Who is Jesus referring to when He says: "Neither pray I for these alone, but for them also which shall believe on me through their word"?

LIGHT ON THE WORD

Believers United

Jesus prays that we as believers would be together and close, just as the first and second Persons of the Trinity. That is beyond our comprehension. Secondly, Jesus asks that the unity of believers would show the world that Jesus was sent by the Father. The unity of the believers would authenticate whether Jesus was sent from God and would cause the world to believe in Him as Savior.

BIBLE APPLICATION

AIM: Students will know that Christians testify of Christ when nonbelievers ask them about their faith.

The text from today's lesson is considered by biblical scholars to be the real Lord's Prayer as we see the passion of the Christ in prayer for all of us. We have to know the thoughtfulness of our Savior in looking through eternity to see not just those who walked with Him during His earthly ministry, but others who would believe far beyond what they could see themselves. Prayer is the most important discipline in the life of a believer to touch and connect with God in Christ as we truly access His power.

STUDENTS' RESPONSES

AIM: Students will affirm through Christ, believers work in unity as God's agents in proclaiming the gospel of salvation in the world.

God has shown us His love through the sending of His Son to die for us. As the church, we must reflect this love by maintaining our relationship with Him and extending this great love out to others. Christ laid the sure foundation for us to be one with the Father by faith, and this oneness is to be manifested in our relationships with other believers. It has been said that the most segregated hour of the week is on Sunday during church. Show our oneness as believers by inviting other believers who are of a different culture or background into your home for a meal and a time of fellowship and prayer.

PRAYER

Jesus, thank You for praying and interceding for us. Your love for us is amazing and a joy in our lives. In Jesus' Name we pray. Amen.

HOW TO SAY IT

Consecration. kon-se-**KREY**-shun.

Crucifixion. kroo-si-**FIK**-shun.

Intercession. in-ter-**SE**-shun.

Gethsemane. geth-**SE**-ma-nee.

Sanctification. sank-ti-fi-**KA**-shun.

PREPARE FOR NEXT SUNDAY

Read **Hebrews 4:14–5:10** and study "Jesus Intercedes for Us."

DAILY HOME BIBLE READINGS

MONDAY
Revealing the Words of the Lord
(Exodus 4:27–31)

TUESDAY
Treasuring God's Word in Your Heart
(Psalm 119:9–16)

WEDNESDAY
Obey the Words of the Lord
(Jeremiah 35:12–17)

THURSDAY
Abide in My Love
(John 15:1–11)

FRIDAY
This is Eternal Life
(John 17:1–5)

SATURDAY
Making Known the Lord's Name
(John 17:22–26)

SUNDAY
Sanctified in the Truth
(John 17:6–21)

Sources:

Abraham, Kenneth A. *The Matthew Henry Study Bible, King James Version.* Dallas, TX: World Bible Publishers, 1994. 2155–2158.

Brown, Raymond Edward. *The Gospel According to John Xiii–Xxi: A New Introduction and Commentary.* Garden City, NY: Doubleday, 1966.

Bruce, F. F. *The Gospel of John: Introduction, Exposition and Notes.* Grand Rapids, MI: Wm. B. Eerdmans, 1983.

Carson, D. A. *The Farewell Discourse and Final Prayer of Jesus: An Exposition of John 14–17.* Grand Rapids, MI: Baker Book House, 1980. 173–207.

Meyer, F. B. *Gospel of John: The Life and Light of Man, Love to the Uttermost.* Fort Washington, PA: Christian Literature Crusade, 1988.

Morris, Leon. *The Gospel According to John: The English Text with Introduction, Exposition and Notes.* Grand Rapids, MI: Eerdmans, 1971. 716-738.

Unger, Merrill. *Unger's Bible Dictionary.* Chicago, IL: Moody Press, 1981. 596.

Zodhiates, Spiros, Baker, Warren. eds. *Hebrew Greek Key Word Study Bible, King James Version.* 2nd ed. Chattanooga, TN: AMG Publishers, 1991. 1709, 1717.

COMMENTS / NOTES:

JESUS INTERCEDES FOR US

BIBLE BASIS: HEBREWS 4:14–5:10

BIBLE TRUTH: God appointed Jesus, the High Priest, as an intercessor on behalf of His people.

MEMORY VERSE: "For we have not an high priest which cannot be touched with the feeling of our infirmities; but was in all points tempted like as we are, yet without sin" (Hebrews 4:15).

LESSON AIM: By the end of the lesson, we will: review how Jesus fulfills the role of intercessor with God for His people; appreciate that Christians do not stand alone before God with their sins; and pray with thanksgiving for our intercessor with God and tell others about Him.

TEACHER PREPARATION

MATERIALS NEEDED: Quarterly Commentary/Teacher Manual, Adult Quarterly, Adult resources—charts, worksheets, and other teaching tools, paper, pens, pencils, Bibles (several different versions)

OTHER MATERIALS NEEDED / TEACHER'S NOTES:

LESSON OVERVIEW

LIFE NEED FOR TODAY'S LESSON

People often have someone who makes special efforts on their behalf.

BIBLE LEARNING

Jesus was the perfect high priest because He was sinless and offered the perfect sacrifice, Himself, so everyone could be forgiven.

BIBLE APPLICATION

Christians approach God with the assurance of acceptance in Jesus Christ.

STUDENTS' RESPONSES

Christians model Jesus' reverent submission to God.

LESSON SCRIPTURE

HEBREWS 4:14–5:10, KJV

14 Seeing then that we have a great high priest, that is passed into the heavens, Jesus the Son of God, let us hold fast our profession.

15 For we have not an high priest which cannot be touched with the feeling of our infirmities; but was in all points tempted like as we are, yet without sin.

HEBREWS 4:14–5:10, NIV

14 Therefore, since we have a great high priest who has ascended into heaven, Jesus the Son of God, let us hold firmly to the faith we profess.

15 For we do not have a high priest who is unable to empathize with our weaknesses, but we have one who has been tempted in every way, just as we are—yet he did not sin.

16 Let us therefore come boldly unto the throne of grace, that we may obtain mercy, and find grace to help in time of need.

5:1 For every high priest taken from among men is ordained for men in things pertaining to God, that he may offer both gifts and sacrifices for sins:

2 Who can have compassion on the ignorant, and on them that are out of the way; for that he himself also is compassed with infirmity.

3 And by reason hereof he ought, as for the people, so also for himself, to offer for sins.

4 And no man taketh this honour unto himself, but he that is called of God, as was Aaron.

5 So also Christ glorified not himself to be made an high priest; but he that said unto him, Thou art my Son, to day have I begotten thee.

6 As he saith also in another place, Thou art a priest for ever after the order of Melchisedec.

7 Who in the days of his flesh, when he had offered up prayers and supplications with strong crying and tears unto him that was able to save him from death, and was heard in that he feared;

8 Though he were a Son, yet learned he obedience by the things which he suffered;

9 And being made perfect, he became the author of eternal salvation unto all them that obey him;

10 Called of God an high priest after the order of Melchisedec.

16 Let us then approach God's throne of grace with confidence, so that we may receive mercy and find grace to help us in our time of need.

5:1 Every high priest is selected from among the people and is appointed to represent the people in matters related to God, to offer gifts and sacrifices for sins.

2 He is able to deal gently with those who are ignorant and are going astray, since he himself is subject to weakness.

3 This is why he has to offer sacrifices for his own sins, as well as for the sins of the people.

4 And no one takes this honor on himself, but he receives it when called by God, just as Aaron was.

5 In the same way, Christ did not take on himself the glory of becoming a high priest. But God said to him, "You are my Son; today I have become your Father."

6 And he says in another place, "You are a priest forever, in the order of Melchizedek."

7 During the days of Jesus' life on earth, he offered up prayers and petitions with fervent cries and tears to the one who could save him from death, and he was heard because of his reverent submission.

8 Son though he was, he learned obedience from what he suffered

9 and, once made perfect, he became the source of eternal salvation for all who obey him

10 and was designated by God to be high priest in the order of Melchizedek.

LIGHT ON THE WORD

A mysterious biblical character, Melchizedek (also referred to as Melchisedec) is first referenced in the book of Genesis as the king of Salem and "priest of the Most High God" (**Genesis 14:17–20**). His encounter with Abram (who would later be renamed Abraham) was after the defeat of Chedorlaomer and the kings allied with him, including the king of Sodom. Abraham's victory was not a single-handed success but was given by the hand of the Lord, who moved on his behalf. In response to God's goodness and honor, Abram gave King Melchizedek, the high priest of the Most High God, one-tenth of the spoils of his victory. This is the first biblicial instance of the tithe, which was custom of the lesser giving to the greater in reverence of His abundant supply. The high priest receives on behalf of the Lord.

TEACHING THE BIBLE LESSON

LIFE NEED FOR TODAY'S LESSON

AIM: Students will often have someone who makes special efforts on their behalf.

INTRODUCTION

Hebrews—A Sound Doctrine to Follow

Scholars' opinion vary on the authorship of Hebrews. Many believe Paul wrote it, even though he did not sign it like his other letters. Nonetheless, it was counted as an inspired source and included in the Bible. A major theme of the book of Hebrews is showing Jesus as the Christ, the Son of God, in His position in the lives of believers as Savior, Priest, and King through His deity and humanity. It should also be noted that this audience of believers was the second generation of the church, who were enduring persecution for their faith. Hebrews sought to provide sound doctrine for them to follow, to further root them in the faith by teaching Christ's superiority over angels and prophets, including Moses, and His position as the great High Priest.

BIBLE LEARNING

AIM: Students will know that Jesus was the perfect high priest because He was sinless and offered the perfect sacrifice, Himself, so everyone could be forgiven.

I. JESUS THE GREAT HIGH PRIEST (Hebrews 4:14–16)

Jesus in His function as our High Priest puts an end to the need to petition anyone else for the forgiveness of sins. The writer reiterates to his audience that Jesus as the Son of God is the profession of the faith, and that because of Him we are able to approach the throne of God. Through this passage, Christians are invited to stand strong in this belief in the face of those who argue differently.

Jesus is Supreme (verses 14–16)

14 Seeing then that we have a great high priest, that is passed into the heavens, Jesus the Son of God, let us hold fast our profession. 15 For we have not an high priest which cannot be touched with the feeling of our infirmities; but was in all points tempted like as we are, yet without sin. 16 Let us therefore come boldly unto the throne of grace, that we may obtain mercy, and find grace to help in time of need.

The author turns our attention to Jesus as the great High Priest. The adjective "great" (Gk. *megas*, **MEH-gas**) places Him in a different category than any other high priest. He is the High Priest of all high priests. The phrase "passed into the heavens" is similar to what the high priest did on the Day of Atonement. He "passed through" the curtain of the Temple and entered the Holy of Holies, where the Ark of the Covenant was placed. The Holy of Holies was where God resided. Jesus' passing into the heavens suggests that He has gone into the very presence of God.

This passage has two admonitions: to hold fast our profession and approach the throne of grace. Both are possible only through Jesus Christ, our great High Priest. Jesus was "touched with the feeling of our infirmities." This does not mean that He experienced every circumstance that we have experienced. It means He experienced and felt what we have felt in our own particular moments of weaknesses and suffering. He has experienced the same emotions and pain. When we pray, we can also approach God with great hope and expectation because we know we will find forgiveness, mercy, and help to overcome our problems. The mention of the "throne of grace" alludes to the area of the Ark of the Covenant which was called "the mercy seat." This was where the high priest sprinkled the blood of the sacrifice to make atonement with God for the people. The author is saying that unlike those other high priests who went into the Holy of Holies trembling, we can come boldly to God because of the work of Jesus our great High Priest.

SEARCH THE SCRIPTURES

QUESTION 1

Where can we go to receive mercy and the grace to help in times of need?

LIGHT ON THE WORD

More than Qualified

Throughout the opening of Hebrews, the writer makes the point that Jesus is the expressed image of God, just as in the world a child is the very reflection of his father in DNA, behavior, and character (**Hebrews 1:3**). Because of what Jesus accomplished through His death and resurrection, He is seated at the right hand of the Father with all power and majesty. This makes Him more than qualified to represent God.

II. JESUS AND EARTHLY HIGH PRIESTS (Hebrews 5:1–6)

The writer goes on to draw comparisons to the office of high priest to show how Jesus perfects the custom. Under the Mosaic Law, God set apart the high priest to represent Himself to the people and the people to Him.

The Responsibilities of a High Priest (verses 1–6)

5:1 For every high priest taken from among men is ordained for men in things pertaining to God, that he may offer both gifts and sacrifices for sins:

This section does not discuss all the features of this office, but highlights those that correspond with what the author wants to say about Jesus as High Priest (**vv. 1–4**). A high priest must be one of the people in order to fulfill his role effectively. He is taken from among men to mediate between them and God. These points are essential in understanding the priesthood of Jesus. One of the functions of a high priest is to "offer both gifts and sacrifices" or to make atonement for sin. The high priest must be holy in all that he is and does. The life of the high priest was governed by a particular set of rules regulating his behavior even down to his apparel when offering sacrifices for the people. The high priest was a representative for the people in "things pertaining to God." Jesus is also holy and pure and able to represent the people before God not because of what He wears or adhering to certain ritual regulations but because He is holy in His very nature.

2 Who can have compassion on the ignorant, and on them that are out of the way; for that he himself also is compassed with infirmity.

Another function of the priest is to empathize with the people. Even though this is not a specific function stated for Aaron, it is implied in his responsibility. The word translated "compassion" is *metriopathe* (Gk. **me-tree-oh-PAH-they**). It is used only here in the New Testament and means to act in moderation or to control one's emotion. A high priest is expected to have compassion toward those who are ignorant and "on them that are out of the way" ("going astray," NIV; see also **Leviticus 4; Numbers 15:22–31**). The high priest is to be compassionate toward those who have ignorantly sinned against the Lord. He should neither dismiss sin lightly nor severely condemn the sinner. He ought to act in moderation. Jesus is able to have compassion because He was a man, and although He was without sin, He could identify with human weakness.

3 And by reason hereof he ought, as for the people, so also for himself, to offer for sins.

The high priest in the Old Testament also had to offer sacrifices for himself (**Leviticus 16:11**) because, like the people, he had sinned. His task, therefore, was not to condemn sinners but to stand in solidarity with them. In doing this he could offer a sacrifice for them. By recognizing his own weakness, he could be deeply compassionate toward and patient with those who were not walking in the truth.

4 And no man taketh this honour unto himself, but he that is called of God, as was Aaron.

A high priest must be "called" (Gk. *kaloumenos*, **ka-LOO-men-ose**) by God. One cannot just decide to enter into this high office and mediate between God and people. Since sinful humanity has violated God's righteous law, we cannot select the mediator. Only God can decide whom He wants as mediator. Aaron and his sons were appointed as priests by God Himself (**Exodus 28**). The connection between this office and Christ's role as High Priest is clearly stated in verse 5.

5 So also Christ glorified not himself to be made an high priest; but he that said unto him, Thou art my Son, to day have I begotten thee. 6 As he saith also in another place, Thou art a priest for ever after the order of Melchisedec.

Although Christ is compared to the high priest and they are both called by God, Christ is superior. In verse 4, the phrase "he that is called of God" indicates that the calling to the office of the high priest is an honor that God gives to whomever He chooses. However, a stronger word, *doxazo* (**dok-SAD-zo**), which means "to glorify, praise, or honor," is used to describe Jesus' becoming High Priest. Christ is glorified or exalted to this office. In **verse 5**, God's call is expressed in the words of **Psalm 2:7** (which was also quoted in **Hebrews 1:5**).

Verse 6 is a quotation of **Psalm 110** (which was also quoted in **Hebrews 1:13**). Unlike Aaron, Melchisedec was both king and priest. No king in Israel functioned as both a king and a priest. As priest and king, Melchisedec had no predecessor and no successor. Similarly, Christ is our High Priest forever. His perfect work of atonement is perpetual; thus, He cannot be succeeded. Jesus Christ is the Son of God, our High Priest and King.

SEARCH THE SCRIPTURES

QUESTION 2

How does Christ as High Priest compare among the priests of the Old Testament?

LIGHT ON THE WORD

The Son, The High Priest

The point the writer makes is that God the Father established His Son as the high priest when we called Him out in His humanity to represent the people by bearing our sins and glorifying His name (**v. 5, John 12:28**).

III. JESUS AND MELCHIZEDEK HIGH PRIEST FOREVER (vv. 7–10)

The writer closes this phase of his argument by introducing the order of Melchisedec and makes the link that Jesus is the High Priest forever. He draws this conclusion because in Old Testament Scripture, Melchisedec has no recorded father, his priesthood predates Aaron's, he is also a king, and he has no recorded end. **Psalm 110:3–5** is a prophetic foreshadow of Christ saying: "The LORD has taken an oath and will not break his vow: You are a priest forever in the order of Melchizedek" (**v. 4**, NLT).

Tears and Prayers (verses 7–10)

7 Who in the days of his flesh, when he had offered up prayers and supplications with strong crying and tears unto him that was able to save him from death, and was heard in that he feared;

Verse 7 emphasizes the humanity of Jesus, which was previously mentioned in **Hebrews 2:9–18**. The phrase "in the days of his flesh" refers to His earthly ministry. The phrase "offered up prayers and supplications" is a reference to Jesus' "High Priestly" prayer in the Garden of Gethsemane (**Matthew 26:36–46; Mark 14:32–42; Luke 22:40–46**). The Gospel accounts clearly describe the fervency and intensity of this prayer. All this shows Jesus can completely empathize with our human condition of weakness.

Jesus prayed for deliverance from death, and He was heard. God's answer was not that He would escape death, but that He would be resurrected. His prayer was heard because He "feared" God (or because of His "reverent submission," NIV). This does not mean that Jesus was afraid of God. Rather, it means that He had the proper attitude of reverence in His duty.

8 Though he were a Son, yet learned he obedience by the things which he suffered;

Through His suffering, Jesus learned obedience. This does not mean that He was at any time disobedient. Rather, He learned how to submit in obedience, laying down His will and rights. The writer engages in wordplay between "learning" (Gk. *mathein*, **MA-thane**) and "suffering" (Gk. *pathein*, **PA-thane**). In doing so, the writer suggests the falsity of the common understanding that obedience always results in peace and disobedience in suffering. Jesus' life and His death on the Cross prove that obedience can lead to suffering.

9 And being made perfect, he became the author of eternal salvation unto all them that obey him;

The phrase "being made perfect" (a single word in Greek; Gk. *teleiothes*, **teh-lay-oh-THASE**) is not a reference to moral perfection but to the satisfactory completion of Christ's role as High Priest. The same word is used in the Greek translation of the Old Testament to mean "consecrated" or "ordained" (**Leviticus 8:33; Numbers 3:3**). Upon completion of this responsibility, Jesus became the "author" or source of eternal salvation for all who obey Him, just as He learned to obey God. The Greek word for "author" (*aitios*, **EYE-tee-os**) could also be translated as "cause." The term "eternal salvation" is to be equated with eternal life, which Christ offers to those who believe in Him. Therefore, the reference to eternal salvation here is a description of Christ's work. His work of procuring salvation as our High Priest is eternally efficacious—a perpetual priesthood.

10 Called of God an high priest after the order of Melchisedec.

Verse 10 ends this discussion of Jesus as our High Priest the way it began: with God's calling. It also introduces the new thought "after the order of Melchisedec," which points to His role as both Priest and King. He is a High Priest, but a different kind of high priest. As the pre-incarnate Son of God, He is one with royal authority.

LIGHT ON THE WORD

Prayer Submission

Melchisedec is the shadow of Christ as he combined kingship and priesthood in his person; Jesus remains in the office of Priest and King forever, which is why we call Him Lord. Jesus in the days of His humanity remained faithful by staying in a posture of prayerful submission to God. The author of Hebrews writes that Christ entered into the heavenly Holy of Holies to apply His blood on the mercy seat on our behalf and now remains in the presence of God to make intercession for us (**Hebrews 9:11–12**).

BIBLE APPLICATION

AIM: Students will know that Christians approach God with the assurance of acceptance in Jesus Christ.

If you ever have need for a lawyer, it is always good to have one who is able to best represent your interest. Isn't it great to know that in Heaven we have the best representation that money cannot buy, but was purchased with the blood of Christ? **Hebrews 7:25** says He lives forever to intercede with God on their behalf. Praise God, Jesus intercedes for us!

STUDENTS' RESPONSES

AIM: Students will model Jesus' reverent submission to God.

Today and throughout the week, reflect on the fact that Jesus ever lives to intercede on your behalf. Live intentionally with the thought that no matter what you experience, there is grace to help in your time of need, and share this grace with others.

PRAYER

Lord, we pray with great joy and thanksgiving for all that You do. We bless You and bow down before You, the High Priest for us all. In Jesus' Name we pray. Amen.

HOW TO SAY IT

Melchisidec. Mel-ki-si-**DEK**.

Infirmity. In-fir-mi-**TEE**.

PREPARE FOR NEXT SUNDAY

Read **James 5:13–18** and study "We Pray for One Another."

DAILY HOME BIBLE READINGS

MONDAY
The Grace of God Has Appeared
(Titus 2:11–15)

TUESDAY
An Advocate with God
(1 John 2:1–6)

WEDNESDAY
Our Faithful High Priest
(Hebrews 3:1–6)

THURSDAY
Jesus Prayed in Anguish
(Luke 22:39–46)

FRIDAY
Gratitude for God's Steadfast Love
(Psalm 107:1–15)

SATURDAY
Boldness and Confidence through Faith
(Ephesians 3:7–13)

SUNDAY
A Great High Priest
(Hebrews 4:14–5:10)

Sources:

Attridge, Harold, et al. *The Harper Collins Study Bible, New Revised Standard Version*. New York: Harper One, 2006. 23.

Cabal, Ted, et al. *The Apologetics Study Bible, Holman Christian Standard*. Nashville, TN: Holman Bible Publishers, 2007. 1821–1822.

Unger, Merrill. *Unger's Bible Dictionary*. Chicago, IL: Moody Press, 1981. 881-886.

Unger, Merrill. *Unger's Bible Handbook: The Essential Guide to Understanding the Bible*. Chicago, IL: Moody Press, 1967. 747, 756–757.

Zodhiates, Spiros, Baker, Warren, eds. *Hebrew Greek Key Word Study Bible, King James Version*. 2nd ed. Chattanooga, TN: AMG Publishers, 1991. 1695, 1761.

COMMENTS / NOTES:

WE PRAY FOR ONE ANOTHER

BIBLE BASIS: JAMES 5:13–18

BIBLE TRUTH: The writer of James teaches that the prayer of faith brings healing and offers Elijah's prayer as an example of prayer's effectiveness.

MEMORY VERSE: "Confess your faults one to another, and pray one for another, that ye may be healed. The effectual fervent prayer of a righteous man availeth much" (James 5:16).

LESSON AIM: By the end of the lesson, we will: explore James' admonitions for prayer and its power to heal; affirm that prayer is powerful and yields good results; and pray for the sick.

TEACHER PREPARATION

MATERIALS NEEDED: Quarterly Commentary/Teacher Manual, Adult Quarterly, Adult resources—charts, worksheets, and other teaching tools, paper, pens, pencils, Bibles (several different versions)

OTHER MATERIALS NEEDED / TEACHER'S NOTES:

____

____

LESSON OVERVIEW

LIFE NEED FOR TODAY'S LESSON
Illness is part of being human.

BIBLE LEARNING
Prayer is talking to God and waiting to hear what God speaks to us.

BIBLE APPLICATION
Believers join with the church in praying for the sick.

STUDENTS' RESPONSES
Believers pray in all situations, both in joyful times and times of trouble.

LESSON SCRIPTURE

JAMES 5:13–18, KJV

13 Is any among you afflicted? let him pray. Is any merry? let him sing psalms.

14 Is any sick among you? let him call for the elders of the church; and let them pray over him, anointing him with oil in the name of the Lord:

15 And the prayer of faith shall save the sick, and the Lord shall raise him up; and

JAMES 5:13–18, NIV

13 Is anyone among you in trouble? Let them pray. Is anyone happy? Let them sing songs of praise.

14 Is anyone among you sick? Let them call the elders of the church to pray over them and anoint them with oil in the name of the Lord.

15 And the prayer offered in faith will

if he have committed sins, they shall be forgiven him.

16 Confess your faults one to another, and pray one for another, that ye may be healed. The effectual fervent prayer of a righteous man availeth much.

17 Elias was a man subject to like passions as we are, and he prayed earnestly that it might not rain: and it rained not on the earth by the space of three years and six months.

18 And he prayed again, and the heaven gave rain, and the earth brought forth her fruit.

make the sick person well; the Lord will raise them up. If they have sinned, they will be forgiven.

16 Therefore confess your sins to each other and pray for each other so that you may be healed. The prayer of a righteous person is powerful and effective.

17 Elijah was a human being, even as we are. He prayed earnestly that it would not rain, and it did not rain on the land for three and a half years.

18 Again he prayed, and the heavens gave rain, and the earth produced its crops.

LIGHT ON THE WORD

The elders were Christians who presided over the gatherings. The term "elder" was taken from the Jewish synagogue. They were the rulers of synagogue life, and this is the function they had in the life of the church. Elders were not always the oldest in terms of age, but had Christian maturity. They were called on to perform certain functions in the church, such as pastoral care and church discipline. In the New Testament, the terms bishops, elders, and presbyters are used interchangably. Historically, these became separate offices and roles in the church.

The word "anointing" means to smear or rub with oil. It was used to designate and bless those who had been chosen by God to carry out a particular task. In the Old Testament, priests and kings were anointed with oil when they were set apart for their office. Anointing was also done to prepare bodies for burial and to refresh the skin after washing. Because of its sacred and religious connotations, it became a symbol of God's presence and power. This is why anointing the sick became a customary Christian ritual, accompanied by prayer for healing.

Elias is the Greek spelling of Elijah. Elijah means "My God is Jehovah." He was a prophet during the reigns of Ahab and Ahaziah. The Bible says that he came from the region of Thisbe (**1 Kings 17:1**) and challenged idolatry. Known for his bold challenging of the monarchy of Israel at the end of his ministry, Elijah was taken up into Heaven to be with God. For this reason, the Jews expected Elijah to return soon in order to prepare the Israelites for the coming of the Messiah.

TEACHING THE BIBLE LESSON

LIFE NEED FOR TODAY'S LESSON

AIM: Students will know that illness is a part of being human.

INTRODUCTION

James, A Book of Wisdom

James has been called the Proverbs of the New Testament, because it is full of wisdom and practical teaching about the Christian life. This epistle was written prior to 70 A.D., but a more precise date is difficult. James 1:1 identifies the author as "James, a servant of God and of the Lord Jesus Christ" (KJV). If this was James the son of Zebedee, he died in the early 40s A.D. (before 44), if James the brother of Jesus, then he died in the 60s A.D. In **James 1:5**, Christians are admonished to ask God for wisdom if they lack it, because God gives wisdom freely and generously.

Some of the themes that are discussed in this epistle are spiritual growth, maturing in Christ, enduring temptation, and demonstrating the faith. James was calling the church to practice holy living. He was encouraging the church to allow their faith to be demonstrated in their lifestyles.

Historically, **James 5:13–18** has been used to claim healing. While healing is addressed, the main idea of the passage is prayer. From Genesis to Revelation, countless examples are given of people entreating God in prayer. In the Old Testament, we read about prayers that moved God to act powerfully and miraculously. David offered prayers of confession for sin. Prophets like Moses and Elijah offered prayers on behalf of Israel for deliverance. In the New Testament, Jesus gives a model for prayer, and New Testament letters often ended with a focus on prayer. James uses this portion of the letter to apply prayer to illness. **James 5:13–18** deals with various issues involving prayer. James here deals with prayer of the individual (**v. 13**), the prayer of the elders (**vv. 14–15**), the prayer of friends and companions for one another (**v. 16**), and the prayer of the prophet Elijah (**vv. 17–18**). No matter what circumstances believers find themselves in, prayer is the recommended remedy.

BIBLE LEARNING

AIM: Students will affirm that prayer is talking to God and waiting to hear what God speaks to us.

I. THE EXHORTATION TO PRAY (James 5:13–16)

An initial reading of **James 5:13–18** would suggest that this passage is about healing. A deeper study reveals that the overall theme is prayer. **Verse 13** specifically addresses prayers of the individual Christians who have been experiencing suffering. James asks, "Is any among you afflicted?" The Greek word *kakopatheo* (**kah-koe-pa-THEH-oh**) means "to suffer misfortune" and is not used for illness. During suffering or misfortune prayer is the conduit to our strength. As we navigate the trials of life, we may feel tempted to question the goodness of God and others. Prayer will help Christians to stay positive and keep our eyes on God even in our darkest hour. In contrast, the believer is also admonished to sing psalms when things are going good. No matter what the circumstance, the believer's focus is toward God.

Prescription for Life Circumstances (verses 13–16)

13 Is any among you afflicted? let him pray. Is any merry? let him sing psalms.

James advises believers on how to respond to different life circumstances. The believers experienced times of joy and times of sorrow (**vv. 13–18; 1:2–3**). James urged them to turn constantly to communication with God in whatever circumstances life brought their way, even in going through "affliction" (Gk. *kakopatheo*, **kah-koh-pahth-EH-oh**) as well as when "merry" (Gk. *euthumeo*, **yoo-thoo-MEH-oh**). In regards to affliction, it may not be removed, but it certainly can be transformed. Divine help and blessings are conveyed to the

Christian in response either to his or her own prayers or the intercessions of other Christians on the individual's behalf. In all circumstances, it is a Christian's duty and privilege to pray. The Greek word *psallo* (**PSAL-loh**) primarily meant "to play a stringed instrument" and later could also mean "to sing to the harp." It can refer to any sounding of God's praises, alone or in the company of others, vocally with or without musical instrument (cf. **Romans 15:9; 1 Corinthians 14:15; Ephesians 5:19**). Through singing, we can express our thanks to God. It is a natural response to the condition of good health, which is recognized as a gift from God.

14 Is any sick among you? let him call for the elders of the church; and let them pray over him, anointing him with oil in the name of the Lord:

In the case of being severely "sick" (Gk. *astheneo*, **ahs-theh-NEH-oh**), when the body may be tormented with pain and the mind considerably disturbed, it is not easy to turn one's concentration to prayer. The word here means to be without strength and feeble and can be applied to any number of sicknesses. In any case, the exhortation is to call the elders of the church to pray over the sick and anoint the afflicted person with oil in the name of the Lord (cf. **Mark 6:13**). The word "oil" (Gk. *elaion*, **EL-eye-on**) specifically means olive oil (from the root *elaia*, **el-EYE-ah**, "olive"). Oil is the symbol of the Holy Spirit, the divine presence (**1 John 2:20, 27**). In biblical times, it was used for medicinal purposes (**Luke 10:34**). The prayer for sickness is accompanied by the oil as a symbol of the divine presence in healing the body. The emphasis on "in the name of the Lord" reminds the reader that the Lord is the Healer, not the elders. It is neither the oil nor the elders that brings the healing. The Lord Himself is the Healer. The anointing of oil is done in His name.

15 And the prayer of faith shall save the sick, and the Lord shall raise him up; and if he have committed sins, they shall be forgiven him.

The expression "shall raise him up" means to restore to physical health. Physical healing is a form of redemption. Here James is offering God's prescription for healing and the forgiveness of sins. The Greek word used for "the sick" (*ton kamnonta*, **ton KAHM-non-tah**) is from a verb whose primary meaning is to grow weary in the sense of growing weary by reason of sickness. The verb *egeiro* (**eh-GAY-roh**) means to rise up, raise up, or awaken (see **Matthew 1:24** from sleep; **John 11:11–12** from death; **11:29** from sitting). The word is used many times for the resurrection of Christ and of believers. In this case it is used in the sense of being raised up from sickness, in contrast to being weak and without strength, with the implication of not being able to rise.

The clause "and if he have committed sins" does not mean that the sickness is necessarily due to sin. The conditional words "and if" (*kan*, **KAHN**) show that it may or may not be. The Bible does not teach that all sickness is due to sin committed by the person suffering, but it is a possibility (**Mark 2:5–11; 1 Corinthians 11:28–30**).

16 Confess your faults one to another, and pray one for another, that ye may be healed. The effectual fervent prayer of a righteous man availeth much.

Confess is the Greek word *exomologeo* (**ehk-so-mo-LO-geh-o**), which means to speak out and make public or agree with. The believers are to agree with God and with one another concerning their "faults" (Gk. *paraptoma*, **par-AHP-toh-mah**), which means a "deviation from the right path" (see **Matthew 5:23–24**). There is great power in intercessory prayer. The Greek word *deesis* (**DEH-ay-sis**), translated "prayer," has a more restricted meaning. It denotes a petition, a supplication (**Luke 1:13; Romans**

10:1). Sin is the enemy of personal and community life; it must be confessed before the throne of grace (**Proverbs 28:13; 1 John 1:8–10**; see **Psalm 32:1**). The word "healed" (Gk. *iaomai*, **ee-AH-oh-meye**) has both a physical and spiritual meaning. It can mean "to be cured from a sickness" or "to be free from error or sin." It is possible considering the context that James has both in mind in this verse.

A righteous person is one who fears God and obeys His Word. His prayers differ from those of others by virtue of their earnestness and their helpfulness. The word *energeio* (Gk., **en-air-GEH-oh**) is translated "effectual fervent." It can also be rendered "active or operative" or "working." It describes the prayer that has the power to produce the desired effect. The grammar of the word suggests prayer is inwardly working on the righteous person, bringing them in line with the will of God. The Lord listens to the righteous because they fear God and are aligned with His will and purpose. Before prayer changes the situation, prayer changes the person. The prayer from this person produces the desired effect in much the same way as the prayers of Elijah did.

SEARCH THE SCRIPTURES

QUESTIONS 1 & 2

What is the purpose of confession in the life of a believer who is sick?

What does "the effective and fervent prayer of a righteous man availeth much" mean?

LIGHT ON THE WORD

Faith and Prayer

Attention is given to the Christian who experiences sickness. James instructs them to rely upon the leaders of the church. Traditionally oil was used to cleanse wounds. Christians may have used the oil to symbolically entrust the issue to God. Turning the issue over in faith shows trust that God is able to heal and enable the believer to endure present sufferings. James reminds the church that prayer offered in faith will bring results. God is faithful to heal the sick person and forgive sin.

Next, James highlights the relationship between being sick spiritually versus physically. Confession of sin is needed to restore and heal not only the physical body but the spiritual relationship with God. Many do not realize that their illnesses can be due to unconfessed sin in their lives. We are then told that the effectual fervent prayers of a righteous person can accomplish a lot in prayer. Effective prayers are those that line up with God's will and produces results. Knowing and distinguishing God's will require spending consistent time with Him.

II. THE EXAMPLE OF PRAYER (vv. 17–18)

Elijah is mentioned as an example of someone who offered up prayers that received answers from God. He is said to be a "man of like passions." Here James lets us know that Elijah was not a superman, and he did not have any special right to have his prayers answered more than we do. Elijah is shown to be a human with the same types of fears and doubts as we have. This is an encouragement to step out in faith and pray. One of the heroes of the Old Testament is shown to be a normal person who prayed to God in faith.

An Earnest Prayer (verses 17–18)

17 Elias was a man subject to like passions as we are, and he prayed earnestly that it might not rain: and it rained not on the earth by the space of three years and six months.

Here the reader's attention is drawn to one outstanding example of the efficacy of a righteous man's prayer, Elias [Elijah] (see **1 Kings 17–18**).

Being "a man subject to like passions (Gk. *homoiopathes*, **ho-moy-oh-PA-theys**) as we are" means Elijah experienced the same things that all human beings experience. This word is the same used by Paul when explaining to the people of Lystra that he and Barnabas were not gods but men of "like passions" (**Acts 14:15**). In using this word, James says that Elijah was not a super human; he was a human being just as we are. Elijah "prayed earnestly" means literally, he "prayed in prayer." With this phrase, James points to the earnestness of Elijah's prayer by translating a certain Hebrew grammatical construction into Greek. The Hebrew infinitive absolute denotes intensity and sincerity. When found in the Old Testament, the English translation usually renders it as "certainly" or "surely" (**Genesis 2:17** "surely die"; **Luke 22:15** "with desire, I have desired"). It is similar to the African American church where someone describes a sermon or song by saying that person "really preached" or "really sang." In other words, James says Elijah "surely prayed" or "really prayed." James wants his readers to know that they too can pray this same type of prayer. All the true followers of the Lord can effectively pray with intensity and sincerity and see their prayers answered.

18 And he prayed again, and the heaven gave rain, and the earth brought forth her fruit.

Elijah's prayer for rain to return and water the dry land is an illustration of the sick returning to life after the prayer of faith. A time of being sick is like a period of dryness. But the prayers of people made righteous through the blood of Jesus are efficient to bring new life. The example of Elijah praying for rain is intended to show that nothing is impossible for believers who call on God in prayer. Elijah prayed with boldness and waited on God. We are called to pray with boldness and to wait on God in every situation (**Hebrews 4:16**).

LIGHT ON THE WORD

Prayer of Expectation

James states the kind of prayer that Elijah prayed. It was an effectual, fervent prayer; that is, it was a serious and earnest prayer that reached the heart of God. It was a prayer that was full of energy and life, not necessarily a lot of words or vain rambling. The prayer Elijah prayed was a bold and convincing petition to the God who could do the impossible. This prayer opened and closed the heavens. Christians are encouraged to pray in a similar fashion and expect results. The Christian should expect God to heal and forgive sin.

BIBLE APPLICATION

AIM: Students will join with the church in praying for the sick.

We are living in a world with modern conveniences like iPads, smartphones, and GPS. These gadgets are meant to make life easier, but often wind up distracting us from practicing spiritual disciplines like prayer. Our lesson today reminds us to pray regardless of the situation. Praying for our brothers and sisters in Christ will keep us sensitive to one another. Through prayer, we can stay connected to our power source: God. He strengthens us to endure the intrusions that appear in life that we never imagined we would encounter.

STUDENTS' RESPONSES

AIM: Students will pray in all situations, both in joyful times and times of trouble.

This week, spend time praying for the needs of your fellow Bible study members. Please write your prayer request on an index card for distribution to fellow class members.

PRAYER

Lord, the power of prayer is a real and motivating force in our lives. Jesus as You hear and answer our prayers, we are reminded how much You care for us. In Jesus' Name we pray. Amen.

HOW TO SAY IT

Anoint. a-**NOI**-nt.

PREPARE FOR NEXT SUNDAY

Read **Daniel 1:5, 8–17, Matthew 6:16–18** and study "Feasting and Fasting."

DAILY HOME BIBLE READINGS

MONDAY
Let Us Seek God's Favor Together
(Zechariah 8:18–23)

TUESDAY
Pray to the Lord for Us
(Jeremiah 42:1–6)

WEDNESDAY
We Pray to God for You
(2 Thessalonians 1:5–12)

THURSDAY
You Heard My Plea
(Lamentations 3:52–58)

FRIDAY
Never Ceasing to Pray for You
(1 Samuel 12:19–25)

SATURDAY
The Prophets' Suffering and Patience
(James 5:1–12)

SUNDAY
The Prayer of Faith
(James 5:13–18)

Sources:
Davids, Peter H. The Epistle of James, The New International Greek Testament Commentary. Grand Rapids, MI: Eerdmans, 1982.
Vincent, Martin R. Vincent's Word Studies in the New Testament: Matthew, Mark, Luke, Acts, James, 1 Peter, 2 Peter, Jude, King James Version. Peabody, MA: Hendrickson Publishers, 1985.

COMMENTS / NOTES:

FEASTING AND FASTING

BIBLE BASIS: DANIEL 1:5, 8–17; MATTHEW 6:16–18

BIBLE TRUTH: The Scripture teaches that fasting is good stewardship that gives physical and spiritual benefits.

MEMORY VERSES: "But thou, when thou fastest, anoint thine head, and wash thy face; That thou appear not unto men to fast , but unto thy Father which is in secret: and thy Father, which seeth in secret, shall reward thee openly" (Matthew 6:17–18).

LESSON AIM: By the end of this lesson, we will: know and understand what Jesus said about fasting and those who fast; feel the value of being connected with God while fasting; and practice a regular discipline of seeking God by fasting.

TEACHER PREPARATION

MATERIALS NEEDED: Quarterly Commentary/Teacher Manual, Adult Quarterly, Adult resources—charts, worksheets, and other teaching tools, paper, pens, pencils, Bibles (several different versions)

OTHER MATERIALS NEEDED / TEACHER'S NOTES:

LESSON OVERVIEW

LIFE NEED FOR TODAY'S LESSON
People often restrict their diet for both physical and spiritual reasons like Daniel and his friends.

BIBLE LEARNING
To know and understand what Jesus said about fasting and those who fast.

BIBLE APPLICATION
To feel the value of being connected with God while fasting.

STUDENTS' RESPONSES
Christians realize that Christianity requires one to make certain sacrifices.

LESSON SCRIPTURE

DANIEL 1:5, 8–17; MATTHEW 6:16–18, KJV

5 And the king appointed them a daily provision of the king's meat, and of the wine which he drank: so nourishing them three years, that at the end thereof they might stand before the king.

8 But Daniel purposed in his heart that

DANIEL 1:5, 8–17; MATTHEW 6:16–18, NIV

5 The king assigned them a daily amount of food and wine from the king's table. They were to be trained for three years, and after that they were to enter the king's service.

8 But Daniel resolved not to defile himself

he would not defile himself with the portion of the king's meat, nor with the wine which he drank: therefore he requested of the prince of the eunuchs that he might not defile himself.

9 Now God had brought Daniel into favour and tender love with the prince of the eunuchs.

10 And the prince of the eunuchs said unto Daniel, I fear my lord the king, who hath appointed your meat and your drink: for why should he see your faces worse liking than the children which are of your sort? then shall ye make me endanger my head to the king.

11 Then said Daniel to Melzar, whom the prince of the eunuchs had set over Daniel, Hananiah, Mishael, and Azariah,

12 Prove thy servants, I beseech thee, ten days; and let them give us pulse to eat, and water to drink.

13 Then let our countenances be looked upon before thee, and the countenance of the children that eat of the portion of the king's meat: and as thou seest, deal with thy servants.

14 So he consented to them in this matter, and proved them ten days.

15 And at the end of ten days their countenances appeared fairer and fatter in flesh than all the children which did eat the portion of the king's meat.

16 Thus Melzar took away the portion of their meat, and the wine that they should drink; and gave them pulse.

17 As for these four children, God gave them knowledge and skill in all learning and wisdom: and Daniel had

with the royal food and wine, and he asked the chief official for permission not to defile himself this way.

9 Now God had caused the official to show favor and compassion to Daniel,

10 but the official told Daniel, "I am afraid of my lord the king, who has assigned your food and drink. Why should he see you looking worse than the other young men your age? The king would then have my head because of you."

11 Daniel then said to the guard whom the chief official had appointed over Daniel, Hananiah, Mishael and Azariah,

12 "Please test your servants for ten days: Give us nothing but vegetables to eat and water to drink.

13 Then compare our appearance with that of the young men who eat the royal food, and treat your servants in accordance with what you see."

14 So he agreed to this and tested them for ten days.

15 At the end of the ten days they looked healthier and better nourished than any of the young men who ate the royal food.

16 So the guard took away their choice food and the wine they were to drink and gave them vegetables instead.

17 To these four young men God gave knowledge and understanding of all kinds of literature and learning. And Daniel could understand visions and dreams of all kinds.

Matthew 6:16 "When you fast, do not look somber as the hypocrites do, for they disfigure their faces to show others they are fasting. Truly I tell you, they have received

understanding in all visions and dreams.

Matthew 6:16 Moreover when ye fast, be not, as the hypocrites, of a sad countenance: for they disfigure their faces, that they may appear unto men to fast. Verily I say unto you, They have their reward.

17 But thou, when thou fastest, anoint thine head, and wash thy face;

18 That thou appear not unto men to fast, but unto thy Father which is in secret: and thy Father, which seeth in secret, shall reward thee openly.

their reward in full.

17 But when you fast, put oil on your head and wash your face,

18 so that it will not be obvious to others that you are fasting, but only to your Father, who is unseen; and your Father, who sees what is done in secret, will reward you.

LIGHT ON THE WORD

In Hebrew, "pulse" includes everything that is grown from sown seed. This means not only vegetables but also fruit, legumes, grains, and bread. It was very similar to a healthy vegetarian diet. This type of food was eaten in a partial fast as opposed to meat and dairy and other delicate foods. Eating pulse was not a condemnation of meat eating in general, but regarded by the participant as a way to humble themselves before God.

A eunuch was commonly one who was castrated. Eunuchs were common in the royal courts of the Jews, Persians, Babylonians, Romans, and Greeks. In the Law it was forbidden for eunuchs to be a part of public worship (**Deuteronomy 23:1**). Elsewhere, Jesus commends those who have figuratively made themselves eunuchs for the kingdom of God (**Matthew 19:12**).

TEACHING THE BIBLE LESSON

LIFE NEED FOR TODAY'S LESSON

AIM: Students will often restrict their diet for both physical and spiritual reasons like Daniel and his friends.

INTRODUCTION

Resisting Conformity

During the conquest of Jerusalem, Nebuchadnezzar, the Babylonian king, took the royal youths to Babylon to be raised in his courts. This included eating at the king's table and receiving a Babylonian education. These royal captives would then be a part of the Babylonian culture and government. Daniel and his three friends Hananiah, Mishael, and Azariah were taken to Babylon to be a part of the court. They were to be trained in all the arts and sciences of Babylon and eat at the king's table. Despite being subjected to a foreign power the four friends resisted conforming to the aspects of Babylonian culture that jeopardized their faithfulness to God. At the same time they rose in prominence and authority and promoted the Hebrew God as the God of all the earth. They were in Babylon but not of Babylon. These four friends serve as an example to Christians who do not belong to this world although we live in it. The first test that Daniel and his friends would encounter had to do with their training. This would determine the trajectory for their lives as pilgrims in a strange land. Would they choose to become fully absorbed into the Babylonian ways, or would they choose to live distinctive lives even while they were in exile far away from home?

BIBLE LEARNING

AIM: Students will know and understand what Jesus said about fasting and those who fast.

I. THE APPOINTMENT OF THE KING (Daniel 1:5, 8)

Nebuchadnezzar had gathered together some of the best-looking and educated young men of Judah to be a part of his royal court. In order for them to be fully indoctrinated into the Babylonian culture, he started with something basic: food. For three years they were to be fed food and drink from the king's table. We do not know exactly what this food consisted of, but we do know that meat was the main dish. Wine was also served along with the food.

Dietary Restrictions (verses 5, 8)

5 And the king appointed them a daily provision of the king's meat, and of the wine which he drank: so nourishing them three years, that at the end thereof they might stand before the king. 8 But Daniel purposed in his heart that he would not defile himself with the portion of the king's meat, nor with the wine which he drank: therefore he requested of the prince of the eunuchs that he might not defile himself.

The Law of Moses requires that Israelites refrain from eating certain kinds of foods that were not restricted in all other cultures. Only animals with split hooves that chewed cud were allowed, so meat from cattle and sheep was acceptable, but pork was not (**Leviticus 11:3–8**; **Deuteronomy 14:6–8**). Since the foreign rulers did not observe such restrictions, consuming the king's portions was problematic because the meat would not be kosher. Consuming wine was generally acceptable for Israelites, with the exceptions of the priests when they entered the tabernacle or Temple (**Leviticus 10:9**) and those making a Nazarite vow for a certain period of time (**Numbers 6:3**). However, in the ancient world, both the meat and the wine could have been sacrificed to the king's gods, so if Daniel and his fellow Hebrews wanted to be sure they were not engaging in practices related to worship of other gods, it was necessary to refrain from consuming the king's foods.

SEARCH THE SCRIPTURES

QUESTION 1

What did Daniel believe would happen to him if he ate the king's meat?

LIGHT ON THE WORD

The Royal Indoctrination

By starting off with something as basic as food, Nebuchadnezzar was showing that he had complete control and they were dependent on him. This was central to the indoctrination process. The royal youth had to believe that their provision and sustenance came from Nebuchadnezzar and not from God.

II. THE ABSTINENCE OF DANIEL AND HIS FRIENDS (vv. 9–17)

Daniel understood the ways of God and had already decided that he would not defile himself with any of the king's meat or drink. This was the first step in resisting the king's attempts to conform him to the ways of Babylon. Next this decision in the heart became an outward action. Since Daniel had gained favor with the head eunuch, Melzar, he requested that he and his friends Hananiah, Mishael, and Azariah be given only water and pulse for ten days. He wanted to prove that their faces would be fairer and fatter than all the other children who ate the king's meat. By doing this, he was protesting the sovereignty of Nebuchadnezzar over their lives while at the same time promoting the king's interests. He knew the king would be interested more in the results and not the means by which the results came.

Favored by God (verses 9–17)

9 Now God had brought Daniel into favour and tender love with the prince of the eunuchs. 10 And the prince of the eunuchs said unto Daniel, I fear my lord the king, who hath appointed your meat and your drink: for why should he see your faces worse liking than the children which are of your sort? then shall ye make me endanger my head to the king.
11 Then said Daniel to Melzar, whom the prince of the eunuchs had set over Daniel, Hananiah, Mishael, and Azariah, 12 Prove thy servants, I beseech thee, ten days; and let them give us pulse to eat, and water to drink. 13 Then let our countenances be looked upon before thee, and the countenance of the children that eat of the portion of the king's meat: and as thou seest, deal with thy servants. 14 So he consented to them in this matter, and proved them
ten days. 15 And at the end of ten days their countenances appeared fairer and fatter in flesh than all the children which did eat the portion of the king's meat.
16 Thus Melzar took away the portion of their meat, and the wine that they should drink; and gave them pulse.

This was a miraculous event in the ancient world. In antiquity, as in two-thirds of the world today, meat was only available to the wealthiest people, so it was a great privilege to be offered the king's portions, even if they were leftovers from a religious sacrifice. To be thin was a sign of poverty or illness, so the fact that the Hebrew youths have gained weight was a sure sign that God is with them.

17 As for these four children, God gave them knowledge and skill in all learning and wisdom: and Daniel had understanding in all visions and dreams.

God not only strengthens Daniel and his friends physically but also gives them the wisdom and discernment necessary to survive in a foreign culture. The fact that God gives them precisely the skills the king requires indicates even more that God provides the faithful with what they need no matter where they are.

SEARCH THE SCRIPTURES

QUESTION 2

What was the purpose of Daniel asking the eunuch for ten days to eat pulse?

LIGHT ON THE WORD

Mission Accomplished

After Daniel and his friends had completed the ten days with only the water and pulse, their countenances were fairer and fatter than the other young men in the court. Daniel and his friends had chosen to remain loyal to God, and it paid off. Melzar, their guardian, noticed the difference between their physical constitution and the other children. This caused him to take away the king's portion of food and give them a full diet of pulse and water for the next three years. These young Hebrew boys proved their appearance and countenance were looking better than the other young men who had been given the king's portion of meat and drink. The ten-day test had worked!

During their three years there, Daniel and his friends were not only stronger and more good looking, but they also grew stronger mentally. The text says that God gave them "knowledge and skill in all learning and wisdom." Their first step in remaining loyal to God proved to be the foundation of the ministry and calling for their lives. This was all because they chose to eat the cuisine of resistance from the beginning of their time in Babylon.

III. THE APPROVAL OF GOD (Matthew 6:16–18)

In this part of the Sermon on the Mount, Jesus explains the proper ways to observe God's commandments. **Matthew 5:17–7:12** is a collection of instructions. Jesus does not abolish the laws established through Moses, but instead he addresses the distinctions between hypocritical and genuine observance (**Matthew 5:17**). Very little is dictated about fasting in Old Testament law, with only the fast of the Day of Atonement, Yom Kippur, explicitly ordained (**Leviticus 16:29–34; 23:27–32**). In fact, the Old Testament includes instances of fasting in ancient Israel for purposes such as repentance (**Jonah 3:5**), petition (**2 Samuel 12:16**) and mourning (**1 Samuel 31:13**). Fasting served numerous purposes, but in each case the individual or community humbled themselves before God by refraining from food and drink and often by putting on sackcloth instead of their everyday clothing. In **Matthew 6**, Jesus does not eliminate fasting as a religious ritual, but he establishes stipulations concerning the intention of the faster, especially in the case of voluntary fasts, which individuals could practice regularly on Mondays and Thursdays. Such fasts should not be about a public display of piety.

Fasting as addressed in **Matthew 6** and a kosher diet as observed in **Daniel 1** are distinct religious practices associated with eating and drinking. Fasting in antiquity typically involved refraining from all food and drink for a short period of time. Today fasting may involve complete abstention from eating and drinking, or it may involve avoiding certain foods, but in all cases the duration is short and for a specific purpose. In contrast, a kosher diet is to be observed regularly as a daily devotion to God, with occasional abstention from additional foods such as leavened bread during Passover (**Exodus 3:15; Leviticus 23:5–6**). In the Roman period and later, some faithful Christians and Jews further restricted their daily diets as a practice of faith, as with John the Baptist, who ate locusts and honey (**Matthew 3:4**). What is clear from the Bible is that dietary habits are associated with faith practices for Jews and Christians.

Sackcloth and Ashes (verses 16–18)

16 Moreover when ye fast, be not, as the hypocrites, of a sad countenance: for they disfigure their faces, that they may appear unto men to fast. Verily I say unto you, They have their reward. 17 But thou, when thou fastest, anoint thine head, and wash thy face;

In addition to refraining from eating and drinking, the Israelites would sometimes wear sackcloth, put ashes on their heads, and refrain from washing as a way of acknowledging their humble situation when they fasted. Whether they were mourning somebody's death, asking for forgiveness for sin, or pleading for help for a personal or community crisis, fasting was a way of acknowledging their situation of loss or need. This is not the type of fasting that Jesus addresses. Instead, He points out that at times people do not fast with these intentions, but with the purpose of calling attention to themselves as pious. The word "hypocrite" in Greek has the basic meaning of one who pretends that the situation is different from what it really is. To make yourself look mournful or needy when you are not serves the purpose of getting other people to look at you and either pity you for your situation or laud you for your piety. Instead, it is better to wash so that you do not stand out.

18 That thou appear not unto men to fast, but unto thy Father which is in secret: and thy Father, which seeth in secret, shall reward thee openly.

The word for secret in Greek is *kruphaios* (**crew-FIGH-os**), and it refers specifically to hidden things, the types of things that only God can see. This is the crux of Jesus' statement about fasting. Fasting can serve a number of important religious purposes, but it should remain between the believer and God because it is not a performance for all to see. Holiday fasts such as Yom Kippur should be observed as always, but voluntary fasts should be practiced not for public display but for true repentance, mourning, or plea for God's help. Everything we do should come from the heart, and God always knows what is in our hearts because God alone knows our secrets.

LIGHT ON THE WORD

Fasting and God's Approval

Later on in the New Testament, Jesus shows His disciples how to receive approval from God in regards to fasting. He says not to be like the hypocrites who make themselves look miserable in order to display to the world what they are doing. Jesus says that fasting is to be done toward God. It is not to show people how super-spiritual you are, but it is a way to deny yourself in order to seek God and His kingdom. Similar to Daniel and his friends, God will see your secret fasting and reward you.

BIBLE APPLICATION

AIM: Students will feel the value of being connected with God while fasting.

In our society, many people eat all kinds of different diets. Some eat fast food and junk food on an everyday basis. Some are vegetarian or vegan. Others have allergies, while others abstain from carbohydrates. Whatever the diet, food is a constant topic of conversation. Whether it is about the health of food or the taste of food, the topic is always on our minds and in our talk on a daily basis. As Christians, we believe that all of life is under the sovereignty and Lordship of Christ. This can even be reflected in the food that we eat. For the believer, eating is not just a physical act, but also deeply spiritual. We can show this by fasting and abstaining from food altogether or from certain foods. This does not earn any merit or favor with God, but displays the closeness and intimacy that we already have with Him.

STUDENTS' RESPONSES

AIM: Students will realize that Christianity requires one to make certain sacrifices.

Fasting can be a challenging practice for those of us who have grown up in the junk and convenience food culture. Not only do we eat foods that are not good for us, but we also eat way more than is needed. Commit yourself to fasting at least once during this next week. It can be a partial fast like Daniel and his friends or a fast from all food altogether. We can also choose to fast from television or social media. Make sure to accompany this fast with prayer and take note of anything the Lord may say to you during this time.

PRAYER

Direct us, O Lord, on how to fast. Help us to understand and know why we fast. Remind us that we are fasting in ways that pleasing to You and not for show. In Jesus' Name we pray. Amen.

HOW TO SAY IT

Kosher.	**KOH**-shur.
Hananiah.	hah-nah-**NIGH**-ah.
Mishael.	**MEE**-shah-el.
Azariah.	ah-zar-**RIGH**-ah.
Yom Kippur.	yohm kih-**POOR**.
hypocrite.	**HIH**-poh-criht.

PREPARE FOR NEXT SUNDAY

Read **Luke 10:25–34** and study "Serving Neighbors, Serving God."

DAILY HOME BIBLE READINGS

MONDAY
Draw Near to Me, O Lord
(Psalm 69:5–18)

TUESDAY
Help Me, O Lord My God
(Psalm 109:21–27)

WEDNESDAY
Humility Before God
(Luke 18:9–14)

THURSDAY
If My People Humble Themselves
(2 Chronicles 7:11–18)

FRIDAY
Humble Yourselves Before God
(2 Chronicles 34:24–33)

SATURDAY
An Appropriate Time for Fasting
(Matthew 9:9–17)

SUNDAY
To Honor God
(Daniel 1:5, 8–17; Matthew 6:16–18)

Sources:

Boring, M. Eugene. "Matthew." Vol. VIII. New Interpreter's Bible Commentary. 12 vols. Edited by Leander E. Keck, et al. Nashville: Abingdon Press, 1995. 87–506.

Gowan, Donald E. Daniel: Abingdon Old Testament Commentaries. Nashville: Abingdon Press, 2001.

Miller, Steven R. The New American Commentary: Daniel. Nashville, TN: Broadman and Holman, 1994.

Senior, Donald W. Matthew: Abingdon New Testament Commentaries. Nashville: Abingdon Press, 1998.

Smith-Christopher, Daniel L. "The Book of Daniel: Introduction, Commentary, and Reflections." Vol. VII. New Interpreter's Bible Commentary. 12 vols. Edited by Leander E. Keck, et al. Nashville: Abingdon Press, 1996. 17–152.

Towner, W. Sibley. Daniel, Interpretation, a Biblical Commentary for Teaching and Preaching: New International Commentary on the New Testament. Atlanta, GA: John Knox Press. 1984.

COMMENTS / NOTES:

SERVING NEIGHBORS, SERVING GOD

BIBLE BASIS: LUKE 10:25–34

BIBLE TRUTH: The parable of the good Samaritan teaches that when the faithful serve their neighbor, they serve God.

MEMORY VERSES: "Which now of these three, thinkest thou, was neighbour unto him that fell among the thieves? And he said, He that shewed mercy on him. Then said Jesus unto him, Go, and do thou likewise" (Luke 10:36–37).

LESSON AIM: By the end of the lesson, your students will: examine Jesus' teaching about compassion for our neighbors; reflect on the connection between serving our neighbors and serving God; and expand our vision and application of service to neighbors and to God.

TEACHER PREPARATION

MATERIALS NEEDED: Quarterly Commentary/Teacher Manual, Adult Quarterly, Adult resources—charts, worksheets, and other teaching tools, paper, pens, pencils, Bibles (several different versions)

OTHER MATERIALS NEEDED / TEACHER'S NOTES:

___

___

LESSON OVERVIEW

LIFE NEED FOR TODAY'S LESSON
People of goodwill take care of and serve their neighbors.

BIBLE LEARNING
For Jesus and Luke, a neighbor is anyone in need.

BIBLE APPLICATION
Believers understand that neighborliness is an expression of one's love of God and love of others.

STUDENTS' RESPONSES
Christians affirm that those who show mercy without expecting rewards or repayment are indeed heirs of the kingdom of God.

LESSON SCRIPTURE

LUKE 10:25–34, KJV

25 And, behold, a certain lawyer stood up, and tempted him, saying, Master, what shall I do to inherit eternal life?

26 He said unto him, What is written in the law? how readest thou?

LUKE 10:25–34, NIV

25 On one occasion an expert in the law stood up to test Jesus. "Teacher," he asked, "what must I do to inherit eternal life?"

26 "What is written in the Law?" he

27 And he answering said, Thou shalt love the Lord thy God with all thy heart, and with all thy soul, and with all thy strength, and with all thy mind; and thy neighbour as thyself.

28 And he said unto him, Thou hast answered right: this do, and thou shalt live.

29 But he, willing to justify himself, said unto Jesus, And who is my neighbour?

30 And Jesus answering said, A certain man went down from Jerusalem to Jericho, and fell among thieves, which stripped him of his raiment, and wounded him, and departed, leaving him half dead.

31 And by chance there came down a certain priest that way: and when he saw him, he passed by on the other side.

32 And likewise a Levite, when he was at the place, came and looked on him, and passed by on the other side.

33 But a certain Samaritan, as he journeyed, came where he was: and when he saw him, he had compassion on him,

34 And went to him, and bound up his wounds, pouring in oil and wine, and set him on his own beast, and brought him to an inn, and took care of him.

replied. "How do you read it?"

27 He answered, "'Love the Lord your God with all your heart and with all your soul and with all your strength and with all your mind'; and, 'Love your neighbor as yourself.'"

28 "You have answered correctly," Jesus replied. "Do this and you will live."

29 But he wanted to justify himself, so he asked Jesus, "And who is my neighbor?"

30 In reply Jesus said: "A man was going down from Jerusalem to Jericho, when he was attacked by robbers. They stripped him of his clothes, beat him and went away, leaving him half dead.

31 A priest happened to be going down the same road, and when he saw the man, he passed by on the other side.

32 So too, a Levite, when he came to the place and saw him, passed by on the other side.

33 But a Samaritan, as he traveled, came where the man was; and when he saw him, he took pity on him.

34 He went to him and bandaged his wounds, pouring on oil and wine. Then he put the man on his own donkey, brought him to an inn and took care of him.

LIGHT ON THE WORD

Lawyers or experts in law (Gk. *nomikos*, **no-mee-KOCE**) are generally believed to be scribes who specialized in studying, teaching, and defending the Law of Moses. They may have been associated with the Pharisees who were well-versed in Mosaic Torah, and Luke groups them together several times (**7:30; 11:53**). Therefore, they were considered religious and moral authorities, and highly revered among common Jews. As proclaimed "protectors" of the Law, lawyers (scribes) are often found in Scripture questioning Jesus on religious matters. Luke uses the term frequently. They are often portrayed as arrogant, unbelieving, and hypocritical (see **Matthew 23:23–28**).

The journey from Jerusalem to Jericho was 17 miles long and on a steep decline of approximately 3,000 feet (thus the term "going down from Jerusalem"). The winding road was filled with rocky places and caves that served as hiding places for robbers. It was known to be a dangerous route, as robberies were common, especially for lone travelers.

In 721 B.C., the Northern Kingdom of Israel was defeated by Assyria, and its people were deported. The king of Assyria repopulated the area with foreigners, and those people intermarried with Jews. The result was Samaritans, a mixed race of people with some Jewish ancestry, and "impure" religion, being a combination of Jewish traditions and pagan/idol worship. Samaritans were, therefore, despised by Jews, and the relationship between the two people groups was a hostile one.

TEACHING THE BIBLE LESSON

LIFE NEED FOR TODAY'S LESSON

AIM: Students will reflect on how people of goodwill take care of their neighbors.

INTRODUCTION

A Test Question

Jesus has just sent out His disciples to preach the kingdom of God and to heal the sick and cast out demons. He gave them instructions for the mission, and they faithfully followed them, and saw the power of God in tangible signs. They were amazed and came back rejoicing when giving Jesus the full report of their ministry. This causes Jesus to rejoice and thank God. Jesus thanks God that what He has told them has been kept from the wise and the proud of this world. In contrast, it has been given to those who are "babes" in understanding.

This sets the stage for a teacher of the law to ask a question. Many times the teachers of the law, along with the scribes and Pharisees, questioned Jesus in order to test and trap Him. This was done to discredit Jesus' ministry. The questions were usually popular questions of the day or ones in which whatever answer was given would place you in a particular theological camp. Jesus was a master at not only giving the right answer but challenging the scribes and Pharisees to live a more God-pleasing life through the answers He gave.

BIBLE LEARNING

AIM: Students will learn that for Jesus and Luke, a neighbor is anyone in need.

I. THE TEST (Luke 10:25–29)

This conversation is considered a typical one between rabbis and their students. Questions about eternal life were common. Rabbis would often answer a question with a question ("How do you read it?") and affirm responses ("You have answered correctly"). However, the lawyer, coming from a mentality of authority, was not seeking to learn, but to test. As a learned, religious Jew, his response quoting **Deuteronomy 6:5** and **Leviticus 19:18** was the correct verbal response, but the motive behind his follow-up question (to justify himself) revealed the flaw in his heart. There was no intention to love his neighbor, only to maintain his reputation.

An Expert Questions Jesus (verses 25–29)

25 And, behold, a certain lawyer stood up, and tempted him, saying, Master, what shall I do to inherit eternal life?

Many readers bypass this initial story of the lawyer (Gk. nomikos, **no-mee-KOCE**; cf. **Mark 12:28–34**, the expert of the law "scribe," Gk. *grammateus*, **gra-ma-te-OOS**)—who tested Jesus as they rush to the more popular story of the parable of the Good Samaritan. However, this dialogue between Jesus and the lawyer is not only a prelude to the parable, it has its own important place in Jesus' work with His disciples. In the Matthean and Marcan parallels, the scribe asks which is the greatest commandment (**Matthew 22:34–40**) or which is the first (**Mark 12:28–34**). In Mark's account, Jesus answers the question, and the scribe approves of Jesus' answer. Matthew's account is a shorter version and includes only the scribe's question and Jesus' answers. However, in Luke's writing here, the lawyer asks Jesus, "What shall I do to inherit eternal life?" Matthew and Luke say that the lawyer tested (Gk. *ekpeirazo*, **ek-pah-RAHD-zo**, to put to the test, try, tempt) Jesus. The lawyer was a recognized religious authority, and he tested Jesus, the unskilled Galilean lay and unofficial teacher, to see if He could give correct answers to tough theological questions. Thus, the lawyer tried to entrap Jesus, wanting to discredit Him if He gave a wrong answer.

Luke's version does not seek to say which of the Torah commandments is the greatest, but rather inquires about the fundamental principle of all the commandments. "What shall I do to inherit eternal life?" One who knew the Mosaic law tested Jesus, not as in Matthew about individual laws, but about what he must do to inherit "eternal life," which is the goal of the entire law (Marshall 442). This question also appears in **Luke 18:18**, where Jesus had a conversation with the rich young ruler. It was a common theme in rabbinical debates of that time (Marshall 442). The word "inherit" (Gk. *kleronomeo*, **klay-ro-no-MEH-o**, to receive an allotted share) is key to understanding that many Jews of the time thought that their eternal destiny was based on their Jewish descent plus their good deeds. They believed that their good deeds qualified them to receive a future blessing from God (Marshall 442).

26 He said unto him, What is written in the law? how readest thou? 27 And he answering said, Thou shalt love the Lord thy God with all thy heart, and with all thy soul, and with all thy strength, and with all thy mind; and thy neighbour as thyself.

Jesus answers the lawyer's question with two questions, taking him to the Old Testament whose authority the lawyer would not question, being an expert in the same. Marshall observes that some scholars believe that Jesus' question is actually, "How do you recite?" Thus the lawyer recalls the Shema from **Deuteronomy 6**, which he probably recited daily. However, Jesus is asking for more than just a recitation. He wants the lawyer to state his own interpretation of the Scriptures, thereby shifting the dialogue from Jesus' teaching to the lawyer's interpretation of the law. Correctly, the lawyer recited two commandments: love God (**Deuteronomy 6:5**) and love your neighbor (**Leviticus 19:18**). Together these two commandments formed the heart of the Jewish religion (Marshall 443–444), but they also formed the core of Jesus' own teaching. Thus, Jesus and the lawyer end up at the same place in their conversation.

28 And he said unto him, Thou hast answered right: this do, and thou shalt live. 29 But he, willing to justify himself, said unto Jesus, And who is my neighbour?

Jesus observes that the lawyer is right in his interpretation, and tells him, "Do this, and you will live." However, having answered the question correctly, the lawyer asks for clarification, possibly to test Jesus further. Since loving your neighbor is a matter of life and death, the correct definition of a neighbor is of extreme importance. So, the lawyer asks,

"Who is my neighbor?" In other words, he was saying, "Whom do I love?" Scholars agree that the general Jewish sense of the neighbor at the time was limited to members of the same people, religious communities, fellow Jews, or fellow members of the covenant (Marshall 444, 446). Marshall adds that there was a tendency among the Pharisees to exclude Samaritans, foreigners, and other ordinary people from the definition (444). Plummer observes that a Jew "except[ed] all Gentiles when he spoke of his neighbor" (285). Since the lawyer might have been a Pharisee, he could easily interpret the commandments in this exclusive manner. He agreed on loving neighbor, but he sought to define neighbor to include only Jews. He wanted to define neighbor—which then defines for him who is not a neighbor.

Consequently, this question is of extreme relevance in our world where segregation tears the Body of Christ apart just as much as it does any other community. Unity in diversity is a thorny subject even among Christians. Divisions take many forms and are prevalent in our communities. Black, White, Hispanic, Asian, Orthodox, Pentecostal, Roman Catholic, Lutheran, male, female, rich, poor, educated, and uneducated are just a few among the categories we use to classify our neighbors, usually to choose which neighbor to recognize or not recognize. Unfortunately, these discriminating definitions of neighbors affect the church's understanding of its mission in the world. God's mission is to invite all people into His kingdom without regard to our man-made qualifiers.

SEARCH THE SCRIPTURES

QUESTION 1

What does the lawyer say is the way to inherit eternal life? How consuming is the pursuit?

LIGHT ON THE WORD

Love, Faith, and Obedience

Jesus' response, "You have answered correctly," is not implying that eternal life is based upon works. It is by faith in Christ alone. One who loves God with all His heart, soul, strength, and mind is one who has faith in Him, and desires to please Him through obedience. One cannot say that they love God, without obeying Him and loving others (**John 15:9–14, 1 John 4:20–21**).

II. THE PARABLE (vv. 30–34)

As an illustration of neighborly love, Jesus tells this parable. During Jesus' time, Jewish religion and culture dictated that "good" Jews avoid impure things and people. Samaritans, as "mixed breeds," would fall into this category. Priests and Levites (along with Pharisees) were considered "holy" ones, striving to maintain the appearance of righteousness.

The Neighborly Act of Compassion (verses 30–34)

30 And Jesus answering said, A certain man went down from Jerusalem to Jericho, and fell among thieves, which stripped him of his raiment, and wounded him, and departed, leaving him half dead. 31 And by chance there came down a certain priest that way: and when he saw him, he passed by on the other side. 32 And likewise a Levite, when he was at the place, came and looked on him, and passed by on the other side.

The conversation takes a twist as Jesus brings in a parable to drive the lesson home.

In the parable, a man (supposedly a Jew) went down from Jerusalem to Jericho—a journey along a road that descends over 3,000 feet through treacherous desert and dangerous rocky country that could easily hide bandits.

On his way, the man met robbers who vandalized him, stripped him, and left him half-dead. While he lay half-conscious on the wayside, a priest and a Levite passed by, and upon seeing him, they went on the other side of the road. Both the priest and the Levite were well-known religious figures. The priests were descendants of Aaron and were responsible for everything to do with Temple worship. Levites were a tribe of descendants of Levi but not of Aaron (who was also a descendant of Levi), and they assisted the priests in the Temple. The Levite in this story seems overly inconsiderate as he "came and looked" at the wounded man and proceeded without offering help. Jesus' audience, however, might have expected that at the sight of a wounded fellow Jew, both the priest and the Levite would stop by to help him. There could be several reasons for their lack of action, among them: (1) their religious responsibilities may have prevented them from helping the wounded man since he might have appeared dead, as the law prohibited them from touching a corpse, (2) they might have been afraid of being attacked by the same robbers, and (3) they might have simply wanted nothing to do with the wounded person. It is possible that they were not indifferent to the wounded man, but their compassion might have been overcome by their commitment to religious purity.

33 But a certain Samaritan, as he journeyed, came where he was: and when he saw him, he had compassion on him, 34 And went to him, and bound up his wounds, pouring in oil and wine, and set him on his own beast, and brought him to an inn, and took care of him.

The plot of the story invites the audience to expect a Jewish layman to be the third traveler who responds to the wounded man, but Jesus brings a very unlikely person from a community hated by the Jews into the story—a certain Samaritan. The relationship between Jews and Samaritans was one of constant hostility. The Jews considered the Samaritans to be second-class citizens, the half-breed descendants of Jews who had intermarried with foreigners (see **2 Kings 17:24–40**). Still, we have here a Samaritan traveling in Jewish territory. His attending to the wounded Jew jeopardized his life, because he could have been easily blamed for the robbery. In addition, the Samaritans were bound by the same religious laws that bound the Jews, and therefore, the Samaritan risked defilement to take care of the possibly dead man—bandaging his wounds, pouring on oil and wine. Being a Samaritan, he could not expect any such kindness from the Jews. However, unlike the priest and the Levite, he fulfilled the law, showed compassion, and helped the wounded man.

He was moved by compassion—the same powerful emotion that moved Jesus to ministry, feeding the hungry and healing the sick, when He saw the multitudes weary and scattered like sheep without a shepherd (**Matthew 9:36–38, 14:14; Mark 8:2**). The word "compassion" here comes from the Greek word splangchizomai (**splonk-NEED-zo-meye**) which means "to be moved in one's gut, hence to be moved with compassion, have compassion" (the guts—inward parts, entrails—were thought to be the seat of love and pity). Jesus uses the story to contrast the lack of compassion shown by two members of the Jewish priesthood toward an unknown and unfortunate sufferer with the obedience to the law shown in practical compassion by the most unlikely of men, a Samaritan. Any Jew would be deeply humiliated for such an enemy of the Jews to show compassion to an injured Jew and pay expenses for his recuperation, while two Jewish religious officials did not. The mercy of the Samaritan made him give generously of his own supplies for the life of the wounded stranger: his oil and wine to cleanse and soothe the wounds, his bandage to bind them, and his own animal to carry the man. He also used his own money to pay for his care at the inn, promising to pay for any further expenses the man's care would require. The personhood of priest and the Levite would be diminished for not giving of themselves to help the needy. Love humanizes both the giver and the receiver—and that is what it takes to be a neighbor. Jesus finishes the conversation by telling the lawyer, "Go and do likewise." In other words, Jesus is saying, "Go and be a good neighbor; this is how you inherit eternal life."

SEARCH THE SCRIPTURES

QUESTION 2

What is implied to be one way for the lawyer to show love toward his neighbor?

LIGHT ON THE WORD

The Unexpected Good Neighbor

A person would expect the priest or Levite to come to the aid of an injured fellow Jew. For many possible reasons, both of them selfishly and intentionally avoided the injured traveler. Unexpectedly, the Samaritan set aside cultural animosity to show compassion and serve another. He uses his time by going out of his way (takes him to an inn, and plans to return), his resources (his animal, oil, wine, money), and his energy (walks while allowing the man to ride). He is a picture of agape-love (love without commonalities or friendship) and mercy (compassion at seeing another's misery). It is undeniable that the Samaritan is the better person—the true neighbor. He illustrated that a neighbor is one who sees another who is in need, and using whatever resources he has, meets that need.

BIBLE APPLICATION

AIM: Students will understand that neighborliness is an expression of one's love of God and love of others.

There are many examples of the lack of mercy and love in our society. There are executives who choose to lay off hard-working employees while accepting million-dollar bonuses. Some people take advantage of funds designated to help those in need. However, the opposite is true as well. There are tales of "heroes," people who rise up during tragedies to rescue, tend to, and provide for complete strangers. It is often said that this is the reflection of the good in humanity. In actuality, it is a reflection of God's love and mercy. Without Him, there would be no "good" in humanity.

STUDENTS' RESPONSES

AIM: Students will affirm that those who show mercy without expecting rewards or repayment are indeed heirs of the kingdom of God.

We are often faced with unexpected opportunities to serve our neighbors. There are people with needs all around us, and we have specific resources to help. Whom is God impressing upon you to serve? What opportunities have you been presented with that you have chosen to ignore because it will cost you time, money, energy, or comfort? Ask God to reveal these to you. Pray that He would give you greater awareness of those around you and a boldness to serve in spite of difficulty.

PRAYER

Lord, serving others is what we are called to do. Give us the resources and the compassion to care for others. Guide us put our faith into action. In Jesus' Name we pray. Amen.

HOW TO SAY IT

Compassion.	com-**PA**-shun.
Empathy.	em-pa-**THEE**.
Samaritan.	sa-**MARE**-ih-tin.
Levite.	**LEE**-vite.
Ubuntu.	u-boon-**TOO**.

PREPARE FOR NEXT SUNDAY

Read **Matthew 25:31–46** and study "Serving the Least."

DAILY HOME BIBLE READINGS

MONDAY
Faith Must Express Itself in Works
(James 2:14–26)

TUESDAY
Mercy Triumphs Over Judgment
(James 2:8–13)

WEDNESDAY
Jesus and the Religious Leaders
(Matthew 23)

THURSDAY
Love God with All Your Heart
(Deuteronomy 6:1–8)

FRIDAY
The Widow Who Gave Her All
(Luke 21:1–4)

SATURDAY
The Canaanite Woman's Faith
(Matthew 15:21–28)

SUNDAY
Serving Neighbors, Serving God
(Luke 10:25–34)

Sources:

Cosby, Michael R. Portraits of Jesus: An Inductive Approach to the Gospels. 1st ed. Louisville, KY: Westminster John Knox Press, 1999. 86–87.

Dunn, James D. G., and J. W. Rogerson. Eerdmans Commentary on the Bible. Grand Rapids, MI: W.B. Eerdmans, 2003.

Hebrew-Greek Key Word Study Bible, King James Version. Chattanooga, TN: AMG Publishers, Inc., 1991.

Josephus. The Antiquities of the Jews. 18.2.2.

Keener, Craig S. The IVP Bible Background Commentary: New Testament. Downers Grove, IL: Intervarsity Press, 1993. 217–218.

Marshall, I. Howard. The Gospel of Luke: A Commentary on the Greek Text. Grand Rapids, MI: Eerdmans, 1978. 440–450.

Plummer, Alfred. A Critical and Exegetical Commentary on the Gospel According to St. Luke. 5th ed. Edinburgh: T. & T. Clark, 1975. 283–288.

Radmacher, Earl D., ed. Nelson Study Bible, New King James Version. Nashville, TN: Thomas Nelson Publishers, 1997. 1618–1619, 1714–1715.

Ryrie, Charles C. Ryrie Study Bible, New International Version. Chicago, IL: Moody Press, 1986. 1423.

Thompson, Richard P., and Thomas E. Phillips. Literary Studies in Luke-Acts: Essays in Honor of Joseph B. Tyson. Macon, GA: Mercer University Press, 1998.

Unger, Merrill F. The New Unger's Bible Dictionary. Chicago, IL: Moody Press, 1988. 762–765, 1116–1119.

Walvoord, John F., and Roy B. Zuck, eds. The Bible Knowledge Commentary: New Testament. Wheaton, IL: Victor Books, SP Publications, Inc., 1983. 233–234.

COMMENTS / NOTES:

SERVING THE LEAST

BIBLE BASIS: MATTHEW 25:31–46

BIBLE TRUTH: Believers should serve others as if they were the Lord, and God will judge the believers accordingly.

MEMORY VERSE: "And the King shall answer and say unto them, Verily I say unto you, Inasmuch as ye have done it unto one of the least of these my brethren, ye have done it unto me" (Matthew 25:40).

LESSON AIM: By the end of the lesson, your students will: understand Jesus' comments on our obligation to meet the needs of the less fortunate; experience how God's love for all inspires us to meet others' needs; and participate in serving the needs of others.

TEACHER PREPARATION

MATERIALS NEEDED: Quarterly Commentary/Teacher Manual, Adult Quarterly, Adult resources—charts, worksheets, and other teaching tools, paper, pens, pencils, Bibles (several different versions)

OTHER MATERIALS NEEDED / TEACHER'S NOTES:

____

____

LESSON OVERVIEW

LIFE NEED FOR TODAY'S LESSON

There are opportunities for serving others all around us, even though believers do not always recognize or respond to them.

BIBLE LEARNING

The righteous (sheep) will be separated from the unrighteous (goats).

BIBLE APPLICATION

Christians understand God's commitment to the poor.

STUDENTS' RESPONSES

People of faith participate in God's commitment to the poor through service and compassion.

LESSON SCRIPTURE

MATTHEW 25:31–46, KJV

31 When the Son of man shall come in his glory, and all the holy angels with him, then shall he sit upon the throne of his glory:

32 And before him shall be gathered all nations: and he shall separate them one from another, as a shepherd divideth his sheep from the goats:

MATTHEW 25:31–46, NIV

31 "When the Son of Man comes in his glory, and all the angels with him, he will sit on his glorious throne.

32 All the nations will be gathered before him, and he will separate the people one from another as a shepherd separates the sheep from the goats.

33 And he shall set the sheep on his right hand, but the goats on the left.

34 Then shall the King say unto them on his right hand, Come, ye blessed of my Father, inherit the kingdom prepared for you from the foundation of the world:

35 For I was an hungred, and ye gave me meat: I was thirsty, and ye gave me drink: I was a stranger, and ye took me in:

36 Naked, and ye clothed me: I was sick, and ye visited me: I was in prison, and ye came unto me.

37 Then shall the righteous answer him, saying, Lord, when saw we thee an hungred, and fed thee? or thirsty, and gave thee drink?

38 When saw we thee a stranger, and took thee in? or naked, and clothed thee?

39 Or when saw we thee sick, or in prison, and came unto thee?

40 And the King shall answer and say unto them, Verily I say unto you, Inasmuch as ye have done it unto one of the least of these my brethren, ye have done it unto me.

41 Then shall he say also unto them on the left hand, Depart from me, ye cursed, into everlasting fire, prepared for the devil and his angels:

42 For I was an hungred, and ye gave me no meat: I was thirsty, and ye gave me no drink:

43 I was a stranger, and ye took me not in: naked, and ye clothed me not: sick, and in prison, and ye visited me not.

44 Then shall they also answer him, saying, Lord, when saw we thee an

33 He will put the sheep on his right and the goats on his left.

34 "Then the King will say to those on his right, 'Come, you who are blessed by my Father; take your inheritance, the kingdom prepared for you since the creation of the world.

35 For I was hungry and you gave me something to eat, I was thirsty and you gave me something to drink, I was a stranger and you invited me in,

36 I needed clothes and you clothed me, I was sick and you looked after me, I was in prison and you came to visit me.'

37 "Then the righteous will answer him, 'Lord, when did we see you hungry and feed you, or thirsty and give you something to drink?

38 When did we see you a stranger and invite you in, or needing clothes and clothe you?

39 When did we see you sick or in prison and go to visit you?'

40 "The King will reply, 'Truly I tell you, whatever you did for one of the least of these brothers and sisters of mine, you did for me.'

41 "Then he will say to those on his left, 'Depart from me, you who are cursed, into the eternal fire prepared for the devil and his angels.

42 For I was hungry and you gave me nothing to eat, I was thirsty and you gave me nothing to drink,

43 I was a stranger and you did not invite me in, I needed clothes and you did not clothe me, I was sick and in prison and you did not look after me.'

hungred, or athirst, or a stranger, or naked, or sick, or in prison, and did not minister unto thee?

45 Then shall he answer them, saying, Verily I say unto you, Inasmuch as ye did it not to one of the least of these, ye did it not to me.

46 And these shall go away into everlasting punishment: but the righteous into life eternal.

44 "They also will answer, 'Lord, when did we see you hungry or thirsty or a stranger or needing clothes or sick or in prison, and did not help you?'

45 "He will reply, 'Truly I tell you, whatever you did not do for one of the least of these, you did not do for me.'

46 "Then they will go away to eternal punishment, but the righteous to eternal life."

LIGHT ON THE WORD

Christ refers to Himself as the Son of Man approximately 80 times throughout the Gospels. Although Matthew's main focus was to portray Christ as the King (**vv. 34, 40**), Son of Man is intended to show Christ's humanity—i.e., He has flesh, He suffers and dies. Whereas the name Son of David connects Him to Jews and Son of God connects Him to Heaven, Son of Man qualifies Him to be the representative for all mankind as the perfect sacrifice and later, our advocate. He knows what it is to be rejected, hungry, thirsty, homeless, tempted, etc.

The Mount of Olives is a limestone ridge of hills that covers the eastern side of Jerusalem. There are several significant events associated with this mountain in the Old and New Testaments, among them this discussion, found in **Matthew 24:1–25:46** and **Luke 21:5–38**.

TEACHING THE BIBLE LESSON

LIFE NEED FOR TODAY'S LESSON

AIM: Students will understand how opportunities for serving others are all around us, even though believers do not recognize or respond to them.

INTRODUCTION

The End Times

After discussions with Jewish leaders, the disciples asked Christ two follow-up questions in **24:3**: "...When will this (the destruction of the Temple) happen and what will be the sign of your coming and of the end of the age?" **Matthew 24:4–25:46**, known as the Olivet Discourse, is His response. Christ describes end times for both Jews and Gentiles. He begins by prophesying the destruction of the Temple in Jerusalem, lays out some of the signs of the end, informs them of His return, and shares parables to encourage preparation. He concludes with this passage on the actions and judgement of the righteous and unrighteous.

There is a debate based on the story's implication that our actions earn us eternal life or eternal punishment. It is written, "For God so loved the world..., that whosoever believeth in him should... have eternal life" (**John 3:16**). Paul says, "For it is by grace you have been saved, through faith—and this is not from yourselves, it is the gift of God—not by works, so that no one can boast" (**Ephesians 2:8–9**, NIV). Faith in Christ leads to eternal life. Showing mercy and serving the poor is a by-product of a life of faith. This passage is an illustration of James' writing "What good is it, dear brothers and sisters, if you say you have faith but don't show it by your actions?... So you see, faith by itself isn't enough. Unless it produces good deeds, it is dead and useless" (**James 2:14, 17**, NLT). Those who love Christ demonstrate it by their actions—by loving others.

BIBLE LEARNING

AIM: Students will learn that the righteous (sheep) will be separated from the unrighteous (goats).

I. THE SEPARATION (Matthew 25:31–33)

Jesus is describing His future return as the Son of Man "in his glory," accompanied by angels. This verse shows how He is both man and God. During that time, He will come as King, judging all people from all nations, based upon their righteousness.

Jesus' Second Coming (verses 31–33)

31 When the Son of man shall come in his glory, and all the holy angels with him, then shall he sit upon the throne of his glory: 32 And before him shall be gathered all nations: and he shall separate them one from another, as a shepherd divideth his sheep from the goats: 33 And he shall set the sheep on his right hand, but the goats on the left.

This passage of Scripture is not so much a parable as it is prophecy. It does, however, have some parabolic traits in that it details the shepherd, sheep, and goats. The point here is to describe the events of Jesus' second coming. When Christ returns, He will come back in His full glory, the same glory that clothed Him before He descended from Heaven. His angels will accompany Him and will help gather all the people together at the same time. The Jews and Gentiles will not assemble in two different groups. Every nation will receive the same judgment before God.

Once more, Jesus teaches in a context with which the Jews were familiar. Sheep are usually milder and gentler while goats are more unruly and boisterous. Both animals grazed together during the daytime but were separated at night. In this passage, the sheep go one way and the goats go another. The right side symbolizes blessing, honor, and favor; the left side symbolizes worthlessness and condemnation.

LIGHT ON THE WORD

Sheeps and Goats

Christ uses the division of sheep and goats to illustrate His point. Jewish shepherds were in the habit of grazing their sheep and goats together during the day. However, the animals had different temperaments and needs, which would warrant separation at night. Even though together during the day, at night they were separated because sheep preferred open air, whereas goats needed to be kept warm. Sheep tend to flock together, while goats are more independent. However, sheep are generally more aloof even though they will stay inside fences more readily than goats. Both served important domestic and religious purposes in ancient Israel, so the eternal blessing of the sheep and condemnation of the goats is somewhat arbitrary here. If anything, it may be the characteristic of acting independently which could result in not caring for those in need that is the problem (however, see Ezekiel 34 where the rams and bucks are condemned for not leaving suitable grazing for the rest of the flocks and herds).

II. THE BLESSED (vv. 34–40)

Christ speaks well of those who are righteous, saying they are blessed heirs with rights to the kingdom. This blessing is connected to the outward expression of their faith: caring for strangers in need. His disciples would have understood this to be a basic expectation: Jews were commanded to care for those less fortunate—the hungry, thirsty, naked, imprisoned.

Jesus is the King (verses 34–40)

34 Then shall the King say unto them on his right hand, Come, ye blessed of my Father, inherit the kingdom prepared for you from the foundation of the world:

Here, Jesus refers to Himself as "King" for the first and only time in Scripture. He called Himself by other titles, and in so doing used the first person, e.g., "I am the good shepherd." In this verse, He uses the third person. Although this is in the third person, we know that Jesus is referring to Himself since the King in this passage refers to God as "my Father."

Once the sheep completely separated, Jesus will address them, inviting them into God's kingdom. Matthew uses the Greek word *kleronomeo* (**klay-roe-no-MEH-o**), meaning "to inherit or possess," signaling to the sheep to take possession of the kingdom. Jesus calls them blessed, not because of what they received (grace), but for what they did with what they received. He further says that this place has been prepared specifically for them since the beginning of the world.

35 For I was an hungered, and ye gave me meat: I was thirsty, and ye gave me drink: I was a stranger, and ye took me in: 36 Naked, and ye clothed me: I was sick, and ye visited me: I was in prison, and ye came unto me.

Jesus lists some of the acts of compassion the sheep performed. The need for compassion still exists today, and many people feed the hungry, satisfy the thirsty, house the homeless, clothe the destitute, and visit the sick and imprisoned. In all of these actions Jesus said they encountered Him.

37 Then shall the righteous answer him, saying, Lord, when saw we thee an hungered, and fed thee? or thirsty, and gave thee drink? 38 When saw we thee a stranger, and took thee in? or naked, and clothed thee? 39 Or when saw we thee sick, or in prison, and came unto thee?

Few people have seen Jesus with unmistakable certainty. Though possible, it is a bit unlikely that anyone living today has had a face-to-face encounter with the Savior. Conversely, we may have seen Christ in others or recognized an opportunity to serve Him by ministering to others.

Here the righteous ask the King some questions. According to what they knew about Christ, He was never hungry, thirsty, a stranger, naked, sick, or imprisoned, and as a result they were confused. Evidently, they sacrificed themselves to attend to someone else, and their charity pleased God.

40 And the King shall answer and say unto them, Verily I say unto you, Inasmuch as ye have done it unto one of the least of these my brethren, ye have done it unto me.

Jesus calms the sheep by referring them to their merciful deeds born of God's love for them. The brethren of Christ were not only His siblings; they included all people who inhabited the land and shared a bond with Christ through His sufferings and afflictions. Jesus stresses the "least" of His brethren, highlighting the humility exercised by the righteous in serving those thought unworthy of service. He then identifies with those people, making their pain, sorrow, and tribulation His own.

SEARCH THE SCRIPTURES

QUESTION 1

What does Christ promise those who are at His right hand?

LIGHT ON THE WORD

Representatives of Christ

Regardless of whether the "brothers" are Jews or Gentile Christians, Christ's point is that the recipients were regarded as representatives of Him. As they were served, He was served. Even more commendable, the righteous cared for "the least"—those without authority or power, without any previous relationship, as they are called strangers. This implies that no agenda existed beyond serving.

III. THE CURSED (vv. 41–45)

In contrast to the blessed, those on the left are marked for destruction. Instead of being commended by the King, they are rejected. Their sin is one of inaction. Their failure to provide for the needs of others served as a reflection of their lack of faith in God, and love for Him and His people. They are assigned a place along with the devil, known for his selfish and evil ways. Their unrighteous acts (or lack of righteous acts) reflect a disregard for others (much like Satan). In the end, they will find themselves cast into eternal punishment.

Judgment and Punishment (verses 41–45)

41 Then shall he say also unto them on the left hand, Depart from me, ye cursed, into everlasting fire, prepared for the devil and his angels: 42 For I was an hungered, and ye gave me no meat: I was thirsty, and ye gave me no drink: 43 I was a stranger, and ye took me not in: naked, and ye clothed me not: sick, and in prison, and ye visited me not.

The Lord uses the same standards for both groups and parallels them to each other. Whereas Jesus invited those on the right to come, He commands those on the left to depart. Because the goats chose not to serve those in need, they were condemned to death. Just as God made the kingdom of Heaven ready for the righteous, He made the everlasting fire ready for the unrighteous (**Revelation 20:11–15**).

Originally the everlasting fire was designated for Satan and his followers. But since the entrance of sin into the world and the introduction of death by sin, man was destined to join Satan in this inferno. God did not prepare this place for mankind because He is "not willing that any should perish" (**2 Peter 3:9**). But since God is just, man's disobedience demanded that he be punished unless he made proper atonement. Christ made that atonement, so man must live through the One who paid his debt. Otherwise, he must suffer God's judgment.

44 Then shall they also answer him, saying, Lord, when saw we thee an hungered, or athirst, or a stranger, or naked, or sick, or in prison, and did not minister unto thee? 45 Then shall he answer them, saying, Verily I say unto you, Inasmuch as ye did it not to one of the least of these, ye did it not to me.

The goats' reply echoes the sheep's, but there may be a difference in the tone. While the sheep may have been pleasantly surprised by Jesus' report, the goats were desperately shocked by His convicting words. They pleaded hopelessly after hearing their sentence, but the King had rendered His ruling.

This contrast brings another issue to the surface. Neither the sheep nor the goats appear puzzled by their destination, but they seem bewildered by the reason for going there. None of them expected to live or die based on how they treated Jesus because no one believed they ever had the opportunity.

SEARCH THE SCRIPTURES

QUESTION 2

In contrast, what does He promise those on His left?

LIGHT ON THE WORD

Serving Jesus by Serving Others

A similar circumstance exists today. Many people are not aware of the good they do through the Holy Spirit, and many don't recognize the chance to love as Christ loved and to serve Him by serving others.

Furthermore, some people believe they are sheep, when God sees them as goats. Jesus reiterates that the service done to others was also done to Him. Our service to our fellow man is not just leftover charity for those who are destitute but an act of service to Christ Himself.

BIBLE APPLICATION

AIM: Students will understand God's commitment to the poor.

Our society is keen on assigning places of honor based on certain criteria—looks, money, popularity, charisma, etc. As a result, those who are without these things often get overlooked. This is true even for believers. It is easier to serve those who we feel deserve our help—starving children in Africa or our friends, for example. However, we often ignore and make assumptions about the homeless man we see daily. It is important to note that Christ did not "fit in" with His community. He was not attractive (**Isaiah 53:2**), did not have money (**Luke 8:1–3**), and was homeless (**Matthew 8:20**). When we choose to serve "the least," we are often choosing to serve those who may be in similar situations as Christ when He walked the earth.

STUDENTS' RESPONSES

AIM: Students will participate in God's commitment to the poor through service and compassion.

We are often faced with opportunities to serve those who are less fortunate than we are. Our care for those in need is a reflection of our heart and relationship with Christ. Christ is serious about this reality and teaches that there are places of eternal honor and eternal punishment reserved. Pray that God shows you ways to serve others. Be open to His challenging you to think out of the box and beyond your comfort zone. It could be serving the homeless in your community, traveling to serve people in a different country, fostering or adopting a child, or caring for a missionary. However He leads, remember His words that whatever you do to the least of these, you do to Him.

PRAYER

Jesus, as we serve and care for others, may we always give from our hearts. In Jesus' Name we pray. Amen.

HOW TO SAY IT

Recipient. ri-**CIP**-ee-ent.

PREPARE FOR NEXT SUNDAY

Read **Ephesians 6:10–20** and study "Clothed and Ready."

DAILY HOME BIBLE READINGS

MONDAY
You Must Be Ready
(Matthew 24:37–44)

TUESDAY
Compassion and Justice for the Poor
(Leviticus 19:9–15)

WEDNESDAY
Open Your Hand to the Poor
(Deuteronomy 15:7–11)

THURSDAY
Celebrate with Presents for the Poor
(Esther 9:19–23)

FRIDAY
Do Not Forget the Oppressed
(Psalm 10:12–18)

SATURDAY
Share Resources with the Poor
(Romans 15:22–28)

SUNDAY
Minister to the Least
(Matthew 25:31–46)

Sources:

Hebrew-Greek Key Word Study Bible, King James Version. Chattanooga, TN: AMG Publishers, Inc., 1991.

Keener, Craig S. *The IVP Bible Background Commentary: New Testament*. Downers Grove, IL: Intervarsity Press, 1993. 118–119.

Radmacher, Earl D., ed. *Nelson Study Bible, New King James Version*. Nashville, TN: Thomas Nelson Publishers, 1997. 1620–1625.

Ryrie, Charles C. *Ryrie Study Bible, New International Version*. Chicago, IL: Moody Press, 1986. 1358.

Unger, Merrill F. *The New Unger's Bible Dictionary*. Chicago, IL: Moody Press, 1988. 72, 940–994, 1211.

Walvoord, John F., and Roy B. Zuck, eds. *The Bible Knowledge Commentary: New Testament*. Wheaton, IL: Victor Books, SP Publications, Inc., 1983. 80–81.

COMMENTS / NOTES:

CLOTHED AND READY

BIBLE BASIS: EPHESIANS 6:10–20

BIBLE TRUTH: Christians can better serve God as they fortify themselves with truth, righteousness, peace, faith, salvation, the Word of God, and prayer.

MEMORY VERSE: "Put on the whole armour of God, that ye may be able to stand against the wiles of the devil" (Ephesians 6:11).

LESSON AIM: By the end of the lesson, your students will: examine the epistle's teaching to put on the whole armor of God; value the feeling of being prepared to serve God; and arm themselves with those character traits needed to best serve God.

TEACHER PREPARATION

MATERIALS NEEDED: Quarterly Commentary/Teacher Manual, Adult Quarterly, Adult resources—charts, worksheets, and other teaching tools, paper, pens, pencils, Bibles (several different versions)

OTHER MATERIALS NEEDED / TEACHER'S NOTES:

____

____

LESSON OVERVIEW

LIFE NEED FOR TODAY'S LESSON

Only proper preparation can give assurance that certain things are accomplished.

BIBLE LEARNING

Christians are divinely armed in their struggle against spiritual forces of evil.

BIBLE APPLICATION

Believers know that God has greater powers than the spiritual forces of evil.

STUDENTS' RESPONSES

Students will value the feeling of being prepared to serve God.

LESSON SCRIPTURE

EPHESIANS 6:10–20, KJV

10 Finally, my brethren, be strong in the Lord, and in the power of his might.

11 Put on the whole armour of God, that ye may be able to stand against the wiles of the devil.

12 For we wrestle not against flesh and blood, but against principalities, against

EPHESIANS 6:10–20, NIV

10 Finally, be strong in the Lord and in his mighty power.

11 Put on the full armor of God, so that you can take your stand against the devil's schemes.

12 For our struggle is not against flesh and blood, but against the rulers, against

powers, against the rulers of the darkness of this world, against spiritual wickedness in high places.

13 Wherefore take unto you the whole armour of God, that ye may be able to withstand in the evil day, and having done all, to stand.

14 Stand therefore, having your loins girt about with truth, and having on the breastplate of righteousness;

15 And your feet shod with the preparation of the gospel of peace;

16 Above all, taking the shield of faith, wherewith ye shall be able to quench all the fiery darts of the wicked.

17 And take the helmet of salvation, and the sword of the Spirit, which is the word of God:

18 Praying always with all prayer and supplication in the Spirit, and watching thereunto with all perseverance and supplication for all saints;

19 And for me, that utterance may be given unto me, that I may open my mouth boldly, to make known the mystery of the gospel,

20 For which I am an ambassador in bonds: that therein I may speak boldly, as I ought to speak.

the authorities, against the powers of this dark world and against the spiritual forces of evil in the heavenly realms.

13 Therefore put on the full armor of God, so that when the day of evil comes, you may be able to stand your ground, and after you have done everything, to stand.

14 Stand firm then, with the belt of truth buckled around your waist, with the breastplate of righteousness in place,

15 and with your feet fitted with the readiness that comes from the gospel of peace.

16 In addition to all this, take up the shield of faith, with which you can extinguish all the flaming arrows of the evil one.

17 Take the helmet of salvation and the sword of the Spirit, which is the word of God.

18 And pray in the Spirit on all occasions with all kinds of prayers and requests. With this in mind, be alert and always keep on praying for all the Lord's people.

19 Pray also for me, that whenever I speak, words may be given me so that I will fearlessly make known the mystery of the gospel,

20 for which I am an ambassador in chains. Pray that I may declare it fearlessly, as I should.

LIGHT ON THE WORD

Principalities and powers are the evil and malicious spirits that oppose God and His people, both in the earthly realm and the heavenly realm (**1:3, 20–21; 3:10**). These powers were created by God and appear to be fallen angels that have rebelled against Him. Scripture declares that Jesus is the ultimate authority over them and that He disarmed them through His death on the Cross. Believers are called to resist and defeat these powers in our lives through the wisdom and power of God.

Armor has been used in battle since ancient times. The pieces of armor included resources for both offense and defense. The equipment of a Roman soldier was consistent for every soldier: a breastplate, a girdle or belt, a large door-like shield, a helmet, sword, spears, and sandals. In Paul's description of the Christian armor, it can be noted that there is no mention of a spear.

TEACHING THE BIBLE LESSON

LIFE NEED FOR TODAY'S LESSON

AIM: Students will know that proper preparation can give assurance that certain things are accomplished.

INTRODUCTION

A Spiritual Battle

Ephesians is unique among the epistles, as it does not explicitly address a particular problem or concern in the church of Ephesus. It can best be described as a model for what the church is supposed to be. In Ephesians, Paul has written a treatise defining what it means to be the church. He communicates to them that they are recipients of every spiritual blessing in Jesus Christ. They are saved by God's grace and mandated to practice good works and walk in a manner worthy of the calling they have received. Paul then proceeds to let them know how to live as the church. They are to exhibit morally pure lives and be filled with the Spirit. With this comes the ability to walk wisely and use their time for godly purposes. They are to mutually submit to one another, and this submission encompasses their home and work life. Paul then concludes his letter with an exhortation to battle. The church is now described in a military perspective. Paul exhorts the Ephesian believers to be strong in the Lord and to put on the whole armor of God. He lets them know that they have a spiritual enemy who is out to destroy them. Then he proceeds to list the pieces of armor they will need in this battle.

BIBLE LEARNING

AIM: Students will affirm that they are divinely armed in their struggle against spiritual forces of evil.

I. THE CALL TO ARMS (Ephesians 6:10–13)

Paul exhorts the Ephesian believers to be strong in the Lord and in His power. He gives them this exhortation for two reasons. The first is that with all the things he said they have been blessed with and all the duties they have been given, Satan will most definitely want to destroy them. Therefore, they need to be plugged into God's mighty power. The second reason is that they are not fighting a physical fight. Paul says that they do not wrestle against flesh and blood but against a hierarchy of evil spiritual forces.

Be Strong in the Lord (verses 10–13)

10 Finally, my brethren, be strong in the Lord, and in the power of his might. 11 Put on the whole armor of God, that ye may be able to stand against the wiles of the devil.

Paul begins by addressing his readers as "my brethren," which emphasizes the bond and intimate relationship that exists between him and the Ephesian church. It also calls for their serious attention and intensifies the importance of the subject matter. He urges them to be strong (Gk. *endunamoo*, **en-doo-nah-MAH-oh**, to empower, to increase in strength) in the Lord and in the power (Gk. *kratos*, **KRAH-tos**, vigor or strength) of His might (Gk. *ischuos*, **iss-KHOO-os**, ability, power, or strength). Using these synonyms, Paul calls on the church to rely totally on the Lord for the strength and ability to face the onslaught of the enemy that surrounds them.

Jesus told His disciples that without Him, they could do nothing (**John 15:1–5**), but Paul writes, "I can do all things through Christ which strengtheneth me" (**Philippians 4:13**; cf. **2 Corinthians 12:9–10; 1 Timothy 1:12**). We must totally rely on God's strength and power because He is all-powerful and His might is infinite, as evidenced in creation and in history. By His power and strength, God not only created the heavens and the earth, but He caused the Red Sea and the Jordan River to be driven back, the moon to stand still, the mountains to tremble, and the rocks to melt. He raised Christ from the dead (**Ephesians 1:20**) and made alive those who were dead in trespasses and sins (**2:1**). In view of these and other deeds which reveal God's omnipotence in history, Paul exhorts believers to hold fast in the Lord, the one who "is able to do exceeding abundantly above all that we ask or think, according to the power that worketh in us" (**3:20**).

Although we rely totally on the strength and might of God, we must equip ourselves with the whole armor (Gk. *panoplia*, **pan-op-LEE-a**, full, total, or complete armor) of God, that ye may be able to stand against the wiles of the devil. We must recall at this point that Paul is writing from prison in Rome and probably guarded by a well-dressed and completely equipped soldier or soldiers. He has a complete picture and image of a soldier in military regalia and readiness for battle. He, therefore, writes to the brethren in Ephesus, and indeed Christians of all times, to be completely dressed and ready for battle. However, the Christian's armor is not like the Roman's, which is physical—it is God's armor, which is spiritual. It is this type of military regalia we use to withstand and overcome the wiles or craftiness of the devil.

There are a few things to learn here about the devil. First, it is a fact that demons, evil spirits, Satan, devils, or whatever name given them exist contrary to the belief of many today who say that evil spirits are a myth. However, we must be careful not to give the devil a place he does not deserve by attributing to him everything adverse that happens. We must not be afraid of him. This often leads to the worship of Satan and his agents. We must acknowledge their existence as Paul did, but we are not to be afraid of them or pay them homage.

Second, we must acknowledge that Satan, the devil, is cunning and crafty, full of fury, and prowls around like a roaring lion looking for someone to devour (**1 Peter 5:8**, NIV). Having been cast out of Heaven, he is full of fury and envy. His hatred is against God, His people, and all they stand for. He has a well-organized army and is out to destroy God's kingdom and to bring with him as many people as possible into hell. Satan's craftiness can be seen throughout Scripture. He mixes falsehood with some truth to make it plausible (**Genesis 3:4, 5, 22**); quotes Scripture out of context (**Matthew 4:6**); and masquerades as an angel of light (**2 Corinthians 11:14**). Therefore, we must be properly equipped to fight him, not with human armor but God's, Paul says. The call here is urgent.

12 For we wrestle not against flesh and blood, but against principalities, against powers, against the rulers of the darkness of this world, against spiritual wickedness in high places. 13 Wherefore take unto you the whole armour of God, that ye may be able to withstand in the evil day, and having done all, to stand.

After Paul establishes the fact of the devil's existence and power and urges his audience to be fully equipped with God's own armor, Paul now gives them the reason they should be so equipped: we are not fighting against "flesh and blood," i.e., against mere, frail humans (**Galatians 1:16**), with all their physical and mental weakness (**Matthew 16:17; 1 Corinthians 15:50**). Rather, we are fighting against all types of forces in all realms of life. However, the enemy knows how to use humans to do his work, so we are often deceived into thinking that the fight is against another human being.

Paul categorizes these forces as "principalities and powers" (Gk. Gk. *arche*, **ar-KHAY**, realm, principality; *exousia*, **eks-oo-SEE-ah**, authorities; cf. **Ephesians 1:21**), as the "rulers of the darkness of this world," which speaks of those who are in tyrannical control of the world of ignorance and sin. We are also fighting against spiritual forces of "wickedness in high places" (Gk. *epouranios*, **ep-oo-RAH-nee-os**, heavenly places). Heavenly places here is the same word and therefore the same realm where Christ is enthroned at God's right hand and therefore has a special position and power above all others inhabiting this realm (**1:20**). It is also where the redeemed are seated with Him (**2:6**) as well as the home of the obedient angels (**3:10**). It is the region above the earth but below the Heaven, referred to as the "domain of the air" (**2:2**).

Paul, in effect, says that since we are contending against an innumerable host of spiritual forces, we must be fully equipped and put on the full armor of God (**v. 11**). Paul repeats this call in **verse 13**. The repetition of this call intensifies its urgency. The word "wrestle" used in **verse 12** can be misleading; since wrestling is viewed as a sport, it therefore can erroneously minimize the magnitude of the battle that is facing the Christian. The explanation is probably that the battle is so intense and violent that it is like hand-to-hand combat. It is only with such divine armament that we would "be able to withstand in the evil day," that is, in the day of severe trial and temptation and onslaught of the evil one (cf. **Psalm 49:5**). The implication here is that we must always be ready and on guard since we do not know when these crises will occur.

SEARCH THE SCRIPTURES

QUESTION 1

Whom does Paul identify as the believers' opponent in battle?

LIGHT ON THE WORD

Prepared for the Enemy

Paul calls the believers to not only arm themselves with God's power, but further explains that believers ought to put on the full armor of God. This will enable followers of Jesus to resist the assaults of the enemy in the evil day. This evil day is the time of trial and testing that we all will experience in our walk with Jesus. Paul concludes his call to arms with an exhortation to stand. This is the final act of resistance. After preparing, Paul admonishes the believer to stand fully armed in the day of trouble.

II. THE SOLDIER'S ARMOR (vv. 14–17)

Next Paul describes the armor of God. This armor resembles the armor of a Roman soldier. It consists of a belt, breastplate, sandals, shield, helmet, and sword. Paul describes these items as the virtues the Christian must put on in the fight against their spiritual adversaries. The equipment is listed in the exact order the Roman soldier would put them on. The first piece of armor is the belt of truth. The next piece of armor is the breastplate of righteousness. After the breastplate is the footgear, the readiness of the Gospel of peace.

Spiritual Armor (verses 14–17)

14 Stand therefore, having your loins girt about with truth, and having on the breastplate of righteousness;

To "stand," here and in verse 11, does not imply passivity, where a soldier is pictured standing like a brick wall waiting for Satan's attack. Rather, Paul paints a picture of a soldier equipped and drawn up in battle array, rushing into war making full use of God's weapons of war for attacks and defense. It is then that the soldier would be able to stand his ground and resist the evil one, and the devil will flee from him (**James 4:7**; cf. **Matthew 10:22**). The picture is that of a soldier who is alert, vigilant, one that is never asleep and never taken unaware by the devil, who cunningly likes to attack at odd times. This is the picture of the Christian Paul paints here, a strong and stable Christian who remains firm against the wiles of the devil (**v. 11**), even in a time of crisis or pressure.

In the next five verses, Paul details the six major pieces of the soldier's armor and gives the function of each one of them: the belt, the breastplate, the boots, the shield, the helmet, and the sword. They represent truth, righteousness, the Gospel of peace, faith, salvation, and the Word of God, respectively. All these pieces of spiritual armor equip us to battle against the evil powers.

The first piece of equipment which Paul lists is the belt of truth: "having your loins girt about with truth." The belt or the girdle, usually made of leather, is tied around the waist and used to brace the armor tight against the body. As the soldier buckles the belt, he feels a sense of hidden strength and confidence. One can see this watching people prepare to fight. One of the first things the fighters can do is take off their hair scarf or neck piece, tie it around their waist, and confidently beckon the other for a fight. As he or she waits for the other person to make a move, one could sense his or her feeling of confidence and inner strength. The belt is also used to hold daggers, swords, and other weapons to give the soldier freedom of movement when marching.

Paul says that the Christian's belt is truth. The two possible types of truth meant here are (1) the truth, as God's revelation in Christ and the Scripture, and (2) truth, as in honesty or integrity. Only the truth can dispel the devil's lies and set us free (**John 8:31–36, 43–45**). The psalmist says that God requires truth in the inward being (**Psalm 51:6**), and Paul says that we are to speak the truth in love (**Ephesians 4:15**). A common piece of advice is that if you speak the truth the first time, you will not worry to find another lie in future. Truth will always prevail, and lies and dishonesty will always be exposed. Honesty and integrity are marks of bravery, but lies are a sign of cowardice. The opposite of truth is lies, and the Bible says that Satan is the father of lies (**John 8:44**, NIV). Therefore we cannot beat him at his own game. Truth is the only thing that will dispel him, because he hates truth.

The second piece of the Christian's weaponry Paul mentions here is the breastplate (Gk. *thorax*, **THO-raks**) of righteousness. A breastplate is described as the armor that covers the body from neck to the thighs, the vital parts of the body. It consists of two parts, one for the back and the other for the front. Here, Paul says that the equipment for protection is righteousness (Gk. *dikaiosune*, **dee-keye-o-SOO-neigh**), which is often translated in Pauline epistles as "justification." This is theologically explained as the process whereby God through Christ puts the sinner in a right relationship with Himself. The most amazing gift for unjust sinners is to stand before the almighty, just God and not to be condemned, but accepted and clothed with God's righteousness through Christ as if they had not sinned. It is the believer's assurance that through Christ, all of our sins are forgiven and the barrier between God and us has been removed (**Isaiah 59:1–2**). This is the work of grace, which God wrought through the death of His Son Jesus on the Cross.

One of Satan's greatest weapons is slander, to accuse us through our conscience. Therefore, there is no greater defensive weapon for the Christian against the slanderous attack of the devil than the assurance of a right relationship with the Father through His Son (**2 Corinthians 5:21**). Paul assures the Roman believers of this fact: "There is therefore now no condemnation to them which are in Christ Jesus, who walk not after the flesh, but after the Spirit . . . . Who shall lay any thing to the charge of God's elect? It is God that justifieth. Who is he that condemneth? It is Christ that died, yea rather, that is risen again, who is even at the right hand of God, who also maketh intercession for us" (**Romans 8:1, 33–34**). This relationship disarms the devil and offers protection for the Christian.

To successfully ward off the devil's unceasing slanderous attack, we must maintain that relationship with the Father by using the weapons of righteousness for the right hand and for the left (**2 Corinthians 6:7**). The righteousness referred to here, as well as in **Ephesians 4:24 and 5:9**, is a moral righteousness. Just as the Christian is to cultivate truth to overcome the deceptions of the devil, he also has to cultivate righteousness (i.e., moral integrity) in order to overcome the devil's slanderous attacks. Without integrity and a clear conscience, one cannot defend oneself against the accusations of the devil, who accuses the brethren night and day (**Revelation 12:10**).

15 And your feet shod with the preparation of the gospel of peace;

The next weapon in the apostle's list for warfare is the boot: the preparation of the Gospel of peace. The word translated "preparation" is the Greek word *hetoimasia* (**heh-toy-mah-SEE-ah**), which means "readiness, the act of preparedness." Paul says that the Christian should put on the Gospel of peace as his army boots. Boots protect soldiers from slipping, and from thorns or objects that can pierce through their feet and thereby hinder them from marching forward into battle. The Gospel (Good News) of peace is the protective mechanism by which we are shielded from the dangerous gimmicks the devil lays in our path to hinder our walk with the Lord. The more we are ready and prepared to testify about or confess Christ to others, the better we are protected from backsliding and falling into Satan's traps and temptation. This verse is also an allusion to the prophet Isaiah's proclamation, "How beautiful upon the mountains are the feet of him that bringeth good tidings, that publisheth peace" (from **Isaiah 52:7**, cf. **Romans 10:15**). The devil hates the Gospel (Good News) of Jesus Christ, because it is the power of God and salvation to everyone that believes (**Romans 1:16**).

Boots are a vital part of a soldier's armor, and with them securely strapped on, the soldier feels a certain amount of confidence and is ready for action. Without boots, the soldier will be ill-equipped and unprepared for battle.

16 Above all, taking the shield of faith, wherewith ye shall be able to quench all the fiery darts of the wicked.

The fourth weapon is the shield of faith, which we must take above all (Gk. *en pasin*, **en PA-sin**) in the sense that it is an indispensable part of the whole armor, rather than the most important part. The phrase can be rendered: "along with or besides all these, take also the shield of faith." The Greek word here, *thureos* (**thoo-reh-OCE**), was a large oblong, four-cornered shield, which covered the whole body, rather than the small round one that covered only a smaller part of the body. The thureos is specially designed to ward off all types of dangerous darts or missiles thrown, such as the arrows, javelins, spears, or stones that were used then.

The fiery darts also probably refer to the combustible arrowheads that set fire to the enemy's fortifications, boats, houses, or wooden shields. In order to quench the fiery darts, the shields are covered with metals. What are the fiery darts of the devil as they relate to the Christian warfare? They no doubt include the following: evil thoughts, lusts, false guilt, sinful passions, temptation of various kinds, doubts, disobedience, rebellion, malice, and fear (cf. **1 Corinthians 10:13–14; 2 Corinthians 10:4–6; James 1:13–15**, etc.). The devil ceaselessly launches all these deadly, fire-tipped darts at us daily in different forms and combinations. There is one weapon to quench or extinguish them: the shield of faith. **Proverbs 30:5** says that God is a shield to them that put their trust in Him. Faith here is reliance in and taking hold of the promises of God in the work Christ fulfilled on the Cross (**Ephesians 1:20–22**). In times of temptation, doubts, and depression, faith is claiming the power of God (**Philippians 4:13**). With faith, we can move mountains, Jesus told His disciples (**Matthew 17:20; Luke 17:6**).

17 And take the helmet of salvation, and the sword of the Spirit, which is the word of God:

Paul adds two more pieces of warfare equipment to the list: the helmet of salvation and the sword of the Spirit. We are to take these as weapons to fight the wicked one. Paul calls the helmet "the hope of salvation" in **1 Thessalonians 5:8**, while here it is the "helmet of salvation." There seems to be no apparent difference in these passages, since salvation is both a present and a future reality. Hence, salvation is anchored in hope. This metaphor is used in the Old Testament, where the Lord wears the helmet of salvation on His head as He goes to vindicate His people, who had been oppressed (**Isaiah 59:17**). Therefore, just as soldiers receive a helmet from their army superiors in charge of supplies, Paul says we are to take (Gk. *dechomai*, **DE-kho-meye**, to receive or accept) salvation through faith as a gift from God (**2:8**). The ancient helmets were cast from iron and brass (**1 Samuel 17:5, 38**) and they offered protection for the head like the breastplate provided for the heart. Salvation is also a protective (defensive) gear that assures the Christian in both the present and the future during times of crisis and persecutions. The assurance of God's salvation, which He has wrought through Christ in us, strengthens and carries the Christian to go on fighting without giving up, even in very difficult situations. It is the confidence that what God has begun in him, He will surely bring to completion (**Philippians 1:6**; cf. **Psalm 138:8**).

The final weapon that Paul urges the Christian to take is the sword of the Spirit. While all the other five listed are primarily weapons for defense or protection, the sword is the only weapon which can clearly be used for both offense and defense. The word translated "sword" is the Greek word *machaira* (**MA-kheye-rah**), which specifically refers to a small or short sword as opposed to a large or long one. Therefore, the combat envisaged here is in close quarters. The Christian's weapon of offense is the sword of the Spirit (or "spiritual sword"), which Paul identifies immediately as the Word (Gk. *rhema*, **RAY-ma**, the spoken word) of God. Jesus foreshadowed the importance of the Spirit's words when He promised His disciples that He would fill their lips with words through the Spirit when they are brought before magistrates (**Matthew 10:17–20**).

The Bible says that the Word of God is powerful and sharper than a double-edged sword (**Hebrews 4:12**), and so we ought to use it with confidence. The Word of God refers to both the written Word (the Scripture) inspired by the Holy Spirit (**2 Timothy 3:16; 2 Peter 1:21**) and the spoken word (*rhema*), the confession and testimony which will stand forever (**Isaiah 40:8**). Jesus applied the Word to fight Satan's temptations in the wilderness of Judea (**Luke 4:1–13**). John records the victory of the saints against Satan, saying, "And they overcame him by the blood of the Lamb, and by the word of their testimony" (from **Revelation 12:11**). The Word of God is the greatest weapon with which we can fight the devil and his gimmicks. It is amazing what victory we can have when we apply the Word of God. Through it, we dispel doubts, fears, and guilt; by it Satan is put to flight, and assurance of salvation is secured in our hearts.

The complete armor of God is made available to every Christian: truth as the girdle, righteousness as the breastplate, the Gospel as the boots, faith as the shield, salvation as the helmet, and the Word of God as the Spirit's sword (or the spiritual sword). Since the battle is not against humans, but spirits, we need all the specified weapons without leaving any out, so that we can withstand and stand firm against Satan's ceaseless onslaught against us. We must be fully equipped, always ready for battle.

SEARCH THE SCRIPTURES

QUESTION 2

What is the purpose of taking up the shield of faith?

LIGHT ON THE WORD

Christian Armor

Paul admonishes the Ephesian believers to take up the shield of faith. He also tells them to take the helmet of salvation. Next he calls them to take up the sword of the Spirit. He further explains that this is the Word of God. Being furnished with all these items, the Christian is completely armored and prepared for the battle.

III. THE CALL TO PRAYER (vv. 18–20)

The secret weapon of prayer is the last piece of the Christian's equipment for battle. Paul exhorts them to use all kinds of prayers in the battle against the spiritual forces of darkness. This praying and supplication is to be done "in the Spirit"; that is, these prayers should be motivated and directed by the Spirit of God, not selfish and man-centered ramblings. These prayers also are to be directed toward all the saints. We are called not only to look after ourselves but to stand with all of our brothers and sisters in Christ. We see here that our secret weapon consists of all kinds of prayers, being prayed in the Spirit, for all the saints.

Paul's Prayer Request (verses 18–20)

18 Praying always with all prayer and supplication in the Spirit, and watching thereunto with all perseverance and supplication for all saints; 19 And for me, that utterance may be given unto me, that I may open my mouth boldly, to make known the mystery of the gospel, 20 For which I am an ambassador in bonds: that therein I may speak boldly, as I ought to speak.

After listing all the armor the Christian should put in use to fight against the wiles and wickedness of the devil, Paul explains how to use them by praying. Prayer and the Word are the two most important aspects of Christian living. Without either or both of them, the Christian's life is in jeopardy, and his life may even be at the mercy of Satan and his agents. No soldier of Christ can do anything on his or her own power without seeking strength and blessing from God, the all-powerful Father, even though he or she may have all their weapons. As a believer puts each piece of the armor on and makes use of it, he or she must rely on God through prayer. Hence, Paul says, put on the whole armor while praying and watching (**vv. 18–20**).

Prayer is not a one-time exercise, but should be done always (at all times), that is, constantly or habitually with all variety of prayers being "all prayer and supplication." The phrase "all prayer" (Gk. *pas*, **PAS**, prayer; proseuche, **pro-sew-KHEE**, prayer) probably includes both public and private, church and family prayer. It will consist of supplication (Gk. *deesis*, **dee-AY-sis**), i.e., making a special request or seeking favor for some special necessity from God. It speaks of being specific instead of general in prayer. It should be done at all times, as we have already intimated, and it should be done through the Holy Spirit, who makes intercession for us even when we do not know how or what to pray (**Romans 8:26–27, 34**).

Paul calls on us to be alert (Gk. *agrupneo*, **ah-groop-NEH-o**, to watch, be attentive) as we pray and with perseverance (Gk. *proskarteresis*, **pros-kar-TEH-ray-sis**) as we make supplication for the saints. This means we must be persistent and resolute in our prayer, not only for ourselves, but also for all members of the family of God in which we now belong. We shall not only be alert and watchful of Satan's strategies; we should be alert to know or be aware of the needs of others so that we can pray objectively, instead of rambling away without tangible things to pray for as we intercede for others.

Paul now, for the first time in the entire letter, makes a request for himself. He asks that when prayer is made on behalf of all the saints, they should remember him in a special way in their prayers. His two-fold request is clear, simple, and noble. First, he asks that God might give him the utterance (*logos*, i.e., the word) or the correct message when he opens his mouth to speak (**Matthew 10:19**); and second, that God might give him the courage at all times to deliver the message in a proper manner (**Acts 4:13**). The prayer request is important to him since it is for the sake of the Gospel, he says, "for which I am an ambassador in chains" (**from v. 20, NKJV**). This echoes his request in **Colossians 4:2–3**, that he be endowed with power and boldness so that he could continue to make known the mystery of the Gospel. What is that mystery of the Gospel? That through Christ, there is full salvation for everyone who comes to Him in faith, both Jew and Gentile, and it is free. That through Christ the barrier of hostility which formerly existed between the Jews and Gentiles has now been removed and they are now one in God's new family (**Ephesians 3:3–7, 9**; cf. **Romans 16:25; Colossians 1:26; 2:2**). The Gospel is the mystery, which God through Christ made known, and Paul, though imprisoned at the time in a Roman jail, is an ambassador charged to proclaim this Good News.

LIGHT ON THE WORD

Paul's Prayer Request

Lastly, Paul makes a prayer request. He asks for them to pray for him. He is chained to a Roman guard and awaiting trial. His obvious prayer request would be that he would be released. Instead, Paul asks them to pray that he would preach the Gospel boldly. He wants the Lord to give Him not only courage but also the right words to say. His mind is on the Gospel being advanced. This is the true battle for the believer. It is not about managing our sin or maintaining our religious piety. It is a battle for the hearts and minds of those who do not know Jesus as Lord. This is the reason we need to make sure we are clothed and ready for battle.

BIBLE APPLICATION

AIM: Students will know that God has greater powers than the spiritual forces of evil.

The world is filled with fighting and hostility. Groups are often pitted against each other in opposition. Many lines are drawn in the sand, and we often resort to uncharitable words and even physical violence. The people of God are called to fight, but not against flesh and blood. We are engaged in a war against spiritual forces of darkness. Wherever we see opposition to God and His Gospel, we must know that it cannot be defeated by mere human methods. We must put on the full armor of God and rely on His power. It is our duty in these times to be clothed and ready.

STUDENTS' RESPONSES

AIM: Students will value the feeling of being prepared to serve God.

The next time you are in a situation where your faith is being challenged or you are experiencing persecution, be sure to see the real enemy. Pray that the Lord would fill you with "the power of his might" and put on the whole armor of God. Create a checklist and examine whether you are clothed and ready with the full armor of God. If you are lacking a piece of equipment, pray that God would give it to you and share this with another Christian brother or sister who can mentor you in this area.

PRAYER

Dear Jesus, we want to grow in our relationship with You. As we pray, forgive, love, act justly, and live Your Word, the stronger we are standing against the devil. Help us to know You and obey Your way and Your will in our lives. In Jesus' Name we pray. Amen.

HOW TO SAY IT

Principality. prin-ci-**PA**-li-tee.

PREPARE FOR NEXT SUNDAY

Read **John 1:29–34** and study "The Lamb of God."

DAILY HOME BIBLE READINGS

MONDAY
Ready with the Word
(Luke 4:1–12)

TUESDAY
The Battle Lines Drawn
(1 Samuel 17:19–30)

WEDNESDAY
Choosing the Right Equipment
(1 Samuel 17:31–39)

THURSDAY
The Battle is the Lord's
(1 Samuel 17:40–50)

FRIDAY
Put on the Lord Jesus Christ
(Romans 13:8–14)

SATURDAY
The Dress for God's Chosen Ones
(Colossians 3:12–17)

SUNDAY
The Whole Armor of God
(Ephesians 6:10–20)

Sources:

Lincoln, Andrew T. *Word Biblical Commentary Ephesians*. Dallas, TX: Word Books, 1990.

Martin, Ralph P. *Interpretation: Ephesians, Colossians, and Philemon*. Louisville, KY: John Knox Press, 1991.

COMMENTS / NOTES:

TEACHING TECHNIQUES

THE COMING OF THE SPIRIT

BY ELDER ERIC JAMES GRÉAUX SR., PH.D.

Associate Professor of Religion, Winston-Salem State University, North Carolina

Pastor, Triad Ministries Church Of God In Christ, Kernersville, NC

INTRODUCTION

The topic of the Holy Spirit is one of the most important in the life of Pentecostal believers. This commentary serves as a very brief biblical pneumatology (study of the Person and work of the Holy Spirit) for studying the background of Jesus' words of promise in John's Gospel (John 14–16), and anticipating the teachings of the other New Testament writers. It is not intended to be comprehensive; such a work would be enormous. Rather, we want to examine some of the most salient points for coming to a fuller understanding of the coming of the Holy Spirit and His work in the lives of believers.

The Prophecy of the Spirit's Coming

Any survey of the Bible's teaching on the Holy Spirit would be incomplete without a consideration of what the Old Testament says. Often it is stated that the difference between the Holy Spirit in the Old and the New Testaments is that the Holy Spirit came *on/upon* people in the Old Testament, but came *into* people in the New Testament and today, or they are *filled* with the Spirit. What is the evidence for this assertion? Within Israel, the Spirit was said to be in or with Israel's leaders, enabling them to act with God's power or to reveal His will. Accordingly, God's Spirit was portrayed as a charismatic endowment on judges. For example, the text tells us that after the children of Israel cried to the Lord, He raised up Othniel. When the Spirit of the Lord came upon him, he judged Israel and prevailed against their enemies (Judges 3:9–10). Likewise, when the Spirit came upon Gideon (Judges 6:34) and then Jephthah (Judges 11:29), each was empowered to lead the people and defeat their enemies. One of the last judges, Samson, also was Spirit-empowered and given extraordinary strength; the text says that when the Spirit of the Lord came mightily upon him, he tore a lion asunder as one tears a young goat (Judges 14:6), slew thirty men of Ashkelon (Judges 14:19), and slew one thousand men in Lehi with the jawbone of an ass (Judges 15:14–15).

The Old Testament says that the Holy Spirit was also given to prophets (for example, Ezekiel 2:2, 3:24, 11:5; Daniel 4:18, 5:11, 14), and kings (for example, Saul and David). Finally, the evidence of the Old Testament also demonstrates that the Holy Spirit was given to those who were ordained to carry out a specific task for a specific period in redemptive history (for example, Bezaleel [Exodus 31:2-3] and the seventy elders [Numbers 11:25]).

So the question arises, "What is the difference between Old Testament and New Testament pneumatology in relation to individuals?" In other words, is it correct to say that the Holy Spirit came *into* New Testament people while merely resting upon Old Testament characters? The evidence of the Scriptures seems to indicate the contrary. Speaking of Joseph, Pharaoh asks the question, "Can we find anyone like this man, one *in whom* is the spirit of God?" (from Genesis 41:38, NIV). Before the demise of Moses, the Lord commanded him, "Take Joshua, son of Nun, a man *in whom* is the spirit of leadership, and lay your hand on him" (Numbers 27:18, NIV). On two occasions, Ezekiel speaks of the Spirit coming *into* him, raising him to his feet and speaking to him (Ezekiel 2:2, 3:24). Finally, in the book of Daniel, there are five references to the holy gods (i.e., God) *in him* by which Daniel is able to interpret the dreams of Nebuchadnezzar (Daniel 4:18) and Belshazzar (Daniel 5:11).

In addition, one could also include Bezaleel (Exodus 31:2-3), and Joshua (Deuteronomy 34:9; Numbers 27:18). The Bible speaks of them as having been *filled* with the Spirit. This observation is important because the New Testament uses the same Greek word (*plerein*) used in the Septuagint (the Greek translation of the Hebrew Bible) to translate the filling of the 120 with the Holy Spirit on the Day of Pentecost. Theologically, what may be concluded from this brief analysis of biblical pneumatology in relation to individuals? Numbers 11 is a key passage for this understanding. After the Spirit comes upon the seventy elders, Eldad, and Medad, Moses expresses his wish that the same would be the experience of *all* God's people (v. 29). Later, during the ministry of Joel, he prophesied of a day when the Lord would pour out of His Spirit upon all flesh resulting in the prophesying of His elect:

"And it shall come to pass afterward, that I will pour out my Spirit upon all flesh; and your sons and your daughters shall prophesy, your old men shall dream dreams, your young men shall see visions: And also upon the servants and upon the handmaids in those days will I pour out my spirit" (Joel 2:28–29).

On the Day of Pentecost, Peter declared that this prophecy of Joel 2:28 was now being fulfilled. In response to the mockeries of the crowd gathered in Jerusalem on that auspicious day, Peter says, "For these are not drunken, as ye suppose, seeing it is but the third hour of the day. But this is that which was spoken by the prophet Joel" (Acts 2:15–16). In other words, Peter equates their being filled with the Holy Spirit as the fulfillment of Joel's prophecy of God's pouring out of His Holy Spirit upon all flesh. Therefore, it may be concluded that the difference between the coming of the Spirit to individuals in the Old Testament and the New Testaments is not a matter of distinction between *upon/on* and *in/filled*. Rather, the distinction lies in the scope of the fulfillment of God's promises (for example, Joel 2:28): that the Spirit would no longer be limited to a particular class of people but available for all His people—"as many as the LORD our God shall call" (from Acts 2:39). The future was thus expected to be an epoch characterized by the lavish outpouring of God's Spirit.

"For I will pour water upon him that is thirsty, and floods upon the dry ground: I will pour my spirit upon thy seed, and my blessing upon thine offspring" (Isaiah 44:3; cf. 32:15; Ezekiel 39:29).

When we turn our attention to the New Testament, we see that both John the Baptist and Jesus prophesy of the coming of the Holy Spirit on believers. Each Gospel records the promise of John the Baptizer that he baptized in water, but the one coming after him would baptize in the Holy Spirit (Mark 1:8; John 1:33) and with fire (Matthew 3:11; Luke 3:16).

The Practice of the Spirit's Arrival

The book of Acts records several events that followed the Passion and Resurrection of Jesus. Luke tells us that Jesus was with His disciples forty days and then led them out to the Mount of Olives. Shortly preceding His ascension to Heaven, He gave them the command to return to Jerusalem and wait for the promised Holy Spirit (Luke 24:49). This promise was fulfilled ten days later on the Day of Pentecost.

The Spirit comes with power. The fulfillment of the various prophecies from Old Testament prophets, John the Baptist, and Jesus is recorded in the book of Acts. The Apostle Luke tells his readers that on the Day of Pentecost, the disciples "were all filled with the Holy Ghost, and began to speak with other tongues, as the Spirit gave them utterance" (Acts 2:4). The result is that they were empowered to give bold witness to the things that they had seen Jesus do and heard Him teach. Bold, open speech in the name of Jesus is a consistent theme in the book of the Acts of the Holy Spirit (Act 9:27, 18:26, 19:8). In other words, in Acts the primary function of the coming of the Spirit is to empower and embolden believers to evangelize the world and witness for Jesus.

The New Testament is a narrative of God's grace. When God acts, He is demonstrating His favor, which we do not deserve, cannot earn or repay, and cannot achieve through our own effort. As such, the New Testament speaks of three kinds of grace: saving grace (i.e., the faith that receives Christ as Savior and Lord), sanctifying grace (i.e., developing Christian character), and serving grace (i.e., receiving and using gifts given to us by the Holy Spirit for the growth of the Kingdom of God).

The sanctifying grace of the Spirit. When the Spirit comes, He causes believers to grow in holiness. In other words, the Holy Spirit works in the lives of God's people to such an extent that they are being conformed to the image of His Son, Jesus (Romans 8:29). This is demonstrated on a regular basis as believers put away sin and put on godly virtues

(Ephesians 4:17–32; Colossians 3:5–17). In other words, the Spirit causes the believer to become sanctified. Sanctification is that progressive work of the Holy Spirit begun at conversion which enables the believer to be separated from evil, dedicated to God, and to become more holy.

One image that Apostle Paul uses to illustrate the sanctifying work of the Holy Spirit is slavery. He reminds believers that as a result of being united with Christ and filled with His Spirit, they are no longer slaves to sin.

"For if we have been united with [Christ Jesus] in a death like his, we shall certainly be united with him in a resurrection like his. We know that our old self was crucified with him in order that the body of sin might be brought to nothing, so that we would no longer be enslaved to sin" (Romans 6:5–6, ESV).

Submission to the sanctifying work of the Spirit enables the believer to live sin-free to the extent that he or she yields to the Spirit's inner work. The promise of the Scripture is that "sin shall not have dominion over you" (from Romans 6:14). Again, John tells us that as a result of the Spirit's work in the lives of believers, they begin to keep Jesus' commandments and to walk as He walked. The emphasis is this: Believers in Jesus do not practice sin as a lifestyle; they do not keep on sinning (1 John 3:6, 9). This statement by no means implies entering into a sinless state. Rather one is clearly on the road to becoming more like Christ. If they sin and confess the sin, they can receive forgiveness (1 John 1:9) and receive that ongoing cleansing work of the Spirit.

Of special concern to Paul was maintaining sexual purity. Such a high standard of morality is possible only through the enabling of the Holy Spirit.

"This is the will of God, your sanctification: that you abstain from sexual immorality; that each one of you know how to control his own body in holiness and honor … For God has not called us for impurity, but in holiness. Therefore whoever disregards this, disregards not man but God, who gives his Holy Spirit to you" (1 Thessalonians 4:3–4, 7–8, ESV).

Yielding to the work of the Spirit will produce His fruit—love, joy, peace, patience, kindness, goodness, faithfulness, gentleness, and self-control—in the lives of believers (Galatians 5:22–23, ESV).

The serving grace of the Spirit. The writers of the New Testament make it quite clear that when the Spirit comes, He comes bearing gifts—spiritual gifts. These gifts can be defined as the ability or skill that enables the recipient to perform a spiritual function in the Body of Christ with ease and effectiveness. According to 1 Corinthians, every believer receives a spiritual gift (12:13–14, 18). The Epistles of the New Testament provide lists of these spiritual gifts, no two of which match, and these lists are not exhaustive (Romans 12:6–8; 1 Corinthians 12:8–9, 28–30; Ephesians 4:11; 1 Peter 4:11). The purpose of these gifts is to equip the saints to do the work of the ministry (Ephesians 4:12).

The Spirit prays for us. When the Spirit comes, He prays for us. Paul reminds the believers in Rome that they are not alone in their efforts to live a life pleasing to God. Rather, they have that very same Helper to which Jesus referred (John 14–16).

"Likewise the Spirit helps us in our weakness. For we do not know what to pray for as we ought, but the Spirit himself intercedes for us with groanings too deep for words. And he who searches hearts knows what is the mind of the Spirit, because the Spirit intercedes for the saints according to the will of God" (Romans 8:26–27, ESV).

One of the issues of interpretation that New Testament scholars discuss regarding this text is whether or not the "groanings too deep for words" may refer to speaking in tongues. If so, perhaps Jude's admonition to believers to pray "in the Holy Spirit" (from Jude 1:20, ESV) may be an exhortation to allow the Spirit to pray through them in this heavenly language.

How wonderful it is to experience the work of the Spirit in our lives! We have been adopted into the family of God by the indwelling of the Spirit (Galatians 4:5f; Ephesians 1:5). That is why we can cry "Abba, Father" (Romans 8:15). We have been sealed by the Spirit. Its image used by Paul (Ephesians 1:13) is meant to demonstrate ownership (as one would brand animals or mark property) and safety. Therefore true believers never need to fear losing their salvation. We are protected by God through His Spirit.

Frank Bottome penned the hymn "The Comforter Has Come." Indeed his word from the nineteenth century rings as a continual reminder of our responsibility as Spirit-filled believers.

O, spread the tidings 'round, wherever man is found,
Wherever human hearts and human woes abound;
Let every Christian tongue proclaim the joyful sound:
The Comforter has come!

The Comforter has come,
The Comforter has come,
The Holy Ghost from heaven,
The Father's promise given;
Oh, spread the tidings 'round
Wherever man is found—
The Comforter has come!

For Further Research

The literature on biblical pneumatology is quite vast. However, the following monographs are quite insightful for anyone wanting to pursue further study of this subject.

Dunn, James D.G. *Baptism in the Holy Spirit: A Re-examination of the New Testament Teaching on the Gift of the Spirit in Relation to Pentecostalism Today.* Philadelphia: Westminster, 1970.

---------. *Jesus and the Spirit: A Study of the Religious and Charismatic Experience of Jesus and the First Christians as Reflected in the New Testament.* Grand Rapids, MI: Eerdmans, 1997.

Fee, Gordon D. *God's Empowering Presence: The Holy Spirit in the Letters of Paul.* Peabody, MA: Hendrickson, 1994.

Green, Michael. *I Believe in the Holy Spirit.* Grand Rapids, MI: Eerdmans, 1975.

Hildebrandt, Wilf. *An Old Testament Theology of the Spirit of God.* Peabody, MA: Hendrickson, 1995.

Keener, Craig S. *3 Crucial Questions about the Holy Spirit.* Grand Rapids, MI: Baker, 1996.

---------. *Gift and Giver: The Holy Spirit for Today.* Grand Rapids, MI: Baker Academic, 2001.

---------. *The Spirit in the Gospels and Acts: Divine Purity and Power.* Peabody, MA: Hendrickson, 1997.

SANCTIFICATION

BY DR. LINDA SMITH

According to Encarta Dictionary, sanctify means to set apart for special use, or to make holy! "Without holiness no one will see the Lord" (from Hebrews 12:14, NIV). "For I am the LORD your God: ye shall therefore sanctify yourselves, and ye shall be holy; for I am holy" (from Leviticus 11:44). God is holy and His children are holy also. "But as he which hath called you is holy, so be ye holy in all manner of conversation" (1 Peter 1:15).

I. ***"Sanctify yourselves therefore, and be ye holy: for I am the LORD your God. And ye shall keep my statutes, and do them: I am the LORD which sanctify you"*** (Leviticus 20:7–8).

II. In the Old Testament, sanctification (or holiness) means following the laws of purification as pertaining to food, washings, sacrifices, and cleanliness, as in Leviticus 7:21, Leviticus 20:25, and Deuteronomy 14:3–20. Sanctification and holiness also mean being pure and obeying the commandments of the Lord, as described in Exodus 20.

III. ***"Now therefore, if ye will obey my voice indeed, and keep my covenant, then ye shall be a peculiar treasure unto me above all people: for all the earth is mine"*** (Exodus 19:5). God told the Children of Israel that if they would sanctify themselves and obey His commandments, then He would be their God and they would be His special people.

IV. Sanctification and holiness comtinues to be discussed in the New Testament as a lifestyle; it's how we as believers are to walk and live. Sanctification is the work of the Holy Spirit in the life of the believer.

- ***"Furthermore then we beseech you, brethren, and exhort you by the Lord Jesus, that as ye have received of us how ye ought to walk and to please God, so ye would abound more and more. For ye know what commandments we gave you by the Lord Jesus. For this is the will of God, even your sanctification, that ye should abstain from fornication. That every one of you should know how to possess his vessel in sanctification and honor; Not in the lust of concupiscence, even as the Gentiles which know not God"*** (1 Thessalonians 4:1–5).

- In the New Testament, sanctification means living a life that is pleasing to God. Living a sanctified life means to present your body as "a living sacrifice, holy, acceptable unto God, which is your reasonable service" (from Romans 12:1). The Bible teaches us that once we become sanctified, sin has no more dominion over us and we are to no longer live a sinful lifestyle (Romans 6). The sinful lifestyle we lived before we received Christ, we don't live that way any longer. The sinful places we used to go, we don't go there anymore. The sinful things we used to do, we don't do them anymore.

- *"Know ye not that the unrighteous shall not inherit the kingdom of God? Be not deceived: neither fornicators, nor idolaters, nor adulterers, nor effeminate, nor abusers of themselves with mankind, Nor thieves, nor covetous, nor drunkards, nor revilers, nor extortioners, shall inherit the kingdom of God. And such were some of you: but ye are washed, but ye are sanctified, but ye are justified in the name of the Lord Jesus, and by the Spirit of our God"* (1 Corinthians 6:9–11).

  In holiness we don't live the ungodly lifestyle as we did in the past. We are to live holy lives.

V. Sanctification/holiness also teaches us to love God and one another.

- "*Thou shalt love the Lord thy God with all thy heart, and with all thy soul, and with all thy mind. This is the first and great commandment. And the second is like unto it, Thou shalt love thy neighbor as thyself. On these two commandments hang all the law and the prophets"* (from Matthew 22:37–40).

VI. In Sanctification/holiness, we are to work honestly with people.

- *"That no man go beyond and defraud his brother in any matter: because that the Lord is the avenger of all such, as we also have forewarned you and testified"* (1 Thessalonians 4:6).

VII. Sanctification/holiness teaches us to live a quiet life and handle our own business.

- *"And that ye study to be quiet, and to do your own business, and to work with your own hands, as we commanded you"* (1 Thessalonians 4:11).

- *"If any would not work, neither should he eat"* (from 2 Thessalonians 3:10).

VIII. Jesus is coming back, and we must be sanctified/holy.

- *"But of the times and the seasons, brethren, ye have no need that I write unto you. For yourselves know perfectly that the day of the Lord so cometh as a thief in the night"* (1 Thessalonians 5:1–2).

- ***"Therefore let us not sleep, as do others; but let us watch and be sober"*** (1 Thessalonians 5:6).

IX. We can't live sanctified/holy lives on our own, we need the Holy Ghost.

- The Holy Ghost enables the believer to live a sanctified/holy life.
- ***"For John truly baptized with water; but ye shall be baptized with the Holy Ghost not many days hence"*** (Acts 1:5).
- ***"But ye shall receive power, after that the Holy Ghost is come upon you: and ye shall be witnesses unto me both in Jerusalem, and in all Judaea, and in Samaria, and unto the uttermost part of the earth"*** (Acts 1:8).
- ***"For the promise is unto you, and to your children, and to all that are afar off, even as many as the LORD our God shall call"*** (Acts 2:39).

Dr. Linda L. Smith is the Jurisdictional Field Representative for Eastern Missouri First Jurisdiction Bishop R.J. Ward, Jurisdictional Prelate and Mother Theresa E. Bolden, Jurisdictional Supervisor. Dr. Smith is a member of Bostick Temple COGIC, where the pastor is Superintendent Terrell and the First Lady is Mother Terrell. Dr. Smith is a Gifted Educational Specialist for the Riverview Gardens School District.

QUARTERLY QUIZ

The questions on this page may be used in several ways: as a pretest at the beginning of the quarter; as a review at the end of the quarter; or as a review after each lesson. The questions are based on the Scripture text of each lesson (King James Version).

LESSON 1

1. What did John see happening to Jesus that caused him to marvel at His presence (**John 1:32**)?

____

____

2. Complete the following Scripture from **John 1:34**, "And I saw, and _____ _____ that this is the ______ ____ ______."

____

____

LESSON 2

1. Name two characteristics (or titles) that John lists about the Holy Spirit in **John 14:16–17**.

____

____

2. If a believer _____ Jesus, then what will happen according to **John 14:23**?

____

____

LESSON 3

1. After Jesus spoke with the disciples, what is their response to His departure (**John 16:6**)?

____

____

2. If Jesus does not leave the disciples, who will not be able to come and guide them (**John 16:7**)?

____

____

LESSON 4

1. Define the word "remit" in **John 20:23**.

2. Jesus showed the disciples His _____ and _____ (**John 20:20**).

____

____

LESSON 5

1. What type of animal did Jesus ask two disciples bring to Him (**Mark 11:7**)?

____

____

2. Jesus came into _____ and went into the _______ (**Mark 11:11**).

____

____

LESSON 6

1. Who has risen from the dead and has become the firstfruits for those who have fallen asleep (**1 Corinthians 15:20**)?

____

____

QUARTERLY QUIZ

2. In Adam, all men died, but Christ makes all what **(1 Corinthians 15:22)**?

____

____

LESSON 7

1. Believers should not be like ____ because he was with the "wicked one," and he _____ his brother **(1 John 3:12)**.

____

____

2. Paul tells the believers that they are to love through ______ and ____ _____ **(1 John 3:18)**.

____

____

LESSON 8

1. We love God because ____ ______ ______ ____ **(1 John 4:19)**.

____

____

2. If a person claims to love God, but hates his brother, then the person is a ______ **(1 John 4:20)**.

____

____

LESSON 9

1. John greets people with ______, ______, and _______ **(2 John 3)**.

____

____

2. "And now I ______ ____, lady, not as though I wrote a ___ __________ unto thee, but that which we had from the beginning, that __ ____ ____ ________" **(2 John 5)**.

____

____

LESSON 10

1. Who does John say has arrogant and unhospitable behavior **(3 John 9–10)**?

____

____

2. John encourages believers to ____ _______ because it is of God and not to do evil **(3 John 11)**.

____

____

LESSON 11

1. Paul does not want the Corinthians to be _____ in their understanding **(1 Corinthians 12:1)**.

____

____

2. List some of the gifts that Paul shares that are from the Spirit **(1 Corinthians 12:10)**.

____

____

LESSON 12

1. Is the body made up of one member or many **(1 Corinthians 12:14)**?

____

____

QUARTERLY QUIZ

2. How does Paul convey his point of the body of the church as one **(1 Corinthians 12:16)**?

___

___

LESSON 13

1. What spiritual event was celebrated during this time **(Acts 2:1)**?

___

___

2. The people were so _______, they asked: "Behold, are not all these which speak Galilaeans?" **(Acts 2:7)**.

___

___

LESSON 14

1. "Though I speak with the _______ __ ___ and of angels, and have not _______, I am become as sounding brass, or a tinkling cymbal" **(1 Corinthians 13:1)**.

___

___

2. Paul "profiteth nothing" if he does not have _____ **(1 Corinthians 13:3)**.

___

___

ANSWERS TO THE QUARTERLY QUIZ

LESSON 1 1. The Spirit, like a dove, descended on Jesus and remained on Him; 2. bare record, Son of God

LESSON 2 1. Comforter and (Spirit of) truth; 2. loves Jesus, then the believer will keep Jesus' words (or commandments)

LESSON 3 1. Jesus realizes that their hearts are full of sorrow; 2. the Comforter

LESSON 4 1. send away (forsake, leave, to forgive debts or sins); 2. hands and side

LESSON 5 1. colt; 2. Jerusalem and temple

LESSON 6 1. Christ; 2. In Christ shall all be made alive

LESSON 7 1. Cain, slew; 2. action, in truth

LESSON 8 1. He first loved us; 2. liar

LESSON 9 1. Grace, mercy, and peace; 2. beseech thee, new commandment, we love one another

LESSON 10 1. Diotrephes; 2. do good

LESSON 11 1. ignorant; 2. miracles, prophecy, distinguishing between spirits, speaking in tongues, interpretation of tongues

LESSON 12 1. many; 2. He says that every individual part of the body has a purpose and belongs to the greater whole.

LESSON 13 1. day of Pentecost; 2. amazed

LESSON 14 1. tongues of men, charity; 2. charity

THE WORD OF GOD

BIBLE BASIS: JOHN 1:29–34

BIBLE TRUTH: John testifies that the baptism of the Holy Spirit surpasses water baptism and that the Spirit surpasses water baptism and that the Spirit bears witness that Jesus is God the Son.

MEMORY VERSE: "And I saw, and bare record that this is the Son of God" (John 1:34).

LESSON AIM: By the end of the lesson, your students will: explore John's account of Jesus' baptism, relive emotions felt while observing or participating in a baptism; and assess how Christians live out their baptismal covenant.

TEACHER PREPARATION

MATERIALS NEEDED: Quarterly Commentary/Teacher Manual, Adult Quarterly, Adult resources—charts, worksheets, and other teaching tools, paper, pens, pencils, Bibles (several different versions)

OTHER MATERIALS NEEDED / TEACHER'S NOTES:

___

___

LESSON OVERVIEW

LIFE NEED FOR TODAY'S LESSON
Christians will develop a closer relationship with Christ and discern the many competing religious and political values in the world.

BIBLE LEARNING
People of faith testify to the power of the Spirit that Jesus is God's Son.

BIBLE APPLICATION
Christians are stirred in heart, mind, and spirit when they witness to who Christ is.

STUDENTS' RESPONSES
Students will seek to live consistently with the covenant made at baptism.

LESSON SCRIPTURE

JOHN 1:29–34, KJV

29 The next day John seeth Jesus coming unto him, and saith, Behold the Lamb of God, which taketh away the sin of the world.

30 This is he of whom I said, After me cometh a man which is preferred before me: for he was before me.

JOHN 1:29–34, NIV

29 The next day John saw Jesus coming toward him and said, "Look, the Lamb of God, who takes away the sin of the world!

30 This is the one I meant when I said, 'A man who comes after me has surpassed me because he was before me.'

31 And I knew him not: but that he should be made manifest to Israel, therefore am I come baptizing with water.

32 And John bare record, saying, I saw the Spirit descending from heaven like a dove, and it abode upon him.

33 And I knew him not: but he that sent me to baptize with water, the same said unto me, Upon whom thou shalt see the Spirit descending, and remaining on him, the same is he which baptizeth with the Holy Ghost.

34 And I saw, and bare record that this is the Son of God.

31 I myself did not know him, but the reason I came baptizing with water was that he might be revealed to Israel."

32 Then John gave this testimony: "I saw the Spirit come down from heaven as a dove and remain on him.

33 And I myself did not know him, but the one who sent me to baptize with water told me, 'The man on whom you see the Spirit come down and remain is the one who will baptize with the Holy Spirit.'

34 I have seen and I testify that this is God's Chosen One."

LIGHT ON THE WORD

The act of baptism was a common Jewish practice. Ritual washing and immersion were used to symbolize purity and preparation for holy use or service. Priests were required to bathe themselves before entering the Temple. For this reason, ritual baths were located nearby. Baptism was also used to indicate a change in status or membership, and was used when Gentiles converted to the Jewish faith. John the Baptist used the ritual in conjunction with repentance of sin, to prepare believers for the coming Messiah.

TEACHING THE BIBLE LESSON

LIFE NEED FOR TODAY'S LESSON

AIM: Students will develop a closer relationship with Christ and discern the many competing religious and political values in the world.

INTRODUCTION

John the Baptist—A Holy Man

John the Baptist was a Nazarite, the son of Zacharias the priest and Elisabeth. His birth was foretold by the angel Gabriel. Gabriel told Zacharias and Elisabeth of John's birth and explained that he would be "great in the eyes of the Lord" and would be "filled with the Holy Ghost" (**Luke 1:15**). He was meant to lead many Israelites to the Lord and would prepare them for the coming of the Messiah. Gabriel also gave instructions that their son was never to drink wine or hard liquor, and that they should name him John. This news was surprising to Zacharias and Elisabeth, because they were very old and Elisabeth wasn't able to have children. Their baby was born, strong in the Spirit just as Gabriel had said. Prior to beginning his ministry in Israel, John lived in the Judean wilderness, between Jerusalem and the Dead Sea. Other accounts about John in the Gospels indicate that he wore camel hair and a leather belt, and ate locusts and honey (**Mark 1:6**). He lived in the wilderness until he began his ministry in Israel, around 26 or 27 A.D. John's ministry focused on calling for repentance, administering baptism, and prophesying about the coming Messiah. John's speaking style was bold and fearless. He urged people to confess their sins and repent. He was also critical of sin in the lives of local religious and political leaders. Shortly after bearing witness to Christ's arrival, John was imprisoned by Herod and beheaded. Jesus refers to John's witness and ministry in **John 5:35**, saying that "he was a burning and shining light."

BIBLE LEARNING

AIM: Students will testify to the power of the Spirit that Jesus is God's Son.

I. JOHN ANNOUNCES CHRIST'S ARRIVAL (John 1:29–31)

John presents Jesus as the "Lamb of God." The phrase alludes to the image of the sacrificial Passover lamb. More specifically, the phrase points to the redemptive nature of Christ's sacrifice. Animals were regularly used in Judaism as a sacrifice to cleanse sin. While the sacrifice of animals was an ongoing, repetitive process, John announces that Christ's atoning sacrifice would be a permanent solution. Furthermore, Christ's redemptive work is for everyone.

The Lamb of God (verses 29–31)

29 The next day John seeth Jesus coming unto him, and saith, Behold the Lamb of God, which taketh away the sin of the world.

As Jesus approached John, John saw something, a sign, that affirmed the identity of the One John was paving the way for. The Lamb of God, being divine, would take away the sin of the whole world. Jesus was the sacrificial Lamb who offered Himself without spot to God (**Hebrews 9:24–28**). The word for "taketh away" is *airo* (Gk., **EYE-row**), which means to take away, bear away, or carry off. It was language that would remind the listeners of Yom Kippur, the Day of Atonement, in which the scapegoat would be set loose into the wilderness to carry off the sin of the nation (**Leviticus 16:20–22**). The language here in John suggests that Jesus is not only the Passover Lamb, serving as a reminder of God's protection of His people in Egypt (**Exodus 12**), but that He is also an atoning sacrifice, accomplishing more than a normal Passover lamb ever could.

30 This is he of whom I said, After me cometh a man which is preferred before me; for he was before me.

John points out that Jesus is the One whom he was referring to in **verse 27**. He also adds that Jesus is "preferred before" (Gk. *emprosthen*, **EM-prohs-thehn**) John in rank, because He existed "before" (Gk. *protos*, **PRO-toss**) John in time. John is speaking of Christ as the eternal Word who existed before creation. This is the basis of Christ's ranking above John. As the preincarnate Christ, Jesus will always be superior to every created thing because He is the Creator (**John 1:1–3**).

31 And I knew him not; but that he should be made manifest to Israel, therefore am I come baptizing with water.

John did not know the identity of the Christ, but that did not prevent him from carrying out his duty to baptize. He knew that through his ministry, the Christ would be "manifest" to Israel. The word "manifest" (Gk. *phanero*, **fah-neigh-RAH-oh**) means more than just to appear. One may appear in a false identity, but to be made manifest is to appear as one truly is. This is significant because Jesus assumed the identity of an everyday Jewish man. Now His true identity would be revealed.

SEARCH THE SCRIPTURES

QUESTION 1

How do you think it felt for John to finally be able to declare Jesus' identity to everyone?

LIGHT ON THE WORD

Jesus is Greater than John

John had risen to popularity in the region. Crowds of people gathered to hear him speak and to be baptized (**Mark 1:4–5; Luke 3:3, 7–17**). His popularity had attracted the interest of the local religious leaders who sent a group of priests and Levites to determine John's identity (**John 1:19–27**). John had denied being the Christ or Elijah, and went on to explain that there would be a much greater man than himself who would be arriving soon after. A day after his explanation to the church leaders, John is now announcing that this is the man he had spoken of. Jesus is the greater one he had been waiting for.

II. JESUS IS THE SON OF GOD (vv. 32–34)

Here John is reflecting on an event that is recorded in **Matthew 3:13–17, Mark 1:9–11**, and **Luke 3:21–22**. Jesus went to John to be baptized in the Jordan River. While John was baptizing Jesus, he witnessed the Holy Spirit rest on Jesus in the form of a dove. This event was significant, not only because of its spectacular nature, but because John had been told that this sign would mark the man who would baptize with the Holy Spirit. John clearly indicates God's direction in his baptism ministry and his testimony to Jesus' identity. God instructed him to baptize to prepare the people for Jesus' arrival.

The Spirit, Like a Dove (verses 32–34)

32 And John bare record, saying, I saw the Spirit descending from heaven like a dove, and it abode upon him.

This was the sign by which John was told he would know the identity of the Christ. We do not know whether it was an actual dove or if the emphasis is on the manner of the Spirit's descension. That is, it could be that John is describing the way in which the Spirit came down and hovered over Jesus. Doves were associated with God in various way in Jewish tradition. A dove was used to let Noah know when the water had receded enough to reveal dry land (**Genesis 8**). They also announce God's presence (**Isaiah 60:8; Psalm 68:13**).

33 And I knew him not; but he that sent me to baptize with water, the same said unto me, Upon whom thou shalt see the Spirit descending, and remaining on him, the same is he which baptizeth with the Holy Ghost.

John did not know who the Son of God would be. This does not mean that John did not know Jesus. John and Jesus were cousins, but John did not know that Jesus was the Christ, the one whom God would send after him. The Lord instructed John to baptize and look for the sign of the Spirit descending as the indicator of the Messiah's identity. John affirms that Jesus came to do more than baptize with water: He came to baptize with the Holy Spirit.

34 And I saw, and bare record that this is the Son of God.

In this concluding sentence of John the Baptist's testimony, John affirmed that he was an eyewitness to that which he had spoken. This language is from court language when testifying. All that John did not know before was made plain by the sign, and John knew that Jesus is the Son of God. This could only be known through revelation given by God.

SEARCH THE SCRIPTURES

QUESTION 2

John states that the Holy Spirit remained on Jesus. What is the significance of this distinction?

LIGHT ON THE WORD

John's a Witness

John would certainly have known Jesus before baptizing Him; they were cousins. John's statement "I knew him not" probably refers to the fact that he didn't yet know Jesus' identity as the Lamb of God, the Son of God (**vv. 31, 33**). It was at the moment of Jesus' baptism that this was revealed to him. After his experience at Jesus' baptism, John was able to report definitively that Jesus is God's Son.

BIBLE APPLICATION

AIM: Students will experience a stirring in their hearts, mind, and spirit when they testify to who Christ is.

People still "bear witness" today. Have you ever asked someone to provide you with a reference or letter of recommendation for a new job? Or maybe a former colleague has asked if you would share your experience of how they performed as a worker. These are modern-day examples of testifying to someone's identity or character. The Holy Spirit within each believer testifies to the fact that we are God's children (**Romans 8:16**). As His children, we have been charged with witnessing to the power and person of Christ. We are meant to be living recommendations of Christ's love.

STUDENTS' RESPONSES

AIM: Students will seek to live consistently with the covenant made at baptism.

John the Baptist provided witness testimony to the identity of Jesus as the Son of God and the redemptive sacrifice for the sins of humanity. Consider ways in which you could testify to the person of Christ this week. Ask God to reveal opportunities to share the love of Christ with your family, friends, and coworkers.

If you don't feel like you're a very reliable witness to the person and ministry of Christ, ask God what changes you can make in your life. Ask the Holy Spirit to give you strength to make those changes in your life.

PRAYER

Dear Lord, we are blessed to experience a wonderful baptism in Jesus as we stay connected to You through the Holy Spirit. Bless us and keep us as we witness to others about the goodness and transforming power of Jesus in our lives. In Jesus' Name we pray. Amen.

HOW TO SAY IT

Nazirite.	**NA**-ze-rite.
Bethabara.	Beth-a-**BA**-ra.
Esaias.	Es-**I**-as.

PREPARE FOR NEXT SUNDAY

Read **John 14:15–26** and study "Jesus Promises an Advocate."

DAILY HOME BIBLE READINGS

MONDAY
The Spirit and Joseph
(Genesis 41:38–43)

TUESDAY
The Spirit and Bezalel
(Exodus 31:1–6)

WEDNESDAY
The Spirit and the Elders
(Numbers 11:11–25)

THURSDAY
Would That All Had the Spirit!
(Numbers 11:26–30)

FRIDAY
Make the Way Straight
(John 1:19–23)

SATURDAY
Why are You Baptizing?
(John 1:24–28)

SUNDAY
I Saw the Spirit Descending
(John 1:29–34)

Sources:

Alexander, David, and Pat Alexander. *Zondervan Handbook to the Bible.* Grand Rapids, MI: Zondervan, 1999. 240–241.

Barker, Kenneth L. and Kohlenberger III, John R., eds. *The Expositor's Bible Commentary.* Abridged Edition: New Testament. Grand Rapids, MI: Zondervan, 1994. 299–300.

Butler, Trent C., ed. "John the Baptist." *Holman Bible Dictionary.* Electronic Edition, Quickverse. Nashville, TN: Holman Bible Publishers, 1991.

Butler, Trent C., ed. "Passover." *Holman Bible Dictionary.* Electronic Edition, Quickverse. Nashville, TN: Holman Bible Publishers, 1991.

Easton, M. G. "John the Baptist." *Easton's Bible Dictionary.* 1st ed. Oklahoma City, OK: Ellis Enterprises, 1993.

Elwell, Walter A. and Robert W. Yarbrough. *Encountering the New Testament: A Historical and Theological Survey.* Grand Rapids, MI: Baker Books, 1998. 42–43.

McGrath, Allister E. and James I. Packer, eds. *Zondervan Handbook of Christian Beliefs.* Grand Rapids, MI: Zondervan, 2005. 240–241.

Thayer, Joseph. "Baptizo." *Thayer's Greek Definitions.* 3rd ed. Electronic Edition, Quickverse. El Cajon, CA: Institute for Creation Research, 1999.

Thayer, Joseph. "Martureo." *Thayer's Greek Definitions.* 3rd ed. Electronic Edition, Quickverse. El Cajon, CA: Institute for Creation Research, 1999.

Walvoord, John F. and Roy B. Zuck, eds. *The Bible Knowledge Commentary: An Exposition of the Scriptures.* Wheaton, IL: Victor Books, 1983. 274–275.

COMMENTS / NOTES:

JESUS PROMISES AN ADVOCATE

BIBLE BASIS: John 14:15–26

BIBLE TRUTH: Jesus said that He would send the Holy Spirit to help His followers to love God and live according to God's commandments.

MEMORY VERSE: "But the Comforter, which is the Holy Ghost, whom the Father will send in my name, he shall teach you all things, and bring all things to your remembrance, whatsoever I have said unto you" (John 14:26).

LESSON AIM: By the end of the lesson, your students will: understand the significance of the Holy Spirit; recognize the power available through the Holy Spirit; and pray for the guidance of the Holy Spirit in making decisions.

TEACHER PREPARATION

MATERIALS NEEDED: Quarterly Commentary/Teacher Manual, Adult Quarterly, Adult resources—charts, worksheets, and other teaching tools, paper, pens, pencils, Bibles (several different versions)

OTHER MATERIALS NEEDED / TEACHER'S NOTES:

____

____

LESSON OVERVIEW

LIFE NEED FOR TODAY'S LESSON
Christians know what is right, but struggle to follow through as they should.

BIBLE LEARNING
Christians recognize that their reliance on and submission to the "Spirit of truth" will sometimes distinguish them from the world.

BIBLE APPLICATION
Disciples rely on the power of the Holy Spirit to enable them to do what they otherwise could not do.

STUDENTS' RESPONSES
Believers seek to express their love for Jesus through their obedience to His commands.

LESSON SCRIPTURE

JOHN 14:15–26, KJV

15 If ye love me, keep my commandments.

16 And I will pray the Father, and he shall give you another Comforter, that he may abide with you for ever;

17 Even the Spirit of truth; whom the world cannot receive, because it seeth

JOHN 14:15–26, NIV

15 "If you love me, keep my commands.

16 And I will ask the Father, and he will give you another advocate to help you and be with you forever—

17 the Spirit of truth. The world cannot accept him, because it neither sees him

him not, neither knoweth him: but ye know him; for he dwelleth with you, and shall be in you.

18 I will not leave you comfortless: I will come to you.

19 Yet a little while, and the world seeth me no more; but ye see me: because I live, ye shall live also.

20 At that day ye shall know that I am in my Father, and ye in me, and I in you.

21 He that hath my commandments, and keepeth them, he it is that loveth me: and he that loveth me shall be loved of my Father, and I will love him, and will manifest myself to him.

22 Judas saith unto him, not Iscariot, Lord, how is it that thou wilt manifest thyself unto us, and not unto the world?

23 Jesus answered and said unto him, If a man love me, he will keep my words: and my Father will love him, and we will come unto him, and make our abode with him.

24 He that loveth me not keepeth not my sayings: and the word which ye hear is not mine, but the Father's which sent me.

25 These things have I spoken unto you, being yet present with you.

26 But the Comforter, which is the Holy Ghost, whom the Father will send in my name, he shall teach you all things, and bring all things to your remembrance, whatsoever I have said unto you.

nor knows him. But you know him, for he lives with you and will be in you.

18 I will not leave you as orphans; I will come to you.

19 Before long, the world will not see me anymore, but you will see me. Because I live, you also will live.

20 On that day you will realize that I am in my Father, and you are in me, and I am in you.

21 Whoever has my commands and keeps them is the one who loves me. The one who loves me will be loved by my Father, and I too will love them and show myself to them."

22 Then Judas (not Judas Iscariot) said, "But, Lord, why do you intend to show yourself to us and not to the world?"

23 Jesus replied, "Anyone who loves me will obey my teaching. My Father will love them, and we will come to them and make our home with them.

24 Anyone who does not love me will not obey my teaching. These words you hear are not my own; they belong to the Father who sent me.

25 "All this I have spoken while still with you.

26 But the Advocate, the Holy Spirit, whom the Father will send in my name, will teach you all things and will remind you of everything I have said to you.

LIGHT ON THE WORD

Orphans were particularly vulnerable. In a patriarchal society where the family was reliant on the father, being orphaned was a difficult existence. Without a father, orphans had no one to provide for them and no representation in court. It was common for orphans to be mistreated and even murdered. Many relied on begging, or were sold into slavery. However, throughout Scripture, God instructs His people to be kind to orphans. He is sympathetic to their plight. In James' epistle, he describes pure and genuine religion as "to look after orphans and widows in their distress and to keep oneself from being polluted by the world" **(James 1:27, NIV).**

TEACHING THE BIBLE LESSON

LIFE NEED FOR TODAY'S LESSON

AIM: Students know what is right, but struggle to follow through as they should.

INTRODUCTION

Jesus Prepares the Disciples

It was just prior to the Passover Festival, and Jesus was dining with the disciples in the Upper Room. Jesus knew that His time on earth was coming to a close. The announcement of His departure and pending arrival of the Holy Spirit follows several events that surprised and confused the disciples.

BIBLE LEARNING

AIM: Students will recognize that their reliance on and submission to the "Spirit of truth" will sometimes distinguish them from the world.

I. THE ADVOCATE IS THE HOLY SPIRIT (John 14:15–17)

Jesus describes the relationship that exists between Himself and the disciples. The Greek verb translated as "keep" is *tereo* (Gk. **tay-REH-oh**), which has a sense of watching over or guarding. Tereo is in the future tense and can be translated "You will obey" (Mounce, 420). Obeying Jesus' commandments is a natural result of their love for Him. This is a statement of relationship, rather than a command. The disciples' love for Jesus will result in their adherence to His teachings.

Keeping the Commandments (verses 15–17)

15 If ye love me, keep my commandments.

Jesus begins this segment of the discourse with a conditional clause using the word "if" and ends with a a statement about the future ("keep my commandments"). The KJV and NIV translate this like a command, but it is a conditional with a simple future tense verb, not an imperative ("if you love me, you will keep"). The sense of the Greek is that the events of the conditional are not certain. As a result, Jesus is indicating that the disciples have a choice in the matter. They may choose to love Him, resulting in them keeping His commandments, or they may choose not to. It is not a lack of omniscience on Jesus' part that is of concern here but the free will of the disciples to love or not love Jesus. Jesus is saying that the proof of their love for Him is the keeping of His commandments. He would repeat this in various ways both in this chapter (**vv. 21, 23**) and in several other passages (e.g., **15:10**). John also reiterates this in his first epistle (**1 John 5:3**).

In **John 13:34**, Christ defines His "new" commandment as loving one another, and all that He has been teaching them is summed up in this one commandment of love. Keeping all of

His commandments can be done by keeping this single one: love one another.

16 And I will pray the Father, and he shall give you another Comforter, that he may abide with you for ever;

The promise that follows seems to be directly linked with the preceding verse and the theme of loving obedience. It seems that His praying to the Father and the sending of the Comforter are conditional on the apostles' relationship with Him, evidenced by keeping His commandments. This relationship would motivate Him to pray (Gk. *erotao*, **eh-roh-TAH-oh**) to the Father on their behalf, and "he shall give you another Comforter."

Because of Jesus' prayer, "another Comforter" will come to the disciples. The word for "another" sheds light on the relationship of the Spirit to the Father and Son. It is not the word for "another of a different kind," *heteros* (Gk. **HEH-teh-ross**), but for "another of the same kind," which is *allos* (Gk. **AH-loss**). The word "Comforter" (Gk. *parakletos*, **pa-RAH-klay-tose**) has the idea of one called alongside to help. Hence, the New American Standard Bible translates it as "Helper." It has the idea of one who stands by another and exhorts or encourages. It is also translated "Advocate" (NIV), meaning one called particularly in a law court to plead one's case (**1 John 2:1**), not as a professional pleader but as a friend.

This is the first of five times the function and activities of the Holy Spirit are mentioned in the discourse (see **14:25–26, 15:26–27, 16:5–15**). The idea here is that since Jesus is about to leave them, the Father will send the Holy Spirit, who will "abide with them forever." The duration of the presence of the Comforter on earth with the disciples and believers is not temporary as Jesus' presence was, but permanent—forever. He assures them that it is to their advantage that He depart so that the Holy Spirit would come and be with them permanently (**16:7**).

17 Even the Spirit of truth; whom the world cannot receive, because it seeth him not, neither knoweth him: but ye know him; for he dwelleth with you, and shall be in you.

This Comforter is called "the Spirit of truth." This defines one of the functions of the Holy Spirit. The word "Spirit" used here (Gk. *pneuma*, **puh-NEHOO-mah**, literally "wind" or "breath") is the same word Jesus used to describe to Nicodemus the function of the Spirit in conversion (**John 3:8**).

Truth is one of the characteristics of the Holy Spirit. This is not surprising, since truth is a recurrent theme in the Gospel of John (**1:17**). Jesus says earlier in this chapter that He is "the way, the truth, and the life" (**14:6**; cf. **8:32**). From these and other passages, we learn that Christ is the embodiment of truth. Here the Spirit shares the same nature with Christ and communicates truth (**15:26; 16:13**), testifying about Christ.

Jesus says the "world" (Gk. *kosmos*, **KOZ-mose**), here meaning the "unsaved," cannot receive this Spirit and gives two reasons for it. Firstly, they do not see Him because they are spiritually blind (see **2 Corinthians 4:4**). Secondly, they do not know Him because they refuse to believe or understand Him (see **1 Corinthians 2:14**).

Christ says the sinful nature of the world causes people to prefer darkness rather than light (**John 3:19**), and calls this kind of people children of the devil, for they desire to do their father's will (**John 8:44**). Only those who believe in the Gospel of Christ are able to receive and know the Spirit of truth (**1 John 4:6**). In contrast to the world, the disciples know the Spirit or have experienced Him because He dwells in them, Jesus says. They have this privilege of knowing Him because of their belief and relationship with Christ.

The next point of interest in this verse is the use of the present and the future tenses, "for he dwelleth with you, and shall be in you." Some interpret this as a continuation of the presence or indwelling of the Holy Spirit in the believer. This agrees with the previous verse: "that He may abide with you forever." Another interpretation is that while the Spirit dwells with them in a measure now, they would receive the Spirit in greater measure when He comes into their lives in His fullness at the baptism of the Holy Spirit (see **John 3:34**; cf. **Matthew 3:11; Luke 11:13; John 1:31–33**). It is believed that this was fulfilled on the day of Pentecost in Acts.

SEARCH THE SCRIPTURES

QUESTION 1

What future event is Jesus referring to when He says that the Spirit will be in them?

LIGHT ON THE WORD

Our Counselor-Advocate Forever

Jesus will ask the Father to send another Advocate who will remain with them forever. The counselor-advocate is the Holy Spirit. In Jesus' physical absence, the Spirit will guide them in the truth. Their relationship with the Holy Spirit is only possible because of their relationship with Jesus, because their love of Christ will allow them to recognize and receive the Spirit when He arrives. Here again, Jesus points to the future when the Holy Spirit will reside both *within* them and *beside* them.

II. THE DISCIPLES ARE NOT ABANDONED (vv. 18–25)

Jesus doesn't intend to leave them fatherless. He will reveal Himself to the disciples after His death, burial, and resurrection. Not only will He visit them physically, but He will send His Spirit. His resurrection ensures that they will have new life (**vv. 19–20**). Modern-day believers also have this new life in Christ because of His sacrificial death and resurrection.

Jesus Reassures the Disciples (verses 18–25)

18 I will not leave you comfortless: I will come to you.

Jesus then assures His disciples of His continued presence. The word "comfortless" is the Greek *orphanos* (**or-fan-OSE**), from which we derive its English equivalent, "orphan." Other renderings of this word include "desolate" or "helpless." The next use of the word is found in **James 1:27**, where KJV renders it "fatherless."

Jesus promises to them further, saying, "I will come to you." Is He referring to His immediate appearance after His resurrection, which happens approximately three days after this speech (**John 20; Acts 1:3**)? Or, is He talking about His coming in the Person of the Holy Spirit, therefore carrying forward the same trend of thought of **verses 16 and 17**? Alternatively, is He talking about His Second Coming, a thought He started with in this chapter (**vv. 1–3**)? All three are possible, and all three might be included in His thought.

19 Yet a little while, and the world seeth me no more; but ye see me: because I live, ye shall live also.

Jesus states that the world would not see Him because He would soon die and ascend into Heaven. He further clarifies that the disciples will be able to see Him, because He would live again and give them access to eternal life through the power of the Holy Spirit.

20 At that day ye shall know that I am in my Father, and ye in me, and I in you.

Here Jesus describes the nature of the relationship He would have with the disciples and all who would subsequently follow Him. He says that they would know experientially that He was in the nature, soul, and thought of the Father; they would be in Him and He would be in them in the same manner. Although He would be away, the Spirit or Comforter would be in them and this would be their relational connection to Him.

21 He that hath my commandments, and keepeth them, he it is that loveth me: and he that loveth me shall be loved of my Father, and I will love him, and will manifest myself to him.

Jesus says that if the disciples not only have His commandments but obey them, it is proof that they love Him. This love for Him will be rewarded with love from both the Father and Son. Jesus says that He will manifest (Gk. *emphanizo*, **em-fa-NEED-zoh**) Himself to those who love Him. The word "manifest" means "to exhibit for view, to show one's self." This would happen through the coming of the Comforter, the Holy Spirit.

22 Judas saith unto him, not Iscariot, Lord, how is it that thou wilt manifest thyself unto us, and not unto the world?

This Judas shares his name with the disciple who betrayed Jesus. He asks how Jesus can show Himself to the disciples and not to the world. Jesus gives His answer in the next verse.

23 Jesus answered and said unto him, If a man love me, he will keep my words: and my Father will love him, and we will come unto him, and make our abode with him.

Jesus says that if a person loves Him and obeys His words, then the Father will love them, and Jesus and the Father will come to and make their abode with that person. Here Jesus is speaking of the indwelling of the Holy Spirit in the life of the believer. This will be the method in which Jesus will manifest Himself to His disciples.

24 He that loveth me not keepeth not my sayings: and the word which ye hear is not mine, but the Father's which sent me. 25 These things have I spoken unto you, being yet present with you.

Jesus goes back to the love motif again. Stating it negatively (cf. **v. 15**), He reinforces the truth about loving Him and keeping His "sayings" (Gk. *logos*, **LAH-goss**) or teachings. He says anyone who does not love Him would not keep His teachings. This is akin to **verse 17**, where we learned that the world cannot receive the Holy Spirit because they do not know Him.

In essence, he who rejects Christ will not even listen to His teachings, and in effect also rejects the Father since Jesus' teachings are the Father's (**Luke 10:16; John 3:36; 13:20**). Jesus refuses to take glory for Himself and says, "for all that I have heard of my Father I have made known to you" (from **John 15:15**). Again He gives the Father total credit for His teachings.

SEARCH THE SCRIPTURES

QUESTION 2

How do you think the disciples might have felt as they heard Jesus talk about leaving them?

LIGHT ON THE WORD

A New Relationship

When Christ returns, the disciples will begin to understand the relationship between Jesus and the Father, and consequently, their new relationship with the Father. In **verse 21,** Jesus again speaks of the relationship between Himself and those who keep His commandments. People who love the Lord indicate as much by adhering to His teachings.

Additionally, God loves those who love Jesus and keep His commandments. Loving Jesus and doing His commandments results in Jesus revealing Himself to the individual.

III. THE HOLY SPIRIT IS JESUS' REPRESENTATIVE (v. 26)

The Father will send the Holy Spirit to represent Christ in the world in the same way that Christ was sent to the world to represent God. In Jesus' absence, the Holy Spirit will remind the disciples of His teachings.

The Comforter Will Come (verse 26)

26 But the comforter, which is the Holy Ghost, whom the Father will send in my name, he shall teach you all things, and bring all things to your remembrance, whatsoever I have said unto you.

The conjunction "but" at the beginning of this verse clarifies the point of the previous verse. There Jesus seems to say, "Although I have been teaching you in person and will soon leave you, you are not losing anything, since you are about to receive the Comforter, the Holy Spirit, whose work includes bringing to your remembrance all My teachings." Here Christ mentions both the office and name of the Holy Spirit, both of which we have come across in the earlier verses of the chapter (**vv. 16–18**).

In **verse 17**, Jesus referred to the Third Person of the Trinity as the Spirit of Truth, but here He calls Him the Holy Spirit, intentionally distinguishing Him from any other spirit. As we have already noted in **verse 16**, the Holy Spirit is from the Father. The new thing here is that Jesus is the medium through whom the Holy Spirit will be sent. This is the significance of the Father sending the Spirit "in [Jesus'] name."

The function of the Holy Spirit is to comfort, encourage, and communicate the truth. He also teaches (**v. 26**). He will both teach and remind us of Jesus' teachings. The work of the Holy Spirit is referenced here again in order to give the disciples confidence and encouragement to face Jesus' imminent departure. The Holy Spirit would have a dual function. He would both aid the disciples by recalling all that Jesus had taught them, and would also teach them Himself—even about future events (cf. **16:13**).

LIGHT ON THE WORD

A Teacher and a Guide

The Spirit will help them to more fully understand all that Christ taught them during His ministry. This clearly indicates that the Holy Spirit was to be more than just a reminder to the disciples; the Holy Spirit would be an active teacher and guide to them.

BIBLE APPLICATION

AIM: Students will rely on the power of the Holy Spirit to enable them to do what they otherwise could not do.

Life is more enjoyable when we walk alongside others who are willing to encourage and support one another. Have you ever encountered a problem that seemed impossible to solve until you asked for help from someone? Remember how relieved you felt when you didn't have to figure it out on your own? This is similar to the Holy Spirit's ministry in believers' lives. He has been given to come alongside us and instruct us in how to live. We are not alone.

STUDENTS' RESPONSES

AIM: Students will seek to express their love for Jesus through their obedience to His commands.

Ask God to reveal ways in which you can actively seek out the guidance of the Holy

Spirit in your life. This might be as simple as praying for the guidance of the Holy Spirit in a situation.

Or, you might find yourself relying solely on your own understanding when making decisions. Instead, prayerfully consider what the Holy Spirit is leading you to do.

PRAYER

Sweet Holy Spirit, guide us in knowing what to do, and how to share God's love for us. Sweet Holy Spirit, we thank You for protecting us, and loving us. Allow us to actively seek Your faithful ways as we live and build God's Kingdom through Jesus. In Jesus' Name we pray. Amen.

HOW TO SAY IT

Motif. mo-**TEEF**.

Iscariot. Is-**KAIR**-ee-ut.

PREPARE FOR NEXT SUNDAY

Read **John 16:4b–15** and study "The Spirit of Truth."

DAILY HOME BIBLE READINGS

MONDAY
Is There No Balm in Gilead?
(Jeremiah 8:18–22)

TUESDAY
No One to Comfort Me
(Lamentations 1:17–21)

WEDNESDAY
Here is Your God!
(Isaiah 40:1–10)

THURSDAY
This is My Comfort
(Psalm 119:49–64)

FRIDAY
The Shepherd's Comfort
(Psalm 23)

SATURDAY
When the Advocate Comes
(John 15:18–26)

SUNDAY
An Advocate with You Forever
(John 14:15–26)

Sources:

Barker, Kenneth L. and John R. Kohlenberger III, eds. *The Expositor's Bible Commentary*. Abridged Edition, New Testament. Grand Rapids, MI: Zondervan, 1994. 346, 349.

Barker, Kenneth L. *Zondervan Study Bible*. TNIV. Grand Rapids, MI: Zondervan, 2006. 1807–1810.

Butler, Trent C., ed. "Fatherless." *Holman Bible Dictionary*. Electronic Edition, Quickverse. Nashville, TN: Holman Bible Publishers, 1991.

Butler, Trent C., ed. "Passover." *Holman Bible Dictionary*. Electronic Edition, Quickverse. Nashville, TN: Holman Bible Publishers, 1991.

Carson, D. A. *The Gospel According to John: Pillar New Testament Commentary*. Grand Rapids, MI: Wm. B. Eerdmans Publishing Company, 1991. 498–510.

Mounce, William D. and Mounce, Robert H., eds. *The Zondervan Greek and English Interlinear New Testament*. Grand Rapids, MI: Zondervan, 2008. 420.

Thayer, Joseph. "Entole." *Thayer's Greek Definitions*. 3rd ed. Electronic Edition, Quickverse. El Cajon, CA: Institute for Creation Research, 1999.

Thayer, Joseph. "Parakletos." *Thayer's Greek Definitions*. 3rd ed. Electronic Edition, Quickverse. El Cajon, CA: Institute for Creation Research, 1999.

Walvoord, John F. and Zuck, Roy B., eds. *The Bible Knowledge Commentary: An Exposition of the Scriptures*. Wheaton, IL: Victor Books, 1983. 323–324.

THE SPIRIT OF TRUTH

BIBLE BASIS: JOHN 16:4b–15

BIBLE TRUTH: Jesus promised the disciples that the Holy Spirit would be a real presence to them and this promise is true for all believers.

MEMORY VERSE: "Nevertheless I tell you the truth; It is expedient for you that I go away: for if I go not away, the Comforter will not come unto you; but if I depart, I will send him unto you" (John 16:7).

LESSON AIM: By the end of the lesson, your students will: learn what Jesus says about how the Holy Spirit works on our behalf; express their feelings about the loss of those close to them; and find ways to tell others about how the Holy Spirit works on our behalf.

TEACHER PREPARATION

MATERIALS NEEDED: Quarterly Commentary/Teacher Manual, Adult Quarterly, Adult resources—charts, worksheets, and other teaching tools, paper, pens, pencils, Bibles (several different versions)

OTHER MATERIALS NEEDED / TEACHER'S NOTES:

____

____

LESSON OVERVIEW

LIFE NEED FOR TODAY'S LESSON
To allow the Holy Spirit to guide us and to trust Him to find people who can help us.

BIBLE LEARNING
Believers trust that the Holy Spirit is helping them just as surely as if Jesus is present in the flesh to give them aid.

BIBLE APPLICATION
Christians grow to understand the role of the Holy Spirit in their lives through the study of the Scriptures.

STUDENTS' RESPONSES
Students will tell others about the presence and transforming power of the Holy Spirit in their lives.

LESSON SCRIPTURE

JOHN 16:4b–15, KJV

4b And these things I said not unto you at the beginning, because I was with you.

5 But now I go my way to him that sent me; and none of you asketh me, Whither goest thou?

6 But because I have said these things unto you, sorrow hath filled your heart.

JOHN 16:4b–15, NIV

4b I did not tell you this from the beginning because I was with you,

5 but now I am going to him who sent me. None of you asks me, 'Where are you going?'

6 Rather, you are filled with grief because I have said these things.

7 Nevertheless I tell you the truth; It is expedient for you that I go away: for if I go not away, the Comforter will not come unto you; but if I depart, I will send him unto you.

8 And when he is come, he will reprove the world of sin, and of righteousness, and of judgment:

9 Of sin, because they believe not on me;

10 Of righteousness, because I go to my Father, and ye see me no more;

11 Of judgment, because the prince of this world is judged.

12 I have yet many things to say unto you, but ye cannot bear them now.

13 Howbeit when he, the Spirit of truth, is come, he will guide you into all truth: for he shall not speak of himself; but whatsoever he shall hear, that shall he speak: and he will shew you things to come.

14 He shall glorify me: for he shall receive of mine, and shall shew it unto you.

15 All things that the Father hath are mine: therefore said I, that he shall take of mine, and shall shew it unto you.

7 But very truly I tell you, it is for your good that I am going away. Unless I go away, the Advocate will not come to you; but if I go, I will send him to you.

8 When he comes, he will prove the world to be in the wrong about sin and righteousness and judgment:

9 about sin, because people do not believe in me;

10 about righteousness, because I am going to the Father, where you can see me no longer;

11 and about judgment, because the prince of this world now stands condemned.

12 "I have much more to say to you, more than you can now bear.

13 But when he, the Spirit of truth, comes, he will guide you into all the truth. He will not speak on his own; he will speak only what he hears, and he will tell you what is yet to come.

14 He will glorify me because it is from me that he will receive what he will make known to you.

15 All that belongs to the Father is mine. That is why I said the Spirit will receive from me what he will make known to you."

LIGHT ON THE WORD

Jesus and the disciples were in Jerusalem preparing for the Passover, one of the three annual Israelite festivals. During the Passover, an unblemished lamb was sacrificed, and its blood sprinkled on the altar and in the Temple. This sacrifice served as a memorial of Israel's preservation during the exodus from Egypt, when the last plague of death "passed over" the Israelites' homes. It also pointed to sin and holy offerings required to be in right standing with God. It is no coincidence that these events, including the Crucifixion and Resurrection, occur during Passover season, when Christ became the sacrifice that protects God's people from death.

John 13–17 occurs after Jesus' triumphant entry into Jerusalem. By this time, the religious leaders (Pharisees and chief priests) have successfully begun turning the tide against Him. They have met with Judas, and agreed to pay him to identify Jesus and hand him over to be tried for His "sin"—claiming to be God. Jesus uses this time to prepare His disciples for what is to come in what is commonly known as the Upper Room Discourse. Several well-known passages are found in this portion of Scripture: **John 14:1–7** (I am the way, truth, and life), **John 14:15–21** (You are not orphans), **John 15:1–17** (the true vine), **John 17** (Christ's High Priestly prayer).

TEACHING THE BIBLE LESSON

LIFE NEED FOR TODAY'S LESSON

AIM: Students will allow the Holy Spirit to guide us and trust Him to find people who can help us.

INTRODUCTION

Expect the Holy Spirit

This Gospel is attributed to John, son of Zebedee and one of Christ's closest disciples. His purpose for writing the book is found in **John 20:31**: "But these are written, that ye might believe that Jesus is the Christ, the Son of God; and that believing ye might have life through his name."

In this particular passage, Christ tells His disciples to expect the Holy Spirit, who will reveal more of the truth of who He is (His glory). The immediate recipients of His instructions were His apostles, but the principles also apply to His future followers.

BIBLE LEARNING

AIM: Students will trust that the Holy Spirit is helping them just as surely as if Jesus is present in the flesh to give them aid.

I. THE COMING OF THE HOLY SPIRIT (JOHN 16:4b–7)

Continuing His instructions, Jesus tells the disciples that after He leaves them, an Advocate will arrive—the Holy Spirit. While they were understandably sad, He pointed out that they were so consumed with how His leaving affected them in the present, they were missing the future benefit—the Holy Spirit, who will abide with them forever (**14:16**). Jesus says that it would be expedient for Him to leave, because this would prepare the way for the Holy Spirit to come.

Persecution and Trouble Ahead (verses 4b–7)

4b And these things I said not unto you at the beginning, because I was with you.

Jesus had not needed to tell them about persecution and future troubles because He was present with them. From the very beginning, they had walked with Jesus and learned from Him. They had assisted Him in performing miracles and witnessed signs and wonders. They were His disciples. The Pharisees and the teachers of the law confronted Him and not His students. He was there to take the brunt of the attacks and be a shield to protect them. Soon He would leave, and they would be confronted as the ones who followed and learned from Him.

5 But now I go my way to him that sent me; and none of you asketh me, Whither goest thou?

In **John 14:5**, Thomas had asked, "Lord, we don't know where you are going, so how can we know the way?" (NIV). He doesn't ask Jesus where He is going but makes a statement about how confused he is by Jesus' pronouncement of going away. Jesus states that He is going "to him that sent me." This should have aroused curiosity within the disciples. If they followed Jesus for such a long time, they should have been hungry to know who sent Him. Jesus was speaking of His ascension to Heaven to return to the Father. The confusion of the disciples indicates that they must have only thought of Jesus' departure on a purely physical level.

6 But because I have said these things unto you, sorrow hath filled your heart.

The disciples were sad because Jesus was leaving them. They didn't understand that He was referring to His ascension and that He was going to the Father. They were merely thinking on an earthly level and did not realize that Jesus is the Son of God, sent to earth to die and rise again. At this point they were only thinking of Him as an earthly rabbi who taught them things and performed some miracles. As a result, when Jesus talks about leaving, sorrow fills their hearts. They don't understand the broader spiritual implications.

7 Nevertheless I tell you the truth; It is expedient for you that I go away: for if I go not away, the Comforter will not come unto you; but if I depart, I will send him unto you.

In this section, Jesus tells them how important and necessary it is that He should leave them. Unless He departs, the Spirit will not come. He has already told them about the persecution they will encounter and the sorrow they will have at His leaving. There is a definite advantage for the disciples that He departs, because then the Spirit (Counselor) would come. "Expedient" (Gk. *sumphero*, **soom-FAIR-oh**) means profitable, beneficial, or for one's good. This word is used two other times in John (**11:50; 18:14**), and in both of these passages, the verb refers to Jesus' death and the fact that it will benefit everyone. After Jesus ascends to Heaven, the Spirit would then be with the disciples and those who came after Him, no matter where they found themselves. It was also expedient because as Jesus explains in the next verse, the Comforter would come with a definite agenda of convicting the world. This was something that could not happen until the ascension of Christ into Heaven.

The use of the word "Comforter" adds another specific dimension in the activities of the Holy Spirit in view of the persecution that would come to them. The word in Greek is *parakletos* (**pah-RAH-klay-tose**), which can mean comforter, advocate or helper. In this passage, the Spirit takes on all of these roles in different ways as one who convicts the world and serves as God's messenger to believers and the world.

The phrase "I will send him unto you" and other passages indicate the manner in which the Holy Spirit is sent to us. He is the gift of God who emanates from the Father (**14:16, 26**) and is sent by the Son (**15:26, 16:7**; cf. **Luke 24:49**). Humans have no part in initiating the process. God takes the initiative. Furthermore, the coming of the Spirit, as we have noted, depends on the departure of Jesus (**16:7**; cf. **7:39**).

LIGHT ON THE WORD

Joy Renewed

Until this point, Christ was the main target of the world's wrath. After His resurrection, the disciples would be. As such, they would need a Helper, an Encourager and Advocate who did not have the physical limitations of a body, and would indwell and equip all believers. After Jesus' departure, they would no longer be sad. The Holy Spirit would comfort them and bring them joy in the absence of Jesus' physical presence.

II. WORK OF THE HOLY SPIRIT: CONVICTION (vv. 8–11)

This Advocate would have a different role in believers' and unbelievers' lives. Ultimately He would function as a guide for both. The guidance of the Holy Spirit for unbelievers would be in the direction of initially submitting to the Lordship of Christ and turning away from sin. John refers to those who don't believe as "the world." This does not refer to the physical creation, but everyone who does not follow Jesus.

Judgment and the Holy Spirit (verses 8–11)

8 And when he is come, he will reprove the world of sin, and of righteousness, and of judgment: 9 Of sin, because they believe not on me; 10 Of righteousness, because I go to the Father, and ye see me no more; 11 Of judgment, because the prince of this world is judged.

These four verses constitute some of the fundamental beliefs in the Christian doctrine concerning the work of the Holy Spirit in the process of conversion. In them, Jesus reveals what hitherto has not been stressed, i.e., the Spirit's work to reprove or convict. The word "reprove" (Gk. *elegkho*, **el-ENG-kho**) means to convict, convince, or expose.

Jesus describes the threefold work of conviction by the Holy Spirit. Firstly, He will convict the world of sin. The Holy Spirit will cause people to recognize their sinfulness in the sight of God. This includes the major sin of not believing in Christ. This rejection of the Gospel of Christ (and the rejection of His person) is the most serious offense because without Christ, all the other sins committed by a person cannot be forgiven.

Secondly, the Spirit convicts the world of righteousness. Here He will bring to their consciousness the standard of righteousness that God demands from all. That standard of righteousness is Christ, and without His presence in the world, we are at a loss for the true standard of what God requires for humanity. The "righteousness" here that God requires is communicated by the Greek word *dikaiosune* (**dee-keye-oh-SOO-nay**), which can also be translated "justification." It means being judicially right in the sight of God. Human justification is the gift of God through our belief in Christ. It is not earned; it is the work of faith.

The third work of the Spirit is to convict the world of judgment, "because the prince of this world is judged." The prince or ruler of this world refers to Satan (see **John 12:31, 14:30; 2 Corinthians 4:4; Ephesians 2:2; 1 John 4:4**). Satan is the author and source of all evil and unbelief. The word "judged" (Gk. *krino*, **KREE-no**) is the language of a court of law and has the idea of being condemned. The noun form speaks of decision, passing a judgment, or verdict by a jury or a tribunal. The world, of course, is the world system ruled by Satan and devil, whom Jesus referred to as their father (see **John 8:44**). Therefore, Jesus says that those who refuse to believe in the Gospel face the same fate of condemnation as their master the devil has already received (see **Luke 10:18–20; John 3:36; Revelation 20:11–15, 21:8**). The actual condemnation or defeat of the prince of this world will be accomplished on the Cross. We see the work of the Holy Spirit is to reveal or expose not only the sin of unbelief, but also its result of judgment or condemnation, which awaits unbelievers. The Holy Spirit, on the one hand, brings people to the consciousness of their sins and leads them to repent and believe in the Gospel, while on the other hand, He also condemns those who refuse to repent, just like their master the devil.

SEARCH THE SCRIPTURES

QUESTION 1

What is the Holy Spirit's role to the world?

LIGHT ON THE WORD

The Spirit Convicts

The Spirit would bring conviction to the world in three areas: sin, righteousness, and judgment. The Spirit reveals the things that people say, think, and do that offend God, working to convince them to turn away from sin and turn toward God. He is also the One who convinces the world that not only are they sinners, but that righteousness (or right standing) before God only comes from Christ's sacrifice—His death, resurrection, and return to Heaven to reign with His Father. Finally, the Holy Spirit reveals that those who insist on rejecting God through unbelief stand condemned along with Satan, the prince of the world.

III. WORK OF THE HOLY SPIRIT: GUIDANCE (vv. 12–15)

The Holy Spirit would come not only to convict the world, but guide believers as the Spirit of truth. The apostles were used to having Christ as their rabbi, teaching and guiding them. Now, they would have to rely on the Holy Spirit. Jesus comments that He has more to tell them but they could not bear it. When the Holy Spirit comes then He would lead them and guide them into all the truth that they could not handle at that moment.

Teachings from the Holy Spirit (verses 12–15)

12 I have yet many things to say unto you, but ye cannot bear them now.

The above sayings are no doubt hard to understand even to the disciples. They are perplexed and cannot make sense of what He is saying. Jesus recognizes their plight and says that He understands their situation. He realizes that they cannot comprehend all that He has been teaching—either the teachings are so highly spiritual that the disciples cannot fully understand them, or the disciples are so filled with emotion that they find it hard to bear the news of His imminent departure. Therefore, Jesus tells them that although He still has lots of things to tell them, He will not do so. The reason is they "cannot bear them now." "Bear" (Gk. *bastazo*, **bahs-TAD-zoh**) translates to carry, or bear something heavy or burdensome. In view of their emotional state, they could not carry the weight of what He wanted to say to them. It would be too much for them to take it all in. What are the things that would be too hard for them? They include "things to come" (**v. 13**), both to the immediate future and the end time events.

13 Howbeit when he, the Spirit of truth, is come, he will guide you into all truth: for he shall not speak of himself; but whatsoever he shall hear, that shall he speak: and he will shew you things to come. 14 He shall glorify me: for he shall receive of mine, and shall shew it unto you. 15 All things that the Father hath are mine: therefore said I, that he shall take of mine, and shall shew it unto you.

In this section, Jesus continues to explain to them the work of the Holy Spirit, whom He names the Spirit of Truth (**14:17, 26**; cf. **1 John 4:6**). His mission here is to guide the believer into all truth about Christ, not of Himself. He will be the medium of God's communication to mankind. Through the communication of the Holy Spirit, Christ will be glorified (cf. **vv. 8–11; 15:26**), because the Holy Spirit will not speak on His own authority, but whatever Christ reveals to Him (cf. **14:24**). The word "glorified" (*doxadzo*, **dok-SAHD-zo**) means to cause the dignity and worth of some person or thing to become manifest and acknowledged.

Whatever can be known about Jesus, the Spirit will reveal to the disciples. Because Jesus is God incarnate, the Spirit will glorify Him by communicating for Him and about Him to believers.. What would the Spirit receive from Jesus? The truth about Jesus. He would communicate the truth about Jesus to the disciples and to the world. This would lead to Jesus being glorified.

In **verse 15**, Jesus equates Himself with the Father since the revelation is from both the Father and the Son through the Spirit. Here we see that God's Word—all truth—is a combined work of the Trinity.

SEARCH THE SCRIPTURES

QUESTION 2

What is one of the Holy Spirit's roles to the apostles and believers?

LIGHT ON THE WORD

The Holy Spirit Speaks God's Truth

During this time, the Pharisees lived by and enforced their version of truth, unable to grasp the real truth that was before them—Christ, as the Son of God. Christ tells His disciples that the Holy Spirit would come "and guide you into all truth." Not only would the Spirit come to help them understand and remember the things Christ taught (**14:26**), He would speak God's Words to them, and tell them what is to come. They would go on to share these truths with the world, bringing glory to God. As a result, they helped to shape the New Testament Scriptures and led the church as it spread in the ancient Roman world.

BIBLE APPLICATION

AIM: Students will trust that the Holy Spirit is helping them just as surely as if Jesus is present in the flesh to give them aid.

We live during a time when people mistakenly believe they can create their own truths depending upon how they feel, what they believe, and how much energy they put toward it. However, not believing something is true does not make it false. If a person does not believe the sky is blue, it does not change the reality that it is. The Holy Spirit is as living and active now as He was in John's day. He still points people to truth, using God's Word and other people. The Spirit of truth still convicts of sin, righteousness, and judgment. He still guides into all truth—not just those truths that make people comfortable.

STUDENTS' RESPONSES

AIM: Students will tell others about the presence and transforming power the Holy Spirit in their lives.

The Holy Spirit still reveals sinners' need for Christ and works to convince them to believe in Him. If there are people in your life who do not believe in Christ, pray for them. Ask God for opportunities, grace, and wisdom through the Holy Spirit to share His truth with them.

PRAYER

Dear Jesus, the Comforter is a reminder of Your love and sacrifice for us and the world. As we allow the Holy Spirit to teach us and show us the way, let us ever be mindful of how we are to care for one another. In Jesus' Name we pray. Amen.

HOW TO SAY IT

Expedient.	eks-**PEE**-dee-ent.
Reprove.	ri-**PROOV**.
Zebedee.	**ZEH**-buh-dee.

PREPARE FOR NEXT SUNDAY

Read **John 20:19–23** and study "Receive the Holy Spirit."

DAILY HOME BIBLE READINGS

MONDAY
Where There is No Prophecy
(Proverbs 29:12–18)

TUESDAY
The Lord Has Closed Your Eyes
(Isaiah 29:8–14)

WEDNESDAY
Speak, for Your Servant is Listening
(1 Samuel 3:1–10)

THURSDAY
A Trustworthy Prophet of the Lord
(1 Samuel 3:11–21)

FRIDAY
I Commit My Spirit
(Psalm 31:1–8)

SATURDAY
Worship in Spirit and Truth
(John 4:21–26)

SUNDAY
The Spirit of Truth Will Guide You
(John 16:4b–15)

Sources:

Grudem, Wayne. *Bible Doctrine.* Grand Rapids, MI: Zondervan, 1999. 104-110.

Hebrew-Greek Key Word Study Bible. King James Version. Chattanooga, TN: AMG Publishers, Inc., 1991.

Keener, Craig S. *The IVP Bible Background Commentary: New Testament.* Downers Grove, IL: Intervarsity Press, 1993. 260–263, 302–303.

Radmacher, Earl D., ed. *Nelson Study Bible.* New King James Version. Nashville, TN: Thomas Nelson Publishers, 1997. 1754–1755, 1792–1800.

Ryrie, Charles C. *Ryrie Study Bible.* New International Version. Chicago, IL: Moody Press. 1986. 1480–1481.

Unger, Merrill F. *The New Unger's Bible Dictionary.* Chicago, IL: Moody Press, 1988. 410–411.

Walvoord, John F., and Roy B. Zuck, eds. *The Bible Knowledge Commentary: New Testament.* Wheaton, IL: Victor Books, SP Publications, Inc., 1983. 327–329.

Zondervan Study Bible. *New International Version.* Grand Rapids, MI: Zondervan Publishers, 2002. 1661–1662.

COMMENTS / NOTES:

RECEIVE THE HOLY SPIRIT

BIBLE BASIS: JOHN 20:19–23

BIBLE TRUTH: Jesus speaks peace to and empowers all His disciples with the gift of the Holy Spirit.

MEMORY VERSE: "And when he had said this, he breathed on them, and saith unto them, Receive ye the Holy Ghost" (John 20:22).

LESSON AIM: By the end of the lesson, your students will: explore the importance of Jesus' appearance to the disciples; describe their feelings from times when the words of others calmed their fears; and perform the mission God has for their lives as empowered by the Holy Spirit.

TEACHER PREPARATION

MATERIALS NEEDED: Quarterly Commentary/Teacher Manual, Adult Quarterly, Adult resources—charts, worksheets, and other teaching tools, paper, pens, pencils, Bibles (several different versions)

OTHER MATERIALS NEEDED / TEACHER'S NOTES:

____

____

LESSON OVERVIEW

LIFE NEED FOR TODAY'S LESSON

Christians know that there is power in the tongue and that Jesus speaks power into our lives.

BIBLE LEARNING

Believers receive and claim the power of the Holy Spirit in their work for the Lord.

BIBLE APPLICATION

Christians, convinced that the risen Christ appeared to the disciples, serve Him with the conviction that He is alive.

STUDENTS' RESPONSES

Students will speak words of reassurance to those whose faith is weak or faltering.

LESSON SCRIPTURE

JOHN 20:19–23, KJV

19 Then the same day at evening, being the first day of the week, when the doors were shut where the disciples were assembled for fear of the Jews, came Jesus and stood in the midst, and saith unto them, Peace be unto you.

20 And when he had so said, he shewed unto them his hands and his side. Then

JOHN 20:19–23, NIV

19 On the evening of that first day of the week, when the disciples were together, with the doors locked for fear of the Jewish leaders, Jesus came and stood among them and said, "Peace be with you!"

20 After he said this, he showed them his

were the disciples glad, when they saw the Lord.

21 Then said Jesus to them again, Peace be unto you: as my Father hath sent me, even so send I you.

22 And when he had said this, he breathed on them, and saith unto them, Receive ye the Holy Ghost:

23 Whose soever sins ye remit, they are remitted unto them; and whose soever sins ye retain, they are retained.

hands and side. The disciples were overjoyed when they saw the Lord.

21 Again Jesus said, "Peace be with you! As the Father has sent me, I am sending you."

22 And with that he breathed on them and said, "Receive the Holy Spirit.

23 If you forgive anyone's sins, their sins are forgiven; if you do not forgive them, they are not forgiven."

LIGHT ON THE WORD

The Resurrection occurred on the third day after Christ's crucifixion, and was an awesome demonstration of God's power and Christ's deity. While it had been prophesied, it was not necessarily expected, even by the disciples. In fact, John writes, "They still did not understand from Scripture that Jesus had to rise from the dead" (**20:9**, NIV). There has been age-old debate regarding whether the Resurrection was bodily or spiritual. However, several facts point to bodily. First, the grave was empty. Next, there were witnesses. He appeared to Mary, the disciples and more than five hundred other people over forty days (see **Acts 1:3, 1 Corinthians 15:3–7**). Finally, when He appeared, His body still had the actual wounds, He was able to be touched, and He ate (**John 21:9–15**).

TEACHING THE BIBLE LESSON

LIFE NEED FOR TODAY'S LESSON

AIM: Students will will know that there is power in the tongue and that Jesus speaks power into our lives.

INTRODUCTION

Jesus Visits the Disciples

After spending several years with the man claiming to be the Messiah and Son of God, and seeing Him perform untold numbers of miracles (so many that "if they should be written every one … the world itself could not contain the books that should be written," **John 21:25**), it was disheartening for the disciples to witness His death. The disciples knew Christ's miraculous power. They had seen Him escape from His enemies several times. They, like many Jews, were expecting Him to be a triumphant King who would free them from their oppressors, the Romans, and usher in a new worldly kingdom (**Luke 24:21, John 6:15**). But He was dead. Not only that, but because of the hostility of the Jewish leaders, they feared for their lives, locking themselves behind closed doors. Christ's promises that they would go on to "greater works" (**John 14:12**) looked grim.

BIBLE LEARNING

AIM: Students will receive and claim the power of the Holy Spirit in their work for the Lord.

I. CHRIST APPEARS TO THE DISCIPLES (John 20:19–20)

After appearing to Mary Magdalene at the tomb very early Sunday morning, Christ paid a visit to the majority of His disciples, although Thomas was not there (**v. 24**). This would be one of many visits that Christ would give to His disciples before ascending to Heaven. What makes this visit special is the words that Christ speaks to them that foretell their upcoming mission. As they gathered in fear, Jesus arrives—despite locked doors—and brings a greeting of peace. While "peace be with you" was a common Jewish greeting in those days, Christ's words carry several meanings.

Jesus Visits the Disciples (verses 19–20)

19 Then the same day at evening, being the first day of the week, when the doors were shut where the disciples were assembled for fear of the Jews, came Jesus and stood in the midst, and saith unto them, Peace be unto you.

In these verses, the resurrected Jesus appears to a group of His followers for the first time. In the previous verses, the Resurrection was only witnessed by individuals. First, Jesus appears to Mary alone as she visits the tomb. Then Peter and the other disciple (assumed to be John) arrive at the empty tomb. Although they do not see Jesus, the empty tomb and His grave clothes neatly wrapped and laid to the side are enough to cause them to believe. This occurs on Sunday, suggesting the practice of Christians gathering on that day, the first day of the week, corresponding with **verse 1**. Ten of the 11 disciples were gathered together after the crisis of seeing their rabbi Jesus arrested and executed by the Jewish rulers and Roman government. As a result, the disciples were fearful of the Jewish leaders and hid themselves from public sight. They did not want to risk being seen in public since their previous association with Jesus was widely known.

The doors were shut. Having the doors locked was a measure of precaution, but here it is mentioned with a reference to the appearance of Jesus. Locked doors proved to not be a barrier to His resurrected body. This suggests that the normal limitations of our bodies will be removed in the resurrection. It also suggests that nothing can keep Jesus from engaging our human condition. Our fears and anxieties cannot keep Jesus from coming to stand with us in whatever situation we find ourselves in. "Peace be with you" was a common Jewish greeting (Shalom), meaning "May all be well with you." As a Jew speaking to Jews, this word had additional connotations of prosperity, health, and blessing. Although this word was common in Jewish culture, when spoken by the Messiah, it means infinitely more. When Jesus says "peace," He actively gives what the word means. Peace is here presented as a gift from the risen Christ.

20 And when he had so said, he showed unto them his hands and his side. Then were the disciples glad, when they saw the Lord.

The risen Christ now reveals the genuineness of this gift before the eyes of the disciples. Jesus shows them the price with which He bought their peace: His pierced hands, His spear-pierced side, evidence of His death by crucifixion. These holy wounds proclaim that Jesus is at peace with the believers. The word *deiknumi* (Gk., **DAYK-noo-me**), to show, is a word that also means to give evidence or proof of thing. Showing His hands and His side would be unmistakable evidence that the same Jesus walked with them and who was crucified was now appearing among them. The disciples were glad because they saw the Lord. Doubt did not disappear all at once. Jesus appeared again and again, intensifying faith and joy, until nothing could ever disturb the solid certainty of their belief.

LIGHT ON THE WORD

Jesus Lives!

First, He who was dead is now alive. The disciples can be at peace and relieved from grief and mourning. Next, they can rest knowing that the man with them is still God and in spite of having a physical body, capable of dying, He still transcends time and space, unhindered by locked doors. Finally, it was common to believe in ghosts and spirits. His greeting of "peace," followed by revealing His wounds, assured them that He was not a ghost, so they had no need to be afraid. They were overjoyed!

II. CHRIST COMMISSIONS THE DISCIPLES (vv. 21–23)

In the Bible, phrases that are repeated are often important. In this short passage, Christ exhorts His disciples to be at peace twice. He has proven that He has risen. He now encourages them: "Peace to you!" They no longer need to fear their persecutors, because God is with them. And, despite abandoning Him, they are not disqualified from service. He assures them that just as God sent Him to earth to fulfill a mission, He is sending them into the world to do the same. But He not only sends them, He equips them.

Greetings in Peace (verses 21–23)

21 Then said Jesus to them again, Peace be unto you: as my Father hath sent me, even so send I you.

"Peace be unto you" is a repetition of the first greeting. Jesus repeats this phrase for a number of possible reasons. One possibility is that the first time was intended to take away fear, while the second time was to call attention to the seriousness of His commission. Another possibility is that Jesus wanted to encourage them in the mission that He was sending them to do. He wanted them to know that although they would experience trials and difficulties, His peace would be with them. Jesus then commissions the disciples using relational analogies: "As the Father has sent me, I am sending you." By this commission, the believers now bear the same divine authorization as Christ. Jesus has been sent into the world for a specific task and purpose, mainly His death and resurrection. The disciples are now authorized for the specific purpose of witnessing to His death and resurrection. They are authorized and commissioned to the task of dispensing this gift of peace in a troubled world. Jesus' Gospel is the Gospel of peace. Jesus Himself is our peace. He gives it to the disciples because those who bring peace must have peace.

Here the word *apostello* (Gk. **ah-po-STELL-oh**) is used for the Father sending Jesus. Jesus uses another word for His sending of the disciples into the world: *pempo* (Gk. **PEHM-po**). This word means to send or thrust, but does not carry authoritative connotation. The emphasis is on the specific action of sending or thrusting out. Jesus is saying just as the Father authorized and commissioned Him for a specific task, He would send or thrust His disciples out into the world.

22 And when he had said this, he breathed on them, and saith unto them, Receive ye the Holy Ghost.

He who sends enables those whom He sends, by the empowerment of the Holy Spirit. "Breathed on them" (Gk. *emphusao*, **em-foo-SAH-oh**) recalls the ancient association of spirit with breath and invokes **Genesis 2:7**. Jesus breathes on them in the same way that God breathed on Adam after shaping and forming him from the dust. This signifies that the church would be a new humanity created in the image of Christ. By breathing on them, Jesus foreshadows what would happen some weeks later on the day of Pentecost as the Spirit filled the house where they were praying like a mighty rushing wind. They would be empowered by the Holy Spirit for the commission that He has just given them. Jesus was filled with the Spirit at the start of His ministry; it would be no less so for the disciples.

The word for receive (Gk. *lambano*, **lam-BAH-no**) is in the imperative mood, which indicates a command. Jesus is not inviting them to receive the Holy Spirit. It is not an option. He is commanding them to receive the Holy Spirit. By using this form of the verb, Jesus implies that the Holy Spirit is indispensable, necessary for the task that He has given them.

23 Whose soever sins ye remit, they are remitted unto them; and whose soever sins ye retain, they are retained.

With this act comes responsibility to execute the divine will among believers and all humanity in the form of forgiveness. By this act, the risen Christ transforms fear into a great joy. The gift of the Spirit is to empower the disciples to exercise the right and authority with which He now clothes them in their sending. Jesus wants the remission of sins dispensed to sinners through the believers as His church on earth, excluding only those who refuse remission.

Two words are significant: "remit" and "retain." To remit (Gk. *aphiemi*, **ah-FEE-ey-mee**) means to send away. Here the sins are removed from the sinner, as far as the east is from the west (see **Psalm 103:12**), blotting out the transgressions so that the Lord Himself will not remember them (see **Isaiah 43:25**). Forgiveness is infinite. To retain (Gk. *krateo*, **krah-TEH-oh**) is to hold fast with strength. The sins committed are not able to be let go. The moment a sin is committed, that sin with all its guilt adheres to the sinner, and no human effort can possibly blot it out. Only one person is able to remove that sin, to remove it as though it had never existed: Jesus Christ our Lord. It is still Jesus who dismisses or holds sins, yet by this act that empowers the disciples, He makes them His agents. He acts through them.

SEARCH THE SCRIPTURES

QUESTIONS 1 & 2

What phrase does Christ use twice?

What is the disciples' mission?

LIGHT ON THE WORD

The Breath of God

The word used for Spirit here is *pneuma* (Gk., **puh-NEW-ma**), as opposed to *parakletos* (Gk., **pa-RAH-klay-tose**, helper) in last week's lesson. Pneuma is also translated as breath and wind. In a play on words reminiscent of God breathing life into Adam, Christ breathes on the disciples and equips them with the Holy Spirit, who He previously told them would lead, guide, instruct, and comfort them. Now is the time for them to go forth to fulfill their mission—sharing the Gospel. Those who choose to believe their message would be forgiven and granted eternal life. Those who reject Christ, would not.

BIBLE APPLICATION

AIM: Students will be convinced that the risen Christ appeared to the disciples and serve Him with the conviction that He is alive.

We have the tendency to underestimate the power of one and the power of the tongue. Genocide has occurred because one person determined that certain people were not worthy of living and convinced others to go along with his views. In other instances, one man or woman with a vision has sparked movements, inspired change, and positively altered the course of history. Just one.

STUDENTS' RESPONSES

AIM: Students will speak words of reassurance to those whose faith is weak or faltering.

There is work to be done for God's glory. What passion has God given you? What problems do you see that you sense God has wired you to be part of solving? What stops you? Write this out, and place it somewhere you will see it often. Pray that God would equip you with His Spirit to fulfill the mission He has given you.

PRAYER

Dear Lord, let us live out the varied experiences that You have for us that molds and shapes our many purposes in life and honors You. Through the many skills, talents, and gifts that You have provided for us, let us give glory to Your name. In Jesus' Name we pray. Amen.

HOW TO SAY IT

Pentecost.	**PEN**-teh-cost.
Shalom.	sha-**LOME**.

PREPARE FOR NEXT SUNDAY

Read **Mark 11:1–11** and study "The One Who Comes."

DAILY HOME BIBLE READINGS

MONDAY
The Holy Spirit Speaks
(Mark 13:5–11)

TUESDAY
Gentiles Receive the Holy Spirit
(Acts 10:39–48)

WEDNESDAY
Full of the Spirit and Faith
(Acts 11:19–26)

THURSDAY
Joy in the Holy Spirit
(Romans 14:13–19)

FRIDAY
Power from the Holy Spirit
(Acts 1:4–8)

SATURDAY
Be Filled with the Spirit
(Ephesians 5:15–21)

SUNDAY
Receive the Holy Spirit
(John 20:19–23)

Sources:

Hebrew-Greek Key Word Study Bible. King James Version. Chattanooga, TN: AMG Publishers, Inc., 1991.

Keener, Craig S. *The IVP Bible Background Commentary: New Testament*. Downers Grove, IL: Intervarsity Press, 1993. 315–317.

Radmacher, Earl D., ed. *Nelson Study Bible*. New King James Version. Nashville, TN: Thomas Nelson Publishers, 1997. 1807–1808.

Ryrie, Charles C. *Ryrie Study Bible*. New International Version. Chicago, IL: Moody Press. 1986. 1487-1489.

Unger, Merrill F. *The New Unger's Bible Dictionary*. Chicago, IL: Moody Press, 1988. 1074–1075.

Walvoord, John F., and Roy B. Zuck, eds. *The Bible Knowledge Commentary: New Testament*. Wheaton, IL: Victor Books, SP Publications, Inc., 1983. 341–343.

Zondervan Study Bible. New International Version. Grand Rapids, MI: Zondervan Publishers, 2002. 1669–1670.

THE ONE WHO COMES

BIBLE BASIS: MARK 11:1–11

BIBLE TRUTH: Followers of Christ celebrate Jesus' arrival in Jerusalem as the coming of God's kingdom.

MEMORY VERSE: "And they that went before, and they that followed, cried, saying, Hosanna; Blessed is he that cometh in the name of the Lord" (Mark 11:9).

LESSON AIM: By the end of the lesson, your students will: survey the story of Jesus' Triumphal Entry into Jerusalem; discuss their feelings about the kingdom of God; and find creative ways to pay homage to Jesus.

TEACHER PREPARATION

MATERIALS NEEDED: Quarterly Commentary/Teacher Manual, Adult Quarterly, Adult resources—charts, worksheets, and other teaching tools, paper, pens, pencils, Bibles (several different versions)

OTHER MATERIALS NEEDED / TEACHER'S NOTES:

____

____

LESSON OVERVIEW

LIFE NEED FOR TODAY'S LESSON
To celebrate God's victory in Christ on a daily basis.

BIBLE LEARNING
Believers accept Jesus as the ruler of a spiritual realm and believe they are part of the spiritual realm.

BIBLE APPLICATION
Disciples make certain sacrifices for the Lord's sake.

STUDENTS' RESPONSES
Students will tell others about the kingdom of God and the joy they have found by being part of it.

LESSON SCRIPTURE

MARK 11:1–11, KJV

1 And when they came nigh to Jerusalem, unto Bethphage and Bethany, at the mount of Olives, he sendeth forth two of his disciples,

2 And saith unto them, Go your way into the village over against you: and as soon as ye be entered into it, ye shall find a colt

MARK 11:1–11, NIV

1 As they approached Jerusalem and came to Bethphage and Bethany at the Mount of Olives, Jesus sent two of his disciples,

2 saying to them, "Go to the village ahead of you, and just as you enter it, you will find a colt tied there, which no one has ever ridden. Untie it and bring it here.

tied, whereon never man sat; loose him, and bring him.

3 And if any man say unto you, Why do ye this? say ye that the Lord hath need of him; and straightway he will send him hither.

4 And they went their way, and found the colt tied by the door without in a place where two ways met; and they loose him.

5 And certain of them that stood there said unto them, What do ye, loosing the colt?

6 And they said unto them even as Jesus had commanded: and they let them go.

7 And they brought the colt to Jesus, and cast their garments on him; and he sat upon him.

8 And many spread their garments in the way: and others cut down branches off the trees, and strawed them in the way.

9 And they that went before, and they that followed, cried, saying, Hosanna; Blessed is he that cometh in the name of the Lord:

10 Blessed be the kingdom of our father David, that cometh in the name of the Lord: Hosanna in the highest.

11 And Jesus entered into Jerusalem, and into the temple: and when he had looked round about upon all things, and now the eventide was come, he went out unto Bethany with the twelve.

3 If anyone asks you, 'Why are you doing this?' say, 'The Lord needs it and will send it back here shortly.'"

4 They went and found a colt outside in the street, tied at a doorway. As they untied it,

5 some people standing there asked, "What are you doing, untying that colt?"

6 They answered as Jesus had told them to, and the people let them go.

7 When they brought the colt to Jesus and threw their cloaks over it, he sat on it.

8 Many people spread their cloaks on the road, while others spread branches they had cut in the fields.

9 Those who went ahead and those who followed shouted, "Hosanna!" "Blessed is he who comes in the name of the Lord!"

10 "Blessed is the coming kingdom of our father David!" "Hosanna in the highest heaven!"

11 Jesus entered Jerusalem and went into the temple courts. He looked around at everything, but since it was already late, he went out to Bethany with the Twelve.

LIGHT ON THE WORD

The palm tree was a symbol of victory. The Romans carried palm leaves during their victory processions. Each day of the Feast of Tabernacles, a Jewish holiday that commemorates the harvest and God's protection in the wilderness after the Jews escaped bondage in Egypt, participants wave palms and shout "Hosanna." Our Palm Sunday is so called because the people laid palm branches on the road before Jesus as He entered Jerusalem, signifying that He is the Messiah. In Revelation 7:9, "Apostle John beheld in vision those who had overcome by the blood of the lamb standing 'before the Lamb, clothed with white robes, and palms in their hands'" (Watson and Bangs, 927).

Mark, Peter's interpreter mentioned in **Acts 12:12, 25; 15:37–39; Colossians 4:10; Philemon 24; 2 Timothy 4:11**; and **1 Peter 5:13**, penned his Gospel in Rome between 66 and 70 A.D., during the Jewish war with Rome that ended with the destruction of the Temple. During that time, many Jewish people were claiming that the Messiah would come to defeat the Romans and restore their national independence. Mark's Gospel reaffirmed for Christians that Jesus was and is the Messiah, whose purpose was to suffer, die, and rise again to ensure eternal salvation for believers.

TEACHING THE BIBLE LESSON

LIFE NEED FOR TODAY'S LESSON

AIM: Students will celebrate God's victory in Christ on a daily basis.

INTRODUCTION

The Journey into Jerusalem

Jesus and His disciples journeyed to Jerusalem for the upcoming Passover. At this point in Jesus' earthly ministry, whenever He went, crowds gathered, curious about the miracles He has performed. During one such stop, a few Pharisees in the crowd questioned Jesus about divorce to trap Him, but instead He clarified the issue for them. He later gave private teaching on divorce to the disciples. As Jesus and the disciples continued to journey on, parents brought their children to Him for a blessing, and a rich man approached, inquiring what he should do to gain eternal life. Once they reached the direct road to Jerusalem, Jesus pulled the twelve aside and predicted His death a third time. James and John requested to be leaders in Jesus' kingdom, but He taught them all that in His kingdom, the leader must serve all. Finally, Jesus healed blind Bartimaeus who sat on the road just outside of Jericho. Once healed, he joined the crowd that had been following Jesus to Jerusalem.

BIBLE LEARNING

AIM: Students will accept Jesus as the ruler of a spiritual realm and believe they are part of the spiritual realm.

I. SUPERNATURAL KNOWLEDGE CONFIRMED (Mark 11:1–6)

Jesus and His disciples were finally within reach of Jerusalem as they approached Bethphage and Bethany at the Mount of Olives. Instead of continuing, He stopped and sent two disciples ahead to find a colt, or young donkey. At this moment in the story, Jesus is poised to reveal a crucial fact about Himself. Perhaps He is very detailed with His instructions because those currently with Him and those who would read of Him later would need to understand that these details revealed His identity. Saying the colt would be tied speaks to Jesus' identity because it mirrors one of the earliest Messianic prophecies: "The sceptre shall not depart from Judah, nor a lawgiver from between his feet, until Shiloh come; and unto him shall the gathering of the people be. Binding his foal unto the vine, and his ass's colt unto the choice vine; he washed his garments in wine, and his clothes in the blood of grapes" (**Genesis 49:10–11**, KJV).

The Preparation Begins (verses 1–6)

1 And when they came nigh to Jerusalem, unto Bethphage and Bethany, at the Mount of Olives, he sendeth forth two of

his disciples,

Jesus and the disciples arrive at Bethphage and Bethany. These two villages were a Sabbath day's journey (approximately 1,000 yards) from Jerusalem. It was a fitting staging point for Jesus' next act of ministry. The Mount of Olives held a special significance in the history of Israel. It was the place that David fled to when Absalom took over Jerusalem. This same place would be the launching pad for Jesus' entry to Jerusalem as its rightful King and Lord. He would not conquer with an army, but with His death on the Cross and subsequent Resurrection. Now it was time for Jesus to enter Jerusalem and fulfill what was spoken about Him in the Old Testament.

The Greek word *apostello* (**ah-poh-STELL-oh**), "sendeth," denotes the sending of a messenger with a special task or commission, and full authority. The disciples were sent as ambassadors with a precise message, speaking in the name of their Master. They were not going in their own authority, but that of Jesus. Their mandate is described in the next verse. Jesus sent the two in order to accomplish a prophecy from **Zechariah 9:9**, thus giving this event messianic significance.

2 and saith unto them, Go your way into the village over against you: and as soon as ye be entered into it, ye shall find a colt tied, whereon never man sat; loose him, and bring him.

The Greek word *polos* (**POH-lahss**) means a young colt. The description of the young animal as one "whereon never man sat" is significant in the light of many Old Testament passages. Animals that were unyoked and unused were sometimes consecrated to a unique and holy use (see **Numbers 19:2; Deuteronomy 21:3; 1 Samuel 6:7**). This animal was fitting to be the one the Messiah would ride on as He entered Jerusalem. In Western countries, the donkey is considered to be stubborn and dumb. However, in the Middle East, the donkey is considered to possess the qualities of patience, intelligence, and submission. It was also ridden by royalty and nobility. The donkey was usually mounted during peacetime, as opposed to a horse mounted and used during times of war. We read of the prophet Balaam riding on a donkey (**Numbers 22:21**) and of the seventy sons of the judge Abdon riding on seventy donkeys (**Judges 12:13–14**). It was the animal used for nobility in peacetime and also for those who stood in the office of judge. Jesus chose an animal that fit into the bigger picture of His role as Messiah. He was coming as a King but with a different kind of kingdom. His kingdom was a kingdom of peace, not war. He would ride into Jerusalem not as a conquering lion, but the Prince of Peace.

What is also fascinating is Jesus' knowledge of the age and location of the colt. This event was not only messianic but supernatural. By describing the colt and predicting that it would be given to Him, Jesus exercised the wisdom and knowledge from the Holy Spirit. This foreknowledge of the location and age of the colt would be seen as further proof that Jesus truly is the Messiah. The disciples would definitely be amazed at finding the young donkey in the right location and condition, unused. In their minds this would have solidified Jesus' claim to being Messiah. Here, Jesus is acting as the now reigning King of the Jews, and His prophetic insight into how to fulfill this symbolic act supported that claim, and confirmed to the disciples that God was confirming this claim as well.

3 And if any man say unto you, Why do ye this? say ye that the Lord hath need of him; and straightway he will send him hither.

The Greek word *kurios* (**KOO-ree-ose**), meaning "Lord," refers to Jesus Himself, showing

His supreme authority over all things. In any case, Jesus armed His two emissaries against possible difficulties by furnishing them with what to say. He predicted that they would send the animal promptly after the disciples gave this answer. The colt is already under the authority and ownership of the Lord, who now needed him.

4 And they went their way, and found the colt tied by the door without in a place where two ways met; and they loosed him. 5 And certain of them that stood there said unto them, What do ye, loosing the colt? 6 And they said unto them even as Jesus had commanded: and they let them go.

Jesus' ambassadors found the young animal exactly as He had said. It was outside the house and fastened by the door. Precisely what Jesus said would happen did happen. The two disciples wasted no time and loosed the colt. They were obedient to their Master and probably were encouraged by seeing the colt exactly as described. They did encounter some difficulty as some nearby people—the owners or villagers—questioned them regarding the colt. The people were satisfied with the disciples' answer probably because Jesus was well-known for His miraculous deeds and for teaching with authority (see **John 7:46; Mark 11:18**). They knew that this Master could be trusted. They might even have been proud that He wanted to use the young colt.

SEARCH THE SCRIPTURES

QUESTION 1

What were Jesus' instructions for finding the colt?

LIGHT ON THE WORD

Jesus Has All Authority

Mark primarily depicts Jesus as the Suffering Servant (cf. **Isaiah 53**). However, in this passage, we witness His authority in His detailed instructions and supernatural knowledge. The two found everything to be as Jesus said it would be. Who but the Messiah, the everlasting King, could speak with such authority and know that everything would be aligned to the smallest detail? For the first-century Christian, this would have been reassurance that the One they served is the true Messiah.

II. THE PROMISED ONE COMES (vv. 7–11)

Jesus sitting on the colt was fulfillment of Messianic prophecy as well (see **Zechariah 9:9**). Often, Jesus would not reveal His identity (**Mark 1:34, 7:36, 8:26, 11:33**), but now His actions declared that He is the Messiah. The people treated Him as a king by throwing their garments on the road (cf. **2 Kings 9:13**). They also showed that they recognized that He was not just any king, but rather the One promised to save, by laying down palm branches on the road and shouting the praise word "Hosanna" (Save now! or Please save us!). This is reminiscent of the Feast of Tabernacles, during which this praise is said with the waving of palms. In the context of this holiday, "Hosanna" means salvation is coming, and in the context of Jesus' entry, the Messiah is here. Victory is imminent. To further emphasize that the crowd believed Jesus was the Messiah, the people shouted, "Blessed is he that cometh in the name of the Lord: Blessed be the kingdom of our father David, that cometh in the name of the Lord: Hosanna in the highest" (**Mark 11:9–10**). This is part of the Hallel praise taken from **Psalm 118:25–26**, which is spoken during Passover and Pentecost holidays as well as the Feast of Tabernacles.

Praise Him! (verses 7–11)

7 And they brought the colt to Jesus, and cast their garments on him; and he sat upon him. 8 And many spread their

garments in the way: and others cut down branches off the trees, and strawed them in the way.

The disciples placed their outer garments on the colt in place of a saddle. Jesus sat and began His ride to the gates of Jerusalem. He was met by a spontaneous expression of homage. The crowd provided "a red carpet" for Him, their King. They threw their garments "in the way." The Greek word here, *eis* (**ACE**), meaning "into," denotes that the crowd threw their garments into the way and spread them there for Jesus to ride over. The picture of Christ riding into Jerusalem on a donkey provoked immediate action, as the people were inspired by this show of humility.

The carpeted way was not made of garments only. The crowd also cut down branches off the trees and strewed them on the road. The Greek word *stibas* (**stee-BAHSS**) speaks of a mass of straw, rushes, or leaves beaten together or strewn loosely so as to form a carpet. John's Gospel account speaks specifically of palm branches being spread out and waved (**12:12–13**). This may have come from the memory of Judas Maccabeus, or Judah the Hammer, who lived almost 200 years before Christ. When Judas defeated the Seleucid Empire and gained control of the Temple, the crowds celebrated by waving palm branches.

9 And they that went before, and they that followed, cried, saying, Hosanna; Blessed is he that cometh in the name of the Lord:

The Greek word Hosanna comes from the Aramaic phrase *Hoshiah na* (**hoh-SHEE-ah NAH**). Its original meaning is a cry for help: "O save" or "Help, I pray," as in **Psalm 118:25**. Coupled with the blessing that follows, as in Mark, it denotes an expression of praise, rejoicing, or greeting. This psalm is one of the Hallel psalms of praise. It is also known as the "Egyptian Hallel" because it praises God's saving act of delivering Israel from Egypt. The Greek word *eulogeo* (**ehoo-loh-GEH-oh**) or "blessed" means to speak well of or to praise. The blessing is from God, the source of all blessings. He who comes is blessed by the Lord God to whom He belongs. Jesus was "eulogized" by the crowd, which subjected itself to Him and recognized Him as the Messiah (cf. **Psalm 118:26**). Some evidence suggests the phrase "he who comes" refers to the Messiah, especially as one who rides a young donkey's colt (**Genesis 49:10**). The crowd recognized Jesus' riding on a donkey as the fulfillment of the prophecy in **Zechariah 9:9** and **Genesis 49:11**.

This event showed that Jesus was indeed coming as a King and Messiah. Many of the Jewish people were eager for freedom from Roman rule. The garments and branches in the road and the cries of "Hosanna" in the air were the responses of a people who needed and sought a Savior. Jesus' riding into Jerusalem on a donkey is more than just a fulfillment of Messianic prophecy; it was also a symbolic action in the manner of the Old Testament prophets. By riding into Jerusalem on a donkey, He was publicly showing that He was the King the Jews had been waiting for. This act defied the Romans, who had political authority over Palestine at the time. It also defied the local Jewish ruler Herod and the high priests who also ruled alongside Rome.

Many refer to this as the Triumphal Entry, but it was very different from the triumphal entry of a Roman general. The Romans honored generals who had won a complete and decisive victory over a foreign enemy with a "triumph." This consisted of riding into Rome in a parade followed by captured treasure, enemy prisoners, and all of his military units. At the end of the parade, some of the enemy prisoners were ritualistically executed or thrown to wild animals for the crowd's entertainment.

10 Blessed be the kingdom of our father David, that cometh in the name of the

Lord: Hosanna in the highest.

The crowds understood this entry to be a sign that God was now in charge. The expectation was that the Messiah would rule as a representative of God and that He would come from the line of David. Their cries focused on the kingdom because they understood that this new King would not continue with business as usual. The Jewish expectation of a Messiah was that God would now be King and turn the whole world upside down.

Hosanna means "O save" or "Help, I pray," but this time it is in the superlative: "Hosanna in the highest." The Greek word *hupsistos* (**HOOP-sis-tose**) means to the highest regions or highest degree possible. It is a word that is often used for God as "the Most High." The crowds gave Jesus praise to the highest degree possible. It was praise that was reserved for God. This was a measure of how much the Jewish people were expecting a Messianic Deliverer and how much they believed that right now, Jesus was that Deliverer.

11 And he entered Jerusalem and went into the temple. And when he had looked around at everything, as it was already late, he went out to Bethany with the twelve.

Jesus goes into the Temple and looks around. The reign of the Messiah was intricately bound with the Temple, since the Temple was a symbol of God's presence on earth. It was fitting for Jesus to go into the Temple although He did not cleanse it at the moment. He and the disciples had journeyed for a day uphill and the text says that it was "already late." With this and after so much excitement had been created with His entry into Jerusalem, Jesus decided to conclude His day. So after looking into the Temple and inspecting the premises, He and the twelve spend the night in Bethany. Business in the Temple would have to wait.

SEARCH THE SCRIPTURES

QUESTION 2

What were the people doing and shouting as Jesus entered Jerusalem?

LIGHT ON THE WORD

The People Didn't Understand

The fact that the Triumphal Entry had all the fanfare of a victory procession conveys the crowd's misunderstanding that the Messiah was a political leader bringing salvation through militaristic means. They seem to want to crown Jesus king immediately. However, He merely enters the Temple, looks around, and returns to Bethany for the night. This emphasizes that Jesus will not be the Messiah they were expecting. He came on a donkey, not a horse, which meant He had come with a peaceful agenda to procure eternal salvation. Although many of those present would later develop disdain for Jesus' brand of salvation, the first-century Christians in Mark's initial audience would find comfort in it while living in a society that was hostile to their beliefs.

BIBLE APPLICATION

AIM: Students will learn to make certain sacrifices for the Lord's sake.

We live in a society that engages in celebrity worship. We spend hundreds of dollars buying tickets to see our star athletes. We camp out for hours to hear our favorite singers. We stand in long lines to get our pictures taken with movie stars. We want to dress and act like celebrities. We love and honor them. However, Jesus is the only One who truly loves us. He loved us so much He suffered, died, and rose again for our salvation. We should strive to live lives that honor Him.

STUDENTS' RESPONSES

AIM: Students will tell others about the

kingdom of God and the joy they have found by being part of it.

We often pray for a house, a promotion, or a mate. There is nothing wrong with looking to God to take care of our every need. However, we should not only limit Him to what we perceive is important. Jesus came so that we could have eternal life, and for this, we should honor Him. For your daily devotion, ask God to show you ways you can honor Him and whatever He reveals, do it.

PRAYER

Jesus, thank You for giving us eternal life and peace that will last forever. In Jesus' Name we pray. Amen.

HOW TO SAY IT

Bethphage.	**BAYTH**-fah-gay.
Bethany.	**BE**-tha-nee.
Hosanna.	ho-**ZA**-na.

PREPARE FOR NEXT SUNDAY

Read **1 Corinthians 15:1–11, 20–22** and study "Resurrection Guaranteed."

DAILY HOME BIBLE READINGS

MONDAY
God Judges the Peoples with Equity
(Psalm 67)

TUESDAY
A Righteous God and a Savior
(Isaiah 45:20–25)

WEDNESDAY
God Highly Exalted Him
(Philippians 2:9–16)

THURSDAY
Beware, Keep Alert
(Mark 13:30–37)

FRIDAY
The Coming Son of Man
(Mark 14:55–62)

SATURDAY
The World Has Gone After Him
(John 12:14–19)

SUNDAY
Blessed is the Coming Kingdom
(Mark 11:1–11)

Sources:

Black, Clifton. "Gospel According to Mark: Introduction and Mark 11: 1–11 notes." *The Harper Collins Study Bible.* NRSV. San Francisco, CA: Harper Collins Publishers, 2006. 1722–24, 1745–46.

Henry, Matthew. "Mark 11." *Matthew Henry's Commentary on the Whole Bible.* Vol. 5: Matthew to John.

Hurtado, Larry W. "Jesus Enters Jerusalem and the Temple." *Understanding the Bible Commentary Series: Mark.* Grand Rapids, MI: Baker Books, 2011.

Jensen, Richard A. *Preaching Mark's Gospel: A Narrative Approach.* Lima, OH: CSS Publishing Co., Inc. 1996. 168–170.

Shanks, Hershel, ed. *Ancient Israel from Abraham to the Roman Destruction of the Temple.* Washington, DC: Prentice Hall, 1999. 286.

Unger, Merrill F. "Festivals: Feast of Booths (or Tabernacles)." *The New Unger's Bible Dictionary.* R.K. Harrison, ed. Chicago, IL: Moody Press, 1988. 417–421.

----------. "Mark, Gospel of." *The New Unger's Bible Dictionary.* R.K. Harrison, ed. Chicago, IL: Moody Press, 1988. 816.

----------. "Palm Tree." *The New Unger's Bible Dictionary.* R.K. Harrison, ed. Chicago, IL: Moody Press, 1988. 957–958.

Watson, Richard and Nathan Bangs. *A Biblical and Theological Dictionary: Explanatory of the History, Manners, and Customs of the Jews, and Neighbouring Nations.* New York: B. Waugh and T. Mason, 1832. 927.

RESURRECTION GUARANTEED

BIBLE BASIS: 1 CORINTHIANS 15:1–11, 20–22

BIBLE TRUTH: Jesus' resurrection provided tangible evidence of the possibility of resurrection for those whose identity is formed by Christ Jesus.

MEMORY VERSE: "For as in Adam all die, even so in Christ shall all be made alive" (1 Corinthians 15:22).

LESSON AIM: By the end of the lesson, your students will: explore the meaning of Christ's Resurrection; value and appreciate our identity in Jesus Christ; and witness personally and corporately to the Resurrection of Jesus Christ.

TEACHER PREPARATION

MATERIALS NEEDED: Quarterly Commentary/Teacher Manual, Adult Quarterly, Adult resources—charts, worksheets, and other teaching tools, paper, pens, pencils, Bibles (several different versions)

OTHER MATERIALS NEEDED / TEACHER'S NOTES:

____

____

LESSON OVERVIEW

LIFE NEED FOR TODAY'S LESSON
Christians need to be reminded of the importance of Jesus' life, death, and resurrection in the lives of believers.

BIBLE LEARNING
Christians experience the effects of God's grace.

BIBLE APPLICATION
Believers value the scriptural record of eyewitness testimony.

STUDENTS' RESPONSES
Students will expand their opportunities to personally identify with Christ as they share the good news of the love of Christ with others.

LESSON SCRIPTURE

1 CORINTHIANS 15:1–11, 20–22, KJV

1 Moreover, brethren, I declare unto you the gospel which I preached unto you, which also ye have received, and wherein ye stand;

2 By which also ye are saved, if ye keep in memory what I preached unto you, unless ye have believed in vain.

1 CORINTHIANS 15:1–11, 20–22, NIV

1 Now, brothers and sisters, I want to remind you of the gospel I preached to you, which you received and on which you have taken your stand.

2 By this gospel you are saved, if you hold firmly to the word I preached to you. Otherwise, you have believed in vain.

3 For I delivered unto you first of all that which I also received, how that Christ died for our sins according to the scriptures;

3 For what I received I passed on to you as of first importance: that Christ died for our sins according to the Scriptures,

4 And that he was buried, and that he rose again the third day according to the scriptures:

4 that he was buried, that he was raised on the third day according to the Scriptures,

5 And that he was seen of Cephas, then of the twelve:

5 and that he appeared to Cephas, and then to the Twelve.

6 After that, he was seen of above five hundred brethren at once; of whom the greater part remain unto this present, but some are fallen asleep.

6 After that, he appeared to more than five hundred of the brothers and sisters at the same time, most of whom are still living, though some have fallen asleep.

7 After that, he was seen of James; then of all the apostles.

7 Then he appeared to James, then to all the apostles,

8 And last of all he was seen of me also, as of one born out of due time.

8 and last of all he appeared to me also, as to one abnormally born.

9 For I am the least of the apostles, that am not meet to be called an apostle, because I persecuted the church of God.

9 For I am the least of the apostles and do not even deserve to be called an apostle, because I persecuted the church of God.

10 But by the grace of God I am what I am: and his grace which was bestowed upon me was not in vain; but I laboured more abundantly than they all: yet not I, but the grace of God which was with me.

10 But by the grace of God I am what I am, and his grace to me was not without effect. No, I worked harder than all of them—yet not I, but the grace of God that was with me.

11 Therefore whether it were I or they, so we preach, and so ye believed.

11 Whether, then, it is I or they, this is what we preach, and this is what you believed.

20 But now is Christ risen from the dead, and become the firstfruits of them that slept.

20 But Christ has indeed been raised from the dead, the firstfruits of those who have fallen asleep.

21 For since by man came death, by man came also the resurrection of the dead.

21 For since death came through a man, the resurrection of the dead comes also through a man.

22 For as in Adam all die, even so in Christ shall all be made alive.

22 For as in Adam all die, so in Christ all will be made alive.

LIGHT ON THE WORD

Paul is often called the great apostle because of his extensive mission to bring the Gospel to the Gentiles, but prior to his conversion, he was a member of the Pharisees. With as much zeal as he would later exhibit in spreading the Gospel, Paul persecuted Christians. He not only sought imprisonment but favored death for men and women who defected from Judaism to Christianity. He condoned the stoning of Stephen (**Acts 8:1, 22:20**). Paul not only wanted to end Christianity in Jerusalem, but wanted to end it throughout the whole known world. He was on the road to Damascus because he heard there were Christians there (**Acts 9:1–2**), and he had asked for special permission to bring them to Jerusalem for punishment. But on that road he encountered Christ and the trajectory of his life was forever changed.

TEACHING THE BIBLE LESSON

LIFE NEED FOR TODAY'S LESSON

AIM: Students will be reminded of the importance of Jesus' life, death, and resurrection in the lives of believers.

INTRODUCTION

Church Issues

Throughout 1 Corinthians, Paul deals with issue after issue. He addressed the divisions in the church (**1:10–4:21**), sexual immorality including incest (**5:1–13**) and fornication (**6:12–20**), marriage and divorce (**7:1–40**), idolatry (**8:1–11:1**), and different aspects of public worship (**chapters 11–13**). In **1 Corinthians 14**, Paul addresses the spiritual gifts of speaking in tongues and prophecy. The apostle instructed that the Corinthians should pursue love and the gift of prophecy because it builds up the whole church. Tongues only build up the individual. The only way tongues can edify the church is if the one speaking has the gift to interpret. Paul writes that proper worship will result in even unbelievers admitting, "God is truly here among you" (**1 Corinthians 14:25**). The chapter ends with Paul describing the proper order of worship. With all of these other issues dealt with, Paul finally launches into explaining the significance of Christ's Resurrection.

BIBLE LEARNING

AIM: Students will experience the effects of God's grace.

I. RESURRECTION CLARIFIED (1 Corinthians 15:1–5)

There were some in the Corinthian church who did not believe in the resurrection of the dead. Paul reminds them that he had already preached the Good News to them and they had, or so it seemed, fully accepted it. He writes, "By which also ye are saved, if ye keep in memory what I preached unto you, unless ye have believed in vain" (**1 Corinthians 15:2, KJV**).

The Good News (verses 1–5)

1 Moreover, brethren, I declare unto you the gospel which I preached unto you, which also ye have received, and wherein ye stand; 2 By which also ye are saved, if ye keep in memory what I preached unto you, unless you have believed in vain.

The opening of this chapter introduces Paul's concerns and lays the foundation for the argument he develops in the verses that follow. Some in the Corinthian church exalted the spiritual so much that they devalued the physical. Consequently, this path led to denial of bodily resurrection.

Paul begins with what they have in common. Paul uses the Greek word *euaggelion* (**ehoo-an-GHEL-ee-on**), which means good news message or Gospel, to describe what he preached and they in turn received as a means for salvation. They owe their existence as a community of faith to the Gospel he brought them (Fee 1987; Horsley 2011). He warns if they cannot hold on to the same Gospel that saved them, their faith is in jeopardy of being ineffective and producing no fruit.

3 For I delivered unto you first of all that which I also received, how that Christ died for our sins according to the scriptures; 4 And that he was buried, and that he rose again the third day according to the scriptures: 5 And that he was seen of Cephas, then of the twelve:

Paul presents the basics of the Gospel by highlighting three points of emphasis: Jesus died, was buried, and rose again on the third day, all in accordance with the Scriptures. This essence of the Gospel was passed down to Paul. It is generally accepted that these verses reflect an early creed. Being of primary importance, he in turn passed it along to the church in Corinth (Fee 1987).

Although Paul covered a wide range of subjects, not everything he discussed was central to the Gospel. Nor does every instruction carry equal weight. In this passage, Paul highlights the elements of the Gospel message that are critical to the church and its health and vitality.

The death, burial, and resurrection of Jesus are presented as an objective reality. There is a grave, and there were witnesses. It is not merely a spiritual phenomenon.

In addition to misconceptions about the Resurrection, it is likely that the church in Corinth had some misgivings about Paul's authority. Paul grounds his argument in tradition, Scripture, and apostolic authority. First, he appeals to tradition by referencing an early church creed. Then, he asserts that these things have hapened according to Scripture. Last, he states that Cephas, or Peter, and the twelve can attest to the validity of his claims. The twelve apostles had an especially close relationship with Jesus and a special role in the founding of the church. Perhaps Peter was singled out because he had followers in the church of Corinth.

SEARCH THE SCRIPTURES

QUESTION 1

What is the Gospel message?

LIGHT ON THE WORD

The Foundation of the Gospel

Before explaining the foundation of the Gospel message, Paul asserts that the message he had given them and he had received himself was valid. He then explains the foundation of the Christian faith: 1) "God presented Christ as a sacrifice of atonement, through the shedding of his blood—to be received by faith" (from **Romans 3:25**, NIV). 2) Christ was buried. To ensure Jesus was dead, a rock was sealed across the tomb and guards placed outside (**Matthew 27:62–66**). 3) Christ rose on the third day. Death needed to be conquered so that salvation could be secured (**2 Timothy 1:10**).

II. RESURRECTION WITNESSED (vv. 6–11)

Paul offers even more validity to the Resurrection by listing the witnesses. Peter and the Twelve saw the resurrected Jesus (**John 20:19–29**). They had been chosen to be witnesses (**Acts 10:40–43**). More than five hundred of His followers saw Jesus, including James, Jesus' brother and other apostles (**Luke 24:33, 36–53**). Perhaps a criterion for being an apostle, from Paul's perspective, was that one had to have been divinely chosen to see the resurrected Christ. They were sent out to preach the Gospel because they could personally testify to its truth (Soards).

Eyewitness Accounts (verses 6–11)

6 After that, he was seen of above five hundred brethren at once; of whom the greater part remain unto this present, but some are fallen asleep. 7 After that, he was seen of James; then of all the apostles. 8 And last of all he was seen of me also, as of one born out of due time.

Paul continues to build the credibility of his position by adding an additional source of authority-eyewitness testimony of believers, apostles, and him. Paul affirms that Jesus was seen by a number of people in a variety of settings after his burial, more than 500 believers, according to Paul. Many of the witnesses were still alive the time of the writing and their accounts could be verified first hand, although some had already "fallen asleep," a common euphemism at the time for death.

Next Paul says that the resurrected Jesus was seen by James, Jesus' half-brother. He was also a major leader in the Jerusalem church. This would have given Paul even more credibility, as James had major influence with the church at large due to his natural relation to Jesus. Paul also speaks of the resurrected Jesus being seen by the apostles. This is obviously not the twelve because they were just mentioned in **verse 5**. Paul must have been referring to others outside of the twelve who had been commissioned to represent Christ, perhaps those mentioned in **Luke 10:1–20**.

Paul establishes a connection between the apostolic tradition and himself, even though there is no evidence he was regarded as one of the Twelve. He is likely referring to his encounter with the risen Lord on the road to Damascus. Paul uses the Greek word *ektroma* (**EK-troh-ma**), which is often translated abnormally born, to describe his apostolic calling. The Twelve had years of mentoring and close relationship with Jesus during His time on earth. Paul, however, did not become an apostle this way. He may have been expressing feelings of being born out of season since his apostolic calling was out of the ordinary.

9 For I am the least of the apostles, that am not meet to be called an apostle, because I persecuted the church of God. 10 But by the grace of God I am what I am: and his grace which was bestowed upon me was not in vain; but I laboured more abundantly than they all: yet not I, but the grace of God which was with me. 11 Therefore whether it were I or they, so we preach, and so ye believed.

Paul explains that he is "least" of the apostles because he formerly persecuted the church. He is unworthy of the calling, and did nothing to earn it. His standing before God as the "least" of the apostles and later as the "chief" of sinners provide the foundation for his deep experience of the grace of God in Jesus Christ.

The grace Paul discusses is best understood as twofold: saving and empowering. By the saving grace of God, Paul was transformed from an enemy of God and the church to a friend. His faith flourished and he was empowered to bear fruit. Paul mentions he "laboured more abundantly" than all the Twelve. Grace should not be confused with meritorious effort, as indicated by his assertion that the agent of these works is "yet not I, but the grace of God which was with me." Hard work is not the means of achieving results in his ministry, but a manifestation of God's empowering grace.

The language he uses in **verse 11**, "I or they," hints that there was debate in the Corinthian church about the authority of various itinerant apostles. He ties what he preached to their faith and all apostles, suggesting it is commonly accepted by all believers. His point is that they all preached the same thing! It allows him to show they were departing from the Gospel message and traditional sources of authority for the church, not him.

SEARCH THE SCRIPTURES

QUESTION 2

How does Paul describe himself?

LIGHT ON THE WORD

Jesus Chose the Least of These

Paul was the last witness. Although, he had not lived and journeyed with Jesus, he too had been chosen when Jesus appeared to him on the road to Damascus. Of himself, Paul writes "last of all he was seen of me also, as of one born out of due time" (**v. 8**). The phrase "born out of due time" refers to a miscarried or still-born baby. In essence, Paul was someone who was spiritually dead and therefore unfit to be an apostle because he had persecuted believers. However, God, in His grace, still chose Paul to be a witness. This fact was in response to those in Corinth who were questioning his authority (**1 Corinthians 9**). Whether the other apostles or Paul preached the Gospel, it was the same message that the Corinthians had already believed.

III. RESURRECTION GUARANTEED (vv. 20–22)

In **verses 12–19**, Paul refutes the people's belief that there is no resurrection of the dead with a line of reasoning that in essence concludes that if there is no resurrection, Christ did not rise and their faith would be useless. They would all still be in their sin, condemned forever. However, Paul reassures his audience, that indeed Jesus had risen from the dead.

The Benefits of the Resurrection (verses 20–22)

20 But now is Christ risen from the dead, and become the firstfruits of them that slept. 21 For since by man came death, by man came also the resurrection of the dead. 22 For as in Adam all die, even so in Christ shall all be made alive.

Paul emphasizes the benefits of the Resurrection for believers. Christ's Resurrection made the resurrection of the dead necessary and inevitable. God raised Christ from the dead based on His own authority and sovereignty. It is required for the final victory over death so God can be "all in all."

Paul uses the Greek word *aparkhe* (**ah-par-KHAY**), meaning a sacrifice of the harvest's firstfruits to sanctify the whole harvest, to describe the work of Christ. He is the first fruit of a larger harvest (**2 Thessalonians 2:13, NIV; 1 Corinthians 16:15, KJV**). This agricultural metaphor has eschatological significance, Christ's resurrection is not bound to one annual harvest, but it sanctifies the resurrection of all believers for eternity. For this to happen, Christ had to be human because death is a part of humankind, not God. Christ reversed what Adam set in motion, ushering in a new order. New life and resurrection for believers is inevitable because we share in the new nature of the Resurrected Christ through the grace of God.

SEARCH THE SCRIPTURES

QUESTION 3

How do Jesus and Adam differ?

LIGHT ON THE WORD

The Joy of the Great Sacrifice

Paul continues to explain the benefit of Jesus' Resurrection. Jesus did not conquer death only for Himself. He is the first of all who have died. His resurrection ensures that all who believe in Him shall have eternal life. To illustrate this truth, Paul compares Jesus to Adam. Just as Adam brought death for all, Jesus has brought eternal life for those who believe in Him. This was Christ's purpose all along; the Father sent Him so "that whosoever believeth in him should not perish, but have everlasting life" (**John 3:16**).

BIBLE APPLICATION

AIM: Students will value the scriptural record of eyewitness testimony.

Certain events define our identities. On the wedding day, we become a spouse. Giving birth to a child, we become a parent. We cherish these life-changing events and commemorate them every year with anniversaries and birthday celebrations. As believers, another event that deserves our devotion is the Resurrection of Christ. The Resurrection is the foundation of our faith. It is the fuel that motivates us to want to live right and treat others with love and kindness. Without it, we would be eternally lost. Let's remember to celebrate the Resurrection not just once a year, but everyday of our lives.

STUDENTS' RESPONSES

AIM: Students will expand their opportunities to personally identify with Christ as they share the good news of the love of Christ with others.

We love to celebrate life-changing events with others. We book banquet halls a year in advance and hire the best caterers so people can spend a few hours with us on our special day. The greatest event to ever happen to us is the Resurrection, and we should find ways to share it. Pray about at least three people with whom you can share the Good News and create a special occasion for the sharing. For example, meet for breakfast, schedule time at the gym, or invite them to a church function.

PRAYER

Thank You and bless You, our wonderful Lord and Savior. Thank you for sacrificing Your life so that we are forgiven of our sins, and have eternal life. In Jesus' Name we pray. Amen.

HOW TO SAY IT

Apostolic.	ah-po-**STOL**-ik.
Eschatological.	es-ka-to-**LAH**-gi-cal.

PREPARE FOR NEXT SUNDAY

Read **1 John 3:11–24** and study "Love One Another."

DAILY HOME BIBLE READINGS

MONDAY
Jesus Has Died
(Matthew 27:45–50)

TUESDAY
Christ Has Risen
(Matthew 28:1–8)

WEDNESDAY
Christ Will Come Again
(1 Thessalonians 4:13–18)

THURSDAY
The Resurrection and the Life
(John 11:20–27)

FRIDAY
The Hope of Eternal Life
(Titus 3:1–7)

SATURDAY
If Christ Has Not Been Raised
(1 Corinthians 15:12–19)

SUNDAY
In Fact, Christ Has Been Raised
(1 Corinthians 15:1–11, 20–22)

Sources:

Keener, Craig S. The IVP Bible Background Commentary: New Testament. Downers Grove, IL: InterVarsity Press, 1993. 647–650, 670–671.

Lane, William L. Hebrews 9–13. Word Biblical Commentary, Vol. 47B. Dallas, TX: Word Inc., 1991.

Life Application Study Bible. King James Version. Wheaton, IL: Tyndale House Publishers, Inc., 1997. 2154–55, 2170–72.

Radmacher, Earl D., ed. Nelson's New Illustrated Bible Commentary: Spreading the Light of God's Word into Your Life. Nashville, TN: Thomas Nelson Publishers, 1999. 1648–53.

Furnish, Paul Victor. "First Letter of Paul to the Corinthians: Introduction and 1 Corinthians 15:1–11; 20–22 notes." The Harper Collins Study Bible. NRSV. San Francisco, CA: Harper Collins Publishers, 2006. 1932–34, 1952–53.

Soards, Marion L. "Back to the Basics: 1 Corinthians 15: 1-11." Understanding the Bible Commentary Series. Grand Rapids, MI: Baker Books. 2011.

Unger, Merrill F. "Corinth." The New Unger's Bible Dictionary. R.K. Harrison, ed. Chicago, IL: Moody Press, 1988. 255–256.

----------. "1 Corinthians." The New Unger's Bible Dictionary. R.K. Harrison, ed. Chicago, IL: Moody Press, 1988. 256.

----------. "Paul." The New Unger's Bible Dictionary. R.K. Harrison, ed. Chicago, IL: Moody Press, 1988. 968–969.

COMMENTS / NOTES:

LOVE ONE ANOTHER

BIBLE BASIS: 1 JOHN 3:11–24

BIBLE TRUTH: John's letter indicates that the measure of people's lives is calculated by their faith in Christ and their love for one another.

MEMORY VERSE: "For this is the message that ye heard from the beginning, that we should love one another" (1 John 3:11).

LESSON AIM: By the end of the lesson, your students will: understand John's message about loving one another; affirm the fundamental discipleship principle of love for God and others; and express unconditional love to others.

TEACHER PREPARATION

MATERIALS NEEDED: Quarterly Commentary/Teacher Manual, Adult Quarterly, Adult resources—charts, worksheets, and other teaching tools, paper, pens, pencils, Bibles (several different versions)

OTHER MATERIALS NEEDED / TEACHER'S NOTES:

____

____

LESSON OVERVIEW

LIFE NEED FOR TODAY'S LESSON
People of faith experience the hatred of the world and counter it with God's love.

BIBLE LEARNING
Believers see Jesus' selfless love as the highest model of friendship and the opposite of the evil example of Cain.

BIBLE APPLICATION
Christians value the abiding nature of God's presence.

STUDENTS' RESPONSES
Students will develop ways for believers to express their love for God and others.

LESSON SCRIPTURE

1 JOHN 3:11–24, KJV

11 For this is the message that ye heard from the beginning, that we should love one another.

12 Not as Cain, who was of that wicked one, and slew his brother. And wherefore slew he him? Because his own works were evil, and his brother's righteous.

1 JOHN 3:11–24, NIV

11 For this is the message you heard from the beginning: We should love one another.

12 Do not be like Cain, who belonged to the evil one and murdered his brother. And why did he murder him? Because his own actions were evil and his brother's were righteous.

13 Marvel not, my brethren, if the world hate you.

14 We know that we have passed from death unto life, because we love the brethren. He that loveth not his brother abideth in death.

15 Whosoever hateth his brother is a murderer: and ye know that no murderer hath eternal life abiding in him.

16 Hereby perceive we the love of God, because he laid down his life for us: and we ought to lay down our lives for the brethren.

17 But whoso hath this world's good, and seeth his brother have need, and shutteth up his bowels of compassion from him, how dwelleth the love of God in him?

18 My little children, let us not love in word, neither in tongue; but in deed and in truth.

19 And hereby we know that we are of the truth, and shall assure our hearts before him.

20 For if our heart condemn us, God is greater than our heart, and knoweth all things.

21 Beloved, if our heart condemn us not, then have we confidence toward God.

22 And whatsoever we ask, we receive of him, because we keep his commandments, and do those things that are pleasing in his sight.

23 And this is his commandment, That we should believe on the name of his Son Jesus Christ, and love one another, as he gave us commandment.

24 And he that keepeth his commandments

13 Do not be surprised, my brothers and sisters, if the world hates you.

14 We know that we have passed from death to life, because we love each other. Anyone who does not love remains in death.

15 Anyone who hates a brother or sister is a murderer, and you know that no murderer has eternal life residing in him.

16 This is how we know what love is: Jesus Christ laid down his life for us. And we ought to lay down our lives for our brothers and sisters.

17 If anyone has material possessions and sees a brother or sister in need but has no pity on them, how can the love of God be in that person?

18 Dear children, let us not love with words or speech but with actions and in truth.

19 This is how we know that we belong to the truth and how we set our hearts at rest in his presence:

20 If our hearts condemn us, we know that God is greater than our hearts, and he knows everything.

21 Dear friends, if our hearts do not condemn us, we have confidence before God

22 and receive from him anything we ask, because we keep his commands and do what pleases him.

23 And this is his command: to believe in the name of his Son, Jesus Christ, and to love one another as he commanded us.

24 The one who keeps God's commands lives in him, and he in them. And this is how we know that he lives in us: We know it by the Spirit he gave us.

dwelleth in him, and he in him. And hereby we know that he abideth in us, by the Spirit which he hath given us.

LIGHT ON THE WORD

In previous books in the Bible, specifically the Gospels, our Lord had already charged His disciples to love their enemies (**Matthew 5:43–45**) and love their neighbors as themselves (**Luke 10:25–37**). The "new commandment" required that Christians love each other (**John 15:12, 17**). This did not overrule the other two love commandments. Jesus' command to love those within the church was initiated to create persuasive evidence for those outside the church. It would provide them discernible proof (1) that His followers were Christ-like in their love toward one another, (2) that the foundation for vigorous human community could be found in Christ, and (3) that, by extension, Jesus' declaration about Himself in concert with the miracles He accomplished were really true (**John 13:35; 17; 21:24–25**).

TEACHING THE BIBLE LESSON

LIFE NEED FOR TODAY'S LESSON

AIM: Students will experience the hatred of the world and counter it with God's love.

INTRODUCTION

Our Actions Reflect Our Love

This letter is written to members of the churches in Asia Minor. The epistle serves as a reminder to the children of God to love one another. The devil is the originator of sin and has sinned from the beginning of time. Those who belong to Satan reveal their essential nature by living lawless lives. This lawlessness is clearly seen in the blatant disregard for human life. John restates that Jesus laid the foundation on how we should treat one another. When Jesus died on the Cross, He demonstrated the greatest, truest, and most unselfish kind of love. His death validated that love is more than mere words; it must be followed by actions. When we say we love someone, our actions should prove our declaration. Displaying love for one another is evidence that we belong to God. Children of God should live to please the Lord in accordance with His commandments. To show indifference to the needs of others is in complete contradiction to the teachings of Christ.

In Jesus' day, many assumed that by obeying the commandments, they could show themselves worthy of God's blessings (**Galatians 3:2**). However, Jesus made it very clear that love was a natural result of God's blessing, not a pre-condition for it. The commandment to love is an expression of how Christ's disciples should act. The disciples were commanded to love in the same sense that branches were "commanded" to bear fruit (**John 15:4**).

BIBLE LEARNING

AIM: Students will see Jesus' selfless love as the highest model of friendship and the opposite of the evil example of Cain.

I. OPERATING IN LOVE (1 John 3:11–20)

Caring for others in accordance to God's will usually means doing the opposite of what is favorable in the eyes of the world. Some may retaliate against our good works, especially if our deeds glorify and illuminate the righteousness of Christ. Showing love toward another person should be prompted by genuine sincerity. In these Scriptures, Cain's reaction to God's rejection was murderous intent. An unchecked attitude of anger, jealousy, and hatred can harden the heart, making it implacable. Our harsh words may not result in a person's death; however, words and actions can assassinate someone's character and destroy their self-esteem.

Love and Obedience (verses 11–20)

11 For this is the message that ye heard from the beginning, that we should love one another.

In this verse, John states that love should not be an afterthought. Obedience to Jesus' command to love one another as He loves us is expected of anyone who accepts the Gospel message. Love shows us that the Gospel includes both the benefits of salvation and the responsibility of Christians to love one another. It goes hand in hand and is not separate or tangential to the Christian faith. Love is the message of the Christian faith, obedience to the command and imitation of the life of Jesus Christ.

12 Not as Cain, who was of that wicked one, and slew his brother. And wherefore slew he him? Because his works were evil, and his brother's righteous.

Cain is cited here as an example of one who did not show love for his brother. Cain is characterized as "that wicked one." The word "wicked" (Gk. *poneros*, **poh-ney-ROCE**) is also translated as "hurtful" or "evil" and refers to someone who is bad or would cause harm. John is explicitly saying that Cain belonged to Satan. Saying Cain belonged to Satan is John's way of pointing out that the way we treat each other is part of the larger cosmic battle between good and evil. If we are characterized by love, it will affect our behavior. Likewise, if we are characterized by hatred, it will certainly show in our behavior. Hence the saying that we sin because we are, by nature, sinners. We are not sinners because we sin.

Cain slew his brother Abel because his "works were evil." Notice that same Greek word, *poneros* (**poh-ney-ROCE**), translated earlier in the verse as "wicked one," is now also used to describe the quality of Cain's works. Cain's murderous act was most assuredly not motivated by love, like his brother Abel, but by hatred.

From the example of Cain, we see that hatred facilitates envy, violence, and murder. While we may not literally murder people, we may assassinate their character and reputation because of hatred (cf. **Matthew 5:21–22**). We must avoid hating others, especially Christians, because of the murderous and devilish nature of hatred.

13 Marvel not, my brethren, if the world hate you. 14 We know that we have passed from death unto life, because we love the brethren. He that loveth not his brother abideth in death.

"The world" here is representative of all those opposed to God. John is saying that we as Christians should not be surprised because the world hates us. It is the expectation for Christians to love one another in obedience to Christ's command. Such acts of love, then, translate into acts of righteousness.

Obeying Christ's command to love one another gives Christians an inner knowledge and assurance of their passage from spiritual death to spiritual life. Love for fellow Christians is a dynamic experience that testifies to the reality of the spiritual journey from death to life in Christ. Metaphorically, John compares brotherly love as a rite of passage representative of a significant change or progress in one's spiritual life. It is crucial to note that John does not say that one can pass simply by loving others—that would be salvation by works. Rather, his point is that having love for others is evidence of one's maturity and passage from death of sin to a life based on faith in Christ. So love is the evidence of, and not the means of, salvation.

15 Whosoever hated his brother is a murderer: and ye know that no murderer hath eternal life abiding in him.

This is an echo of Cain's experience from **verse 12**. John presents to his readers the serious consequence of hatred and establishes the parallel between hate and murder: anyone who, like Cain, hates his brother is also a murderer. One could assume that this verse means that a true Christian cannot hate his fellow Christian. But it is a fallacy to believe that the people of God are incapable of hatred and murder. The Bible records several instances of murder by those who were His people. Moses, who killed an Egyptian (**Exodus 2:12**), and David, who had Uriah killed to conceal his adultery with Bathsheba (**2 Samuel 12:9**), are two major examples. Having established this link with Cain, John now concludes that hatred of others is the spiritual equivalent of murder and that no murderer is entitled to eternal life.

The word for "abiding" is from the Greek word *meno* (**MEH-noh**), which means to remain, last, or endure. Its use here by John is very important. John was saying that although believers possess eternal life, those who hate or murder do not have Christ's Spirit residing within them. Thus, hatred is the equivalent of moral murder.

16 Hereby perceive we the love of God, because he laid down his life for us: and we ought to lay down our lives for the brethren.

The love of God for others is made known not just in words, but in concrete acts of love. The Greek word *ginosko* (**ghin-OCE-koh**), translated here as "perceive," refers to obtaining knowledge. John is saying that we will obtain knowledge of the love of God by looking at the life of Jesus. Very practically, God demonstrated His love to us by sending His Son to lay down His life on our behalf. This demonstration of divine love is the heart of the Gospel. Christ gave His own sinless life to pay the penalty incurred by our sins. He now offers the pardon resulting from this sacrificial act of love to all who will accept it by faith in Him. Divine love is a giving love. God gave His Son for love. The Son gave His life for love. The Greek word *agape* (**ah-GAH-pay**), translated here as "love," finds its ultimate definition in Jesus' unconditional act of giving.

If Christians follow this model of divine love, then they too ought to give something of themselves to express their love for one another. Jesus says, there is no greater love than this self-sacrificing love (**John 15:13**). That is why Christians are called to a self-sacrificing love rather than a self-preserving love. As beneficiaries of this kind of love, it is incumbent on us to love others in the same way.

17 But whoso hath this world's good, and seeth his brother have need, and shutteth up his bowels of compassion from him, how dwelleth the love of God in him?

John says when anyone has the material means to help the needy but refuses to give compassionately, the existence of a Christ-like love in such a Christian is open to question. Using a rhetorical question, John shows that God's love does not exist in anyone who can refuse to help those in need. At issue is not whether God loves the person, but whether such a person possesses God's kind of love toward others.

Our material possessions are not given to us only for self-indulgence. God's command to love others requires that we use our possessions to obey that command. Some regard worldly possessions as an end in themselves. But John says they are a means for expressing God's love in us, opening the door of compassion in us, enabling us to reach out to others in need.

The Greek word *splagchnon* (**SPLANGKH-non**) literally means "bowels" or "intestines," but figuratively means "tender mercy or inward affection" and here indicates that compassion is a quality of one's inner emotions. Now, we use similar metaphors when we talk about feeling something deep down, in our "gut," or with our heart. As such, love must unlock it from inside before it can show outwardly. Anybody can perceive a need, but not everybody has the compassion to help others.

18 My little children, let us not love in word, neither in tongue; but in deed and in truth.

Addressing his readers as children not only suggests that John was advanced in years, but also shows the family atmosphere he was trying to create among his readers. There is no better institution that reflects the kind of sacrificial love John is writing about than the family. Including himself in the admonition, he says, "let us not love in word, neither in tongue." The construction suggests like a father giving advice, John was asking them to stop merely talking about love, but show it in deed and truth.

Christian love is more than a feeling: It involves the essential ingredient of giving. Many times when people say they love another, their only real action is from their mouth (i.e., "in tongue"). An expression of love that is backed up by only the tongue is not true love like Christ's self-sacrificing love. True love engages in actions centered on others. The world is tired of passive love; only active love will attract outsiders and make them want to join God's family.

19 And hereby we know that we are of the truth, and shall assure our hearts before him.

The word "hereby" (Gk. *houtos*, **HOO-tose**, here meaning "by this") refers to verse 18 and points to an active expression of love that corresponds to Christ's self-sacrifice. When Christians demonstrate this kind of active love, they know they belong to the "truth" (Gk. *aletheia*, **ah-LAY-thay-ah**, what is true in things pertaining to God and the duties of man, morality, and religious truth). In the parable of the sheep and the goats, the sheep on Christ's right were commended for their acts of love toward others and were rewarded accordingly by Christ (**Matthew 25:31–46**). In the future, when Christ returns, we will all stand before Him to be judged and rewarded according to our deeds.

20 For if our heart condemn us, God is greater than our heart, and knoweth all things.

The Greek word *kardia* (**kar-DEE-ah**) refers to the heart organ, but here it figuratively denotes the center of all physical and spiritual life. Therefore, if the testimony of our hearts is negative, then we have not been sacrificially reaching out to love others like Christ. Fortunately, God is greater than our hearts and knows our motives for service. The Greek word for "condemn" is *kataginosko* (**ka-ta-gi-NOH-skoh**), which means to find fault, blame, accuse, or condemn. Our motives may be unknown to others, but deep inside we know our reasons. Just as we cannot deceive ourselves, we cannot deceive God, who knows all things.

SEARCH THE SCRIPTURES

QUESTIONS 1 & 2

What proves that we have passed from death to life?

What shows that we love one another?

LIGHT ON THE WORD

Love Is Action

The Holy Spirit is a filtering system that checks the contents of our hearts and purifies us through the Word of God. Real love is an attribute of God, seen magnificently in the life of Christ. When we lay down our lives for someone else, it means we serve expecting God to reward us. Love is action, not just words. Those of us who can give generously to support the needs of others ought to do so with an honest heart, not grudgingly or expecting favors in return. Our actions indicate our connection and affiliation to Christ.

II. MOTIVATED BY LOVE (vv. 21–24)

When our actions are motivated by love, we can approach God in boldness and confidence. Pure intentions glorify and please God, and a clean heart gives room for His love to flourish. When genuine love occupies our hearts, prayers that encompass both personal and community needs are expressed. These kinds of prayers include fellow Christians, our nation, the church, and the less fortunate. God answers prayers from hearts willing to see the fulfillment of His Word in both private and public arenas.

Love One Another (verses 21–24)

21 Beloved, if our heart condemn us not, then have we confidence toward God. 22 And whatsoever we ask, we receive of him, because we keep his commandments, and do those things that are pleasing in his sight.

As Christians, we must learn to listen to our inner voice so we can have confidence before God. The Greek word for "confidence" is *parresia* (**par-ray-SEE-ah**), which means openness, or speaking or acting without concealment. It may be easy to deceive others, but God knows our hearts. Therefore, John says, if our hearts are open and honest, we can go confidently before the throne of grace and petition God.

Verse 22 discusses the benefits of a positive testimony of the heart. If we have a confident heart because we keep God's commandments and do the things that please Him, then we also have assurance that we shall receive whatever we pray for that is in line with His will. John's point is that disobeying Christ's command to love can hinder our prayers, so we should obey Him.

23 And this is his commandment, that we should believe on the name of his Son Jesus Christ, and love one another, as he gave us commandment.

In this verse, John provides the crux of his epistle. When Christians act in obedient, self-sacrificing love, we gain confidence toward God. Faith in Christ and love for one another bring us into a new relationship with God where we become His children. Believing on the name of Jesus Christ includes accepting the fact that He is the Son of God who gave His life to pay the penalty for our sins, reconciling us back to God.

The second part of the commandment is to love one another. The sequence is important. The command is that we have both faith in Christ and also love one another. Faith in Jesus Christ is the basis of our new relationship with God, and love for one another is the expression of that saving faith in us.

24 And he that keepeth his commandments dwelleth in him, and he in him. And hereby we know that he abideth in us, by the Spirit which he hath given us.

To keep God's commands, which includes loving one another, is to abide in Him and to have Him abide in us. As referenced previously in verse 15, the word "abideth" (Gk. *meno*, **MEH-noh**) means to continually be present. This mutual indwelling characterizes the relationship between God and His Son Jesus and points to their unity (**John 17:21**). The believers' mutual indwelling with God is also a reference to the familial union between God and His believing children.

God is present in believers through His Holy Spirit, who dwells in them (cf. **Romans 8:9, 11**). Through the presence of the Holy Spirit within believers, they have a sense of belonging in God's family. Paul says, "For ye have not received the spirit of bondage again to fear; but ye have received the Spirit of adoption, whereby we cry, Abba, Father" (**Romans 8:15**). This context shows that by the Spirit we know we are children of God (**Romans 8:16**).

LIGHT ON THE WORD

Following God's Commandment

The love commandment requires that we believe in the name of Jesus, and acknowledge that He is the Son of God, our Savior and Lord. This commandment also requires that we love each other, especially those in the Body of Christ. This command also states that we remain in fellowship with God, which means staying connected to Him, through personal devotion, meditating on the Word, and in prayer. This also includes staying connected with other Christians. Sometimes we are tempted to "do church" via the Internet; however, fellowship cannot be accomplished via satellite. We need to affirm one another through physical human sight and touch! Sometimes a person's smile and embrace can make a world of difference in someone's life.

BIBLE APPLICATION

AIM: Students will value the abiding nature of God's presence.

Tragedy dominates media attention. The more horrific the crime, the more news coverage it receives. With this kind of media frenzy, wickedness appears to have taken an exalted position in our society, leaving many to question the true value of love. It is no wonder so many of us feel love is trivial and irrelevant. Yet, this lesson tells us no matter what goes on in the world, we are commanded to love one another.

STUDENTS' RESPONSES

AIM: Students will develop ways for believers to express their love for God and others.

Love is a basic human desire and the evidence that we belong to the Body of Christ. Love is more than a word, it is a repeated commandment from the Creator: love one another. How can you express love? Make a list of things you can do in your church and community. Volunteer and serve today.

PRAYER

Your sacrifice through Your shed blood, death, and resurrection is true love. Therefore, loving You, Jesus, is a joy that we must treasure. In Your Name we pray. Amen.

HOW TO SAY IT

Sacrificial. sa-kri-**FI**-shul.

Bowels. **BOW**-uls.

PREPARE FOR NEXT SUNDAY

Read **1 John 4:13–5:5** and study "Believe God's Love."

DAILY HOME BIBLE READINGS

MONDAY
God So Loved the World
(John 3:16–21)

TUESDAY
Love Given Us by God
(1 John 3:1–5)

WEDNESDAY
Loved to the End
(John 13:1–15)

THURSDAY
Great Love Shown
(Luke 7:44–48)

FRIDAY
Those Who Do Not Love
(1 John 3:6–10)

SATURDAY
A New Commandment
(John 13:31–35)

SUNDAY
Love Made Possible by the Spirit
(1 John 3:11–24)

Sources:

Key Word Study Bible. New International Version. Grand Rapids, MI: Zondervan Bible Publishers, 1996. 1437.

Life Application Study Bible. New International Version. Wheaton, IL: Tyndale House Publishers, 1991. 1909, 2279–80.

The New Oxford Annotated Bible. New Revised Standard Version, New York: Oxford University Press, 2001. 386.

Rainbow Study Bible. New International Version. Grand Rapids, MI: Zondervan Bible Publishers, 1992. 1375.

Tyndale Bible Dictionary. Philip W. Comfort and Walter A. Elwell, eds. Wheaton, IL: Tyndale House Publishers, 2001. 719–728.

Unger, Merrill F. *The New Unger's Bible Handbook.* Chicago, IL: Moody Press, 1998. 634.

COMMENTS / NOTES:

BELIEVE GOD'S LOVE

BIBLE BASIS: 1 JOHN 4:13–5:5

BIBLE TRUTH: Believers are made complete when as a community they abide in God's love and the Spirit of God's love abides in them.

MEMORY VERSE: "Whosoever believeth that Jesus is the Christ is born of God: and every one that loveth him that begat loveth him also that is begotten of him" (1 John 5:1).

LESSON AIM: By the end of the lesson, your students will: comprehend what is required to live in community; talk about experiences of love within the community that exemplify faith and love in God; and celebrate the community's contribution to our formation as disciples of Jesus.

TEACHER PREPARATION

MATERIALS NEEDED: Quarterly Commentary/Teacher Manual, Adult Quarterly, Adult resources—charts, worksheets, and other teaching tools, paper, pens, pencils, Bibles (several different versions)

OTHER MATERIALS NEEDED / TEACHER'S NOTES:

LESSON OVERVIEW

LIFE NEED FOR TODAY'S LESSON
To better understand how to live in community that is built on unity and mutuality in God's love.

BIBLE LEARNING
To know and understand God's commandments.

BIBLE APPLICATION
Believers model their lives after God's love when they love their neighbors.

STUDENTS' RESPONSES
Students will explore different ways that Christians live in God's love in unity and community.

LESSON SCRIPTURE

1 JOHN 4:13–5:5, KJV

13 Hereby know we that we dwell in him, and he in us, because he hath given us of his Spirit.

14 And we have seen and do testify that the Father sent the Son to be the Saviour of the world.

1 JOHN 4:13–5:5, NIV

13 This is how we know that we live in him and he in us: He has given us of his Spirit.

14 And we have seen and testify that the Father has sent his Son to be the Savior of the world.

15 If anyone acknowledges that Jesus

15 Whosoever shall confess that Jesus is the Son of God, God dwelleth in him, and he in God.

16 And we have known and believed the love that God hath to us. God is love; and he that dwelleth in love dwelleth in God, and God in him.

17 Herein is our love made perfect, that we may have boldness in the day of judgment: because as he is, so are we in this world.

18 There is no fear in love; but perfect love casteth out fear: because fear hath torment. He that feareth is not made perfect in love.

19 We love him, because he first loved us.

20 If a man say, I love God, and hateth his brother, he is a liar: for he that loveth not his brother whom he hath seen, how can he love God whom he hath not seen?

21 And this commandment have we from him, That he who loveth God love his brother also.

5:1 Whosoever believeth that Jesus is the Christ is born of God: and every one that loveth him that begat loveth him also that is begotten of him.

2 By this we know that we love the children of God, when we love God, and keep his commandments.

3 For this is the love of God, that we keep his commandments: and his commandments are not grievous.

4 For whatsoever is born of God overcometh the world: and this is the victory that overcometh the world, even our faith.

5 Who is he that overcometh the world, is the Son of God, God lives in them and they in God.

16 And so we know and rely on the love God has for us. God is love. Whoever lives in love lives in God, and God in them.

17 This is how love is made complete among us so that we will have confidence on the day of judgment: In this world we are like Jesus.

18 There is no fear in love. But perfect love drives out fear, because fear has to do with punishment. The one who fears is not made perfect in love.

19 We love because he first loved us.

20 Whoever claims to love God yet hates a brother or sister is a liar. For whoever does not love their brother and sister, whom they have seen, cannot love God, whom they have not seen.

21 And he has given us this command: Anyone who loves God must also love their brother and sister.

5:1 Everyone who believes that Jesus is the Christ is born of God, and everyone who loves the father loves his child as well.

2 This is how we know that we love the children of God: by loving God and carrying out his commands.

3 In fact, this is love for God: to keep his commands. And his commands are not burdensome,

4 for everyone born of God overcomes the world. This is the victory that has overcome the world, even our faith.

5 Who is it that overcomes the world? Only the one who believes that Jesus is the Son of God.

but he that believeth that Jesus is the Son of God?

LIGHT ON THE WORD

The writer of the book of 1 John is thought to be John the apostle. John, along with his brother James, was a fisherman until he was called by Jesus to join the other eleven disciples. For three years, he followed and learned from Christ. He is known as the one apostle who died a natural death, although it is also reported that he was thrown in a pot of boiling oil.

The Day of Judgment refers to the final and ultimate judgment of God. It involves the final appearance of Christ when He judges the actions of all humankind. This phrase finds its roots in the Old Testament concept of the Day of the Lord. The Hebrews believed this would be the day when God would judge the nations and vindicate His people. In the New Testament, it loses its nationalistic tone and refers to God's solemn condemnation of all evil. On that day, Christians will inherit eternal life and unbelievers the ill-fated choice of eternal damnation (hell).

TEACHING THE BIBLE LESSON

LIFE NEED FOR TODAY'S LESSON

AIM: Students will better understand how to live in community that is built on unity and mutuality in God's love.

INTRODUCTION

Christian Spiritual Fundamentals

The letters of John are three brief epistles. The succinctness is misleading, for they deal with insightful and significant questions about the fundamental nature of Christian spiritual experience. The Johannine letters also provide fascinating insight to the condition of the church at the end of the first century. Heresy played a critical and deceptive role in the church. Autonomy and church organization are reflected. The genuine nature of a committed and obedient relationship to God through Christ is strongly and affectionately depicted and commanded.

BIBLE LEARNING

AIM: Students will know and understand God's commandments.

I. LIVING PROOF (1 John 4:13–17)

All Christians can receive the Holy Spirit as living proof of God's presence in our lives. The Holy Spirit gives us power to love and confess Jesus Christ as Lord, and provides assurance that we are connected to our Heavenly Father. Perfect love does not mean we love perfectly; it is a description of our Savior's love for us. Jesus loves flawlessly because He accepts us with all our imperfections and mistakes, and regardless of our gender; sex; race; marital, educational, or economic status; physical, mental, or emotional qualities; age; or cultural background. He loves us!

God's Spirit Manifested in Our Lives (verses 13–17)

13 Hereby know we that we dwell in him, and he in us, because he hath given us of his Spirit.

Two themes dominate John's exhortation in **verses 13–21**: faith and love. In **verse 13**, John affirms that the assurance of the presence of God in the life of a Christian (cf. **vv. 12, 15**) is proved by the residence of the Holy Spirit in him or her. Since love is the first of the fruit produced by the Spirit, John's connection of love with the Holy Spirit is obvious, in addition to the other work of the Spirit in the life of a believer.

14 And we have seen and do testify that the Father sent the Son to be the Saviour of the world.

Although no one has seen God, He has revealed Himself visibly in His Son Jesus Christ. As one of the apostolic eyewitnesses, John bears testimony to this fact (cf. **1:1–3**). The Greek word *soter* (**soh-TAYR**), which means savior or deliverer, defines both the purpose and the result of Christ's mission (cf. **Matthew 1:21; John 1:29**).

15 Whosoever shall confess that Jesus is the Son of God, God dwelleth in him, and he in God.

Emphasis is placed on the test of (doctrinal) faith in Christ as evidence of God's indwelling. The Greek word *homologeo* (**ho-mo-lo-GEH-oh**, confess) indicates that confession involves the intellectual acknowledgment of the human-divine nature of Christ and a personal acceptance of Him.

16 And we have known and believed the love that God hath to us. God is love; and he that dwelleth in love dwelleth in God, and God in him.

John effectively connects faith with works (action). Belief must find expression in behavior. Here, believing and loving are intimately joined. They are proof of God's Spirit in the believer.

17 Herein is our love made perfect, that we may have boldness in the day of judgment: because as he is, so are we in this world.

By dwelling in love and consequently in God, and by God dwelling in us, love will be perfected (Gk. *teleioo*, **teh-lay-OH-oh**, to complete or accomplish). This word refers to completion of a goal or maturity. Love will be made complete, mature, and perfect once for all in us. This perfection refers to a complete, fully accomplished state. John is stating that the on-going action of God abiding in us and we abiding in God perfects our love. The phrase "because as he is, so are we in this world" refers to God's abiding in us (**v. 17**). If we abide in God and God in us, despite being in this imperfect world, we are like God, who is love. This should give us confidence on the day of judgment which comes from loving as Jesus loved us. It does not mean that we will love perfectly, but that we will have evidence that we are believers, and we will have confidence that our hearts are right before God.

SEARCH THE SCRIPTURES

QUESTIONS 1 & 2

How do we know God lives in us?

What gives proof that we love God?

LIGHT ON THE WORD

The Freedom in Love

Knowing we are loved by God diminishes our apprehension of Judgment Day, increases our need to see others saved, and supplies us freedom to love indiscriminately and do the work God called us to do. The confidence we receive in acknowledging God's love is not arrogant. Arrogance is when we depend and boast in our own abilities. The confidence that the Bible describes is a declaration of our relationship with Jesus and evidence of the abiding Holy Spirit within us.

II. LOVING PROOF (vv. 18–19)

The love of God eradicates all fear. If we operate from fear, it is a sign that we have not fully grasped the concept of God's unconditional love. Even many Christians function in fear and live as prisoners of anxiety, even though the Lord cannot use us when we walk in apprehension. If we fear Judgment Day, are we certain of our salvation? There needs to be a level of confidence in knowing we are saved and eternally secure with Christ.

Love Without Fear (verses 18–19)

There is no fear in love; but perfect love casteth out fear: because fear hath torment. He that feareth is not made perfect in love.

John then goes on further to clarify that love is absent of fear. Mature and complete love casts out all fear. The word for "casts out" literally means to lay or throw aside something. Christians should not experience fear of punishment in their life. The punishment that John refers to is the judgment, which is clear because it is mentioned in the context of the day of judgment. Because fear has punishment (the two are inevitably intertwined), the person who fears punishment does not have the love in **vv. 16–17**. The same Greek verb appears again here as "perfect" (*teleioo*), confirming the connection. John seals his point by stating that whoever fears has not matured in love. The one who fears that they will receive the Final Judgment has not experienced the complete work of God's love in their life.

19 We love him, because he first loved us.

Next we see the motivation behind the Christian's love. It is because we have experienced the love of God in Jesus Christ. This verse points to the detailed description and explanation of the preceding verses. It summarizes what John has said concerning the love of Christ and its effect in the life of a believer. We love God because He has shown His love to us in Christ. We love one another because we have experienced God's love in our hearts.

LIGHT ON THE WORD

God Loves Imperfect People

We cannot explain why God loves us; He just does! It is human nature to want justification for our feelings and actions; however, the Bible tells us Jesus loved us before we became Christians (**Romans 5:8**). So if a sovereign God can love imperfect people, then who are we to refuse to love another imperfect being? Christians have experienced the fullness of Christ's love and have testimonies of His kindness. The greatest tragedy is to hoard the love of God and miss opportunities to pour this precious gift into the lives of others.

III. LASTING PROOF (vv. 4:20–5:5)

John's emphasis on loving others is nowhere more clearly reflected than in this passage of Scripture. We are lying if we say we love God, but actually hate our brothers and sisters in Christ. Many biblical teachers skate over these verses because they are too direct. Yet, these verses force us to examine our actions. How can we claim to love the invisible Lord and still be seen to hate the visible inhabitants of His kingdom? We cannot love God apart from loving one another.

Love and Hate (verses 20–5:5)

20 If a man say, I love God, and hateth his brother, he is a liar: for he that loveth not his brother whom he hath seen, how can he love God whom he hath not seen?

John says that if anyone says they love God and hates their brother, they are more than a walking contradiction: they are a liar. This may not mean they are intentionally deceiving others. At the most basic level, they are deceiving themselves. They are not walking consistent with the truth. Anyone who does not love someone who is physically visible to them cannot love God, who is invisible to their natural senses. For John, the real test of true love is loving those who are right in front of you. Loving people whom you can see is the litmus test of loving the God whom you cannot see.

21 And this commandment have we from him, That he who loveth God love his brother also.

Not only is loving your brother a litmus test for loving God, but not loving your brother is disobedience to the Lord's command. John appeals to the direct command of Jesus (**John 13:34**). If we do not love our brother, we are not obeying the command of Jesus. Jesus has given us this command, and Christians must fulfill it or risk disobeying the Lord who loves them.

1 John 5:1–5

This Scripture passage is a part of John's final elaboration of the three principle tests of authentic Christianity: belief (faith), righteousness (obedience), and love. He has devoted sections of his letter to treating the subjects in turn. Here, all three are closely related, integrated, and woven together into one theological fabric, within the overriding idea of Christian confidence and assurance through the new birth. The text shows the Christian's confidence in victory, witnesses, eternal life, and prayer.

5:1 Whosoever believeth that Jesus is the Christ is born of God: and every one that loveth him that begat loveth him also that is begotten of him.

John connects belief and love mutually and spiritually. The Greek word *pisteuo* (**pih-STEHOO-oh**) means to trust or to believe. It is more than a mere profession of a creed; it means personal faith in and personal union with Christ. Our proof of the new birth is shown as a continual belief in the humanity and deity of Christ and His redemptive mission. The logical consequence of the new birth is an expression of love for God, who is the source of the spiritual birth, as well as to all who have been given birth by Him.

2 By this we know that we love the children of God, when we love God, and keep his commandments.

In the preceding verse, John connects belief and love. In this verse and the next, the connection is made between love and obedience (righteousness), indicating how intertwined the themes are. John reverses the relationship by stating that our love for one another is made manifest when we love God and keep His commandments. Previously John declared that we cannot love God if we hate one another. Now John is saying that loving God reveals our love for one another. The two are intimately related, so that both should flow from each other.

3 For this is the love of God, that we keep his commandments: and his commandments are not grievous.

John takes a step further to link love and obedience. This verse is obviously an echo of the precept of Christ Himself: "If ye love me, keep my commandments... He that hath my commandments, and keepeth them, he it is that loveth me..." (**John 14:15, 21**). Love for God is both a basis and motivation for obedience. The Greek word *barus* (**ba-ROOS**), translated as "grievous," also carries the idea of something difficult or burdensome. For example, some of the regulations of the scribes and the Pharisees were heavy burdens hard to bear. Jesus' yoke, on the contrary, is easy and His burden light (**Matthew 11:30**). Furthermore, divine resources are made available to equip

Christians to do the will of God. John directly references the impartation of divine nature and the indwelling presence of the Holy Spirit in all who have been born of God (see **1 John 3:24**).

4 For whatsoever is born of God overcometh the world: and this is the victory that overcometh the world, even our faith. 5 Who is he that overcometh the world, but he that believeth that Jesus is the Son of God?

John's confidence in the believer's victory is contagious. Within two verses he uses the words "overcome" and "victory" four times (**vv. 4–5**). The Greek verb *nikao* (**nih-KAH-oh**) means to conquer, to overcome, or to prevail, while its related noun *nike* (**NI-kay**) means victory or conquest. Anything that has been born of God conquers the world, but here John focuses on our faith as the victory that has already conquered the world.

Two aspects of the believers' conquest are implied in these verses. First, Christ's victory becomes the believers' own upon their belief in the person and work of Christ, acceptance of Christ as Lord and Savior by faith, and consequent union with Christ (cf. **John 1:12, 16:33**). Second, the abiding presence of the Holy Spirit enables the believer to live in daily victory over the flesh, the world, and the devil. In everyday experience, the Christian can constantly express thanks to God "which giveth us the victory through our Lord Jesus Christ" (from **1 Corinthians 15:57**; cf. **1 John 4:4; Romans 8:37**).

BIBLE APPLICATION

AIM: Students will model their lives after God's love when they love their neighbors.

Society teaches us to love conditionally. Some people live in fear of rejection from those who claim to love them. This is not real love. One of the most remarkable attributes of God is His ability to love unconditionally and completely. No matter what we face in life, God's love is everlasting and nothing can separate us from His love! Not only do we have God's promise of love but also the promise of eternal life. With this kind of reassurance, what keeps us from loving others?

STUDENTS' RESPONSES

AIM: Students will explore different ways that Christians live in God's love in unity and community.

The Lord has high regards for the community of believers, and we should too. All we can do is learn to love and obey God's command. Pray and ask God to reveal where you can extend love to someone in the family of God. After God shows you, act! Write in a journal about how the incident impacted your life and share your experience with the class.

PRAYER

Lord, we pray that we are giving our best in love to others. Help us to learn how and to love one another. Love, faith, and hope are qualities that we should give to one another. In Jesus' Name we pray. Amen.

HOW TO SAY IT

Johannine.	joe-**HA**-nine.
Grievous.	**GREE**-vus.

PREPARE FOR NEXT SUNDAY

Read **2 John** and study "Watch Out for Deceivers!"

DAILY HOME BIBLE READINGS

MONDAY
Prophetic Discernment by Christ's Spirit
(1 Peter 1:8–12)

TUESDAY
Seeking Unity of Spirit
(1 Peter 3:8–12)

WEDNESDAY
Be Steadfast in the Spirit
(Romans 12:9–18)

THURSDAY
Nothing Can Separate Us
(Romans 8:31–39)

FRIDAY
Test the Spirits
(1 John 4:1–6)

SATURDAY
Since God Loved Us So Much
(1 John 4:7–12)

SUNDAY
Love God, Love Others
(1 John 4:13–5:5)

Sources:

International Bible Lesson Commentary. King James Version. Colorado Springs, CO: Dave C. Cook Publishers, 2008.

Key Word Study Bible. New International Version. Grand Rapids, MI: Zondervan Bible Publishers, 1996. 1440–41.

Life Application Study Bible. New International Version. Wheaton, IL: Tyndale House Publishers, Inc., 1991. 1909, 2282–83.

The New Oxford Annotated Bible. New Revised Standard Version, New York: Oxford University Press, Inc., 2001, 386–387.

Rainbow Study Bible. New International Version. Grand Rapids, MI: Zondervan Bible Publishers, 1992. 1378–79.

Tyndale Bible Dictionary. Wheaton, IL: Tyndale House Publishers, Inc., 2001. 719–728.

Unger, Merrill F. *The New Unger's Bible Handbook.* Chicago, IL: Moody Press, 1998. 635–636.

COMMENTS / NOTES:

WATCH OUT FOR DECEIVERS!

BIBLE BASIS: 2 JOHN

BIBLE TRUTH: Believers who remain faithful in their belief in Christ will have eternal life; and beware of deceivers who will corrupt the community of believers.

MEMORY VERSE: "Look to yourselves, that we lose not those things which we have wrought, but that we receive a full reward" (2 John 8).

LESSON AIM: By the end of the lesson, your students will: research John's caution to beware of those who do not abide in Christ's teachings; reflect on the emotional response to teachings that are contrary to what they have been previously taught; and testify that walking in Jesus' commandment to love protects the faith community from deceivers and corruption.

TEACHER PREPARATION

MATERIALS NEEDED: Quarterly Commentary/Teacher Manual, Adult Quarterly, Adult resources—charts, worksheets, and other teaching tools, paper, pens, pencils, Bibles (several different versions)

OTHER MATERIALS NEEDED / TEACHER'S NOTES:

____

____

LESSON OVERVIEW

LIFE NEED FOR TODAY'S LESSON
To understand how belief and actions in God's love and eternal life, provides strength and care for believers.

BIBLE LEARNING
Believers understand that behavior and belief are interconnected.

BIBLE APPLICATION
Believers affirm that observing the commandments protects the community of faith in love.

STUDENTS' RESPONSES
Student will identify false teachings against the commandments of Christ and ways to respond to these false teachings.

LESSON SCRIPTURE

2 JOHN, KJV

1 The elder unto the elect lady and her children, whom I love in the truth; and not I only, but also all they that have known the truth;

2 For the truth's sake, which dwelleth in us, and shall be with us for ever.

2 JOHN, NIV

1 The elder, To the lady chosen by God and to her children, whom I love in the truth—and not I only, but also all who know the truth—

2 because of the truth, which lives in us and will be with us forever:

3 Grace be with you, mercy, and peace, from God the Father, and from the Lord Jesus Christ, the Son of the Father, in truth and love.

4 I rejoiced greatly that I found of thy children walking in truth, as we have received a commandment from the Father.

5 And now I beseech thee, lady, not as though I wrote a new commandment unto thee, but that which we had from the beginning, that we love one another.

6 And this is love, that we walk after his commandments. This is the commandment, That, as ye have heard from the beginning, ye should walk in it.

7 For many deceivers are entered into the world, who confess not that Jesus Christ is come in the flesh. This is a deceiver and an antichrist.

8 Look to yourselves, that we lose not those things which we have wrought, but that we receive a full reward.

9 Whosoever transgresseth, and abideth not in the doctrine of Christ, hath not God. He that abideth in the doctrine of Christ, he hath both the Father and the Son.

10 If there come any unto you, and bring not this doctrine, receive him not into your house, neither bid him God speed:

11 For he that biddeth him God speed is partaker of his evil deeds.

12 Having many things to write unto you, I would not write with paper and ink: but I trust to come unto you, and speak face to face, that our joy may be full.

13 The children of thy elect sister greet thee. Amen.

3 Grace, mercy and peace from God the Father and from Jesus Christ, the Father's Son, will be with us in truth and love.

4 It has given me great joy to find some of your children walking in the truth, just as the Father commanded us.

5 And now, dear lady, I am not writing you a new command but one we have had from the beginning. I ask that we love one another.

6 And this is love: that we walk in obedience to his commands. As you have heard from the beginning, his command is that you walk in love.

7 I say this because many deceivers, who do not acknowledge Jesus Christ as coming in the flesh, have gone out into the world. Any such person is the deceiver and the antichrist.

8 Watch out that you do not lose what we have worked for, but that you may be rewarded fully.

9 Anyone who runs ahead and does not continue in the teaching of Christ does not have God; whoever continues in the teaching has both the Father and the Son.

10 If anyone comes to you and does not bring this teaching, do not take them into your house or welcome them.

11 Anyone who welcomes them shares in their wicked work.

12 I have much to write to you, but I do not want to use paper and ink. Instead, I hope to visit you and talk with you face to face, so that our joy may be complete.

13 The children of your sister, who is chosen by God, send their greetings.

LIGHT ON THE WORD

Many scholars believe the term "chosen lady" refers to a Christian matron named Lady Electa (a Greek name meaning "chosen"). This matron lived somewhere in the Johannine churches located in Asia Minor. t's also possible that this is the title John uses to address the church itself, with the children being the church members. One reason for writing this missive is to warn this cherished lady (**vv. 1–2**) against deceitful teachers. She apparently hosted meetings with visiting preachers in her home (**v. 10**), similar to Nympha in Laodicea (**Colossians 4:15**). John encourages her and cautions against erroneous doctrine. He proposes that she not support anyone who teaches less than the full deity and humanity of Christ.

TEACHING THE BIBLE LESSON

LIFE NEED FOR TODAY'S LESSON

AIM: Students will understand how belief and actions in God's love and eternal life, provides strength and care for believers.

INTRODUCTION

Teach the Truth

In **2 John**, the issue lies with those who do no profess Jesus to be fully human (such as the docetists who thought Jesus' physical form was a phantasm of God). John's second epistle battles this ungodly perspective and the wicked behavior that stems from its teaching. The apostle encourages true believers to keep the faith. He reiterates God's commandment of love and the necessity of walking in love and truth. He gingerly reminds the congregation of his desires to visit them soon. His message is not written in a stern, threatening, supervisory voice, yet is concise and powerful. This epistle is relevant not only to the Johannine Christians, but also to modern-day Christians. To obscure the truth, practice erroneous doctrine, and partner with deceitful instructors violates the fundamental principles of the Gospel. This principle does not originate with the apostle John; it is traceable to an idea Jesus established (**John 3:20–21**).

BIBLE LEARNING

AIM: Students will understand that behavior and belief are interconnected.

I. WALK IN TRUTH (2 John 1–3)

The truth John refers to is the acknowledgment that Jesus Christ is the Son of God, fully human and fully divine; to recognize that Jesus, who is the one true God, came in the flesh so that we can know God, and through Him attain eternal life (**1 John 5:20**).

Love In Truth (verses 1–3)

1 The elder unto the elect lady and her children, whom I love in the truth; and not I only, but also all they that have known the truth; 2 For the truth's sake, which dwelleth in us, and shall be with us for ever. 3 Grace be with you, mercy, and peace, from God the Father, and from the Lord Jesus Christ, the Son of the Father, in truth and love.

John begins this letter with the common introductory greeting of an epistle. He addresses himself as the elder. The recipient is the elect lady. This woman could have been the host or leader of a particular Christian church. John declares his love for her and "her children." This love is qualified by being in the truth. It is not clear whether these are her biological children or children in the Lord. He then states that this love is not particular to him but universal to all who know the truth. This love is motivated by the truth that dwells in all who know it. John here gives personal qualities to "the truth," perhaps as a way to refer to Jesus Christ, who described Himself as "the Way, the Truth, and the Life."

John says this "truth" will be with us forever. It is an eternal truth that lives with them. It is more than just objective facts; it is living, breathing truth. John concludes his introductory greeting with the standard well wishes of grace, mercy, and peace. What distinguishes him from other New Testament writers is that he includes himself in the well wishes. He says this "grace, mercy, and peace will be with us"—the ones who know the truth (**v. 3**). This grace, mercy, and peace is not just from John and does not rest in his mere human words; it comes from God the Father and the Lord Jesus Christ.

LIGHT ON THE WORD

The Divinity and Humanity of Christ

Understanding that Christ is both God and human is of great importance to the author. Believers need to know this truth and remain in it. Holding on to this understanding of who Christ is allows us to abide in the Son of God and not be taken away from Him by heretical teachings. False prophets are easily identified because one of their major christological mistakes is the renunciation of Christ's humanity and the insinuation that He is not the Messiah.

II. WALK IN LOVE (vv. 4–6)

The love described in this epistle is not the love portrayed in cinema. It is unconditional love that nullifies selfishness and epitomizes genuine concern for others. We cannot mimic God's love without the sustaining power of the Holy Spirit. John understood that love is a powerful motivation. Our capacity to love is often fashioned by our experiences. John penned declarations about God's loving character because he experienced His love firsthand. He called himself "the disciple whom Jesus loved" (**John 21:20**). Jesus' love is clearly communicated by all the Gospel writers, yet it is more prominent in John's literature. John was sensitive to those words and actions of Jesus that illustrated how the One who is love loved others.

Belief and Actions (verses 4–6)

4 I rejoiced greatly that I found of thy children walking in truth, as we have received a commandment from the Father.

Characteristically as a shepherd, John's heart was highly elated at the consistent Christian life of members of the congregation to whom he wrote. "Walking" here is from the Greek word *peripateo* (**peh-ree-pah-TEH-oh**), which literally means to walk around, and is figuratively used to signify the habits of the individual life. The use of the word "truth" (*aletheia*, **ah-LAY-thay-ah**) implies its doctrinal and ethical denotations. To walk in the truth involves belief and behavior. Walking in the truth conveys the imagery of a path that one walks on and keeps on course without deviating. The tense of the word indicates a perpetual pattern of healthy spiritual life. The truth that John talks about did not originate with humankind, not even with the apostles themselves, who originally received it. The truth originated in divine revelation, and so is the command (Gk. *entole*, **en-tow-LAY**) to obey it. Indeed, in John's epistle, both the truth and the commandments are synonymous (cf. **vv. 5–6**).

5 And now I beseech thee, lady, not as though I wrote a new commandment unto thee, but that which we heard from the beginning, that we love one another.

John proceeds from commendation to exhortation, based on personal request (Gk. *erotao*, **eh-roh-TAH-oh**, to ask, beg, appeal, or entreat). The commandment he affirms and urges on his readers was not new; it was as old as the Gospel (cf. **John 13:34–35**) or the time of their hearing and receiving of the same. Here, the command to believe is added to the command to love. To believe in the full humanity and divinity of Christ and His redemptive mission, and to demonstrate brotherly love, is proof of the new birth (**1 John 4:7, 5:1**).

6 And this is love, that we walk after his commandments. This is the commandment, That, as ye have heard from the beginning, ye should walk in it.

John pursues the line of argument of his first letter—that Christian love is more than emotion; it is action (demonstration). Love for God and Christ is expressed in practical obedience (**John 14:15, 21, 15:10; 1 John 5:2–3**; cf. **Romans 8:8**). Jesus summarized the whole Law in the greatest commandment: love (**Matthew 22:37–40**). Here, John urges a continual walk in love: "that you follow love" (RSV).

In the second part of this message (**vv. 7–11**), John draws the attention of the church to the threat from without: false teaching. He shifts focus from the true believers to the false teachers—from the wheat to the tares (**Matthew 13:24–30, 36–43**). John describes the heretics, identifies their error, and warns to neither be deceived by them nor give any encouragement to them. In this Scripture passage, John commands watchfulness. He urges the believers to remain loyal not only in love, but also to the teaching of Christ.

SEARCH THE SCRIPTURES

QUESTION 1

What is the meaning of love?

LIGHT ON THE WORD

Sacrifice and Obedience

Christians have an obligation to love. When we focus on the enormous sacrifice Jesus made on the Cross, how can we not love one another?

III. WALK IN OBEDIENCE (vv. 7–13)

False teachers do not walk in obedience to God's truth. Moral irresponsibility, acceptance of sin, and disregard for the spiritual, mental, and emotional welfare of others are common outcomes of fallacious doctrine. John's letter reminds Christians to live ethically, compassionately, and discerningly. To deny the humanity and deity of Jesus Christ is heresy. The apostle warns faithful believers to forfeit all association with false teachers. His message is relevant in our communities today. We should not lend ourselves to opposing philosophies. The company of false teachers allows them to propagate their doctrine and can signify our approval of what they do.

False Teachers (verses 7–13)

7 For many deceivers are entered into the world, who confess not that Jesus Christ is come in the flesh. This is a deceiver and an antichrist.

John affirms the appearance of false teachers in the world. He describes the false teachers as "deceivers" and "an antichrist." The Greek word *planos* (**PLAH-nohs**), translated as "deceiver," implies an impostor or corrupter, signifying wandering or leading astray. This is a repeat of his earlier warning against "deceivers" and "many antichrists" (**1 John 2:18, 26; 4:1–6**). An antichrist is literally someone who is against the Messiah (Gk. *anti*, **ahn-TEE**, against, instead of; *Christos*, **khreess-TOSE**, Messiah, anointed one). This is not a separate category of people from the decievers, but instead those who deceive concerning Christ's nature are opposed to Christ and are described with both of these terms. The errors of the heretic are both moral and doctrinal; the latter is in focus here. The Greek word *homologeo* (**ho-mah-lo-GEH-oh**), translated as "confess," also means to acknowledge, admit, or affirm. A heretic denies the incarnation of Christ as fully man and fully deity.

8 Look to yourselves, that we lose not those things which we have wrought, but that we receive a full reward.

This is the first command of the letter: a warning to be on guard. The present imperative of the

Greek word, *blepo* (**BLEH-poh**), implies continual watchfulness to prevent disaster. John commands readers to reject the enticement of error for two reasons: to prevent the ruin of what both they and John had worked for, and to ensure that they would be paid their reward in full.

9 Whosoever transgresseth, and abideth not in the doctrine of Christ, hath not God. He that abideth in the doctrine of Christ, he hath both the Father and the Son.

Two contradictory consequences of heterodoxy (or false doctrine) and orthodoxy are stated. The negative is first mentioned. The Greek word *proago* (**pro-AH-goh**), rendered "transgresseth," literally means to lead before. The false teachers were trying to change the core doctrine the Christians had received—he who fails to abide (Gk. *meno*, **MEHN-oh**, to stay or remain) by the doctrine cannot have the Christ and His salvation. The opposite is also true. To remain continually in the doctrine (Gk. *didache*, **dih-dah-KAY**) or teaching of Christ, showing belief in and obedience of the same, is the proof of the believer's personal relationship to both the Father and the Son.

10 If there come any unto you, and bring not this doctrine, receive him not into your house, neither bid him God speed: 11 For he that biddeth him God speed is partaker of his evil deeds.

John adds a practical note after warning about deceivers. He says that the church is not to receive (Gk. *lambano*, **lam-BAH-noh**) these deceivers into their houses. He then goes even further to say that they should not even bid them "God speed" (Gk. *chairo*, **KHEYE-roh**). This is the word for "rejoice" or "be glad." It became a common greeting or salutation that essentially meant to be well.

The reason behind this action toward false teachers is that by receiving them into your home or wishing them well, you partake (Gk. *koinoneo*, **koy-noh-NEH-oh**) in the false teachers' evil deeds.

12 Having many things to write unto you, I would not write with paper and ink: but I trust to come unto you, and speak face to face, that our joy may be full. 13 The children of thy elect sister greet thee. Amen.

John concludes the letter by letting the church know that he has so much he wants to say that he would rather tell them in person. He does not want any confusion or misunderstanding concerning what he says so that "our joy may be full." He includes himself in the experience of having this joy full (Gk. *pleroo*, **play-RAH-o**). This word means to be complete or filled to the brim. John and the church's joy will be completed once they talk face to face. John finally ends with a salutation from the children of the elect sister. These might have been the biological children of a woman related to the elect lady or fellow converts of the church.

SEARCH THE SCRIPTURES

QUESTION 2

What are the consequences of wandering from the truth?

LIGHT ON THE WORD

Meditate on God's Word

We should not be disrespectful or condemn cordiality toward unbelievers. However, fellowship with apostates is a serious matter to God. This letter serves as a warning to cherish sound doctrinal truth. To identify an imposter is to know the truth. Meditating on God's Word opens our spiritual eyes to learning the truth.

BIBLE APPLICATION

AIM: Students will affirm that observing the commandments protects the community of faith in love.

Financial scandals, fueled by deception and greed, have crushed the American people's perception on our nation's financial stability. Financial crises caused many to lose their livelihood, sense of security, self-esteem, and dignity. Lives were ruined and many never recovered economically or emotionally. Believing a lie is dangerous and costly. Christ's teaching is in direct opposition to the deception and selfishness that are rampant in our society. Jesus commands that we live in love and honesty. Anyone who claims devotion to Christ must live by these directives.

STUDENTS' RESPONSES

AIM: Students will identify false teachings against the commandments of Christ and ways to respond to these false teachings.

To remain faithful to Jesus' teaching requires tenacity and a commitment to study God's Word. It also means obeying His commandments. We can also help others who do not know the truth through our testimonies and sharing the Good News of the Gospel. Make a decision to share your testimony about how God transformed your life!

PRAYER

Dear God, open our eyes to false teachings that draw us away from You. Allow us to see and be active participants with Jesus in our hearts, minds, and bodies. In Jesus' Name we pray. Amen.

HOW TO SAY IT

Transgresseth. trans-**GRESS**-ith.

Beseech. bih-**SEECH**.

PREPARE FOR NEXT SUNDAY

Read **3 John** and study "Coworkers with the Truth."

DAILY HOME BIBLE READINGS

MONDAY
They Refuse to Know the Lord
(Jeremiah 9:1–7)

TUESDAY
Don't Listen to Impostors
(Acts 15:22–35)

WEDNESDAY
False Prophets Will Lead Many Astray
(Matthew 24:3–14)

THURSDAY
Avoid Those Who Cause Dissensions
(Romans 16:16–20)

FRIDAY
The Boldness We Have in Christ
(1 John 5:6–15)

SATURDAY
God Protects Those Born of God
(1 John 5:16–21)

SUNDAY
Be on Your Guard
(2 John 1–13)

Sources:

Key Word Study Bible. New International Version. Grand Rapids, MI: Zondervan Bible Publishers, 1996. 1442.

Life Application Study Bible. New International Version. Wheaton, IL: Tyndale House Publishers, Inc., 1991. 1909, 2285–87.

The New Oxford Annotated Bible. New Revised Standard Version, New York: Oxford University Press, Inc., 2001. 395–400.

Rainbow Study Bible. New International Version, Grand Rapids, MI: Zondervan Bible Publishers, 1992. 1381

Tyndale Bible Dictionary. Wheaton, IL: Tyndale House Publishers, Inc., 2001. 719–728.

Unger, Merrill F. *The New Unger's Bible Handbook*. Chicago, IL: Moody Press, 1998. 640.

COWORKERS WITH THE TRUTH

BIBLE BASIS: 3 JOHN

BIBLE TRUTH: Hospitality is one way that Christians express their faith in Christ to others, making them faithful coworkers with the truth.

MEMORY VERSE: "We therefore ought to receive such, that we might be fellowhelpers to the truth" (3 John 8).

LESSON AIM: By the end of the lesson, your students will: learn the importance of hospitality as written in 3 John; tell of experiences of hospitality and the reactions to it; and practice acts of hospitality.

TEACHER PREPARATION

MATERIALS NEEDED: Quarterly Commentary/Teacher Manual, Adult Quarterly, Adult resources—charts, worksheets, and other teaching tools, paper, pens, pencils, Bibles (several different versions)

OTHER MATERIALS NEEDED / TEACHER'S NOTES:

LESSON OVERVIEW

LIFE NEED FOR TODAY'S LESSON
Most people really appreciate the kindness and generosity they have experienced because of good hospitality.

BIBLE LEARNING
John explained that showing hospitality shows truth and encourages others to be coworkers with the truth.

BIBLE APPLICATION
Believers learn the importance of showing hospitality to other believers as they study and live the commandment to love.

STUDENTS' RESPONSES
Students will commit to live their lives so that others can see they are walking in the truth.

LESSON SCRIPTURE

3 JOHN, KJV

1 The elder unto the wellbeloved Gaius, whom I love in the truth.

2 Beloved, I wish above all things that thou mayest prosper and be in health, even as thy soul prospereth.

3 For I rejoiced greatly, when the brethren came and testified of the truth that is in

3 JOHN, NIV

1 The elder, To my dear friend Gaius, whom I love in the truth.

2 Dear friend, I pray that you may enjoy good health and that all may go well with you, even as your soul is getting along well.

3 It gave me great joy when some believers came and testified about your

thee, even as thou walkest in the truth.

4 I have no greater joy than to hear that my children walk in truth.

5 Beloved, thou doest faithfully whatsoever thou doest to the brethren, and to strangers;

6 Which have borne witness of thy charity before the church: whom if thou bring forward on their journey after a godly sort, thou shalt do well:

7 Because that for his name's sake they went forth, taking nothing of the Gentiles.

8 We therefore ought to receive such, that we might be fellowhelpers to the truth.

9 I wrote unto the church: but Diotrephes, who loveth to have the preeminence among them, receiveth us not.

10 Wherefore, if I come, I will remember his deeds which he doeth, prating against us with malicious words: and not content therewith, neither doth he himself receive the brethren, and forbiddeth them that would, and casteth them out of the church.

11 Beloved, follow not that which is evil, but that which is good. He that doeth good is of God: but he that doeth evil hath not seen God.

12 Demetrius hath good report of all men, and of the truth itself: yea, and we also bear record; and ye know that our record is true.

13 I had many things to write, but I will not with ink and pen write unto thee:

14 But I trust I shall shortly see thee, and we shall speak face to face. Peace be to thee. Our friends salute thee. Greet the friends by name.

faithfulness to the truth, telling how you continue to walk in it.

4 I have no greater joy than to hear that my children are walking in the truth.

5 Dear friend, you are faithful in what you are doing for the brothers and sisters, even though they are strangers to you.

6 They have told the church about your love. Please send them on their way in a manner that honors God.

7 It was for the sake of the Name that they went out, receiving no help from the pagans.

8 We ought therefore to show hospitality to such people so that we may work together for the truth.

9 I wrote to the church, but Diotrephes, who loves to be first, will not welcome us.

10 So when I come, I will call attention to what he is doing, spreading malicious nonsense about us. Not satisfied with that, he even refuses to welcome other believers. He also stops those who want to do so and puts them out of the church.

11 Dear friend, do not imitate what is evil but what is good. Anyone who does what is good is from God. Anyone who does what is evil has not seen God.

12 Demetrius is well spoken of by everyone—and even by the truth itself. We also speak well of him, and you know that our testimony is true.

13 I have much to write you, but I do not want to do so with pen and ink.

14 I hope to see you soon, and we will talk face to face. Peace to you. The friends here send their greetings. Greet the friends there by name.

LIGHT ON THE WORD

Gaius' name could mean "lord" or "man of the earth." He was a Christian in Asia Minor who was highly commended by John. John speaks of him as "beloved." He also appreciates that Gaius is "walking in the truth" and "doing a faithful work." He was known for his hospitality "toward them that are brethren and strangers." Gaius has been identified by some scholars as the Gaius mentioned in the Apostolic Constitution and may have been ordained as the Bishop of Pergamum.

Diotrephes' name means "nourished by Jupiter." Diotrephes is mentioned by John as resisting John's authority. He also used his authority in the church to refuse hospitality to Christian workers. John writes that he is one who "loveth to have the preeminence among them." From this we can assume that Diotrephes was a leader in the church. Diotrephes was also known for speaking malicious words against John and other leaders in the church.

TEACHING THE BIBLE LESSON

LIFE NEED FOR TODAY'S LESSON

AIM: Students will really appreciate the kindness and generosity they have experienced because of good hospitality.

INTRODUCTION

John, the Elder

John names himself "the Elder" in his outreach to Gaius. Although not explicit in his epistle, tradition suggests that he is writing from Ephesus. What is clear, however, in this letter is the importance of strong relationships within the early church. Far different from modern Western culture's obsession with individualism and isolation, the world of John, Gaius, and even Diotrephes depended heavily on a network of closely intertwined community connections. While we are able to choose how deeply we will become involved with people different from ourselves, the early church was a blend of people from various walks of life. As John writes this third epistle, his words convey a key element of hospitality, which is genuine appreciation. He is both a spiritual elder in the church, and a physical elder of advanced age. This has earned him a wealth of experience with people at their best and worst.

BIBLE LEARNING

AIM: Students will know that that showing hospitality shows truth and encourages others to be coworkers with the truth.

I. THE HEART OF HOSPITALITY (3 John 1–4)

In John's Gospel and letters, "truth" (Gk. *aletheia*, **ah-LAY-thay-ah**) includes freedom from affectation, pretense, simulation, falsehood, and deceit. Since John greets his friend in the truth, loves him in truth, walks with him in truth, and encourages the church to be cooperative in the truth, we know that truth is at the heart of Christian hospitality (**vv. 1–4**). This recognition of truth may tempt us to say that we should only associate with others who walk likewise in the truth. While it is important that we as believers connect ourselves with others who hold the truth of Christ at heart, we should also be mindful that our Christian obligation is not just to hold the truth secret. Our job as ministers of Christ is to take and share His truth (**vv. 3–4**).

The Truth of Jesus Christ (verses 1–4)

1 The elder unto the wellbeloved Gaius, whom I love in the truth. 2 Beloved, I wish above all things that thou mayest prosper and be in health, even as thy soul prospereth.

John addresses this letter to Gaius, who appears to be a leader in the church. He states his love for Gaius in the same way that he states his love for the elect lady and her children in **2 John**. His love is "in the truth." This is the truth of Jesus Christ. He adds to his well wishes toward Gaius by saying that he wishes "above all things that thou mayest prosper and be in health, even as thy soul prospereth." Many have used this to justify the prosperity teaching that God wants all people to be rich, when in fact this verse does not communicate material prosperity for all. These are actually general well wishes and not a promise from God. John puts these general well wishes in a Christian context by also desiring the prosperity or health of Gaius' soul.

3 For I rejoiced greatly, when the brethren came and testified of the truth that is in thee, even as thou walkest in the truth. 4 I have no greater joy than to hear that my children walk in truth.

John was overwhelmed with joy (twice in two verses) over the report of the balanced spiritual life of Gaius. The first characteristic of the latter's faith is underscored in these verses: he possessed and lived the truth, the fact of which was attested by the external testimony of fellow Christians.

SEARCH THE SCRIPTURES

QUESTION 1

What does it mean to walk in the truth?

LIGHT ON THE WORD

The Cost of Sharing the Truth

The heart of hospitality is to have something good and be willing to share it without concern for loss. To share the truth of Christ costs us nothing. Yes, there are expenses for traveling and preparing materials and facilities for the spread and study of the Gospel. Yet, to give to Christ is to increase the family of faith, rather than to lose resources. John desires prosperity and health for his friends and spiritual children. It is important to note that this is John's desire and not necessarily a mandate or promise from God to all believers. This prosperity is not for their own selfish desires but so that they may have strength and ability to continue sharing the most important truth of all (**vv. 1–2**).

II. WORKING TOGETHER REQUIRES WORK (vv. 5–8)

John continues his epistle by providing specific recognition of the hard work Gaius and his congregation have performed. Often in church life we find ourselves giving until it hurts. Sometimes this is financial. Other times, our contributions are in large amounts of time spent or in providing supplies and resources for the work at hand. Still, we are human and it is quite normal for us to feel that our great sacrifices are not recognized. John acknowledges that Gaius' flock is diligent and faithful to the ministers and missionaries they have served. He has received good reports from them and he has firsthand knowledge of their good reputation for superior care (**vv. 5–6**). Knowing that there may be challenges to their ability to provide accommodations, John praises the church for what they have done, confirming their reputation is sure. He reminds them, however, that whatever the cost of their hospitality, it is still no greater than the price Jesus paid for our sins.

Beloved Community (verses 5–8)

5 Beloved, thou doest faithfully whatsoever thou doest to the brethren, and to strangers; 6 Which have borne witness of thy charity before the church: whom if thou bring forward on their journey after a godly sort, thou shalt do well:

The second characteristic of the balanced spiritual life of Gaius is his love, demonstrated practically among Christians, especially in warm and rich hospitality toward Christian missionaries. Such care for missionaries was a great service, particularly at a time when inns and guest houses were scarce and uncomfortable (cf. **Hebrews 13:2**).

Beneficiaries of Gaius' hospitality gave testimonies, confirming the quality of his faith and love publicly in the assembly (Gk. *ekklesia*, **eck-klay-SEE-uh**, the church).

He is further encouraged to remain committed to this labor of love. The Greek word *propempo* (**pro-PEHM-poh**), translated "bring forward," indicates that the missionaries are to be provided with necessities and escorts for the next stage of their journey.

The phrase translated "after a godly sort" or "in a manner worthy of God" (NIV) describes the manner in which the traveling missionaries are to be sent on their journey They are messengers of God, and as such, they are to be treated with the same type of honor that God is worthy of. This is an extraordinary standard of hospitality!

7 Because that for his name's sake they went forth, taking nothing of the Gentiles.

John here offers as examples reasons for encouraging such support. First, the traveling Christians were missionaries: they went out on a Gospel mission. Christ, not money, was their motive. The phrase "for his name's sake" is a common Semitic (or Hebrew) reference to God. Because God's actual name was so holy, Jews would say "the name" rather than "Yahweh" when talking about God. Thus, the verse could be translated "Because that for Yahweh's sake..." Second, they were not "funded" by the Gentiles. They had no means of support other than the Christians.

8 We therefore ought to receive such, that we might be fellowhelpers to the truth.

The pronoun "we" (referring to Christians) is emphatic. The Greek word *opheilo* (**ah-FAY-loh**, "ought") carries a sense of obligation. Christians have the moral duty to actively support the work of God. A third reason is that such support is actually a partnership in the truth.

SEARCH THE SCRIPTURES

QUESTION 2

What was significant about acting faithfully toward the brethren and to strangers?

LIGHT ON THE WORD

Believers Must Care for Other Believers

Verse 7 reminds us of the early church's limitations, as "they went forth, taking nothing of the Gentiles." In John's day, the average person could literally go only as far as a day's walk. They would eat generally what they could carry, then rely on the kindness of strangers for sustenance each night of their journey. The church could have asked for support from "the Gentiles" (**v. 7**), but the implication is that believers should not have to seek financial support from non-believers. John emphasizes this in **verse 8**, saying that we should be "fellowhelpers to the truth." Notice that John focuses attention on the mission, not the missionary. He gives preference to the cargo, not the caravan. The Bible certainly allows for the care and feeding of ministers, but the reason for that is the overall mission to spread the truth.

III. CHALLENGES TO THE TRUTH (vv. 9–14)

John boldly calls out Diotrephes (**v. 9**), who is in church leadership, yet defies the commandment of hospitality. This is a most distressing error that unfortunately can happen even today. Diotrephes represents an even worse threat to the church than the false teachers John warned against in his earlier epistles. As a result, although Diotrephes has taken position and no doubt made himself lord within the church, we should be cautious not to allow our earthly authority to supersede the truth of Christ, which encompasses Jesus' examples and explicit teaching. To call oneself Christian yet refuse hospitality to believers is to commit a disastrous sin. The church needs to reflect God, who welcomes us all to the table. Diotrephes needed to be a better example like Gaius and Demetrius (**v. 12**), remembering that despite rank, there is no division in Christ; we are all one (**Galatians 3:28**).

A True Servant's Heart (verses 9–14)

9 I wrote unto the church: but Diotrephes, who loveth to have the preeminence among them, receiveth us not.

Now John cites a contrast to shun: Diotrephes is the self-seeking church leader who exhibited a bad example. He refused hospitality to delegates from John. He was motivated not by truth and love like Gaius, but by personal ambition.

10 Wherefore, if I come, I will remember his deeds which he doeth, prating against us with malicious words: and not content therewith, neither doth he himself receive the brethren, and forbiddeth them that would, and casteth them out of the church.

Other antitheses of truth and love demonstrated by Diotrephes are listed here. First, he spread slanderous gossip against John. Second, he went from words to action: he refused hospitality to delegates who came from John. Third, he prevented others in the church from entertaining the traveling missionaries. And finally, he expelled those who resisted his authority.

11 Beloved, follow not that which is evil, but that which is good. He that doeth good is of God: but he that doeth evil hath not seen God.

The first command of this letter is contained in this verse. John's exhortation to Gaius in view of the bad example of Diotrephes is expressed negatively and positively. The Greek word *mimeomai* (**mih-MEH-oh-my**) means to use as a model, imitate, emulate, or follow. Negatively, Gaius is to forsake the bad example just cited. The Greek word *kakos* (**kah-KOHSS**) describes what is bad, evil, or harmful. Positively, he is to follow the good model (i.e., Demetrius in the next verse).

The Greek word *agathos* (**ah-gah-THOHSS**) defines what is morally and spiritually good. John also states the reason for his command: A tree is known by its fruit (cf. **Matthew 7:20**). A Christian's behavior is evidence of his or her spiritual condition.

12 Demetrius hath good report of all men, and of the truth itself: yea, and we also bear record; and ye know that our record is true.

There is much speculation on the identity of Demetrius. Some believe that he was the one who carried this letter to the congregation. As such, John wanted the local church to give him a good reception. The phrase "hath good report" is a single verb in Greek (*martureo*, **mar-too-REH-oh**, to confirm or testify to). A better translation would be "well spoken of." This verb is in the perfect tense and implies that this good report of Demetrius had been given over a period of time and continued to be up to date. John also adds that not only do people in the church speak well of Demetrius, but his life and teaching is also aligned with the truth of the Gospel itself. To complete the list of Gaius' recommendation, John lets Gaius know that Demetrius is well spoken of by John and the local church. This personal recommendation along with all the others would carry weight in the eyes of Gaius and the recipients of the letter.

13 I had many things to write, but I will not with ink and pen write unto thee: 14 But I trust I shall shortly see thee, and we shall speak face to face. Peace be to thee. Our friends salute thee. Greet the friends by name.

John concludes the letter by stating there is more to be said. He writes that he will tell them in person rather than by letter. This may be due to the credibility attached to speaking in person rather than in writing. John uses the word "friends" twice. The Epicurean philosophers of the time also called each other "friends." John could be utilizing this terminology to emphasize the unity and harmony that he and the local churches shared in regards to the truth.

LIGHT ON THE WORD

Share Communion

John closes his message with the same sense of fellowship with which he began. He specifically mentions that he has many things to write, but he prefers to meet in person—something we sometimes lack in our modern world of text messages, e-mails, and other impersonal methods of communication. He closes by expressing peace, friendship, and a desire to share communion.

BIBLE APPLICATION

AIM: Students will learn the importance of showing hospitality to other believers as they study and live the commandment to love.

John the elder desires that his friends prosper. He writes a message of love and encouragement and expects that they treat others with the same kindness and compassion. Despite our good intentions or the results of our good works, the task of caring for others can still present risks. Whether we care for traveling evangelists, orphaned children, relatives, or even non-believers who ask for our help, there will always be challenges to our Christian compassion. Thankfully, as God presents us with opportunities to minister, He will open doors for us to include others who desire to help. We are not alone in our time of need or of sharing with others.

STUDENTS' RESPONSES

AIM: Students will commit to live their lives so that others can see they are walking in the truth of Christ.

We have all missed opportunities to show hospitality. Whether we overlooked someone's need or deliberately ignored a situation we could have easily assisted, we have all dropped the ball at some point. With John's message in mind, take time this week to show hospitality to strangers. Invite someone who is not like you to your home for a meal. At the end of the meal, offer to pray for them.

PRAYER

Jesus, You are kind, gracious, and caring. We learn from You how to show hospitality, kindness and care for those who struggle or need Your reassuring grace. Thank You and bless You. In Your Name we pray. Amen.

HOW TO SAY IT

Malicious.	ma-**LIH**-shus.
Preeminence.	pre-**EM**-in-ins.

PREPARE FOR NEXT SUNDAY

Read **1 Corinthians 12:1–11** and study "Gifts of the Spirit."

DAILY HOME BIBLE READINGS

MONDAY
All God's Works are Truth
(Daniel 4:34–37)

TUESDAY
Walk Before God in Faithfulness
(1 Kings 2:1–4)

WEDNESDAY
Truth is in Jesus
(Ephesians 4:17–25)

THURSDAY
Knowledge of the Truth
(Hebrews 10:23–27)

FRIDAY
Rightly Explain the Word of Truth
(2 Timothy 2:14–19)

SATURDAY
A Teacher in Faith and Truth
(1 Timothy 2:1–7)

SUNDAY
Coworkers with the Truth
(3 John)

Sources:

Akin, Daniel, ed. *The New American Commentary.* Nashville, TN: Broadman and Holman. 2001.

Anders, Max and David Walls, eds. *Holman New Testament Commentary.* Nashville, TN: Broadman and Holman, 2000.

Keener, Craig S, ed. *IVP Bible Background Commentary.* Downers Grove, IL: InterVarsity Press, 1991.

COMMENTS / NOTES:

GIFTS OF THE SPIRIT

BIBLE BASIS: 1 CORINTHIANS 12:1–11

BIBLE TRUTH: One person does not possess all of the spiritual gifts; therefore, believers must work together for the church's common good.

MEMORY VERSE: "But the manifestation of the Spirit is given to every man to profit withal" (1 Corinthians 12:7).

LESSON AIM: By the end of the lesson, your students will: outline the purpose of spiritual gifts according to 1 Corinthians 12:1–11; appreciate individual spiritual gifts and the ways they are used; and uncover the spiritual gifts of the faith community and the ways they can be used for its benefit.

TEACHER PREPARATION

MATERIALS NEEDED: Quarterly Commentary/Teacher Manual, Adult Quarterly, Adult resources—charts, worksheets, and other teaching tools, paper, pens, pencils, Bibles (several different versions)

OTHER MATERIALS NEEDED / TEACHER'S NOTES:

____

____

LESSON OVERVIEW

LIFE NEED FOR TODAY'S LESSON

Most people seek opportunities to become loyal contributing members of their societies.

BIBLE LEARNING

Paul was responding to the tendency of some in the Corinthian church to boast in their spiritual sophistication and power.

BIBLE APPLICATION

Believers put the common good of the church above their personal interests.

STUDENTS' RESPONSES

Students will distinguish between spiritual gifts and natural abilities or talents.

LESSON SCRIPTURE

1 CORINTHIANS 12:1–11, KJV

1 Now concerning spiritual gifts, brethren, I would not have you ignorant.

2 Ye know that ye were Gentiles, carried away unto these dumb idols, even as ye were led.

3 Wherefore I give you to understand, that no man speaking by the Spirit of God

1 CORINTHIANS 12:1–11, NIV

1 Now about the gifts of the Spirit, brothers and sisters, I do not want you to be uninformed.

2 You know that when you were pagans, somehow or other you were influenced and led astray to mute idols.

3 Therefore I want you to know that no

calleth Jesus accursed: and that no man can say that Jesus is the Lord, but by the Holy Ghost.

4 Now there are diversities of gifts, but the same Spirit.

5 And there are differences of administrations, but the same Lord.

6 And there are diversities of operations, but it is the same God which worketh all in all.

7 But the manifestation of the Spirit is given to every man to profit withal.

8 For to one is given by the Spirit the word of wisdom; to another the word of knowledge by the same Spirit;

9 To another faith by the same Spirit; to another the gifts of healing by the same Spirit;

10 To another the working of miracles; to another prophecy; to another discerning of spirits; to another divers kinds of tongues; to another the interpretation of tongues:

11 But all these worketh that one and the selfsame Spirit, dividing to every man severally as he will.

one who is speaking by the Spirit of God says, "Jesus be cursed," and no one can say, "Jesus is Lord," except by the Holy Spirit.

4 There are different kinds of gifts, but the same Spirit distributes them.

5 There are different kinds of service, but the same Lord.

6 There are different kinds of working, but in all of them and in everyone it is the same God at work.

7 Now to each one the manifestation of the Spirit is given for the common good.

8 To one there is given through the Spirit a message of wisdom, to another a message of knowledge by means of the same Spirit,

9 to another faith by the same Spirit, to another gifts of healing by that one Spirit,

10 to another miraculous powers, to another prophecy, to another distinguishing between spirits, to another speaking in different kinds of tongues, and to still another the interpretation of tongues.

11 All these are the work of one and the same Spirit, and he distributes them to each one, just as he determines.

LIGHT ON THE WORD

An idol is anything that is worshiped other than God. In ancient times and in some cultures now, many worship at the feet of statues. These statues represent the deity that they worship and serve. The city of Corinth was full of idolatry, or the worship of idols and the false gods they represent.

Gentiles are non-Jewish people. Initially, God dealt more with the Jews in His plan of salvation. After the death and resurrection of Christ, the Gentiles were welcomed into the family of God without having to become Jews themselves. The task of preaching this Good News was given to the Apostle Paul. Paul's journeys led him to

Corinth, where he preached to a mostly Gentile audience. Consequently, although some Jews received Paul's message at Corinth, the majority of the converts were Gentiles.

TEACHING THE BIBLE LESSON

LIFE NEED FOR TODAY'S LESSON

AIM: Students will seek opportunities to become loyal contributing members of their societies.

INTRODUCTION

A Proper Perspective on Spiritual Gifts

The Corinthian church had been wrapped up in all kinds of immorality and unethical practices. Although it was a very gifted church in one of the most cosmopolitan cities in the Roman Empire, they were lacking in some basic Christian theology and behavior. In order to help them, Paul wrote the letter that we know as **1 Corinthians**. In **1 Corinthians**, we see Paul address a list of issues in the life of the church. This list of issues included celebrity worship of Christian ministers, sexual immorality, eating foods offered to idols, head covering for women, and the proper way to host communion. Next he addresses the spiritual gifts and specifically the gift of tongues. In order to introduce the topic, Paul teaches the Corinthians the proper perspective on spiritual gifts.

BIBLE LEARNING

AIM: Students will respond to the tendency of some in the church to boast in their spiritual sophistication and power.

I. THE TEST OF THE SPIRIT (1 Corinthians 12:1–3)

Paul starts off this chapter by stating that he does not want the Corinthians to be ignorant about spiritual gifts. His desire is that they would be mature in their knowledge about what spiritual gifts are and how they operate in the church. He then reminds them of their life as Gentiles. As Gentiles, they worshiped idols. Many of them probably participated in the worship of Aphrodite and Poseidon, two popular gods. Paul said they were led and guided to worship these mute idols. By a Jewish mindset, these idols were blind and could not speak in the same dynamic way as the God of Israel (**Habakkuk 2:18–20; Psalm 135:16**).

Spiritual Guidance (verses 1–3)

1 Now concerning spiritual gifts, brethren, I would not have you ignorant.

To be "ignorant" (Gk. *agnoeo*, **ag-no-EH-o**) means not only a lack of knowledge, but also a lack of understanding that leads to error or even sin through mistake. In this instance, to be ignorant is to be wrong. Often we sin because we do not know or understand correctly. Concerning spiritual matters, this can have grave consequences for the Body of Christ. Most disunity, bigotry, and other errors in the Body of Christ are committed by well-meaning, devoted Christians who are either ignorant of the truth or wrong, concerning spiritual or other things of God. This is especially true concerning "spiritual gifts" (Gk. *pneumatikos*, **puh-nehoo-mah-teek-OSE**).

2 Ye know that ye were Gentiles, carried away unto these dumb idols, even as ye were led.

Paul was not impressed by their enthusiastic worship and religious frenzy. Idol worshipers (which many of them were) could boast of the same religious excitement. Spirited worship services are not necessarily evidence of the Holy Spirit. There are many kinds of spirits related to pagan idols. The Holy Spirit is the Spirit of Christ. Only one's attitude toward Christ and consideration for those in the body can distinguish which spirit you worship. Some who worship are gifted in music, others with enticing speech, many with elegant liturgical dance, and still others lively praise while paying little attention to the doctrines being taught—whether they are of Christ or not.

3 Wherefore I give you to understand, that no man speaking by the Spirit of God calleth Jesus accursed: and that no man can say that Jesus is the Lord, but by the Holy Ghost.

Under persecution, distress, or religious frenzy, believers were often forced or led to curse the name of Jesus. "Accursed be Jesus" could not come from the lips of one under the influence of the Holy Spirit (the Spirit of Christ). On the other hand, "Jesus is Lord" (Gk. *kurios*, **KOO-ree-ose**) was the battle cry of Christians. Kurios was the same title that the Romans demanded everybody who came under their power ascribe to Caesar, saying "Caesar is Lord!" But kurios was also the title given to Yahweh by Jews, God-fearers, and Christians alike. To say "Jesus is Lord" was to commit to ultimate loyalty to Jesus. Thus, those who would not be ignorant or wrong about the Holy Spirit must examine their confession of faith.

SEARCH THE SCRIPTURES

QUESTION 1

What is the reason Paul says "no man can say that Jesus is the Lord, but by the Holy Ghost"?

LIGHT ON THE WORD

The Gifts from the Holy Spirit

Paul lets the Corinthians know the litmus test of whether someone is speaking by the Spirit of God so they can discern the activity of the Holy Spirit in their gatherings. Paul says that no one can speak by the Spirit of God and at the same time call Jesus cursed. To do so would mean that they were not really speaking by the Spirit of God. In contrast, he says that no one can say that Jesus is Lord except through the Holy Spirit. The purpose of the Holy Spirit is to glorify Jesus (**John 15:26, 16:14**) and therefore proclaiming His Lordship is the approved sign of the Spirit's activity.

II. THE UNITY OF THE SPIRIT (vv. 4–7)

The argument is furthered with a discussion centered on the unity of the Spirit. God grants many different spiritual gifts, which operate and serve the Body of Christ in different ways. Paul underscores the fact that they all have the same source and they are all working toward the same purpose under the same leadership.

One Spirit, Many Gifts (verses 4–7)

4 Now there are diversities of gifts, but the same Spirit.

There are "diversities" (Gk. *diairesis*, **dee-EYE-reh-sis**) of allocations of gifts, but they are derived from the same Holy Spirit. Paul wants to make it plain that there can be unity in diversity. It is the Spirit's function to connect, not divide. These gifts are given not for individual glory, but to glorify or edify the Body of Christ as a whole. If one does not want to be ignorant or go wrong, one must understand the underlying unity of the operations of the Holy Spirit, remembering that these people once worshiped many gods according to their function (i.e., war gods, fertility gods, gods of the harvest). This was not so with the Spirit of Christ. With the Holy Spirit, there is unity in diversity.

5 And there are differences of administrations, but the same Lord.

There are a variety or "differences" (the same Greek word as "diversities" in **v. 4**) of "administrations" (Gk. *diakonia*, **dee-ah-koh-NEE-ah**) rendered at the command of the same Lord. As each has a different gift given by the same Spirit, each performs a different service command by the same Lord and Master. Once again, Paul emphasizes unity in diversity because the church was in danger of being fractured by the very instruments of God that should have brought them together. Monotheism (belief in one God) was relatively new outside of the Jewish faith in this region of the world. Thus, among the Corinthian church, who were largely not former Jews but instead former Greeks who worshiped many gods, it was necessary to emphasize oneness of the Lord and operations of the Holy Spirit.

6 And there are diversities of operations, but it is the same God which worketh all in all.

There is again the same diairesis of "operations" (Gk. *energema*, **en-ER-gay-mah**, energy, efficacy, actions, or activities), but it is the same God that is active in all that happens. The Corinthians were divided by those who brought them to Christ and baptized them (**1 Corinthians 3:5–9**). Paul faults their immaturity in the faith. Using the metaphor of building a house, he shows how God is the general contractor, and he, Apollos, Cephas (Peter), and others who brought them the Gospel and nurtured them were mere subcontractors in building the Temple of God (**1 Corinthians 3:10–23**).

The same principle is at work in Paul's rhetorical argument that all gifts are mere tools put into their hands by God to build up the Body of Christ. Each member is a part of God's construction crew.

7 But the manifestation of the Spirit is given to every man to profit withal.

The spiritual gifts are given by the Spirit to be used in service of the Lord. With power and efficacy made possible by God, they are the manifestation of the Spirit in the Christian community for the good of all. It is not a benefit to the individual, but the whole community. It is a benefit to the individual only insofar as it enhances one's value to the community. However, the manifestation of the Spirit is given to each expressly for the benefit of the whole community. The Body of Christ is Paul's metaphor for the functioning Christian community.

SEARCH THE SCRIPTURES

QUESTION 2

How can spiritual gifts be used to defend the doctrine of the Trinity?

LIGHT ON THE WORD

Unity in the Spirit

Here Paul is highlighting the unity of the spiritual gifts. They are given out to every believer and work in different ways, but they are all for the same purpose of glorifying Jesus as Lord and building up the Body of Christ. Different people can exercise the same gifts multiples different ways, but it is all for one purpose and from one source. God through the Holy Spirit uses the gifts to proclaim Jesus as Lord and build up His church.

III. THE GIFTS OF THE SPIRIT (vv. 8–11)

Paul then lists the gifts of the Spirit. These gifts come from the Holy Spirit as opposed to natural talents and endowments. He begins with the word of wisdom. Next is the word of knowledge. After this, Paul mentions the gift of faith. Next Paul lists supernatural healing. Then he goes on to mention the working of miracles. Prophecy is listed after this. Then Paul mentions discerning of spirits. Lastly he mentions the gifts of tongues and interpretation of tongues.

Diverse Spiritual Tools (verses 8–11)

8 For to one is given by the Spirit the word of wisdom; to another the word of knowledge by the same Spirit;

Paul begins to list the toolbox of gifts given by the Spirit to build the Temple of God, the Body of Christ. He painstakingly emphasizes to these newcomers in Christ (**1 Corinthians 3:2**), who saw their gifts as a source of personal pride, that spiritual unity is the foundation for these diverse spiritual tools that have been given as gifts.

The first gifts are the tools for the teaching ministry of the church. The word or utterance of "knowledge" (Gk. *gnosis*, **GNO-sis**) is to know what to do in any given situation, and "wisdom" (Gk. *sophia*, **soh-FEE-ah**) is the knowledge of the best things to do according to God's will. They both come from the same Spirit and are used to build up the church with knowledge of what Jesus Christ would do in any given situation (**John 14:26**), and wisdom to understand the will of God for their mission in the world (**2 Peter 3:9**). This is the wisdom and knowledge that did not come from academic achievement alone, but from communion with God and the study of His Word.

9 To another faith by the same Spirit; to another the gifts of healing by the same Spirit;

Paul names faith as a gift and tool. Everyone has a measure of faith, especially those who claim personal salvation, which comes by faith. Paul has in mind here an all-encompassing trust in God that can move mountains (**Matthew 17:20–21**), cause blind people to see (**Matthew 9:29**), and lame people to walk (**Mark 2:5–12**). It was the faith of former slaves in America that built institutions of higher learning and great churches while bearing the burden of racism and slavery. This kind of faith is a gift and a mighty tool.

The gifts of faith and healing are closely associated throughout the Gospels. The gifts of healing, along with faith and prayer, are important tools in building Christian fellowship because they demonstrate the unity of the mind, body, and spirit. Even more than that, the laying on of hands, anointing with oil, and mutual prayer build intimacy as they bring healing both individually and communally.

10 To another the working of miracles; to another prophecy; to another discerning of spirits; to another divers kinds of tongues; to another the interpretation of tongues:

The Greek word for "miracles" is *dunamis* (**DOO-nah-mis**), or power. Miracles were a demonstration of power as evidenced by the Messianic age. When John sent his disciple to inquire whether Jesus was the Messiah or not, Jesus responded with a recitation of His demonstrations of power as evidence (**Matthew 11:2–5**).

The gift of prophecy is the ability to reveal the will of God for our lives and communities. The prophet through the Spirit knows the mind of God and speaks it into the lives of His people. The Spirit works either to rebuke those people or institutions who are not in the will of God by foretelling the dire consequences of their actions, or by advising people or institutions who seek God's guidance to live according to His will.

The discerning of spirits is the ability to distinguish whether one's performance of miracles is by the Holy Spirit or some other spirit. It is necessary to understand the source of a demonstration or power to know its intent.

Diverse kinds of "tongues" (Gk. *glossa*, **GLOH-sah**) were not exactly the same as the Pentecost experience (**Acts 2:4**), where the Spirit enabled them to speak known foreign languages. In Corinth, they spoke unlearned languages that no one understood, except perhaps the one speaking or someone who had the gift of interpreting unknown tongues.

11 But all these worketh that one and the selfsame Spirit, dividing to every man severally as he will.

Again Paul reminds us that all the diversity of gifts has one source: the Spirit of God, who chooses who gets what gift. Therefore, no one has reason to boast. More importantly, one does not choose a gift; the Spirit chooses the person for the gift. The same Spirit that gives the gift, gives according to the will of God.

LIGHT ON THE WORD

Unite and Glorify Christ

Paul concludes this list with a reminder that it is the Spirit of God that gives out these gifts. They cannot be possessed at our whim, but are given by the will of the Holy Spirit. They are given to each person as the Holy Spirit sees fit. He also highlights the fact that they all are given by the same Spirit. They are not given to divide the church, but to unite it in glorifying Christ. This is a reminder to us as believers not to be divisive when it comes to spiritual gifts, but to celebrate and receive the gifts of others as they endeavor to build up the Body of Christ and testify to His Lordship.

BIBLE APPLICATION

AIM: Students will put the common good of the church above their personal interests.

Those who are gifted often use their talents for their own profit and success. We can see this in the lives of famous entertainers and politicians. The gifts that God has given them are used to glorify themselves and afford extravagant, luxurious lifestyles. This way of thinking has infiltrated the church, and many have sought to use their spiritual gifts to amass wealth and fame. Paul lets us know this is not what the gifts are for. They are for building up the church and serving others. The spiritual gifts are not ours. We are called to steward what the Holy Spirit has given us for the good of others.

STUDENTS' RESPONSES

AIM: Students will distinguish between spiritual gifts and natural abilities or talents.

Our spiritual gifts are learned in community and experience. If you are not involved in a ministry of your church, then volunteer for a limited time to serve in a ministry you have been interested in. It could be the children's ministry, hospitality, or outreach to the community. After serving for a while, ask for feedback from the leader of the ministry and others who you have served with about what spiritual gift they may see in you. Be sure to let others know what spiritual gifts you see in them and encourage them as well.

PRAYER

Gracious God, You continue to bless in so many ways. We want to serve You as we serve others through the gifts and talents that You have given us. Thank You for allowing us to care for others as You continue to care for us. In Jesus' Name we pray. Amen.

HOW TO SAY IT

Discerning. dih-**SER**-ning.

Diversities. di-**VER**-si-tees.

PREPARE FOR NEXT SUNDAY

Read **1 Corinthians 12:14–31** and study "The Spirit Creates One Body."

DAILY HOME BIBLE READINGS

MONDAY
Not Exalted Over Other Members
(Deuteronomy 17:14–20)

TUESDAY
God's Gifts and Calling are Irrevocable
(Romans 11:25–32)

WEDNESDAY
God Distributed Gifts of the Spirit
(Hebrews 2:1–9)

THURSDAY
Grace Gifts Given to Us
(Romans 12:1–8)

FRIDAY
Understanding the Gifts God Bestows
(1 Corinthians 2:11–16)

SATURDAY
Gifts That Build Up the Church
(1 Corinthians 14:1–5)

SUNDAY
One Spirit, a Variety of Gifts
(1 Corinthians 12:1–11)

Sources:

Hays, Richard B. *First Corinthians: Interpretation, A Bible Commentary for Teaching and Preaching*. Louisville, KY: John Knox. 1997.

Henry, Matthew. *Matthew Henry's Commentary on the Whole Bible: Complete and Unabridged in One Volume*. Peabody, MA: Hendrickson, 1994.

Utley, Robert James. *Paul's Letters to a Troubled Church: I and II Corinthians*. Study Guide Commentary Series, vol. 6. Marshall, TX: Bible Lessons International, 2002.

COMMENTS / NOTES:

THE SPIRIT CREATES ONE BODY

BIBLE BASIS: 1 CORINTHIANS 12:14–31

BIBLE TRUTH: The church needs all the spiritual gifts to work together to function effectively and efficiently.

MEMORY VERSE: "For by one Spirit are we all baptized into one body, whether we be Jews or Gentiles, whether we be bond or free; and have been all made to drink into one Spirit" (1 Corinthians 12:13).

LESSON AIM: By the end of the lesson, your students will: learn how each member of the body supports the other members; value the different gifts operating within the church; and use spiritual gifts in cooperation with others for building up the Body of Christ.

TEACHER PREPARATION

MATERIALS NEEDED: Quarterly Commentary/Teacher Manual, Adult Quarterly, Adult resources—charts, worksheets, and other teaching tools, paper, pens, pencils, Bibles (several different versions)

OTHER MATERIALS NEEDED / TEACHER'S NOTES:

____

____

LESSON OVERVIEW

LIFE NEED FOR TODAY'S LESSON
Why is it important for Christians to know and operate in unity within their spiritual gifts?

BIBLE LEARNING
Believers trust that love governs the exercise of all the gifts of the Spirit.

BIBLE APPLICATION
Christians recognize and support all parts of the Body of Christ.

STUDENTS' RESPONSES
Students will strive to identify and understand their gifts and how they can best be used for the glory of God.

LESSON SCRIPTURE

1 CORINTHIANS 12:14–31, KJV

14 For the body is not one member, but many.

15 If the foot shall say, Because I am not the hand, I am not of the body; is it therefore not of the body?

16 And if the ear shall say, Because I am not the eye, I am not of the body; is it

1 CORINTHIANS 12:14–31, NIV

14 Even so the body is not made up of one part but of many.

15 Now if the foot should say, "Because I am not a hand, I do not belong to the body," it would not for that reason stop being part of the body.

16 And if the ear should say, "Because I am

therefore not of the body?

17 If the whole body were an eye, where were the hearing? If the whole were hearing, where were the smelling?

18 But now hath God set the members every one of them in the body, as it hath pleased him.

19 And if they were all one member, where were the body?

20 But now are they many members, yet but one body.

21 And the eye cannot say unto the hand, I have no need of thee: nor again the head to the feet, I have no need of you.

22 Nay, much more those members of the body, which seem to be more feeble, are necessary:

23 And those members of the body, which we think to be less honourable, upon these we bestow more abundant honour; and our uncomely parts have more abundant comeliness.

24 For our comely parts have no need: but God hath tempered the body together, having given more abundant honour to that part which lacked.

25 That there should be no schism in the body; but that the members should have the same care one for another.

26 And whether one member suffer, all the members suffer with it; or one member be honoured, all the members rejoice with it.

27 Now ye are the body of Christ, and members in particular.

28 And God hath set some in the church, first apostles, secondarily prophets, thirdly teachers, after that miracles, then

not an eye, I do not belong to the body," it would not for that reason stop being part of the body.

17 If the whole body were an eye, where would the sense of hearing be? If the whole body were an ear, where would the sense of smell be?

18 But in fact God has placed the parts in the body, every one of them, just as he wanted them to be.

19 If they were all one part, where would the body be?

20 As it is, there are many parts, but one body.

21 The eye cannot say to the hand, "I don't need you!" And the head cannot say to the feet, "I don't need you!"

22 On the contrary, those parts of the body that seem to be weaker are indispensable,

23 and the parts that we think are less honorable we treat with special honor. And the parts that are unpresentable are treated with special modesty,

24 while our presentable parts need no special treatment. But God has put the body together, giving greater honor to the parts that lacked it,

25 so that there should be no division in the body, but that its parts should have equal concern for each other.

26 If one part suffers, every part suffers with it; if one part is honored, every part rejoices with it.

27 Now you are the body of Christ, and each one of you is a part of it.

gifts of healings, helps, governments, diversities of tongues.

29 Are all apostles? are all prophets? are all teachers? are all workers of miracles?

30 Have all the gifts of healing? do all speak with tongues? do all interpret?

31 But covet earnestly the best gifts: and yet shew I unto you a more excellent way.

28 And God has placed in the church first of all apostles, second prophets, third teachers, then miracles, then gifts of healing, of helping, of guidance, and of different kinds of tongues.

29 Are all apostles? Are all prophets? Are all teachers? Do all work miracles?

30 Do all have gifts of healing? Do all speak in tongues? Do all interpret?

31 Now eagerly desire the greater gifts. And yet I will show you the most excellent way.

LIGHT ON THE WORD

Helps is the special ability to aid, assist, and support others. It is closely related to the gift of mercy, which is caring for those who are distressed and disadvantaged. In **1 Thessalonians 5:14**, the phrase "support the weak" could refer to this ministry in particular. The men who were selected to feed the poor widows in Jerusalem could have possessed this gift (**Acts 6:1–7**). This gift could also be used in an unofficial capacity as those who gave alms and fed the poor without an official role or title.

"Governments" is related to the word for a captain or pilot of a ship. It is the special ability to organize and make decisions that lead to the church operating efficiently and effectively. It is the ability to administrate people and details in order to accomplish goals. Those with this gift usually have an eye for detail and an ability to problem solve.

TEACHING THE BIBLE LESSON

LIFE NEED FOR TODAY'S LESSON

AIM: Students will understand the importance for Christians to operate in unity within their spiritual gifts.

INTRODUCTION

A Common Source for a Common Goal

Paul likens the church to a human body. He emphasizes that every member has an important function just like the parts of the body. Each and every member contributes to the health and functioning of the whole body. This makes every believer a necessary part of the Body of Christ. He reminds them that God is the provider of all gifts, and that the Holy Spirit is the source (**1 Corinthians 12:2–5**). As a balance, he illustrates the similarity of the human body to the Body of Christ (**1 Corinthians 12:13**). By breaking down the importance of each member, he makes it clear that the church's body cannot afford to be divided for any reason, whether from outside influence or internal disagreement. Even as the various parts serve differing functions, they have a common source and a common goal and cannot operate separate from one another.

BIBLE LEARNING

AIM: Students will trust that love governs the

exercise of all the gifts of the Spirit.

I. THE PURPOSE OF THE PARTS (1 Corinthians 12:14–20)

Paul begins his analogy of the Body of Christ by using very common language regarding the human body. He blends humor and a hint of irony to describe the rather silly way that people can treat each other. Paul uses rhetorical questions to state the fact that the church is one body. If the church is made up of only one member or one spiritual gift, then it would miss out on some important things that it needed. In contrast, God has placed all of the members of the church into one body; thus the diversity of gifts can profit the whole church.

Strength in Diversity (verses 14–20)

14 For the body is not one member, but many.

The body metaphor was widely used in the ancient world. Many politicians used it to create peace and harmony between the different social classes. The argument was usually that the lower parts needed to be subordinated under the more superior or noble parts. In other words, the poor and working classes must submit to the rich and noble classes. This was not the case with Paul. The metaphor of the body is used in a more egalitarian way for Paul to show what true Christian community looks like. It can be safe to infer that for Paul, the idea of the church as the Body of Christ was more than a metaphor but an actual reality.

Here Paul uses the body metaphor to highlight the necessity of diversity. Everyone cannot have the same gift if the Body of Christ is to operate effectively. The body must consist of many members with diverse gifts. The oneness of the body does not take away from the diversity of its members.

15 If the foot shall say, Because I am not the hand, I am not of the body; is it therefore not of the body? 16 And if the ear shall say, Because I am not the eye, I am not of the body; is it therefore not of the body?

In many cultures, the foot is regarded as being very lowly. To touch another person with the foot would be considered disrespectful, if not insulting. But the touching of hands is considered a gesture of friendship. Thus, if the foot did not wish to belong to the body, because it did not have the status of a hand, that would not change that it is still a vital part of the body in reality.

The ear and the eye both occupy a position upon the head, so there is not as great a difference in status as the foot and the hand. However, the difference lies in function. These two organs have distinct purposes, neither of which the body would gladly do without.

17 If the whole body were an eye, where were the hearing? If the whole were hearing, where were the smelling?

The argument for diversity continues. The Body of Christ cannot function properly with prophecy only, but also healing, hospitality, teaching, etc. Paul's point is that if the whole consisted of only one thing, the body would lose many functions, if not its very existence. The body was not meant to just pursue one function. Paul argues that a diversity of gifts are needed for the church to do all the work it is meant to do.

18 But now hath God set the members every one of them in the body, as it hath pleased him. 19 And if they were all one member, where were the body? 20 But now are they many members, yet but one body.

Paul credits God with having arranged each member of the body by plan. The body is organized for God's purpose. There would not be a body if He had not planned it, if all the members were the same. Diversity is necessary. According to God's purpose, many diverse members work together for the good of the whole body.

SEARCH THE SCRIPTURES

QUESTION 1

What is the reason that God set the members in one body?

LIGHT ON THE WORD

The Blessing in Sharing Gifts

Paul says that these many members are a part of one body. These many members are necessary for the whole body to function; without them, the body would be incapacitated. All the members with all of their gifts are a part of the one body. This shows the diversity as well as the unity of the church.

II. THE DANGER OF DIVISION (vv. 21–26)

Paul continues his conversation among the body parts by shedding light on very common attitudes. He supposes the eye and hand suffer a disagreement in which they attempt to cast each other off (**v. 21**). While it is quite possible for a body to survive an amputation of an eye or hand (or foot or arm, etc.), the point is that a seeing eye still has nothing with which to grasp. Likewise, a hand without an eye to guide it will do more bumbling and destruction rather than productive handiwork. Far too often, arguments rise in the church wherein members work harder to find fault in each other than they do to find alternate solutions to a common problem. More serious is the idea of "schism" (Gk. *schisma*, **SKHIZ-mah**). This word describes a division or dissention. More seriously, it represents a tear or a rip, as in a garment. Whenever we look upon our brothers and sisters as being less valuable—either to God or mankind—we are forgetting our own personal need for salvation.

The Body of Christ as One (verses 21–26)

21 And the eye cannot say unto the hand, I have no need of thee: nor again the head to the feet, I have no need of you.

One member or body part does not equal a body. Paul ties the existence of the body to the diversity of its members such that the Corinthian church could not protest his argument for diversity and interdependence. The many members make up the one body. Since the existence of the body is wrapped up in its diversity, then interdependence becomes necessary. None of the parts can exist alone; they all need each other to function as one body.

22 Nay, much more those members of the body, which seem to be more feeble, are necessary: 23 And those members of the body, which we think to be less honourable, upon these we bestow more abundant honour; and our uncomely parts have more abundant comeliness.

Here Paul overturns the Corinthians' attitude of pride and boasting. The parts of the body that seem weakest and least important are the most necessary. The parts with less honor and dignity are also the ones given the most care. Those that are weakest are those we clothe with the greatest care. The parts that are stronger do not receive the same kind of care and attention.

For the Corinthian church, this means that those members they deem less dignified and lacking in knowledge are the ones to be treated with honor. The ones they despised for being weaker and an embarrassment were actually placed there by God to receive greater honor and care. This profound statement was rooted in the design of the body and therefore a part of God's plan.

24 For our comely parts have no need: but God hath tempered the body together, having given more abundant honour

to that part which lacked. 25 That there should be no schism in the body; but that the members should have the same care one for another.

Continuing with the theme of interdependence and unity, Paul says that God has mixed the body together and given more honor to the parts that naturally lack it so that there would not be a schism in the body. The opposite of division is that the different members would provide the same care for one another. There would be no member who was isolated and did not receive the same care as the others. That would be detrimental for the health of the body and contrary to their existence as the Body of Christ.

26 And whether one member suffer, all the members suffer with it; or one member be honoured, all the members rejoice with it.

With our physical bodies, an injury to any part is felt throughout the body. So it is with the Body of Christ. Similarly, if one member exercises his or her gifts for the glory of the Lord, the whole of the church is edified. We see this edification in how the presence of a single member in a church can make an enormous difference in the quality of worship, in the feeling of hospitality visitors receive, even in the effectiveness of the church's administrative functions.

SEARCH THE SCRIPTURES

QUESTION 2

What is the reason Paul gives for honoring less honorable members in the Body of Christ?

LIGHT ON THE WORD

Togetherness Among Christians

After the argument between the eye and the hand, the head and feet erupt into an outright dismissal of one another. As ludicrous as it would be for one body part to dismiss another, we are quick to seek separation from other Christians, regardless of our common call to life in Christ. Paul acknowledges that there are those among us who may have less favorable attributes **(vv. 23–24)**, yet we have no right to dismiss them or devalue their presence within the body. Schism represents a painful rip among humans, and also rips us from God's will.

III. THE MISSION OF MEMBERSHIP (vv. 27–31)

As Paul concludes this portion of his letter, he calls the discorporated body parts into a unified vision of hope. He addresses them directly, saying, "Now ye are the body of Christ; and members in particular" **(v. 27)**. As such he outlines that rather than lowly feet or eye or hand, the members of the church are actually far more vital. Naming gifts like prophecy, teaching, healing, preaching, and administration, he makes it clear that there is no person or gift that is without value in God's eyes **(vv. 27–31)**.

Connected as One Body (verses 27–31)

27 Now ye are the body of Christ, and members in particular.

Paul underlines what he has been teaching throughout this passage. The members of the Corinthian church were the Body of Christ. As individuals, they were members or parts of that body. Their existence as the Body of Christ is based on their unity and interdependence. It was not an either/or proposition, but a both/and proposition.

28 And God hath set some in the church, first apostles, secondarily prophets, thirdly teachers, after that miracles, then gifts of healings, helps, governments, diversities of tongues. 29 Are all apostles? are all prophets? are all teachers? are all workers of miracles? 30 Have all the gifts of healing? do all speak with tongues? do

all interpret?

Now Paul goes back to the beginning of his argument in **1 Corinthians 12:12**. There are many members but one body. He states that God has set some in the church with different gifts. Four gifts are mentioned here that are not mentioned in the beginning of the chapter: apostles, prophets, teachers, and governments. All four are stated as roles or leadership positions with the final one potentially encompassing a number of types of leadership including administration. Paul includes them all here as spiritual gifts.

To be an apostle (Gk. *apostolos*, **ah-PO-stel-ose**) is literally to be "one who is sent." This applies to the twelve apostles who traveled with Jesus during His earthly ministry, as well as others, including Paul, who came after Jesus who have been specially commissioned by Him to be His witness and lay the foundation for the church. The other three gifts Paul mentions here have similarly important roles in spreading the Gospel. The prophet is one who hears from and speaks for God. Teachers regularly educate the members of the emerging church. "Governments" can be defined as the gift of administration or organizing.

He next asks some rhetorical questions. All of them can be answered with an emphatic "No!" The main point he is making is that not everyone can be every gift. He is continuing his argument for the diversity of gifts within the church. Everyone should not have the same gifts, or the church would cease to be a functioning body. This is the practical application of Paul's earlier statements about the whole body being an ear or an eye; there would be a loss of function. Paul is now making it plain that we do not all have, and should not all seek to have, the same gifts.

31 But covet earnestly the best gifts: and yet shew I unto you a more excellent way.

The word for covet earnestly (Gk. *zeloo*, **zeh-LO-oh**) means to burn with zeal. Here Paul says to seek after the best gifts with intense passion. We can see that Paul wants to encourage spiritual gifts actively functioning in the church. He says to covet earnestly the best gifts. From this text, we cannot see what the best gifts are. It could be a way to appeal to the Corinthians' fascination with the more ecstatic supernatural gifts, or linked to his preference of prophecy as the best gift (cf. **1 Corinthians 14:1**).

Paul adds a qualifier to his encouragement to seek out the best gifts. He says that he will show them a more excellent (Gk. *hyperbole*, **hoo-pair-bow-LAY**) way. Literally, this Greek word means "throwing beyond." Metaphorically it is an adjective describing something beyond measure. Paul is now about to show them a way that is beyond all measure of goodness. This is a transition into Paul's famous passage about love. It is clear from this transition that Paul's chapter on the qualities and the importance of love are set in the context of the spiritual gifts and his teaching on the diversity and unity of the Body of Christ.

LIGHT ON THE WORD

Individuals Building Collectively

More than a simple call to mend fences, Paul is actually empowering each individual to know their place in the Body of Christ so that their individual gifts may be put to their best use for God, rather than personal or individual gain. To be a member of the Body of Christ is a serious responsibility, but that responsibility is made bearable by support and care from the other members connected to us.

BIBLE APPLICATION

AIM: Students will recognize and support all parts of the Body of Christ.

Often people separate from a church after a negative experience. Sometimes people can be put off by a well-intentioned but poorly placed comment. The news is unfortunately replete with accounts of people suffering tragic abuse at the hands of church leaders. Our natural reaction may be to say how much better we are than a particular denomination. We may go so far as to speak negatively about that particular group's theology based on human failures. Our task in striving for unity is not to condone or cover misdeeds done in or around the church. Instead, we should hold each other up via upholding standards and accountability. While it is hard to subject ourselves to each other, it is best that we determine that we will submit together to the will of God.

STUDENTS' RESPONSES

AIM: Students will strive to identify and understand their gifts and how they can best be used for the glory of God.

In some church cultures, the idea of spiritual gifts is only understood to be evident by certain worship activities. In the African American culture, it is no secret that exuberant singing, shouting, dancing, or displays of emotion may indeed reflect the power of the Holy Spirit upon someone's life and physical body. Still, Paul's letter makes certain that our gifts are not simply to be seen or heard within the assembly. Seek out those people in your church body who contribute behind the scenes. Make a point to show them appreciation through words of encouragement, a card, or a gift.

PRAYER

Praises and honor to the Creator of all gifts. We are excited and rejoice at knowing that each of us has a gift from God to glorify Jesus, our true Savior. In Jesus' Name we pray. Amen.

HOW TO SAY IT

Schism. **SKIH**-zim.

Feeble. **FEE**-bul.

PREPARE FOR NEXT SUNDAY

Read **Acts 2:1–7, 12; 1 Corinthians 14:13–19** and study "Gift of Languages."

DAILY HOME BIBLE READINGS

MONDAY
Speaking with One Voice
(Exodus 19:1–8)

TUESDAY
We Will Be Obedient
(Exodus 24:1–7)

WEDNESDAY
Sincere and Pure Devotion
(2 Corinthians 11:1–5)

THURSDAY
Living in Harmony
(Romans 15:1–7)

FRIDAY
One Spirit, One Mind
(Philippians 1:21–30)

SATURDAY
One in Christ Jesus
(Galatians 3:23–29)

SUNDAY
Many Members, One Body
(1 Corinthians 12:14–31)

Sources:

Hays, Richard B. *First Corinthians: Interpretation, A Bible Commentary for Teaching and Preaching.* Louisville, KY: John Knox. 1997.

Henry, Matthew. *Matthew Henry's Commentary on the Whole Bible: Complete and Unabridged in One Volume.* Peabody, MA: Hendrickson, 1994.

Prime, Derek. *Opening Up 1 Corinthians.* Opening Up Commentary. Leominster, UK: Day One Publications, 2005.

Utley, Robert James. *Paul's Letters to a Troubled Church: I and II Corinthians.* Study Guide Commentary Series, vol. 6. Marshall, TX: Bible Lessons International, 2002.

GIFT OF LANGUAGES

BIBLE BASIS: ACTS 2:1–7, 12; 1 CORINTHIANS 14:13–19

BIBLE TRUTH: The need for finding a common understanding is necessary whether people are speaking in different native languages as in Acts 2 or unknown spiritual languages as in 1 Corinthians 14.

MEMORY VERSE: "What is it then? I will pray with the spirit, and I will pray with the understanding also: I will sing with the spirit, and I will sing with the understanding also" (1 Corinthians 14:15).

LESSON AIM: By the end of the lesson, your students will: discover how the Holy Spirit helped people communicate in both different native and spiritual languages; empathize with people in situations in which language inhibits communication; and find ways to communicate with diverse people to foster common understanding.

TEACHER PREPARATION

MATERIALS NEEDED: Quarterly Commentary/Teacher Manual, Adult Quarterly, Adult resources—charts, worksheets, and other teaching tools, paper, pens, pencils, Bibles (several different versions)

OTHER MATERIALS NEEDED / TEACHER'S NOTES:

____

____

LESSON OVERVIEW

LIFE NEED FOR TODAY'S LESSON

Communication is important as believers work together through worship, praise, and programs to build the church.

BIBLE LEARNING

Believers affirm the reality of spiritual gifts.

BIBLE APPLICATION

Believers participate with the church in recognizing and celebrating its founding on the day of Pentecost.

STUDENTS' RESPONSES

Students will affirm the importance of mutual edification in church life.

LESSON SCRIPTURE

ACTS 2:1–7, 12; 1 CORINTHIANS 14:13–19, KJV

1 And when the day of Pentecost was fully come, they were all with one accord in one place.

2 And suddenly there came a sound from

ACTS 2:1–7, 12; 1 CORINTHIANS 14:13–19, NIV

1 When the day of Pentecost came, they were all together in one place.

2 Suddenly a sound like the blowing of a violent wind came from heaven and filled

heaven as of a rushing mighty wind, and it filled all the house where they were sitting.

3 And there appeared unto them cloven tongues like as of fire, and it sat upon each of them.

4 And they were all filled with the Holy Ghost, and began to speak with other tongues, as the Spirit gave them utterance.

5 And there were dwelling at Jerusalem Jews, devout men, out of every nation under heaven.

6 Now when this was noised abroad, the multitude came together, and were confounded, because that every man heard them speak in his own language.

7 And they were all amazed and marvelled, saying one to another, Behold, are not all these which speak Galilaeans?

2:12 And they were all amazed, and were in doubt, saying one to another, What meaneth this?

1 Corinthians 14:13 Wherefore let him that speaketh in an unknown tongue pray that he may interpret.

14 For if I pray in an unknown tongue, my spirit prayeth, but my understanding is unfruitful.

15 What is it then? I will pray with the spirit, and I will pray with the understanding also: I will sing with the spirit, and I will sing with the understanding also.

16 Else when thou shalt bless with the spirit, how shall he that occupieth the room of the unlearned say Amen at thy giving of thanks, seeing he understandeth not what thou sayest?

the whole house where they were sitting.

3 They saw what seemed to be tongues of fire that separated and came to rest on each of them.

4 All of them were filled with the Holy Spirit and began to speak in other tongues as the Spirit enabled them.

5 Now there were staying in Jerusalem God-fearing Jews from every nation under heaven.

6 When they heard this sound, a crowd came together in bewilderment, because each one heard their own language being spoken.

7 Utterly amazed, they asked: "Aren't all these who are speaking Galileans?

2:12 Amazed and perplexed, they asked one another, "What does this mean?"

1 Corinthians 14:13 For this reason the one who speaks in a tongue should pray that they may interpret what they say.

14 For if I pray in a tongue, my spirit prays, but my mind is unfruitful.

15 So what shall I do? I will pray with my spirit, but I will also pray with my understanding; I will sing with my spirit, but I will also sing with my understanding.

16 Otherwise when you are praising God in the Spirit, how can someone else, who is now put in the position of an inquirer, say "Amen" to your thanksgiving, since they do not know what you are saying?

17 You are giving thanks well enough, but no one else is edified.

18 I thank God that I speak in tongues more than all of you.

17 For thou verily givest thanks well, but the other is not edified.

18 I thank my God, I speak with tongues more than ye all:

19 Yet in the church I had rather speak five words with my understanding, that by my voice I might teach others also, than ten thousand words in an unknown tongue.

19 But in the church I would rather speak five intelligible words to instruct others than ten thousand words in a tongue.

LIGHT ON THE WORD

The phenomenon of speaking in tongues is prominent in the book of Acts and refers to the ability to speak in a known or unknown language. This was first seen at Pentecost, where the twelve apostles experienced the empowerment of the Holy Spirit and praised God in different languages that were understood by the pilgrims residing in Jerusalem at the time. The ability to speak in tongues is also referenced throughout Acts and the book of 1 Corinthians. In these instances, it refers to the ability to speak to God in a language unknown to man. Some in the congregation were not only gifted by the Spirit to speak in unknown tongues, but also gifted to give the interpretation of what was said.

TEACHING THE BIBLE LESSON

LIFE NEED FOR TODAY'S LESSON

AIM: Students will learn that communication is important as believers work together through worship, praise, and programs to build the church.

INTRODUCTION

Chaos in Communication

After the chapter on love, Paul turns to the place of tongues in the church gathering. Some had prided themselves on speaking in tongues. This led them to cause chaos in their gatherings. Those who were new to the church could not understand what was going on. Paul attempts to guide the Corinthian church in how to use the gift of tongues and what gifts they ought to be seeking. His main goal in the whole matter is that any contribution a member makes in the church would be strengthened and encouraged.

BIBLE LEARNING

AIM: Students will affirm the reality of spiritual gifts.

I. A CASE OF CLEAR COMMUNICATION (Acts 2:1–7, 12)

At the beginning of Acts, we see God's heart communicate clearly His salvation to all the nations. The apostles were told to wait in Jerusalem until they were empowered by the Holy Spirit. The sign of this was tongues of fire resting over their heads. We do not know whether these tongues actually consisted of real fire or were just a metaphor. Regardless, these tongues of fire were a symbol of the fact that the apostles were empowered to speak for the Lord. Immediately they began to praise

God as "the Spirit gave them utterance," and the crowd of Jewish pilgrims who had come from all over for the feast of Pentecost heard them speak in their own language (**vv. 4–6**).

The Outpouring of the Spirit (verses 1–7, 12)

1 And when the day of Pentecost was fully come, they were all with one accord in one place.

The narrative opens with a reference to the time and place of the coming of the Holy Spirit. The time is precise: "when the day of Pentecost was fully come." The word "Pentecost" (Gk. *pentekoste*, **pen-tay-kos-TAY**) literally means "fiftieth," because it was celebrated 50 days after Passover. It was the second of the three great Jewish annual festivals (**Deuteronomy 16:16**), falling between Passover and the Feast of Tabernacles, or Feast of Booths. Pentecost was also called the Feast of Weeks because it was held seven weeks after Passover (**Exodus 34:22**). It had a double meaning. Pentecost celebrated the end of the grain harvest and was also known as the Feast of Harvest (**Exodus 23:16**). In later Judaism (toward the 1st century A.D.), it was observed as the anniversary of the giving of the Law to Moses at Sinai. It is possible to draw out from the two meanings of Pentecost a double symbolism for Christians. The coming of the Holy Spirit occurred 50 days after the crucifixion and resurrection of Christ, marking the beginning of the new covenant and the harvesting of the firstfruits of the Christian missionary enterprise.

The Day of Pentecost "was fully come" (Gk. *sumpleroo*, **soom-play-RAH-oh**), which means that it was in the process of fulfillment or coming to an end.

The expression "in one place" probably refers to their usual meeting place somewhere within the Temple area, such as one of the many rooms or halls of the Temple (cf. **Acts 2:46; 3:11; 5:12**).

2 And suddenly there came a sound from heaven as of a rushing mighty wind, and it filled all the house where they were sitting.

The place where the disciples were gathered was suddenly filled with what sounded like "a rushing mighty wind" from Heaven. The word "wind" (Gk. *pnoe*, **pno-AY**) is frequently used in the Bible as a symbol of the Spirit (**1 Kings 19:11; Ezekiel 37:9-14; John 3:8**). The Spirit came upon them with great power. This was the power promised by Jesus for witnessing (**Luke 24:49; Acts 1:8**).

3 And there appeared unto them cloven tongues like as of fire, and it sat upon each of them.

The disciples not only heard the sound of a rushing mighty wind, but they saw "tongues like as of fire." The word "fire" (Gk. *pur*, **poor**) also denotes the divine presence (**Exodus 3:2**) and the Spirit who purifies and sanctifies (cf. **Matthew 3:11; Luke 3:16**).

The expression "cloven tongues" (Gk. *diamerizo glossa*, **dee-ah-meh-REED-zo GLOH-sah**) refers to tongues dividing, distributing, or parting themselves. Then the tongues "sat" (Gk. *kathizo*, **kah-THEED-zo**) on the disciples. The verb is singular, giving the understanding that a tongue of fire sat on each person.

4 And they were all filled with the Holy Ghost, and began to speak with other tongues, as the Spirit gave them utterance.

The disciples were all filled with the Holy Spirit (cf. **Acts 4:8; 13:9; Ephesians 5:18**), and they "began to speak with other tongues." Speaking in tongues is also called glossolalia, from two Greek words: *glossa* (**GLOH-sah**), tongue, and *laleo* (**lah-LEH-oh**), to speak. It was not an unparalleled manifestation (cf. **Acts 10:46; 19:6**). It was also a spiritual gift that was highly valued by the church of Corinth (**1 Corinthians 12–14**). Without denying that it was a manifestation of the Holy Spirit, Paul denounced the undue importance that some people of the Corinthian church attached to it. The glossolalia in Corinth was uttered in speech that could not be understood until someone present received the corresponding spiritual gift of interpretation. Speaking in tongues is similar to the prophetic utterances of people possessed by the Spirit of God in the Old Testament (**Numbers 11:25–29; 1 Samuel 10:5–6**).

In **Acts 2**, however, the disciples were speaking in tongues that were completely different from their native languages, as prompted by the Holy Spirit. The words they were speaking were immediately recognized by immigrants and visitors from many parts of the world. The following verse (**v. 5**) shows that the purpose of the Spirit-inspired glossolalia was to symbolize the universality of the Gospel (**Acts 1:8**). It shows that people from all nations will be brought into a unity of understanding through the preaching of the Gospel in the power of the Holy Spirit.

5 And there were dwelling at Jerusalem Jews, devout men, out of every nation under heaven.

The verb translated as "were dwelling" (Gk. *katoikeo*, **kat-oy-KEH-oh**) is used for temporary dwellers who came for Pentecost. They had come from "every nation under heaven" to stay in Jerusalem near the Temple within the city walls as permanent residents. The expression "every nation under heaven" also stresses the international nature of the crowd. The crowd was composed of permanent residents of Jerusalem and visitors who had come to celebrate the feast.

6 Now when this was noised abroad, the multitude came together, and were confounded, because that every man heard them speak in his own language.

They "were confounded" (Gk. *suncheo*, **soon-KHEH-oh**) as they heard loud praises to God uttered by the disciples in the indigenous languages and dialects of their native lands. The word "language" (Gk. *dialektos*, **dee-AH-lek-toce**) means the language of a particular nation or region. It can refer to a whole language or even dialects within a language. The diversity of language is stressed here and in the following verses (**v. 7–12**). The desire of God is that every tribe and nation will be reached with the Gospel (cf. **1 Timothy 2:4–7; Revelation 5:9**).

7 And they were all amazed and marvelled, saying one to another, Behold, are not all these which speak Galilaeans?

They were "amazed" (Gk. *existemi*, **ex-IS-tay-mee**), which literally means to be beside oneself or out of place, denoting an overwhelming surprise. They "marvelled" (Gk. *thaumazo*, **thow-MAHD-zo**), denoting a continuing wonder and speculation as they heard loud praises to God uttered in languages and dialects other than the speakers' native Galilaean. The Galilaeans used a peculiar dialect that distinguished them from other Judeans (cf. **Matthew 26:73; Mark 14:70**).

12 And they were all amazed, and were in doubt, saying one to another, What meaneth this?

Again we see that the visitors present on the Day of Pentecost are amazed. This verse also adds that they were in doubt (Gk. *diaporeo*, **dee-ah-poh-REH-oh**). This word means to be totally at a loss. They were at a loss for an explanation of the events they were experiencing. As a result, they ask themselves "What meaneth (Gk. *thelo*, **THEH-lo**) this?" Thelo can specifically mean to intend or to purpose.

In essence, the travelers are asking, "What is the purpose of our being able to hear and see this phenomenon?"

LIGHT ON THE WORD

Speaking to Be Understood

The Jewish pilgrims had two questions regarding this encounter. First they questioned that the apostles, who were not educated, could speak in their language. "Behold, are not all these which speak Galilaeans?" they asked with amazement. The apostles were from Galilee and the Galilean accent was famous among the Jews as being distinctive (cf. **Matthew 26:73; Mark 14:70**). Hearing Galileans speak their language clearly and fluently excited them and must have aroused their curiosity. The next question they asked was "What meaneth this?" (**v. 12**). To hear untrained Galileans speak in Persian, Arabic, Egyptian, Libyan, and a multitude of other languages had to mean something. This was a case of God using the apostles to cross language barriers to communicate to humanity. Through this scene at Pentecost, we see a demonstration of clear communication and also the need to take it a step further as the Jewish pilgrims needed to have this event interpreted for them.

II. THE CALL TO CLEAR COMMUNICATION (1 Corinthians 14:13–15)

Years later, in the Corinthian church, Paul discusses the need for clear communication. The church had been blessed with miraculous gifts, including the ability to speak in unknown tongues. From the text here and in **1 Corinthians 12**, we can see that this ability to speak in unknown tongues was different from what the apostles experienced at Pentecost. These were tongues that were not known and needed miraculous or supernatural interpretation (**1 Corinthians 12:10, 14:5, 27**). The Corinthians had placed a higher priority on speaking in tongues than other gifts that brought more clarity and built up the whole church. They were more interested in gifts that built up and elevated self.

Order for Speaking in Tongues (verses 13–15)

13 Wherefore let him that speaketh in an unknown tongue pray that he may interpret.

The "wherefore" (Gk. *dio*, **dee-OH**) connects this sentence with Paul's preceding thoughts. Since those who earnestly desire spiritual gifts must seek to edify the church, then the one speaking in an unknown tongue must pray for God to give him or her the interpretation of what he or she is saying. The word for tongue here is glossa, the generic word for tongue or language. This is translated as "unknown" tongue because the one speaking it does not need to study a known foreign language to understand what is being said. Instead, the one speaking in a tongue is encouraged to pray or ask for divine help to interpret what he or she is saying.

14 For if I pray in an unknown tongue, my spirit prayeth, but my understanding is unfruitful. 15 What is it then? I will pray with the spirit, and I will pray with the understanding also: I will sing with the spirit, and I will sing with the understanding also.

Next Paul describes the dynamics of unknown tongues. When worshipers speak in unknown tongues, their spirit or inner self is praying. At the same time, they have not understood anything that they have said. The word "unfruitful" is *akarpos* (Gk. **AH-kar-poce**), and means to be barren or not yielding what it ought to yield. Paul is saying that speaking in tongues is unproductive as far as the mind's understanding is concerned.

Paul then states his own approach to unknown

tongues. He will pray "with the spirit," another way of saying praying in unknown tongues. This will be accompanied by praying with understanding as well. He also states that he will sing in unknown tongues, but with understanding.

SEARCH THE SCRIPTURES

QUESTION 1

What did Paul tell the Corinthians to pray for when they spoke in unknown tongues?

LIGHT ON THE WORD

What are You Saying?

Paul instructs the Corinthians that whoever speak in tongues needs to pray for interpretation. He further explains that when a person speaks in an unknown tongue, their spirit prays, but their mind has no idea what is being communicated. Here we see Paul is not forbidding speaking in tongues, but regulating it so that the church would benefit from clarity in communication.

III. THE CONVICTION FOR CLEAR COMMUNICATION (vv. 16–19)

Paul's point is that the gift of tongues is not worth anything unless it brings about clarity in communication. They can speak in unknown tongues in a public meeting, and it wouldn't help anyone but themselves.

Sharing for Understanding (verses 16–19)

16 Else when thou shalt bless with the spirit, how shall he that occupieth the room of the unlearned say Amen at thy giving of thanks, seeing he understandeth not what thou sayest? 17 For thou verily givest thanks well, but the other is not edified.

The results of speaking in unknown tongues are obvious. The one who is a novice or unlearned in the Christian faith will not be able to understand what is being said. Paul uses the word *eulogeo* (Gk. **ehoo-loh-GEH-oh**), which means to speak well of someone or something. It is commonly translated as bless. Here he is saying that the person speaking in tongues is doing a good thing by speaking well of God, but at the same time, it is not good for the assembly or worship gathering when no one understands.

18 I thank my God, I speak with tongues more than ye all: 19 Yet in the church I had rather speak five words with my understanding, that by my voice I might teach others also, than ten thousand words in an unknown tongue.

Here we see that Paul participated in speaking in unknown tongues. In order to drive the point home to the Corinthian church, he boasts that he speaks in tongues more than all of them. Although this is the case, he would rather speak a small amount with understanding so that he can teach others, than ten thousand words in an unknown tongue which neither he nor his hearers could understand. The word for ten thousand (Gk. *murios*, **MOO-ree-oce**) was the largest number the Greek language of the time had. Paul uses this hyperbole to show just how much he desired communication in the church to be intelligible.

SEARCH THE SCRIPTURES

QUESTION 2

What is the goal of our communication in a church setting?

LIGHT ON THE WORD

Good Communication is a Necessity

Paul then takes it a step further and makes it more personal by stating his own experience of speaking in tongues. He says he thanks God that he speaks in tongues more than them all.

Here we see Paul again not advocating for abolishing this practice. He says that this is part of his own experience of the Holy Spirit. The point is not to stop speaking in tongues, but to encourage clear communication when the people of God are gathered together.

BIBLE APPLICATION

AIM: Students will participate with the church in recognizing and celebrating its founding on the day of Pentecost.

There are approximately 6,500 languages in the world, not counting unspoken languages or codes. There is also the particular dialect and slang of numerous subcultures. With all of these different languages, it is not hard to believe that we live in a world where people do not understand one another. As followers of Christ, we are called to bridge the language gap. Whether it is a spoken language or what some may call "Christianese," we are called to interpret and make clear what God wants to say to the world. If people cannot understand at first, it is our responsibility to relay God's message so that they can receive it.

STUDENTS' RESPONSES

AIM: Students will affirm the importance of mutual edification in church life.

We as Christians have our own theological and church language. This week, make a list of those words or phrases that would sound strange to those who have no understanding of the Christian faith. Write out ways that you can communicate these concepts to others who are not in the church without losing the meaning.

PRAYER

Dear Lord, help us to listen, appreciate, learn, and affirm one another. Let us be cautious and respectful of those who speak or listen through different cultural and language experiences. May we strive to work together in unity and love. In Jesus' Name we pray. Amen.

HOW TO SAY IT

Galileans. ga-lih-**LEE**-ins.

Occupieth. ok-yu-**PIE**-ith.

PREPARE FOR NEXT SUNDAY

Read **1 Corinthians 13** and study "The Greatest Gift is Love."

DAILY HOME BIBLE READINGS

MONDAY
Made You Hear God's Voice
(Deuteronomy 4:32–40)

TUESDAY
A Small Member, Great Boasting
(James 3:1–5)

WEDNESDAY
All Languages, One Loud Voice
(Revelation 7:9–12)

THURSDAY
We Hear in Our Own Languages
(Acts 2:8–13)

FRIDAY
They Shall Prophesy
(Acts 2:14–21)

SATURDAY
Excel in Your Gifts
(1 Corinthians 14:6–12)

SUNDAY
Building Up Others
(Acts 2:1–7, 12; 1 Corinthians 14:13–19)

Sources:

Hays, Richard B. *First Corinthians: Interpretation, A Bible Commentary for Teaching and Preaching*. Louisville, KY: John Knox. 1997.

Henry, Matthew. *Matthew Henry's Commentary on the Whole Bible: Complete and Unabridged in One Volume*. Peabody, MA: Hendrickson, 1994.

Prime, Derek. *Opening Up 1 Corinthians*. Opening Up Commentary. Leominster, UK: Day One Publications, 2005.

Utley, Robert James. *Paul's Letters to a Troubled Church: I and II Corinthians*. Study Guide Commentary Series, vol. 6. Marshall, TX: Bible Lessons International, 2002.

COMMENTS / NOTES:

THE GREATEST GIFT IS LOVE

BIBLE BASIS: 1 CORINTHIANS 13

BIBLE TRUTH: Love is needed to fully achieve the benefit of all spiritual gifts.

MEMORY VERSE: "And now abideth faith, hope, charity, these three; but the greatest of these is charity" (1 Corinthians 13:13).

LESSON AIM: By the end of this lesson, your students will: explore the meaning of love as seen in 1 Corinthians 13; feel appreciation for one another in love; and seek a variety of ways to express love.

TEACHER PREPARATION

MATERIALS NEEDED: Quarterly Commentary/Teacher Manual, Adult Quarterly, Adult resources—charts, worksheets, and other teaching tools, paper, pens, pencils, Bibles (several different versions)

OTHER MATERIALS NEEDED / TEACHER'S NOTES:

____

____

LESSON OVERVIEW

LIFE NEED FOR TODAY'S LESSON

Love is the primary requirement for societies attempting to make a dramatic influence on the world around them.

BIBLE LEARNING

Believers affirm with Paul that love is the guarantee of the manifestations of the Spirit for the building up of the church.

BIBLE APPLICATION

Christians experience love as the difference in living a faithful life of obedience to God.

STUDENTS' RESPONSES

Believers develop spiritually in their ability to express and live in Christian love.

LESSON SCRIPTURE

1 CORINTHIANS 13, KJV

1 Though I speak with the tongues of men and of angels, and have not charity, I am become as sounding brass, or a tinkling cymbal.

2 And though I have the gift of prophecy, and understand all mysteries, and all knowledge; and though I have all faith, so that I could remove mountains, and have not charity, I am nothing.

1 CORINTHIANS 13, NIV

1 If I speak in the tongues of men or of angels, but do not have love, I am only a resounding gong or a clanging cymbal.

2 If I have the gift of prophecy and can fathom all mysteries and all knowledge, and if I have a faith that can move mountains, but do not have love, I am nothing.

3 And though I bestow all my goods to feed the poor, and though I give my body to be burned, and have not charity, it profiteth me nothing.

4 Charity suffereth long, and is kind; charity envieth not; charity vaunteth not itself, is not puffed up,

5 Doth not behave itself unseemly, seeketh not her own, is not easily provoked, thinketh no evil;

6 Rejoiceth not in iniquity, but rejoiceth in the truth;

7 Beareth all things, believeth all things, hopeth all things, endureth all things.

8 Charity never faileth: but whether there be prophecies, they shall fail; whether there be tongues, they shall cease; whether there be knowledge, it shall vanish away.

9 For we know in part, and we prophesy in part.

10 But when that which is perfect is come, then that which is in part shall be done away.

11 When I was a child, I spake as a child, I understood as a child, I thought as a child: but when I became a man, I put away childish things.

12 For now we see through a glass, darkly; but then face to face: now I know in part; but then shall I know even as also I am known.

13 And now abideth faith, hope, charity, these three; but the greatest of these is charity.

3 If I give all I possess to the poor and give over my body to hardship that I may boast, but do not have love, I gain nothing.

4 Love is patient, love is kind. It does not envy, it does not boast, it is not proud.

5 It does not dishonor others, it is not self-seeking, it is not easily angered, it keeps no record of wrongs.

6 Love does not delight in evil but rejoices with the truth.

7 It always protects, always trusts, always hopes, always perseveres.

8 Love never fails. But where there are prophecies, they will cease; where there are tongues, they will be stilled; where there is knowledge, it will pass away.

9 For we know in part and we prophesy in part,

10 but when completeness comes, what is in part disappears.

11 When I was a child, I talked like a child, I thought like a child, I reasoned like a child. When I became a man, I put the ways of childhood behind me.

12 For now we see only a reflection as in a mirror; then we shall see face to face. Now I know in part; then I shall know fully, even as I am fully known.

13 And now these three remain: faith, hope and love. But the greatest of these is love.

LIGHT ON THE WORD

The city of Corinth is a major trade city located on an isthmus that connects mainland Greece with the Peloponnesian peninsula. Its location made Corinth a bustling trade and cultural center. As a result, there was a mixture of religious beliefs in Corinth. During the time in which Paul wrote, Corinth was a Roman colony. The ancient city of Corinth, known for its artistry, wealth, and rampant sexual immorality, was destroyed in 146 B.C. It was reestablished by Rome in 44 B.C. Under Roman rule, Corinth continued to be known for its wanton sexuality.

TEACHING THE BIBLE LESSON

LIFE NEED FOR TODAY'S LESSON

AIM: Students will accept that love is the primary requirement for societies attempting to make a dramatic influence on the world around them.

INTRODUCTION

The Divine Love

First Corinthians 13 is often misinterpreted, which leads to improper application. This is not a mere ode to the virtues of love. Paul is using these words to address specific issues in the Corinthian church: selfishness, division, abuse of gifts, and envying of others' gifts.

The Greek term for love used in this chapter is *agape* (**ah-GAH-pay**). This word is closely associated with the Hebrew word *khesed* (**KHESS-ed**) which refers to God's covenant love for His people. Because of this association, agape became a key word for describing God's character and took on the meaning of a divine love that is deeply loyal. Believers should emulate this love, and Paul highlights its importance in this letter to the Corinthians.

BIBLE LEARNING

AIM: Students will affirm with Paul that love is the guarantee of the manifestations of the Spirit for the building up of the church.

I. LOVE IS SUPERIOR TO OTHER SPIRITUAL GIFTS (1 Corinthians 13:1–3)

Paul begins by demonstrating the superiority of love. The Corinthians held eloquence in especially high esteem and were somewhat preoccupied with the gift of tongues. However, even the most sophisticated gift of tongues, speaking the languages of men and angels, is just noise if not exercised in love.

The Necessity of Love (verses 1–3)

1 Though I speak with the tongues of men and of angels, and have not charity, I am become as sounding brass, or a tinkling cymbal.

The word "charity" here means love, heavenly love, affection, goodwill, or benevolence. Agape love means the decentering of the ego. The person is no longer the center of his or her universe or ultimate concern; "the other" is now in the center. Love is a radical reordering of priorities and ultimate values. Without love, everything we do is for our own self-glorification and benefit. With love, what we do is for God and others. Love is not a feeling; it is what we do for others without regard for self. It is partaking in the very nature of God, because He is love (**1 John 4:8**).

Spirit-inspired speech spoken in ecstasy, different languages, brilliant human rhetoric, or superhuman entities means nothing if it is not of God. Any intention whose source is not the God of love is in vain. If the Spirit of God animates the body, love holds it together. Tongues without love are only noise.

2 And though I have the gift of prophecy, and understand all mysteries, and all knowledge; and though I have all faith, so that I could remove mountains, and have not charity, I am nothing.

The gift of prophecy or preaching is mere entertainment or scolding and has no effect if the speaker is not motivated by love. The gift of intellectual accomplishment without love leads to contempt and snobbery. The gift of great faith that achieves or sacrifices much can lead to false pride. Without love, none of these gifts edifies the Body of Christ or pleases God.

3 And though I bestow all my goods to feed the poor, and though I give my body to be burned, and have not charity, it profiteth me nothing.

Benevolence and even self-sacrifice done with ill intention or with the wrong spirit might as well not be done at all. To give out of obligation, self-promotion, or even contempt is worse than not giving at all. It does not build up the Body of Christ. Likewise, to seek persecution or make sacrifice for selfish intentions may very well hurt one's cause more than it helps.

Paul has made it clear that agape love is more important than spiritual gifts. In this passage, he explains exactly what agape is. Love is that which connects us to God and one another. Like the blood that circulates through the body's veins carrying oxygen and nutrients from cell to cell, so love also brings us into a life-giving relationship to God and one another.

LIGHT ON THE WORD

Love is Essential

The use and exercise of the other spiritual gifts is pointless without love. Prophecy, though a desirable gift (**14:1**), is useless without love. Knowledge of the deepest mysteries of God has no value apart from love. Faith, even when great enough to move mountains, is nothing apart from love. Likewise, boundless generosity is not profitable without love. Willingness to suffer, even to the point of martyrdom, is worthless in the absence of love.

Love is essential. Spiritual gifts are nothing without love; they can even be destructive when not practiced in love. Love is what enriches the gifts and gives them value. Therefore, spiritual gifts must be founded and exercised only in genuine love for God and His people.

II. CHARACTERISTICS OF LOVE (vv. 4–7)

In the King James Version, *agape* is translated "charity." When we think of charity, we usually think of giving to others, an active expression of Christian love. This was not the limit of the meaning of "charity" in King James' time, however. Back then, "charity" was understood as it related to the similar word "cherish." To show charity to someone was to show that you cherished them. This includes, but also goes far beyond, giving alms, as Paul further explains.

Love is incompatible with ill will. It does not seek its own honor, profit, or pleasure. Instead, love focuses on the well-being of others. It is not quarrelsome or vindictive. Instead, love "thinketh no evil," meaning that it keeps no account of wrongs.

Love is Amazing (verses 4–7)

4 Charity suffereth long, and is kind; charity envieth not; charity vaunteth not itself, is not puffed up,

Love "suffereth long" (Gk. *makrothumeo*, **mah-kro-thoo-MEH-oh**), or endures patiently the errors, weaknesses, and even meanness of people. Love makes us slow to anger or repay hurt for hurt. It will suffer many things for the sake of the relationship. Love is kind (Gk.

chresteuomai, **khray-STEH-oo-oh-meye**); it shows kindness whenever possible. Love does not "envieth" (Gk. *zeloo*, **zay-LAH-oh**); it does not earnestly covet another's good fortune. Love does not get angry at another's success. Love does not "vaunteth" (Gk. *perpereuomai*, **per-per-EHOO-oh-meye**), or brag, about oneself. It is not boastful or stuck up. Love does not have a swollen head and is not "puffed up" (Gk. *phusioo*, **foo-see-AH-oh**), snobbish, or arrogant. A loving person esteems others higher than themselves.

5 Doth not behave itself unseemly, seeketh not her own, is not easily provoked, thinketh no evil;

Love is never rude; it is full of grace and charm. It does not go around hurting others' feelings. It always uses tact and politeness whenever possible. Love never demands its rights, but seeks its responsibilities toward others. It is not self-centered or self-assertive. Love does not fly off the handle. It does not lose its temper. It is not easily exasperated at people. Love does not keep the books on the wrong done to it. Love does not keep score in order to repay wrong for wrong. It forgives the evil that people do to it. It does not carry a grudge.

6 Rejoiceth not in iniquity, but rejoiceth in the truth;

Love does not like to hear about the moral failures of others. It does not get pleasure out of the misfortune of others. There is a sick joy from witnessing or hearing gossip about the misdeeds of others. We often judge our own righteousness and well-being as measured by the failings of others. However, love is happy to hear the truth (or what is right), no matter how painful. Love rejoices when what is true, correct, and righteous wins the day regardless of how that may impact it directly.

7 Beareth all things, believeth all things, hopeth all things, endureth all things.

If God is love and He created all things good, then love also is the progenitor of all things good. Love is our participation in God's nature. Thus, love is the only foundation for Christian community and relationships. Love, like God, is eternal. It "beareth" (Gk. *stego*, **STEH-goh**) the errors and faults of others. Love does not expose one's weakness because it does not rejoice in the misfortune of others. Yet it does not excuse sin or wrongdoing, because it equally rejoices in truth. Instead, as Christ bore our sin on the Cross, we take on the weakness and faults of others as though they were our own.

Love believes the best, trusts in the object of its love, has confidence in him or her, and gives credit to the object of love that may not be self-evident except through the eyes of love. Love can bear all things because it believes all things with the special insight that only a loving relationship can bring. Love "hopeth" (Gk. *elpizo*, **el-PID-zo**) with joy, full confidence in eager expectation the salvation of the Lord to come. It bears all things because it believes with only the insight of God the maker, thus it can wait for the true nature of people to reveal itself. Love trusts in the eventual reconciliation with God. It "endureth" (Gk. *hupomeno*, **hoo-po-MEN-oh**) and continues to be present; it does not perish or depart in spite of errors, faults, or wrongs done.

SEARCH THE SCRIPTURES

QUESTION 1

What are some of the characteristics of love?

LIGHT ON THE WORD

Love is Transforming

In **verse 7**, Paul writes that love bears, believes, hopes, and endures all things. His use of language implies that love does these things at all times. Love "beareth all things." It covers and protects. Love "believeth all things." It has faith in others and is always willing to give the benefit of the doubt. Love "hopeth all things." It does not despair, but is always hopeful for the growth and development of other believers. Love "endureth all things." This communicates a strong sense of enduring temptation or testing. Love does not retaliate or reject, but is patient.

Paul highlights the character of love as it should be expressed by Christians. His descriptions of love are active, indicating that love is something one does, not merely an emotion. As Christians who have received the love of God, we are to love others. The indwelling Holy Spirit empowers us to demonstrate this kind of love.

III. LOVE ENDURES (vv. 8–13)

Love surpasses all the other spiritual gifts because they will pass away, but it endures forever. Prophecy, tongues, and knowledge are limited (**v. 9**). Further, a time will come when those gifts will not be necessary. They are given by the Spirit for the building and maturation of the church. We will not need such things in Heaven, but will experience love there.

Love is Forever (verses 8–13)

8 Charity never faileth: but whether there be prophecies, they shall fail; whether there be tongues, they shall cease; whether there be knowledge, it shall vanish away.

Love is eternal; it never comes to an end. It is absolutely permanent. Whereas all the gifts in which the Corinthians pride themselves are transitory at best, love is transcendent. Love is—exists only in and for—relationship, yet is more than the sum of its parts; like life itself, it is always renewed, even in the age to come.

The gifts, on the other hand, have no such guarantee. They were given by the Spirit as instruments to be used in this age. Paul anticipates that these gifts will no longer be needed when the next age occurs, marked by the return of Christ and fulfillment of the reign of God. They will pass away with the old age. Love, on the other hand, is essential, not instrumental; it will never pass away. In contrast, when all prophecy has been fulfilled, tongues will no longer be necessary as a language; signs, missions, and knowledge will vanish because there will be no more mysteries.

9 For we know in part, and we prophesy in part.

Love like God, is complete. On the other hand, we are imperfect creatures who can only comprehend reality—both material and spiritual—in an incomplete manner. Therefore, we can only preach or prophesy in an imperfect and partial way. For Paul, the kingdom of God was near, but not yet. It was not fully revealed in this age, so our knowledge and prophecy of it could only be partial.

10 But when that which is perfect is come, then that which is in part shall be done away.

The "perfect" (Gk. *teleios*, **TEL-ay-os**) maturity or completeness will come with the end of this present, imperfect age and the beginning of the new, perfect age—namely the "eschaton" (Gk. *eschatos*, **ES-khah-toce**, last, uttermost). Paul describes the times the Corinthians lived in as transitory at best. Thus they should not make gods or idols out of the gifts they esteem so highly, because their gifts are both imperfect and temporary.

11 When I was a child, I spake as a child, I understood as a child, I thought as a child: but when I became a man, I put away childish things.

Paul uses the metaphor of the maturing spiritual human being who grows from childhood to adulthood. The spiritual gifts become mere toys or childish things in people who do not love. Paul, who had called the Corinthians "babes in Christ," chided them once again to grow up and put away their toys, in this case, using their gifts for the wrong reasons (**1 Corinthians 3:1**).

12 For now we see through a glass, darkly; but then face to face: now I know in part; but then shall I know even as also I am known.

Mirrors were a primary industry in the city of Corinth. Mirrors made in Corinth were made of finely polished silver and bronze. The image was often concave and distorted, much like the amusement park house of mirrors. Thus we see only dimly through the distorted reflections of our own limited apprehensions. However, when Jesus returns and God makes His dwelling place among His people, we will see face to face (**Revelation 21:22–23**).

When we look through a mirror, we see only a reflection of ourselves and have only a knowledge that is filtered through our senses. However, when we come face-to-face with another, we see clearly, but are also seen. We not only come to know, but also are known by another.

13 And now abideth faith, hope, charity, these three; but the greatest of these is charity.

After everything that has been said, we come to the conclusion of the matter. Spiritual gifts are transient, given to a particular community, for a particular purpose, and for the particular time. It is childish to esteem them too highly. However, by faith we are saved according to the grace of God. In hope, we wait upon the return of Jesus and the coming of the reign of God. All this is due to God's love for us. These are what remain when one matures in Christ.

Love has revealed itself completely in the revelation of Jesus Christ in His life, death, and resurrection. Thus we can love the Holy One. Jesus says, "This is my commandment, That ye love one another, as I have loved you. Greater love hath no man than this, that a man lay down his life for his friends" (**John 15:12–13**). Love is the greatest.

SEARCH THE SCRIPTURES

QUESTION 2

Why is love superior to the other spiritual gifts?

LIGHT ON THE WORD

Imperfect Gifts

Corinth was well known for its bronze artistry and bronze mirrors. Paul's illustration in **verse 12** would have been particularly meaningful for the Corinthians. We exercise our gifts imperfectly. Our knowledge is imperfect, like seeing indirectly, as if through a bronze mirror. However, imperfection will give way to perfection, enabling us to see perfectly.

In the perfection of Heaven, we will experience love eternally. Because love is eternal and is superior to the other spiritual gifts, it is childish to focus on spiritual gifts in the absence of love.

Not only is love superior to the spiritual gifts, but also faith and hope. Just as in Heaven we will no longer need prophecy or tongues, we will also no longer need faith (because we will see God) or hope (because all hopes will be fulfilled; cf. **Romans 8:24**). Since love outlasts all of these good things, it is the greatest.

BIBLE APPLICATION

AIM: Students will experience love as the difference in living a faithful life of obedience to God.

The Holy Sprit is the source of all the spiritual gifts and He decides which gifts each person will have (**1 Corinthians 12:11**). The spiritual gifts are given to strengthen other believers (**1 Corinthians 12:7**), not to gain personal status and position.

The gifts themselves should not be our primary focus. Love is an essential element in the exercise of spiritual gifts. It is good to desire spiritual gifts (**1 Corinthians 14:1**). However, love is superior to every gift. Prophecy, knowledge, and the demonstration of great faith must all reflect a genuine love and affection for people.

Websites and bookstores abound with assessments to help people discover their spiritual gifts. While the understanding and use of spiritual gifts is important, we must always exercise them in love.

STUDENTS' RESPONSES

AIM: Students will develop spiritually in their ability to express and live in Christian love.

Spiritual gifts cannot be effective if not used in love. Grow in your relationship with Christ. Show His love to those around you. Demonstrate the love of God as you use your spiritual gifts to help others grow and mature.

PRAYER

In times like these, Lord, we need to know Your powerful and wonderful love. Thank You for loving us as we grow in loving the church and others. In Jesus' Name we pray. Amen.

HOW TO SAY IT

Vaunteth. **VON**-teth.

Bestow. bi-**STOW**.

PREPARE FOR NEXT SUNDAY

Read **Amos 2:4–8** and study "Judgment on Israel and Judah."

DAILY HOME BIBLE READINGS

MONDAY
Love and the Knowledge of God
(Hosea 6:1–6)

TUESDAY
Abounding in Steadfast Love
(Jonah 3:10–4:11)

WEDNESDAY
Guided by the Spirit
(Galatians 5:19–26)

THURSDAY
Increasing Love for One Another
(2 Thessalonians 1:1–5)

FRIDAY
Love and Steadfastness
(2 Thessalonians 3:1–5)

SATURDAY
Filled with the Fullness of God
(Ephesians 3:14–21)

SUNDAY
Love Never Ends
(1 Corinthians 13)

Sources:

English Standard Version Study Bible. Wheaton, IL: Crossway, 2007.

Henry, Matthew. *Matthew Henry's Commentary on the Whole Bible: Complete and Unabridged in One Volume*. Peabody, MA: Hendrickson, 1994.

Prime, Derek. *Opening Up 1 Corinthians*. Opening Up Commentary. Leominster, UK: Day One Publications, 2005.

Utley, Robert James. *Paul's Letters to a Troubled Church: I and II Corinthians*. Study Guide Commentary Series, vol. 6. Marshall, TX: Bible Lessons International, 2002.

Walvoord, John F., and Roy B. Zuck. *The Bible Knowledge Commentary: An Exposition of the Scriptures*. Dallas Theological Seminary. Wheaton, IL: Victor Books, 1985.

Wiersbe, Warren W. *The Bible Exposition Commentary*. Wheaton, IL: Victor Books, 1996.

TEACHING TECHNIQUES

GOD'S PROPHETS DEMAND JUSTICE

BY EVANGELIST GLENDA WILLIAMS GOODSON, EXECUTIVE DIRECTOR

The Center for African American Church History and Research, Inc., Dallas, Texas

School shootings. Terrorism. Torture and persecution of Christians in North Korea and Sudan. Much, if not all, of the rationale for any negative reactions arise out of a sense of injustice had not been addressed by individuals, the community, the race, or the nation. Both the individual and the country want justice! Humanity, grappling as best they can, takes a secular approach to what really is a problem resulting from sin. As part of the global village, Christians must examine and begin to understand the nature of justice through the lens of what God expects and indeed demands from His people.

This synopsis of the Summer 2015 Annual Commentary, "God's Prophets Demand Justice," develops ideas on inherent individual ideals of justice, modern concepts of social justice, and finally God's definition and revelation of His justice through Old Testament prophets.

Justice as Inherent in the Individual

In creating humankind in His own image, Creator God hardwired within each individual a part of His essence—in thought, emotions, intellect—along with the intrinsic ability to develop a sense of right and wrong. We feel inherently that God's world should be "fair," so within our being we have the capacity to sense good and evil, what is just or unjust.

> *Known unto God are all his works from the beginning of the world (Acts 15:18).*
>
> *Because that which may be known of God is manifest in them; for God hath shewed it unto them (Romans 1:19).*

The significance of God's justice has been shared by individuals from hunter-gatherers who worked together to benefit families, to communities codifying a sense of impartiality for the benefit of the whole.

When one considers the word "justice," the concept of what is fair to all comes to mind. We have all heard toddlers cry out "no fair!" when a toy is taken, for example. Social scientists wished to understand the age a child recognized a sense of fairness and studied infants as young as fifteen months to determine their capacity of fairness. One such study discovered through controlled experiments that some of these infants indeed show a sense of fairness prior to their ability to articulate it either negatively or positively. ("Are We

Born With a Sense of Fairness," Alan Honick with Gordon Orians, December 26, 2012, www.psmag.com/culture/are-we-born-with-a-sense-of-fairness-50925)

By the time we have developed normally as adults, our fair/unfair or justice/injustice radar has been finely attuned so that we accept social mores and act on the norm for our family, culture, community, and nation. On a basic level, we recognize that social justice must be addressed to prevent anarchy or mayhem. The late Jewish author and Holocaust survivor Elie Wiesel summed it up in this way: "There may be times when we are powerless to prevent injustice, but there must never be a time when we fail to protest."

The Modern Development of Social Justice as a Means of World Order in the 21st Century

From a sociological perspective, a working definition of justice is "the view that everyone deserves equal economic, political, and social rights and opportunities" (*Encyclopedia of Social Work*, 20th ed, Terry Mizrahi and Larry E. Davis, eds.: Oxford University Press, 2008). However, the words "social justice" teem with emotional, political, and philosophical points of view depending on the individual or governing body. Definitions include those adopted by social scientists, social workers, socialists, leftists, conservatives, and every ideology in between. In its Preamble, the 1945 United Nations Charter states that the world's nations would work:

> *to reaffirm faith in fundamental human rights, in the dignity and worth of the human person, in the equal rights of men and women and of nations large and small, and*
>
> *to establish conditions under which justice and respect for the obligations arising from treaties and other sources of international law can be maintained, and*
>
> *to promote social progress and better standards of life in larger freedom.*

The statement, of course, fits snugly within the frame of social justice as defined by the United Nations, to wit,

> *an underlying principle for peaceful and prosperous coexistence within and among nations. We uphold the principles of social justice when we promote gender equality or the rights of indigenous peoples and migrants. We advance social justice when we remove barriers that people face because of gender, age, race, ethnicity, religion, culture or disability.*

(World Day of Social Justice, 20 February, www.un.org/en/events/socialjusticeday)

But no matter the noble goals of individuals or world governing bodies, they fall short of achieving the mission. The world's poorest populations grapple with tuberculosis, polio, and other diseases eradicated for decades in the First World, modern-day slaves worldwide are estimated in the millions, and the United Nations estimates that 80 percent of the world's population displaced by war are found in developing countries. In his 2014 World Day of Social Justice Address, United Nations Secretary General Ban Ki-Moon stated, "The gap between the poorest and the wealthiest around the world is wide and growing. … We must do more to empower individuals through decent work, support people through social protection, and ensure the voices of the poor and marginalized are heard." This statement can be confirmed by events such as the 2010 birth of the Arab Spring movement, launched in Tunisia when 26-year-old Mohamed Bouazizi protested inhumane conditions by setting himself on fire in front of a government building. This event set off demonstrations in the Middle East leading to governments toppling like dominoes across the region.

Do we look to governments only when we seek to understand and fashion our lives in a fecund manner? Or are individuals responsible, not only to God, but also to their fellow human beings to act justly when confronting issues concerning the poor, the fatherless, the innocent who are incarcerated, and the otherwise marginalized among us? In America, does empowerment give government a right to play the role of Robin Hood, to take from the rich in the form of taxes and give to the poor through social assistance? What role does the 21st century Christian or Christian church play in defining and demanding justice for all based on Old and New Testament doctrine?

God Defines Justice and Proclaims It Through His Prophets

To properly define justice, we must turn to Creator God. He called men and women to speak for Him as prophets. Through His Old Testament prophets, we first hear God's heart concerning the subject. The Word of the Lord was revealed to the prophet (1 Samuel 3:21; Ezekiel 18:1; Zephaniah 1:1), after which the prophet spoke in the Word of the Lord (1 Kings 20:35; Isaiah 28:14), and saw the Word that God sent performed (2 Kings 1:17; 2 Chronicles 6:10). Some prophets, as in the case of Jeremiah, risked their lives to proclaim the Word of the Lord.

God is a just God, and in His divine order, He demands justice. Justice is at the core of the human approach to community. The Word of justice the prophets proclaimed was meant to provide equity for the rights of others (between rich and poor, toward strangers, in business dealings, and through a fair court system).

Each time the nation of Israel fell short, God called His people back to Himself through the prophet. In Psalms, the Temple poet/prophet Asaph admonishes rulers that judges will be judged, providing a good explanation of what God expects of the household of faith:

> *How long will ye judge unjustly, and accept the persons of the wicked? Selah. Defend the poor and fatherless: do justice to the afflicted and needy. Deliver the poor and needy: rid them out of the hand of the wicked (Psalm 82:2–4).*

The summer lessons provide further insight into how we should conduct ourselves with justice by examining God's heart through the prophets Amos, Micah, Isaiah, Jeremiah,

Ezekiel, Zechariah, and Malachi. Examination of the prophet's words that both warn and comfort will assist us in our 21st century sensibilities to respond to real and urgent demands from God to impact our world for His glory.

In Unit 1, "Amos Rails Against Injustice," the prophet Amos (Heb. *'Amos)* is called to reform the nation. Born in the nation of Judah, Amos prophesied to the nations around Israel. More telling is that he took God's people to task by proclaiming the Word of the Lord during the reigns of the wicked King Jeroboam II of Israel and Uzziah in Judah. His name is related to the Hebrew for "carry" or "burden." It was his burden to move out of his occupation as a shepherd and enter into covenant with God to warn His people that the Lord's mercy toward them was near an end. Amos told them that God sees. This sentiment resonates throughout Scripture.

> *The eyes of the LORD are in every place, beholding the evil and the good (Proverbs 15:3).*
>
> *If thou seest the oppression of the poor, and violent perverting of judgment and justice in a province, marvel not at the matter: for he that is higher than the highest regardeth; and there be higher than they (Ecclesiastes 5:8).*

But the land was prosperous, and who was Amos? He did not have the pedigree or distinction of being related to any prophets! Yet God called him to denounce the wealthy who gained their prosperity by robbing the poor. They were rich in material goods but were poor—they lacked justice, had forsaken mercy, and disregarded those who lacked the material resources to provide for their families. His warning of Assyrian conquest went unheeded.

Compared to many nations, America is prosperous. America has been blessed with an abundance of wealth, and even the poorest among us have a safety net of protection if they choose to access it. Yet there are discrepancies. Even among American Christian churches, a spirit has crept in that reasons, "Because one prospers, that person is within the will of God." The spirit and insistence of Amos would tell us of God's mercy and warn of His judgment. Amos would say to us that God sees every individual who becomes rich by using selfish schemes or other means to capitalize on people who are desperate. By promising a quick way out of poverty or implementing prophecy schemes, for example, individuals put themselves in danger of God's wrath.

The prophet Micah was a contemporary of Isaiah and prophesied during the reigns of some of Judah's good kings and evil kings—Jotham, Ahaz, and Hezekiah—speaking to both Judah and Israel. His name means "who is like Jehovah?"

Unit 2 is titled "Micah Calls for Justice Among Unjust People." The Lord's people had fallen into grave corruption. The mercy of God raised up yet another prophet who spoke in the Word of the Lord. He was courageous amid a society that ignored God's justice. He spoke against idolatry, covetousness, wicked officials, and the corruption that permeated society.

If individuals override, from the core of their being, the fact that God calls for justice, then anything can happen in society. Children shoot other children in schools, modern-day slavery increases, victims of depression and despair murder their spouses and children, and worse.

> *Righteousness makes a nation great, but sin degrades any people (Proverbs 14:34, CJB).*

Micah was not politically correct. He did not conduct a survey to ascertain what the majority of the people wished to hear. He spoke as an oracle of God, and delineated in detail the scope of the wickedness prevailing in Judah and Israel. As the mouthpiece of the Almighty, he explained what the Lord required and reminded them of God's mercy.

As people of God, we must, like the Old Testament prophets, give prophetic witness to the truth of God's Word. Can any person connected to the Spirit honestly state that God is pleased with all our society's doings? As the salt and light of the nation, are we bold enough to declare that enough is enough? That we will not only pray in our homes and churches but demand high standards in our schools, on our nation's airwaves, and in our communities according to the principles of righteousness as described in Scripture? As Micah was called to confess personal and national sins, saints today should be honest enough to declare that in whatever way we have participated in sin in the past, we will leave those ways and heed the Word of the Lord to avert further national disaster.

The last summer unit offers a cornucopia of evidence from major and minor prophets of the love God has for His people. As we study Unit 3, "Advocates of Justice for All," the prophets Isaiah, Jeremiah, Ezekiel, Zechariah, and Malachi will speak to us of the hope that God offers.

Isaiah is generally regarded as the greatest of the Old Testament prophets because he is preeminently the prophet of redemption. Isaiah means "salvation of Jehovah." He prophesied during the reigns of Uzziah, Jotham, Ahaz, and Hezekiah. In great literary style, the prophet points to a Redeemer whom Jehovah sends to sustain and protect His people.

Jeremiah, called the "Weeping Prophet," was one of the most courageous prophets of the Old Testament. He spoke boldly of the sins of oppression committed by God's people against God's people. Because of his divine commission, he called out kings, denounced their backsliding, and warned them of coming judgment, but also gave them hope that a merciful God gave them choices. For his obedience to God, Jeremiah was rejected by family, neighbors, priests, friends, and the king. He was even threatened with death.

Ezekiel's name means "God strengthens." Probably in his 30s, he was a priest of the most high God. And God called him to be fearless in his proclamation of His Word. His book, like those of Daniel and Revelation, are difficult to understand. In our lesson, though, Ezekiel, after listing the high crimes of oppression and corruption by the people of God, offers a way out through repentance.

One of the most insidious ways a people can fall under the spell of the enemy is through spiritual indifference. True justice among God's people cannot be divorced from how the widow, the fatherless, or the stranger is treated, says the prophet Zechariah. Young men and women can find in the youthful Zechariah an example of faithfulness to God in proclaiming a prophetic witness to their society, that a just God demands a just people to do justly for the people around them.

The last prophet in the unit is the prophet Malachi, "my messenger." Little is known of him except that he was probably a contemporary of Nehemiah. Malachi spoke of the continuing sins of the disobedient people of God. Malachi also said a spiritual reformer was coming prior to the coming of the Lord! The reformer would purify the people, especially the priests, so that offerings would be presented to God in righteousness (justice).

The people to whom Malachi prophesied did not fear God. So they acted with injustice. They would be taken to task for their failure to respond to God's divine love, evidenced in their treatment of their wives, their lackadaisical attitudes in giving sacrifice so that they robbed God, their priests' evil worship and behavior, and their treachery in oppressing their brothers who struggled with daily life. Evil was prevalent, and there was little justice in the land at this time. Their worship had become ritual.

Conclusion

God has work to do with us, and work to do on us. He demands that we examine ourselves to determine whether we address the concerns of justice, not in the way the world responds, but by His standards. He wants to refine, cleanse, and prepare us for His purposes. We cannot be part of the camp that overextends its actions to personal piety and ignores social justice, or the camp that extols social justice to the detriment of personal holiness. God wants us to live balanced, fruitful lives. He wants to raise up prophets who will bring us back to Him through their proclamation of His divine love *and* divine wrath.

DEALING WITH CHILD ABUSE AND NEGLECT IN THE CHURCH

BY ISSD ASSISTANT FIELD REPRESENTATIVE MISSIONARY EVANGELIST CHARLA V. JOHNSON

- A report of child abuse is made every ten seconds
- Child abuse occurs at every socioeconomic level, across ethnic and cultural lines, within all religions and at all levels of education.

The first step in helping abused or neglected children is learning to recognize the signs of child abuse and neglect. The presence of a single sign does not prove child abuse is occurring in a family, but a closer look at the situation may be warranted when these signs appear repeatedly or in combination.

If you do suspect a child is being harmed, reporting your suspicions may protect the child and get help for the family.

Sunday School teachers, especially the women of the church, work closely with our children. Sunday School is a key outreach for children for many churches in the community. It is vital that those working with children recognize signs of physical and mental abuse, including neglect.

RECOGNIZING CHILD ABUSE[1]

There are key signs that may signal the presence of child abuse or neglect.

The Child:

- Shows sudden changes in behavior or school performance
- Has not received help for physical or medical problems brought to the parents' attention
- Has learning problems (or difficulty concentrating) that cannot be attributed to specific physical or psychological causes
- Is always watchful, as though preparing for something bad to happen
- Lacks adult supervision

---

1 Child Welfare Information Gateway. www.childwelfare.gov/pubs/factsheets/signs.cfm

- Is overly compliant, passive, or withdrawn
- Comes to school or other activities early, stays late, and does not want to go home

The Parent:

- Shows little concern for the child
- Denies the existence of—or blames the child for—the child's problems in school or at home
- Asks teachers or other caregivers to use harsh physical discipline if the child misbehaves
- Sees the child as entirely bad, worthless, or burdensome
- Demands a level of physical or academic performance the child cannot achieve
- Looks primarily to the child for care, attention, and satisfaction of emotional needs

The Parent and Child:

- Rarely touch or look at each other
- Consider their relationship entirely negative
- State that they do not like each other

Proper ways of documentation and reporting for incidents should be discussed and a standard operating procedure should be designated for each church. Your plan of operation should include but not be limited to:

- Ways that the children can be helped in an immediate situation
- Understanding the chain of command for reporting incidents
- Possibly requiring online training for those working with children within the local Sunday Schools

Every church should have a background screening for anyone who is going to work within the Sunday School or Children's Church prior to that employee or volunteer's start!

Periodically, every worker in the church that interacts with children should have an in-service and sign-in sheet indicating attendance and comprehension of what will and will not be tolerated. This in-service also helps workers to know what they should do if there is a negative incident that occurs.

The church has to be proactive in the protection of our children. It needs to be accentuated in each church that bad behavior will not be tolerated by volunteers or employees who interact with our children. The church is obligated to involve the authorities in these situations.

Professional educators, childcare workers, social workers, and medical personnel are trained to look for signs of abuse. These persons bear a heavier burden for mandatory reporting according to federal and state law. It is time that the church enhances its safety concerns for our children.

This article is not intended to scrutinize internal workers for bad behavior; however, as a powerful force within the community, your church should not have workers who would destroy the life of a child giving them a distorted image of our Lord and Savior Jesus Christ.

This discussion is to recognize certain types of abuse that may be occurring with our children whether inside or outside the church. If your church has a vital strategic evangelistic Sunday School program, it is possible your ministry may attract a child from the local community who may be suffering with a problem at home that is affecting them negatively.

It is quite disconcerting to think or believe that a child in a supposedly devout Christian home would be suffering abuse, but this taboo subject is set to expose the Enemy wherever he would lurk in or outside the church setting.

Our innocent children need to be protected from all hurt, harm, or danger. Jesus assured us in His Word that "whoso shall offend one of these little ones which believe in me, it were better for him that a millstone were hanged about his neck, and that he were drowned in the depth of the sea" (from Matthew 18:6).

This topic has been presented by a medical professional, Dr. Dwight Owens, a forensic psychologist, through the Women's Directorship during the Sunday School University of the International AIM Convention. The subject is paramount to me because I believe the house of God should be a safe haven for all who come to find refuge.

DEFINITION OF CHILD ABUSE

The Federal Child Abuse Prevention and Treatment Act (CAPTA) (42 U.S.C.A. § 5106g), as amended by the CAPTA Reauthorization Act of 2010, defines child abuse and neglect as, at minimum:

"Any recent act or failure to act on the part of a parent or caretaker which results in death, serious physical or emotional harm, sexual abuse or exploitation"; or

"An act or failure to act which presents an imminent risk of serious harm."

This definition of child abuse and neglect refers specifically to parents and other caregivers. A "child" under this definition generally means a person who is younger than age 18 or who is not an emancipated minor.[2]

MANDATED REPORTING

As mentioned earlier, there are those who are considered mandatory reporters. Although Cain asked the rhetorical question of God "Am I my brother's keeper?" (from Genesis 4:9), because of the love of God in our hearts, we should care for those who cannot care for themselves. Jesus desired the children to come to Him and even used a child as an example for how we are to receive the Kingdom of God (Matthew 19:14; Luke 18:16–17). It is both morally appropriate and legally required for us to protect our children as best we can.

I would suggest that if you suspect a child in a Sunday School class has been abused or the child reports something to you as a teacher, your first course of action should be to ***notify*** your local Sunday School superintendent, the pastor, and the appropriate authorities! The pastor's involvement is critical here to determine policy on what to do. It is always great to pray in situations such as this; however, faith without works is truly dead in this type of incident. Taking what you have seen or heard to your pastor and the appropriate authorities may save a child's life!

What steps should you take to prevent or deal with a bad situation?

Reassure the child that it is okay to talk with you about what is happening to them. Let them know that you are going to help them and assure their protection.

You need to write down incidents you see if you notice that the child is in your class with recurrent injuries. The first incident, unless severe, should coyly be inquired about with the child and the parent if possible. Some children may have health issues like cerebral palsy, or they are very rambunctious and fall a lot. This is why gentle inquiry of the cause of an accident is necessary for both child and parent prior to simply reporting one incident.

An established policy of the "Two Adult Rule"[3] is good for the children and the volunteers working with children. If it is established that there should be two adults at all times to work with or be with children at church-sponsored functions, then all parties involved will feel protected. It is less likely for there to be any false accusations toward the church or its volunteers this way.

---

2 "Definitions of Child Abuse and Neglect in Federal Law," U.S. Department of Health and Human Services. Child Welfare Information Gateway. Administration for Children and Families. 2013, accessed January 16, 2014. https://www.childwelfare.gov/can/defining/federal.cfm.

3 Joy Thornburg Melton, *Safe Sanctuaries: Reducing the Risk of Abuse in the Church for Children and Youth.* (Nashville, TN: Discipleship Resource, 2012), 45.

Churches and individual volunteers may feel like it is overkill to have a criminal background check system in place. However, the safety of our children should never be held hostage by feelings of being hurt or one's integrity being questioned.

Volunteers who want to work with children and have their safety at heart will follow through with the church policy. The church should obtain a written agreement to obtain a background search. Most states have a public website that exposes registered sex offenders. Though this is public record, the church should still alert the volunteer to the background check.

Sources:

Melton, Joy Thornburg. *Safe Sanctuaries: Reducing the Risk of Abuse in the Church for Children and Youth*. Nashville, TN: Discipleship Resource, 2012.

Owens, Dwight, M.D. "Dealing With Child Abuse in the Church" (presentation for Baltimore, MD AIM Convention), July 2013.

Evangelist Charla V. Johnson serves within the International Sunday School Department as the Assistant International Field Representative to Mother Cleolia Penix, Director of Education for Women's Ministry in the International Sunday School University, and Jurisdictional Field Representative for the South Central Georgia Jurisdiction. She is also a license certified physician assistant pursuing her Masters Degree in Theology at Liberty University. Her bishop and pastor is Bishop Norman O. Harper and her supervisor is Mother Edith L. McGrew. She is active in her local Sunday School with an outreach program for day laborers. She has been a Sunday School teacher for the primary through adult classes for over 22 years. Her passions are teaching and writing.

INTERNATIONAL SUNDAY SCHOOL DEPARTMENT

Solutions and Strategies for a Distressed and Troubled World through the Ministry of Sunday School

According to Elmer L. Towns, noted author on the principles of church growth and the ministry of Sunday School, "Sunday School is the ***Reaching***, ***Teaching***, ***Winning*** and ***Nurturing*** arm of the church."[1]

We are living in a deeply distressed and troubled world, and the church can no longer ignore the effects of this world's ills on our people. Both the churched and unchurched are encountering devastating situations in our homes and families, to name a few:

-Drug and substance abuse

-Physical, emotional, and sexual abuse

-Unparalleled gun violence and murders

-Elder abuse and neglect

-Homelessness

-Absence of college-age and young adults (18–29) in our congregations

When members and visitors (both children and adults) walk through our church's doors, the local Sunday School ***can*** and ***must*** be ready to impact their world, giving hope, solutions, and tools to implement change through the Word of God.

This may mean that rather than spending our lesson time on the written lesson for that Sunday, it might be used to educate our students on a particular area of concern to all, i.e., child abuse and neglect or concerns of aging.

1. How does your church currently handle a concern regarding child abuse or neglect?

2. Is there a written policy?

3. Are the seniors in your church aware of the various programs and services available to them?

Sunday School is the one place each week where people gather and meet with the same individuals to learn and grow. Why not use this prime opportunity to educate, enlighten, empower, and in some cases, rescue our students by bringing life and ***solutions*** to their everyday life challenges through … ***THE MINISTRY OF SUNDAY SCHOOL!***

---

1 Dr. Elmer L. Towns, *What Every Sunday School Teacher Should Know: 24 Secrets That Can Help You Change Lives* (Ventura, CA: Gospel Light, 2001).

Sometimes we have to push the envelope or think outside of the box in order for true and total change to take place. It is said that the definition of insanity is ***"doing things the same way, expecting different results."***

Our goal this year, through the following articles, is to initiate the process for creating ***solutions*** and ***strategies***, to assist in ***identifying tools*** that will empower and positively impact lives, stimulate Sunday School and church growth, as well as win our communities to Christ in this ***distressed*** and ***troubled world.***

SOLUTIONS, STRATEGIES, AND TOOLS:

"MOTIVATION: HOW TO INSPIRE AND MOTIVATE OTHERS TO DO THEIR BEST" By Dr. Jeannette H. Donald

One of Sunday School's greatest assets is its volunteer workforce. Men and women who, week after week, give of their wisdom, time, and talent that lives might be changed through the Word of God. We must learn how to continually motivate them to continue working for the Kingdom.

"FORMULATING A WORKING STRATEGY FOR SUNDAY SCHOOL GROWTH" By Evangelist Betty J. Byrd

Our ministries must become and remain current and relevant. Do you know where your Sunday School is going? What will your Sunday School be like in two or three years? If you do not change anything, will the future be any different than the past? One sure way to impact your Sunday School's future is to use an old tool called The Strategic Plan.

"KEYS TO SUCCESSFUL AGING" By Evangelist Jo Ann Davis

According to the US Census, 77 million people were born between 1946 and 1964, which is defined as the baby boomer era. The first baby boomer turned 65 on January 1, 2011. The senior age group is now, for the first time, the largest in terms of size and percent of the population in the U.S. By 2015, those aged 50 and older will represent 45% of the U.S. population (AARP). Seniors are living longer than their predecessors. A knowledge of available resources to live a continued fulfilling life is key to successful aging.

"DEALING WITH CHILD ABUSE AND NEGLECT IN THE CHURCH" By Evangelist Charla Johnson

Sunday School teachers, especially the women of the church, work closely with our children. Sunday School is a key outreach for children for many churches in the community. It is vital that those working with children recognize signs of physical and mental abuse, which include neglect, for children from both churched and unchurched homes.

"A DISCIPLESHIP PRIMER ON SANCTIFICATION"
By Dr. Linda Smith

Lessons on the basic tenets of our faith can always be a bonus to any Sunday School class. As so many "unchurched" individuals are being saved, this is a vital and clear presentation on what it means, according to the Scriptures, to live a sanctified life.

"ISSD 'LOVE ALIVE' CAMPUS MINISTRY– COLLEGE STUDENT/YOUNG ADULT MINISTRY"
By Pastor A.L. Shaw, Director

Another choice feature is our ***ISSD "Love Alive" campus ministry for college-aged youth ages 16–29,*** *providing the how-to's of building a successful ministry to reach teens and young adults within your local church—a missing population gap in most local churches today—and how to successfully build a campus ministry.*

Our young people are the church of not only the future, but today. As they experience new challenges and face many big decisions, letting them know that "The LORD himself goes before you and will be with you; he will never leave nor forsake you" (from Deuteronomy 31:8, NIV) is so very vital. It is imperative that we share this good news with a hurting world.

Special Articles:

"THE SHIFT"

COLLEGE MINISTRY TRAINING FOR CHURCH LEADERS
By Pastor A.L. Shaw

"DEVELOPING COLLEGE MINISTRY"

ESSENTIALS OF DEVELOPING, IMPLEMENTING & BUILDING COLLEGE MINISTRY WITHIN YOUR LOCAL CHURCH
By Tyrone Williams

“UNDER PRESSURE, BUT NOT PERSUADED”

CAMPUS MINISTRY SWAG

(SAVED WILLING AGENTS FOR GOD)

How to maintain your Christian “swag” during college life challenges
By Alethea Nichols

As you read, study and prayerfully implement these solutions, strategies, and tools, believe God for increase in your local Sunday School and church!

Vice President Althea Sims serves as a member of the Executive Team of the International Sunday School Department (ISSD). Sims also serves as the Jurisdictional Sunday School Superintendent of the First Ecclesiastical Jurisdiction of Southern California under the leadership of Bishop Joe L. Ealy. Assistant General Supervisor, Mother Barbara McCoo Lewis is her Jurisdictional Supervisor.

QUARTERLY QUIZ

The questions on this page may be used in several ways: as a pretest at the beginning of the quarter; as a review at the end of the quarter; or as a review after each lesson. The questions are based on the Scripture text of each lesson (King James Version).

LESSON 1

1. What type of punishment will God send to Judah and the palaces of Jerusalem (**Amos 2:5**)?

2. The people would ____ the ____ of the condemned in the house of their god (**Amos 2:8**).

LESSON 2

1. How did God respond to the people celebrating their feast days (**Amos 5:21**)?

2. Write the famous words of justice declared by the prophet Amos (**Amos 5:24**).

LESSON 3

1. What type of houses will be destroyed in **Amos 6:11**?

2. Amos declares that the people have changed righteousness into ____________ (**Amos 6:12**).

LESSON 4

1. In **Amos 8:5**, the merchants would be glad when the new moon would be gone. Why?

2. The merchants cheated the poor by creating new "money" by making the _____ ______ and the _____ _______ (**Amos 8:5**).

LESSON 5

1. The rich were not open to hearing Micah's judgment from God against them. What was their response to Micah (**Micah 2:6**)?

2. The rich were about to be evicted from their land—true or false (**Micah 2:10**)?

LESSON 6

1. In **Micah 3:7**, what will happen to the lips of the various "speakers of truth"?

2. Micah prophesied that Zion and Jerusalem will experience _________ (**Micah 3:12**).

QUARTERLY QUIZ

LESSON 7

1. Why do you think the Lord asked the people to testify against Him in **Micah 6:3**?

____

____

2. What does the Lord require of His people (**Micah 6:8**)?

____

____

LESSON 8

1. The _____ will be _____ by what God will do (**Micah 7:16**).

____

____

2. What image is used in **Micah 7:17** to describe how the nations will respond to God's movement?

____

____

LESSON 9

1. Why was God displeased (**Isaiah 59:15b**)?

____

____

2. God saw no ____ and no ___________ to intervene for the people (**Isaiah 59:16**).

____

____

LESSON 10

1. The Lord instruct Jeremiah to stand at the ______ of the Lord's house, the Temple (**Jeremiah 7:2**).

____

____

2. Name the city that God challenged the people to visit and see where He allowed the Temple to be destroyed (**Jeremiah 7:12**).

____

____

LESSON 11

1. Write one of the just actions of the righteous father in **Ezekiel 18:7**.

____

____

2. Complete the following Scripture: "For I have no pleasure ______________________________ ______________________________" (**Ezekiel 18:32**).

____

____

LESSON 12

1. Name the prophet that God speaks to in **Zechariah 7:8**.

____

____

2. The prophet proclaims in **Zechariah 7:9** that the Lord expects the people to do what?

____

____

QUARTERLY QUIZ

LESSON 13

1. What type of messenger will be sent to the Temple (**Malachi 3:1**)?

____

____

2. State the characteristic God shares about Himself in **Malachi 3:6**.

____

____

ANSWERS TO THE QUARTERLY QUIZ

LESSON 1 1. Fire upon Judah and the palaces of Jerusalem; 2. drink, wine

LESSON 2 1. God despised their celebrations; 2. "But let judgment run down as waters, and righteousness as a mighty stream."

LESSON 3 1. a great house and a little house; 2. hemlock

LESSON 4 1. They wanted to sell more corn to the people and not celebrate the festival (or any religious festivals); 2. ephah small, shekel great

LESSON 5 1. They wanted Micah to stop talking; 2. True

LESSON 6 1. They will need to cover their lips because there will be no answer from God; 2. destruction

LESSON 7 1. Because they had no case and they could only show the many ways that God protected, loved, and delivered them; 2. "… to do justly, and to love mercy, and to walk humbly with thy God."

LESSON 8 1. nations, ashamed; 2 "They will lick dust like a snake, like creatures that crawl on the ground."

LESSON 9 1. There was no judgment; 2. man, intercessor

LESSON 10 1. gate; 2. Shiloh

LESSON 11 1. does not oppress anyone, returns what he took in pledge for a loan, does not commit robbery, gives his food to the hungry, provides clothing for the naked; 2. "For I have no pleasure in the death of him that dieth, saith the Lord GOD: wherefore turn yourselves, and live ye."

LESSON 12 1. Zechariah; 2. "Administer true justice; show mercy and compassion to one another."

LESSON 13 1. The messenger of the covenant; 2. God does not change.

JUDGMENT ON ISRAEL AND JUDAH

BIBLE BASIS: AMOS 2:4–8

BIBLE TRUTH: God will not overlook injustice, but will punish the unjust.

MEMORY VERSE: "Thus saith the LORD; For three transgressions of Judah, and for four, I will not turn away the punishment thereof; because they have despised the law of the LORD, and have not kept his commandments, and their lies caused them to err, after the which their fathers have walked" (Amos 2:4).

LESSON AIM: By the end of the lesson, your students will: review God's judgment of Judah and Israel; encourage sensitivity toward social injustice; and address issues of injustice in their local and global communities.

TEACHER PREPARATION

MATERIALS NEEDED: Quarterly Commentary/Teacher Manual, Adult Quarterly, Adult resources—charts, worksheets, and other teaching tools, paper, pens, pencils, Bibles (several different versions)

OTHER MATERIALS NEEDED / TEACHER'S NOTES:

____

____

LESSON OVERVIEW

LIFE NEED FOR TODAY'S LESSON

Even though people know right from wrong, some people treat others unjustly.

BIBLE LEARNING

Believers learn that God hates injustice and oppression of the poor.

BIBLE APPLICATION

People of faith are called to stand for justice even though this may necessitate standing against others.

STUDENTS' RESPONSES

Discuss how Christians are involved in corporate injustices.

LESSON SCRIPTURE

AMOS 2:4–8, KJV

4 Thus saith the LORD; For three transgressions of Judah, and for four, I will not turn away the punishment thereof; because they have despised the law of the LORD, and have not kept his commandments, and their lies caused them to err, after the which their fathers have walked:

AMOS 2:4–8, NIV

4 This is what the LORD says: "For three sins of Judah, even for four, I will not relent. Because they have rejected the law of the LORD and have not kept his decrees, because they have been led astray by false gods, the gods their ancestors followed,

5 But I will send a fire upon Judah, and it shall devour the palaces of Jerusalem.

6 Thus saith the LORD; For three transgressions of Israel, and for four, I will not turn away the punishment thereof; because they sold the righteous for silver, and the poor for a pair of shoes;

7 That pant after the dust of the earth on the head of the poor, and turn aside the way of the meek: and a man and his father will go in unto the same maid, to profane my holy name:

8 And they lay themselves down upon clothes laid to pledge by every altar, and they drink the wine of the condemned in the house of their god.

5 I will send fire on Judah that will consume the fortresses of Jerusalem."

6 This is what the LORD says: "For three sins of Israel, even for four, I will not relent. They sell the innocent for silver, and the needy for a pair of sandals.

7 They trample on the heads of the poor as on the dust of the ground and deny justice to the oppressed. Father and son use the same girl and so profane my holy name.

8 They lie down beside every altar on garments taken in pledge. In the house of their god they drink wine taken as fines.

LIGHT ON THE WORD

The concept of slavery depicted in the Old Testament is not the equivalent of the North Atlantic slave trade, although there are certain parallels between the two. Slavery was a customary practice throughout the ancient Near East. Individuals could be sold into slavery to repay a personal debt or a debt to society. In war, citizens of conquered countries were often made slaves. Mosaic Law governed how Israel was to treat slaves, given the practice was already a custom in Near Eastern culture. These laws detailed how masters were to treat slaves humanely, and how slaves could be freed. For example, in **Exodus 21:2–4,** it is indicated that a Hebrew who sold himself to another Hebrew should be released after six years of service.

TEACHING THE BIBLE LESSON

LIFE NEED FOR TODAY'S LESSON

AIM: Students will know that even though people know right from wrong, some people treat others unjustly.

INTRODUCTION

The Prophet Amos

The prophet Amos was born in the city of Tekoa. He prophesied in Israel around 750 B.C. He was not the descendant of prophets; rather he was from "among the herdsman of Tekoa" (**Amos 1:1**). He was a shepherd and also tended and gathered sycamore figs. He received his call to ministry while he was out in the pastures, with his sheep (**Amos 7:14–15**). His career as a shepherd and a common working man informed his view of the world and the way he communicated his prophetic message. He used images from nature and agriculture in his prophecies. Amos lived during an era of relative peace and prosperity. This prosperity led to an atmosphere of indulgent luxury, corrupt power, and moral depravity in Israel. Many had turned to the worship of idols and other gods. Some religious practices were still maintained; however, these had deteriorated into empty rituals. Israel's religion didn't have the intended impact on how they lived their lives.

BIBLE LEARNING

AIM: Students will learn that God hates injustice and oppression of the poor.

I. JUDAH'S SIN AND GOD'S JUDGMENT (Amos 2:4–5)

Amos delivers his message from the Lord, explaining the sins that Judah has committed. Judah's sin is repetitive; a continual pattern of disobedience. Their sins are numerous and God's patience with Judah has run out. In this regard, Judah is no different than the other nations that God has judged. The same pattern, "for three transgressions ... and for four" used to judge pagan nations, is used here as well. However, Judah's sin is different in that they had received God's laws and chosen not to follow them. Rather than keeping His laws, they have "despised the Law of the LORD." The word translated "despised" in the KJV is the Hebrew word *ma'as* (**mah-AHS**), also meaning to reject or refuse. Judah knew what to do, but refused to do it.

Judah's Judgment and Punishment (verses 4–5)

4 Thus saith the LORD; For three transgressions of Judah, and for four, I will not turn away the punishment thereof; because they have despised the law of the LORD, and have not kept his commandments, and their lies caused them to err, after which their fathers have walked.

By moving from neighboring nations on to Judah, Amos begins to zero in on the goal of prophesying against Israel. Judah is condemned for rejecting the Law of God and for idolatry. Although the actual word "idolatry" is not mentioned, we can infer this from the reference to lies (Heb. *kazab*, **kah-ZAHV**) making them err. The word "lies" is often used in reference to idols or anything that gives them false hope (**Psalm 4:2; Ezekiel 13:6**). The idols of the nations only lead people into deception. The sin of idolatry is also alluded to with the phrase "after which their fathers have walked." "Walking after" is often used in reference to idol worship or following the commands and statutes of Yahweh (**Deuteronomy 8:19; Jeremiah 8:2**). It is obvious Amos is referring to the former since he has already stated that Judah has "despised" (Heb. *ma'as*, **mah-AHS**) God's Law.

This oracle against Judah stands out from the prophetic oracles against the other nations because Judah is closest to Israel and Judah's sins are of a covenantal nature, not just crimes against humanity. They are indicted for their breach of covenant with God by going after idols. This is something that God does not take lightly with His covenant people.

5 But I will send a fire upon Judah, and it shall devour the palaces of Jerusalem.

Amos announces that Judah's sins will not go unpunished. The Lord will send a fire on Judah and the palaces (Heb. *'armon*, **ar-MONE**) of Jerusalem. Most likely, Amos is referring to the citadels and strongholds that made up the king's palace and Temple complex, since this word for "palace" can also mean citadel or fortress. The word comes from a root meaning high and lofty. These high and lofty places would be brought down by fire. This happened in 586 B.C. when

Nebuchadnezzar and the Babylonian army defeated Jerusalem through siege.

SEARCH THE SCRIPTURES

QUESTION 1

What conditions do you think contributed to Judah's rejection of God's Law and reliance on the false teaching of their ancestors?

LIGHT ON THE WORD

Lying People

Judah has chosen to follow in the lies and falsehoods of their ancestors. They have continued a historical pattern of prefering false teaching over the divine instruction provided to them. For their sin, Judah will be judged in the same manner as the surrounding pagan nations: They will be destroyed in warfare, consumed by fire.

II. ISRAEL'S SIN (vv. 6–8)

Amos completes his message with a stern rebuke of Israel. Israel's spiritual climate has fallen to the point that they resemble the foreign nations around them. Their sin and rejection of God's Law places them squarely in the company of nations that haven't even received it. Again, the prophecy indicates an identical pattern of judgement: "For three transgressions ... and for four."

The innocent and the poor are being abused in Israel. Though slavery is a customary practice, Amos speaks to the rigged and unjust practice of driving debtors to slavery for the sole purpose of benefiting the powerful and wealthy. Rather than being merciful and allowing them more time to repay, people are driven into slavery. For as little as the cost of a pair of sandals, the poor and innocent are dealt with harshly. Additionally, those sold into slavery are abused within the households of the wealthy. A man and his son lying with the same servant woman is a violation of Moses' Law and profanes God's name (**Exodus 20:17**). A servant given in marriage to a son is to be treated as a daughter by the master of the house (**Exodus 21:9**).

Injustice and Pain (verses 6–8)

6 Thus saith the LORD; For three transgressions of Israel, and for four, I will not turn away the punishment thereof; because they sold the righteous for silver, and the poor for a pair of shoes.

Now Amos turns his prophetic gaze toward Israel. As Amos prophesied against the other nations like Tyre, Edom, Moab, and Judah, Israel must have savored and enjoyed hearing their neighbors' condemnation. Now it was their turn. The Lord would not be partial but would judge fairly. If the other nations received prophetic pronouncements of judgment, then Israel would receive judgment as well.

Amos repeats the same prophetic formula "for three transgressions of Israel and for four." This was an acknowledgment of God's patience toward their sin. Adding "for four" showed that God was at His limit and could not restrain His punishment for their wrongdoing. This wrongdoing manifested itself in selling "the righteous for silver, and the poor for a pair of shoes." The word "righteous" (Heb. *tsaddiyq*, **tsah-DEEK**) here may be used in a legal sense, referencing those who are innocent in Israel's law courts but who nevertheless are found guilty by corrupt judges. It could also be referring to those sold into slavery for a debt. Both meanings could be in view here. A pair of sandals could be referring to land transfer (see **Ruth 4**) or a very small, insignificant debt. Amos was pointing out how the Israelites were devaluing human life.

7 That pant after the dust of the earth on the head of the poor, and turn aside the

way of the meek: and a man and his father will go in unto the same maid, to profane my holy name.

Israel is accused of having little or no regard for the poor. The word "pant" (Heb. *sha'ap*, **shah-AHF**) is often rendered "swallow up" or "trample." They trample the head of the poor into the earth, meaning they provide no means for the poor to better themselves. Instead, Israel is accused of wanting the poor to remain poor for their own benefit and personal gain. They also push the meek or afflicted out of the way and do not give alms or financial, social, or physical assistance.

Their social evils extend into the realm of sexual immorality as well. The sexual sin presented breaches proper familial relationship and is condemned (**Leviticus 18:15, 20:12**). The word used for girl (Heb. *na'arah*, **nah-ah-RAH**) can also be rendered female servant. For both father and son to have sexual relations with the same slave girl would be a misuse of power by exploiting those who have no rights to speak up for themselves. This abuse of power made their acts an even greater violation of God's covenant. Such acts profane, defile, or stain the Lord's holy name. The Hebrew word *chalal* (**khih-LEL**) expresses the hideous act of desecrating that which belongs to God. It is making unholy that which is deemed holy. The Israelites are particularly accused of defiling the Lord's name through sexual and social sins.

8 And they lay themselves down upon clothes laid to pledge by every altar, and they drink the wine of the condemned in the house of their god.

Amos continues to show how Israel has sinned. They are accused of "laying themselves down upon clothes laid to pledge by every altar." Their sexual immorality and injustice (**v. 7**) was connected to their religious sin and unfaithfulness to their covenant with God. Part of their idolatrous practices was to worship through sexual acts. Their crime is even more serious, as they commit these acts on clothes that have been taken as collateral for a loan. The law stated that these garments (usually the outer garments or cloaks) were to be returned for the night (**Exodus 22:26**). Instead they were kept to be used for shameful acts. The perpetrators also drank wine, which was paid for by "unjust fines" (NLT). It is not clear whether these fines are unjust taxes or part of the tithe to the "house of their god." During this time, ancient Israel had set up shrines and temples to replace the Temple of Yahweh at Jerusalem. At these shrines, Yahweh was represented as a bull, which was also the representation of Baal. It is not surprising that because of this syncretistic mix of ideas, their worship was also patterned after the worship of Baal to include orgiastic rituals.

SEARCH THE SCRIPTURES

QUESTION 2

The poor are sold into slavery for what amounted to the cost of a pair of sandals. Do you think greed motivated the actions of the wealthy? What other evil rationale may have driven their actions?

LIGHT ON THE WORD

Deeply Rooted Sins

Israel's sin is not merely negligent abuse. The innocent are actively being denied justice in the courts and are taken advantage of in the name of power and greed (**v. 7**). The poor, rather than being helped and protected, are pushed down even further. These practices have become commonplace in Israel.

Israel's rejection of God's Law has resulted in horrible abuses against its people. The majority of these involve the powerful using the system to benefit themselves and push down the needy and less powerful. They have perverted legitimate political and legal systems to enrich themselves.

BIBLE APPLICATION

AIM: Students will know they are called to stand for justice even though this may necessitate standing against others.

The powerful and wealthy in Israel used legitimate political and legal systems to enrich themselves and hold down the less fortunate. A parallel to this type of behavior is the modern-day practice of predatory lending in America. Predatory lending occurs when wealthy banking institutions provide loans under terms that are misleading or abusive. Often the loan terms make it impossible for a borrower to repay the loan or make the required payments. This results in the debtor losing land, money, or property to the bank. The poor and less educated are often the primary targets of such lending practices. Rather than taking advantage of the less fortunate, God calls us to minister to those that need help (**Matthew 25:34–35**).

STUDENTS' RESPONSES

AIM: Students will discuss how Christians are involved in corporate injustices.

As a nation and as the church, when it comes to social injustice, we often point the finger at others. Prayerfully make a list of the ways our nation and the church contribute to social injustice. Commit to practicing justice in these areas of life as an individual.

PRAYER

God of justice, we are sorry for any injustices that we have actively or unknowingly committed in our lives. We seek justice for all and thank You for allowing Your justice to prevail in us. In Jesus' Name we pray. Amen.

HOW TO SAY IT

Devour. di-**VOW**-er.

Profane. pro-**FAYN**.

PREPARE FOR NEXT SUNDAY

Read **Amos 5:14–15, 18–27** and study "God is Not Fooled."

DAILY HOME BIBLE READINGS

MONDAY
I Will Judge with Equity
(Psalm 75)

TUESDAY
I Will Press You Down
(Amos 2:9–16)

WEDNESDAY
I Will Punish Your Iniquities
(Amos 3:1–8)

THURSDAY
I Will Punish Your Transgressions
(Amos 3:9–15)

FRIDAY
Judgment is Surely Coming
(Amos 4:1–6)

SATURDAY
You Did Not Return to Me
(Amos 4:7–13)

SUNDAY
I Will Not Revoke Punishment
(Amos 2:4–8)

Sources:

Alexander, David and Pat Alexander. *Zondervan Handbook to the Bible*. Grand Rapids, MI: Zondervan, 1999. 490.

Burge, Gary M. and Andrew E. Hill, eds. *Baker Illustrated Bible Commentary*. Grand Rapids, MI: Baker Books, 2012. 834.

Butler, Trent C., ed. *Holman Bible Dictionary*. Electronic Edition, Quickverse. Nashville, TN: Holman Bible Publishers, 1991. S.vv. "Amos," "Slavery in the Old Testament," and "Tekoa."

Carson, D. A., R. T. France, J. A. Motyer, and G. J. Wenham, eds. *New Bible Commentary*. Downer's Grove, IL: InterVarsity Press, 1994. 796–797.

Easton, M. G. *Easton's Bible Dictionary*. 1st ed. Oklahoma City: Ellis Enterprises, 1993. S.vv. "Amos," "Slave," and "Tekoa."

Motyer, J. A. The Message of Amos. Downers Grove, IL: InterVarsity Press, 1974. 49–60.

Orr, James, ed. "Tekoa." *International Standard Bible Encyclopedia. Electronic Edition*. Omaha, NE: Quickverse, 1998.

Strong, James. *The New Strong's Exhaustive Concordance Of The Bible Expanded Edition*. Nashville, TN: Thomas Nelson, 2001. S.vv. "Ma'ac" and "Pasha."

Stuart, Douglas. *Word Biblical Commentary: Hosea–Jonah*. Nashville, TN: Thomas Nelson, 1987. 304–305, 315–318.

Walton, John H., Victor H. Matthews, and Mark W. Chavalas. *The IVP Bible Background Commentary: Old Testament*. Downers Grove, IL: InterVarsity Press, 2000. 764.

COMMENTS / NOTES:

GOD IS NOT FOOLED

BIBLE BASIS: AMOS 5:14–15, 18–27

BIBLE TRUTH: Amos declared to the people that God will not be fooled by insincere offerings and will severely punish all sinners.

MEMORY VERSE: "But let judgment run down as waters, and righteousness as a mighty stream" (Amos 5:24).

LESSON AIM: By the end of the lesson, your students will: know how God establishes justice for the righteous and punishes deceivers; recognize and reflect on actions of injustice within the community of faith; and identify unjust practices, commit to stop our participation in them, and help others do the same.

TEACHER PREPARATION

MATERIALS NEEDED: Quarterly Commentary/Teacher Manual, Adult Quarterly, Adult resources—charts, worksheets, and other teaching tools, paper, pens, pencils, Bibles (several different versions)

OTHER MATERIALS NEEDED / TEACHER'S NOTES:

LESSON OVERVIEW

LIFE NEED FOR TODAY'S LESSON
Some people cover their evil ways with outward acts of goodness.

BIBLE LEARNING
Judah and Israel's expression of faith is inconsistent with the ways they treated others and is a reminder of how our faith should be aligned with God's justice.

BIBLE APPLICATION
People of faith discover that acting for justice requires putting aside self-interest.

STUDENTS' RESPONSES
Worshipers listen to God's calls for justice and respond with a commitment to justice.

LESSON SCRIPTURE

AMOS 5:14–15, 18–27, KJV

14 Seek good, and not evil, that ye may live: and so the LORD, the God of hosts, shall be with you, as ye have spoken.

15 Hate the evil, and love the good, and establish judgment in the gate: it may be that the LORD God of hosts will be gracious unto the remnant of Joseph.

AMOS 5:14–15, 18–27, NIV

14 Seek good, not evil, that you may live. Then the LORD God Almighty will be with you, just as you say he is.

15 Hate evil, love good; maintain justice in the courts. Perhaps the LORD God Almighty will have mercy on the remnant of Joseph.

18 Woe unto you that desire the day of the LORD! to what end is it for you? the day of the LORD is darkness, and not light.

19 As if a man did flee from a lion, and a bear met him; or went into the house, and leaned his hand on the wall, and a serpent bit him.

20 Shall not the day of the LORD be darkness, and not light? even very dark, and no brightness in it?

21 I hate, I despise your feast days, and I will not smell in your solemn assemblies.

22 Though ye offer me burnt offerings and your meat offerings, I will not accept them: neither will I regard the peace offerings of your fat beasts.

23 Take thou away from me the noise of thy songs; for I will not hear the melody of thy viols.

24 But let judgment run down as waters, and righteousness as a mighty stream.

25 Have ye offered unto me sacrifices and offerings in the wilderness forty years, O house of Israel?

26 But ye have borne the tabernacle of your Moloch and Chiun your images, the star of your god, which ye made to yourselves.

27 Therefore will I cause you to go into captivity beyond Damascus, saith the LORD, whose name is The God of hosts.

18 Woe to you who long for the day of the LORD! Why do you long for the day of the LORD? That day will be darkness, not light.

19 It will be as though a man fled from a lion only to meet a bear, as though he entered his house and rested his hand on the wall only to have a snake bite him.

20 Will not the day of the LORD be darkness, not light—pitch-dark, without a ray of brightness?

21 "I hate, I despise your religious festivals; your assemblies are a stench to me.

22 Even though you bring me burnt offerings and grain offerings, I will not accept them. Though you bring choice fellowship offerings, I will have no regard for them.

23 Away with the noise of your songs! I will not listen to the music of your harps.

24 But let justice roll on like a river, righteousness like a never-failing stream!

25 "Did you bring me sacrifices and offerings forty years in the wilderness, people of Israel?

26 You have lifted up the shrine of your king, the pedestal of your idols, the star of your god—which you made for yourselves.

27 Therefore I will send you into exile beyond Damascus," says the LORD, whose name is God Almighty.

LIGHT ON THE WORD

There were three major feast days in the nation of Israel: the Feast of Unleavened Bread (Passover), the Feast of Harvest (Pentecost), and the Feast of Ingathering (Tabernacles).

These were pilgrimage festivals that required participation from the entire Israelite community. All work was to cease and travelers made their way from all over Israel to celebrate these festivals in Jerusalem.

Sikkuth is another name for the Mesopotamian astral deity Sakkut (Ninib). This god was also associated with the planet Saturn. It was commonly believed that this god was not introduced until after the Assyrian conquest, but recent scholarship has revealed that Aramean merchants and other foreign travelers helped to spread the worship of Sikkuth in Israel.

Kaiwan (Chiun) was the Babylonian Saturn god. The name actually means "the steadiest one" and is taken from the planet Saturn's slow moving orbit. The differences in spelling are likely because when foreign gods were referenced, the original vowels were often replaced with the vowels from the Hebrew word for "abomination." The Phoenicians were thought to offer human sacrifices to this god.

TEACHING THE BIBLE LESSON

LIFE NEED FOR TODAY'S LESSON

AIM: Students will know some people cover their evil ways with outward acts of goodness.

INTRODUCTION

The Death of Israel

Amos begins **chapter 5** as a eulogy for the "dead" nation of Israel. Israel isn't yet dead, but the lament is meant to impress on the nation the severe danger it is in. The death of Israel is described as the death of a virgin (**Amos 5:2**). The death of a virgin would have been considered particularly tragic because she had no children to carry on her memory. This type of death is distinctly permanent. Furthermore, the dead virgin is described as having been left lying in a field, unburied. To leave a body unburied would have been a shocking and appalling image to consider, yet this is how the demise of Israel is described. Its depraved moral climate and refusal to turn back to God have indeed set it on the path of destruction.

BIBLE LEARNING

AIM: Students will reflect on how Judah and Israel's expression of faith was inconsistent with the ways they treated others and is a reminder of how our faith should be aligned with God's justice.

I. LOVE GOOD, HATE EVIL (Amos 5:14–15)

Israel has become complacent in their presumption of God's favor (**v. 14**). Israel has mistakenly believed that, despite their sinful ways and their worship of other gods, they can still count on God's protection. However, Amos has declared to them that their actions have displeased God and will result in the destruction of their nation.

Choose Good Over Evil (verses 14–15)

14 Seek good, and not evil, that ye may live: and so the LORD, the God of hosts, shall be with you, as ye have spoken.

Amos continues with the refrain of seeking. The word seek (Heb. *darash*, **dah-RASH**) is used in **5:4** and **5:6** to refer to the people seeking the idol sanctuaries and then to refer to seeking God. Now Amos uses it in reference to good as opposed to evil. The good that the people were to seek was justice for the poor. Amos holds out the promise of the Lord's presence if they seek good. This highlights the fact that the Lord is not with them to begin with because of their injustice and oppression.

15 Hate the evil, and love the good, and establish judgment in the gate: it may be that the LORD God of hosts will be gracious unto the remnant of Joseph.

This seeking of good is more than just an outward action. It must radiate from an attitude of the heart. Amos uses strong words here. Seeking good is spelled out as hating (Heb. *sane'*, **sah-NAY**) evil. In other passages of the Old Testament, this word is used to refer to an enemy. The Israelites had been friends with evil and stood on the side of injustice. By using this word, Amos confronts them and challenges them to choose sides. Being on the side of good means establishing "judgment in the gate." The gates of the town were often used for courts of justice and centers of trade, and there the Israelites did most of their oppression of the poor. So this is where they could show that they loved good and hated evil instead.

If the people would seek Him and seek good instead of seeking the sanctuaries at Bethel and Gilgal, then maybe he would be gracious (Heb. *chanan*, **khah-NAHN**) to them. Amos is communicating that there is still the possibility of God showing favor and mercy to them. A remnant of Joseph is offered grace. After breaking away from the Southern Kingdom of Judah, the ten tribes were often referred to as Joseph. To refer to the remnant of Joseph is to appeal to those who will choose to seek good, although most of Israel will not.

SEARCH THE SCRIPTURES

QUESTION 1

What do you think it would have looked like for an Israelite to love good and hate evil during this time in Israel's history?

LIGHT ON THE WORD

Loving Good

In order for some to be spared, Israel must both seek good and avoid evil. The two-fold action of seeking and avoiding is emphasized in verse 15. They are to "hate" the evil and "love" the good. The terms "hate" and "love" indicate decisions that one must make. Seeking good is connected with choosing to love good. Avoiding evil is connected to choosing to hate evil.

II. A DAY OF DARKNESS (vv. 18–20)

Again, the prophet's message seizes on Israel's presumption of God's favor. It was common in times of trouble for the Israelites to long for "the day of the Lord," when God would rescue them from their enemies. But "the day of the Lord" will now be a day of reckoning.

God's Holy War Against Israel (verses 18–20)

18 Woe unto you that desire the day of the LORD! to what end is it for you? the day of the LORD is darkness, and not light. 19 As if a man did flee from a lion, and a bear met him; or went into the house, and leaned his hand on the wall, and a serpent bit him. 20 Shall not the day of the LORD be darkness, and not light? even very dark, and no brightness in it?

"The day of the Lord" is a term that refers to the Lord appearing and waging a holy war with His enemies. This is the first reference to the Day of the Lord in the Old Testament. Amos implies that those Israelites who were involved in oppressing the poor longed for this Day of Judgment. He lets them know that it will not be a good time for them; it will be darkness and not light. The images of running from a lion only to meet a bear or running into a house only to be bitten by a serpent describe the Day of the Lord as a time where they will not be able to escape God's judgment.

LIGHT ON THE WORD

Nowhere to Hide

For those who have turned to idols and denied justice to the poor, there will be no rescue, but rather darkness and judgment waiting for them. This will be a jarring turn of events for Israel. It is described metaphorically like escaping a lion, only to find that you must escape a bear; then resting at home, only to find that a snake is waiting to bite you.

III. GOD DESIRES JUSTICE, NOT EMPTY RITUALS (vv. 21–24)

The worship of other gods had seeped into Israel's religious practices, but the people still maintained their Israelite rituals and festivals too. However, God is not fooled by their empty worship. True worship flows out of the hearts of those who earnestly seek to follow God's will. A true worshiper's relationships and personal life will be consistent with their public worship.

Israel's Despicable Acts (verses 21–24)

21 I hate, I despise your feast days, and I will not smell in your solemn assemblies.
22 Though ye offer me burnt offerings and your meat offerings, I will not accept them: neither will I regard the peace offerings of your fat beasts.

Outwardly impressive religious acts of good will that are selfishly done, do not move the heart of God. The phrase "your feast days" (Heb. *chag*, **KHAG**) refers to the three main festivals that God established in Israel: Passover, Pentecost, and the Feast of Tabernacles (**Exodus 23:14–19; Deuteronomy 16:16–17**). Israel was abusing all of these festivals at this time. God rejected what Israel did in these feasts, which had a form of godliness but lacked the power thereof. The implication is that God Himself may establish events, activities, or procedures, but His people can pervert, abuse, and misuse them to achieve their own selfish ends. The Lord says He will not smell in their assemblies (Heb. *atsarah*, **at-sa-RAH**). Amos is possibly referring to the solemn assembly on the seventh day of the Feast of Unleavened Bread and the eighth day of the Feast of Tabernacles (**Leviticus 23:8, 36**). The Lord would not be pleased with any of the worship practiced on those days because of the absence of justice and right living.

None of the offerings prescribed in the law would please God. The Lord would not accept their burnt offerings (Heb. *'olah*, **oh-LAH**), in which the whole animal was consumed with fire. This was a symbol of the total commitment of the worshiper's life to God. He would not accept their meat offerings (Heb. *minchah*, **min-KHAH**). These were sacrifices devoid of blood and intended as gifts to the Lord. Lastly, He would not accept their peace offerings (Heb. *shelem*, **SHEH-lem**), as these gifts were a sign of reconciliation or friendship, and this was not the state of their relationship with God. All of the worship rituals here were to be symbols of the people's real-life walk with the Lord, and offering them without the true reality behind them was hypocritical. This made their offerings unacceptable to the Lord.

23 Take thou away from me the noise of thy songs; for I will not hear the melody of thy viols.

Celebrations and rejoicing in God's presence played an important part in Israel's Temple worship, which God had established. The Israelites used many kinds of musical instruments to praise God for His goodness and faithfulness (**2 Chronicles 7; Psalm 149**). In this instance the Lord actually calls their songs noise (Heb. *hamon*, **hah-MONE**). It is not the joyful noise of Psalm 100:1, but the noise and confusion of a host of people—noise that the Lord does not want to hear.

24 But let judgment run down as waters, and righteousness as a mighty stream.

God illustrates the nature of judgment (justice) and righteousness by using the phrases "run down as water" and "as a mighty stream," which speak of the ongoing and unobstructed movement of an ever-flowing body of water. The word for stream, *nakhal* (Heb. **NAH-khal**), is the word for the desert wadi. These small narrow valleys laid dry and barren for much of the year until a torrent of rain flooded them and made them into flowing streams. The Lord has already laid out the stipulations of justice in His covenant, and He is waiting for His people to fill the dry and barren land with justice and righteousness as the rains fill up a desert wadi.

SEARCH THE SCRIPTURES

QUESTION 2

What were the attitudes and motives of the Israelite worshipers? Why did God refuse their worship?

LIGHT ON THE WORD

Justice Rejected

Israel's worship was hypocritical. They publicly gave offerings to God and worshiped Him with their music, but they continued to reject justice and righteousness in their everyday lives. Their religious practices had become distasteful to God, and He refused their show of piety. Rather than continued injustice and hypocrisy, the Lord desires a continual, daily flow of justice and righteousness.

IV. ISRAEL'S IDOLATRY RESULTS IN EXILE (vv. 25–27)

Israel's unfaithfulness is called out here. In addition to making offerings to Yahweh, they have begun worshiping foreign deities. Idol worship often included parades in which the people would carry handmade representations of their gods.

Judgment Against Hypocritical Worship (verses 25–27)

25 Have ye offered unto me sacrifices and offerings in the wilderness forty years, O house of Israel? 26 But ye have borne the tabernacle of your Moloch and Chiun your images, the star of your god, which ye made to yourselves. 27 Therefore will I cause you to go into captivity beyond Damascus, saith the LORD, whose name is The God of hosts.

The Lord ends His pronouncement of judgment upon Israel's hypocritical worship with a rhetorical question. He asks if the Israelites have offered sacrifices to Him in the wilderness. While there were sacrifices made to the Lord in the wilderness, they were not a regular feature in Israel's religious life until after the conquest. The Lord is affirming that His relationship with them was not dependent on sacrifices and offerings. He had been with them in the wilderness without regular sacrifices.

Next He confronts them on their worship of idols. They have paraded images of Sikkuth and Kaiwan through their streets to their shrines. Sacrifices, sacred dancing, and other perverse forms of worship followed this parade. Many translations say the "tabernacle of Moloch and Chiun your images." Other translations say "Sikkuth your king and Kaiwan your star god." The second translation is more probable as Sikkuth and Kaiwan were worshiped as astral deities in Mesopotamia connected to the planet Saturn. In ancient times, Saturn was observed as being a star and influencing agriculture. This explains the reference to "the star of your god" (**v. 26**). In the next verse, Amos predicts that instead of them carrying their gods to the shrine to worship, they will be carried away captive. The phrase "beyond Damascus" points toward the coming Assyrian invasion that would take place, and the resulting demise of the Northern Kingdom.

LIGHT ON THE WORD

Punishment and Exile

Amos described an image that depicts Israel, the chosen people of Yahweh the one true God, carrying around idols made to worship other gods (**v. 26**). It is a sad betrayal of the God that had redeemed them. Idolatry leads to injustice. It is at the root of their oppression of others and their choosing to love evil and not good. As a result, the Lord will send them into exile—what happens to all those who choose other gods.

BIBLE APPLICATION

AIM: Students will discover that acting for justice requires putting aside self-interest.

Most Christians have no problem determining the difference between good and evil. In fact, even non-believers often choose to do the right thing. But merely choosing not to do evil is different than actively opposing evil. Opposing evil requires a level of conviction that goes beyond a simple understanding of right and wrong. It is often the case that only certain individuals will go out of their way to oppose an injustice. Most people are content to sit by while others are treated unfairly. It is God's desire that Christians would not only seek to do good, but also oppose evil and injustice. We are charged with standing for justice in our communities and in our world.

STUDENTS' RESPONSES

AIM: Students will listen to God's calls for justice and respond with a commitment to do justice.

It is often difficult in the moment to choose to love good and hate evil. One way to be prepared for those times and situations where we have decisions to make is to determine what is good or evil. Get a piece of paper and on one side write "Love Good" and on the other side write "Hate Evil." On the "Love Good" side, write all the ways that you can seek good in your daily life. On the "Hate Evil" side, write all the ways that you can hate evil in your daily life. Thinking about these things beforehand can help us to not only avoid falling into sin, but also move us forward in serving others in our community.

PRAYER

Lord, we worship You in spirit and in truth. May Your majestic and awesome power continue to give us the courage and strength that we need to choose good over evil. In Jesus' Name we pray. Amen.

HOW TO SAY IT

Tabernacle. **TA**-ber-na-hul.

Damascus. da-**MAS**-kus.

PREPARE FOR NEXT SUNDAY

Read **Amos 6:4–8, 11–14** and study "Rebuked for Selfishness."

DAILY HOME BIBLE READINGS

MONDAY
Fools Say, "There is No God"
(Psalm 14)

TUESDAY
Can You Deceive God?
(Job 13:7–12)

WEDNESDAY
Full of Hypocrisy and Lawlessness
(Matthew 23:23–28)

THURSDAY
To Obey is Better than Sacrifice
(1 Samuel 15:7–23)

FRIDAY
I Know Your Transgressions and Sins
(Amos 5:7–13)

SATURDAY
Seek the Lord and Live
(Amos 5:1–6)

SUNDAY
Love Good and Establish Justice
(Amos 5:14–15, 18–27)

Sources:

Alexander, David, and Pat Alexander. *Zondervan Handbook to the Bible.* Grand Rapids, MI: Zondervan, 1999. 490.

Burge, Gary M., and Andrew E. Hill, eds. *Baker Illustrated Bible Commentary.* Grand Rapids, MI: Baker Books, 2012. 834–835, 837–838.

Butler, Trent C., ed. *Holman Bible Dictionary.* Electronic Edition, Quickverse. Nashville, TN: Holman Bible Publishers, 1991. S.vv. "Kaiwan" and "Prophet."

Easton, M. G. "Chiun." *Easton's Bible Dictionary.* 1st ed. Oklahoma City: Ellis Enterprises, 1993.

Kaiser, Walter C., and Duane Garrett, eds. "Prophets in the Bible and Pagan Nations." *Archaeological Study Bible.* Grand Rapids, MI: Zondervan, 2005.

Keck, Leander, ed. *The Twelve Prophets.* The New Interpreter's Bible. Vol. 7. Nashville, TN: Abingdon Press, 1996. 384–397.

Orr, James, ed. "Chiun." *International Standard Bible Encyclopedia.* Electronic Edition. Omaha, NE: Quickverse, 1998.

Strong, James. *The New Strong's Exhaustive Concordance Of The Bible Expanded Edition.* Nashville, TN: Thomas Nelson, 2001. S.vv. "Chanan" and "Tsadaqah."

Stuart, Douglas. *Word Biblical Commentary: Hosea–Jonah.* Nashville, TN: Thomas Nelson, 1987. 340–356.

Walton, John H., Victor H. Matthews, and Mark W. Chavalas. *The IVP Bible Background Commentary: Old Testament.* Downers Grove, IL: InterVarsity Press, 2000. 769–771.

COMMENTS / NOTES:

REBUKED FOR SELFISHNESS

BIBLE BASIS: AMOS 6:4–8, 11–14

BIBLE TRUTH: God will dispossess the greedy and selfish and thus demonstrate God's justice.

MEMORY VERSE: "Shall horses run upon the rock? will one plow there with oxen? for ye have turned judgment into gall, and the fruit of righteousness into hemlock" (Amos 6:12).

LESSON AIM: By the end of the lesson, your students will: explore God's response to injustice as recorded by Amos; reflect on ways people practice greed and selfishness; and uncover and discover ways God does justice amid injustice and ways humans can join God in the fight against injustice.

TEACHER PREPARATION

MATERIALS NEEDED: Quarterly Commentary/Teacher Manual, Adult Quarterly, Adult resources—charts, worksheets, and other teaching tools, paper, pens, pencils, Bibles (several different versions)

OTHER MATERIALS NEEDED / TEACHER'S NOTES:

____

____

LESSON OVERVIEW

LIFE NEED FOR TODAY'S LESSON
Some people care only about accumulating lavish possessions for themselves and care nothing for those who possess little.

BIBLE LEARNING
True prosperity comes through obedience to God's commands.

BIBLE APPLICATION
People of faith, responding to God's desire for justice, examine their ways of life.

STUDENTS' RESPONSES
People of faith grieve and repent when God's people live unjustly.

LESSON SCRIPTURE

AMOS 6:4–8, 11–14, KJV

4 That lie upon beds of ivory, and stretch themselves upon their couches, and eat the lambs out of the flock, and the calves out of the midst of the stall;

5 That chant to the sound of the viol, and invent to themselves instruments of musick, like David;

AMOS 6:4–8, 11–14, NIV

4 You lie on beds adorned with ivory and lounge on your couches. You dine on choice lambs and fattened calves.

5 You strum away on your harps like David and improvise on musical instruments.

6 You drink wine by the bowlful and use

6 That drink wine in bowls, and anoint themselves with the chief ointments: but they are not grieved for the affliction of Joseph.

7 Therefore now shall they go captive with the first that go captive, and the banquet of them that stretched themselves shall be removed.

8 The Lord GOD hath sworn by himself, saith the LORD the God of hosts, I abhor the excellency of Jacob, and hate his palaces: therefore will I deliver up the city with all that is therein.

11 For, behold, the LORD commandeth, and he will smite the great house with breaches, and the little house with clefts.

12 Shall horses run upon the rock? will one plow there with oxen? for ye have turned judgment into gall, and the fruit of righteousness into hemlock:

13 Ye which rejoice in a thing of nought, which say, Have we not taken to us horns by our own strength?

14 But, behold, I will raise up against you a nation, O house of Israel, saith the LORD the God of hosts; and they shall afflict you from the entering in of Hemath unto the river of the wilderness.

the finest lotions, but you do not grieve over the ruin of Joseph.

7 Therefore you will be among the first to go into exile; your feasting and lounging will end.

8 The Sovereign LORD has sworn by himself—the LORD God Almighty declares: "I abhor the pride of Jacob and detest his fortresses; I will deliver up the city and everything in it."

11 For the LORD has given the command, and he will smash the great house into pieces and the small house into bits.

12 Do horses run on the rocky crags? Does one plow the sea with oxen? But you have turned justice into poison and the fruit of righteousness into bitterness—

13 you who rejoice in the conquest of Lo Debar and say, "Did we not take Karnaim by our own strength?"

14 For the LORD God Almighty declares, "I will stir up a nation against you, Israel, that will oppress you all the way from Lebo Hamath to the valley of the Arabah."

LIGHT ON THE WORD

Hamath was situated on the Orontes river and was the northern boundary of ancient Israel. Hamath represented the farthest north you could go before you ventured outside of Israel (**Numbers 13:21**). The river of wilderness was a desert wadi or brook that ran through the Arabah valley, which was a barren depression on the southern side of the Dead Sea. This brook flowed on the border of Moab and Edom. The river of the wilderness represented the furthest southern border of undivided Israel that could be inhabited. Thus the phrase "from

Hamath to the river of the wilderness" encompassed the entirety of the undivided kingdom of Israel.

TEACHING THE BIBLE LESSON

LIFE NEED FOR TODAY'S LESSON

AIM: Students will discuss that some people care only about accumulating lavish possessions for themselves and care nothing for those who possess little.

INTRODUCTION

Warning of Judgment

Amos proclaims prophecies from God that convict leaders for a lack of social justice and warning them of the "day of the Lord" when judgment would come to Israel. He has opposed the nation's sins and has encouraged them to repent for their evil and unjust ways. However, Israel has refused to turn away from their wickedness and remember the God they worshiped when they were in bondage. They are at risk for God's divine punishment.

BIBLE LEARNING

AIM: Students will affirm that true prosperity comes through obedience to God's commands.

I. A SELFISH LIFESTYLE (Amos 6:4–8)

The rich leaders of Samaria had completely turned all of their attention to their material wealth. They had become consumed with a lifestyle that was rich, elegant, exquisite, lavish, and excessive. They were only concerned with a higher standard of living that required the finest and best. From dining selections, fine clothing, wild parties, extravagant celebrations, grand mansions and expensive skin creams, the influential people of Israel had grown accustomed to a lifestyle that only served an elite class. Their lifestyle had caused them to lose focus on real-life issues around them. They were blind to the fact that as the elite became richer, the poor became poorer.

Loving Things Instead of God (verses 4–8)

4 That lie upon beds of ivory, and stretch themselves upon their couches, and eat the lambs out of the flock, and the calves out of the midst of the stall; 5 That chant to the sound of the viol, and invent to themselves instruments of musick, like David; 6 That drink wine in bowls, and anoint themselves with the chief ointments: but they are not grieved for the affliction of Joseph.

Verse 4 continues the woe that was declared in **verse 1**. In essence, he is saying, "Woe to you who put far off the day of doom . . . who sing idly to the sound of stringed instruments . . . who drink wine from bowls . . . but are not grieved." Amos had earlier prophesied against the houses of ivory, and now, it was the beds overlaid with ivory that invoked judgment (**Amos 3:15**). The eating of meat (lambs) with any regularity was the privilege of the wealthy. "The general population lived on wheat and barley and whatever fruits and vegetables were at hand, and if they had meat at all, they reserved it for times of high celebration. ... In contrast, Samaria's elite not only ate animals at random but also put their calves in special stalls to fatten them, undoubtedly on grain wrested from the poor" (Hubbard 193). Of course, Amos had earlier said that this luxury is obtained through robbery and violence against the poor (**3:10**).

The reclining (or lying down) and sprawling in **verses 4 and 7** depict not just comfort but drunken torpor—possibly of the religious kind like those mentioned in **Isaiah 65:11** and **Jeremiah 44:17**. The traditional custom in Israel at the time was to eat while sitting on rugs or seats. The practice of reclining at meals that Amos describes here is foreign. The Hebrew *sarach* (**sah-RAHKH**), translated "sprawl" (NLT), means to "go free, unrestrained," and is used in Arabic for camels left loose to pasture where they choose and of hair hanging loose (Snaith 112). Hubbard adds that it may also mean "free fall" from weakness or fatigue (Hubbarb 193). The word *parat* (Heb., **pah-RAHT**), generally translated "to chant," "to improvise," or "to sing extemporaneously," suggests a flow of trivial words in which the rhythm of words and music was everything but the sense and meaning nothing (Hubbard 193). Overall, scholars have concluded that this might have been a cultic banquet that was associated with specific deities and met periodically to celebrate with food and drink, and sometimes with sacred sexual orgies (Hubbard 192). These feasts were practiced for centuries across the Mediterranean basin and were known for their lavish consumption (Dunn 694). *Mizraq* (Heb., **miz-RAHK**) suggests that they used special bowls or basins for their wine-drinking, not ordinary cups. However we understand Amos' imagery, their parties featured extreme extravagance and careless ease.

The whole chapter pictures an upper class too self-centered and intent on its own pleasure as to find Amos' prediction of catastrophe credible. We see their apathy expressed in the clause, "they are not grieved for the affliction of Joseph," i.e., their own Northern Kingdom. Hubbard interprets this to say they have been sick for the wrong reasons: their drunkenness and their mourning of the dead (**6:9–10**). As they enjoyed all their luxuries, they had not even the slightest concern for the broken-down state of the nation of Israel. Much like today, selfishness and greed caused people to only look for their own comfort, often at the expense of the needy.

7 Therefore now shall they go captive with the first that go captive, and the banquet of them that stretched themselves shall be removed. 8 The Lord GOD hath sworn by himself, saith the LORD the God of hosts, I abhor the excellency of Jacob, and hate his palaces: therefore will I deliver up the city with all that is therein.

The prophet's "therefore" begins to conclude the rebuke. Everything—all their drunken gluttonous orgies—will come to an end. Just as He rejects the sound of their worship (**Amos 5:21–24**), God also finds the noise of their amusement nauseous. These careless leaders of today will tomorrow lead the pitiful column of captives who go into exile. Thus, with tragic irony, Amos declares that they will be first to the bitter end. These notables of the "first of nations" (**v. 1**) who used "first quality oils" (**v. 6**) are now to be "first of the exiles." Where revelry filled the air, there shall remain only ominous silence (Mays 117). This prophecy emphasizes the unusually strong announcement of judgment that Amos also gives in **4:2** and **8:7**, "The Lord has sworn by himself." Mays observes, "That Yahweh takes oath on his own person (as in **Jeremiah 22:5, 49:13, 51:14**) makes the decree more final, because the total force of Yahweh's integrity is invested in this solemn oath—the ancient Near East's most binding form of commitment" (Mays 118).

The language used here is "the strongest possible language God used to express wrath … the language of abhorrence, hatred and chiasm" (Hubbard 195). The Lord abhors the "pride of Jacob." This pride of Jacob—which might actually be the city of Samaria (Dunn 694)—speaks of Israel's national self-confidence, which meant their displacement of Yahweh as the foundation of their national existence. However, God was about to judge their pride by sending an army that would bring them low. In addition, God hates the strongholds of Jacob—the strongholds that gave Israel a sense of self-sufficiency and security but were filled with the spoils of robbery and violence. They were like a monument before God as constant reminders of the pride of the rich and the plight of the poor. Mays adds, "The city and its strongholds ... enshrines the worst of Israel's guilt. The powerful rich may think themselves invulnerable against any foe, but when Yahweh is against them, their strength is useless and their defenses already breached (Mays 119). This chapter concludes with the promise that God will raise up a nation against Israel to afflict them (**v. 14**). Assyria defeated Israel in 721/722 B.C., during the reign of King Hoshea of Israel.

SEARCH THE SCRIPTURES

QUESTIONS 1 & 2

What are the the signs of Israel's selfishness?

What does the Lord despise and hate about Israel?

LIGHT ON THE WORD

The Israelites Forgot About God

Often when we experience an increase of wealth, we forget about God and the plight of others. The elite of Israel had only used their wealth for selfish and luxurious needs, forsaking those who were suffering among them. Amos declares an oath from the Sovereign Lord that God is angry at their conceited and arrogant way of living. God holds the wealthy accountable for the use of their resources and whether they use it for the blessing of others instead of selfishness.

II. PUNISHMENT FOR THE SELF-INDULGENT (vv. 11–14)

The Lord has promised to enact severe punishment on Israel because of their refusal to repent. God will not only punish individuals, but plans to completely destroy their houses and buildings.

Disobedience and Destruction (verses 11–14)

11 For, behold, the LORD commandeth, and he will smite the great house with breaches, and the little house with clefts.

In judgment, God will smite the great house with breaches and the small house with clefts. Some scholars have said that the great house stands for Israel and the small house is Judah. For instance, Jerome interprets the former being reduced to branches or ruins, literally, "small drops"; the latter, though injured with "clefts" or rents, which threaten its fall, is still permitted to stand (Mays 120). Other scholars believe that "great house" and "small house" have nothing to do with Israel and Judah. This is because Amos primarily prophesied to the former and not the latter, and there is no other evidence of these terms being used for Israel and Judah. A better interpretation of the verse is that the judgment would come to both wealthy and poor. Why? Because rich and poor alike were guilty of turning away from Jehovah to serve their appetites. Destruction and death did not spare anyone.

12 Shall horses run upon the rock? will one plow there with oxen? for ye have turned judgment into gall, and the fruit of righteousness into hemlock: 13 Ye which rejoice in a thing of nought, which say, Have we not taken to us horns by our own strength?

Horses do not run on cliffs like mountain goats, nor can one plough through boulders with an ox. These are both absurd scenarios. In turning "justice into poison, and . . . righteousness into wormwood" (or hemlock, which is bitter and noxious), the Israelites were acting perversely. Thus, as horses and oxen are useless on a rock, so the Israelites are making justice poisonous. The absurd is happening in Israel. Arnold Schultz interprets this verse as saying, "There is a spiritual and moral order in the universe that is just as impossible to ignore as the natural order. It is as senseless to pervert justice as it is to expect horses to run on the rocks, or for oxen to plow on rock" (835). It is, thus, easier to change the course of nature than the course of God's providence or the laws of His just retribution.

The national leaders felt proud and confident because under Jeroboam, Israel had recaptured some territory that it had formerly lost to Aram (**2 Kings 14:25**). These recaptured lands included the town of Lodebar in Transjordan (**2 Samuel 9:4, 17:27**). Amos, however, cleverly made light of this feat by deliberately misspelling the city's name as "Lo-debar," which means "not a thing" (Mays 122). They had taken nothing of much value. The people were also claiming that they had taken the town of Karnaim (whose name means "a pair of horns," symbols of strength) by their own strength. It was not they but Yahweh, however, who had strengthened them to achieve this victory over a symbolically strong town. Therefore, Israel's leaders celebrate the capture of nothing and think they have captured it by their own strength (Mays 122).

14 But, behold, I will raise up against you a nation, O house of Israel, saith the LORD the God of hosts; and they shall afflict you from the entering in of Hemath unto the river of the wilderness.

Archaeological reports suggest that the capture was exactly and terribly fulfilled just as God had promised. Less than forty years after Amos wrote this prophecy, the Northern Kingdom was destroyed by Sargon of Assyria. "Behold" indicates God's resolute emphasis, as Yahweh had sworn by Himself (**v. 8**). God, through His power and sovereignty, raises up Sargon and the Assyrian empire to defeat and oppress the nation of Israel. "With power, he identifies himself as the Lord of all armies and with specificity, he directs his announcement to the whole house of Israel" (Hubbard 200). Selfishness, greed, and pride do not only affect the leaders of the nation; they affect everyone. The influence of Israel's leaders has corrupted the nation. Thus, the whole house of Israel is doomed to disaster by the complacency and corruption of their leaders.

LIGHT ON THE WORD

Twisted Justice

The prophet explains that God will punish them because they twisted justice into a poison doing more harm than good. God mocks Israel for their prideful celebration over smaller cities that they had successfully conquered. Finally, their ultimate judgment is given as God announces that another force will be raised up against them to return the oppression that they have afflicted on others. Selfishness always ends with judgment; the selfish can expect to reap the fruits of what they have sown.

BIBLE APPLICATION

AIM: Students will acknowledge that people of faith, responding to God's desire for justice, examine their ways of life.

In many places around the world, people are living in underserved and impoverished areas. They are suffering from lack of clean water, fresh produce, safe living conditions, and other resources that affect their everyday lives. There is not an equal distribution of wealth in our world. The powerful will continue to get rich, while the poor and working class will continue to suffer. The issue with wealth that is mentioned in this text is not the possession of wealth, but the dangers of being selfish, prideful, and sinful in the ways we use it. If we choose to ignore the injustices of the poor and needy, then we are at risk of God's punishment.

STUDENTS' RESPONSES

AIM: Students will discover that people of faith grieve and repent when God's people live unjustly.

We are tempted to ignore injustice because we are wealthy and comfortable. To combat this tendency, we can show solidarity with those who are disadvantaged. As a class, make a commitment to eat only one meal a day as an act of solidarity with those who live in hunger. While you are doing that, research ways in which you as a class can help fight global hunger. You can find many resources for this at the Bread for the World website (http://www.bread.org/help).

PRAYER

Lord, we do not always choose to love good, seek justice, and walk humbly before You. Thank You for another chance to love good, seek justice, and walk humbly before You. In Jesus' Name we pray. Amen.

HOW TO SAY IT

Lo-Debar. lo-de-**BAR**.

Karnaim. kar-**NAH**-yim.

PREPARE FOR NEXT SUNDAY

Read **Amos 8:1–6, 9–10** and study "God Will Never Forget."

DAILY HOME BIBLE READINGS

MONDAY
Israel's Guilt and Punishment
(Amos 3:1–11)

TUESDAY
Jeroboam II's Reign
(2 Kings 14:23–28)

WEDNESDAY
Israel Carried Captive to Assyria
(2 Kings 17:5–23)

THURSDAY
Judah Carried Captive to Babylon
(2 Kings 25:1–21)

FRIDAY
Warning to Rich Oppressors
(James 5:1–6)

SATURDAY
The Deserted City
(Lamentations 1)

SUNDAY
God Has Got a Plan for This
(Jeremiah 29:10–14)

Sources:

Anderson, Francis I., and David Noel Freedman. *The Anchor Bible.* 1st Edition. New York: Doubleday, 1989.

Bitrus, Daniel. *Africa Bible Commentary.* Ed. Tokunboh Adeyemo. Grand Rapids, MI: Zondervan, 2006.

Boling, Robert G. *The Anchor Bible: Judges.* Vol. 6A. Garden City, NY: Doubleday & Company, Inc., 1975.

Dunn, James D. G., and J. W. Rogerson. *Eerdmans Commentary on the Bible.* Grand Rapids, MI: W.B. Eerdmans, 2003.

Gowan, Donald E. *The New Interpreter's Bible: A Commentary in Twelve Volumes.* Nashville, TN: Abdingdon Press, 1996.

Hubbard, David Allan. *Joel and Amos: An Introduction and Commentary.* Downers Grove, IL: InterVarsity Press, 1989.

Mays, James Luther. *Amos: A Commentary.* Philadelphia: Westminster, 1969.

Schultz, Arnold. *Wycliffe Bible Commentary.* Chicago: Moody Press, 1962.

Snaith, Norman Henry. *The Book of Amos.* London: Epworth Press, 1945.

GOD WILL NEVER FORGET

BIBLE BASIS: AMOS 8:1–6, 9–10

BIBLE TRUTH: Amos says that God will no longer overlook their misdeeds and will destroy them for all time.

MEMORY VERSE: "And he said, Amos, what seest thou? And I said, A basket of summer fruit. Then said the LORD unto me, The end is come upon my people of Israel; I will not again pass by them any more" (Amos 8:2).

LESSON AIM: By the end of the lesson, your students will: explore unjust practices and their consequences during Amos' time; reflect on how the church practices injustices and seems to be oblivious; encourage the church to address injustices practiced within our community of faith.

TEACHER PREPARATION

MATERIALS NEEDED: Quarterly Commentary/Teacher Manual, Adult Quarterly, Adult resources—charts, worksheets, and other teaching tools, paper, pens, pencils, Bibles (several different versions)

OTHER MATERIALS NEEDED / TEACHER'S NOTES:

____

____

LESSON OVERVIEW

LIFE NEED FOR TODAY'S LESSON

People must be careful and not allow their deceit and cheating of others to become their way of life and miss the warning signs of the consequences of their wicked ways.

BIBLE LEARNING

Celebrations by the oppressors becomes clearly hypocritical and focused on selfish gain.

BIBLE APPLICATION

People of faith live to obey God rather than to test God.

STUDENTS' RESPONSES

People of faith will reflect on and analyze the root causes of injustice and their involvement in that injustice.

LESSON SCRIPTURE

AMOS 8:1–6, 9–10, KJV

1 Thus hath the Lord GOD shewed unto me: and behold a basket of summer fruit.

2 And he said, Amos, what seest thou? And I said, A basket of summer fruit. Then said the LORD unto me, The end is come

AMOS 8:1–6, 9–10, NIV

1 This is what the Sovereign LORD showed me: a basket of ripe fruit.

2 "What do you see, Amos?" he asked. "A basket of ripe fruit," I answered. Then the LORD said to me, "The time is ripe for my people Israel; I will spare them no longer.

upon my people of Israel; I will not again pass by them any more.

3 And the songs of the temple shall be howlings in that day, saith the Lord GOD: there shall be many dead bodies in every place; they shall cast them forth with silence.

4 Hear this, O ye that swallow up the needy, even to make the poor of the land to fail,

5 Saying, When will the new moon be gone, that we may sell corn? And the sabbath, that we may set forth wheat, making the ephah small, and the shekel great, and falsifying the balances by deceit?

6 That we may buy the poor for silver, and the needy for a pair of shoes; yea, and sell the refuse of the wheat?

9 And it shall come to pass in that day, saith the Lord GOD, that I will cause the sun to go down at noon, and I will darken the earth in the clear day:

10 And I will turn your feasts into mourning, and all your songs into lamentation; and I will bring up sackcloth upon all loins, and baldness upon every head; and I will make it as the mourning of an only son, and the end thereof as a bitter day.

3 "In that day," declares the Sovereign LORD, "the songs in the temple will turn to wailing. Many, many bodies—flung everywhere! Silence!"

4 Hear this, you who trample the needy and do away with the poor of the land,

5 saying, "When will the New Moon be over that we may sell grain, and the Sabbath be ended that we may market wheat?"—skimping on the measure, boosting the price and cheating with dishonest scales,

6 buying the poor with silver and the needy for a pair of sandals, selling even the sweepings with the wheat.

9 "In that day," declares the Sovereign LORD, "I will make the sun go down at noon and darken the earth in broad daylight.

10 I will turn your religious festivals into mourning and all your singing into weeping. I will make all of you wear sackcloth and shave your heads. I will make that time like mourning for an only son and the end of it like a bitter day.

LIGHT ON THE WORD

Amos' personal name means "one who is carried," and he was a prophet from Judah who ministered in Israel around 750 B.C. Some might describe the prophet Amos as a "burden bearer." He carried a heavy burden for his people, or his people were a burden he carried.

The New Moon was a festival held at the beginning of every lunar month. The priests would offer a burnt offering. This consisted of two male calves, one ram, and seven spotless lambs combined with a drink offering of wine. These offerings were accompanied by the blowing of the trumpet or shofar. All trade and commerce were stopped as on the Sabbath. The spiritual significance of the New Moon festival can be found in the setting apart of a natural division of time.

TEACHING THE BIBLE LESSON

LIFE NEED FOR TODAY'S LESSON

AIM: Students will learn to be careful and not allow their deceit and cheating of others to become their way of life and miss the warning signs of the consequences of their wicked ways.

INTRODUCTION

The Lord's Visions for Amos

The Lord gave Amos a series of visions that described Israel's complete destruction. The first vision that Amos receives is a swarm of locusts. These locusts would come at the most inopportune time, right after the king's portion had been harvested and the next crop was beginning to grow. If locusts came, then there would be a famine for the people. After Amos pleaded to spare the people, the Lord relented and showed him a devouring fire that consumed the land. Amos pleaded again and the Lord relented. Next Amos was shown a plumb line. This was a weight that builders used to make sure that walls were constructed properly. Israel would be shown to not be in line with God's standards and torn down. Before Amos could plead for God's mercy, the Lord confirmed that the nation of Israel would be judged.

Then Amos is confronted by Amaziah, the priest of Bethel. This confrontation results in Amos being charged with conspiracy against the king. Amos had denounced the legitimacy of the shrine at Bethel and the people's worship. As a result, Amaziah told Amos to go back to Judah and earn a living as a prophet there. Amos responds to this by stating that he is a farmer and a shepherd and that his prophetic calling is not for monetary gain, but a divine mandate from the Lord. He prophesies that Amaziah's family would die and that foreigners would claim his property. Amos adds that Amaziah himself would die in a foreign land. After this the Lord shows Amos a vision of a basket of ripe fruit and predicts the end of Israel.

BIBLE LEARNING

AIM: Students will know celebrations by the oppressors becomes clearly hypocritical and focused on selfish gain.

I. HUMAN GRIEF (Amos 8:1–3)

Amos' vision begins with a basket of summer fruit. This fruit was a symbol for Israel's impending judgment. The summer fruit was the fruit gathered in the harvest season. God was communicating a message to Israel through Amos: the time is ripe. The end had come for Israel and they were ripe for God's wrath. The Lord would spare them no longer. He could no longer offer them grace and show patience in the face of their persistent injustice and disobedience.

An Imminent Devastation (verses 1–3)

1 Thus hath the Lord GOD shewed unto me: and behold a basket of summer fruit. 2 And he said, Amos, what seest thou? And I said, A basket of summer fruit. Then said the LORD unto me, The end is come upon my people of Israel; I will not again pass by them any more. 3 And the songs of the temple shall be howlings in that day, saith the Lord GOD: there shall be many dead bodies in every place; they shall cast them forth with silence.

In the closing verses of **chapter 7**, Amos had confronted the priest Amaziah and pronounced an oracle of judgment against him for his failure to believe the Word of God (**Amos 7:16–17**). Now he resumes where he left off and continues the account of his visions. He begins by authenticating his fourth vision the same way as the previous ones, by declaring that the Lord showed him a vision (**7:1, 4, 7**). In the last vision in **7:7–9**, Amos declared that the end was certain but here he declares its imminence. The present vision is to reiterate and make final the previous one. He saw a basket of summer fruit (Heb. *qayits*, **KAH-yits**) and heard a response from the Lord that the "end" (Heb. *qets*, **KATES**) has come. Usually, summer fruit was not preserved but eaten as soon as it was gathered. So the Lord hints by this symbol and the pun on the word "end" that the kingdom of Israel was now ripe for destruction, and punishment must descend on it without delay. The Lord "will not again pass by them any more," that is, he will spare them no longer. However, the Hebrew word "end" here does not merely refer to its ripeness for judgment in a temporal sense, but its destruction and devastation.

There will be two responses. First, all the joy shall be turned into mourning. The songs of joy would be turned into yells, that is, into sounds of lamentation because of the multitude of the dead on the ground on every side. The word "howling" describes an inarticulate, shattering scream common during funerals, particularly in times of sudden devastation. Second, there will be silence, an appropriate response to God's severe judgment, accompanied by a destruction of untold proportions—"there shall be many dead bodies in every place."

SEARCH THE SCRIPTURES

QUESTION 1

What did God show Amos?

LIGHT ON THE WORD

The Songs of Misery

The Lord goes on to say that Israel's Temple songs would turn into the sounds of grief and misery. The Temple in Bethel was the foundation of the nation. It was the spiritual foundation to the political kingdom. The destruction of this Temple would definitely mean the destruction of the Northern Kingdom. The "dead bodies" everywhere would only elicit the response of silence. It suggests that because of the horror of this scene, anyone who was left would be at a loss for words.

II. COSMIC GRIEF (vv. 4–6, 9–10)

After the Lord shows them the grief they will experience, He shows them the reason for the coming judgment. They will be grieved because He has been grieved. He has put up with their trampling of the poor and needy. They anticipated the end of the New Moons and Sabbaths so they could go on cheating the people by selling inferior products and creating dishonest scales so they could make a profit. Instead of seeking justice for the poor, they sought ways to enslave them for negligible amounts of money: the price of sandals. They clearly had a low perspective on human life.

The Greedy Swallow Up the Needy (verses 4–6, 9–10)

4 Hear this, O ye that swallow up the needy, even to make the poor of the land to fail, 5 Saying, When will the new moon be gone, that we may sell corn? And the sabbath, that we may set forth wheat, making the ephah small, and the shekel great, and falsifying the balances by deceit? 6 That we may buy the poor for silver, and the needy for a pair of shoes; yea, and sell the refuse of the wheat?

Amos gives the reasons for the judgment and punishment. Israel failed to take care of its needy and poor, but instead exploited them and swallowed them up. The poor, vulnerable, and unprotected members of the society were treated harshly and unjustly. The rich grew richer on the back of the poor, and the poor became poorer. Yet these oppressive merchants kept going on with their religious activities, observing the Sabbath and other festivals. Worship, fraud, exploitation, and oppression went on simultaneously. Their worship was superficial, formal, and hypocritical. They detested the rest of the Sabbath, wanting to keep it as short as possible if they could, so as not to rest from their frauds. They considered the time spent for the festivals as business time lost. Amos quoted the merchants to show their attitude toward worship, "When will the new moon be gone, that we may sell corn and the Sabbath, that we may set forth wheat . . . ?" Their greed caused them to use deception to increase their profits. On the one hand, they reduced the weight, "made the ephah small," and on the other hand, they "made the shekel great," that is, increased the prices both ways by paring down the quantity which they sold and by obtaining more silver by fictitious weights, and weighing in uneven balances. Customers had no choice but to pay more than what the items they purchased were worth. Merchants bought the poor and confiscated their property as payment for debts. It sounds like modern-day "payday lending." Israel's sins are descriptive of our contemporary society.

For those living in the Western world, materialism is another god. Possessiveness is a great challenge. It is a world of opulence, one drowned in affluence. It raises several questions: At whose expense are we being enriched? Are workers being underpaid? What of those who rig the market, speculate with currency, or specialize in the financial subterfuge that falls only just short of outright theft? We must also remember that human greed for profit at the expense of the innocent destroys a society in the just desserts of divine repayment. It is indeed akin to a kind of religion, evoking profound love of self and happy acceptance of the ruin of others, neglecting God's command to love God and neighbors first (**Matthew 22:36–40**). But insatiable greed is so fundamentally foreign to the whole truth of God that it must not be tolerated but seriously condemned. But as Amos sees it, the foundations of avarice are so firm that only something earth-shattering could weaken its proud structures.

9 And it shall come to pass in that day, saith the Lord GOD, that I will cause the sun to go down at noon, and I will darken the earth in the clear day:

The first phrase "and it shall come to pass" in **v. 9** translates the Hebrew word wehaya (**we-haw-YAH**), usually denoting that what follows as occurring in the future. "In that day" points to a time of the Lord's visitation to bring additional judgment and disasters on Israel. Israel needed to know that what was going to happen to them was the Day of the Lord. Amos refers to a devastation, namely a total eclipse of the sun. The Lord would create a day of darkness that would turn their merriment into misery, and transform their happy days into lamentation and mourning. The day of light would become a day of darkness, the eclipsed sun symbolizing that the light of God's face would be hidden from Israel. There are similar images of the Lord bringing darkness in times of judgment in several passages (see **Isaiah 59:10; Jeremiah 13:16, 15:9**). The imagery here of darkness on a clear day is shocking and symbolically expresses the sudden and unexpected end of Israel's prosperity and the darkening of her glory days, just when the nation seemed at its pinnacle of power. Nations today must be warned because God has not changed.

10 And I will turn your feasts into mourning, and all your songs into lamentation; and I will bring up sackcloth upon all loins, and baldness upon every head; and I will make it as the mourning of an only son, and the end thereof as a bitter day.

The consequences of Israel's failure to follow the Lord continue to reverberate in **verse 10**. Because of God's judgments, happy days will become harrowing days, festivals will be turned into mourning and joy to sadness. Because Israel had turned God's justice and righteousness into bitterness and poison (cf. **5:7; 6:12**), He would turn their joy into grief. One cannot celebrate light and live in darkness. Baldness on every head suggests that every person in Israel would be touched by the grief-causing calamity. The Lord vowed to make the coming grief "like mourning for an only son." The loss of an only son produces an unspeakable grief. Such great sorrow attends the loss of an only son because not only is all hope for continuing one's family gone, but also the provision for one's old age (cf. **Jeremiah 6:26; Zechariah 12:10**). Mourning an only son is always a bitter experience—it is a picture of hopelessness. The day that starts out with mourning an only son is sure to end as bitter as it began. If we really desire the light of God to shine on us, then we must walk in the light.

SEARCH THE SCRIPTURES

QUESTIONS 2 and 3

When will God cause the sun to go down and what will happen to the earth?

What was God going to turn their feasts into?

LIGHT ON THE WORD

God's Power in Darkness

The Lord announces what will happen to them on the day of punishment. It will be cosmic in scope. The sun will go down at noon. The earth will be darkened in broad daylight. Aside from the fact that this actually happened in 763 B.C., when there was an eclipse of the sun along with an earthquake, these words carry additional significance. The darkness announced here would remind Israel of the judgment on Egypt. Where before the Lord's judgment fell on Pharaoh and his kingdom, now the Lord's judgment falls on the Northern Kingdom for their own stubbornness and disobedience. It will be a day of mourning. Feasting and celebration will cease; all the songs they sing will be gloomy funeral dirges. The Lord's judgment will cause them to wear sackcloth and shave their heads, a sign of repentance toward God. By then it will be too late. They will mourn just like the Egyptians mourned for their firstborn children. God will remember their sins of injustice and oppression and judge accordingly.

BIBLE APPLICATION

AIM: Students will accept to live and obey God rather than to test God.

The profit motive drives most of what we do in a capitalist economy. While this has created many blessings for those with no opportunity, it has also created a culture in which we worship at the god of "profit." Whatever will sell, we will sell it regardless of whether it affects our fellow citizens negatively. As long as we can find a way to boost our finances, we buy and sell with no regard for the consequences. The Lord calls us to seek justice even in our commerce. These things brought judgment on the nation of Israel and may bring judgment on us as well.

STUDENTS' RESPONSES

AIM: Students will reflect on and analyze the root causes of injustice and their involvement in that injustice.

The greed and injustice of many corporate and business leaders is all around us if we open our eyes to see it. In the coming week, find an example online or in a newspaper of the ways that people's greed has led to oppression of the weak and vulnerable. Come back to class ready to share what you have discovered and an idea for combating this injustice.

PRAYER

Oh God! You brought us through so many troubled waters of racism, economic exploitation, and other isms. Yet, we do not always honor and worship You for all of the many blessings You have given us, and the justice that has prevailed in our lives. Help us keep focused on Your justice and not just-us. In Jesus' Name we pray. Amen.

HOW TO SAY IT

Amaziah. am-uh-**ZEE**-uh.

Ephah. ee-**FAH**.

PREPARE FOR NEXT SUNDAY

Read **Micah 2:4–11** and study "No Rest for the Wicked."

DAILY HOME BIBLE READINGS

MONDAY
A Famine of Hearing God's Word
(Amos 8:11–14)

TUESDAY
Reaping the Whirlwind
(Hosea 8:7–14)

WEDNESDAY
Days of Punishment Have Come
(Hosea 9:5–9)

THURSDAY
Israel's Sin Shall Be Destroyed
(Hosea 10:1–8)

FRIDAY
Israel Refused to Return to Me
(Hosea 11:1–7)

SATURDAY
God Will Remember Their Iniquity
(Jeremiah 14:1–10)

SUNDAY
A Day of Mourning and Lamentation
(Amos 8:1–6, 9–10)

Sources:

Achtemmeier, Elizabeth. *Minor Prophets 1.* Understanding the Bible Commentary Series. Grand Rapids, MI: Baker Books, 1996.

Craigie, Peter C. *Twelve Prophets.* The Daily Study Bible Series. Vol. 1. Louisville, KY: Westminster John Knox Press, 1984.

Nogalski, James D. *The Book of the Twelve: Hosea–Jonah.* Macon, GA: Smyth and Helwys Publishing, Inc., 2011.

Smith, Billy K., and Franklin S. Page. *Amos, Obadiah, Jonah. The New American Commentary.* Vol. 19B. Nashville, TN: Broadman & Holman Publishers, 1995.

Stuart, Douglas. *Hosea–Jonah.* Word Biblical Commentary. Vol. 31. Dallas: Word Publishers, 2002.

de Waard, Jan, and William Allen Smalley. *A Translator's Handbook on the Book of Amos.* UBS Handbook Series. Stuttgart, Germany: United Bible Societies, 1979.

NO REST FOR THE WICKED

BIBLE BASIS: MICAH 2:4–11

BIBLE TRUTH: God gives no rest to those who practice evil against His faithful ones.

MEMORY VERSE: "O thou that art named the house of Jacob, is the spirit of the LORD straitened? are these his doings? do not my words do good to him that walketh uprightly?" (Micah 2:7).

LESSON AIM: By the end of the lesson, your students will: explore Micah's depiction of people who deny their wrongdoing in the community; express feelings about people who attempt to justify the evil and harm they commit; and respond with appropriate opposition to those engaged in wrongdoing in the community.

TEACHER PREPARATION

MATERIALS NEEDED: Quarterly Commentary/Teacher Manual, Adult Quarterly, Adult resources—charts, worksheets, and other teaching tools, paper, pens, pencils, Bibles (several different versions)

OTHER MATERIALS NEEDED / TEACHER'S NOTES:

LESSON OVERVIEW

LIFE NEED FOR TODAY'S LESSON
People do not want to be confronted with their social and moral abuse of others.

BIBLE LEARNING
Micah confronted those whose evil actions resulted in the suffering of innocent people.

BIBLE APPLICATION
Believers affirm that God is in control despite the presence of evil and suffering.

STUDENTS' RESPONSES
Students will step out in God's power to speak and act for justice.

LESSON SCRIPTURE

MICAH 2:4–11, KJV

4 In that day shall one take up a parable against you, and lament with a doleful lamentation, and say, We be utterly spoiled: he hath changed the portion of my people: how hath he removed it from me! turning away he hath divided our fields.

MICAH 2:4–11, NIV

4 In that day people will ridicule you; they will taunt you with this mournful song: 'We are utterly ruined; my people's possession is divided up. He takes it from me! He assigns our fields to traitors.'"

5 Therefore you will have no one in the

5 Therefore thou shalt have none that shall cast a cord by lot in the congregation of the LORD.

6 Prophesy ye not, say they to them that prophesy: they shall not prophesy to them, that they shall not take shame.

7 O thou that art named the house of Jacob, is the spirit of the LORD straitened? are these his doings? do not my words do good to him that walketh uprightly?

8 Even of late my people is risen up as an enemy: ye pull off the robe with the garment from them that pass by securely as men averse from war.

9 The women of my people have ye cast out from their pleasant houses; from their children have ye taken away my glory for ever.

10 Arise ye, and depart; for this is not your rest: because it is polluted, it shall destroy you, even with a sore destruction.

11 If a man walking in the spirit and falsehood do lie, saying, I will prophesy unto thee of wine and of strong drink; he shall even be the prophet of this people.

assembly of the LORD to divide the land by lot.

6 "Do not prophesy," their prophets say. "Do not prophesy about these things; disgrace will not overtake us."

7 You descendants of Jacob, should it be said, "Does the LORD become impatient? Does he do such things?" "Do not my words do good to the one whose ways are upright?

8 Lately my people have risen up like an enemy. You strip off the rich robe from those who pass by without a care, like men returning from battle.

9 You drive the women of my people from their pleasant homes. You take away my blessing from their children forever.

10 Get up, go away! For this is not your resting place, because it is defiled, it is ruined, beyond all remedy.

11 If a liar and deceiver comes and says, 'I will prophesy for you plenty of wine and beer,' that would be just the prophet for this people!

LIGHT ON THE WORD

Micah's name is actually a sentence that befittingly proclaims "Who is like Yah(weh)?" Micah boldly proclaims in **3:8**, "I am filled with authority, justice and courage," all of which are reflected in his oracles (messages from God). These oracles concerned the destruction of Jerusalem and Samaria due to injustice, corrupt government, idolatry, and dishonest economic principles. One of Micah's most amazing feats was that even within his prophecy of doom, he was able to remain hopeful regarding Jerusalem's future. He foretold of the Messiah and even the city of His birth. Micah is known as one of the twelve minor prophets, a category based solely on the length of the author's work, not their importance or status.

TEACHING THE BIBLE LESSON

LIFE NEED FOR TODAY'S LESSON

AIM: Students will learn that people do not want to be confronted with their social and moral abuse of others.

INTRODUCTION

God Rewards the Oppressors

Micah ministered during a time in which Assyria enjoyed great power and influence. The Northern Kingdom of Israel had already fallen. King Ahaz of Judah made an arrangement with Assyria to prevent the fall of Judah. The Southern Kingdom would pay large tribute and honor Assyria's gods. As a result, idol worship spread throughout Judah.

Samaria would be destroyed. The walls would be broken down, the foundations would be laid bare, and vineyards would be planted where their streets once were (**Micah 1:6**). Her destruction came in 722 B.C., after a three year siege by the Assyrian army.

The Lord also names specific cities in Judah where His judgment will be visited. The Lord gives His reasons for His judgment against Judah: the greed and covetousness of the rich and the oppression of the lower class.

Micah 2 begins with the description of the deeds of the wealthy land barons and their wanton greed. The rich seized the houses and land of the poor and stole their possessions. The Lord promises to reward their evil with evil and that the oppressors would themselves be oppressed.

BIBLE LEARNING

AIM: Students will discover that Micah confronted those whose evil actions resulted in the suffering of innocent people.

I. THE LAND DIVIDED (Micah 2:4–5)

The rich were getting richer at the expense of the poor. Greedy land barons were confiscating the lands, homes, and goods of the poor. The Lord promised judgment for this injustice, and tells them that they will suffer the same injustice (**vv. 4–5**). Assyria would confiscate the lands, homes, and goods that the rich had taken. Further, they would taunt Judah with their own lamentations.

Justice is Served! (verses 4–5)

4 In that day shall one take up a parable against you, and lament with a doleful lamentation, and say, We be utterly spoiled: he hath changed the portion of my people: how hath he removed it from me! turning away he hath divided our fields. 5 Therefore thou shalt have none that shall cast a cord by lot in the congregation of the LORD.

Beginning with **verse 2**, the prophet Micah presents a portrait of God's reversal of Judah's situation. In **verses 1–2**, the oppressing classes ruined others; they had used violence to deprive others of their possessions and take the fields of the poor. Now in **verse 4**, the tables are turned: the oppressors will become the oppressed, and their enemies will divide up their land. The Lord will take the fields away from the scheming land-grabbers in Israel, and give them to the treacherous Assyrians. The rich had seized the fields of their helpless victims (**v. 2**); now the Lord will take those fields and turn them over to enemies. So the rich are dispossessed of their ill-gotten property. Micah quotes the rich as saying, "We be utterly spoiled: he hath changed the portion of my people: how hath he removed it from me!" When the disaster comes, the rich landowners will be mocked. "Men will ridicule you" (NIV) is literally "he will lift up against you a parable." The Hebrew word *mashal* (**maw-SHAWL**), translated as "parable," is used here with the negative sense of a byword.

The prophet speaks on behalf of God (**v. 5**). He uses the word "therefore" to link this verse with the preceding verses, showing both the result and extent of the judgment. In the Old Testament, there were two ways in which land was returned to its original owner: first in the year of Jubilee (**Leviticus 25**), second by lot at the time of Joshua (**Joshua 14:2**), a practice that continued and was alluded to in **Psalm 16:6** (KJV). The latter is what Micah refers to here. The families of the oppressors will have no representation. The punishment fits the crime. What a solemn warning against greed, materialism and oppression. Because the guilty parties have dealt with their neighbors' fields unjustly, none of their descendants will be left in the Lord's covenant community who can use a cord (measuring line) to divide up the land by lot. So they will be cut off from the promises of the Lord's people. They will have no one to claim their inheritance, either because their family will be completely wiped out or they will all be in exile. People who have a desperate greed for land and material wealth turn their personal goals into their god, but such people will also learn the emptiness of riches, lands, and materials at their loss.

SEARCH THE SCRIPTURES

QUESTION 1

How does the Lord punish Judah for their evil practices?

LIGHT ON THE WORD

No Justice for the Unjust

The people of Judah would lament that they are "utterly spoiled" and that the Lord has taken away their inheritance. Their lands would be taken from them and given to their enemies. The "fields" that had been unjustly acquired would be divided among their conquerors.

II. THE LORD INCITED (vv. 6–9)

The people of Judah had no interest in Micah's message of judgment. "Don't prophesy like that," they said. They did not believe that any calamity would befall them. During this time, there were false prophets in Judah that only prophesied peace and blessing. The wealthy people of Judah preferred to hear the false messages. They did not want to hear any prophecies that exposed their faults or demanded change.

Micah—Stop Talking! (verses 6–9)

6 Prophesy ye not, say they to them that prophesy: they shall not prophesy to them, that they shall not take shame. 7 O thou that art named the house of Jacob, is the spirit of the LORD straitened? are these his doings? do not my words do good to him that walketh uprightly?

How true is the axiom that truth hurts! It is hardly surprising that Micah's stern message to the rich did not bring him popularity. The message sounded offensive to them, so they commanded him to stop saying such things as he had said in **2:1–5**. The verb used for prophesy is *nataf* (Heb., **naw-TAWF**), which means "to drip." Used in this context, it has a connotation of driveling or foaming at the mouth. The false prophets are really telling the Lord's prophets, "Stop foaming at the mouth," which shows their scorn for the message. The same is true today: charlatans reject all judgment, prophecy, and proclamation. They could not believe that disaster and disgrace would overtake them because they thought God would not do such things. It was, to them, a figment of Micah's imagination, but they were wrong. The greedy oppressors were confident that no evil would trouble them.

Micah's opponents used rhetorical questions to say, "Do not even mention judgment. God is not annoyed." The word *qatsar* (Heb.,

kaw-TSAR), translated "straitened" (KJV), literally means "short." Here Micah turns the words of the evildoers against them by asking of the Lord is "short of spirit," an idiom for "impatient" or "quick-tempered." The false prophets were teaching erroneously that the Lord's patience had no limits (cf. **Exodus 34:6–7a**). They cannot believe that the Lord would really lose His patience, especially with them. Surely, He must be able to put up easily with them despite their sins. So, they asked, "Is the Lord short-tempered," "Does the Lord get angry quickly?" Without waiting for an answer, they ask another question, "Are these things that you say will happen the deeds of God?" The final question admits that God is righteous, but if this question comes from the mouths of the oppressors, it shows that they assume that they also are among those who walk uprightly, and can thus expect that God will speak kindly to them. This assumption underlines their moral blindness. The point is that God's words or promises cause good to happen to the one who walks uprightly.

8 Even of late my people is risen up as an enemy: ye pull off the robe with the garment from them that pass by securely as men averse from war. 9 The women of my people have ye cast out from their pleasant houses; from their children have ye taken away my glory for ever.

Micah continues to describe the offenses of his hearers. He lists the specific sins of the people. God calls them "my people." However, their behavior did not reflect that of those that belong to God. It was a sad case of God's people living ungodly lives. He said, "Even of late," that is, only recently you have pulled off the robe of those who walked securely and men who were averse to war, a reference to the innocent and peaceful travellers. The women and children were not spared the humiliation and atrocities. The former were driven away from their houses, suggesting that these women might have been widows. The wealthy not only dispossessed women but also disinherited their children. Thus, the children were left without property, money, or security. Doubtless, a society could not be in a lower state of morality than when it oppresses and exploits the vulnerable in it. Micah's denouncements retain a pressing relevance in a world where such conditions continue. Covetousness and greed still have the same devastating results for defenseless women and children and the unprotected poor. For those who are called Christians, it is important that our character mirrors that of Christ.

SEARCH THE SCRIPTURES

QUESTION 2

What evil does the Lord judge them for?

LIGHT ON THE WORD

The Lord's Challenege

The Lord challenges the people of Judah: "Is the spirit of the Lord straitened? are these his doings?" (**v. 7**). In other words, "Has the patience of the Lord run short? Are these His deeds?" The false prophets had been preaching messages of the Lord's patience and long-suffering without preaching about His willingness to judge and discipline His people. When God established His covenant with Israel on Mount Sinai, He stated that He is "slow to anger" (**Exodus 34:6**). The belief that God is patient and forgiving was central to Israel's theology. Many believed that love would prevent the Lord from punishing them, and false teachers of Micah's time encouraged this belief (**v. 11**). The people did not want to be confronted with their sin and preferred to continue in their wicked ways.

The Lord continues, "Do not my words do good to him that walketh uprightly?" The righteous have no fear of judgment; those who walk uprightly can expect to be rewarded. This also implies that judgment could be averted with a behavioral change. Judah, however, had not been walking uprightly; they had engaged in wicked behavior characterized by greed and covetousness.

III. THE LIES INVITED (vv. 10–11)

The Lord gives His sentence against Judah: "Up! Begone! This is no longer your land and home, for you have filled it with sin and ruined it completely" (**v. 10**). The powerful land barons would be evicted from the very property they had stolen. In the same way that they stripped the poor, widows, and orphans of their lands and possessions, the Lord would strip them.

The Destiny of the Rich is Sealed (verses 10–11)

10 Arise ye, and depart; for this is not your rest: because it is polluted, it shall destroy you, even with a sore destruction.

This verse takes up again the theme of **verse 4** and announces the fate of the rich oppressors. The rich must get up and go into exile. The oppressors among God's people rose up like an enemy to increase their wealth and power at the expense of others among their own people; now the Lord tells them to prepare to leave their ill-gotten land and possessions behind. They who had evicted others from their land were about to be evicted themselves; they would go away into exile. Their wrongfully acquired land will no longer be their possession. The reason is that they defiled it with their sins and ruined it beyond all remedy. Others will take over their property acquired by fraud and oppression.

11 If a man walking in the spirit and falsehood do lie, saying, I will prophesy unto thee of wine and of strong drink; he shall even be the prophet of this people.

The section ends in **verse 11** as the prophet returns to practice of false prophecy. Micah says that his hearers are so deluded that if a preacher or prophet were to come along preaching the gospel of wine and strong drink, or prosperity gospel as we know it today, they would hire him immediately. Here, such a prophet is called a liar and deceiver, obviously because he does not tell the truth and so leads others astray. His message is one of peace and prosperity, "plenty of wine and beer" (NIV). The sinful, covenant-breaking people deserve that kind of prophet. Anyone who promises greater affluence will gain a hearing. False prophets are happy to oblige with "feel-good messages" so long as their hearers feed them and fill the coffers of the church or ministry with money (**3:5, 11**). The tests of true prophets are given in **Deuteronomy 13:1–3, 18:17–22**: A prophet's message must not contradict or disagree with the previous revelation of truth through true prophets (cf. **Isaiah 8:19–20**), and his predictions must come true. These prophets failed on both counts.

Today there are still false prophets and teachers both inside and outside the church. In recent years, some preachers throughout the world have not only made predictions about the coming of the Lord but also about those who might be elected to certain political offices. Unfortunately they have been proven wrong. There are still swindlers and hucksters who "peddle the word of God for profit" **(2 Corinthians 2:17, NIV)**. Jesus issued a warning about them **(Matthew 24:4–5, 10–11, 23–24)**; so did Paul and John **(1 Timothy 4:1–2; 1 John 2:18–19, 4:1–3)**. Such so-called ministers may masquerade as "apostles of Christ," but in reality they are "false apostles" and servants of Satan (**2 Corinthians 11:13–15**). They will exist as long as there are people who "will gather around them a great number of teachers to say what their itching ears want to hear" (from **2 Timothy 4:3**).

SEARCH THE SCRIPTURES

QUESTION 3

What is the message the people would like to hear?

LIGHT ON THE WORD

The Prosperity of Lies

The people of Judah had no regard for the Lord's message (**v. 11**). They preferred the false teachings of the prophets. Wine and strong drink represent prosperity. The people were looking for someone that would give only messages of peace and prosperity, rather than change and judgment. Instead of the truth, they would rather hear lies. This is a definite sign that they were truly not interested in doing God's will and seeking justice; they only sought their own selfish ends.

BIBLE APPLICATION

AIM: Students will affirm that God is in control despite the presence of evil and suffering.

The effects of greed can be felt throughout our society. Corporations have crushed the lives of countless people in their quest to make a profit. As a society, we have sought luxuries at the expense of workers and their wages. We put our material comforts ahead of justice for others. God is not pleased with this. Instead of wanting to hear the truth, we would rather hear preachers tell us about how much more money we are going to get or what expensive house or car God is going to give us. The Lord wants us to repent of our evil ways so we can hear the truth and seek justice for the oppressed.

STUDENTS' RESPONSES

AIM: Students will step out in God's power to speak and act for justice.

Greed was the driving force behind Judah's unjust ways. So often, the world prompts us to get all we can, even at the expense of others. Instead God calls us to seek out the welfare of the poor and weak. One way that we can do that is fight against modern slavery. Take some time to learn more about the conditions and what you can do at the "Not For Sale" website (http://www.notforsalecampaign.org/about/slavery/slavery-faq).

PRAYER

Jesus, we seek to learn more or grow deeper in what we do for others. Lord, let us be receptive to people caring for us when we are in need, so that we in turn will be refreshed and ready to care for others. In Jesus' Name we pray. Amen.

HOW TO SAY IT

Doleful.	**DOL**-ful.
Averse.	a-**VERS**.

PREPARE FOR NEXT SUNDAY

Read **Micah 3:5–12** and study "No Tolerance for Corrupt Leaders and Prophets."

DAILY HOME BIBLE READINGS

MONDAY
Good Deeds for the Oppressed
(Job 29:7–17)

TUESDAY
Attention to the Needs of Others
(Job 31:13–22)

WEDNESDAY
Judge Me, O Lord
(Psalm 7:1–8)

THURSDAY
Test My Mind and Heart
(Psalm 7:9–17)

FRIDAY
The Lord Executes Judgment
(Psalm 9:15–20)

SATURDAY
The Righteous and the Wicked
(Proverbs 11:1–10)

SUNDAY
A Day of Bitter Lamentation
(Micah 2:4–11)

Sources:

Allen, Leslie C. *The Books of Joel, Obadiah, Jonah and Micah*. New International Commentary of the Old Testament. Grand Rapids, MI: Wm. B. Eerdmans, 1976.

Barker, Kenneth L. *Micah, Nahum, Habakkuk, Zephaniah*. The New American Commentary. Vol. 20. Nashville, TN: Broadman & Holman Publishers, 1999.

Boice, J. M. *The Minor Prophets*. 2 vols. Complete in one edition. Grand Rapids, MI: Kregel, 1996.

Clark, David J. and Norm Mundhenk. *A Translator's Handbook on the Book of Micah, UBS Handbook Series*. London: United Bible Societies, 1982.

Craigie, P. C. *Twelve Prophets*. 2 vols. Philadelphia: Westminster, 1985. S.v. 2:19.

Dockery, David S., ed. *Holman Concise Bible Commentary*. Nashville, TN: Broadman & Holman Publishers, 1998.

Easton, M. G. *Easton's Bible Dictionary*. New York: Harper & Brothers, 1893.

Feinberg, Charles L. *The Minor Prophets*. Chicago: Moody Press, 1976.

Henry, Matthew. *Matthew Henry's Commentary on the Whole Bible: Complete and Unabridged in One Volume*. Peabody, MA: Hendrickson, 1994.

Jamieson, Robert, A. R. Fausset and David Brown. *Commentary Critical and Explanatory on the Whole Bible*. Oak Harbor, WA: Logos Research Systems, Inc., 1997.

Myers, Allen C. *The Eerdmans Bible Dictionary*. Grand Rapids, MI: Eerdmans, 1987.

Smith, James E. *The Minor Prophets*. Old Testament Survey Series. Joplin, MO: College Press, 1994.

Smith, Ralph L. *Micah–Malachi*. Word Biblical Commentary. Vol. 32. Dallas: Word, Incorporated, 1998.

Walvoord, John F., Roy B. Zuck, and Dallas Theological Seminary. *The Bible Knowledge Commentary: An Exposition of the Scriptures*. Wheaton, IL: Victor Books, 1985.

COMMENTS / NOTES:

NO TOLERANCE FOR CORRUPT LEADERS AND PROPHETS

BIBLE BASIS: MICAH 3:5–12

BIBLE TRUTH: God will judge and punish corrupt leaders and prophets.

MEMORY VERSE: "But truly I am full of power by the spirit of the LORD, and of judgment, and of might, to declare unto Jacob his transgression, and to Israel his sin" (Micah 3:8).

LESSON AIM: By the end of the lesson, your students will: explore how Micah confronted corrupt leaders; reflect on reactions to leaders who mislead and deceive people; and address corruptions in leadership within the church and the broader community.

TEACHER PREPARATION

MATERIALS NEEDED: Quarterly Commentary/Teacher Manual, Adult Quarterly, Adult resources—charts, worksheets, and other teaching tools, paper, pens, pencils, Bibles (several different versions)

OTHER MATERIALS NEEDED / TEACHER'S NOTES:

LESSON OVERVIEW

LIFE NEED FOR TODAY'S LESSON

Some leaders are corrupt and lie to the people they are charged to protect.

BIBLE LEARNING

People of faith understand that sins against others affect their relationship to God.

BIBLE APPLICATION

Christians realize that the truth must always be told, even if the message is not pleasant.

STUDENTS' RESPONSES

People of faith can find comfort in knowing that God will bring justice where there is corruption.

LESSON SCRIPTURE

MICAH 3:5–12, KJV

5 Thus saith the LORD concerning the prophets that make my people err, that bite with their teeth, and cry, Peace; and he that putteth not into their mouths, they even prepare war against him.

6 Therefore night shall be unto you, that ye shall not have a vision; and it shall be dark unto you, that ye shall not divine;

MICAH 3:5–12, NIV

5 This is what the LORD says: "As for the prophets who lead my people astray, they proclaim 'peace' if they have something to eat, but prepare to wage war against anyone who refuses to feed them.

6 Therefore night will come over you, without visions, and darkness, without

and the sun shall go down over the prophets, and the day shall be dark over them.

7 Then shall the seers be ashamed, and the diviners confounded: yea, they shall all cover their lips; for there is no answer of God.

8 But truly I am full of power by the spirit of the LORD, and of judgment, and of might, to declare unto Jacob his transgression, and to Israel his sin.

9 Hear this, I pray you, ye heads of the house of Jacob, and princes of the house of Israel, that abhor judgment, and pervert all equity.

10 They build up Zion with blood, and Jerusalem with iniquity.

11 The heads thereof judge for reward, and the priests thereof teach for hire, and the prophets thereof divine for money: yet will they lean upon the LORD, and say, Is not the LORD among us? none evil can come upon us.

12 Therefore shall Zion for your sake be plowed as a field, and Jerusalem shall become heaps, and the mountain of the house as the high places of the forest.

divination. The sun will set for the prophets, and the day will go dark for them.

7 The seers will be ashamed and the diviners disgraced. They will all cover their faces because there is no answer from God."

8 But as for me, I am filled with power, with the Spirit of the LORD, and with justice and might, to declare to Jacob his transgression, to Israel his sin.

9 Hear this, you leaders of Jacob, you rulers of Israel, who despise justice and distort all that is right;

10 who build Zion with bloodshed, and Jerusalem with wickedness.

11 Her leaders judge for a bribe, her priests teach for a price, and her prophets tell fortunes for money. Yet they look for the LORD's support and say, "Is not the LORD among us? No disaster will come upon us."

12 Therefore because of you, Zion will be plowed like a field, Jerusalem will become a heap of rubble, the temple hill a mound overgrown with thickets.

LIGHT ON THE WORD

The heads of Israel were the heads of families. The elders of the tribes became the judges. This system was based on the cultural custom of the time. During the Exodus, Moses established a system that organized the heads in groups of ten, fifties, and hundreds in order to better manage and give leadership to the people **(Exodus 18:13–24)**. By the time of David, these heads or judges began to be organized as a circuit court with delegated royal authority **(1 Chronicles 23:4, 26:29, 28:1)**. This made it easy for them to become corrupt and dishonest. By the time of the prophets, the heads were known for taking bribes and being partial to the rich.

While there were many true prophets in Israel, there were also false prophets. These false prophets often offered messages of hope and peace. These messages comforted the people without pointing out their sin and challenging them to repent from their evil ways. The false prophets became rich from the fees they charged for their services. Often they would use pagan methods of divination or fortune telling, which were strictly forbidden in the Law of the Old Testament. The Lord had given the people of Israel ways to evaluate a false prophet: one was if the message they had spoken came to pass (**Deuteronomy 18:21–22**), the other if they enticed the people to worship idols (**Deuteronomy 18:20**).

TEACHING THE BIBLE LESSON

LIFE NEED FOR TODAY'S LESSON

AIM: Students will affirm that some leaders are corrupt and lie to the people they are charged to protect.

INTRODUCTION

Deceptive Rulers

The Neo-Assyrian Empire was a very dominant and real threat to Jerusalem at Micah's time. One of many ways Jerusalem prepared for conflict was to strengthen the economy so they would have the necessary resources to fight off both foreign and domestic threats. As today's text suggests, the ways they pursued economic stability were immoral and did not align with the precepts of the Lord. Their stimulus plan was based on greed, exploitation, and senseless taxes, and as a result, moral corruption slowly crept in.

BIBLE LEARNING

AIM: Students will understand that sins against others affect their relationship with God.

I. CORRUPT PROPHETS (Micah 3:5–7)

Micah is speaking on behalf of God and unveiling the sinister practices of the prophets in Jerusalem and Samaria. Micah not only classifies them as deceivers, but specifically identifies their transgressions (wrongdoings). War was imminent and the prophets were capitalizing on Jerusalem's concerns by structuring their messages to benefit their paying audience, while those who could not pay received detrimental messages.

Oppressive Prophets (verses 5–7)

5 Thus saith the LORD concerning the prophets that make my people err, that bite with their teeth, and cry, Peace; and he that putteth not into their mouths, they even prepare war against him.

After an analogy comparing the leaders of Judah to cannibalistic shepherds, Micah then focuses on Judah's prophets, who are causing the people to err (Heb. *ta'ah*, **ta-AH**) or wander. The prophets were causing the people to go astray and wander from God and His truth—the opposite of their true role as spokesmen for God. Instead of speaking for God, they are speaking on their own and drawing people away from God. Micah says that they "bite with their teeth." The word "bite" can also be used figuratively as "to vex" and "to oppress." The prophets were vexing and oppressing the people by offering prophecies for money. This is further confirmed by the next clause. The word "putteth" (Heb. *natan*, **na-TAN**) is more often rendered "to give." The prophets' message of peace was their selling point; they told the people that everything would be well and received the people's money and applause. However, this was a false peace; those who would not give to them would be the objects of their hostility.

6 Therefore night shall be unto you, that ye shall not have a vision; and it shall be dark unto you, that ye shall not divine; and the sun shall go down over the prophets, and the day shall be dark over them.

As a result of their false prophecies and oppression, God would judge the prophets, manifesting itself in their lack of prophetic sight. Micah says that the prophets will experience darkness, and they will not be able to divine (Heb. *qasam*, **kah-SAM**). Divination was a common way to understand the will of the gods. This was done through various methods; some would read and interpret the liver of animals or the position of fired arrows, while others studied dreams and visions. The latter is probably the method used by these false prophets of Judah. The sun going down and the day turning dark are metaphors for the loss of the prophet's gifts.

7 Then shall the seers be ashamed, and the diviners confounded: yea, they shall all cover their lips; for there is no answer of God.

Micah announces the fate of the seers (Heb. *chozeh*, **kho-ZEH**) and diviners (Heb. *qasam*, **kah-SAM**): they will be ashamed and confounded, and experience the humiliation of lepers by having to cover their lips (**Leviticus 13:45**). The prophets would be considered unclean like lepers because they had "no answer of God." Their lack of honesty and true relationship with God would be evident. Because their falsehood was on display, they would cover their lips and feel the same shame as those considered outcasts to the covenant community.

SEARCH THE SCRIPTURES

QUESTION 1

What were the prophets doing to the people?

II. THE MAN OF GOD (vv. 8–10)

Amid all of this, Micah stands up for justice. He proclaims his strength and courage so all will know he knows the depth of their corruption. He also informs them he understands the magnitude of the danger that he is in by speaking out. The eighth century B.C. was not very different from today's society as far as the extent of corruption; someone seeking to change the economic and social structure would face social, political, and religious opposition much as Jesus, Medgar Evers, and Martin Luther King Jr. did.

A True Prophet of God (verses 8–10)

8 But truly I am full of power by the spirit of the LORD, and of judgment, and of might, to declare unto Jacob his transgression, and to Israel his sin.

Micah declares his distinction from the false prophets. He says that he is full of power (Heb. *koach*, **KOH-akh**) by the spirit of the Lord. He is also full of judgment (Heb. *mishpat*, **mish-PAWT**) and might (Heb. *geburah*, **geh-voo-RAH**). Micah's "judgment" here is the establishment of right through fair and legal procedures in accordance with the will and laws of God. Micah has aligned himself with the cause of justice, and by using the word's power and might, he states that this cause is God's cause and he is equipped to be victorious.

9 Hear this, I pray you, ye heads of the house of Jacob, and princes of the house of Israel, that abhor judgment, and pervert all equity.

Micah particularly addresses the political and religious groups of Judah. He calls out the heads and princes responsible for establishing the religious and political moral standards for the people. The Lord, through Micah, accuses them of hating or abhorring what is just. The word "abhor," or *ta'ab* (Heb., **tah-AV**, to loathe, detest, or make abominable) is a strong indication of how far those who rule over the Hebrews have fallen from God. They are not instructing people with fairness, but seeking their own gain and pursuing personal agendas.

Not only do these rulers and chiefs abhor justice, they also pervert equity (Heb. *yashar*, **yah-SHAWR**, that which is straight, right, or just). This word also denotes fairness and being honest and aboveboard. Those who rule over Judah do not practice such honesty.

10 They build up Zion with blood, and Jerusalem with iniquity.

The prophet continues to personalize the accusation against Judah. In the name of religion and sacrifice to God, the people have erected buildings using perverse and deceitful means. Instead of using tithes and offerings to establish places of worship, the religious leaders have taken from the poor and, in some instances, killed to expand Jerusalem. Archaeology testifies to the building activities underway in Jerusalem during Micah's prophecy. Such capital activities were performed at the expense of the oppressed and less fortunate. Jeremiah makes reference to similar activities, mentioning those who build their homes by unrighteousness (**22:13**). The prophet Habakkuk (**2:12**) also records official building with bloodshed.

The name "Zion" refers to the hill between the Kidron and Tyropean valleys that David captured from the Jebusites (**2 Samuel 5:7**). After the building of the Temple to the north of the hill, Zion became the center of the Lord's activity, since the Temple was where Yahweh dwelt. The term "Zion" may refer specifically to the Temple vicinity or Jerusalem in general. Thus, Micah's reference to the people building Zion up with blood shows how this holy habitation had been defamed and desecrated.

LIGHT ON THE WORD

Misusing the Gifts

Micah explained that the punishment for misusing their gifts would be to stop hearing from God altogether. Those who continued to communicate these messages would be shown to have no knowledge of God and false. Those who claim to speak for the Lord and only talk of peace in order to gain a profit are not speaking for the Lord but only for themselves.

III. CORRUPT LEADERS (vv. 11–12)

Micah says the leaders are attempting to build up the city, but at the expense of the poor. There was no respect for justice or righteousness. The false prophets were not the only corrupt citizens in Samaria and Jerusalem; leaders in almost every area of their society had gone astray (**vv. 9–12**). As a nation and individually for many leaders, the focus quickly became prosperity by any means necessary.

Corrupt Leaders of Judah (verses 11–12)

11 The heads thereof judge for reward, and the priests thereof teach for hire, and the prophets thereof divine for money: yet will they lean upon the LORD, and say, Is not the LORD among us? none evil can come upon us.

Micah again compels Judah to reexamine its political and social ethics. The rulers who govern civic and state affairs are corrupt. The priests who dictate religious standards practice evil. The prophets who speak the Word of the Lord only do it for money. Micah contends that Judah's leadership have turned away from the Lord. Those in power only want to be compensated by humankind for what God has gifted and instructed them to do. Rulers give judgment for a bribe, priests teach for a price, and prophets give oracles for money. Micah stresses the greed and insatiable materialism pervading Judah.

These leaders, however, believe that what they do is good and pleasing in the eyes of the Lord. They are convinced that since Zion is the dwelling place of God and that since the Hebrews are God's chosen people, all is well and their transgressions can be overlooked. Speaking rhetorically, Micah states that those in authority did not lean on the Lord. The word "lean" (Heb. *sha'an*, **shah-AWN**), means to lie, rely on, or rest on, often with reference to God (**2 Chronicles 14:11**). Isaiah uses another verb for leaning in stating how Judah must depend on God (**48:2**). Such leaning implies a need to find favor and obtain support. Judah wishes to engage in wrongdoing while depending on the Lord for safety. The leaders, despite their unscrupulous conduct, believe that God will protect them because of His faithfulness and promises. The people do not see the error of their ways; they are so obstinate and spiritually blind that they are convinced that because the Lord dwells in Zion, no harm can come to them even when they sin against God.

12 Therefore shall Zion for your sake be plowed as a field, and Jerusalem shall become heaps, and the mountain of the house as the high places in the forest.

Because Judah has become prideful and sinful, the Lord, through Micah, predicts its ensuing destruction. The crassness of the leaders will result in the leveling of Jerusalem and its Temple. Micah made a similar pronouncement earlier stating that Samaria would be a heap and a place for planting vineyards, i.e., a desolate, open land (**1:6**). This prophecy is remembered a century later when the people of Israel observe its fulfillment (**Jeremiah 26:18–19**). Both prophets were foretelling the captivity of Judah by the Babylonians and the exile afterward. Judah, during Micah's time, was already a vassal state of the Assyrians; further enslavement was the next step.

Again the prophet specifically names Zion and Jerusalem, the center of Israelite worship, as places to be destroyed. No place was beyond God's wrath when evil had been committed. Micah personalizes the message and the plans of God to show Judah's leaders their ill behavior.

SEARCH THE SCRIPTURES

QUESTION 2

Based on Micah's prophecy, what was the primary source of motivation during this period in Jerusalem?

LIGHT ON THE WORD

False Sense of Grandeur

Despite the fact that the nation had adopted a culture of cheating, lying, stealing, and marginalizing the poor, they professed that their "growth and success" was due to their dependence on and protection by God. Micah ends by telling people that the city they were working so hard to build would ultimately be destroyed.

BIBLE APPLICATION

AIM: Students will realize that the truth must always be told, even if the message is not a pleasant one.

It can be very difficult to speak against leadership at any level. Some people naturally believe that if someone has been given a title or responsibility, they have integrity and will maintain the best interest of the people they represent. However, the Bible and life have provided us with many examples of leaders who have ill intentions, succumb to temptation, and take advantage of their positions. As children of God, our instructions are simple: do justice, love kindness, and walk humbly with our God (**Micah 6:8**). Every group that we are members of—our country, civic organization, religious institution, or sorority/fraternity—should follow the same statutes.

STUDENTS' RESPONSES

AIM: Students will find comfort in knowing that God will bring justice where there is corruption.

After reading the lesson, discuss what we should do as Christians if we suspect a political leader is corrupt. Make a list of appropriate and inappropriate response methods. One way to respond is to confront the leader and withhold votes or cooperation with unjust policies and practices. With this in mind, consider your own community and whether this response is needed.

PRAYER

Dear God, we pray for all leaders. We pray that they will do what You have called them to do. Protect us from those leaders who want to harm us. Give us the courage and wisdom to challenge unjust leadership. In Jesus' Name we pray. Amen.

HOW TO SAY IT

Diviners.	di-**VIE**-ners.
Equity.	**EH**-kwi-tee.

PREPARE FOR NEXT SUNDAY

Read **Micah 6:3–8** and study "Justice, Love, and Humility."

DAILY HOME BIBLE READINGS

MONDAY
Do Not Pervert Justice
(Exodus 23:1–8)

TUESDAY
False Prophecies of Peace
(Ezekiel 13:15–20)

WEDNESDAY
Act in the Fear of the Lord
(2 Chronicles 19:4–10)

THURSDAY
Walk Blamelessly, Do Right, Speak Truth
(Psalm 15)

FRIDAY
Known by Their Fruits
(Matthew 7:15–20)

SATURDAY
Woe to Those Striving with God
(Isaiah 45:5–13)

SUNDAY
Sold Out Religion
(Micah 3:5–12)

Sources:

Achtemeier, Paul J., ed. *The HarperCollins Bible Dictionary*. New York: HarperCollins Publishing, 1996. 680, 888.

Smith, Ralph L. *Micah–Malachi*. Word Biblical Commentary. Waco, TX: World Books Publishers, 1984. 32–34.

Waltke, Bruce K. *A Commentary on Micah*. Grand Rapids, MI: Eerdmans 2007. 181–183.

COMMENTS / NOTES:

JUSTICE, LOVE, AND HUMILITY

BIBLE BASIS: MICAH 6:3–8

BIBLE TRUTH: God instructs the unjust to be just, to love kindness, and to walk humbly with Him.

MEMORY VERSE: "He hath shewed thee, O man, what is good; and what doth the LORD require of thee, but to do justly, and to love mercy, and to walk humbly with thy God?" (Micah 6:8).

LESSON AIM: By the end of the lesson, your students will: know how to honor God gratefully by exhibiting the character traits that God requires; express feelings about living up to God's expectations for us to be just, loving, and humble; and lead the community into making God's requirements a reality.

TEACHER PREPARATION

MATERIALS NEEDED: Quarterly Commentary/Teacher Manual, Adult Quarterly, Adult resources—charts, worksheets, and other teaching tools, paper, pens, pencils, Bibles (several different versions)

OTHER MATERIALS NEEDED / TEACHER'S NOTES:

____

____

LESSON OVERVIEW

LIFE NEED FOR TODAY'S LESSON

People sometimes forget what a benefactor has done for them or they make insincere efforts to show gratitude.

BIBLE LEARNING

The Israelites' disrespect toward God and disobedience of His commands arose from their lack of regard and gratitude for His saving acts for them.

BIBLE APPLICATION

Christians understand that because of all that God has done for them, they must live upright lives to show their gratitude to Him.

STUDENTS' RESPONSES

Students will recognize that true worship of God goes beyond the performance of ritual.

LESSON SCRIPTURE

MICAH 6:3–8, KJV

3 O my people, what have I done unto thee? and wherein have I wearied thee? testify against me.

4 For I brought thee up out of the land of Egypt, and redeemed thee out of the house of servants; and I sent before thee Moses, Aaron, and Miriam.

MICAH 6:3–8, NIV

3 "My people, what have I done to you? How have I burdened you? Answer me.

4 I brought you up out of Egypt and redeemed you from the land of slavery. I sent Moses to lead you, also Aaron and Miriam.

5 O my people, remember now what Balak king of Moab consulted, and what Balaam the son of Beor answered him from Shittim unto Gilgal; that ye may know the righteousness of the LORD.

6 Wherewith shall I come before the LORD, and bow myself before the high God? shall I come before him with burnt offerings, with calves of a year old?

7 Will the LORD be pleased with thousands of rams, or with ten thousands of rivers of oil? shall I give my firstborn for my transgression, the fruit of my body for the sin of my soul?

8 He hath shewed thee, O man, what is good; and what doth the LORD require of thee, but to do justly, and to love mercy, and to walk humbly with thy God?

5 My people, remember what Balak king of Moab plotted and what Balaam son of Beor answered. Remember your journey from Shittim to Gilgal, that you may know the righteous acts of the LORD."

6 With what shall I come before the LORD and bow down before the exalted God? Shall I come before him with burnt offerings, with calves a year old?

7 Will the LORD be pleased with thousands of rams, with ten thousand rivers of olive oil? Shall I offer my firstborn for my transgression, the fruit of my body for the sin of my soul?

8 He has shown you, O mortal, what is good. And what does the Lord require of you? To act justly and to love mercy and to walk humbly with your God.

LIGHT ON THE WORD

In the ancient Near East, many cultures practiced human sacrifice. The nations surrounding Israel also worshiped fertility gods who demanded a portion of what they helped produce: crops, animals, and children. The child sacrifice was usually the firstborn son, because he would be the most precious thing to a family as the heir of all the wealth and possessions of the family. This practice was a temptation for the Israelites and forbidden by the Lord (**Deuteronomy 18:9–12; Jeremiah 7:31**). Although the firstborn of every man and animal belonged to the Lord, Israel was given specific commands for redeeming the firstborn (**Numbers 18:15–17**). This was Israel's way of distinguishing themselves from the different nations around them.

TEACHING THE BIBLE LESSON

LIFE NEED FOR TODAY'S LESSON

AIM: Students will sometimes forget what a benefactor has done for them or they make insincere efforts to show gratitude.

INTRODUCTION

God's Court Case

Micah's prophecy begins with a general announcement to Samaria and Jerusalem that God has a case to present against the nations of Israel and Judah. He then lays out the first of two series of judgments against Israel and Judah. Micah describes the sins that they have committed against God as well as their fellow man.

Israel has allowed the worship of idols and other gods to take root in their religious practices. Pagan practices have become a part of Israel's worship to Yahweh. For example, they have engaged in the pagan ritual of temple prostitution. They have presented the money earned by prostitutes to God as an offering (**Micah 1:7**; cf. **Deuteronomy 23:17–18**).

The wealthy have oppressed the poor to gain more wealth and power. They lie awake at night, devising how they will collect more land by defrauding others (**Micah 2:1–2**).

Israel's leaders have neglected their duties and led the people astray. Rather than protecting and instructing their citizens, they have exploited and misled them. Similarly, the prophets have chosen to seek after money, rather than speak God's truth to the people. They prophesy according to how much money their words might bring them. Israel's leaders are not directed by God; their actions are driven by greed and ambition (**Micah 3:11**).

Micah's first series of judgments is followed by a hopeful look to a distant future, when Israel will be restored. God will eventually redeem His exiled people once again. He will lift Israel up above all other nations.

It is against this backdrop that Micah's second series of judgments begins in chapter 6. This second series of judgments also concerns the issue of social justice in Israel.

BIBLE LEARNING

AIM: Students will understand that the Israelites' disrespect toward God and disobedience of God's commands arose from their lack of regard and gratitude for God's saving acts for them.

I. GOD REMINDS ISRAEL OF HIS BENEVOLENCE (Micah 6:3–5)

Through the prophet Micah, God questions why Israel has turned against Him. Why have they turned to false gods? What did God do to deserve their indifference? He recounts how He delivered Israel from the slavery of Egypt. It would seem that Israel has forgotten the significance of their freedom from Egypt and His hand in delivering them. God has done nothing to provoke their negative attitude toward Him. He graciously rescued them from a life of cruel slavery, and provided leaders to guide them.

Clarifying the Issues (verses 3–5)

3 O my people, what have I done unto thee? and wherein have I wearied thee? testify against me.

Here the Lord pleads His case. He asks the people of Judah the reason they have become so unfaithful as His covenant people. Specifically, He asks what He has done to them and how He has wearied (Heb. *la'ah*, **la-AH**) them. This word means to be tired or to give up. The Lord asks, "How have I offended you? How could you become dissatisfied with me?" He gives them an opportunity to testify (Heb. *'anah*, **ah-NAH**, literally to answer or, in a legal suit, to provide opposing testimony) against Him.

4 For I brought thee up out of the land of Egypt, and redeemed thee out of the house of servants; and I sent before thee Moses, Aaron, and Miriam.

Next the Lord rehearses His blessings and how gracious He has been toward His people. He brought them out of Egypt. He redeemed them from slavery. He sent Moses, Aaron, and Miriam. They were not left without leaders, but were guided to the Promised Land.

5 O my people, remember now what Balak king of Moab consulted, and what Balaam the son of Beor answered him from Shittim unto Gilgal; that ye may know the righteousness of the LORD.

Next the Lord brings up the incident with Balak the King of Moab and Balaam the prophet. Balak feared the Israelites coming out of Egypt, so he hired Balaam to pronounce a curse on them (**Numbers 22:1–6**). Quite the opposite happened, as the Lord caused a donkey to speak to Balaam and refuse to go any further (**Numbers 22:22–30**). This opened Balaam's eyes to an angel of the Lord in the middle of the road, who told him not to follow through with the king's orders (**Numbers 22:31–35**). After this, Balaam could do nothing but bless them. Each time he opened his mouth, he blessed God's people. The Lord here shows them that even when their enemies tried to curse them, God fulfilled His promise and they were blessed instead.

Shittim and Gilgal are references to the Israelites' conquest of the land. Shittim was the place where Joshua camped east of the Jordan River, and Gilgal is where they crossed to take over the land. It was quite common in military annals of the ancient Near East to summarize the itinerary of the conquering king as a way to summarize the whole conquest. The reference to these places was God's way of reminding them of all that He had done to give them the land they now enjoyed.

SEARCH THE SCRIPTURES

QUESTION 1

Why do you think Israel had forgotten the significance of their miraculous deliverance from Egyptian slavery?

LIGHT ON THE WORD

God's Faithfulness to Israel

God also acted on the Israelites' behalf with those who sought to harm them. He recounts how He disrupted King Balaak's plot to have Balaam curse Israel. God's intervention resulted instead in a blessing over Israel. He has rescued Israel, and acted to assure their continued freedom. He has maintained his commitment to the Israelites. These accounts are a reminder of what God has done for them in the past, as well as a reminder of His continued presence among them.

II. GOD REQUIRES JUSTICE, LOVE, AND HUMILITY (vv. 6–8)

What can Israel do to correct their broken relationship with God? Their immediate response is to offer sacrifices to God. They first suggest reasonable sacrifices of calves and burnt offerings. However, they exponentially increase their offer of sacrifice to ridiculous levels. They ultimately offer the human sacrifice of a firstborn child, which was customary of pagan sacrifice but prohibited by the covenant law (**Leviticus 18:21, 20:2–5**). The ridiculous nature of their offers seems to imply that there might be no pleasing Yahweh. However, Micah's prophecy, in keeping with other Israelite prophecies, clearly indicates that the inward condition of one's heart is of more concern to God than outward religiosity.

Honor and Respect God (verses 6–8)

6 Wherewith shall I come before the LORD, and bow myself before the high God? shall I come before him with burnt offerings, with calves of a year old?

Micah establishes a courtroom setting in which the Lord is the accuser (plaintiff) who charges Israel, the accused (defendant), with social and religious injustice. Judah attempts to respond to God's indictment by asking how they can approach God, who is so high and mighty under the shadow of their own sin and transgressions.

The people of Judah acknowledge the royal and lofty nature of God and realize that the King of kings is worthy to receive their obeisance. Because of the greed of the religious and political leadership, they have not paid God the respect and honor He deserves.

Not only does God deserve their honor as the King of kings, He must be offered sacrifices, particularly burnt offerings. The burnt offering (Heb. *'olah*, **oh-LAH**) is a gift that ascends to the heavens. A portion is given to the priest to offer to God and the remainder is consumed or burned. The offering is dedicated completely to God. Young calves, or any animal less than a year old, were often sacrificed to render this type of offering. By their question, Judah knows they should have been engaging in these sacrifices. Yet their questions also indicate how far they have strayed from the Lord's covenant promise.

7 Will the LORD be pleased with thousands of rams, or with ten thousands of rivers of oil? shall I give my firstborn for my transgression, the fruit of my body for the sin of my soul?

Judah continues an arrogant defense of their crimes by sarcastically asking what the Lord requires. The people know that sacrifices of rams are pleasing to the Lord. Yet they exaggerate how many sacrifices they should give to God by asking if thousands of rams will do. The Hebrews are aware that oil is used in anointing royalty and in presenting gifts to God. Yet they are overzealous in their need to repent and ask if many rivers, not vials, of oil will suffice. Micah again uses this rhetorical line of reasoning to show how far the people are removed from God. They are not aware repentance needs to occur.

The line of questioning and sarcasm continues with Judah even offering their firstborn as restitution for sin. Micah alludes to the importance of the Lord receiving the firstfruits of the harvest for sacrifice. This passage also alludes to God delivering the firstborn of the Hebrew children from the angel of death during Israel's enslavement in Egypt (**Exodus 12**). This giving of the firstborn also refers to human sacrifices practiced in Judah under kings Ahaz (**2 Kings 16:3**) and Manasseh (**2 Kings 21:6**).

8 He hath shewed thee, O man, what is good; and what doth the LORD require of thee, but to do justly, and to love mercy, and to walk humbly with thy God?

Micah now offers a response to the questions of **verses 6 and 7**. None of what Judah has offered is what the Lord desires. God does not seek sacrifices, offerings, or rituals. The Lord wants the people to treat each other fairly and to walk according to His way. Obedience is better than sacrifice (**1 Samuel 15:22**).

To do justly or carry out justice comes from the Hebrew word *mishpat* (**mish-PAWT**). It means judgment or a right sentence. It is the establishment of right through fair and legal procedures in accordance with the will of God. Mercy is translated from the Hebrew word *chesed* (**KHEH-sed**, pity, loving kindness, or doing good for those in a lower position) and is similar to the New Testament concept of grace. The idea of walking humbly with God is juxtaposed with Judah's arrogance and refusal to lean on the Lord (**Micah 3:11**). Because the people have allowed their lust for money to interfere with their relationship with God and have chosen their own selfish gain, Micah warns that He wants them to submit, to return to the commandments and the way of the Lord.

SEARCH THE SCRIPTURES

QUESTION 2

Why do you think their first response was outward sacrifice, rather than inward change?

LIGHT ON THE WORD

Justice, Love, and Humility

God doesn't require outrageous sacrifice; He has already told them what He requires. As communicated earlier in Micah's prophecy, God requires that His people would once again be a just society that loves mercy. He desires protection for the oppressed and poor. He desires that His people would act mercifully toward one another. He requires that they would continue to walk in covenant fellowship with Himself.

BIBLE APPLICATION

AIM: Students will understand that because of all that God has done for them, they must live upright lives to show their gratitude to Him.

We live in a world where we are bombarded with advertisements daily. It has been said that the average person today sees more ads in a day than someone in the 1950s saw in their lifetime. These ads have a subtle way of making us ungrateful and dissatisfied, so we crave new products and luxuries and pursue them no matter what the cost—even injustice. God wants us to be satisfied with the blessings He has given us. By remembering what God has already done for us and who He is, we will be motivated to seek justice for others, not wealth and comfort for ourselves.

STUDENTS' RESPONSES

AIM: Students will recognize that true worship of God goes beyond the performance of ritual.

Consider the ways that God has blessed you. Do you sometimes forget all that He has done in your life? In order to get out of yourself this week and focus on God, create a list of things that God has done for you. As you create this list, think about one thing that you can do for others who are treated unjustly.

PRAYER

God, we want to walk in Your justice, and live our lives in love and mercy with one another. Thank You for first loving us and caring for us even when we do not follow Your ways of justice. In Jesus' Name we pray. Amen.

HOW TO SAY IT

Shittim. shee-**TEEM**.

Beor. be-**OR**.

PREPARE FOR NEXT SUNDAY

Read **Micah 7:14–20** and study "God Shows Clemency."

DAILY HOME BIBLE READINGS

MONDAY
What Does the Lord Require?
(Deuteronomy 10:12–22)

TUESDAY
Who Gives Speech to Mortals?
(Exodus 4:10–17)

WEDNESDAY
The Word the Lord Speaks
(Numbers 22:1–14)

THURSDAY
Do Only What I Tell You
(Numbers 22:15–21)

FRIDAY
Speak Only What I Tell You
(Numbers 22:31–38)

SATURDAY
You Have Blessed My Enemies
(Numbers 23:1–12)

SUNDAY
Justice, Kindness, and Humility
(Micah 6:3–8)

Sources:

Brown, Francis, S. R. Driver, and Charles Briggs. *The Brown-Driver-Briggs Hebrew and English Lexicon*. Peabody, MA: Hendrickson Publishers, 2007. S.vv. "Chesed" and "Padah."

Burge, Gary M. and Andrew E. Hill, eds. *Baker Illustrated Bible Commentary*. Grand Rapids, MI: Baker Books, 2012. 860–870.

Butler, Trent C., ed. "Balaam." *Holman Bible Dictionary*. Electronic Edition, Quickverse. Nashville, TN: Holman Bible Publishers, 1991.

Carson, D. A., R. T. France, J. A. Motyer, G. J. Wenham, eds. *New Bible Commentary*. Downer's Grove, IL: Intervarsity Press, 1994. 830.

Easton, M. G. "Balaam." *Easton's Bible Dictionary*. 1st ed. Oklahoma City, OK: Ellis Enterprises, 1993.

Hill, Andrew E. and John H. Walton. *A Survey of the Old Testament*. Grand Rapids, MI: Zondervan. 2009. 642–647.

Keck, Leander, ed. *The Twelve Prophets*. The New Interpreter's Bible. Vol. 7. Nashville, TN: Abingdon Press, 1996. 533–534, 577–580.

Orr, James, ed. "Balaam." *International Standard Bible Encyclopedia*. Electronic Edition. Omaha, NE: Quickverse, 1998.

COMMENTS / NOTES:

GOD SHOWS CLEMENCY

BIBLE BASIS: MICAH 7:14–20

BIBLE TRUTH: God will show compassion and faithfulness to His people, even to the unjust.

MEMORY VERSE: "Where is another God like you, who pardons the guilt of the remnant, overlooking the sins of his special people? You will not stay angry with your people forever, because you delight in showing unfailing love" (Micah 7:18).

LESSON AIM: By the end of the lesson, your students will: learn of God's mercy even when punishment seems in order; reflect on experiences when God's mercy and compassion were more than expected; and carry out acts of mercy and compassion.

TEACHER PREPARATION

MATERIALS NEEDED: Quarterly Commentary/Teacher Manual, Adult Quarterly, Adult resources—charts, worksheets, and other teaching tools, paper, pens, pencils, Bibles (several different versions)

OTHER MATERIALS NEEDED / TEACHER'S NOTES:

____

____

LESSON OVERVIEW

LIFE NEED FOR TODAY'S LESSON
Sometimes evil and injustice are not met with corrective justice, but are trumped by mercy.

BIBLE LEARNING
Micah describes the uniqueness of the Lord, who among all gods forgives sin.

BIBLE APPLICATION
Christians believe that God's forgiveness is unconditional. God forgives completely.

STUDENTS' RESPONSES
Believers praise God because of His mercy.

LESSON SCRIPTURE

MICAH 7:14–20, KJV

14 Feed thy people with thy rod, the flock of thine heritage, which dwell solitarily in the wood, in the midst of Carmel: let them feed in Bashan and Gilead, as in the days of old.

15 According to the days of thy coming out of the land of Egypt will I shew unto him marvellous things.

MICAH 7:14–20, NIV

14 Shepherd your people with your staff, the flock of your inheritance, which lives by itself in a forest, in fertile pasturelands. Let them feed in Bashan and Gilead as in days long ago.

15 "As in the days when you came out of Egypt, I will show them my wonders."

16 The nations shall see and be confounded at all their might: they shall lay their hand upon their mouth, their ears shall be deaf.

17 They shall lick the dust like a serpent, they shall move out of their holes like worms of the earth: they shall be afraid of the LORD our God, and shall fear because of thee.

18 Who is a God like unto thee, that pardoneth iniquity, and passeth by the transgression of the remnant of his heritage? he retaineth not his anger for ever, because he delighteth in mercy.

19 He will turn again, he will have compassion upon us; he will subdue our iniquities; and thou wilt cast all their sins into the depths of the sea.

20 Thou wilt perform the truth to Jacob, and the mercy to Abraham, which thou hast sworn unto our fathers from the days of old.

16 Nations will see and be ashamed, deprived of all their power. They will put their hands over their mouths and their ears will become deaf.

17 They will lick dust like a snake, like creatures that crawl on the ground. They will come trembling out of their dens; they will turn in fear to the LORD our God and will be afraid of you.

18 Who is a God like you, who pardons sin and forgives the transgression of the remnant of his inheritance? You do not stay angry forever but delight to show mercy.

19 You will again have compassion on us; you will tread our sins underfoot and hurl all our iniquities into the depths of the sea.

20 You will be faithful to Jacob, and show love to Abraham, as you pledged on oath to our ancestors in days long ago.

LIGHT ON THE WORD

The area east of the Jordan River was divided into three parts: the plain, Gilead, and Bashan. Bashan is most known from a passage in **Deuteronomy 3**. In the text, Moses was facing war with King Og of Bashan and God's instructions were, "Do not be afraid of him, for I have delivered him into your hands, along with his whole army and his land" (from **v. 2**, NIV). And that is exactly what transpired.

Gilead is the land that borders Bashan. It was also among the land seized during the battle with King Og, but it is famous for other reasons. The Bible talks about the healing balm that was able to soothe and remedy sickness and this is what the area was known for (**Jeremiah 8:22**). Gilead became synonymous for God's healing power. Both David and Jesus knew it as a place of retreat.

TEACHING THE BIBLE LESSON

LIFE NEED FOR TODAY'S LESSON

AIM: Students will discover that evil and injustice are not met with corrective justice, but are trumped by mercy.

INTRODUCTION

God's Mercy for His People

Micah speaks a psalm of trust and salvation for Israel. He lets them know that the Lord will not let their enemies gloat over them. This is probably a prophecy of the fall of Jerusalem in 586 B.C. Additionally, he informs them that one day their walls will be rebuilt and foreigners from Assyria to Egypt will come to be part of Israel. At the same time, the rest of the nations will be uninhabited as punishment for what they did to God's people. This leads Micah to speak of God's mercy and faithfulness to His people.

BIBLE LEARNING

AIM: Students will describe the uniqueness of the Lord, who among all gods forgives sin.

I. THE LORD IS MY SHEPHERD (Micah 7:14–15)

Micah is asking God to care for His people in the same tender and affectionate manner that a shepherd oversees his flock. More specifically, he requests divine provision because they are God's children. He uses the imagery of lush pastures in Gilead and Bashan to further urge God to restore not only the people, but the land.

God Cares for the People (verses 14–15)

14 Feed thy people with thy rod, the flock of thine heritage, which dwell solitarily in the wood, in the midst of Carmel: let them feed in Bashan and Gilead, as in the days of old.

Starting with the relational image of a shepherd, Micah prays for the fulfillment of the promised salvation and restoration of **vv. 11–14**. The prayer is reminiscent of **Psalm 23:4**, where David portrays the Lord as a Shepherd, who with loving care, leads His sheep with the rod and the staff. The people of God are called the flock of His inheritance or possession. They belong to Him (**cf. v. 18; Psalms 94:14, 100:3**). But Israel was dwelling solitarily in the field. Dwelling "solitarily in the woods" is probably used to stress that they were not living in a good situation. Not only is their ground poor, but they are also cut off from other peoples and cannot get goods or help from them. So, Micah prays that their Shepherd will once again let them feed in Bashan and Gilead, cities that had proverbially fruitful pasturelands. This may also have been a prayer for the return of that rich and fertile land to the people of Zion (**Zechariah 10:10**).

15 According to the days of thy coming out of the land of Egypt will I shew unto him marvellous things.

God gives an answer to the prophet's prayer. He will protect, save, defend, and work miracles for them in their restoration, such as He did for their fathers in their return from Egypt to the Promised Land. God showed them His wonders then, and He will do it again. His future acts for them will include similar displays of His redemptive grace and power on their behalf. With the restoration of Israel, Micah anticipated manifestations of God's power and leadership like those at the Red Sea, Sinai, and other cities along the Exodus out of Egypt.

SEARCH THE SCRIPTURES

QUESTION 1

What is the writer comparing God's people to?

LIGHT ON THE WORD

Micah's Plea for God's Intervention

Although Micah's plea may appear to be a monologue, God responds. He interjects a quick, comforting word to assure Micah that He will forgive and restore. Similar to Micah drawing from their history, God cites a past experience to confirm that He will continue to intervene on the side of Israel.

II. EMBARRASSMENT (vv. 16–17)

After Micah requests favor for Israel, he then asks God to punish their enemies by shaming them and having them acknowledge the limitations of their power compared to the Lord. Micah is very specific when he relays to God the wrath he wants them to receive. Micah's petition is for all of their enemies to experience God in such a way that His dominance and authority cannot be doubted or disputed.

The Awesomeness of God's Power (verses 16–17)

16 The nations shall see and be confounded at all their might: they shall lay their hand upon their mouth, their ears shall be deaf.

When the Lord begins to work miracles for His people again, His activity will have a dramatic effect on the nations around them, just as it did on the Egyptians at the time of the Exodus. They will see this and be confounded in spite of all their might, because when they see the mighty acts of God, they will realize how weak they really are. The nations, who thought they were so strong, will realize that their strength is nothing compared to God's power, and they will be ashamed of their strength instead of proud. They will be so dismayed that they can neither speak nor hear. They will lay their hands on their mouths in awe and amazement. Their ears will become deaf, perhaps meaning that they will turn a deaf ear to all this; they do not want to hear anything more about the Lord's powerful redemptive acts for His people.

17 They shall lick the dust like a serpent, they shall move out of their holes like worms of the earth: they shall be afraid of the LORD our God, and shall fear because of thee.

Micah continues with his description of the heathen nations' reaction to the Lord's miracles, and again uses symbolic actions. "They shall lick the dust like a serpent, they shall move out of their holes like worms of the earth" are two parallel lines expressing a single idea. It is a graphic way to show the humiliation of the nations, and lying with their faces in the dust (like snakes) shows how weak and lowly they are. The expression "lick dust like a snake" may have **Genesis 3:14** as its background and may also be compared to the modern idiom "to bite the dust," symbolizing death in defeat (cf. **Psalm 72:9**). Finally the nations will come trembling out of their hiding places, and they will turn in fear to the Lord and will be afraid of him.

LIGHT ON THE WORD

Humbled Before God

When Micah suggests "They will come trembling out of their dens" (**v. 17**, NIV), this could signify repentance because the nations would have to change their ways. However, Micah wants them to approach God as humbly as snakes, which symbolize the lowest position possible.

III. WHO IS LIKE GOD? (vv. 18–20)

How fitting is it that Micah would begin to praise God? He recognizes that there is no being on Earth or in Heaven as merciful as God, and begins praising Him. After considering the nation's immorality in comparison to

God's grace, Micah boasts of the love and compassion God repeatedly extends through His never-ending forgiveness.

God Delights in Mercy (verses 18–20)

18 Who is a God like unto thee, that pardoneth iniquity, and passeth by the transgression of the remnant of his heritage? he retaineth not his anger for ever, because he delighteth in mercy.

Verse 18 opens with a rhetorical question, "Who is a God like unto thee ...?" The answer expected is clearly that there is no one like God. The question here is a way of affirming God's incomparability, particularly in His forgiving love and grace. The characteristic that sets Him apart is His ability and willingness to forgive sin. God's forgiveness "that pardoneth iniquity" is suitable to His greatness. It is not like the imperfect forgiveness that people offer, but instead full, free, bottomless, boundless, and absolute. The magnitude of God's forgiveness is underscored by the use of three different, common words in this verse and the next for sin ("iniquity" and "transgression" in **verse 18**, and "iniquities" and "sins" in **verse 19**), their purpose and effect are to emphasize the completeness of God's ability to forgive all kinds of sin.

God does not retain His anger forever. He may be angry with His people when they sin, but once they have repented or been punished, He instead takes pleasure in showing mercy. He is more ready to save than to destroy. Nothing can please Him better than having the opportunity to show mercy to the sinner.

19 He will turn again, he will have compassion upon us; he will subdue our iniquities; and thou wilt cast all their sins into the depths of the sea. 20 Thou wilt perform the truth to Jacob, and the mercy to Abraham, which thou hast sworn unto our fathers from the days of old.

Because He is such a God as described in **verse 18**, "he will turn again." His face has been long turned from His people because of their sins. But He will have compassion on them, pitying our state and feeling for our sorrows. He will defeat the iniquities of His people, and demonstrate His complete victory over their sin. Though they have been mighty, He will bring them down. The theme recalls the treatment of their enemies in **verse 10**. To further accentuate the extent of His forgiveness, He will cast all their sins into the depths of the sea—He will fully pardon them. The word "compassion" suggests a tender, maternal love. The word "subdue" paints the picture of sin as an enemy that God conquers and liberates His people from (**cf. Romans 6:14**). God overcomes sin and sets His people free.

The book of Micah, despite its threats of punishment and judgment in the earlier chapters, ends on a note of joy and confidence that the nation will eventually enjoy a restored relationship with the Lord. In concluding his prophecy, Micah sees God's future work as a continuation of His covenants and promises to the Israelites' ancestors. He knew that the same love, compassion, and mercy He showed to their parents was available to them, if they received it in faith. Regardless of the moral and spiritual decline of His people, God can be relied on to be faithful to His covenant promises.

SEARCH THE SCRIPTURES

QUESTION 2

What does God take delight in doing?

LIGHT ON THE WORD

The Covenantal Love

Micah rejoices in the covenant between his

ancestors and God. He knows that God will honor His promises to Abraham and Jacob, and as such Israel will always know the covenantal love of God.

BIBLE APPLICATION

AIM: Students will believe that God's forgiveness is unconditional. God forgives completely.

Just like chivalry, some may say that compassion is a thing of the past. While this may appear true at first glance, innumerable examples of empathy, forgiveness, and reconciliation suggest otherwise. Every day we face situations where we can turn the other cheek and extend compassion, or subject someone to the consequences of their actions. In the same way, although God demands justice, He also has mercy for those who repent. This is fully demonstrated by Jesus' work on the Cross.

STUDENTS' RESPONSES

AIM: Students will praise God because of His mercy.

Think of a specific person you know who has done something wrong. Should that person receive mercy or punishment? Make a point to offer forgiveness for this person, and if possible, alleviate the consequences of their actions.

PRAYER

Lord, we do not always want to forgive, but we know that You forgive us. We serve a God who knows that we are sometimes slow to accept forgiveness or give forgiveness to others. Take care of us and our hearts that we may always do what is right and pleasing before You. In Jesus' Name we pray. Amen.

HOW TO SAY IT

Solitarily.	so-li-**TA**-ri-lee.
Pardoneth.	**PAR**-dun-ith.
Retaineth.	ree-**TAYN**-ith.

PREPARE FOR NEXT SUNDAY

Read **Isaiah 59:15b–21** and study "Our Redeemer Comes."

DAILY HOME BIBLE READINGS

MONDAY
I Trusted in Your Steadfast Love
(Psalm 13)

TUESDAY
My Sheep Were Scattered
(Ezekiel 34:1–6)

WEDNESDAY
The Lord Will Shepherd His Sheep
(Ezekiel 34:7–16)

THURSDAY
You are My Sheep
(Ezekiel 34:23–31)

FRIDAY
Troubling Times of Woe
(Micah 7:1–6)

SATURDAY
I Will Look to the Lord
(Micah 7:7–11)

SUNDAY
God Delights in Showing Clemency
(Micah 7:14–20)

Sources:

Achtemeier, Paul J., ed. *The HarperCollins Bible Dictionary.* New York: HarperCollins Publishing, 1996. 919, 923, 1026.

Allen, Leslie C. *The Books of Joel, Obadiah, Jonah and Micah.* New International Commentary of the Old Testament. Grand Rapids, MI: Wm. B. Eerdmans, 1976.

Barker, Kenneth L. *Micah, Nahum, Habakkuk, Zephaniah.* The New American Commentary. Vo. 20. Nashville, TN: Broadman & Holman Publishers, 1999.

Boice, J. M. *The Minor Prophets.* Complete in one edition, 2 volumes. Grand Rapids, MI: Kregel, 1996. S.v. 2:24.

Clark, David J. and Norm Mundhenk. *A Translator's Handbook on the Book of Micah, UBS Handbook Series.* London: United Bible Societies, 1982.

Craigie, P. C. *Twelve Prophets.* 2 vols. Philadelphia: Westminster, 1985. 2:19.

Smith, Ralph L. *Micah–Malachi.* Word Biblical Commentary. Vol. 32. Dallas: Word Books Publishers, Inc., 1984. 58–59.

Wolfendale, James. "Minor Prophets." *The Preacher's Homiletical Commentary.* New York: Funk and Wagnalls, 1892.

Waltke, Bruce K. *A Commentary on Micah.* Grand Rapids, MI: Eerdmans 2007. 181-183.

COMMENTS / NOTES:

OUR REDEEMER COMES

BIBLE BASIS: ISAIAH 59:15b–21

BIBLE TRUTH: Isaiah and the psalmist promise a time when God will come as a Redeemer with a foundation of righteousness and justice and will place God's spirit on those who repent of their sins.

MEMORY VERSE: "And the Redeemer shall come to Zion, and unto them that turn from transgression in Jacob, saith the LORD" (Isaiah 59:20).

LESSON AIM: By the end of the lesson, your students will: explore how God promises a renewed covenant relationship; reveal their feelings about the cruelty and violence of society; and express gratitude and joy for God's salvation from worldly dangers and work toward a renewed community.

TEACHER PREPARATION

MATERIALS NEEDED: Quarterly Commentary/Teacher Manual, Adult Quarterly, Adult resources—charts, worksheets, and other teaching tools, paper, pens, pencils, Bibles (several different versions)

OTHER MATERIALS NEEDED / TEACHER'S NOTES:

____

____

LESSON OVERVIEW

LIFE NEED FOR TODAY'S LESSON

Sometimes everything around us seems violent, cruel, and immoral.

BIBLE LEARNING

People of God will learn to praise God and know that the Lord will not be angry with the chosen people forever.

BIBLE APPLICATION

People of faith understand that disobedience causes God pain.

STUDENTS' RESPONSES

Students will praise God for His mercy and forgiveness.

LESSON SCRIPTURE

ISAIAH 59:15b–21, KJV

15b The LORD saw it, and it displeased him that there was no judgment.

16 And he saw that there was no man, and wondered that there was no intercessor: therefore his arm brought salvation unto him; and his righteousness, it sustained him.

ISAIAH 59:15b–21, NIV

15b The LORD looked and was displeased that there was no justice.

16 He saw that there was no one, he was appalled that there was no one to intervene; so his own arm achieved salvation for him, and his own righteousness sustained him.

17 For he put on righteousness as a breastplate, and an helmet of salvation upon his head; and he put on the garments of vengeance for clothing, and was clad with zeal as a cloak.

18 According to their deeds, accordingly he will repay, fury to his adversaries, recompence to his enemies; to the islands he will repay recompence.

19 So shall they fear the name of the LORD from the west, and his glory from the rising of the sun. When the enemy shall come in like a flood, the Spirit of the LORD shall lift up a standard against him.

20 And the Redeemer shall come to Zion, and unto them that turn from transgression in Jacob, saith the LORD.

21 As for me, this is my covenant with them, saith the LORD; My spirit that is upon thee, and my words which I have put in thy mouth, shall not depart out of thy mouth, nor out of the mouth of thy seed, nor out of the mouth of thy seed's seed, saith the LORD, from henceforth and forever.

17 He put on righteousness as his breastplate, and the helmet of salvation on his head; he put on the garments of vengeance and wrapped himself in zeal as in a cloak.

18 According to what they have done, so will he repay wrath to his enemies and retribution to his foes; he will repay the islands their due.

19 From the west, people will fear the name of the LORD, and from the rising of the sun, they will revere his glory. For he will come like a pent-up flood that the breath of the LORD drives along.

20 "The Redeemer will come to Zion, to those in Jacob who repent of their sins," declares the LORD.

21 "As for me, this is my covenant with them," says the LORD. "My Spirit, who is on you, will not depart from you, and my words that I have put in your mouth will always be on your lips, on the lips of your children and on the lips of their descendants—from this time on and forever," says the LORD.

LIGHT ON THE WORD

The "islands" were not just simply dry lands in the middle of the sea. This term was used to denote the Mediterranean coastlands or a maritime region. For the Israelites, these coastlands, such as Greece and Italy, represented the far ends of the earth. Gentiles inhabited these lands, so they were also known as the isles of the Gentiles (**Genesis 10:5**).

In the Old Testament, the word "redeemer" can have one of three meanings. The first meaning refers to a person who recovers ownership by purchasing something that has been sold, usually property or a family member who has fallen into slavery. The second meaning is of the avenger of blood who takes revenge for the murder of a deceased relative. The third use applies solely to God acting in relation with His people and reestablishing relationship after acts of rebellion, disobedience, or transgression.

TEACHING THE BIBLE LESSON

LIFE NEED FOR TODAY'S LESSON

AIM: Students will know that there are times when everything around us seems violent, cruel, and immoral.

INTRODUCTION

God's Vision for Isaiah

The events that were transpiring around him inspired Isaiah to give His prophecies during a crucial time in the history of Judah. In approximately 791 B.C., Uzziah became king of Judah. Forty years into his reign, he was stricken with leprosy, so his son Jotham became co-regent, helping him rule. Around 745 B.C., Assyria, a dominant and opposing empire, began to shift their focus in an attempt to conquer the Mediterranean area, including Judah and many other nations. In the year that King Uzziah died, Jotham began to rule alone and Isaiah had one of his greatest visions.

BIBLE LEARNING

AIM: Students will praise God and know that the Lord will not be angry with the chosen people forever.

I. INTERCESSION (Isaiah 59:15b–16)

The writer discloses that there was a paradigm shift in the land. His report reveals that the people abandoned truth and embraced wickedness because harsh retaliation was the consequence for siding with righteousness. The historical truth is that people were physically persecuted and even killed for following the Lord. However, this is not a foreign or antiquated premise because even today, people suffer and die for righteousness in countries like China and Syria.

Abandoned Truth (verses 15b–16)

15b The LORD saw it, and it displeased him that there was no judgment. 16 And he saw that there was no man, and wondered that there was no intercessor: therefore his arm brought salvation unto him; and his righteousness, it sustained him.

These verses portray the social degradation of the people of God. They directly follow **verses 14–15a**, where we see the consequence of what happens when people live in lies and assume that it is alright to oppress those who are weaker, neglect God, and turn away from His commandments and the path of righteousness. First, "truth faileth," which means that truth has been left behind or abandoned. People do not care for the truth but tell lies with impunity. Although not limited to politicians, people say the lies over and over until they are somehow convinced that the lies are truth. Second, whoever turns away from sin is considered out of sorts or insane. One would expect that everyone departing from evil would not feel hatred and censure, but commendation and appreciation. Unfortunately, this is not the case; on the contrary, the person who takes this step will "make himself a prey." In a society that is increasingly morally bankrupt, turning aside from evil could easily make one seem the most apparent loser. Third, there was injustice—that is, no social justice, no sense of the "right" manifestly ruling in the common relations of life.

God sees the helplessness of His people and cares about it. The word "intercessor," from the Hebrew root word paga' (**pah-GAH**), which also occurred in **53:12,** means to cover the breach with one's body. In the same manner as in **Isaiah 53**, God has to intervene on behalf of His people. God looked down and saw the degenerate and hopeless condition of His people. He knew how far the evil spread, until the whole people were corrupted. To make matters worse, God saw no one stood for truth and righteousness—none such as Abraham, Moses, or Phinehas (**Genesis 15:6; Exodus 33:11–14; Numbers 25:7–8**). That God wondered does not suggest a surprise or ignorance of the situation, but rather astonishment. As no human intercessor could be found among the exiles, God Himself brought salvation. He was patient and waited for a disobedient Israel to turn to Him. He waited and longed for a man to lead them back to Him, but none defended His cause or proclaimed His truth, so the Lord did it Himself. If an intercessor had stepped forth, it would have saved Israel a lot of calamity, but the lack of an intercessor did not derail God's plan. His work would still go forth if none arose (cf. **Esther 4:14**). The Lord put on His armor and went forth to destroy His enemies, protect His people, and glorify His name.

LIGHT ON THE WORD

God Intervenes

According to Isaiah, God would survey the situation and realize that human intervention was not possible because the people lacked the strength and tenacity to oppose injustice. God would act on behalf of the oppressed with extraordinary power and ensure their recovery.

II. GOD'S WRATH (vv. 17–21)

God's intervention will not be diplomatic; Judah's adversaries will know God's wrath and fury. Here we get our first glimpse of the armor of God. Paul tells his readers that they should guard themselves by donning this holy battle gear (**Ephesians 6:10–18**), but in this text it is used as a metaphor to describe the intensity with which God will admonish the enemy. It is no surprise that Isaiah uses warrior metaphors to describe God; He was often known as a battle-ax, conqueror, and divine warrior to the people of Israel, and they were confident that He would intervene on their behalf.

God's Armor (verses 17–21)

17 For he put on righteousness as a breastplate, and an helmet of salvation upon his head; and he put on the garments of vengeance for clothing, and was clad with zeal as a cloak.

Using metaphorical language, Isaiah continues showing how the Lord will help His people. God appears as a man of war and puts on His arms—righteousness as breastplate, helmet and garments of salvation, and zeal as a cloak. The imagery is a prototype of **Ephesians 6:13–17**, where Paul exhorts his hearers to prepare for spiritual battle. The absence of offensive weapons such as bows or spears is striking; perhaps all God needs to execute vengeance on His enemies is His mighty arm. He will proceed in righting the wrongs and avenging the injuries of His people. Both in saving them and destroying their enemies, He will secure the honor of His faithfulness and justice, and by preserving His people, He maintains the honor and glory of His name. Since the heart and inward parts are protected by the breastplate, He calls righteousness His breastplate, to show the justness of His cause and His faithfulness in making good on His promises. In putting on the garments of vengeance, He is determined to punish His and His people's enemies. In this verse, God comes to the defense of His people.

18 According to their deeds, accordingly he will repay, fury to his adversaries, recompence to his enemies; to the islands he will repay recompence.

The Lord will deal with the enemies of His people according to the laws of retribution and retaliation. God will judge and repay His foes; He will execute vengeance on all those who have opposed Him. Sin's havoc on creation will be fully and richly repaid. Nothing will be left unrequited.

19 So shall they fear the name of the LORD from the west, and his glory from the rising of the sun. When the enemy shall come in like a flood, the Spirit of the LORD shall lift up a standard against him.

The negative picture gives way to positive results. The verse begins with a general statement that people from all over the world will fear the Lord. Here "fear" is understood as godly, reverent, childlike fear from the acknowledgement of His name. The last part of the verse gives further reasons for the reverential awe displayed toward the Lord—whenever the enemy comes to attack God's people, the Lord Himself raises a standard, showing that He is in control of the situation. No enemy can conquer God's people because He is ever-present to both demonstrate His care for His people and show His sovereignty. For this reason, people from across the world will fear the name of the Lord. God's name is His reputation and character; to fear His name is to fear Him, as He has revealed Himself in His acts on earth (**Psalm 86:11**). In the Scriptures, fear has both negative and positive connotations. Those who oppose the power and holiness of God have every reason to be afraid because He will judge them and consume them; on the other hand, those who know and revere Him enjoy the benefits of a personal relationship.

20 And he the Redeemer shall come to Zion, and unto them that turn from transgression in Jacob, saith the LORD. 21 As for me, this is my covenant with them, saith the LORD; My spirit that is upon thee, and my words which I have put in thy mouth, shall not depart out of thy mouth, nor out of the mouth of thy seed, nor out of the mouth of thy seed's seed, saith the LORD, from henceforth and for ever.

Verses 15–19 provided a description of how the Lord deals with the enemies of His people. He will be stern and just. There is a marked shift in tone in **verse 20**. Now He describes how differently He will deal with His own people and the generations that follow. First, God, acting as the Redeemer, shall come to Zion, but only to those who turn and repent from their sins. As such, turning from sin is the entry point into the covenant. God's judgment on His people was a foreshadowing of that final Day of the Lord, when all the nations will be judged. When it is ended, then "the Redeemer shall come to Zion" and the glorious kingdom will be established. Israel will be God's chosen and purified people, and the glory of the Lord will radiate from Mt. Zion. God's dealings are based on the covenant, which embodies the mercies that he has repeatedly promised to them. The substance of the covenant is encapsulated in two words—spirit and words. The words here may be the Torah. Israel will become a people that truly meditate on the Torah day and night. Both the words and the spirit belong together and constitute testimony that characterizes God's people not only in its momentary fulfillment but "from henceforth and for ever." The people of God must continue to embrace the Word by constantly hearing, saying, and learning it. They also have the responsibility to teach the word to their "seeds" and their "seeds' seeds," that is, to their children and grandchildren, as in the case of Timothy (cf. **2 Timothy 1:5**).

SEARCH THE SCRIPTURES

QUESTIONS 1 & 2

What is the purpose of the Lord putting on armor and robes of vengeance?

What did God promise would not depart out of their mouth and why is this important?

LIGHT ON THE WORD

God's Justice Prevails

Isaiah makes it clear that those who oppose justice and truth will be held accountable. The Lord's vengeance will be swift and strong. The prophet paints a vivid picture of the Lord's retribution. Isaiah, like so many other prophets, makes the claim that as a result of God's judgment, they will fear and acknowledge the Lord.

BIBLE APPLICATION

AIM: Students will understand that disobedience causes God pain.

Morals and socioeconomic perspectives are two of the primary contributors to ideas of justice. Apart from individual premises of justice, nations have a prevailing interpretation of justice that shapes policy, governance, and culture. Justice does not solely address law; it addresses moral questions of right and wrong in humanity. Words such as accountability, equity, access, representation, and opportunity are key when analyzing justice in a society.

STUDENTS' RESPONSES

AIM: Students will praise God for His mercy and forgiveness.

Israel was to be very diligent in sharing their experiences with God with their children. **Isaiah 59:21** says, "[The words I have given you] will be on your lips and on the lips of your children and your children's children forever" (NLT). For this to happen, there must be an exchange of information from one generation to the next. Share your spiritual encounters and experiences in seeking justice with your children or others in the neighborhood. Not only will they know God through their personal experience, but they will know God through yours as well.

PRAYER

God, Your truth and love are amazing. We need to walk in Your truth and care for justice with passion and deliverance in our lives. Bless us and keep us. In Jesus' Name we pray. Amen.

HOW TO SAY IT

Phinehas. **PHI**-nee-us.

Recompence. **REH**-kum-pence.

PREPARE FOR NEXT SUNDAY

Read **Jeremiah 7:1–15** and study "A Chance to Be Just."

DAILY HOME BIBLE READINGS

MONDAY
Our Sins Testify Against Us
(Isaiah 59:1–14)

TUESDAY
Taught for Our Own Good
(Isaiah 48:12–19)

WEDNESDAY
God's Everlasting Love
(Isaiah 54:1–8)

THURSDAY
Our Redeemer is Strong
(Jeremiah 50:28–34)

FRIDAY
Walking in the Light
(Psalm 89:11–18)

SATURDAY
Redeemed with Outstretched Arm
(Exodus 6:2–8)

SUNDAY
The Lord Will Come as Redeemer
(Isaiah 59:15–21)

Sources:

Achtemeier, Paul J., ed. *The HarperCollins Bible Dictionary*. New York: HarperCollins Publishing, 1996. 918.

Brueggemann, Walter. *Isaiah 40-66*. Louisville, KY: Westminster John Knox Press, 1998.

Goldingay, John. *Isaiah*. New International Bible Commentary. Peabody, MA: Hendrickson Publishers, 2001.

Hanson, Paul D. *Isaiah 40–66*. Interpretation. Louisville, KY: Westminster John Knox Press, 1995.

Leupold, H, C. *Exposition of Isaiah*. Grand Rapids, MI: Baker Books House, 1976.

Oswald, John N. *The Book of Isaiah, Chapters 44–66*. The New International Commentary on the Old Testament. Grand Rapids, MI: Wm. B. Eerdmans, 1998.

Simeon, Charles. *Isaiah, XXVII–LXVI*. Horae Homileticae. Vol. 8. London: Holdsworth and Ball, 1832.

Spence-Jones, H. D. M., ed. *Isaiah, Vol. II*. The Pulpit Commentary. London: Funk & Wagnalls Company, 1910.

Warren W. Wiersbe. *Be Comforted*. "Be" Commentary Series. Wheaton, IL: Victor Books, 1996.

Watts, John D. *Isaiah 34–66*. Word Biblical Commentary. Waco, TX: World Books Publishers., 1987. 286-287.

Young, Edward J. *The Book of Isaiah, Vol. 3*. Grand Rapids, MI: Wm. B. Eerdmans, 1972.

COMMENTS / NOTES:

A CHANCE TO BE JUST

BIBLE BASIS: JEREMIAH 7:1–15

BIBLE TRUTH: Through Ezra and Jeremiah, God sent messages of hope to those who will amend their ways and messages of doom to those who will not.

MEMORY VERSE: "Thus saith the LORD of hosts, the God of Israel, Amend your ways and your doing, and I will cause you to dwell in this place" (Jeremiah 7:3).

LESSON AIM: By the end of the lesson, your students will: review the messages of doom and hope found in Jeremiah; regret the error of their ways and resolve to change; and address their personal unfaithfulness and their community's corruption.

TEACHER PREPARATION

MATERIALS NEEDED: Quarterly Commentary/Teacher Manual, Adult Quarterly, Adult resources—charts, worksheets, and other teaching tools, paper, pens, pencils, Bibles (several different versions)

OTHER MATERIALS NEEDED / TEACHER'S NOTES:

____

____

LESSON OVERVIEW

LIFE NEED FOR TODAY'S LESSON

Many people show partiality, oppress the weak, and break the law as though they are unaware of the error of their ways.

BIBLE LEARNING

Jeremiah speaks to the issues of oppression and abuse of strangers, orphans, and widows.

BIBLE APPLICATION

Believers acknowledge that the state of one's heart matters to God.

STUDENTS' RESPONSES

Students will respond to the conviction of their sins by repenting.

LESSON SCRIPTURE

JEREMIAH 7:1–15, KJV

1 The word that came to Jeremiah from the LORD, saying,

2 Stand in the gate of the LORD's house, and proclaim there this word, and say, Hear the word of the LORD, all ye of Judah, that enter in at these gates to worship the LORD.

JEREMIAH 7:1–15, NIV

1 This is the word that came to Jeremiah from the LORD:

2 "Stand at the gate of the LORD's house and there proclaim this message: "'Hear the word of the LORD, all you people of Judah who come through these gates to worship the LORD.

3 Thus saith the LORD of hosts, the God of Israel, Amend your ways and your doings, and I will cause you to dwell in this place.

4 Trust ye not in lying words, saying, The temple of the LORD, The temple of the LORD, the temple of the LORD, are these.

5 For if ye throughly amend your ways and your doings; if ye throughly execute judgment between a man and his neighbour;

6 If ye oppress not the stranger, the fatherless, and the widow, and shed not innocent blood in this place, neither walk after other gods to your hurt:

7 Then will I cause you to dwell in this place, in the land that I gave to your fathers, for ever and ever.

8 Behold, ye trust in lying words, that cannot profit.

9 Will ye steal, murder, and commit adultery, and swear falsely, and burn incense unto Baal, and walk after other gods whom ye know not;

10 And come and stand before me in this house, which is called by my name, and say, We are delivered to do all these abominations?

11 Is this house, which is called by my name, become a den of robbers in your eyes? Behold, even I have seen it, saith the LORD.

12 But go ye now unto my place which was in Shiloh, where I set my name at the first, and see what I did to it for the wickedness of my people Israel.

13 And now, because ye have done all these works, saith the LORD, and I spake unto you, rising up early and speaking, but ye heard not; and I called you, but ye

3 This is what the LORD Almighty, the God of Israel, says: Reform your ways and your actions, and I will let you live in this place.

4 Do not trust in deceptive words and say, "This is the temple of the LORD, the temple of the LORD, the temple of the LORD!"

5 If you really change your ways and your actions and deal with each other justly,

6 if you do not oppress the foreigner, the fatherless or the widow and do not shed innocent blood in this place, and if you do not follow other gods to your own harm,

7 then I will let you live in this place, in the land I gave your ancestors for ever and ever.

8 But look, you are trusting in deceptive words that are worthless.

9 "'Will you steal and murder, commit adultery and perjury, burn incense to Baal and follow other gods you have not known,

10 and then come and stand before me in this house, which bears my Name, and say, "We are safe"—safe to do all these detestable things?

11 Has this house, which bears my Name, become a den of robbers to you? But I have been watching! declares the LORD.

12 "'Go now to the place in Shiloh where I first made a dwelling for my Name, and see what I did to it because of the wickedness of my people Israel.

13 While you were doing all these things, declares the LORD, I spoke to you again and again, but you did not listen; I called you, but you did not answer.

answered not;

14 Therefore will I do unto this house, which is called by my name, wherein ye trust, and unto the place which I gave to you and to your fathers, as I have done to Shiloh.

15 And I will cast you out of my sight, as I have cast out all your brethren, even the whole seed of Ephraim.

14 Therefore, what I did to Shiloh I will now do to the house that bears my Name, the temple you trust in, the place I gave to you and your ancestors.

15 I will thrust you from my presence, just as I did all your fellow Israelites, the people of Ephraim.'

LIGHT ON THE WORD

The eastern gate of the Temple in Jerusalem was most likely the place where Jeremiah delivered the sermon found in **Jeremiah 7**. This was the magnificent Temple Solomon had built some 350 years earlier, where the people worshiped and where the Ark of the Covenant, the symbolic presence of God, resided. Jerusalem had withstood many attacks over the years, and the people of Jerusalem believed that because God resided in the Temple, He would never allow His Temple or His people to fall.

TEACHING THE BIBLE LESSON

LIFE NEED FOR TODAY'S LESSON

AIM: Students will know people show partiality, oppress the weak, and break the law as though they are unaware of the error of their ways.

INTRODUCTION

Preach, Jeremiah, Preach!

The occasion for Jeremiah's sermon was most likely the beginning of one of the Israelite pilgrimage festivals, when great crowds of people would be pouring into the Temple courts for worship. Most scholars date the chapter 7 sermon to around 609 B.C., during the first year of the reign of King Jehoiakim (**Jeremiah 26:1**). This is significant because it was some 110 years after the Northern Kingdom of Israel had fallen to the Assyrians. Jeremiah frequently points to the fall of Israel as an example of God's judgment upon a sinful and unrepentant nation, and he repeatedly warns that Judah and Jerusalem are destined for the same fate if they do not repent. The people of Judah were well aware of Israel's fate, but they had come to believe that because they had the Temple, God would never judge them in the same way.

BIBLE LEARNING

AIM: Students will discover how Jeremiah speaks to the issues of oppression and abuse of strangers, orphans, and widows.

I. THE LORD OF THE TEMPLE (Jeremiah 7:1–3)

During the pilgrimage festivals, it would not have been unusual for pilgrims entering the

Temple area to be greeted by a representative of the Temple asking them to examine their lives before going in for worship. On this particular day, that representative was Jeremiah. But his pleas on that day had a sense of urgency about them. Beyond the usual call for repentance, Jeremiah conveyed that their words of repentance must be accompanied by actions of abandoning their evil ways.

Jeremiah's Temple Sermon (verses 1–3)

1 The word that came to Jeremiah from the LORD, saying, 2 Stand in the gate of the LORD's house, and proclaim there this word, and say, Hear the word of the LORD, all ye of Judah, that enter in at these gates to worship the LORD. 3 Thus saith the LORD of hosts, the God of Israel, Amend your ways and your doings, and I will cause you to dwell in this place.

When Josiah became king of Israel, a priest found a copy of the Word of God in the Temple, and Josiah led the nation in a religious revival that sought to restore the people's worship of God to its rightful place. However, King Josiah was slain in a battle with an Egyptian pharaoh, and when Jehoiakim replaced Josiah as king, he immediately began to reverse the religious reforms that had been instituted. Judah was caught in the middle of a battle between Egypt and Babylon over who would control Palestine, raising questions of national security and prosperity. Under Jehoiakim, worship within the Temple had become ritualistic with more emphasis on the external matters of the Temple than proper worship of God. The people had a form of godliness, but it was only external. They attended the Temple as required, paid their tithes, and submitted their sacrificial offerings, but it was only for show. When they were not in the Temple, the people committed the same evils as the heathens around them. It was under these circumstances that God instructs Jeremiah to stand in the "gate" (Heb. *sha'ar*, **SHAH-ar**) of the Lord's "house" (Heb. *bayit*, **BAH-yith**, dwelling or habitation) to proclaim a word to the entering people of Judah. The gate where Jeremiah stood was the gate that led into the court of the women and the outer court of the Temple, or the court of the Gentiles. The prophet's message, then, was directed toward all those religious people within the nation that still attempted to worship God. For preaching this message, called the Temple Sermon, Jeremiah's life was threatened (see **Jeremiah 26:7–9**).

SEARCH THE SCRIPTURES

QUESTION 1

What did it mean for the people of Judah to amend their ways?

LIGHT ON THE WORD

Misplaced Faith

So great was God's anger against the Israelites that their privilege of staying in the land was contingent on radical and immediate amending of their immoral ways. Additionally, in **verse 4,** he challenged them to examine the superficial nature of their worship and their false sense of security associated with the Temple. They were convinced that God would never allow anything bad to happen to His Temple or to the people who worshiped there. They had put their faith in the Temple of the Lord instead of the Lord of the Temple.

II. THE LONGING FOR CHANGE (vv. 4–7)

Through His servant Jeremiah, God makes it very clear that continued blessings are conditional on the people's making drastic changes in their attitudes and actions. If the people stopped their evil deeds, He would allow them to continue to live in the land and have access to the Temple. It was clearly the people's choice: they must choose to do justice, and treat those around and among them with respect and honor. So important was this issue of justice, and its conditional tie to living in the Promised Land, that it was included in the Ten Commandments: "Honor your father and your mother, so that you may live long in the land the LORD your God is giving you" (**Exodus 20:12, NIV**).

The Sins of the People (verses 4–7)

4 Trust ye not in lying words, saying, The temple of the LORD, The temple of the LORD, The temple of the LORD, are these. 5 For if ye throughly amend your ways and your doings; if ye throughly execute judgment between a man and his neighbor; 6 If ye oppress not the stranger, the fatherless, and the widow, and shed not innocent blood in this place, neither walk after other gods to your hurt: 7 Then will I cause you to dwell in this place, in the land that I gave to your fathers, for ever and ever.

The nation of Israel collectively embraced a misunderstanding of God's relationship with them. Because they were His chosen people and He had located His Temple among them, they believed that no harm could befall them. Almost like a charm, the people would reply "the temple of the LORD" whenever they felt threatened. By doing so, they were asserting that they could do as they pleased and "trust" (Heb. *batach*, **bah-TAKH**, to feel safe or confident in) God would protect them because His home was with them. Further, the nation of Israel was under the impression that they could not be displaced from "the land" (Heb. *'erets*, **EH-rets**, land, country or territory) because God had promised it to their "forefathers" (Heb. *'ab*, **AHV**) and they believed it was their inheritance forever. What Jeremiah sought to make them understand was that God did not bestow the nation with a covenant without obligation. Only as the nation faithfully observed the requirements of their covenant with the Lord, would He honor His portion of the covenant with them. They would have to "throughly amend their ways" and "throughly execute judgment." These two phrases are examples of the Hebrew infinitive absolute. This form of verb is meant to convey intensity. In other words, the Lord wanted the people to "really amend their ways" and "truly execute judgment." Jeremiah, here, begins a representative listing of the sins Judah had committed.

LIGHT ON THE WORD

Justice and Mercy

God's requirements of justice comprise a large part of His elaboration on the Law in **Exodus 20–23**. The Israelites in Jeremiah's day were openly violating God's laws of justice, yet He still offered mercy (**v. 7**) if they would turn from their evil ways.

III. THE LITANY OF SINS (vv. 8–11)

Here God shows that He not only knows His people's evil deeds, but He also knows their corrupt view of the Temple and their worship there. The people were guilty of violating at least five of the Ten Commandments, yet they confidently flocked to the Temple, where they believed their mere attendance and participation in rituals would atone for their sins. God is obviously angry both at their sins, and at their attitude that Temple worship gave them indulgence to keep on sinning. He says they have turned His Temple into a "den of robbers" (**Jeremiah 7:11**).

God is Watching (verses 8–11)

8 Behold, ye trust in lying words, that cannot profit. 9 Will ye steal, murder, and

commit adultery, and swear falsely, and burn incense unto Baal, and walk after other gods whom ye know not; 10 And come and stand before me in this house, which is called by my name, and say, We are delivered to do all these abominations? 11 Is this house, which is called by my name, become a den of robbers in your eyes? Behold, even I have seen it, saith the LORD.

It is easy to imagine that as Jeremiah stood in the gate of the Temple and continued his sermon to the nation of Israel, the people and their leadership would have become angrier with him. They had been coming to the Temple to bring their offerings as they believed the Law demanded; what then was God's problem? Jeremiah was trying to show them that they had an outward show of religiosity but were inwardly corrupt. The nation of Judah assumed that their presence in the Temple was all that was needed. "We are delivered" (Heb. *natsal*, **nah-TSAL**, to take away or snatch away, e.g., from violence) was the phrase used as license for them to live as they pleased when not in the Temple. God would deliver them out of harm's way because His house was among them. The list of sins Jeremiah recounts for the people accuses them of violating nearly all the Ten Commandments God had handed down (**Exodus 20; Deuteronomy 5**), and though they retreated to God's house as though it were a "den" (Heb. *me'arah*, **muh-ah-RAH**, hideout) to which robbers would escape once they committed their evil deeds, it was not enough to protect them from God's wrath. God had been watching and had "seen" (Heb. *ra'ah*, **rah-AH**, to inspect, perceive, or consider) their wrong doings.

SEARCH THE SCRIPTURES

QUESTION 2

What did the people's chant say about their attitude toward God and their sin?

LIGHT ON THE WORD

Imminent Judgment

The prophet's audience would have certainly known about the many limestone caves in the mountains surrounding Jerusalem where gangs of thieves sought temporary safety between their robberies. For the people to treat the Temple as a place of sanctuary, where they thought they were safe from the consequences of their sins, was such an abomination in God's eyes that He was about to rain judgment down on them.

IV. THE LAST WARNING (vv. 12–15)

Shiloh, located about thirty miles north of Jerusalem in the Northern Kingdom of Israel, was an important place of worship during the time of the Judges (c. 1,300 B.C.–1,030 B.C.), as the tabernacle was set up there for a time. The hearers of Jeremiah's Temple gate sermon were well aware that the tabernacle, an earlier forerunner to the Jerusalem Temple, had been destroyed in Shiloh many hundreds of years previous. **Psalm 78:59–62** records the fate of that once sacred place of worship: "God … was filled with wrath … so that He abandoned the dwelling place at Shiloh." God would not be bound to any physical building, location, or place of worship.

Rebellious Consequences (verses 12–15)

12 But go ye now unto my place which was in Shiloh, where I set my name at the first, and see what I did to it for the wickedness of my people Israel. 13 And now, because ye have done all these works, saith the LORD, and I spake unto you, rising up early and speaking, but ye heard not; and I called you, but ye answered not; 14 Therefore will I do unto this house, which is called by my name, wherein ye trust, and unto the place which I gave to

you and to your fathers, as I have done to Shiloh. 15 And I will cast you out of my sight, as I have cast out all your brethren, even the whole seed of Ephraim.

Jeremiah now seeks to reinforce for the nation of Judah the truth: trusting in a location will not preserve them from God's wrath. God challenges the people to visit Shiloh (Heb. *Shilo*, **shee-LOH**), a city in Ephraim and temporary home of the Ark of the Covenant and the Tabernacle, and view how He permitted it to be destroyed because of the wickedness of the Jewish nation at that time. The Jews at that time even brought out the Ark of the Covenant before their enemy, the Philistines, in an effort to secure their victory over them. However, the Israelites were defeated and the Ark was carried off into the land of the Philistines (**1 Samuel 4:10**). Jeremiah was seeking to teach the people of Judah that God's favor is not tied to a location, but rather the covenant made with His people. Violation of the covenant, regardless of the location, would result in punishment.

At Shiloh, God demonstrated that He would remove His tabernacle to Jerusalem, where it now resided, and He could just as easily remove His Temple from Jerusalem. God declares then that He tried to reason with the nation of Judah, "rising up early" (implying an earnestness) and speaking to them, only to have His plea for a return to righteousness fall on deaf ears. Therefore, God promises to do two things to them because of their rebellious state: 1) He will permit the enemies of Judah to conquer them, and 2) He will permit His chosen people to be carried off into captivity the same way that He permitted the seed of Ephraim (i.e, the Northern Kingdom) to be carried off.

LIGHT ON THE WORD

Repent Now!

In 722 B.C., God gave all of Israel over to destruction and exile at the hands of the Assyrians. Jeremiah makes it very clear that unless the people of Judah amend their ways and turn from their abominations, their fate will be like that of Shiloh and Israel. Clearly, the choice was theirs. The sad reality of their response is recorded later in Jeremiah's ministry (**26:8–15**).

BIBLE APPLICATION

AIM: Students will acknowledge that the state of one's heart matters to God.

Like the Israelites of Jeremiah's day, each of us daily faces temptations to perpetuate injustices and commit sinful acts. We must make choices and face their consequences. This text should also inform our attitudes and practices concerning worship and redemption. Sometimes we treat our church the way the Israelites treated their Temple. We are sometimes focused on appearances and rituals rather than the God who is supposed to be the object of our worship.

STUDENTS' RESPONSES

AIM: Students will respond to the conviction of their sins by repenting.

Often our attempts at repentance and reform fall short because we simply forget what God requires of us and only talk about change in a general way. In order to combat this tendency, write down a list of resolutions and practices that will specifically help you to "throughly amend your ways" (**Jeremiah 7:5**).

PRAYER

God, help us and guide us to follow Your ways. We do not want to worship our church instead of You. Lord, You truly deserve our praise and adoration. In Jesus' Name we pray. Amen.

HOW TO SAY IT

Throughly. thru-**LEE**.

Shiloh. **SHY**-lo.

PREPARE FOR NEXT SUNDAY

Read **Ezekiel 18:1–13, 31–32** and study "A Call for Repentance."

DAILY HOME BIBLE READINGS

MONDAY
Justice for the Poor
(Psalm 140:6–13)

TUESDAY
My People Have Forgotten Me
(Jeremiah 18:11–17)

WEDNESDAY
Judgment for the Disobedient
(Ezra 7:21–28)

THURSDAY
If You Will Not Listen
(Jeremiah 26:1–7)

FRIDAY
Amend Your Ways and Your Doings
(Jeremiah 26:8–15)

SATURDAY
God Abandoned Shiloh
(Psalm 78:56–62)

SUNDAY
Let Me Dwell with You
(Jeremiah 7:1–15)

Sources:

Brown, Francis. *The Brown-Driver-Briggs Hebrew and English Lexicon.* Peabody, MA: Hendrickson, 2010.

Burton, James. *Coffman Commentaries on the Old Testament and New Testament.* Abilene, TX: Abilene Christian University Press, n.d.

Craigie, Peter, Page Kelley, and Joel Drinkard Jr. *Jeremiah 1–25.* Word Biblical Commentary. Vol. 6. Nashville, TN: Thomas Nelson, 1991.

Dunn, James D. G. and John W. Rogerson. *Commentary on the Bible.* Grand Rapids, MI: Wm. B. Eerdmans, 2003.

English, E. Schuyler and Marian Bishop Bower, eds. *The Holy Bible: Pilgrim Edition.* New York: Oxford University Press, Inc., 1952.

Espinosa, Eddie. *Songs of Faith and Praise.* Alton H. Howard, editor. West Monroe, LA: Howard Publishing, 1994.

Feinberg, Charles. Jeremiah. *The Expositor's Bible Commentary.* Vol. 6. Frank Gaebelein, editor. Grand Rapids: Zondervan, 1986.

Howley, G. C. D., F. F. Bruce, and H. L. Ellison. *The New Layman's Bible Commentary.* Grand Rapids, MI: Zondervan Publishing, 1979.

Life Application Study Bible. New Living Translation. Carol Stream, IL: Tyndale House Publishers, 2007.

Strong, James. *Strong's Exhaustive Concordance of the Bible.* Nashville, TN: Thomas Nelson, 1990.

Wolf, Herbert. Judges. *The Expositor's Bible Commentary. Vol. 3.* Frank Gaebelein, editor. Grand Rapids, MI: Zondervan, 1992.

COMMENTS / NOTES:

A CALL FOR REPENTANCE

BIBLE BASIS: EZEKIEL 18:1–13, 31–32

BIBLE TRUTH: Ezekiel advises confession and, along with Proverbs, exhorts the people to do the right thing and thereby build a just community.

MEMORY VERSES: "Repent, and turn yourselves from all your transgressions; so iniquity shall not be your ruin. Cast away from you all your transgressions, whereby ye have transgressed; and make you a new heart and a new spirit" (from Ezekiel 18:30–31).

LESSON AIM: By the end of the lesson, your students will: review the message of Ezekiel that God holds each person responsible for his or her own actions; feel accountability for personal acts of omission that damage the community; and pray for discernment in how to amend our ways and build communities of justice.

TEACHER PREPARATION

MATERIALS NEEDED: Quarterly Commentary/Teacher Manual, Adult Quarterly, Adult resources—charts, worksheets, and other teaching tools, paper, pens, pencils, Bibles (several different versions)

OTHER MATERIALS NEEDED / TEACHER'S NOTES:

____

____

LESSON OVERVIEW

LIFE NEED FOR TODAY'S LESSON
People are aware of behavior that is harmful to the life of a community.

BIBLE LEARNING
God rewards those who seek to build healthy communities and to please Him.

BIBLE APPLICATION
Believers understand that they are responsible for their actions.

STUDENTS' RESPONSES
Students will respond to conviction of their sins by repenting.

LESSON SCRIPTURE

EZEKIEL 18:1–13, 31–32, KJV

1 The word of the LORD came unto me again, saying,

2 What mean ye, that ye use this proverb concerning the land of Israel, saying, The fathers have eaten sour grapes, and the children's teeth are set on edge?

EZEKIEL 18:1–13, 31–32, NIV

1 The word of the LORD came to me:

2 "What do you people mean by quoting this proverb about the land of Israel: "'The parents eat sour grapes, and the children's teeth are set on edge'?

3 "As surely as I live, declares the

3 As I live, saith the Lord GOD, ye shall not have occasion any more to use this proverb in Israel.

4 Behold, all souls are mine; as the soul of the father, so also the soul of the son is mine: the soul that sinneth, it shall die.

5 But if a man be just, and do that which is lawful and right,

6 And hath not eaten upon the mountains, neither hath lifted up his eyes to the idols of the house of Israel, neither hath defiled his neighbour's wife, neither hath come near to a menstruous woman,

7 And hath not oppressed any, but hath restored to the debtor his pledge, hath spoiled none by violence, hath given his bread to the hungry, and hath covered the naked with a garment;

8 He that hath not given forth upon usury, neither hath taken any increase, that hath withdrawn his hand from iniquity, hath executed true judgment between man and man,

9 Hath walked in my statutes, and hath kept my judgments, to deal truly; he is just, he shall surely live, saith the Lord GOD.

10 If he beget a son that is a robber, a shedder of blood, and that doeth the like to any one of these things,

11 And that doeth not any of those duties, but even hath eaten upon the mountains, and defiled his neighbour's wife,

12 Hath oppressed the poor and needy, hath spoiled by violence, hath not restored the pledge, and hath lifted up his eyes to the idols, hath committed abomination,

Sovereign LORD, you will no longer quote this proverb in Israel.

4 For everyone belongs to me, the parent as well as the child—both alike belong to me. The one who sins is the one who will die.

5 "Suppose there is a righteous man who does what is just and right.

6 He does not eat at the mountain shrines or look to the idols of Israel. He does not defile his neighbor's wife or have sexual relations with a woman during her period.

7 He does not oppress anyone, but returns what he took in pledge for a loan. He does not commit robbery but gives his food to the hungry and provides clothing for the naked.

8 He does not lend to them at interest or take a profit from them. He withholds his hand from doing wrong and judges fairly between two parties.

9 He follows my decrees and faithfully keeps my laws. That man is righteous; he will surely live, declares the Sovereign LORD.

10 "Suppose he has a violent son, who sheds blood or does any of these other things

11 (though the father has done none of them): "He eats at the mountain shrines. He defiles his neighbor's wife.

12 He oppresses the poor and needy. He commits robbery. He does not return what he took in pledge. He looks to the idols. He does detestable things.

13 He lends at interest and takes a profit. Will such a man live? He will not! Because he has done all these detestable things,

13 Hath given forth upon usury, and hath taken increase: shall he then live ? he shall not live: he hath done all these abominations; he shall surely die; his blood shall be upon him.

31 Cast away from you all your transgressions, whereby ye have transgressed; and make you a new heart and a new spirit: for why will ye die, O house of Israel?

32 For I have no pleasure in the death of him that dieth, saith the Lord GOD: wherefore turn yourselves, and live ye.

he is to be put to death; his blood will be on his own head.

31 Rid yourselves of all the offenses you have committed, and get a new heart and a new spirit. Why will you die, people of Israel?

32 For I take no pleasure in the death of anyone, declares the Sovereign LORD. Repent and live!

LIGHT ON THE WORD

Usury is the act of giving a loan with exorbitant interest. The Israelites were forbidden to charge interest to one another, but they could charge interest to strangers. The practice of charging interest became a common sin among the exiles that returned from Babylon. This prompted Nehemiah to command those who had charged interest to give back 1 percent monthly of the interest they took from their fellow Isarelites (**Nehemiah 5:9–12**).

TEACHING THE BIBLE LESSON

LIFE NEED FOR TODAY'S LESSON

AIM: Students will become aware of behavior that is harmful to the life of a community.

INTRODUCTION

The Blame Game

Ezekiel's sermon in this lesson was preached to an audience of Israelites living in exile in Babylonia. They were foreigners living in a strange land, having a very hard time making sense of all the bad things that had happened to them.

They had placed their hope in the Temple and the God of their forefathers. They felt both helpless and hopeless. They blamed their current fate on the failures and sins of the generations before them. They no doubt just felt like giving up on their past, including their faith and their God, and were just trying to make the best of a bad situation.

God had called Ezekiel to minister to these people of little hope. God had told him that this would not be an easy assignment. He had said these people were "rebellious ... obstinate and stubborn" and not likely to listen (**Ezekiel 2:3–5**). Ezekiel would need to employ some creative ways of communicating to the Israelites, including using dramatic object lessons, and speaking in parables, as he does here. Through it all, Ezekiel was fearlessly faithful as God's prophet. We can only hope that some of his original audience heeded his warnings, and that we heed them ourselves today.

BIBLE LEARNING

AIM: Students will learn that God rewards those who seek to build healthy communities and to please God.

I. THE PROVERB FROM THE PAST (Ezekiel 18:1–4)

The people of Judah, exiles in a foreign land, rationalized that they were being punished for the sinful deeds of their ancestors. There was a popular, though not scriptural, proverb in those days that reflected this sentiment: "The fathers have eaten sour grapes, and the children's teeth are set on edge." Apparently God was tired of hearing this proverb tossed about as a fatalistic and irresponsible view of the consequences of sin (**vv. 2–3**). He says He has heard it enough and He doesn't want to hear it any more, so He bans its use.

Father and Son (verses 1–4)

1 The word of the LORD came unto me again, saying, 2 What mean ye, that ye use this proverb concerning the land of Israel, saying, The fathers have eaten sour grapes, and the children's teeth are set on edge?

When things do not go as well as one might want, the natural tendency is to complain and try to put the blame on another. This had occurred so often within the land of Israel that it had developed into a "proverb" (Heb. *mashal*, **mah-SHAHL**, a proverbial saying or aphorism) (see **Jeremiah 31:29–30**). Because of the sins of the "fathers" (Heb. *'ab*, **AHV**, the father, head, or founder of a household, group, or clan), the children were being made to pay the penalty. Some support for the belief that the children were being made to pay the penalty for the sins of their fathers can be found in **Exodus 20:5; 34:7** (cf. **Joshua 7:19–25; 2 Kings 24:1–4**). The nation of Israel was conquered and driven into exile because of the apostasy of Manasseh. Only by this means could the sin be removed. However, within the nation of Israel, the teaching had been carried to excess and was being used to remove personal responsibility for sins.

3 As I live, saith the Lord GOD, ye shall not have occasion any more to use this proverb in Israel. 4 Behold, all souls are mine; as the soul of the father, so also the soul of the son is mine: the soul that sinneth, it shall die.

God as the Creator and Father of all affirms that all "souls" are His (Heb. *nephesh*, **NEH-fesh**, a living being with life in the blood) and that He has the right to impose penalty for wrongdoing. God knew that there was a natural tendency in people for the son to follow the sins of the father and thereby share the father's guilt. For that reason, there was no room for the children to complain that they were being punished unfairly. The prophet Jeremiah offered that the sins of the father would be visited on the children (see **32:18**). If the father lived in rebellion to God and His precepts, then there was every possibility that the son would follow in the same rebellion. Beginning with this verse, Ezekiel begins to offer a corrective to the misunderstanding of God's intent, which had grown into a common proverb by stating that "the soul that sinneth" would be the soul that "died" (Heb. *mut*, **MOOTH**, to perish). In other words, the individual person was responsible for his or her own sin and its consequences.

SEARCH THE SCRIPTURES

QUESTION 1

What does God say about the soul of the father and the son?

II. THE PARABLE; PROMISE OF LIFE FOR A RIGHTEOUS MAN (vv. 5–9)

Ezekiel uses a parable to illustrate his point

about individual responsibility and punishment for sins.

Living a Just Life (verses 5–9)

5 But if a man be just, and do that which is lawful and right,

The laws determining what was "lawful" (Heb. *mishpat*, **mish-PAHT**, justice or fairness) and "right" (Heb. *tsedaqah*, **tseh-dah-KAH**, honesty, loyalty, or justness) were spelled out in Mosaic Torah, including Exodus, Deuteronomy, and the Holiness Code in **Leviticus 17–26**. Many of these laws were more detailed expressions of the Ten Commandments (**Exodus 20:1–17**) and the greatest commandments of loving God and loving your neighbor (**Deuteronomy 6:5, Leviticus 19:18**). In this way, a man was to be righteous in the eyes of God but also dealt justly with those around him.

6 And hath not eaten upon the mountains, neither hath lifted up his eyes to the idols of the house of Israel, neither hath defiled his neighbor's wife, neither hath come near to a menstruous woman,
7 And hath not oppressed any, but hath restored to the debtor his pledge, hath spoiled none by violence, hath given his bread to the hungry, and hath covered the naked with a garment; 8 He that hath not given forth upon usury, neither hath taken any increase, that hath withdrawn his hand from iniquity, hath executed true judgment between man and man, 9 Hath walked in my statutes, and hath kept my judgments, to deal truly; he is just, he shall surely live, saith the Lord GOD.

The righteous man was one who did not participate in ritual meals on mountaintop sanctuaries, which was the practice of the pagans (cf. **Ezekiel 6:2–4; 20:28–29**), nor indulged in the worship of idols (cf. **Leviticus 19:4**), did not commit adultery (cf. **Exodus 20:14**), did not approach a menstruating woman (cf. **Leviticus 18:19**), did not violate the laws governing business practices (cf. **Exodus 22:25**), fed the hungry, clothed the naked, and judged fairly (cf. **Leviticus 19:15**). God declares that this individual shall live.

LIGHT ON THE WORD

Righteousness and Blessings

Ezekiel describes a man who is righteous in conduct and character (**vv. 5–9**). In three broad areas of godly morality (piety, chastity, and charity), he displays the attributes of one who is just and right. For piety, he does not involve himself in any idolatrous acts, or even look upon idols. He is faithful to God's Law and obeys it to the best of his ability. As for chastity, he is faithful to his wife, and treats her with respect. As for charity, he is fair in his business dealing, merciful to those who are poor, and gracious to those in need. He practices justice, and is fair and honest in all his dealings and judgments. As a result, this man, when judged by God, will surely live, and receive blessings from Him.

III. THE PARABLE CONTINUED; PUNISHMENT FOR AN UNRIGHTEOUS SON (vv. 10–13)

Ezekiel continues his parable by presenting the imaginary son who is the antithesis of all his father's good characteristics. He is not faithful to God, and he treats his neighbors with contempt. He is a thief and a liar, oppresses the poor, and withholds justice. Ezekiel says God will judge this man for his sins, and he deserves death. His father's righteousness could not save him from bearing responsibility and punishment for his own actions.

Bad Choices Lead to Bad Consequences (verses 10–13)

10 If he beget a son that is a robber, a shedder of blood, and that doeth the like to any one of these things, 11 And that doeth not any of those duties, but even hath eaten upon the mountains, and defiled his neighbor's wife, 12 Hath oppressed the poor and needy, hath spoiled by violence, hath not restored the pledge, and hath lifted up his eyes to the idols, hath committed abomination, 13 Hath given forth upon usury, and hath taken increase: shall he then live? he shall not live: he hath done all these abominations; he shall surely die; his blood shall be upon him.

However, if the same individual has a son who is guilty of being a thief, a killer, of any of those things expressly forbidden in the Torah, then this son "shall surely die," reinforcing the principle that the consequence of his actions will only be upon him.

LIGHT ON THE WORD

The Next Generation: Guilty

This parable illustrates the fact that the earlier proverb had no application to the Judean people's present circumstance, nor was it a proper understanding of the justice of God. Ezekiel clearly makes the point that although the present exiled generation is indeed suffering because of the sins of the previous generations, they are not guiltless, and they are fully responsible for their own actions. The people of the exiled generation are not innocent bystanders, but actually guilty participants in many sins.

IV. THE PLEADING FOR REPENTANCE (vv. 31–32)

The destruction of Israel, Jerusalem, and the Temple was God's judgment and punishment for the spiritual apostasy and moral decay of the previous generations. But He speaks through Ezekiel to tell the exiled Israelites that their situation is as much a judgment of their sins as a national punishment for their fathers' sins. God justly judges each person individually. One person's sins may affect other lives, even the entire community. But God does not punish anyone for another's sins. Each person is responsible for his own actions.

New Way of Being (verses 31–32)

31 Cast away from you all your transgressions, whereby ye have transgressed; and make you a new heart and a new spirit: for why will ye die, O house of Israel?

Ezekiel pleads on God's behalf for the nation of Israel to turn away from all its "transgressions." They are to do their part to "make a new heart" (Heb. *leb*, **LEV**, heart, mind, or inclination) and also to make a "new spirit" (Heb. ruach, **ROO-akh**, spirit, breath, mental and spiritual essence of the human or divine). The prophet wants the people to understand that the cause of their sin resides within themselves and that the only sure way to escape sin's consequences is to be reconciled to God (see **Romans 7:21–8:2**). Ezekiel implores the people to acquire a new heart, a task that is impossible for us to do, but trying to do so teaches us what God desires of us and brings with it the realization that God alone can make our hearts new. So too with the spirit: man does not have the ability to make a new spirit for himself, but the effort drives man to see his own helplessness and seek God's Holy Spirit to accomplish the task. Ezekiel is telling the people that they need not die, because God will honor their sincere repentance with an abundance of His grace.

32 For I have no pleasure in the death of him that dieth, saith the Lord GOD: wherefore turn yourselves, and live ye.

Ezekiel concludes this entreaty by reminding the nation of Israel that God takes no "pleasure" (Heb. *chapats*, **khah-FAHTS**, to delight or take joy in) in the death of the wicked. All that is required is to sincerely turn from wickedness, repent, and experience God's grace. God is merciful and desires that all find life in Him and "live" (Heb. *chayah*, **khah-YAH**, to restore to life or quicken) (see **2 Peter 3:9**).

SEARCH THE SCRIPTURES

QUESTION 2

What does Ezekiel show as the appropriate response when we are tempted to blame others for our situation?

LIGHT ON THE WORD

Hope

Ezekiel does not leave the people without hope. They can continue to blame their situation on previous generations, and use that as an excuse to continue in their own sin. Or they can repent of their own sins and change course, and the result will be life, not death. It is not too late! When any individual sincerely repents of his sins, God will not only forgive him, but He will give him a new heart and a new spirit. This new heart will move them to be righteous and promote justice.

BIBLE APPLICATION

AIM: Students will understand that they are responsible for their actions.

Perhaps you or someone you know feels like they are suffering because of the actions of others. Perhaps your parents were substance abusers, or were absent during your formative years. Perhaps you were abused physically or emotionally. Perhaps you just don't feel loved and appreciated, and have given up hope for a better future. When people are without hope, it is easy to blame someone else, and turn to gangs, drugs, or alcohol as an escape. Your situation may indeed be miserable. But God's Word assures us that we are not bound to our present condition. There is hope, life, and joy to be found in the loving community of faith that is the family of God.

STUDENTS' RESPONSES

AIM: Students will respond to conviction of their sins by repenting.

Sometimes taking responsibility for our own actions, acknowledging our sin, and turning from it is very difficult to do. If you are struggling with this, seek the guidance of a spiritually mature trusted friend. Jesus has already won the victory over our sin and the penalty of death. What joy there is in allowing Him to transform your thinking from that of victim to victor! He will give you a new heart and a new spirit, one in which you will find joy in helping others, and in building and maintaining healthy relationships in a healthy community.

PRAYER

Lord, create in us a renewed spirit and a willing heart to care for others and ourselves in ways that are pleasing and just before You. You are gracious and kind to give us the opportunity to witness to others about our faith in Christ. In Jesus' Name we pray. Amen.

HOW TO SAY IT

Usury.	**USE**-uh-ree.
Executed.	**EK**-se-kyu-tid.

PREPARE FOR NEXT SUNDAY

Read **Zechariah 7:8–14** and study "God Demands Justice."

DAILY HOME BIBLE READINGS

MONDAY
Justice, Righteousness, and Repentance
(Isaiah 1:24–28)

TUESDAY
Justice: A Joy to the Righteous
(Proverbs 21:10–15)

WEDNESDAY
Avoiding a Parent's Negative Example
(Ezekiel 18:14–19)

THURSDAY
The Consequences of Changing Behaviors
(Ezekiel 18:21–28)

FRIDAY
The Lord Weighs the Heart
(Proverbs 21:2–8)

SATURDAY
Walking in the Lord's Ways
(Hosea 14)

SUNDAY
The Person Who Sins Shall Die
(Ezekiel 18:1–13, 31–32)

Sources:

Brown, Francis. *The Brown-Driver-Briggs Hebrew and English Lexicon*. Peabody MA: Hendrickson, 2010.

Burton, James. *Coffman Commentaries on the Old Testament and New Testament*. Abilene, TX: Abilene Christian University Press, n.d.

Duguid, Iain M. Ezekiel. *The NIV Application Commentary*. Grand Rapids, MI: Zondervan, 1999.

Dunn, James D. G. and John W. Rogerson. *Commentary on the Bible*. Grand Rapids, MI: Wm. B. Eerdmans, 2003.

English, E. Schuyler and Marian Bishop Bower, eds. *The Holy Bible: Pilgrim Edition*. New York: Oxford University Press, 1952.

Howley, G.C.D., F.F. Bruce, and H.L. Ellison. *The New Layman's Bible Commentary*. Grand Rapids, MI: Zondervan, 1979.

Life Application Study Bible. New Living Translation. Carol Stream, IL: Tyndale House Publishers, 2007.

Rainer, Thom S. *Baptist Hymnal*. Nashville, TN: LifeWay, 2008.

Strong, James. *Strong's Exhaustive Concordance of the Bible*. Nashville, TN: Thomas Nelson, 1990.

COMMENTS / NOTES:

GOD DEMANDS JUSTICE

BIBLE BASIS: ZECHARIAH 7:8–14

BIBLE TRUTH: God requires kindness and mercy for the widows, orphans, aliens, and the poor. The Lord will also heal the wounds of the afflicted and shower prosperity on the people.

MEMORY VERSE: "Thus speaketh the LORD of hosts, saying, Execute true judgment, and shew mercy and compassions every man to his brother: and oppress not the widow, nor the fatherless, the stranger, nor the poor; and let none of you imagine evil against his brother in your heart" (Zechariah 7:9–10).

LESSON AIM: By the end of the lesson, your students will: study the punishment meted out by God for those who reject His demands; make confessions concerning how we abandon the weak; and show kindness to the oppressed and the weak.

TEACHER PREPARATION

MATERIALS NEEDED: Quarterly Commentary/Teacher Manual, Adult Quarterly, Adult resources—charts, worksheets, and other teaching tools, paper, pens, pencils, Bibles (several different versions)

OTHER MATERIALS NEEDED / TEACHER'S NOTES:

LESSON OVERVIEW

LIFE NEED FOR TODAY'S LESSON
Some people show no kindness, mercy, or justice to others.

BIBLE LEARNING
God consistently communicates that obedience and justice are more important than any ritualistic act.

BIBLE APPLICATION
Believers expect divine displeasure when they reject divine commands.

STUDENTS' RESPONSES
Believers utilize the resources with which God has blessed them to help others.

LESSON SCRIPTURE

ZECHARIAH 7:8–14, KJV

8 And the word of the LORD came unto Zechariah, saying,

9 Thus speaketh the LORD of hosts, saying, Execute true judgment, and shew mercy and compassions every man to his brother:

ZECHARIAH 7:8–14, NIV

8 And the word of the LORD came again to Zechariah:

9 "This is what the LORD Almighty said: 'Administer true justice; show mercy and compassion to one another.

10 Do not oppress the widow or the

10 And oppress not the widow, nor the fatherless, the stranger, nor the poor; and let none of you imagine evil against his brother in your heart.

11 But they refused to hearken, and pulled away the shoulder, and stopped their ears, that they should not hear.

12 Yea, they made their hearts as an adamant stone, lest they should hear the law, and the words which the LORD of hosts hath sent in his spirit by the former prophets: therefore came a great wrath from the LORD of hosts.

13 Therefore it is come to pass, that as he cried, and they would not hear; so they cried, and I would not hear, saith the LORD of hosts:

14 But I scattered them with a whirlwind among all the nations whom they knew not. Thus the land was desolate after them, that no man passed through nor returned: for they laid the pleasant land desolate.

fatherless, the foreigner or the poor. Do not plot evil against each other.'

11 "But they refused to pay attention; stubbornly they turned their backs and covered their ears.

12 They made their hearts as hard as flint and would not listen to the law or to the words that the LORD Almighty had sent by his Spirit through the earlier prophets. So the LORD Almighty was very angry.

13 "'When I called, they did not listen; so when they called, I would not listen,' says the LORD Almighty.

14 'I scattered them with a whirlwind among all the nations, where they were strangers. The land they left behind them was so desolate that no one traveled through it. This is how they made the pleasant land desolate.'"

LIGHT ON THE WORD

Zechariah was likely a young boy when he first began to prophesy. It appears that the second part of his book belongs to his old age. Zechariah was the son of Berechiah, the son of Iddo the prophet (**1:1**). He was an enthusiast for the rebuilding of the Temple in 520 B.C.

Malachi, Zechariah, and Haggai all prophesied during the post-exilic period. This was a time in Israel's history after the returning of the exiles to Jerusalem in 538 B.C. up until the time of Christ. During the post-exilic period, the people's main concern was the building up of Jerusalem and the second Temple. At various times there were enemies who tried to stop the restoration and rebuilding of the Temple, and the people of Judah's own complacency in worshiping Yahweh and doubt concerning the future of the nation. Because of this, the Lord raised up prophets to stir the people to action and to give them a vision and hope for the future.

TEACHING THE BIBLE LESSON

LIFE NEED FOR TODAY'S LESSON

AIM: Students will know that some people show no kindness, mercy, or justice to others.

INTRODUCTION

Zechariah's Prophetic Oracles

Zechariah prophesied during a time of great upheaval in the Persian Empire. Cambyses, the son of Cyrus the Great, succeeded his father, who died in 530 B.C. Then Darius took the throne after Cambyses' sudden death in 522 B.C. to inherit the job of extinguishing several rebellions that sprang up throughout the empire. At the same time, the Jews who had returned to their homeland were rebuilding the Temple in Jerusalem. Zechariah was a contemporary of Haggai and they both preached to encourage the people to continue the work of rebuilding this second Temple.

It is in this context that a delegation is sent to Zechariah from Bethel, the former site of idolatrous worship in the Northern Kingdom. The delegation is sent to ask whether they should continue fasting now since their seventy-year exile would soon be completed (7:3). Zechariah begins a series of prophetic oracles concerning the time of the Messiah and the renewed righteousness of the people of God.

BIBLE LEARNING

AIM: Students will learn that God consistently communicates that obedience and justice are more important than any ritualistic act.

I. THE CALLING (Zechariah 7:8–10)

This passage begins with God's calling for the Israelites. It is a formula that is often used in reference to their basic duties as God's covenant people. They were to "execute true judgment and shew mercy and compassions every man to his brother." These two admonitions are prominent in Scripture, especially in the prophetic writings (**Micah 6:6–8; Hosea 12:6–7**). Zechariah's prophecy gets at the heart of true covenant loyalty to God, which is not found in blindly following religious rituals such as fasting at a certain time of year, but in dealing justly with others and showing them the kindness and compassion of God.

False Worship (verses 8–10)

8 And the word of the LORD came unto Zechariah, saying,

The people of Bethel (an important and symbolic town; its name means "house of God") had sought out the priest and prophets to see if they should fast during a certain month, as was their custom. Jehovah takes this opportunity to recall to the people's minds the former prophets and their message. Zechariah realizes that Bethel's religious practice is similar to that of Israel and Judah before the exile, who were practicing religious rituals but did not have any true heart involvement or genuine repentance behind it. In light of this suspicion, he reminds the people that the prophets had, for years, warned the people about practicing ritual without true worship.

9 Thus speaketh the LORD of hosts, saying, Execute true judgment, and shew mercy and compassions every man to his brother:

At this point in the book of Zechariah, the building of the Temple is well underway, so that in one sense, God's people are showing responsiveness and obedience to His command. However, it is clear from God's Word through Zechariah that true covenant faithfulness is absent, as evidenced by the failure of the people to demonstrate justice and kindness in community. God's voice thunders with a verb-noun combination: *shapat* (Heb. **shah-FAHT**) and *mishpat* (Heb. **mish-PAHT**). These words are from the same Hebrew tri-consonantal root, sh-p-t, and are linked together in a phrase that might be literally translated as "judge a judgment." This word combination has a variety of meanings that, taken together, speak not only of "judgment" but of "judgment according to truth." Although the people have apparently shown some discernment and wisdom, the forceful repetition of this word group indicates that they have not extended true justice and mercy to their neighbor, even though the Lord has shown remarkable mercy to them. As a result, Jehovah demands conduct that simply reflects the way He has treated His people. "Mercy" and "compassions" do not refer to some heroic act or unreasonable demand, but the natural and proper outgrowth of the mercy the people had received from the Lord's hand.

10 And oppress not the widow, nor the fatherless, the stranger, nor the poor; and let none of you imagine evil against his brother in your heart.

Zechariah's call for justice rather than oppression repeats the calls of the prophets before the exile, as well as God's command to show mercy to the helpless (**Deuteronomy 14:29; 16:11; 24:19–21**). Although the verb *'ashaq* (Heb. **ah-SHAHK**) can often mean "defraud," "oppress" is a better translation here because, in this context, the word emphasizes the position of power in which the Israelites find themselves, relative to the helpless among them. Once again, these commands are full of sad irony: Although the Jews found themselves utterly helpless in Babylon and Persia, God showed them mercy and made a way for them to return to Jerusalem and build the Temple. Yet, shockingly, the Jews have turned and looked on the powerless in their community with contempt, perhaps even taking advantage of their lowly position.

God's covenant people are supposed to mirror the covenant faithfulness He has shown them. In light of the Gospel revealed through Christ, the perfect Covenant Keeper, we understand that our failings are covered in the blood of the new covenant, shed by the Lamb. Because of Christ's sacrifice, we should strive to demonstrate His faithfulness to us in our dealings with each other!

SEARCH THE SCRIPTURES

QUESTION 1

Whom did God command them to show mercy, kindness, and tender compassion toward?

LIGHT ON THE WORD

An Attitude and Behavior of Justice

God's justice and compassion are spelled out in detail in **verse 10**. The poor and marginalized are to be the objects of this justice and compassion. They were commanded to not "oppress the widow, nor the fatherless, the stranger, nor the poor." These groups were landless and without inherited rights in Israelite society and could not plead their case in the courts of law, making them vulnerable to oppression. As a result, the Law of Moses had several stipulations to protect them from those who would take advantage of them (**Exodus 22:22, 23:6–9; Deuteronomy 10:18–19, 24:14**). Zechariah also zeroes in on the internal state of the heart with the words "Let none of you imagine evil against his brother in your heart." It is not just about external righteousness, but the attitude we have toward our fellow brother and sister. These words echo similar admonitions in the Torah (**Leviticus 19:15–18**) and Jesus' focus on the internal attitudes that produce outward sinful actions (**Matthew 5:28, 15:19**).

II. THE REJECTION (vv. 11–12)

Zechariah recalls the people's past disobedience. First he goes over their initial actions in response to the words of God concerning their covenant duties of justice and compassion. The people were stubborn and would not listen to the Word of God concerning their behavior.

A Stubborn People (verses 11–12)

11 But they refused to hearken, and pulled away the shoulder, and stopped their ears, that they should not hear.

The word "hearken" in the King James Version, although not commonly used today, brings out the sense of the Hebrew word *qashab* (**kah-SHAV**), which means more than just listening. It does not merely indicate that the Israelites had failed to hear the prophets' warnings; it means that they had heard these warnings all too well, but had stubbornly refused to repent and obey. Nevertheless, the focus on hearing is obvious; the phrase "pulled away the shoulder" might be expressed in more modern terms as "turned their backs" (implying a breaking of relationship and disobedience, but also making it harder to hear). The phrase translated "they stopped their ears" literally means "they made their ears heavy," suggesting that the act of listening was burdensome to them. The final clause shows the purpose of these actions on their part: They did not want to hear the warnings of the prophets, and although they no doubt heard the warnings, they made every effort to pretend that they hadn't. Zechariah's warning gains added force in that his hearers could hardly claim not to have heard him! The actions of their ancestors and the resulting destruction and despair would have made God's warning utterly impossible to ignore.

12 Yea, they made their hearts as an adamant stone, lest they should hear the law, and the words which the LORD of hosts hath sent in his spirit by the former prophets: therefore came a great wrath from the LORD of hosts.

The description of the covenant people's faithlessness continues, with a natural transition from the ears to the heart (which in the Bible always represents the center of both understanding and affections). There is no doubt who the guilty party is in this covenant violation. God did not harden their hearts, as He did with Pharaoh (**Exodus 9:12, 10:1, 20**); they hardened their own hearts. On the contrary, the prophets before the Exile portray a God longing for His people to return to Him, pining for His adulterous bride. The intentional hardening described here was heartbreaking, coming from a people who had seen the disastrous consequences of disobedience. The word used for "adamant stone" *shamir* (**shah-MEER**) is the word used for the hard point of a stylus, usually made of a kind of quartz. The people had made their hearts as hard as flint.

Zechariah mentions the Spirit as the agent of the former prophets' inspiration. This reference brings out the seriousness of not heeding their commands and warnings—to do so was to deny the very Spirit of God. The New Testament shows us that denying the Spirit is blasphemy (**Mark 3:22–30**). Ananias and Sapphira paid with their lives for what is called "lying to the Holy Spirit" (see **Acts 5:1–10**). It is no wonder that the military phrase "LORD of hosts" reappears, with God pictured as going to war against His own people! Their treason has brought about the King's inevitable response, despite centuries of patience.

SEARCH THE SCRIPTURES

QUESTION 2

What did the people do with the word that they heard through the prophet?

LIGHT ON THE WORD

Hearts of Stone

Zechariah continues his description with the condition of their hearts in light of God's Word to them. He describes their hearts as adamant stone or flint. Flint was a form of quartz that was abundant in the land of Palestine. It is a very sharp, hard stone that can be used for starting fires. This was a picture of Judah's collective heart. They were firm and resolute in turning away from God and rejecting His Law and the words of the prophets. This resulted in the wrath of God on the whole nation.

III. SCATTERING (vv. 13–14)

Zechariah concludes this oracle with a description of God's wrath on the nation of Judah as they refused to hear His Word. Judah's deafness to God's Word receives a reciprocal response from God to their prayers. Since they will not listen to His Word, He will not listen to their prayers. This is similar to the words of **Proverbs 28:9**: "He that turneth away his ear from hearing the law, even his prayer shall be abomination" (KJV). This is a clear example of what happens when we refuse to obey God's Word: He will refuse our prayers.

Hearing, but Not Listening (verses 13–14)

13 Therefore it is come to pass, that as he cried, and they would not hear; so they cried, and I would not hear, saith the LORD of hosts:

The verbs in this passage suggest repeated, customary actions; the Lord's call to His people was, of course, repeated many times over, as was their unbelieving response. God in His mercy patiently offered restoration far beyond what His people deserved. Eventually, however, He executed His justice in a perfectly proportional way. Because He had called to them and they had not listened, He would not hear their cries. Yet, God provided safety and security (albeit in Babylonia) for those who truly repented. Many of these same people returned to Jerusalem and were addressed by Zechariah. For them, the importance of hearing the Lord's call was abundantly clear.

14 But I scattered them with a whirlwind among all the nations whom they knew not. Thus the land was desolate after them, that no man passed through nor returned: for they laid the pleasant land desolate.

The term translated "scattered . . . with a whirlwind" occurs seven times in the Old Testament (cf. **Isaiah 54:11; Habakkuk 3:14**), and in all but two cases, it refers to a violent storm. This is not a literal storm, however, but the worst kind of curse imaginable: exile from the Promised Land, where the people had rest, and forcible removal into the terrible strangeness of foreign lands, with strange customs and foreign gods. It is no accident that the curses of **Deuteronomy 28** focus primarily on assault and capture by a foreign people; this was the worst kind of judgment imaginable for a people whose very lifeblood, blessedness, and peace depended on the land that had been promised to their great forefather Abraham hundreds of years earlier. And so the worst kind of upheaval took place: Whereas back in the glory days of Israel—the reigns of David and Solomon—the whole world traveled through the blessed land, now it had become desolate, without the hum of merchants traveling through it. Given that this land at the eastern end of the Mediterranean was a key crossroads, its desolation would have been a terribly striking reminder of God's rejection of His people.

As Zechariah now stands among the people to whom God has shown great mercy and restored their land, his warnings and promises focus on making sure that the people retain the blessedness promised to them. Such warnings and promises are wonderfully relevant to people who are richly blessed in Christ. Believers must both hear and obey God's commands.

SEARCH THE SCRIPTURES

QUESTION 3

What did God say He would do when the people cried?

LIGHT ON THE WORD

Unfruitful and Unproductive

The Lord eventually cannot tolerate the wickedness of His people and decides to scatter them like a whirlwind "among all nations whom they knew not." This happened in the Babylonian captivity. Judah was invaded by Nebuchadnezzar, and Jerusalem was sacked in 586 B.C. Most of the people were exiled to Babylonia or fled to other surrounding nations. Their disobedience resulted in their livelihood being made unfruitful and unproductive. Instead of being filled with farms and vineyards and people moving about to work and play, this land would remain empty, a symbol of what happens when we do not show justice and compassion to our neighbors.

BIBLE APPLICATION

AIM: Students will expect divine displeasure when they reject divine commands.

There are numerous problems in our society. Gangs and drugs plague our urban areas. Our national economy is unstable. Wars with other nations are a constant threat. We pray and cry out to God and observe all the outward rituals of religion, but we do not have a high priority on justice and compassion for our neighbor. If these two things had priority in our lives, then we would be able to eradicate these problems. Instead we cry out to God without listening to His Word. It is important for us not only to cry out to God, but also do what He says. Sometimes the solution to our problems lies within our own hearts as we turn back to Him.

STUDENTS' RESPONSES

AIM: Students will utilize the resources with which God has blessed them to help others.

Often justice issues are separate from our prayer life. It is possible that we have cried out to God, but He does not hear because we have not obeyed His call to show justice and compassion to those less fortunate. As an experiment, before your private times of prayer, list out ways that you can personally show justice and compassion to those around you. Once you make this list, pray for the people you will serve. Make note in the days to come whether God answers your other requests as well. Sometimes He isn't hearing us because we aren't hearing Him.

PRAYER

God of justice and compassion, Your love for those who need Your guidance is a very present reality. Give us the resources, the hope, and the fortitude to help others. Your love never fails, so let us in love, be the light of hope to others. In Jesus' Name we pray. Amen.

HOW TO SAY IT

Hearken. **HAR**-ken.

Adamant. **AH**-duh-ment.

PREPARE FOR NEXT SUNDAY

Read **Malachi 3:1–10** and study "Return to a Just God."

DAILY HOME BIBLE READINGS

MONDAY
You Behaved Worse than Your Ancestors
(Jeremiah 16:9–13)

TUESDAY
I Call Upon the Lord
(2 Samuel 22:1–7)

WEDNESDAY
Hope in God's Steadfast Love
(Psalm 147:1–11)

THURSDAY
Walking in the Way
(Judges 2:16–23)

FRIDAY
Pursue Justice and Only Justice
(Deuteronomy 16:16–20)

SATURDAY
The Lord Waits to Be Gracious
(Isaiah 30:18–26)

SUNDAY
The Results of Not Listening
(Zechariah 7:8–14)

Sources:

Burton, James. *Coffman Commentaries on the Old Testament and New Testament.* Abilene, TX: Abilene Christian University Press, n.d.

Dunn, James D. G. and John W. Rogerson. *Commentary on the Bible.* Grand Rapids, MI: Wm. B. Eerdmans, 2003.

Howley, G.C.D., F.F. Bruce, and H.L. Ellison. *The New Layman's Bible Commentary.* Grand Rapids, MI: Zondervan, 1979.

COMMENTS / NOTES:

RETURN TO A JUST GOD

BIBLE BASIS: MALACHI 3:1–10

BIBLE TRUTH: God requires justice and faithfulness and will bestow bountiful blessings in many ways.

MEMORY VERSE: "Even from the days of your fathers ye are gone away from mine ordinances, and have not kept them. Return unto me, and I will return unto you, saith the LORD of hosts. But ye said, Wherein shall we return?" (Malachi 3:7).

LESSON AIM: By the end of this lesson, your students will: review Malachi's prophecy about possessions, wealth, and hospitality in light of our faithfulness and justice; confess personal unfaithfulness to God and pray for forgiveness; and institute a personal plan for charitable living.

TEACHER PREPARATION

MATERIALS NEEDED: Quarterly Commentary/Teacher Manual, Adult Quarterly, Adult resources—charts, worksheets, and other teaching tools, paper, pens, pencils, Bibles (several different versions)

OTHER MATERIALS NEEDED / TEACHER'S NOTES:

LESSON OVERVIEW

LIFE NEED FOR TODAY'S LESSON

Fairness and philanthropy are most apparent during times of great tragedy and loss.

BIBLE LEARNING

God expects His people to be just, faithful, and show mercy.

BIBLE APPLICATION

Believers give as a grateful expression of their commitment to God's grace and justice.

STUDENTS' RESPONSES

Believers confess their lack of forgiveness and seek human and divine forgiveness.

LESSON SCRIPTURE

MALACHI 3:1–10, KJV

1 Behold, I will send my messenger, and he shall prepare the way before me: and the Lord, whom ye seek, shall suddenly come to his temple, even the messenger of the covenant, whom ye delight in: behold, he shall come, saith the LORD of hosts.

2 But who may abide the day of his

MALACHI 3:1–10, NIV

1 "I will send my messenger, who will prepare the way before me. Then suddenly the Lord you are seeking will come to his temple; the messenger of the covenant, whom you desire, will come," says the LORD Almighty.

2 But who can endure the day of his

coming? and who shall stand when he appeareth? for he is like a refiner's fire, and like fullers' soap:

3 And he shall sit as a refiner and purifier of silver: and he shall purify the sons of Levi, and purge them as gold and silver, that they may offer unto the LORD an offering in righteousness.

4 Then shall the offering of Judah and Jerusalem be pleasant unto the LORD, as in the days of old, and as in former years.

5 And I will come near to you to judgment; and I will be a swift witness against the sorcerers, and against the adulterers, and against false swearers, and against those that oppress the hireling in his wages, the widow, and the fatherless, and that turn aside the stranger from his right, and fear not me, saith the LORD of hosts.

6 For I am the LORD, I change not; therefore ye sons of Jacob are not consumed.

7 Even from the days of your fathers ye are gone away from mine ordinances, and have not kept them. Return unto me, and I will return unto you, saith the LORD of hosts. But ye said, Wherein shall we return?

8 Will a man rob God? Yet ye have robbed me. But ye say, Wherein have we robbed thee? In tithes and offerings.

9 Ye are cursed with a curse: for ye have robbed me, even this whole nation.

10 Bring ye all the tithes into the storehouse, that there may be meat in mine house, and prove me now herewith, saith the LORD of hosts, if I will not open you the windows of heaven, and pour you out a blessing, that there shall not be room enough to receive it.

coming? Who can stand when he appears? For he will be like a refiner's fire or a launderer's soap.

3 He will sit as a refiner and purifier of silver; he will purify the Levites and refine them like gold and silver. Then the LORD will have men who will bring offerings in righteousness,

4 and the offerings of Judah and Jerusalem will be acceptable to the LORD, as in days gone by, as in former years.

5 "So I will come to put you on trial. I will be quick to testify against sorcerers, adulterers and perjurers, against those who defraud laborers of their wages, who oppress the widows and the fatherless, and deprive the foreigners among you of justice, but do not fear me," says the LORD Almighty.

6 "I the LORD do not change. So you, the descendants of Jacob, are not destroyed.

7 Ever since the time of your ancestors you have turned away from my decrees and have not kept them. Return to me, and I will return to you," says the LORD Almighty. "But you ask, 'How are we to return?'

8 "Will a mere mortal rob God? Yet you rob me. "But you ask, 'How are we robbing you?' "In tithes and offerings.

9 You are under a curse—your whole nation—because you are robbing me.

10 Bring the whole tithe into the storehouse, that there may be food in my house. Test me in this," says the LORD Almighty, "and see if I will not throw open the floodgates of heaven and pour out so much blessing that there will not be room enough to store it.

LIGHT ON THE WORD

In order to separate the dross or impurities from the pure metal, a refiner would heat it until the dross burned off and the metal was purified or refined. The refiner's tools were a crucible or furnace and some bellows or a blow pipe. He would usually sit and carefully watch for the right time to let the melted metal run off (**Malachi 3:3**).

A fuller was someone who cleaned clothes. It literally means "to trample." This referred to how fullers laundered clothes by beating or stepping on them. There were many cleaning agents in biblical times, including white clay, urine, and alkali powder from indigenous plants. **Malachi 3:2** refers to alkali powder. The fuller would take soda powder from the iceplant, found in Mesopotamia, and wash clothes. Afterward he would stomp on them or beat them with sticks. This process would not only clean the clothes but also make them dazzling white (**Mark 9:3**).

A hireling was a hired servant. This servant was different than a slave in that he was paid wages. As a hireling had no land rights of their own, they were vulnerable to exploitation and the Lord provided protection in the Law of Moses for them (**Leviticus 19:13; Deuteronomy 24:14**).

A tithe was a tenth of someone's possessions that was offered to God. Tithing was practiced in patriarchal times and existed before the Law was given on Mount Sinai. Once the Law was established in Israel, tithes were required annually and every third year. These offerings would help provide for the Levites, poor, fatherless, widows, and foreigners in the land. Offerings were the obligatory sacrifices to God that were taken from the flock or herd.

TEACHING THE BIBLE LESSON

LIFE NEED FOR TODAY'S LESSON

AIM: Students will know that fairness and philanthropy are most apparent during times of great tragedy and loss.

INTRODUCTION

The Prophets Speak

Malachi was written during the post-exilic period. This was the time after the Jews returned from exile in Babylonia to rebuild their nation and the Temple of God. Malachi was a contemporary of Zechariah and Haggai. All three prophets were concerned with the people's neglect and complacency concerning the worship of God and the people's repetition of the sins and injustice that caused them to be scattered in the first place. Malachi spoke out against a corrupt priesthood. He also indicted the people of Judah for their lack of faith, which was shown in the neglect of worship particularly in withholding tithes and sacrificial offerings. This meant that the priests who officiated worship were not adequately provided for. It also meant that worship was not continuous and therefore not a priority among the majority of the people. Malachi condemns this attitude and announces that God's messenger will come to refine His people so that they worship Him in righteousness.

BIBLE LEARNING

AIM: Students will know that God expects His people to be just, faithful, and show mercy.

I. THE MESSENGER OF GOD (Malachi 3:1–4)

Malachi begins this oracle with an announcement concerning God's messenger, who will prepare the way before Him. It is a prophecy concerning the time of the Messiah. The people needed to change their ways in order to receive the Messiah, so a messenger would be sent to prepare them for His coming. Although they longed for a Messiah who would bring justice, they were not in a moral state to be ready for Him. Malachi's announcement lets them know that a Messiah is coming, and they need to be ready for Him when He comes.

The Sovereign Ruler Returns (verses 1–4)

1 Behold, I will send my messenger, and he shall prepare the way before me: and the Lord, whom ye seek, shall suddenly come to his temple, even the messenger of the covenant, whom ye delight in: behold, he shall come, saith the LORD of hosts.

The name "Malachi" (Heb. *mal'aki*, **mal-ah-KEE**) means "my messenger." However, scholars generally agree that the prophet who goes by that name is not being referred to here. The message that Malachi the prophet was to deliver to the people seems to be in response to their question in **Malachi 2:17** when they inquire, "Where is the God of Judgment?" Malachi responds that the Lord they were "seeking" (Heb. *baqash*, **bah-KASH**, to seek, demand, or find) and in whom they found "delight" (Heb. *chapets*, **khah-FAHTS**, having pleasure in) would come "suddenly" (Heb. *pit'om*, **pith-OME**, any moment now or unexpectedly) to His Temple. The question of those who were seeking to live and do right is rhetorical. The priests of the Temple were corrupt and many of the people had stopped taking issues of right or wrong seriously. Malachi was warning that the Sovereign Ruler would come unannounced and would bring judgment with Him.

2 But who may abide the day of his coming? and who shall stand when he appeareth? for he is like a refiner's fire, and like fullers' soap:

Because the Lord would bring judgment with Him, Malachi asks the people, who will be able to "abide" (Heb. *kul*, **KOOL**, to survive or endure) the day "of his coming" (Heb. *bow'*, **BO**, to fall or light upon)? Further, he inquires who will be able to "stand" (Heb. *'amad*, **ah-MAHD**, to stand up) when he "appeareth" (Heb. *ra'ah*, **rah-AH**, to present oneself or to be visible). The suggestion is that no one will be able to continue as before, because the Lord will come like a "refiner's" (Heb. *tsarap*, **tsah-RAF**, to purge away or to smelt) fire or even like the "fuller's" (Heb. *kabas*, **kah-VAHS**, to launder or wash by treading) "soap" (Heb. *borit*, **bo-REETH**, lye or potash).

3 And he shall sit as a refiner and purifier of silver: and he shall purify the sons of Levi, and purge them as gold and silver, that they may offer unto the LORD an offering in righteousness. 4 Then shall the offering of Judah and Jerusalem be pleasant unto the LORD, as in the days of old, and as in former years.

Such a "purge" (Heb. *zaqaq*, **zah-KAHK**, to distill or strain) would be harsh on all who were found to be lacking moral or ethical standards. The Lord's purpose, once He appeared, would be to "purify" (Heb. *taher*, **tah-HAR**, to pronounce clean) His Temple, and its leadership, the Levites. Malachi tells the people that the Lord would begin His work of purification with the priests. He would "sit" (Heb. *yashab*, **yah-SHAV**, to dwell or remain) as one who refines silver, because it is more difficult than refining gold. The refining of silver requires hotter fires and takes more time and patience. Once the Temple and its leadership have been cleansed, the expectation is that the priests would once again return to the offering of sacrifices as spelled out in the laws of the Old Testament, and the people would follow their leadership. The end result of all of these actions would be a restoration of the relationship between God and His chosen people (see **Philippians 1:8–11**).

SEARCH THE SCRIPTURES

QUESTION 1

What is the purpose and role of the "messenger of the covenant"?

LIGHT ON THE WORD

The Refinement Process

The Messiah or "messenger of the covenant" would come to the Temple and would refine and purify His people. Malachi shows them that their cries for justice are hypocritical (**Malachi 2:17**) because they themselves would not be able to stand the refining fire of this coming Messiah. He would purify the sons of Levi so that their offerings to God would be pleasant to Him. The Lord wanted to purify them like silver and gold, or the whitening soap of a launderer. He desires pure worship from a righteous people.

II. THE MESSAGE OF GOD (vv. 5–7)

Malachi then takes the people into the heavenly law courts. The Lord is the chief witness testifying against them. He will not be hesitant but swift in His judgment of their unrighteousness. He has seen their adultery, oppression, sorcery, lying, and idolatry. They have no excuse for their behavior, and the Lord will see to it that they are judged accordingly. He then states, "I am the LORD, I change not." He is not a wishy-washy God. His character is steadfast and faithful, therefore they "are not consumed."

Judgment, Repentance, and Mercy (verses 5–7)

5 And I will come near to you to judgment; and I will be a swift witness against the sorcerers, and against the adulterers, and against false swearers, and against those that oppress the hireling in his wages, the widow, and the fatherless, and that turn aside the stranger from his right, and fear not me, saith the LORD of hosts. 6 For I am the LORD, I change not; therefore ye sons of Jacob are not consumed.

Malachi continues to respond to the people's question (**2:17**). He informs them that God will appear, and in addition to being a refining fire on some, will be the God of "judgment" (Heb. *mishpat*, **mish-PAHT**, justice, legal decision before a judge) they asked for. The continual presence of so many within the community of returned exiles practicing acts condemned by the Law served as an indication that they did not fear God and His punishment would be their reward. When God does appear to judge, there will be no need for others to be witnesses against the wrongdoers; God has declared that He Himself will be the witness. However, because God is unchanging and always remains true to His Word, His people will not be "consumed" (Heb. *kalah*, **kah-LAH**, to come to an end) even in their faithlessness and rebellion.

7 Even from the days of your fathers ye are gone away from mine ordinances, and have not kept them. Return unto me, and I will return unto you, saith the LORD of hosts. But ye said, Wherein shall we return?

The rebellion in the Jewish nation had been going on for a very long time. Like their "fathers" (Heb. *'ab*, **AHV**, the head or founder of a household, group, family or clan) before them, the people had turned away from the ordinances of God and embraced the evil ways of men (see **Matthew 15:3**), which resulted in the ruin of the nation. Malachi, speaking for God, implores them to return to the "ordinances" (Heb. *choq*, **KHOKE**, rules or commands) of the Law so that the Lord of hosts would reward them by returning to them. The people have shown themselves deserving of God's wrath, and as the righteous judge, He had every right to consume them, but God demonstrates His patience and graciousness to His chosen people by speaking gently to them and offering for them to return. The people only needed to repent. This was the message of John the Baptist too (see **Matthew 3:2 and 4:17**). However, rather than repentance, the Lord's plea is met with continued denial and rebellion. The self-righteous Pharisees did not feel the need for repentance because they believed that they had kept the whole Law and were blameless before God. In asking "wherein they needed to return" (Heb. *shub*, **SHOOV**, to turn back) to God, they were justifying themselves and their behavior in their own eyes.

LIGHT ON THE WORD

A Broken Covenant

The Lord points out the irony of the situation. He has not changed, but they have changed by not being faithful to His ordinances. He says if they return to Him, then He will return to them. The people of Judah want justice, but God wants them to repent. Now the question on the people's lips is "How shall we return?"

III. THE MAINTENANCE OF GOD'S HOUSE (vv. 8–10)

Malachi points out that they are the ones in the wrong. He pronounces them as cursed by the Lord. Although they demanded justice, they have robbed God by not giving the tithes of their crops and herds and by not giving the proper worship sacrifices or offerings (**Malachi 1:6–14**). They were giving blind, diseased, and sometimes even stolen animals to the Temple. This was shameful and disrespectful in God's eyes. They also had not given the tithe, which was designed to support the priests and others who had no land rights (**Deuteronomy 14:28–29; 26:12**).

A Lack of Gratitude (verses 8–10)

8 Will a man rob God? Yet ye have robbed me. But ye say, Wherein have we robbed thee? In tithes and offerings. 9 Ye are cursed with a curse: for ye have robbed me, even this whole nation.

Through the prophet, God answers their inquiry. The people had become guilty of "robbing" (Heb. *qaba'*, **kah-VAH**, to defraud) God because they had stopped bringing their tithes and offerings for sacrifice to the Temple. The nation was to take care of the needs of the priests and the Levites; however, by not giving their tithes and not offering sacrifices, or by doing either grudgingly, they were guilty of robbing God. The people's lack of giving with a cheerful spirit was viewed by God as a lack of gratitude for how He favored them or lack of acknowledgement of Him as Lord. The "curse" (Heb. *'arar*, **ah-RAR**, to condemn or call judgment down on) God inflicted on them was the withholding of rain so their crops would not grow (see **3:11**).

10 Bring ye all the tithes into the storehouse, that there may be meat in mine house, and prove me now herewith, saith the LORD of hosts, if I will not open you the windows of heaven, and pour you out a blessing, that there shall not be room enough to receive it.

Finally, God challenges the people to put Him to the test. They are to once again bring their tithes to the "storehouse" (Heb. *'otsar*, **oh-TSAR**, treasure-house or armory), a repository which was attached to the Temple and over which the priest exercised control, and "prove" (Heb. *bachan*, **bah-KHAN**, to examine or try) if God would in fact open the windows of Heaven so that an overabundance of "blessing" (Heb. *berakah*, **beh-rah-KAH**, gift, prosperity) might flow down. Malachi suggests that the people who did bring tithes to the storehouse were guilty of withholding a portion of those tithes, thereby robbing God further. He implores the populace to bring all their tithes so that they might receive God's favor.

SEARCH THE SCRIPTURES

QUESTION 2

How could the people properly return to the Lord?

LIGHT ON THE WORD

God's Challenge

The Lord then issues the people a challenge: He calls them to put Him to the test by giving their full tithe. By giving pure whole animals from their flocks and herds and tithing the best of their crops, they would be placing their trust in the Lord. Their tithe would be placed in the storehouse for the priests, and God's house would be properly maintained. The Lord says if they do this, then He would bless them beyond what they would ever need. Instead of being cursed, they would be blessed so much they would not have room for the abundance that He would give them. This is the reward for their returning to Him.

BIBLE APPLICATION

AIM: Students will give as a grateful expression of their commitment to God's grace and justice.

Many people today cry out hypocritically for justice. The same people who demand justice are quick to dish out injustice. We fight with others and look down on those who are disadvantaged. We cheat and steal from others in order to claw our way to success. Then we complain to God when someone cheats and steals from us. We are quick to point the finger and pray to God to make things right. We only pray when we need something and neglect God in our everyday life. The lesson for us today is that making things right has to start with us. We cannot think that God will take care of our house when we do not take care of His house.

STUDENTS' RESPONSES

AIM: Students will know that believers confess their lack of forgiveness and seek human and divine forgiveness.

Oftentimes we want God to be there for us in our time of need, yet we don't ask how we can serve Him. This week in your prayer times, instead of asking the Lord for things that benefit you, ask Him how you can serve Him and be a blessing to those around you. If you are not being faithful in your financial giving to your local church, make a commitment to give. If you have been faithful, consider what charities or non-profits could be blessed by your financial giving. Ask your pastor or church leader whether there is a missionary you can help support through your financial contribution.

PRAYER

Lord, forgive us for not giving You the best that we have in our tithes, offerings, and our compassion for one another. Bless us to have the mind, heart, and spirit that is aligned with Your commandments. In Jesus' Name we pray. Amen.

HOW TO SAY IT

Sorcerer. **SOR**-seh-rer.

Ordinance. **OR**-di-nens.

PREPARE FOR NEXT SUNDAY

Read **Acts 4:23–31** and study "Praying for One Another."

DAILY HOME BIBLE READINGS

MONDAY
Teach Me Your Paths, O Lord
(Psalm 25)

TUESDAY
How Shall We Treat Others?
(Matthew 7:7–14)

WEDNESDAY
How Have We Spoken Against You?
(Malachi 3:11–18)

THURSDAY
How Shall We Be Judged?
(Joel 3:9–16)

FRIDAY
How Shall We Repent?
(Jeremiah 6:26–30)

SATURDAY
The Contrite and Humble in Spirit
(Isaiah 57:10–21)

SUNDAY
The Change Agent
(Malachi 3:1–10)

Sources:

Burton, James. *Coffman Commentaries on the Old Testament and New Testament*. Abilene, TX: Abilene Christian University Press, n.d.

Dunn, James D. G. and John W. Rogerson. *Commentary on the Bible*. Grand Rapids, MI: Wm. B. Eerdmans Publishing House, 2003.

Howley, G.C.D., F.F. Bruce, and H.L. Ellison. *The New Layman's Bible Commentary*. Grand Rapids, MI: Zondervan, 1979.

COMMENTS / NOTES:

GLOSSARY

A

Abomination: A foul and detestable thing
Affliction: Anguish, burden, persecution, tribulation, or trouble
Angels: God's messengers; they are not eternal or all-knowing, and are sometimes referred to as winged creatures known as "cherubim" and "seraphim"
Atonement: To "propitiate" (to satisfy the demands of an offended holy God) or "atone" (being reconciled to a holy God) because of sin
Avenger: One who takes revenge, one who punishes

B

Be Baptized: To dip repeatedly, to immerse, to submerge
Blameless: Irreproachable, faultless, flawless
Blessedness: Happiness, joy, prosperity. It is not based on circumstance but is rooted in the deep abiding hope shared by all who have received salvation through Jesus Christ.
Bless the Lord: To simply speak well of Him
Blood of the Lamb: The blood that Jesus shed on the Cross of Calvary when He suffered and died for humanity's sin
Bowels: The place of emotions, distress, or love

C

Called: Appointed or commissioned by God to fulfill a task
Charge: Admonish, order, command
Chosen: To be elected or selected
Christ: The Anointed One
Commandments: God's mandates; the entire body of Laws issued by God to Moses for Israel
Conduct: Manner of living
Confess: To acknowledge or to fully agree
Consider: To determine, make out
Covenant: An agreement with God based on God's character, strength, and grace; an agreement and promise between God and humankind
Crucifixion: Jesus suffered and died on the Cross

D

Decalogue: The Ten Commandments; the words translated "Ten Commandments" literally mean "ten words"
Desolation: Making something deserted or uninhabited
Disciples: Learners, students, followers
Dominion: Rule or reign
Dwelling place: A location that is a person's refuge, home

E

El: The Hebrew word for "god" or "mighty one"
Even from everlasting to everlasting: "Indefinite or unending future, eternity" (Strong)
Evil: To do "bad, unpleasant, displeasing" things
Evil doer: A malefactor, wrongdoer, criminal, troublemaker
Evil spirits: Messengers and ministers of the devil
Exalt: To raise up; to raise to the highest degree possible
Exhortation: Giving someone motivation to change his or her behavior; it can imply either rebuke or encouragement.

F

Faithfulness: Steadfastness, steadiness
Fear of the Lord: Reverence or awe of who God is

G

Gittith: A musical instrument resembling a Spanish guitar that, in ancient times, provided a musical tune or tempo during a ceremony or festival
Glory: Splendor, unparalleled honor, dignity, or distinction; to honor, praise, and worship
God called: To commission, appoint, endow
God's Bride: The Church
God's own hand: God's strength, power
God's protection: Conveys the idea of staying in God's abode, staying constantly in His presence, getting completely acquainted or connected with Him, and resting permanently in Him
Gospel: "The glad tidings of the kingdom of God soon to be set up, and later also of Jesus the Messiah,

the founder of this kingdom" (Strong).

Graven image: An idol or likeness cut from stone, wood, or metal and then worshiped as a god

Great Tribulation: A time of great suffering (Daniel 12:1, Revelation 6–18)

H

Hallowed: Consecrated, dedicated, or set apart

Hear: Listen to, yield to, to be obedient

Hearken: Pay attention to, give attention to

Heart: The place, figuratively, where our emotions and passions exist

Heathen: Literally means "nations" and is used in the Old Testament to refer to the Gentiles, all those who are not a part of the people of God

Holy: Anything consecrated and set aside for sacred use; the place made sacred because of God's presence; set apart from sin

Honor: To revere, value

Hosts: Those which go forth; armies

I

Idolatry: The worship of anything other than God, our Creator

Infidel: One who is unfaithful, unbelieving, not to be trusted

Iniquities: Perversity, depravity, guilt

In vain: A waste, a worthless thing, or simply emptiness

J

Jesus' ascension: Forty days after Jesus' death, burial, and Resurrection, He ascended or went back to Heaven to sit at the right hand of the Father (Acts 1:9–11).

Jesus' transfiguration: While on the Mount of Olives with His closest disciples—Peter, James, and John—Jesus changed into another form. His face shone with the brightness like the sun and His raiment was white as snow (Matthew 17:2; Mark 9:2; Luke 9:29).

Just: A word often rendered as "righteous"; that which is right and fair

Justice: Righteousness in government

K

Kingdom of Christ: It is the same as the "Kingdom of Heaven" (Matthew 18:1–4); it is where Jesus reigns in "glory" (i.e., in "dignity or honor").

Know: To ascertain by seeing, have understanding, to acknowledge

Knowledge: Discernment, understanding, wisdom

L

Labor: To toil to the point of exhaustion or weariness

Logos (LOG-os): The entire Word of God

M

"Make a joyful noise": A command that literally means "shout"

Manna: Food from Heaven

Messiah: The Promised One; the Anointed One

Minister: "A servant, an attendant, one who executes the commands of another" (Strong)

O

Omnipotent: All powerful

Omnipresent: All present, present everywhere

Omniscient: All knowing

Ordained: Established and founded by God; founded, fixed, appointed, or established

P

Parousia (par-oo-SEE-ah): Christ's Second Coming

Path: Connotes an ongoing process of taking dynamic steps toward an expected end

Peace: Denotes "wholeness, quietness, contentment, health, prosperity" (Strong); it is far more than an absence of conflict or problems, but that every part of life would be blessed.

Pentateuch: The Mosaic Law or Divine Law; the first five books of the Old Testament, as well as the Old Testament as a whole, reveal the entire set of legal and religious instructions which God gave, through Moses, for God's people. Terms that are synonymous for "Law" include commandments, ordinances, statutes, legal regulations, authoritative instructions, and teachings.

People(s): Most English versions translate "people" as "peoples." The New Living Translation goes even further: "Let the whole world bless our God."

Power: Boldness, might, strength, especially God's

Prophets: They were filled with the Spirit of God and under the authority and command of God, pleaded His cause and urged humanity to be saved

Profit: To gain, benefit, avail

Prosperous: To make progress, to succeed, especially in spiritual things. It often did not refer to personal profit. Rather it meant "to move forward or succeed" in one's efforts.

Proved: Examined, tested, and tried

Psalm: A Hebrew title that means "praise"

Purity: "Sinless of life" (Strong)

R

Ransom: To redeem (buy back) from, to pay a price for a person. It is commonly used as a purchase price to free slaves.
Redeemed: Ransomed, purchased
Refuge: Place of shelter; stronghold or fortress—a place to which we can run when the enemy threatens and be secure; a shelter from rain, storm, or danger
Repent: To change (be transformed) or turn back from sin and turn to God in faith
Righteous: To be declared "not guilty"
Righteousness: God's justness and rightness, which He works as a gift also in His people; refers to the right way to live as opposed to a lifestyle that treats others unfairly or unjustly

S

Sabbath: In Hebrew, *shabbath* means "ceasing from work." A day set aside to worship God.
Sanctuary: A word that means "holy" when used as an adjective. The "holy place" of which David speaks is the tabernacle, the portable temple built under Moses' leadership after the Exodus from Egypt
Salvation: Rescue, safety, deliverance
Satan: An adversary or devil
Savior: A defender, rescuer, deliverer
Scribes: They were secretaries, recorders, men skilled in the law
Secret place: A refuge, place of safety and a covering from all forms of destructive elements that seek to attack or destroy the children of God and to prevent us from experiencing the fullness of His blessings, peace, and divine providence
See: To behold, consider, discern, perceive
Selah: This Hebrew expression (**SEH-lah**) is found almost exclusively in the book of Psalms. Some believe that Selah denotes a pause or a suspension in singing of the psalm or recitation, and the insertion of an instrumental musical interlude. The Greek Septuagint renders the word *dia'psalma*, meaning "a musical interlude." Still others think that the word *Selah* signaled a holding back of singing and allowed for silent meditation.
Septuagint: It means "seventy," and it is the ancient Greek translation of the Hebrew Old Testament by 70 Jewish scholars.
Servant: A slave, subject, worshiper
Shalom: Means "peace"
Shekinah Glory: The awesome presence of the Lord; His honor, fame, and reputation
Shofar (sho-FAR): Means "ram's horn" and was used in celebration as well as in signaling armies or large groups of people in civil assembly
Soul: Refers to the immaterial part of the human being (what leaves the body when death occurs), or to the whole being—the self, one's life
Stiffnecked: Obstinate and difficult
Strengthen: To secure, make firm, make strong
Strive: To struggle, to exert oneself
Supplications: Seeking, asking, entreating, pleading, imploring, and petitioning God

T

Tabernacles: Literally means "dwelling places," the name of the portable temple constructed by Moses and the people of Israel
Teaching: Instruction in Christian living
Tetragrammaton: Hebrew name for God (YHWH)
Torah: The Law, which means "instrument" or "direction"; the first five books of the Old Testament (Genesis, Exodus, Leviticus, Numbers, and Deuteronomy)
Transfigured: To change or transform
Transgressions: Include sins, rebellion, breaking God's Law
Tried: Smelted or refined, purified
Trumpet: A ram's horn that was used in celebration as well as in signaling armies or large groups of people in civil assembly

U

Understand: To consider, have wisdom

W

Wisdom: "Prudence, an understanding of ethics" (Strong)
Woe: An exclamation of grief
Worship: Bow down deeply, show obeisance and reverence
Wrath: "Burning anger, rage" (Strong)

Y

Yahweh: Many scholars simply use the Hebrew spelling with consonants only, *YHWH*, which is God's name.

Source:

Strong, James. *New Exhaustive Strong's Numbers and Concordance with Expanded Greek-Hebrew Dictionary.* Seattle, WA: Biblesoft, and International Bible Translators, 1994. 2003.

OUR AFFIRMATION OF FAITH

is a reminder of the basic beliefs of the Church Of God In Christ. It witnesses to the reality that God has been active in creation, history, and our lives. Being Trinitarian, our affirmation focuses on the work of the Father, Son, and Holy Spirit, while proclaiming the Gospel holistically. God tells us through Scripture that salvation is available to all through Jesus Christ.

Our Affirmation of Faith is woven throughout the testifying, singing, praying, preaching, and teaching of the Church. Hence, one can hear the cardinal beliefs through these events.

The affirmation makes no pretense of being exhaustive, or being a complete statement of all our beliefs. It presents a set of key beliefs that are grounded in Scripture.

The affirmation echoes the classic testimony: "Giving honor to God in the highest and to the Lord Jesus Christ, I thank God that I'm saved, sanctified, and filled with the Holy Ghost." Our theology begins with God; the doctrine of God shapes all other doctrines for the Church Of God In Christ.

The Church Of God In Christ — Affirmation of Faith

We Believe the Bible to be the inspired and only infallible written Word of God,

We Believe that there is One God, eternally existent in three Persons; God the Father, God the Son, and God the Holy Spirit.

We Believe in the Blessed Hope, which is the rapture of the Church of God, which is in Christ at His return.

We Believe that the only means of being cleansed from sin, is through repentance and faith in the precious Blood of Jesus Christ.

We Believe that regeneration by the Holy Ghost is absolutely essential for personal salvation.

We Believe that the redemptive work of Christ on the Cross provides healing for the human body in answer to believing prayer.

We Believe that the Baptism in the Holy Ghost, according to Acts 2:4, is given to believers who ask for it.

We Believe in the sanctifying power of the Holy Spirit, by whose indwelling, the Christian is enabled to live a Holy and separated life in this present world.

Amen.

THE SYMBOL OF THE CHURCH OF GOD IN CHRIST

The Symbol of the Church Of God In Christ is an outgrowth of the Presiding Bishop's Coat of Arms, which has become quite familiar to the Church. The design of the Official Seal of the Church was created in 1973 and adopted in the General Assembly in 1981 (July Session).

The obvious GARNERED WHEAT in the center of the seal represents all of the people of the Church Of God In Christ, Inc. The ROPE of wheat that holds the shaft together represents the Founding Father of the Church, Bishop Charles Harrison Mason, who, at the call of the Lord, banded us together as a Brotherhood of Churches in the First Pentecostal General Assembly of the Church, in 1907.

The date in the seal has a two-fold purpose: first, to tell us that Bishop Mason received the baptism of the Holy Ghost in March 1907 and, second, to tell us that it was because of this outpouring that Bishop Mason was compelled to call us together in February of 1907 to organize the Church Of God In Christ.

The RAIN in the background represents the Latter Rain, or the End-time Revivals, which brought about the emergence of our Church along with other Pentecostal Holiness Bodies in the same era. The rain also serves as a challenge to the Church to keep Christ in the center of our worship and service, so that He may continue to use the Church Of God In Christ as one of the vehicles of Pentecostal Revival before the return of the Lord.

This information was reprinted from the book *So You Want to KNOW YOUR CHURCH* by Alferd Z. Hall, Jr.

COGIC AFFIRMATION OF FAITH

We believe the Bible to be the inspired and only infallible written Word of God.

We believe that there is One God, eternally existent in three Persons: God the Father, God the Son, and God the Holy Spirit.

We believe in the Blessed Hope, which is the rapture of the Church of God, which is in Christ at His return.

We believe that the only means of being cleansed from sin is through repentance and faith in the precious Blood of Jesus Christ.

We believe that regeneration by the Holy Ghost is absolutely essential for personal salvation.

We believe that the redemptive work of Christ on the Cross provides healing for the human body in answer to believing in prayer.

We believe that the baptism in the Holy Ghost, according to Acts 2:4, is given to believers who ask for it.

We believe in the sanctifying power of the Holy Spirit, by whose indwelling the Christian is enabled to live a Holy and separated life in this present world. Amen.

The Doctrines of the Church Of God In Christ

THE BIBLE

We believe that the Bible is the Word of God and contains one harmonious and sufficiently complete system of doctrine. We believe in the full inspiration of the Word of God. We hold the Word of God to be the only authority in all matters and assert that no doctrine can be true or essential if it does not find a place in this Word.

THE FATHER

We believe in God, the Father Almighty, the Author and Creator of all things. The Old Testament reveals God in diverse manners, by manifesting His nature, character, and dominions. The Gospels in the New Testament give us knowledge of God the "Father" or "My Father," showing the relationship of God to Jesus as Father, or representing Him as the Father in the Godhead, and Jesus himself that Son (St. John 15:8, 14:20). Jesus also gives God the distinction of "Fatherhood" to all believers when He explains God in the light of "Your Father in Heaven" (St. Matthew 6:8).

THE SON

We believe that Jesus Christ is the Son of God, the second person in the Godhead of the Trinity or Triune Godhead. We believe that Jesus was and is eternal in His person and nature as the Son of God who was with God in the beginning of creation (St. John 1:1). We believe that Jesus Christ was born of a virgin called Mary according to the Scripture (St. Matthew 1:18), thus giving rise to our fundamental belief in the Virgin Birth and to all of the miraculous events surrounding the phenomenon (St. Matthew 1:18–25). We believe that Jesus Christ became the "suffering servant" to man; this suffering servant came seeking to redeem man from sin and to reconcile him to God, His Father (Romans 5:10). We believe that Jesus Christ is standing now as mediator between God and man (I Timothy 2:5).

THE HOLY GHOST

We believe the Holy Ghost or Holy Spirit is the third person of the Trinity; proceeds from the Father and the Son; is of the same substance, equal to power and glory; and is together with the Father and the Son, to be believed in, obeyed, and worshiped. The Holy Ghost is a gift bestowed upon the believer for the purpose of equipping and empowering the believer, making him or her a more effective witness for service in the world. He teaches and guides one into all truth (John 16:13; Acts 1:8, 8:39).

THE BAPTISM OF THE HOLY GHOST

We believe that the Baptism of the Holy Ghost is an experience subsequent to conversion and sanctification and that tongue-speaking is the consequence of the baptism in the Holy Ghost with the manifestations of the fruit of the Spirit (Galatians 5:22–23; Acts 10:46, 19:1–6). We believe that we are not baptized with the Holy Ghost in order to be saved (Acts 19:1–6; John 3:5). When one receives a baptismal Holy Ghost experience, we believe one will speak with a tongue unknown to oneself according to the sovereign will of Christ. To be filled with the Spirit means to be Spirit controlled as expressed by Paul in Ephesians 5:18,19. Since the charismatic demonstrations were necessary to help the early church to be successful in implementing the command of Christ, we, therefore, believe that a Holy Ghost experience is mandatory for all believers today.

MAN

We believe that humankind was created holy by God, composed of body and soul. We believe that humankind, by nature, is sinful and unholy. Being born in sin, a person needs to be born again, sanctified and cleansed from all sins by the blood of Jesus. We believe that one is saved by confessing and forsaking one's sins, and believing on the Lord Jesus Christ, and that having become a child of God, by being born again and adopted into the family of God, one may, and should, claim the inheritance of the sons of God, namely the baptism of the Holy Ghost.

SIN

Sin, the Bible teaches, began in the angelic world (Ezekiel 28:11–19; Isaiah 14:12–20) and is transmitted into the blood of the human race through disobedience and deception motivated by unbelief (I Timothy 2:14). Adam's sin, committed by eating of the forbidden fruit from the tree of knowledge of good and evil, carried with it permanent pollution or depraved human nature to all his descendants. This is called "original sin." Sin can now be defined as a volitional transgression against God and a lack of conformity to the will of God. We, therefore, conclude that humankind by nature is sinful and has fallen from a glorious and righteous state from which we were created, and has become unrighteous and unholy. We therefore, must be restored to the state of holiness from which we have fallen by being born again (St. John 3:7).

SALVATION

Salvation deals with the application of the work of redemption to the sinner with restoration to divine favor and communion with God. This redemptive operation of the Holy Ghost upon sinners is brought about by repentance toward God and faith toward our Lord Jesus Christ which brings conversion, faith, justification, regeneration, sanctification, and the baptism of the Holy Ghost. Repentance is the work of God, which results in a change of mind in respect to a person's relationship to God (St. Matthew 3:1–2, 4:17; Acts 20:21). Faith is a certain conviction wrought in the heart by the Holy Spirit, as to the truth of the Gospel and a heart trust in the promises of God in Christ (Romans 1:17, 3:28; St. Matthew 9:22; Acts 26:18). Conversion is that act of God whereby He causes the regenerated sinner, in one's conscious life, to turn to Him in repentance and faith (II Kings 5:15; II Chronicles 33:12,13; St. Luke 19:8,9; Acts 8:30). Regeneration is the act of God by which the principle of the new life is implanted in humankind, the governing disposition of soul is made holy, and the first holy exercise of this new disposition is secured. Sanctification is that gracious and continuous operation of the Holy Ghost, by which He delivers the justified sinner from the pollution of sin, renews a person's whole nature in the image of God, and enables one to perform good works (Romans 6:4, 5:6; Colossians 2:12, 3:1).

ANGELS

The Bible uses the term "angel" (a heavenly body) clearly and primarily to denote messengers or ambassadors of God with such Scripture references as Revelations 4:5, which indicates their duty in Heaven to praise God (Psalm 103:20), to do God's will (St. Matthew 18:10), and to behold His face. But since Heaven must come down to earth, they also have a mission to earth. The Bible indicates that they accompanied God in the Creation, and also that they will accompany Christ in His return in Glory.

DEMONS

Demons denote unclean or evil spirits; they are sometimes called devils or demonic beings. They are evil spirits, belonging to the unseen or spiritual realm, embodied in human beings. The Old Testament refers to the prince of demons, sometimes called Satan (adversary) or Devil, as having power and wisdom, taking the habitation of other forms such as the serpent (Genesis 3:1). The New Testament speaks of the Devil as Tempter (St. Matthew 4:3), and it goes on to tell the works of Satan, the Devil, and demons as combating righteousness and good in any form, proving to be an adversary to the saints. Their chief power is exercised to destroy the mission of Jesus Christ. It can well be said that the Christian Church believes in demons, Satan, and devils. We believe in their power and purpose. We believe they can be subdued and conquered as in the commandment to the believer by Jesus. "In my name they shall cast out Satan and the work of the Devil and to resist him and then he will flee (WITHDRAW) from you" (St. Mark 16:17).

THE CHURCH

The Church forms a spiritual unity of which Christ is the divine head. It is animated by one Spirit, the Spirit of Christ. It professes one faith, shares one hope, and serves one King. It is the citadel of the truth and God's agency for communicating to believers all spiritual blessings. The Church then is the object of our faith rather than of knowledge. The name of our Church, "CHURCH OF GOD IN CHRIST," is supported by I Thessalonians 2:14 and other passages in the Pauline Epistles. The word "CHURCH" or "EKKLESIA" was first applied to the Christian society by Jesus Christ in St. Matthew 16:18, the occasion being that of His benediction of Peter at Caesarea Philippi.

THE SECOND COMING OF CHRIST

We believe in the second coming of Christ; that He shall come from Heaven to earth, personally, bodily, visibly (Acts 1:11; Titus 2:11–13; St. Matthew 16:27, 24:30, 25:30; Luke 21:27; John 1:14, 17; Titus 2:11); and that the Church, the bride, will be caught up to meet Him in the air (I Thessalonians 4:16–17). We admonish all who have this hope to purify themselves as He is pure.

DIVINE HEALING

The Church Of God In Christ believes in and practices Divine Healing. It is a commandment of Jesus to the Apostles (St. Mark 16:18). Jesus affirms His teachings on healing by explaining to His disciples, who were to be Apostles, that healing the afflicted is by faith (St. Luke 9:40–41). Therefore, we believe that healing by faith in God has scriptural support and ordained authority. St. James's writings in his epistle encourage Elders to pray for the sick, lay hands upon them and to anoint them with oil, and state that prayers with faith shall heal the sick and the Lord shall raise them up. Healing is still practiced widely and frequently in the Church Of God In Christ, and testimonies of healing in our Church testify to this fact.

MIRACLES

The Church Of God In Christ believes that miracles occur to convince people that the Bible is God's Word. A miracle can be defined as an extraordinary visible act of divine power, wrought by the efficient agency of the will of God, which has as its final cause the vindication of the righteousness of God's Word. We believe that the works of God, which were performed during the beginnings of Christianity, do and will occur even today where God is preached, faith in Christ is exercised, the Holy Ghost is active, and the Gospel is promulgated in the truth (Acts 5:15, 6:8, 9:40; Luke 4:36, 7:14, 15, 5:5, 6; St. Mark 14:15).

THE ORDINANCES OF THE CHURCH

It is generally admitted that for an ordinance to be valid, it must have been instituted by Christ. When we speak of ordinances of the church, we are speaking of those instituted by Christ, in which by sensible signs the grace of God in Christ and the benefits of the covenant of grace are represented, sealed, and applied to believers, and these in turn give expression to their faith and allegiance to God. The Church Of God In Christ recognizes three ordinances as having been instituted by Christ himself and, therefore, are binding upon the church practice.

THE LORD'S SUPPER (HOLY COMMUNION)

The Lord's Supper symbolizes the Lord's death and suffering for the benefit and in the place of His people. It also symbolizes the believer's participation in the crucified Christ. It represents not only the death of Christ as the object of faith, which unites the believers to Christ, but also the effect of this act as the giving of life, strength, and joy to the soul. The communicant by faith enters into a special spiritual union of one's soul with the glorified Christ.

FOOT WASHING

Foot washing is practiced and recognized as an ordinance in our Church because Christ, by His example, showed that humility characterized greatness in the Kingdom of God, and that service rendered to others gave evidence that humility, motivated by love, exists. These services are held subsequent to the Lord's Supper; however, its regularity is left to the discretion of the pastor in charge.

WATER BAPTISM

We believe that Water Baptism is necessary as instructed by Christ in St. John 3:5, "UNLESS MAN BE BORN AGAIN OF WATER AND OF THE SPIRIT..."

However, we do not believe that water baptism alone is a means of salvation, but is an outward demonstration that one has already had a conversion experience and has accepted Christ as his personal Savior. As Pentecostals, we practice immersion in preference to sprinkling because immersion corresponds more closely to the death, burial, and Resurrection of our Lord (Colossians 2:12). It also symbolizes regeneration and purification more than any other mode. Therefore, we practice immersion as our mode of baptism. We believe that we should use the Baptismal Formula given to us by Christ for all "...IN THE NAME OF THE FATHER, AND OF THE SON, AND OF THE HOLY GHOST..." (Matthew 28:19).

NOTES

NOTES